PIMLICO

774

# THE NUREMBERG INTERVIEWS

Dr Leon Goldensohn was an American physician and psychiatrist who joined the U.S. Army in 1943 and was posted to France and Germany. He died in 1961.

Robert Gellately is the Earl Ray Beck Professor of History at Florida State University and the author of *The Gestapo and German Society: Enforcing Racial Policy, 1933–1945* and *Backing Hitler: Consent and Coercion in Nazi Germany*. He lives in Tallahassee, Florida.

# THE NUREMBERG INTERVIEWS

## Conversations with the Defendants and Witnesses

Conducted by
### LEON GOLDENSOHN

Edited and Introduced by
### ROBERT GELLATELY

PIMLICO

Published by Pimlico 2007

2 4 6 8 10 9 7 5 3 1

Interviews copyright © 2004 by
The Estate of Leon N. Goldensohn
Introduction copyright © 2004 by Robert Gellately

First published in the United States of America by
Knopf, Borzoi Books, in 2004

First published in Great Britain by
Pimlico in 2006

Published in Great Britain in paperback by
Pimlico in 2007

Pimlico
Random House, 20 Vauxhall Bridge Road,
London SW1V 2SA

www.randomhouse.co.uk

Addresses for companies within The Random House Group Limited can be found at:
www.randomhouse.co.uk

The Random House Group Limited Reg. No. 954009

A CIP catalogue record for this book
is available from the British Library

ISBN 9781845950149

The Random House Group Limited makes every effort
to ensure that the papers used in its books are made from trees that have been
legally sourced from well-managed and credibly certified forests. Our paper procurement
policy can be found at: www.randomhouse.co.uk/paper.htm

Printed and bound in Great Britain by Clays Ltd, St Ives PLC

# CONTENTS

## PART ONE
# DEFENDANTS

PART TWO
# WITNESSES

# Nuremberg—Voices from the Past

Leon Goldensohn was an American physician and psychiatrist at the time the United States entered the Second World War. In 1943 he joined the U.S. Army and was soon posted to France and Germany, where he served in battles in the European theater. Not long after the war ended, he became prison psychiatrist at Nuremberg, the location of the first postwar trials of the major Nazi war criminals. Goldensohn arrived in Nuremberg in early January 1946, about six weeks into the trials, and remained there until late July of that year. As a trained psychiatrist he had responsibility for the mental health of the nearly two dozen German leaders who had survived the war and who were now fighting for their lives before the International Military Tribunal. As a medical doctor who saw the prisoners nearly every day, he also kept careful track of their physical problems. Over a period of seven months in Nuremberg prison he spoke on a regular basis with many of the twenty-one prisoners who were there when he arrived, and he carried out formal and extended interviews with most of them. In addition, he interviewed a large number of defense and prosecution witnesses, some of whom had also been significant Nazi officials.

This book publishes for the first time a broad selection of the interviews Goldensohn conducted during his time in Nuremberg. They represent an important addition to the record of the trials and of the Third Reich. They are unique in that they are systematic interviews conducted by a trained psychiatrist, and they offer new testimony about the mentality and motives of the major Nazi perpetrators.

**Background to the Nuremberg Trials**
The Nuremberg trials came into existence out of a multitude of political and judicial concerns, but are seen by many today as a landmark in international law. They were by no means inevitable, however, and might

never have taken place. During the war, as Allied leaders learned about the vast scale of the Nazi atrocities, President Franklin D. Roosevelt of the United States, Prime Minister Winston S. Churchill of Great Britain, and General Secretary Joseph Stalin of the Soviet Union at one time or another all considered summary execution as the more appropriate response to Nazi crimes.

The concept of the trials was apparently first suggested by Soviet foreign minister Vyacheslav Molotov as far back as October 14, 1942. On that date Molotov wrote to several East European governments in exile in London about Moscow's inclination to try the most prominent leaders of "the criminal Hitlerite government" before a "special international tribunal."[1] Moscow was evidently upset that Britain was not willing to try Rudolf Hess, Hitler's deputy, who had flown to Scotland in May 1941, and the Soviets harbored fears that their allies might even conclude some kind of deal with Germany. For their part, the western Allies gave little thought to postwar trials, but continued to lean toward some kind of summary execution. Their immediate priority was winning the war.

Nevertheless, on November 1, 1943, all three Allies finally issued a joint statement about what should happen to the war criminals, in the so-called Moscow Declaration. It stated several general principles. For example, the declaration laid down that those who had committed crimes would be returned to the localities where these had taken place and be "judged on the spot." Trial and punishment would follow the laws of the land in each locality. There would be different treatment for the major war criminals, however, whose crimes were seen as not restricted to any particular geographic area. The Moscow Declaration left up in the air precisely what ought to happen to these men and did not say whether there would be a trial or summary execution.[2]

Churchill's own views were far from benign. He thought, as he said behind closed doors of a cabinet meeting on November 10, 1943 — just prior to the Tehran Conference — that there was some point to drawing up a short list of specific war criminals. He was inclined to believe that dealing with this group summarily might shorten the war insofar as the named individuals would become isolated figures in their own country. This strategy required that the Allies avoid the entanglements of legal procedures, and Churchill himself favored a list of perhaps fifty to one hundred or so Nazi leaders. Once the list was reviewed by some sort of international committee of jurists, these men would be declared "out-laws" and thus fair game for anyone who wished to kill them. For Churchill, if there was to be anything like a trial for the major war criminals, its job would be to verify the identity of these "outlaws."[3]

One of the most remarkable exchanges on the topic of summary executions took place at a Roosevelt-Churchill-Stalin meeting during the Tehran Conference (November 28–December 1, 1943). Over dinner on November 29, Stalin suggested in passing that if at the end of the war about fifty thousand leaders of the German armed forces were rounded up and liquidated, then Germany's military might would be ended once and for all.[4] Churchill was taken aback by the scale of the liquidations envisioned by Stalin. He said simply that the British Parliament and public would never accept such mass executions. But Roosevelt responded to Stalin more warmly, and when Churchill became upset (or so Churchill recalled), FDR said that the Allies should execute not fifty thousand, but "only 49,000." Elliott Roosevelt, the president's son, who happened to be present, chimed in to say he was sure the United States Army "would support it."[5]

The drift of this conversation bothered Churchill so much that he left the room, but he was chased down by a jovial Stalin, who said that he was, of course, only joking. If we look at the evidence of later discussions, however, and consider that Stalin had already instigated the liquidation of thousands of his own people and even many in the Soviet officer corps, there is reason to believe that had Churchill been in agreement that evening, an important decision might have been taken. Whether this step would have culminated in a large number of executions remains open to speculation and debate. Certainly, Churchill had his doubts that Stalin and Roosevelt were just pulling his leg on the evening in Tehran. Although he let himself be persuaded by Stalin to return to dinner, he was not "fully convinced that all was chaff and there was no serious intent lurking behind."[6]

Inside the government of the United States there was deep division about what should be done about Nazi war crimes. One of the most powerful voices in favor of executions over a trial of any kind was articulated on September 5, 1944, when Secretary of the Treasury Henry Morgenthau Jr. proposed a plan that would have permanently crippled Germany. In the context of that plan he wanted Nazi leaders summarily executed, and on a scale that looked closer to what Stalin had mentioned at Tehran, and not the more "modest" one that Churchill had in mind. U.S. secretary of war Henry L. Stimson, fortunately, offered a voice of reason on the American side.

The seventy-six-year-old Stimson would not accept the notion that Germany's economy should be deindustrialized or destroyed, supposedly in order to save the world from another war, and he was also completely opposed to Morgenthau's approach to war criminals. Stimson insisted, to the contrary, on the need for due process, which had to embody "the rudimentary aspects of the Bill of Rights." In a memorandum of September 9, 1944, he sagely noted that it was not a matter of being hard or soft on Germany, but of adopting an appropriate method for dealing with the Nazi criminals. The approach had to be a product of "careful thought and well-defined procedure." He believed the United States should participate in some kind of international tribunal, one that would charge the main Nazi officials with offenses against "the laws of the Rules of War in that they committed wanton and unnecessary cruelties in connection with the prosecution of the war." He noted that these rules had been upheld by the U.S. Supreme Court and ought to be "the basis of judicial action against the Nazis."[7]

Roosevelt, however, much to Stimson's consternation, continued to side with Morgenthau — who was also a personal friend — and the position of summary execution, without trial, by the military. Indeed, in the wake of the Quebec Conference (August 11–24, 1944), Roosevelt and Churchill issued a statement that said a judicial process was inappropriate for "arch-criminals such as Hitler, Himmler, Goering, and Goebbels." As they put it, "Apart from the formidable difficulties of constituting the Court, formulating the charge, and assembling the evidence, the question of [the Nazi leaders'] fate is a political and not a judicial one. It could not rest with judges however eminent or learned to decide finally a matter like this, which is of the widest and most vital public policy. This decision must be 'the joint decision of the Governments of the Allies.' This in fact was expressed in the Moscow declaration."[8]

Roosevelt and Churchill came to the conclusion that on balance it would be best to execute certain Nazi leaders without any trials, and this was a point of view that Stalin also seemed to share. Churchill was somewhat surprised, therefore, to learn on a visit to Moscow in October 1944 that evidently Stalin had changed his mind. He and other Soviet leaders

now favored a trial, along the lines of an international tribunal as originally suggested by Molotov. It is also possible that once Stalin saw for
himself that Churchill would never go along with the liquidation of tens
of thousands of the German elite, he went over to the idea of holding a
trial of the major war criminals, which could be used for propaganda
purposes. Perhaps Stalin also thought that in advocating trials, he might
be able to polish his tarnished image in the West.[9]

In the meantime the Soviets were taking steps of their own to settle
scores with the invaders. As they liberated their land from the Nazi yoke
in the summer of 1943, they began carrying out their own trials, including trials of their own citizens, for participation in Nazi war crimes. In the
first such trial (July 14–17, 1943), at Krasnodar, the Soviets made public
to the world one of the first cases of mass murder of the Jews. There were
eight death sentences, which were carried out in the city square in front
of a crowd estimated at thirty thousand people.[10] In August and September some smaller Soviet trials followed, but in Kharkov on December
15–18, another large and public trial took place, with a similar result. It
culminated in the hanging of those found guilty, in the market square
before an estimated fifty thousand. The event was widely publicized by
special news films as well as on the radio and in the press. Such proceedings reminded some western observers, as well they might, of the show
trials that were a prominent feature of the Soviet Great Terror in the
late 1930s. The Soviets used these first trials of Nazi sympathizers to
appeal to world opinion as well as to strengthen morale. Soviet practice,
therefore, began to favor some kind of trial over summary execution.
The Soviets' intention, of course, was to use the format of a trial to
demonstrate the guilt of the accused.

The governments of the United States and Great Britain were concerned about these Soviet show trials just behind the lines. They were
especially worried lest the proceedings set off Nazi retaliations and lead
to the execution of American and British prisoners of war who were in
German captivity. Indeed, Hitler was incensed, and in response he
ordered his own show trials, not of Soviet prisoners of war but of what
he called "English-American war criminals" and especially "Anglo-
Saxon terror bombers."[11] Hitler's orders were in fact followed up, but
eventually came to nothing, as often happened to many of his more
destructive orders by war's end.

The U.S. government, prodded by Stimson, gradually came to accept the view that judicial proceedings were preferable to summary executions. Stimson could not simply voice his opposition to Morgenthau, who seemed to have the support of President Roosevelt; he had to come up with an alternative. In September 1944 he gave the task of looking into such a plan to his assistant secretary John J. McCloy, who passed it down the chain of command. Eventually Colonel Murray C. Bernays produced what turned out to be a key document in the evolution of American policy.

Bernays was a lawyer in civilian life. He drew up a paper on what he called the "trial of European war criminals," in which he made strong arguments in favor of due process. He claimed that a trial would have enormous advantages over mere political condemnation — such as had followed the end of the previous war. Bernays argued that the Nazis could and should be charged with conspiracy to commit crime. Moreover, he maintained that certain organizations (such as the Nazi Party, the Gestapo, and the SS) could be indicted, not just a few individual leaders. Such organizations would also be charged with being part of a criminal conspiracy. It would not be necessary to charge every single person in the organization, just "representative individuals." Once the organization was tried and convicted, an individual member could be judged as a criminal coconspirator, and given a summary trial by the Allies. It is important to note, however, that contrary to what some of the defendants said when they spoke with Goldensohn, Article 10 of what became the charter of the International Military Tribunal did not simply declare certain Nazi organizations to be criminal. That decision was left to the tribunal to determine. Moreover, any particular member of those organizations that the tribunal eventually found to be criminal was not automatically deemed to be criminal. Each had the right to a trial.[12]

The political and judicial position of the American administration in favor of trials, along with the conspiracy/organizations approach, was endorsed by Secretary of State Cordell Hull, Secretary of the Navy James Forrestal, and Stimson. On November 11, 1944, they sent a memorandum to President Roosevelt with a view to providing him with guidance for the upcoming Yalta Conference.[13]

Roosevelt was surprisingly slow to come around, however. At Yalta (February 7–12, 1945), the president apparently made no mention of the changed position of his administration. He and Churchill still seemed to prefer summary executions, but no decisions were taken.

It was Stalin and the Soviets who perhaps ultimately did most to per-suade the other Allies that some sort of "judicial procedure was the way forward."[14] Stimson and others kept trying to move the president in that direction. They continued to insist on the need to avoid the impression that the Allies were seeking vengeance. That view was accepted by the new president, Harry S. Truman, after he took over when Roosevelt died suddenly on April 12, 1945.[15]

The demands for summary execution came to naught, as Truman adopted the position in favor of a trial put forward in late 1944 and early 1945 by Stimson, Hull, and other high government officials.[16] In several meetings between the Allies in 1945, the Americans also convinced the reluctant British. By May 3 (at San Francisco), the western Allies and the Soviet Union, along with newly liberated France, all agreed in principle to judicial proceedings. By August 8, after still more months of negotiations in London, they finally worked out a charter for the tri-als. They established in detail how the court would be constituted and what rights the defendants would have. At the same time the Allies worked out and agreed to the four counts of the indictment: conspiracy to commit crimes, crimes against peace, war crimes, and crimes against humanity.[17]

Even after the Allies had agreed in principle to the trials, they had to overcome the last hurdles to holding them. Part of the difficulty lay in the fact that the liberal-democratic Anglo-American powers and the Soviet Union conceived of the trials in very different ways. The Soviets had endured extreme suffering at the hands of the invading Germans. Even by conservative and quite reliable estimates, the German-Soviet war had led to the deaths of around 25 million people in the USSR, most of whom were civilians.[18] For the Soviet leaders, the trials would be more like grand show trials, designed to demonstrate the "measure of guilt" of each of the accused, after which each would get "the necessary punish-ment."[19] For the United States and Great Britain, however, once they finally accepted the notion of a trial, it necessarily followed (at least in theory) that the defendants had certain rights of self-defense. There also had to be an assumption of innocence until they were proven guilty and the possibility that some or all of the accused might be set free or at least found not guilty on some counts.

It was also difficult for the Allies to reach agreement about the form and procedures of the trials because Anglo-American and continental legal traditions are quite different. The United States and Great Britain have an "adversarial" system, whereby relatively open cases go to trial, evidence is presented in court, and witnesses — sometimes also the accused — are cross-examined under oath by defense lawyers and the prosecution, who face each other in court and fight it out. On the European continent, however, there is more of an "inquisitorial" system, in which the investigative work is done by a magistrate who puts together a dossier based on the evidence. If a charge is warranted, copies of the dossier are given to the court and the accused. During the trial, it is the judges who decide whether to hear further testimony. It is they who question witnesses, but rarely cross-examine the accused, who may or may not make a statement at the end of the trial. The Soviet judge at Nuremberg — whose participation in the notorious show trials of the 1930s in Moscow was well known in the West — asked with some consternation at one of the last pre-Nuremberg meetings in 1945, "What is meant in the English by 'cross-examine'?"[20]

The Americans and the British carried the day on how the trials would proceed. They worked out what is sometimes called a clever compromise with the Soviets and the French, but of course the accused had no say whatsoever in any of the pretrial discussions. They were also deprived of many of the most important rights enshrined in the American Constitution. For example, the accused could not invoke the Fifth Amendment, which would have permitted them to refuse to answer a question on the grounds that doing so might tend to incriminate them. The accused could be, and were, questioned in court, each in turn, and they could not decline to testify.

## The Charges

The defendants at Nuremberg were indicted on four counts, the first two of which proved to be particularly controversial for scholars of international law.

*Count one* alleged that the accused had "participated as leaders, organizers, instigators or accomplices in the formulation or execution of a common plan or conspiracy to commit, or which involved the commission of, Crimes Against Peace, War Crimes, and Crimes Against Humanity as defined in the Charter."[21]

*Count two* was related to the first and indicted the defendants and diverse others who, over many years, "participated in the planning, preparation, initiation, and waging wars of aggression, which were also wars in violation of international treaties, agreements and assurances." This count thus indicted what were called "crimes against peace," and obviously had to include acts of aggression like the German invasion of Poland on September 1, 1939, even though that act of war was clearly carried out as part of a joint conspiracy with the Soviet Union, which went unmentioned. The Nazi-Soviet Nonaggression Pact of August 23, 1939, not only opened the door to war but contained secret clauses about the division of Poland, which the Soviet Union also invaded from the east as Germany did so from the west.

Counts one and two, therefore, opened the tribunal to controversy, not least because they failed to indict the Soviet Union for these "crimes against peace"— which would have been politically unpalatable at the time. The very appearance of doing justice was colored also because the Soviets acted as judges and prosecutors at Nuremberg. On balance it might have been better not to have brought the first two counts at all, but to have focused instead on war crimes and crimes against humanity.

*Count three* accused the defendants of having a "common plan or conspiracy to commit War Crimes." Carrying out this plan, it was alleged, involved the practice of "total war," which exceeded "the laws and customs of war." More particularly, this count in the indictment pointed to crimes such as the murder and mistreatment of civilian populations, the deportation and use of slave labor, the murder and mistreatment of prisoners of war, the killing of hostages, and the plunder and wanton destruction of cities, towns, and villages.

*Count four* dealt with "crimes against humanity," which "included murder, extermination, enslavement, deportation and other inhumane acts committed against civilian populations before and during the war." Count four also singled out "persecution on political, racial and religious grounds in execution of and in connection with the common plan mentioned in count one."

None of the accused who were indicted before the International Military Tribunal was charged in a specific count for persecuting and murdering the Jews. Terms such as "genocide" or "the Holocaust" became current only later. "Genocide," which was coined in 1944 by the Polish jurist Raphael Lemkin, was made into a crime by a special United Nations convention in 1948.[22] "Holocaust" had existed earlier, certainly before 1939, but it was not used during the trials.[23] But the unprecedented atrocities committed against the Jews across Europe were mentioned in passing under count three, and more extensively in count four, which charged that the "mass murder" of Jews involved "millions of persons."

These four counts brought serious charges, all of them more or less without precedent in international law. The first two were especially problematical, and without them — also without the continuing and misplaced attempt to link all the crimes to an overall conspiracy — the trials might have been more fruitful for future prosecutions of war crimes and crimes against humanity. In an effort to make its case on all counts, however, and particularly on the first — the long-term conspiracy charge — the prosecution exaggerated the intentionality and coherence of Nazi planning and policy making. The United States was especially enthusiastic about the conspiracy charge, which was somewhat familiar in American law, even if it had previously been used far more restrictively. The idea of such a wide-ranging conspiracy certainly gave the British cause for concern, but from the Americans' perspective it had the advantage of making it possible to link pre-1939 human rights and legal abuses inside Germany to the far more egregious kinds committed during the war.

The idea of a conspiracy — which in fact informed every count in the indictment — opened the door to the defense. The counsels took every opportunity to show, not without some plausibility, that there was enormous confusion of authority in the Third Reich. They said that the regime had a haphazard, incoherent, and inefficient system of administration and government. It became common for the accused to plead ignorance, and to point to the highly compartmentalized system of Nazi administration. The defendants all claimed to have had limited knowledge and to have played no part in any long-term conspiracy.

The prosecution, on the other hand, had to prove there was a clear plan, with shared aims among the accused from early on in the regime. They set out to show that there was an intention from the very beginning to commit specific crimes; that included long-term planning not only for a war of aggression, but for specific events like the murder of the Jews. The prosecution ended up overstating the intentionality, just as the defense unduly played it down, the latter in order to paint a picture of administrative chaos, endless power struggles, and a system without a real leader. For the defense it was logical to insist that no one believed in

Nazi ideology or had read Hitler's book, much less Alfred Rosenberg's books.

To this day there continues to be significant controversy among historians about the nature and extent of Hitler's role and his relations to the Nazi leaders. The picture now supported by many historians is more complex and blends elements from both prosecution and defense claims.[24] However, the prosecution image of Alfred Rosenberg as the main Nazi "theoretician" or "philosopher" is without any merit whatever.

The International Military Tribunal responsible for trying the major war criminals was the product of long political and judicial debates. After a preliminary session in Berlin on October 18, 1945, the trials moved to the Palace of Justice in Nuremberg, where the sessions ran from November 14. The main proceedings, comprising prosecution and defense presentations, lasted just over nine months, from November 22, 1945, to August 31, 1946. The trials were a massive undertaking. There were four judges and four prosecutors (with alternates), each with a team of his own, all of them drawn from the victorious powers — the United States, Great Britain, and the Soviet Union, along with France. The court met in 403 open sessions, heard a total of 166 witnesses, and worked through literally thousands of written affidavits and hundreds of thousands of documents.[25] The trials were cumbersome and slow, not least because they were carried on in four languages and required enormous translation work just to record the testimony, the cross-examinations, the written submissions, and many documents. A sense of the scale of the trials can be gathered from the fact that the transcripts and only a selection of the documents entered as evidence were published (also in four languages) in forty-two large volumes.[26]

Charges were initially brought against twenty-four men deemed on various grounds to be major war criminals. These included Robert Ley, the head of the Labor Front, who committed suicide on October 24, 1945, before the trials began, and the industrialist Gustav Krupp von Bohlen und Halbach, chosen by the Allies as "representative" of big business, who proved to be unfit. Included, in absentia, among the twenty-two defendants was Martin Bormann, Hitler's private secretary. On September 30 and October 1, 1946, the court delivered its judgments. Twelve of the defendants were sentenced to death by hanging (Bormann in absentia, Hans Frank, Wilhelm Frick, Hermann Goering,

Alfred Jodl, Ernst Kaltenbrunner, Wilhelm Keitel, Joachim von Ribbentrop, Alfred Rosenberg, Fritz Sauckel, Arthur Seyss-Inquart, Julius Streicher). Of the remaining ten defendants, three were found not guilty (Hans Fritzsche, Franz von Papen, Hjalmar Schacht), three were sentenced to life imprisonment (Rudolf Hess, Walther Funk, Erich Raeder), two got twenty years' imprisonment (Baldur von Schirach, Albert Speer), one was sentenced to fifteen years (Constantin von Neurath), and one to ten years (Karl Doenitz).

Immediately after sentencing, counsels for two men condemned to hang (Jodl and Keitel) requested that their clients be granted the dignity of a military death by shooting. Counsel for Raeder also requested that he be shot, in place of his sentence of life imprisonment. All three requests were denied. On October 16, 1946, all those condemned to death (with the exceptions of Bormann and Goering) were hanged. Reich Marshal Goering had managed to defy the court by committing suicide in his cell just before the scheduled execution.

## The Goldensohn Interviews

After the United States government finally decided, toward the end of 1944 and into 1945, that trials were necessary and preferable to summary executions, the Americans took the leading role. They insisted almost immediately, with British support, on moving the venue outside the Soviet sector of occupied Germany, and at the end of June 1945 decided on Nuremberg. The city had been nearly obliterated during the war, but it still had facilities where the trials could be held.[27] The occupying powers were very much drawn to the choice of Nuremberg. The city's name was identified with the racist laws of September 1935, and beyond that it had hosted the annual Nazi Party rallies, when hundreds of thousands of people would fill the city and infuse it with wild enthusiasm for Hitler. Thus, holding the trials of the fallen Nazi leaders at Nuremberg had both political and symbolic value.

By September 1945 American prosecutors Robert H. Jackson and Thomas J. Dodd could call on a staff of two hundred. There were legal officers and experts of various kinds, as well as translators and stenographers. Jackson was by far the most active of the prosecutors, followed by Sir David Maxwell Fyfe of Great Britain. The British, however, had at most only thirty-four staffers and usually fewer, while the Soviet and French teams were smaller still.[28] The Americans, therefore, tended to dominate the proceedings in nearly every way, and not only because the trials were held in the American sector of Germany.

In addition to a medical staff, the Americans generally had a psychologist and a psychiatrist on duty during most of the proceedings. The first prison psychiatrist at Nuremberg was Major Douglas M. Kelley, who had previously served at a holding camp for important Nazi prisoners at Mondorf-les-Bains, in Luxembourg. Most of the Nuremberg defendants had been kept there before the trials, and it was not without a touch of victor irony that the camp became known among the Allies simply as "Ashcan." It was run along spartan lines by the strict Colonel Burton C. Andrus, a man known to be a firm disciplinarian. Other Nazi bigwigs, notably Speer and Schacht, were kept in less stringent conditions at Kransberg Castle near Frankfurt am Main, a camp nicknamed "Dustbin." All the leading Nazis were questioned either at Ashcan or Dustbin, and some of the information garnered from them has been preserved. Interesting selections of this material, much of it never used in the trials, have recently been published.[29] Colonel Andrus and Major Kelley were sent from Ashcan to Nuremberg. Kelley stayed only for the first month of the trials, when he left and was replaced by Goldensohn.

Throughout the period of the incarceration, at Mondorf and later at Nuremberg, American guards communicated hardly at all with their prisoners, but maintained a permanent suicide watch. Initially, one guard was assigned to four cells, but after Robert Ley's suicide in October 1945, Colonel Andrus had a guard posted at every cell. They had to check on the prisoners more or less continuously through tiny portholes in each cell door. Before prisoners returned to their very sparse cells they had to remove belts, suspenders, shoelaces, and so on — in short, anything that might be used to commit suicide. Guards were ordered to keep the head and hands of prisoners in view at all times, including when they tried to sleep (on their backs only) during the night. Prisoners were generally isolated from the outside world and not allowed newspapers. Their mail, even with family members, was censored, and they were allowed to move outside their cells only for meals, talks with their lawyers, and a daily exercise period. During those times the defendants colluded whenever possible, in order to plan their strategies against the prosecution. Guards generally did not communicate with the prisoners, even though Colonel Andrus, unbeknownst to them, had recruited some German-speaking GIs for guard duty. They were to report to him anything they found suspicious or that might be useful in the trials. The prisoners were virtually cut off from human contact, except for their defense attorneys, so that it is not surprising they were willing to talk to the psychiatrists and psychologists who worked in the medical detachment of the 685th Internal Security Detachment (ISD) of the U.S. chief counsel in Nuremberg. The doctors had more or less free access at all times.

When Leon Goldensohn was posted to Nuremburg, he was thirty-four years old. Born on October 19, 1911, in New York City, he received a B.A. from Ohio State in 1932 and an M.D. from George Washington University School of Medicine in 1936. He trained in neurology at Montefiore Hospital in New York City and in psychiatry at the William Alanson White Institute of Psychiatry. At the end of the war, Major Goldensohn was assigned to the 121st General Hospital in Nuremberg, and on January 3, 1946, to the 685th Internal Security Detachment. He served as prison psychiatrist until July 26, 1946—which was close to the end of the defense hearings.

In the immediate wake of the defeat of Germany in the spring of 1945, and into the summer, when the International Military Tribunal was announced, there was enormous interest in "what made those Nazis tick."[30] Kelley referred to the "psychological treasure" he and psychologist Gustave Gilbert had at their fingertips, and initially the plan was to publish a Kelley-Gilbert book.[31] Captain Gilbert was an American intelligence officer. He was fluent in German and managed to get an assignment as translator for Major Kelley. He was also a trained psychologist and soon convinced Colonel Andrus to appoint him "official" prison psychologist. Gilbert was apparently of one mind with Kelley, and saw the war criminals "as available to him as laboratory mice."[32] In addition to reporters, psychiatrists and psychologists from around the world tried to gain access to the prisoners. Goldensohn, like Kelley and Gilbert, likely became the envy of his professional peers and the many reporters, all eager to interview the defendants.[33]

The plan for the Kelley-Gilbert book never came to fruition. But Kelley published his own book in 1947. It remains useful in a limited way, though it is now quite dated.[34] His former coworker Gilbert also published a book, which appeared several months after Kelley's. It took the format of a diary, and with it readers can follow the course of the trial from the author's experiences and perspective.[35]

Goldensohn too had intended to write a book. He never wrote it, but his notes survived. Some of these transcripts were typed up not long after the interviews were held. Any plans for a book came to a halt when the doctor died prematurely at age fifty from a coronary heart attack, on October 24, 1961. But a few small notebooks were typed up later under the supervision of Dr. Goldensohn's brother, Dr. Eli Goldensohn, who collated and organized all the original materials. What we have in this volume is an edited and abridged selection of some of Goldensohn's interviews with nineteen defendants and fourteen witnesses.

We are indebted to Goldensohn for his conscientious note taking. Whereas psychologist Gilbert would jot down his impressions at the end of the day, and in that sense relied more on his memory to reconstruct conversations and impressions, psychiatrist Goldensohn insisted on taking detailed notes. Although he spoke little German himself, some of his interviewees knew English and he was able to converse freely with them. However, in his formal interviews he wanted to have the defendants and witnesses express themselves fully in their own language, and so he strongly preferred to employ the services of Howard H. Triest, a translator. He duly recorded both his questions and the defendants' answers, writing these down as he went.

Gilbert's fluency in German would have facilitated conversation with the prisoners, most of whom were talkative and eager for human contact. And yet some prisoners felt that Gilbert hated them, certainly that he entertained dark thoughts about them. One said he taunted them — for example, with pictures of hanged Nazi war criminals in *Stars and Stripes*, assuring them they were going to get the same treatment. The prisoners generally seemed to have had a kindlier attitude toward Goldensohn, whom they considered more detached and professional. On some occasions he and Gilbert made their rounds together, with Gilbert acting as translator.

Goldensohn shared the belief of the times in the "pathology" of the leading Nazis and, though gentle in his approach, was especially interested in trying to account for their "depravities." There was never any pretense of doctor-patient confidentiality, and none was apparently expected by the prisoners. Not all of them were happy with this situation, but the majority seemed resigned to the fact that they were "material" for various book projects. Today, with our concerns about privacy, it might seem troubling that a medical doctor would openly and repeatedly ask one prisoner what he thought of another. On occasion an interviewee might ask Goldensohn to keep something in confidence, but he was not inclined to give any such assurance. Like the other doctors on the American team, Goldensohn saw the Nazi prisoners as subjects to be studied, and rather secondarily, if at all, as patients. He explicitly referred in his interview notes to the "subjects" of his investigations. The prisoners, on the other hand, used their conversations with the doctors as an opportunity to air statements or approaches they would soon use in their defense before the tribunal. Goldensohn was certainly aware of that and even encouraged it. In conversation with the Americans, the defendants rarely let their guard down, especially when it came to confessing to crimes as charged, because they worried that what they said could be used against them in court. Prisoners who resented these professionals accused them of being more interested in collecting material for the books they were all writing than in providing care.[36]

Goldensohn saw the defendants almost every day, but what sets his record apart from the others is his persistent effort to hold formal and often extended interviews. He recorded everything he could of psychiatric and human interest. We can read what the accused and the witnesses had to say about the role of a given defendant in certain specific events, all the way down to details about his family and medical history. Goldensohn asked them what they thought of certain leaders, like Hitler, and even how they regarded one another and their crimes, as well as how they performed before the tribunal on any given day. He followed up with many questions, sometimes to the point of infuriating his subjects, but he kept on digging and digging. He claimed he did not want to cross-examine the defendants, but in fact during these one-on-one encounters, he sometimes did. He often went over a defendant's testimony in court, noting, for example, parts of it that he did not find credible or difficult to understand. In some of these exchanges, Goldensohn was harder to satisfy than the prosecutor in the court.

Goldensohn generally did not record casual conversations, only his formal interviews through the medium of a translator. The note taking and translation meant that the defendants rarely got carried away. Instead, they had plenty of time to think rationally about how to answer Goldensohn's questions, and perhaps that was precisely what the doctor wanted.

A crucial point to keep in mind is that each of the accused was on trial for his life. Like anyone indicted on serious crimes, these men were determined to exculpate themselves. (In at least one important philosophical tradition, every person, no matter how heinous his crimes, reserves a natural right to fight for his life.) For most of the defendants, who were essentially deprived of most legal rights (certainly as these are commonly understood under the United States Constitution), the note taking of Goldensohn must have set off alarm bells. The accused were not protected against self-incrimination, nor were their lawyers present, and it was not unreasonable for them to assume that they might end up in court being faced by their very own words as noted by Dr. Goldensohn. That never happened, but at the very least we have to keep in mind that the defendants would have been uncertain about the status of these interviews, which were not protected by doctor-patient confidentiality. Goldensohn may have regarded himself as a doctor and a scientist first, but from the point of view of any of the accused, he was one of the victors, while they were the vanquished, and so they had to treat him as if he were a member of the prosecution's team. He assured them they had nothing to worry about and that they could talk freely, but he could not give them any real basis for believing him.

The defendants generally tried to get away with everything they could, and as one of them suggested, they sometimes succeeded. That claim was made by Hitler's architect Speer, often regarded as the shrewdest observer among the defendants. He was not pleased at the end of the trial when he saw that Fritzsche, Papen, and Schacht got off, while he was given twenty years. He noted in his diary that their "lies, smokescreens, and dissembling statements had paid off after all." Speer resented not being exonerated by the court, but it was certainly not because he had failed to lie or to cover up the truth.[37] Speer and no doubt other defendants resented people like Goldensohn and Gilbert. So far as we can tell, Speer gave Goldensohn no more than a brief and tersely worded statement (included in this volume). He accused Gilbert of being "always eager to add to his psychological knowledge." In answer to Gilbert's question about his sentence, Speer lied when he said the twenty years he got "was fair enough. They couldn't have given me a lighter sentence, considering the facts, and I can't complain."[38] By his own later admission, Speer was not telling the truth, for in fact he felt unjustly treated by the court.

We can multiply such examples of the cover-ups many times, but they do not mean that everything said by the defendants and witnesses is a pack of lies. In fact what is remarkable is how often the interviews are candid accounts and sometimes even shockingly truthful. At various points at least some defendants and witnesses admit the commission of heinous crimes, even if they also try to offload the guilt to someone else. Their excuses, reasoning, and attempts to avoid the legal consequences of their actions are of interest in their own right. Sometimes we can see that Goldensohn was misled, did not fully grasp the importance of some piece of information, or missed telling clues. In spite of everything, the defendants revealed a great deal about themselves and what attracted them to Hitler and Nazism.

I was contacted by the publisher and asked to edit the interviews. I have done so as carefully as possible. I corrected obvious mistakes, such as dates, and errors in the spelling of names, places, and ranks, all of which were sometimes quite garbled.[39] Goldensohn never reached the stage of checking for and correcting errors in the facts, dates, and names mentioned in an interview, and I have tried to verify everything possible. He sometimes made simple mistakes when taking notes about an interviewee's social, educational, and military experiences. I have put right obvious slips in so far as I could identify them, but some inaccuracies undoubtedly remain. These I trust are not the kinds of mistakes that will detract from the substance of the testimony provided in the interview.

Whenever it has been possible to do so, I have tried to keep the text as close as possible to the original. However, I have also had to make many stylistic changes in order to clarify the prose. I cut the interviews in places where there were obvious repetitions and overlaps, such as when one session went over the same ground as an earlier one. In order to keep the manuscript to a manageable size I also had to exclude entire interviews with some defendants and many witnesses, but my intention was to include whatever was of more importance for the historical record. Sometimes I had to make extensive changes, in order to be true to the substance of what was being communicated by the defendants. Some problems arose from translation difficulties, others from Goldensohn's misinterpretation of what he was being told, for example about the operation of the German political system. Like every editor, I have had to rely on my professional judgment, based on my own and others' research, when trying to resolve issues of interpretation that were not clear-cut.

I have not tried to correct every error or obvious untruth that Goldensohn unwittingly recorded. Sometimes the interviewees played down their own role or their knowledge, or simply tried to rationalize the crimes. Some also tried to minimize their own crimes by maintaining that they were fighting a defensive or preventive war. Some reminded Goldensohn of what the Allies, especially the Russians, did to the Germans during the latter part of war. It is not possible to deal with every single such episode, but we have to be aware of the problem of deliberate falsifications and unconscious untruths.

In the notes to the interviews I provide some guidance and references for readers. I also supply basic information on notable figures and events mentioned in the text when I feel it is necessary. As well, I address the most obvious and important falsehoods, denials, and fabrications, or the repetition of unfounded myths and rumors. I provide more accurate information on some important issues, for example, on the Nazi takeover of power and the number of Jews who were murdered.

Some of the interviewees and Goldensohn himself mention that 5 million Jews were murdered in the Third Reich. Where did they get that number? In fact, that was the figure usually put forward by the prosecution at Nuremberg. For example, American prosecutor Jackson mentioned in his opening statement to the tribunal that out "of 9,600,000 Jews who lived in Nazi dominated Europe, sixty percent are authoritatively estimated to have perished. 5,700,000 Jews are missing from the countries in which they formerly lived, and over 4,500,000 cannot be accounted for by the normal death rate."[40] Later in the trial itself the prosecution tended to round off the number at 5 million.

At various points during the trial, as well as in Justice Jackson's final remarks and in the tribunal's judgment, the larger figure of 6 million victims was also used. One notable witness on this topic was Wilhelm Hoettl, whose testimony appears to have been followed in the judgment. However, he had at best secondhand knowledge. He said in court (and added in a separate affidavit) that he had asked Adolf Eichmann at the end of August 1944 about the number of Jews who had been killed.[41] Eichmann replied that he had recently reported to Himmler that around 4 million Jews had been killed in the camps and another 2 million had died in various ways, especially by shooting. According to Hoettl's recollection of what Eichmann said, Himmler had guessed that even more Jews had been killed by that time. Today most historians would suggest that the numbers apparently given by Eichmann and repeated by

Hoettl in court were likely too high, certainly for the period ending in August 1944.

Several historians, most importantly Raul Hilberg in his definitive account of the destruction of the European Jews, put the figure at just over 5.3 million.[42] Hilberg shows the number of those murdered at Auschwitz at around 1 million, which is staggering, but well below the figure estimated at the trial by Commandant Rudolf Hoess. That larger figure — between 2.5 million and 3 million — though unreliable, continues to be cited, even in scholarly studies of Auschwitz, up to the present day.[43] We need to get the figures as accurately as possible and thereby close the doors to the deniers and the revisionists.

We can also read the interviews from the point of view of what they tell us about the general understandings of Nazism and the Third Reich that existed at that moment on the American side. Goldensohn, for example, fully accepted one of the key American charges, namely that the Nazis had engaged in a wide-ranging conspiracy to commit various crimes, including crimes against peace, war crimes, and crimes against humanity, as these were defined in the charter of the trial. He accepted the view that a vast conspiracy began more or less at the beginning of the Third Reich and continued into the war years. Few historians today would agree with such an "intentionalist" approach to the Third Reich, and most subscribe to the view that many policies, including the policy to murder all the Jews in Europe, were improvised and decided only well into the Second World War. We have had a great deal more time to carry out research into the decision-making process, but beyond that most of us now have different understandings of the Third Reich than did Goldensohn and his contemporaries.

Newer research has made it possible for us to see some of the important documentation presented at Nuremberg in a fuller light and from new perspectives. Sometimes we can see far more in certain documents today than could the Nuremberg prosecution or the judges, who were at times overwhelmed. One of many clever tactics of the defense was to bury the tribunal in a sea of documents, affidavits, and eyewitness testimony.[44] Only much later have we been able to figure out what was meant by some of those who testified at the trial — and others repeated the point in the interviews with Goldensohn — that the Nazis had plans to wipe out 30 million people. There would have been in fact not one, but serial genocides.[45] Key documents about these plans were submitted at the trial, but the whole matter was not fully comprehended.

Although Goldensohn generally kept a neutral demeanor during the interviews, he definitely made his own judgments clear, including his profound skepticism regarding many of the explanations offered by the defendants. Some of his offhand reactions could be quite sharp, as we learn from another source.[46] For example, he interviewed Otto Ohlendorf, who was not among the major war criminals, but who appeared as a witness at this trial. (He was later tried and executed.) Ohlendorf had been head of Action Group D — that is, Einsatzgruppe D — which by his own testimony was responsible for the murder of at least ninety thousand people, most of them Jews.[47] This was one of four such Nazi death squads in the East, but in fact there were many more.[48] He liked to regard himself as one of the "intellectual" leaders of the Security Service (SD), and also thought of himself as an "idealist" and not even an anti-Semite. Therefore, he was particularly bothered one day when Goldensohn accused him of being some kind of sadist, pervert, or lunatic. What other explanation was there, the doctor asked, to explain how Ohlendorf — a man who prided himself on such "integrity and incorruptibility" — could have ordered the murder of so many completely innocent men, women, and children?[49]

As readers will see from the interviews, Goldensohn was not usually quite so blunt, but he does seem to have arrived at Nuremberg convinced that some, perhaps many, Nazis were sadists, even those who did not engage directly in cruel actions. Goldensohn, who wanted answers to his queries about the nature of Nazism, could also be somewhat intrusive in his interviewing technique. He was certainly not shy about trying to pin down defendants when he found their statements unsatisfactory or contradictory, though generally he pulled back when he found himself engaging in too much cross-examination.

With the exception of Rudolf Hess, and in the later stages of the trials, possibly Hans Frank, the defendants at Nuremberg were anything but mentally ill. Alas, most of them were all too "normal," and excluding Hess, they were mentally competent throughout their careers. Most of them turned out to be "good family men," and many had been highly educated or had received some kind of professional training. An intelligence test administered by Dr. Gilbert showed that all defendants but one (Streicher) "were above average intelligence" — average being an IQ that measured between 90 and 110. Of the twenty-one tested, seven had IQs as high as the 130s and two more reached the 140s.[50] These once all-powerful "Reich leaders" resented the idea of being examined by their captors in this way, but as soon as the intelligence test started each of them strove "to do the best he could on it and see his abilities confirmed."[51]

**Nuremberg as Unfinished Project**

There were an additional twelve follow-up trials at Nuremberg between December 1946 and April 1949. Whereas, in the first great trials, the judges and prosecution were drawn from the three Allied powers and France, in the follow-up trials, the United States acted alone against specific individuals and groups who were accused of actually carrying out the crimes.[52] These latter trials were particularly important for bringing to light the broader social participation in human rights abuses and involvement in war crimes and mass murder. Still more trials took place over the years in Germany as each of the occupying powers — the United States, Great Britain, the Soviet Union, and France — prosecuted the Nazis on various counts.[53] The Germans themselves have also prosecuted various crimes committed in the Third Reich, and even though the "politics" of war crimes trials was and remains extremely complex, they have intermittently continued to do so right up to the present.[54]

It was the first great Nuremberg trials of the major war criminals, however, that really shocked public opinion. Although Allied governments had publicized examples of Nazi atrocities during the course of the Second World War, including the mass murder of the Jews, there was a tendency to write off many of these stories as similar to the exaggerated propaganda that was heard about the Germans in the First World War. At the very least, therefore, the massive documentation presented at Nuremberg made the crimes abundantly clear.

The general public, including people inside Germany, were unprepared for what they learned, but on balance favored the trials and learned a great deal from them.[55] We still find it difficult to believe the full extent of the human rights abuses, the sheer scale of the murderousness, and the depths of the unspeakable cruelties.

In the United States, Great Britain, and elsewhere, legal positivists have generally maintained that the trials were invalid because they were not based on existing international law. This position was rejected by pragmatic natural law theorists, who insisted, to the contrary, that the trials were necessary in that civilization had to protect itself in the face of such unprecedented criminality. These two approaches continue to be used in the scholarly debate and they are important for our understanding of contemporary issues such as the debates about the new International Criminal Court (ICC) in The Hague.[56] In 1945, all legal and philosophical objections were overruled, and the trials went ahead, more or less as the pragmatic natural law theorists wished.[57]

— ROBERT GELLATELY

## HOW THE NUREMBERG INTERVIEWS
## WERE OBTAINED AND PRESERVED

Leon Goldensohn's extensive notes, taken in the prisoners' cells during the Nuremberg interviews, were handwritten in notebooks. Each interview was typed within a few days. When Leon left the Army in 1946, he brought his papers back and kept them in his New York City apartment until 1950 and subsequently in his Tenafly, New Jersey, home until his death in 1961.

For many years after Leon's death, his widow, Irene, kept the notebooks, the typed interviews, the lecture notes, and other related materials (including his personal correspondence) intact in their home.

In 1970, when she moved to a small apartment in nearby Fort Lee, she sold most of her library to a dealer from Englewood. Inadvertently included in this lot were several books written by some of the defendants and purchased by Leon in a Nuremberg store. The books were autographed — some authors had written short messages addressed to Leon on the frontispiece; others simply signed their names. These books were purchased later from the Englewood dealer by Dr. John Lattimer (a colleague of mine at the Columbia-Presbyterian Medical Center in New York City). Dr. Lattimer asked if I could tell him about the "Major Goldensohn" on the frontispieces. I explained to him that Leon was my brother, and we had several pleasant meetings, in which I supplied him with information about Leon. Dr. Lattimer sent me photocopies of the frontispieces for my possible use.

In 1983 Irene gave all the remaining Nuremberg materials to her children. In 1994 — responding to my long-standing offer to review the work and discuss possible publication for it — two of Leon's children (Daniel, of San Francisco, California; and Julia, of Jackson, Wyoming) agreed to send me all their material, which arrived piecemeal over a period of several months.

The original typed interviews and original carbon copies are now in my safe deposit box in the M&T Bank in Nyack, New York. Leon's plans for publication, discussed in his letters from abroad, his later lecture notes, and six of his many notebooks are also in my care.

— ELI GOLDENSOHN

## PART ONE

# DEFENDANTS

# Karl Doenitz
## 1891–1980

Karl Doenitz was grand admiral, commander in chief of the navy from 1943. In Hitler's last testament Doenitz was appointed the Führer's designated successor. He was sentenced at Nuremberg to ten years' imprisonment for crimes against peace and war crimes.

## March 3, 1946

Spent afternoon with Karl Doenitz. He is polite, affable in a half-suspicious way, speaks fairly perfect English, but must be given his own reins or he shuts up with mouth firmly compressed. I inquired after his health. He asked me to be seated, made room on his cot for me. We talked of his rheumatism, which is particularly annoying in his left wrist. There is a slight swelling of the left wrist compared with the right, but no marked difference. He asked what I thought of the trials and I said that I had been rather busy in the past few days and had not attended the sessions regularly.

The past week's sessions have been concerned mainly with the indictments against the various organizations. "Your Judge Francis Biddle," said Doenitz, "he sees clearly, very clearly.[1] Did you hear him ask the prosecutors all those questions?" I replied that I had heard some. Doenitz is very impressed with Biddle, who he says towers above the rest of the judges. "He has that little smile about his lips," he said, "when he is listening to something that is questionable. An admirable man. Very fair and sharp." I responded that Biddle was an excellent man, was one of the Roosevelt cabinet. I made that remark quite pointedly, as there has been some talk of bringing anti-Roosevelt propaganda into the defenses when they get started next week.

Doenitz liked particularly the question Biddle asked Justice Robert H. Jackson about how far the responsibility for criminal acts would go, in the event the organizations were found criminal. Doenitz feels it is "very dangerous" to make these organizations criminal because so many thousands of people belonged to them, and every German had at least a relative belonging to the SA, SD, SS, and so forth. "You know what your General Lucius Clay said.[2] He said that should this tribunal find the organizations guilty, he must immediately arrest 500,000 Germans." I replied that I had not been aware of General Clay's statement, but that Justice Jackson had made it quite clear that he did not intend for all members of these organizations to go on trial, but that the leadership and certain individuals be brought to justice.[3] This point was ignored by Doenitz, as it is ignored by Baldur von Schirach, and Wilhelm Frick, and the others to whom I've spoken in the last few days.

We talked of many things. Doenitz's plans for the future, for instance, consist of "I will get myself a little room, and isolate myself with my wife, and I will write my memoirs. I think I should do this for the German people. So they can see for themselves what things went on and how little those of us in the leadership knew about Hitler and Heinrich Himmler's atrocities."[4]

It is hard for an American to understand, said Doenitz, but the watchword of Hitler was "Mind your own business and just do the job you have." Therefore Doenitz knew nothing about plans for an aggressive war, nothing about extermination of the Jews, nothing about the plans for extermination of 30 million Slavs, nothing of the atrocities in Russia and Poland. "I do know that the Russians did the same things when they went through East Prussia." I challenged this by asking how he knew this and what evidence he had. He admitted it was not firsthand information but that much had been carried in the Nazi press about Russian atrocities and some of it was undoubtedly true.

He feels he has had a "hard life." He was in the last war, and at its end was a lieutenant in the submarine division. He remained in the navy all through the years. He went all over the world, but strangely never went to America. He feels this was unfortunate, and he would have liked to see the United States. He has been to Japan and all around the globe. From 1918, until he was summoned by Admiral Erich Raeder in 1935 to reorganize the submarine service, he served on cruisers and other naval craft.[5] It was a tough assignment and one he was quite surprised to get. He remarks on Raeder's telling him he was in charge of submarines and submarine training. He had been out of touch with submarine developments for so long, and there were only young men in the navy, and he had to brush up on the whole subject.

From that time forth he was in submarines daily. "It wasn't good for my rheumatism," he said, "to be in dampness, oil and water, all the time."

Until 1943 he saw Hitler once every two years. After 1943 he saw Hitler twice a month. In the last few months he was in frequent contact with the Fuehrer. When he was informed that the latter had committed suicide and he had been chosen as Hitler's successor as chief of state, he decided to sue for peace "at once, which I did." I said that if I recalled the radio correctly at the time, it was announced at first that Germany would surrender to the British and Americans but not to the Russians. He assented. It was just a token gesture, he said. He knew it was impossible. He did not consider himself Hitler's successor. He felt that he had been selected to sue for peace and arrange the surrender because only a non-political figure could do it. That was the reason he accepted the designation as Hitler's successor as chief of state.

I asked him what he thought of the "Fuehrer principle." He said he had never been in favor of it because a man always needs a "corrective." That is why a chief of state needs a chief of staff and other advisers. Did he oppose Hitler in any way, by any actions or expressed opinions? No. He was a man of the sea and that was all.

Most of the atrocities, he believes, were committed by Austrians, or at least by Bavarians. He seems to dislike Bavarians more than he does Austrians. "They are choleric." He explained this by stating that the Bavarians were overly emotional. For instance, if a group of northern Germans went sleigh riding and the stick between the sleigh and the horse broke going up the mountain, the northern Germans would get out and proceed to repair the stick. But the Bavarian driver would get out, rave and rant, take the broken stick, and wildly beat it against a rock, saying: "You bad stick, you terrible stick!" and so on. He laughed at this description. What about the northern character? I asked.

"The north German is slow, quiet, thinks, maybe stupid." He smiled as he said this. He was obviously trying to give a self-characterization. "The north German does not go in for extremes. He has broader horizons than the men from the mountains of Bavaria and Austria."

I asked him whether he felt that Hermann Goering, too, knew nothing of what went on regarding plans for war, atrocities, and extermination programs. He said he believes Goering is telling the truth and does not know more than he says he knew. "I realize how impossible that must sound to an American. It could not happen in a democracy. But in our type of government, it was possible."

Joachim von Ribbentrop, he feels, is "like a man of wood." He will not express much opinion regarding him, except that "when these trials began, you know, Ribbentrop said his memory was impaired because of sleeping pills." I replied that it was rather improbable that a man's memory could be seriously damaged because of sedatives. Doenitz laughed and said he hardly thought it was likely, either. "My lawyer is a good one. He will show in my defense that I hardly knew any of these men. Ribbentrop I met a couple of times, the first time in 1943, I think. Schirach I met for the first time, I believe, in 1944."

He feels that his lawyer, a naval judge, is very capable. When he was informed that he would have to have a defense counsel, he knew of no one. Then he recalled having been present at a hearing where this naval officer had presided, before the war, concerning an incident in which responsibility was to be placed for the ramming of a naval boat. "I liked the way he handled that affair, so I requested Otto Kranzbuehler. I must say I am not disappointed in him. And the British and Americans are doing everything in their power to assist me in my defense. Last week my second defense counsel, also formerly a naval officer, was flown to London and granted every courtesy to get documents in my behalf. He is expected back this week.

"Did you know," Doenitz continued, "that the British judge, Sir Geoffrey Lawrence, sent me a letter which the court had received from about a hundred U-boat commanders now interned in England, in which they made an affidavit that I had never ordered the shooting of survivors of sunken boats, but that quite the contrary was true?"

Regarding the projected plan for the future, after his release from prison, I queried: What will the theme of your memoirs be? Well, he said in substance, I will take them all through my life, during the empire, during the Weimar Republic days, through the Third Reich days. His main theme, he believes, will be that there should be a United States of Europe, under the direction of Great Britain. "A commonwealth of nations of Europe," he said, "to band together and balance Russia in the east." I asked whether he thought that was actually going to happen. He replied that it was his idea, and that it was not a new idea to him. If Britain should do such a thing, she must invite Germany to be a member of this commonwealth of nations. He said that Germany must do this, because her culture is related to the West and not to the East, like Russian culture.

I asked him whether he was still thinking in terms of a balance of power. Yes, definitely. I asked whether he felt a war with the East was not implicit in his recommendation as to a united commonwealth of Europe to balance the weight of Russia. He replied that he had no idea of what to expect in that regard, but he was not thinking of a war with Russia in recommending a united Europe which would be a commonwealth under British protection.

He asked me where I lived and I told him. He wanted to know if it were a hotel. I said that it was formerly an apartment house. He sighed. "I'm an old man at fifty-four, without teeth, and with rheumatism." He explained by saying that he had mostly false teeth, and that he felt his useful life was more or less passed. "My wife will have to work to get bread for us while I write my memoirs," he said whimsically.

I don't believe this man has any notion of what is going on in the world. He is acute, in no ways dull, but his mind seems to have blocked out the salient features of the trials thus far. He rejects the atrocities, the killing of millions of Jews, the barbarism of the SS, the entire criminal modus operandi of the Nazi Party. He sees only that he was innocent of any crime, past or present, and that any attempt to incriminate him or any of the others on trial with him is political connivery. He feels Germany's actions were the result of oppression after the last war, on the one hand, and on the other takes no cognizance of his own culpability in being a faithful servant to Hitler and his regime. He denies atrocities at sea, and is still doubtful about them on land. What about the evidence? I asked. "Yes," he replied, "Dr. Douglas Kelley and Dr. Gustave Gilbert both said to me when that film was shown, where the people of Weimar had to go to see Buchenwald, that it was evident from the people's faces that they knew nothing of what went on there. In the film their faces were merry as they walked to Buchenwald. When they left the place you could see they were broken."

I asked whether that film itself wasn't sufficient evidence as to war crimes and their existence and the atrocities of the Nazi regime. Did he accept that film as documentary and true? Yes, of course, he said, but regarding the other atrocities he was doubtful still. "That just shows you how much we in the leadership knew of what was transpiring."

During the interview he drew for me a one-man torpedo and explained its workings. I told him that I'd heard it was practically a suicide venture for the pilot. He agreed, but said it was a very effective weapon when the enemy was near shore and implied that it was worth a life to get a big battleship or other craft. I said I wouldn't like to be the pilot of one of those one-man torpedoes. He laughed and said, "To get a big ship, it's worth it."

As I left when called to the phone, he wrote on the paper on which he had drawn the submarine torpedo (in German), "To a pleasant afternoon's conversation," and signed his name. He said he had enjoyed the talk very much and I should drop in again.

**May 2, 1946**
I visited Doenitz this evening. Hjalmar Schacht had been on the stand all day. Doenitz smiled and asked me where I had been all week. I explained that I had flown to London and visited there for five days. He wanted to know how things were in England, the sentiment of the people, what they thought of the trials, was London very much destroyed, and so forth. I explained that my impression was based on a very short stay, and that all I could say was that things seemed better than when I was in London last year about the same time. As far as public opinion concerning the trials, I really didn't know. The British press seemed to give the trials more space than the American papers.

"Ah. What did they have to say about Julius Streicher's defense? Did they have much to say about the beginning of Schacht's case, or were you in London then?" I said that apparently adequate coverage of the trial in the London newspapers was being given the public as I could follow the events in Nuremberg quite reasonably by reading the London *Times*. "Have you noticed the difference between some Englishmen and others? Some look like north Germans. Others are more like Bavarians or easterners." I remarked that I had not paid much attention to these differences.

"I can see it in the court. Most of the time I don't pay much attention to what is being hashed over and over again by defense and prosecution. It doesn't interest me. I watch the faces of the judges. Biddle has a very intelligent, sympathetic face. All the other judges, with the exception of the Frenchmen and the Russians, who are like stone men, watch Biddle and react according to what he whispers in Lawrence's ear. Justice Lawrence is probably trying to conduct the case fairly, but it is Biddle who steps in and makes the Russian prosecution behave decently when it is on one of its wild accusations."

What did Doenitz think of Streicher's defense? "I didn't listen. I drew pictures and watched Biddle." And of Schacht's case? "Well, I don't want to start any camps among us defendants. Schacht is wrong about Hitler. He didn't have to come out so strongly against him. If Schacht knew all along about Hitler ordering the exterminations, why didn't he say so before this trial? I personally don't think Hitler ordered it, despite his last testament."[6] I replied that he was expressing almost verbatim the opinion of Goering, who had the same idea and told me it was probably Martin Bormann who did it in Hitler's name.[7]

Doenitz did not particularly cherish the idea that he had said something which seemed to come out of Goering's mouth. "I'm not a politician. I was a corvette captain when the war started. I hardly knew Hitler until 1942. He always seemed reasonable and his demands seemed for the good of Germany. Now I see that he had too little consideration for other peoples, such as the Jews, or neighbor states. But I never had any idea of the goings-on as far as Jews were concerned. Hitler said each man should take care of his own business, and mine was U-boats and the navy."

As usual, Doenitz turned to a discussion of his own case and the ridiculousness of it. "It's so ridiculous. That American navy officer who presented the case against me did me a favor. My best witnesses were the prosecution's witnesses. It amounts to this: If a submarine torpedoes a boat and can safely take survivors, well and good. But if the submarine is in danger and must leave the scene immediately, survivors can't be rescued. That is as true in the English and American navies as in the German."

He repeated anew his theme about his being apolitical and merely a sailor doing his job. If Germany had won the war there would certainly have been a clamping down on the Nazi Party power, he said. Soldiers and sailors returning to their homes would not allow themselves to be bossed by a block leader, but would want freedom. Probably the National Socialist government would have collapsed soon after a German victory.[8]

Was it not likely that if Hitler had won the war, he would have been politically even stronger than ever? "No. I don't think so. Not after I see what crimes went on in the name of the party, the exterminations, the wholesale murders. No. I think a military party would have come into power almost at once."

I remarked that it seemed to me he was quite satisfied with Hitler in every way if he accepted the leadership of Germany from Hitler after the latter's suicide. "Is that a crime? Is to accept the leadership of a crumbling country a crime? Is to prevent the Russians, the natural enemy of Germany, from obtaining our arms and manpower a crime? In Russian eyes it probably is. But I'm referring to the eyes of a westerner. I knew that we had to capitulate and I wanted it to be to the Americans and British, and not to the East. I'm not even accused of war crimes in the sense of the atrocities. It's clear they have no case against me. I came into a powerful position in 1943. How can I be accused of a conspiracy?

"They have only one point against me — that I gave an order not to rescue survivors. That that was false was proven by the prosecution and its own witness. I also give credit to my lawyer, who is very sharp, critical, and alert. The trial can only end in a mistake because it is founded on one. How can a foreign court try a sovereign government of another country? Could we have tried your President Franklin Delano Roosevelt and Secretary Henry Morgenthau, or Winston Churchill and Anthony Eden, if we had won the war? We could not have done so and would not have. Any trying that went on would have to be done by the nation itself and the courts set up there."

Doenitz became quite excited and his voice rose. "To think of Russians sitting on a bench in Nuremberg, trying German leaders! The Russians sank a German boat with men, women, and children aboard. I know of the case. But is that investigated? You Americans were not completely without fault, either. You armed merchant boats before the U.S.A. was in the war."

I replied that it was not my purpose to debate with him, but that I merely wanted his views so that I could try to understand his actions. He smiled suspiciously. "And write a book about me, telling the world what a stupid fellow I am, eh?" I assured him that if I wrote anything it would have to be approved by proper authorities, and that it was neither my purpose nor aim to portray him as anything but what he actually was.

One of the things which did puzzle me, I said, was Hitler's choosing him as his successor. "Hitler chose me because he felt, doubtlessly, that only a reasonable man with an honest reputation as a sailor could make a decent peace. I gladly accepted. Why not? I didn't know then about Hitler's extermination of Jews, which I learned about for the first time in Nuremberg."

Did Doenitz know of persecutions of Jews at all? "Yes and no. I read sometime around 1938 of Jewish fines and some street actions against them.[9] But I was too concerned with U-boats and the naval problems to be concerned about Jews." Was he concerned about the fate of these Jews now? "My conscience is clear. I did not participate in the brutalities or criminal actions. My aiding Hitler in carrying on a war for my Fatherland does not make me subject to the criticism that I helped him annihilate Jews. It just is not the case."

Had Doenitz known of the concentration camps? "Yes. I knew there were such things in 1933 and 1934. But there were only about twelve thousand people, political enemies, in them at the time.[10] Now in American-occupied Germany alone there are over 600,000 Germans interned. Have you ever thought of that?" He smiled as if he had scored a point.

Then I was correct in understanding that he felt the concentration camps were justified? "In a measure they were justified. If Hitler had not thrown the Communists into camps in 1933 there would have been civil war and bloodshed. The Communists would have revolted against the legally elected government. The greatest danger of civil war in Germany came in 1932 when it was clearly a choice between Communism and National Socialism. So Paul von Hindenburg and the other conservative bourgeois elements chose Hitler. So did I, and I would do it again if a choice between Communism and Nazism arose." He went on to explain that those were revolutionary times, and the herding together into concentration camps of a few thousand political opponents was not a particularly bad thing. "By placing these people with foreign ideas in camps, German blood was saved. Would it have been better to have a civil war?"

**July 14, 1946**
The former grand admiral was lying on his cot with a handkerchief over his head and forehead when I entered his cell. He arose with alacrity and said he was glad to see me, and asked what was new in the world. I

replied that there was nothing striking in the radio news I had heard this morning. He said he had a slight cold, which he attributed to the draft coming into the cell from the open window through the open square vent in the door.

He spoke with his usual incisive evasiveness. Tomorrow his defense counsel, Kranzbuehler, would speak in the final summation of his defense. "A very critical fellow, my lawyer," said Doenitz. "And he tells me that as far as crimes are concerned, the defense is clear and the prosecution hasn't a leg to stand on." His lawyer also told him a few weeks ago, when he was through with his defense, that the chief of staff of an American admiral, who was visiting the trials, had personally conveyed his greetings to Doenitz. "Your American admiral said that he held me in the highest esteem, and thought that I conducted my defense perfectly. He said through his chief of staff that my conduct was beyond reproach and he had the greatest admiration for me."

I recalled seeing a party of naval officers at Doenitz's defense presentation, but I did not know the name of the American admiral. Doenitz did not know his name either, but stressed the importance of the greeting he had received through his lawyer.

"The Russians will cause trouble for you. You will see. I know those Russians. Ernest Bevin said that the Potsdam Agreement was the greatest folly.[11] Harold Laski, the head of the English Labor Party, also said that the borders drawn up by the three powers at Potsdam was a great mistake." Doenitz proceeded to draw a map of Europe on a pad, and the demarcation line between the Russian and the American-British zones. "All of the wheat and potatoes, the very granaries of Germany, lie in the Russian zone. They will never withdraw their troops. They will spread Communism. They will never withdraw from the Balkans either. Poor Turkey is now completely surrounded by Russians. Everything the Russians have done in the past year shows clearly that they are lining up against the western powers, namely against the U.S.A. and Great Britain.

"The Russians make an accusation against me that I sent our armies and navies to the West when I took over command of Germany after Hitler's death. Well, let me tell you, General Dwight Eisenhower and especially General Bedell Smith and Field Marshal Bernard Montgomery were very grateful at the time that I didn't let the Russians get hold of our fleet and 3 million German soldiers and their weapons. It was very clear to me at the time that if I sent the fleet to Leningrad to surrender, for example, or let 3 million soldiers be captured by the Russians, the latter would be that much stronger, and in the end German soldiers would be fighting against Germany."

Russia was the greatest threat to world peace, said Doenitz, and he quoted articles read in the *Reader's Digest* written by Joseph Kennedy, the former American ambassador to England, and other articles.

Did Doenitz believe another war was probable? He replied, shrugging his shoulders, "No. Quite impossible. With the new weapons like the atom bomb, Russia would have it, too, and use it first. It is a very difficult world. But that trouble is imminent is obvious. The *Herald Tribune* had a cartoon which I saw recently showing the world divided by a great ditch, the U.S.A. and Great Britain on one side, and the USSR on the other." Well, how would these difficulties be solved, in Doenitz's opinion? "I can't say now while I am a prisoner. Just let me be freed and I will have plenty to write about, and speak my mind freely. Russia is the greatest criminal nation in the world and Communism the greatest evil. I have to laugh when they accuse me of participating in a conspiracy. The Russians are always conspiring.

"The Russians asked us for a piece of Denmark and parts of Poland before we went to war with them. Now they accuse me of political conspiracy. I was sitting with my fleet in the Bay of Biscay, hardly ever went to Berlin before 1943, when Raeder retired and I was made chief of the navy. I accept responsibility for U-boat warfare from 1933 onward, and of the entire navy from 1943 on, but to make me responsible for what happened to Jews in Germany, or Russian soldiers on the east front — it is so ridiculous all I can do is laugh."

What about the navy itself? Did the navy have any anti-Semitic policies? "None at all. I had four Jewish high officers that I can think of at the moment. One was Rogge, a vice admiral who was in charge of the education of naval cadets all along until the end of the war.[12] Another was a captain. I had an affidavit from Rogge for my defense. If any of those four Jewish officers had known about what was happening to the Jews inside Germany or elsewhere by Himmler and Hitler, they would surely have told me. There was a letter I received from Hitler once in 1943 saying that the party complained because a Jew was in charge of the education of naval cadets. He meant Admiral Rogge. I replied that he should mind his own business.

"Our navy was like on an island. We had complete autonomy. A few times Hitler suggested that jurisdiction over political and criminal offenses among navy personnel be handled by the SS or other agencies of the party. I always declined. I always said that the navy must try its own offenders."

Did not Doenitz know of Jewish persecutions at all? "No. I knew nothing but naval matters. I was busy from morning till night with such affairs. We had no Jewish problem in the navy." What was his attitude toward Jews in general? "I had no prejudices. Once in 1934, I stopped at a Spanish port and was visited by a German Jew who owned some lead mines in the north of Spain. I had a luncheon aboard my vessel and arranged it through the German consul. I mentioned that I wanted to invite, among others, this certain Jew and his daughter. The German consul said it was quite impossible because the man was a Jew. My adjutant grinned at me because he knew my attitudes. I replied that my ship was my domain and I would have aboard it anyone I chose. The man and his daughter came to lunch.

"He was a very decent chap. When I left, he thanked me and was very sympathetic toward Nazism. I was at the time collecting porcelain. In that part of Spain there was a two-hundred-year-old porcelain factory which made a certain type of blue-and-white patterned plate which I wanted for my collection. I couldn't find one to buy. When we were at sea, my adjutant presented me with a beautiful plate of this porcelain, which was a gift from the German Jew. He was very tactful, and didn't want to present it to me personally, but waited until I was at sea to make a gift of it to me. I corresponded with him until 1939. I don't know what happened to him afterward. He once wrote me that his daughter married a Spanish prince."

What did Doenitz think of the trials thus far? "Ach! It's a joke, it seems to me. What they will do to us is of small concern, but that any of us is guilty of conspiracy is ridiculous. My own case is quite clear. So I sit here in my cell with my clear, clean conscience, and await the decision of the judges. There will probably be a difference of opinion between the British and American and French and Russians as to who is guilty and of what and so forth. If these trials confined themselves to who ordered killing of the Jews and other killings of human beings, it would be all right. I wouldn't be kept in this dock three hours. But I sit here from November on, and hear the same stuff over and over again. Half the time I no longer listen. I just draw pictures or jot down my musings."

Did he think any of the twenty-one defendants guilty? He evaded the question. "I am not a judge. I don't want to express my opinion. Before I came to Mondorf[13] I wouldn't shake hands with Goering, I didn't like him. I never saw Streicher before Mondorf, and in the beginning I wouldn't talk with him. Now I do. We all have the same destiny, at least for the present, and I see no reason for not being on friendly terms with each other."

Yes, but did he, within himself, find differences in guilt or lack of guilt among the twenty-one defendants? I persisted. "Certainly inside my heart I know degrees of difference. But I can't blame any of these men who share a common fate with me. The big folly of this trial is that it lacks the two men who are to blame for anything which was criminal, namely Hitler and Himmler."

Did not Hitler and Himmler require assistance to achieve their aims? Wasn't it reasonable to assume that a former corporal in the German army required some expert assistance in his deeds? "Well, in the first place Hitler was no ordinary German corporal. He had a tremendous mind. I can remember nine digits backward in the intelligence test Dr. Gilbert gave me.[14] Hitler could remember things in a phenomenal sort of way. He had the ability to recall everything he had ever read."

Did Doenitz, then, believe that none of the defendants were guilty of anything? Did he mean that they could all transfer the blame to Hitler and Himmler? "Let us put it this way. I assume responsibility for the German submarines from 1933, and of the German navy from 1943. But to make me responsible for a conspiracy is false. Each man must be responsible for his share."

Would it be correct to say, then, that Wilhelm Keitel, for example, was responsible for the misconduct of the German army, insofar as the orders for the misconduct bore his name? "I don't want to say. Keitel was completely under Hitler's influence. My own case is clearer. Your own admiral who sent me his greetings and high esteem bears that out."

And what about Ernst Kaltenbrunner, Himmler's chief of the Reich Security Main Office (RSHA)? "Again I think it was Himmler who was responsible and not Kaltenbrunner. I know that if I had been given orders to do as was done in the SS I would have refused."

Doenitz's "solid front" attitude with the defendants was particularly strong as far as Goering was concerned. "I can't see a thing wrong with Goering's behavior as far as this trial is concerned. They have proven none of the charges. I have mentioned to Goering that the trouble with

National Socialism is that it is a house divided, that we Germans tried to live in a community without considering our neighbors, and Goering agreed with me. So even Goering isn't as bad a fellow as the prosecution would have the world believe."

He smiled cynically and remarked, "Wait and see." I inquired what he was driving at. What would happen? "Just you wait and see. Your President Harry Truman and Secretary James Byrnes will have trouble with Russia. The East is threatening the West. Two varying cultures and kinds of humans are vying for power. They will thank me someday for sending the navy to the West and withdrawing our armies to avoid a surrender to the Russians. I think that's what your American admiral in court here the other day had in mind. It was a very smart move of your president to send General Bedell Smith to Moscow, and General George Marshall to China. Those two places need a military man to smell out and feel the pulse of the countries, to find out, more than any civilian could, what steps are being taken in preparation for war.

"I receive letters from my former naval officers asking me questions. I get pleasure and satisfaction from them. Do you know that several of my submarine designers and engineers have been asked by Russia to work for the Russian government to tell them about plans for the new secret German submarine which could travel underwater all the way from Germany to Japan? Yes. The Russians are after those secrets. Then they will build hundreds of such submarines, which we had just about ready when the war came to an end."

I said that there were a few points in his biography I should like clarification upon. He was smoothly uninformative about many of the matters in which I was interested, particularly about his early childhood.

His mother had died, presumably of tuberculosis of the lungs, at an early age, when he was four years old. His father died at the age of fifty-five of uremia, when Doenitz was twenty-one. His father never remarried. He had but one brother, two years his senior, who was killed during a bombing raid of Berlin in 1943. His childhood was a "happy" one, in Schleswig-Holstein. "Various relatives of my father" served as mother to him at various times.

His own marriage is a happy one. His wife is alive and well in Schleswig-Holstein at present and merely waiting for his release. His oldest child, a daughter, is married and has three small children. The daughter lives in the same town as the mother. Doenitz's two sons were killed in action in the navy, in 1943 and 1944, at ages twenty-one and twenty-three, unmarried.

"My only true friend here in the prison among the defendants is Albert Speer. He is a great architect and has a great genius for organization. When I came to Berlin in 1943 to take charge of the navy, there was a housing shortage. The navy assigned me a poor-looking house in Dahlem. I phoned my friend Speer and told him I needed a house. He said he would do his best. Next day he phoned and said my wife should come over to inspect the house he had for me. It was a beautiful manor house, on a hill, with two wide windows on either side and great gardens all around it. It was two stories high, with a fine broad staircase connecting the two floors. Often in the evenings Speer and his wife would visit me and my wife, and we would return the visits. Speer would bring along his pianists and violinists, who were perfect. We would spend many a musical evening together."

Doenitz played the flute since childhood and can still play "fairly well." He said that his father wanted him to study violin but his brother was learning at that time, and it sounded like a cat with its tail caught in a door, so he refused and chose flute lessons. "Now I'm sorry I didn't learn the violin because I prefer it to any other instrument. It shows I should have listened to my father's advice."

What did he think of the Führer principle? "It's all right, as long as the Führer is a good man. Hitler was good, or so I thought until the end of the war and all these atrocities were brought forth. There isn't anything wrong with the strongman principle in politics. In fact, it's too bad your President Roosevelt isn't alive today. Things would have been different at the Potsdam Conference. There was Churchill, Truman, and Stalin. Churchill had just been defeated and Clement Attlee came.[15] Truman was a new hand and did not know how to handle Stalin. Roosevelt would never have agreed to the boundaries as they now exist due to the Potsdam Conference."

# Hans Frank
1900–1946

Hans Frank, Hitler's personal lawyer, was governor general of Poland during World War II. He was found guilty at Nuremberg of war crimes and crimes against humanity, and was hanged on October 16, 1946.

**February 12, 1946**

Hans Frank was interviewed again this evening. He was in his cell, having come down from court about an hour before. He had just finished his evening meal. It was about 6:30 p.m. He was apparently happy to see me and Mr. Triest (the translator), whom he addressed as "Mr. Translator." Frank cleared his cot and chair of clothing, which was strewn about haphazardly, and invited us to be seated. He spoke some English, but I preferred speaking to him in German through the interpreter. I told him my reasons for this preference, and said that he could answer in German or English as he wished. He seemed pleased by this arrangement, and the conversation proceeded largely in German. I explained that I was concerned with the psychological welfare of the defendants in my capacity as prison psychiatrist, but that I was naturally interested in learning about their individual characters.

He seemed agreeable and said he understood, as Dr. Kelley, my predecessor, had talked with him. "Since you are also a psychiatrist, you will probably find my case interesting." He smiled with his customary leering grimace and cackled. I asked if he had any particular physical or other complaints. "None except this sty on my right eye." This began in December, recurred in January, and was present for the past few days again. He also had "very bad" sties three years ago. He believed that the drafts and strong lighting in court may have caused it. Two years ago it was caused by overwork. It was very painful, he said. Examination today revealed a slight sty on the right lower lid near the external canthus without much inflammation.

He said, too, that several years ago he had a middle ear infection, with some drainage from either ear. As a child, however, he never had ear disease. Because of this infection, he constantly kept cotton plugs in both ears for prophylactic purposes. I asked how long he had been doing that, and he said on and off for two or three years. "My hearing is extraordinarily acute, even with the cotton plugs in the canals. You see, I'm musically inclined. I play the piano and organ." His favorite composers were Brahms, Bach, and Max Reger; he added that the latter was a Bavarian composer. "I did not care for Wagner," he observed seriously. "My tastes are more classical. Der Führer had no musical taste and liked Wagner because of the bombastic Teutonic glories."

At five years of age, he had diphtheria and "almost died." He recalled an appendectomy at the age of thirteen. He remembered a doctor putting a "needle" in his throat when he was twelve. He grimaced, then smiled, at the recollection. He had two scars on his neck, one on either side, at the level of the thyroid cartilage, which he said were self-inflicted the first day he was captured (May 3, 1945), at Tegernsee. He again attempted suicide on May 5, 1945, he said, when he lacerated his left arm at the antecubital space and at the wrist. He still had a tickling sensation of the first three fingers.

"I tried to commit suicide because I sacrificed everything for Hitler. And that man whom we sacrificed everything for left us all alone. If he had committed suicide four years before, it would have been all right."

When had he begun to realize that Hitler was not so good? Frank sighed and answered equivocally: "I lost my official office in 1942 because I was outspoken against concentration camps and against policy by force. My lawyer has copies of those speeches."[1]

And what had he done against these things from 1942 onward? "Hitler took away all my offices but left me as governor of Poland. I remained in Krakow until the end. I wanted to resign twelve times but couldn't get Hitler to accept my resignation. I wanted to return to the army, but Hitler would not allow it." He had held a reserve lieutenancy of infantry in the army since World War I.

Had he had any suicidal thoughts recently? "On the contrary. A man

is responsible for the thousands who worked under him. I consider suicide the greatest sin. I'm glad I didn't succeed."

At this point I offered him a cigarette, and he smiled and accepted,
saying: "Ah! American cigarettes are like the American soul — sweet
and light." It was my impression that he was not being hypocritical or
attempting to be cynical. I believe he meant it for a compliment, and that
the remark in itself was significant from a character standpoint.

We casually discussed his early life. He attended elementary school
from 1906 to 1910 in Munich. During the years 1910 to 1919 he was a student, also in Munich, but in 1916–17 he "couldn't stand" school anymore
and went to Prague. "I wrote about the conflicts I had in school in my
autobiography. It was an inward revolution. I revolted against the out-
moded ways of teaching in school." He said he published a periodical
while in school, called *Deutsche Jugend Zeitung* (*German Youth Newspaper*), which was mimeographed and spread "wildly" among the students — "more than a thousand copies." The paper was banned by the
authorities. Its viewpoint was "that the students should educate themselves — a protest against old and obsolete forms of teaching."

He added: "It was just a development of puberty — I later forgot all
about it and became a lawyer." He spent four years in law school in
Munich and Kiel, graduating in 1926. He became an assistant teacher of
jurisprudence in a school in Munich, and remained a teacher until 1930.
At the same time he had a private practice as a lawyer, and one of his
clients was Hitler. In 1930, "I had to decide between teaching and law,
and I decided on law because of family responsibility." He became a
National Socialist in 1923, the year he met Hitler. His law practice was
"political."

Frank was married in 1925. His wife, Brigitte, was now fifty — four and
a half years his senior. They had five children, three boys and two girls,
ages six to eighteen. His wife was well. For the last three years they have
been separated. They were never happily mated, he says. The only thing
that kept them together was the children, and now the trials. "It's no
fault of my wife — it's my own as well. A difference in temperaments. My
wife was a secretary, has a normal education. But she is uninterested in
anything which I consider interesting. She is practical, I am an idealist."
They lacked a "common ground." She had, for instance, no interest in
music. He knew her but six months before they married. "We are not
well-adjusted sexually. She is a typical north Prussian cold type, not

interested in sex. Just day-to-day happenings." Both were Catholic. Recently, Frank returned to the church. "I would like to tell you more about that when you have time."

### March 5, 1946

The interviewing of Frank continues. Spent about an hour or more with him this evening. In the dock in court he presents a rather bemused picture, a manner which he has presented since I first saw him on my arrival here on January 8, 1946. At times he smiles sardonically at some piece of testimony, and other times he smiles and it is difficult to state whether or not the smile is the result of an appropriate external stimulus or the result of inner fantasy. Once he smiled beamingly when the American judge, Biddle, asked some questions of the American prosecutor, Jackson. This was appropriate in a way, since all of the defendants heartily approved of Biddle's questions (relevant to the cases against the organizations), yet none of the other defendants smiled so beamingly.

In his cell today, in the early afternoon (court recessed to a closed session), he was most cordial, bubbling over with laughter, smiles, and inappropriate good humor. He had been reading when I entered the cell in the company of Triest (the interpreter). He said: "Have you heard? On Thursday begins the defense of the art collector!" He laughed uproariously at his own witticism, high-pitched, almost hysterical laughter; then sudden seriousness, during which his tortuous right temporal vein stood out prominently. "Yes. If his time had been spent more collecting planes, and less time collecting art, we wouldn't be where we are today.

"It's strange. Man can get used to captivity. Back to the feelings when people lived in caves." He again laughed loudly but without humor, with a certain uncontrolled quality. I asked him what he meant, for instance. His face became serious again. "The urge for activity is not great anymore. I live here easily, like a holy man, a hermit." He laughed sharply and harshly. "In a cloister one must voluntarily keep his promises of poverty and virginity. Here you are forced to do it. Are you Catholic?" He addressed the query to Triest and myself. We answered in the negative, and I asked him why he had asked. "Maybe the pope will move to America! There is but one power in the world to stave off Russia. Our power was too small. Pope Pius, who reigns now, was once in America."

Asked about his own religion, he replied: "I'm an accepted Catholic. In Germany the son always adopts the mother's religion. She is Catholic.

It's all in the three-hundred-page autobiography I wrote, which I gave to Dr. Gilbert."[2] He then showed me a thin book called *Cabin Boy of Columbus,* written by him. "My idea was that Columbus had a cabin boy who was really a young man. I dictated this book in ten hours. It was published at Christmas 1944. It's written in the form of an old testament by an old lady. It would have been better if I had stuck to writing such books rather than gone into politics."

Frank's father died on January 16, 1945, the same day that Frank left Krakow. He says he believes there is some significance in these two events occurring on the same date. His father died in Munich, where he was a practicing lawyer. He was seventy-seven years old. He had been ill for three months, "the result of seeing so many people burned and dying from bombing raids."

Frank went on describing his father: "He was very good-humored, a jurist from the Rhine Palatinate. He practiced all kinds of law, but was completely unpolitical. He was good-natured, humorous, liked wine, was well liked, just like a man from the Rhine country would be.

"He was an elder lawyer, a jurist." What was his attitude toward the Nazis? "He was a very strong opponent of the Nazi Party. He was a democrat. He always said, 'You'll see what will happen.' He had many Jewish friends."

How did you happen to become anti-Semitic? "Anti-Semitism was not the reason I joined the party. It was because of Germany." Were there many Jews killed in Poland? "No. In Auschwitz there were; that was in Upper Silesia. I want you to read documentary evidence which proves it was completely out of my hands. For that which I am responsible, I am responsible, but I never had a single Jew put in a concentration camp or burned — that I can prove. You'll be surprised if you see what my defense counsel has. The extermination of the Jews was a personal idea of Hitler's. It was in Hitler's testament. In that he said he had exterminated Jews because they had started the war."

Frank described his mother, age seventy-two, as "a very strong woman, of country stock, from upper Bavaria. She was a temperamental woman, humorous — a very beautiful woman, artistically inclined. She has a large circle of friends who take care of her now. The proverb 'No friends in time of need' does not fit in my case. I'm touched by the care the people around my mother and wife are giving them. My mother is well educated and always writes me quotations from Goethe and

Schiller. It's very amazing for an old woman like that, especially since my only sister was arrested. She had never been a party member — she was arrested just because she was my sister. My wife was not arrested. Maybe they took my sister because they didn't want to take my wife."

His sister is forty, the wife of an employee of the patent office. When her husband came back from the front, he found his wife arrested. His sister's husband was also not politically inclined. "That's the only thing I don't like, taking her a prisoner because of me." She is interned at Straubing on the Danube.

Frank also had a brother, born in 1897, who was killed in action in 1916. The only other sibling is the sister mentioned above.

Asked about his childhood, Frank replied, "It was generally a good childhood, though in the years after the first war it was difficult. Father was not rich and we lived on cabbages and potatoes. When I was twenty-three we drank malt coffee. This makes the Nazi idea understandable. The mark was worth one-billionth at the end.[3] Out of this period arose Nazism."

We then talked of the cases against the organizations which were being discussed in the last few days in court. "Against the SS and the Gestapo they have a case. Against the Supreme Command of the Armed Forces and so forth, they can't do it. As a political measure it's different. But legally, as a legal measure, it can't be done. It doesn't matter that I'm interned or that the trials are taking place. I approve of it all — but I learned most of the history of National Socialism and its crimes during this trial.

"In Germany we heard nothing of Jewish persecution. Other nations had a free press, et cetera, while in Germany we had no free press or radio.

"This trial has one big significance because it shows that the German people are innocent."

At this point Frank smiled broadly, in a forced manner, inclined his head forward, and in a confidential manner, ingratiatingly friendly, said: "You will have plenty to say — as a psychiatrist, who understands people. It's a tragic place, this row of twenty-one persons who ruled a part of the world. Already you can notice preparations which might make for another war more cruel than the last."

For instance? "The atom bomb. But I hope humanity is more sound mentally. My life is over. I have no interest. Not even in looking into

Germany. It's like a dream. How valueless is everything politically! It doesn't matter whether I'm judged criminal. I have a great feeling of guilt — I have a feeling that I ran after Hitler like a wildfire without reason. If I can sacrifice my life to make something good, I'd gladly do it.

"I believed that man. If I knew what I have learned in the trials, I would have protested in a different way than 1942." What protest in 1942? "My famous speech against the concentration camps and against the SS, which I gave at Vienna, Heidelberg, Munich, and Berlin.

"Before I die, I demand you read those speeches in my diary. It created a tremendous uproar and crisis, and I was relieved of all party positions and became just a plain party member. They didn't recognize my request for transfer — they kept me there because it was the most terrible place in Europe. The SS behaved like mad. My headquarters was in Krakow, in the old king's palace. Therefore one can say I was five years a king, but without power.

"It was just like the whole Führer state of Hitler — a façade."

**March 16, 1946**
Frank was in one of his cheerful, smiling, effusive moods. He greeted Mr. Triest, the interpreter, and myself warmly and said that he was delighted to have us visit him again.

"I feel very well; I have been treated too well — it is an honor the way we are all treated. If we had fallen in the hands of Himmler, it would have been different. I only wish I had a pipe because the Americans took my pipe. I hope I can get one."

Frank laughingly stated that when he was arrested, everything he owned was taken from him, including his pipe. After the second of his two suicidal attempts, he stated that the American doctor advised that his wedding ring be removed for "safety's sake," but when Frank recovered later and asked the doctor for it, the latter refused, saying that he wanted it for a souvenir. "That's not right. It shouldn't be done that way. There were other Americans present who said the same thing, that my ring and other possessions shouldn't be taken. This occurred in the Augsburg military hospital."

Frank displays emotional lability. His mood and affect changed from minute to minute. He smiled or laughed raucously at one moment, was depressed and almost tearful at the next moment.

Frank asked me whether there was anything in particular that I cared to ask him today. I said, nothing especially, but that I would like to learn more about his early development and history.

"You remember my telling you of my uncle who played a large part in my youth. In fact, my aunt and uncle played a bigger part in my life than did my father and mother. This aunt and uncle were my mother's sister and brother. Although I never lived with them, I visited them frequently and they exerted a profound influence on my character."

Frank said that he had been thinking about the early years of his life, particularly his first meeting with Hitler. He would rather talk about this today than about his own family, he said. "In November 1918, I was a soldier in Munich. I saw the downfall of the first republic — the Councils Republic — in 1919. This caused fourteen thousand people to lose their lives. I felt that that in itself constituted adequate reason for anti-Semitism. Many Jews were sent from Communist Moscow, and we all knew what a regime of terror existed there. For example, there was the playwright Ernst Toller. He was not from Russia, having been born a German, but his thoughts were influenced by the Communists. There were four fellows who came from Moscow and created the republic in Munich.[4]

"I entered the Freikorps in order to liberate Munich. After three days of fighting, we finally succeeded. In September or October 1919, I met the founder of the National Socialist movement. This, of course, was not Hitler, because the party existed prior to Hitler. The man I am referring to was a worker named Anton Drexler.[5] He was a simple man who had not grown sufficiently to the task of leading the party, and he left it in 1922. I was not yet a member of the party.

"It would be interesting to study the original party because it would then become obvious how in the course of time Hitler falsified the party aims. Goering himself testified that Hitler did not follow through with the party program. For example, in the party program there is no call for the physical extermination of Jews, but rather merely the removal of their influence. The criminal step of exterminating the Jews physically was taken by Hitler during the war. One has only to read the last testament of Hitler — and if one compares this testament with the National Socialist Party program, one can see how far he departed. I feel that behind this departure were Bormann, Joseph Goebbels,[6] and Himmler.

"Drexler told me in 1919 that I should make sure to hear Hitler, who at the time was a young soldier and reported to be a very interesting speaker. I was present when Hitler spoke for the first time before a large group. He appeared sickly, weak, and tired. He gave the impression that he would not live long. Personally, I was not very much impressed by Hitler's statements at that time.

"As I said, Hitler spoke like a sick man who would die at any moment. All the original party members were small people, mostly workers, as well as an amazingly large number of women followers. In 1920 I met Drexler again. He took me to some of the big party rallies and during one of these Hitler read the party program. I believe that was on February 24, 1920, at the Hofbräuhaus in Munich.

"In the summer of 1923 I returned from Kiel. At the time I was an ambitious student. A friend of mine informed me that the National Socialist movement had taken a tremendous upswing and that the party was strongest in Bavaria. This friend of mine said that I should see for myself by attending some of the meetings.

"In the summer of 1923 there was the inflation. As you may remember from history, the French broke into the Ruhr in January 1923. The German economy as a whole broke down. There was a terrible period of hunger. One American dollar was worth 400,000 marks. Later in November 1923, a dollar was worth a billion marks. It was at this crucial time that Hitler rose.[7]

"But I was still not in the party. I was a cavalryman of the Freikorps Franz von Epp. We had a reserved table at one of the large beer halls in Munich. On November 7, 1923, when I came to the table in the beer hall, I found that Adolf Hitler had invited the members of the Freikorps present at the time to come to the Bürgerbräukeller on November 8. The next day, November 8, forty of us went to the *Keller*. We happened to come too late — at about 9:30 p.m. Hitler had already made his putsch, which started at 8:30 p.m.

"At the time the people were enthusiastic about National Socialism because they felt that a new, free government was coming and that Germany would rise again. General Erich Ludendorff was with Hitler and marched at his side. It was because of Ludendorff's presence that we members of the Freikorps von Epp participated. We felt that it must be a good thing if the respectable Ludendorff was there. I remember Goering standing at the door of the Bürgerbräukeller, saying to us, 'We can use you.' We were given weapons and with the others we marched from barracks to barracks. There was real revolutionary feeling in the air. We stayed up all night and felt sure of success. The next day, on November 9, at noon, there was an armed clash, and the result is history; the party was dissolved, and Hitler and a few others were sentenced to prison.

"I remember that during this clash there was a judge by the name of Theodor von der Pfordten who was killed and whom I helped carry off the street dead. After that I went home; the party was banned but not forgotten.

"In 1926 I became a party member for the first time. But I left the party three months later. My father told me, 'I'm surprised you don't see what a fool that man Hitler is. He is impossible and I can't understand why you are attracted to him.' I then wrote Hitler a letter saying that I didn't believe that he was correct in his advocacy of certain party principles and I resigned. I became absorbed in my legal work. On December 27, 1926, I read an announcement in a newspaper that some poor people were looking for a defense counsel." Frank laughs in a cackling fashion at this point. "I became the defense counsel for these poor people, who happened to be some SA men in Berlin. It's ironic that I became defense counsel for party members without myself being a party member.

"In 1928 I rejoined the party to serve as a legal adviser. I became more and more absorbed and finally interested in the movement. In 1929 Hitler came to see me personally and requested that I become his full-time lawyer. I accepted with the provision that I be permitted at any time to take up my personal professional career again. Many years later, in 1942, when I had my great falling-out with Hitler, I reminded him about this provision which we had agreed on in 1929. Hitler didn't want to know anything more about this at that time and brushed aside my request for resignation.

"There is only one explanation. There is a fate that brings people to a road without their actually wanting it. I use this not as an excuse for myself but merely to make it understandable.

"Of course, what I am recounting this afternoon is just the outward frame of the events which led to my present tragedy. I can only tell you one one-thousandth of the things which led up to it. I can assure you that I had no financial advantage during the whole of my career. I had no picture galleries or personal fortune like that man Goering — nothing like that. Therefore, it is easier now for me to see the little that I owned confiscated. Really, the only thing that can be confiscated which belonged to me personally is my little home. When I was captured, the American officers asked me where my castle was located. I'm happy to say that I never owned a castle."

Frank asked me what I thought of Goering's defense. I countered the question by stating that it was difficult for me to judge and that he was in a much better position to comment on it. He replied, "The only thing I like about Goering's defense is his statement that he is not innocent. He has not been innocent. I like that. But I think the prosecution could have been more effective than it has been up to now. If Goering had spent more time on the air force and less time on his bacchanals and looting of art treasures, perhaps Germany would be better off today and I would not be sitting here in this cell.

"My own defense is small. In fact, my defense counsel is small and reminds me of Goebbels. I hope Dr. Seidl has a mouth like Goebbels, although I doubt if it will help me very much.

"The most difficult thing in Goering's defense was his weaknesses regarding art collections, et cetera. Your Justice Jackson is completely equipped with a whole collection of books and documents. Trial psychology is very interesting. I sit in the dock there like a spectator. It is difficult to remember that while we sit in here, the outside world goes on, and now I ruminate on how Hitler started and how the whole bloody movement resulted from hunger in Germany.

"All these things are still apparent today. You Americans can see for yourselves how impossible it is to feed the German people from the German soil itself. From the viewpoint of an historian one can say that Hitler never would have arisen if the Allies had not treated Germany so poorly. Justice Jackson said so himself. Today things are more impossible than ever. The East has been taken away from Germany — in other words, hunger created Hitler, and paradoxically, Hitler created still greater hunger.

"These are the facts of life and one can't disregard them. Germans are being thrown out by the Poles and Russians, and a big catastrophe is occurring. It becomes worse and worse daily.

"This does not explain or justify the crimes which Hitler committed. An astrologist once visited me and read a horoscope of Adolf Hitler in which he called him a criminal. That was about four years ago. I don't believe in astrology, but I do believe implicitly in the power of fate — that all of us mortals are included in the cosmic laws of the universe. We sit in the world, and the world is part of the universe. I believe in what Christ said, that no sparrow falls from a roof unless it is God's will.

"I don't believe this war was the end of controversies. The struggle will go on until all existing cultures are destroyed. The same thing happened in the fall of the Roman Empire. Germany is always the first nation to be built up and the first to collapse completely. The collapse of Europe will eventually take place.

"Europe is nothing — it is merely a question of what Russians and Americans decide to do with it. A complete change will occur. Three hundred years ago, Europe was the dominant part of the world. The next thing that is highly endangered is the British Empire. Forty million Englishmen are not sufficient to govern an empire of four to five hundred million people.

"I was a good friend of Oswald Spengler,[8] and together with Spengler's niece I saved his library during an air raid. Spengler's niece was in charge of the University of Munich library. Spengler was the last great man of Germany. In 1933 he prophesied that the Reich under Hitler would perish. I didn't want to believe it. Now, in my cell, I often think of the letter Spengler wrote to me in 1936, shortly before his death. In it he said that within ten years the German Reich would probably cease to exist. He died in December 1936. He told me that when Hitler screamed, 'Out with the Jews,' he proved that he was no statesman. Spengler felt that if Hitler had been a statesman, he would have said that Germany consisted of more than just Germans or Jews and that anyone of use to Germany should be kept. He quoted the example of Lord Beaconsfield under Queen Victoria, on the Indian question, and he told me of the great deeds of the Jew Cecil Rhodes in South Africa.

"Spengler said that Hitler is doing a good job for the enemies of Germany. You can imagine how strong an influence Hitler must have had, if even a man like myself failed to be influenced by the wisdom of Spengler but was influenced only by Hitler.

"One cannot underestimate the influence of the hypnotic personality of Hitler. That, too, I do not offer as an excuse, but just as an example. After the deed is done, one always becomes clever and philosophical.

"There was a great difference between the fate and personalities of Napoleon and Hitler. In a way, their two fates coincide. I can show you in ten minutes. It is something I've already indicated to Goering. It is surprising how one can make analogies between historical personalities. It is good to be in a cell to be able to think things — it is sensational.

"I met my wife in 1924. The relationship was one of a chance happening and was one of the biggest mistakes of my life. I certainly don't want to say anything against the character of my wife, but she is too old — five years older than I am — and I am of the opinion that it's just too bad. Secondly, her character is the opposite of mine. I was engaged to a nice person who would have suited me perfectly. I believe that if I had stuck to my first sweetheart, I think my life would have taken a new turn. During that time I dictated my doctoral thesis to a typist — and the typist was the woman who became my wife. Although she was five years older than I, I suddenly was seized with a mental desire for this woman.

"The whole thing was difficult because, for one thing, my wife came from a poor family. I think I was in an intoxicated condition, not literally but figuratively. I broke off my engagement to my first sweetheart, who came from a well-to-do, influential family and was a young girl. I married the typist, who is my present wife. In 1926 our first child was born and I had to earn something. That was one of the reasons for my accepting Hitler's offer. I don't want to place the blame on my wife, but there was economic necessity.

"The most outspoken critic of my wife is my mother. Even now when my mother is quite alone, she declines to receive my wife. There is absolutely no bond of friendship between my mother and my wife.

"For many years I had no relationship as a husband with my wife. In 1942 I wanted a divorce, and in fact divorce proceedings were going on. Then Hitler stepped in and prohibited this action. My wife had written Hitler and Hitler said that I could not be divorced because it was not his wish. This is an example to show how far Hitler's influence went in Germany. A week after filing suit for divorce, I was informed by the minister of justice that Hitler disapproved of the proceedings. In the summer of 1943 I accidentally met Hitler, who said that under no conditions would I be allowed to become divorced. Now in captivity, I merely write to her, especially for the children's sake, and because of the short life I am going to have anyway.

"I met the girl I was supposed to marry again in the last few years. She, too, was unhappy. We went together and practically lived together like man and wife. Our not getting married originally was due in part to personal stupidity, but mainly I think it was a trick of fate. The biggest mistake is that I act and speak under emotional influences and do not take an objective view of circumstances.

"My marriage was such that I was always lonely. I could not speak with my wife about things that depressed me. I was virtually a married bachelor. I don't want you to misunderstand me — this has nothing to do with the character of my wife. She would have fit admirably with another kind of man, probably." I asked Frank what kind of a man his wife would have suited, in his opinion. "A practical man, an industrious businessman who likes money, gives parties, and that sort of life."

I asked him how he explained emotionally his originally having fallen in love with his wife. He replied, "There was undoubtedly a physical attraction, which became completely extinguished after two or three years. My wife was a cold beauty. She had no need for physical satisfaction. I think one of the reasons for her desiring that our marriage not be broken by divorce was that she never felt any need for a sex life."

I asked Frank whether he frequently had arguments with his wife. He replied, "There were weeks and sometimes months when I stayed away from home. My political life demanded my going on trips and tours. Of course, social appearances were kept up, but that was about all."

Frank went on to tell me about his mistress. "I had several mistresses at various times. They were always younger girls — ones that I had known from the time of my youth. They were girls I had loved in my youth and childhood. There were never any new ones. For many years I lived secretly with a girl who was an old friend of mine in my boyhood. She was married but her husband was ill and much older than she was, and she was unhappy just like me. I would have married her if she had been a widow and if I could have gotten a divorce. She had everything — comradeship, character. She would have been a perfect partner. She is the girl I told you about — the one I was engaged to when I broke it off to marry my wife. In retrospect, I believe she was the same age as I was, nineteen or twenty — but she came from a rich family and I was but a poor student. I didn't have the power or nerve to ask her to elope with me. I think that was the first tragedy of my life.

"This wonderful woman, who was my girlfriend before I married and also in the last few years, is a very close friend of my mother's. Mother always liked her and both our families were very friendly. I will give you her name — because after I am dead, it doesn't matter." At this point, Frank took an envelope from his pocket and showed me a picture of a young woman who, he said, was the sweetheart of his youth. He did not mention her name at this point, and I did not ask him for it.

He seemed rather depressed after his statements regarding his personal relationship with his wife and mistress and I asked him why he appeared so downhearted at this moment. He said, "I feel that I am obligated to my people — that is not pessimism. If I tried to prove that I was innocent, it would be the same as trying to prove that the German people are guilty. Only one innocent man sits in that dock — and that man is the symbol of the German people. An epoch with such happenings as the murder of 5 million Jews, the projective extermination of millions of Slavs — such an epoch must close up definitely once and for all. It cannot go dragging on and on. Those of us who are guilty must pay the price and set the German people free, no longer to be blamed for our stupidity."

It seemed to me that actually Frank's depressed appearance had more to do with his personal life and fate than with his platitudinous concern about the German people. I said that I was more interested in his personal life from a psychological standpoint, and did he care to tell me anything more about his relationships with his wife or with other women? He again displayed the picture of his sweetheart and gazed at it sentimentally. "In 1937 or '38 I met this old sweetheart of mine again and we became most intimate. This was especially true from 1941 until the end. In the last few months before my arrest I was together again with her almost constantly in Bavaria, near Munich. She is a very clever woman and I say that not because I loved her but because I knew her so well.

"It might interest you to know that when I returned from Krakow I didn't go to my wife but to this woman. I knew at that time that everything was collapsing, and I wanted to say farewell to the beautiful things of life. The only disagreement she ever had with me was the fact that she was a fanatical opponent of Hitler and everything having anything to do with National Socialism. We could not find a mutual understanding politically. That is why I said that if I had married her, I would not have become a Nazi, and I must admit that I am so small and easily influenced, especially by a woman I love, that I can say this with assurance."

### July 20, 1946

Frank was in his blue denim coveralls, reading a magazine, when Mr. Triest and I entered his cell this morning. It was Saturday and there was no court session. The sun streamed in through the open cell window. Most of the other defendants were exercising in the yard. He was grandiosely courteous and eager for company. As usual, he greeted us eloquently, and ceremoniously made place for me on his chair and for Mr. Triest on the cot beside him. He filled his pipe with tobacco, an American brand, and praised it highly. "This blessed Granger tobacco," he said, "it is marvelous." I offered him a cigarette and he accepted it quickly, thanking me profusely.

What had Frank been thinking about in the past few days? What did he think of the trials recently? What about the organizations? He smiled mirthlessly, giggled in a high-pitched manner, then drew his hand over his face in a gesture of changing expression. When he spoke, his face assumed a serious mien. "The case against the organizations is a mistake. It was contemplated in the first white rage after the war. If the Allies were to think about such a case now, they could not have indicted the organizations. You can't indict a government and its organizations as criminal. The conception of the Reich government is a hundred years old. The general staff is several hundreds of years old. The case of the SS is another matter, because it was started with the party and by the party. But it's quite impossible to indict or convict an organization as criminal if it has in its membership millions of innocent people."

He reiterated what so many Nazis in Nuremberg had said. "As a lawyer I feel that only the indictment of individuals is correct or possible. Not organizations or a whole government. I think that the trial will be short as far as the organizations are concerned because the Allies already realize the difficulties. If you will recall, a few weeks ago there was a sharp debate between the French judge, Donnedieu de Vabres, and Mr. Jackson or Mr. Dodd — I forget exactly — regarding the prosecution of the organizations. There was a hectic controversy about it all. The French judge said just about what I have just said — that one can convict an individual, but to convict a government or entire organization is impossible."

What did Frank think of the American prosecutors, Justice Jackson and Mr. Dodd? "They are politicians, not lawyers, as far as this procedure is concerned. Their mission is political. They are mouthpieces of political interests which are directed toward the destruction of National Socialism. I mean they are the tools which the Allies are using to smash Nazism ideologically as well as actually. Neither Jackson nor Dodd, nor the other Allied prosecutors, refer too much to law or legality, because the subject is too difficult. The problem of placing these matters discussed in court in a legal light is left to the tribunal.

"The entire trial affords a picture of a mixture of politics and law. It isn't the fault of Jackson. There is the old controversy between Anglo-Saxon and American legal procedures, on the one hand, and continental law as typified by French and German methods, on the other side. The prosecutor, for example, in a French or German court has quite a different function than the prosecutor in an American court. Personally, I liked Jackson for openly and plainly stating in court that he voiced the sentiment of the world — and not merely represented the law.

"That's why I don't consider him a lawyer in this case. In a way he is also the defense counsel for the victims of Hitlerism. I must attribute to Jackson a position apart and above the law. His is a political, and also a moral and humane, mission. Secondly, did you ever consider how impossible it would be to prosecute by legal means the acts of Hitlerism? Hitler himself didn't keep within the law, so how can the prosecutor of Hitlerism confine himself to legal technique?"

Frank said he'd been thinking something over rather carefully in the past few days, and he wondered if I'd be good enough to tell him my opinion of his ideas. "In my final speech, which I should be working on one of these days, since the trial is going pretty fast now, I have thought of devoting it almost entirely to a new idea. My idea is to defend Hitler. Not in the customary sense of the term. But I feel that here in Nuremberg we have twenty-one defendants, all guilty to a more or less degree, but the man who should be the main defendant is absent because he committed suicide. Now whereas Bormann is absent, he has a defense counsel. But every defense lawyer's strategy has been to place the blame upon Hitler. Therefore, according to a just court procedure, the man who is most highly accused, by defense and prosecution both, should have a lawyer or a defense of some kind.

"Now it isn't a matter of whether Hitler's actions are defensible. They aren't. His last testament alone is a frightful document in which he admits and brags about killing off the Jews. It's the most hideous, frightful document in history. But unless a ghost appears in these last few weeks in court and speaks for Hitler, he is unheard.

"Therefore my idea would be to devote most of my final speech to a so-called defense of Hitler. It would be proper, in the sense that I was his old lawyer for years, and his personal attorney from 1927 to 1933, defending him in over 140 legal suits, mostly for slander, in the courts all over Germany. It would make sense for another reason. It would help to destroy for posterity the possibility of a 'Hitler legend.' If Hitler is accused of so many dastardly things, and if no one speaks up for him to answer the charges, the legend of Hitler's greatness might grow. But if I said, 'Well, I represent Hitler's legal interests. I will answer the charges A, B, C, and D,' et cetera, and proceed to answer them as Hitler would answer them, the nonsense of a Hitler legend would be dissipated forever. Because there is no answer to the things he did and the government he created. There is only one thing which would and should happen, if someone like myself, or Hitler himself, were to answer the charges made against him. The answers would be thrown out and considered trash and nonsense. The tribunal would have to answer only one word to all the stuff I could say in defense of Hitler: the word 'Auschwitz.' That would be enough. Hitler's legend would be done and finished. I cite that as only a small example.

"The problem of who shall defend Hitler has occurred to me often." Frank laughed sardonically in a high-pitched, uncontrolled manner. "Hitler is always attacked and never defended. It's a problem. It would be hard to defend Hitler, but in every trial where manifold charges are made against a man, he should be defended. I repeat, maybe a ghost will yet appear in court who will defend Hitler!" Frank laughed again in his characteristic hysterical manner.

"It is quite interesting from a legal standpoint because up to now, the very end of the trial, nobody has been able to defend that man with even a single meaningful word. Our defense counsels continue to attack Hitler, because their idea is that if you blame Hitler, then their clients will not be so much to blame. The tactic of the defense counsel is to separate Hitler from the defendants. The idea is to toss Hitler into an abyss and say, 'These poor defendants had no idea of what a monster he was, and had nothing to do with him.' Believe me, nothing could be farther from the truth.

"If Hitler is the main defendant in this trial, which he must be, because all the defendants blame him for everything, then this principal accused one should be heard. Personally, I should like to see Hitler among those upon whom a sentence will be passed. Now, if you pass a sentence on a man, he should be heard, and given a chance to defend himself. It would be more effective if we said that Hitler wanted such and such, but that it does not compare with such and such, which was actually done and which was criminal.

"I think of these things frequently, because I know the German people. Among them might arise the legend of Hitler, because Hitler was not heard from in this trial. Time always has some reconciling effect. On every ruin there eventually grows grass, and then some shrubbery, and finally, before you realize it, what is really an old hideous ruin becomes a romantic sight and legend.

"And I want to warn the world on that point in regard to Hitler and these trials. I know Europe and its possibilities. It would interest me greatly, Dr. Goldensohn, if you gave me your opinion." I replied that there seemed to be some reason behind his idea, but I should like to know more about it. For one thing, admitting the important figure of Hitler is not in the dock, what could be done about it, since he committed suicide? Frank replied thoughtfully, "For one thing, the following can be done. One or the other of us, in his final speech before this tribunal, should make a defensive speech for Hitler. Not the lawyers, the defense counsels, but one of us defendants who were Hitler's agents.

"The worst testament in the world is Hitler's own last testament. Goering's so-called faithfulness to Hitler is a joke — nonsense. Criminal nonsense. But one should stand up and say, 'I am attempting to defend Hitler as his attorney or representative.' Then the court should ask questions and let whoever defends Hitler answer. The prosecution, believe me, would have an easy task. They would simply have to say, 'Hitler, here is your last testament. What do you have to say about it?' What can be said in its defense? Not a word that makes sense! It's the confession of the order to kill the Jews. The most horrible document, attesting to the most horrible crime in world history! The prosecution would just have to say, 'What do you say to this, Herr Hitler?' Then one has to imagine an answer or argument for it.

"The court would weigh this argument and answer and label it as nonsense and throw it out. There is, of course, no possible argument to justify it. The whole idea of mine to defend Hitler is just an answer to a psychological problem of combating any possibility of a Hitler legend.

"Of course, one can say there's no use discussing these things. They are criminal and require no discussion. But the Allies removed such an argument themselves when they started these very trials. There is a good possibility of a Hitler legend. The trial drags on, world history continues, and the golden age hasn't yet arrived. The German people are in terrible need.

"In the course of this trial, I collected forty-four degrading names which had been applied to Hitler, calling him a mass murderer, and so on. I have them here in my cell in my notes. These names came not from the prosecution but from the defendants and the defense counsels. Now one must ask himself how Adolf Hitler would defend himself against these accusations. I would try to collect all the arguments, even the most far-fetched ones, which Hitler might try to use.

"I shall consider it further, as to whether I shall put this business in my final speech. Of course, I shall do it with the explanation and introduction I just gave you. I don't know if this is possible in my case. But it should be because I have nothing much to say in my final speech since I told the court quite openly about my guilt and I hid nothing.

"But it's a terrible task to even seek for words of excuse for Hitler. Even in art, there is no light without shadows, and no shadows are cast without some light. Even the shadow of Adolf Hitler is accompanied by some light. I would tell the court that as Hitler's old attorney from 1927 to 1933, I will defend him. Then I would say that all my arguments were not sufficient as a human being and there is no defense except words. Meaningless words.

"I believe this would combat the legend of Hitler. It would answer all the thoughts which the thousands of hidden followers of Hitler still hold. You would have to say, for example, that the Poles have murdered thousands of Germans. That there was hatred and jealousy against Hitler. The answer would be simple and more important than the argument. But Auschwitz remains! That is the answer. One-thousandth of the answer, but enough."

We seemed to have expended the subject of Frank's bright idea of defending Hitler, and his reasons for so contemplating. I asked him if he had any other thoughts recently and whether or not he cared to talk about something in particular.

He said that his mind was constantly "working," but that he had reached a state of being "at peace with the world." I asked him about his family again. His face darkened, then he said lightly, "My mother is still alive, as you know. I've often thought about her here. She is a wonderful woman. All my battling spirit I derive from her. My father was a lawyer, but a weak one, who had much trouble with his practice.

"In 1925 he was disbarred, because he took both sides in a divorce case. He was representing the husband, when the wife appeared before him with tears in her eyes, so he advised her, too. The local court found out that he was acting against the rules, representing both parties, so he was disbarred. But three years later, in 1928, he was reinstated and continued to practice law until his death, on January 15, 1945. That event in 1925 was not the only difficulty my father had with his practice. It was one of many such details. But he was not a criminal or anything like that. It was simply that he wasn't cut out for the practice of law.

"Father came from an old Rhineland family, in the region of the Palatinate. The Franks are a very old family and the blood is worn thin. If I didn't have my mother's battling spirit I would have been like my father, an indecisive man, never amounting to much. But Mother was different. She was a fine woman. Mother and Father never got along well. They remained married until I was ten years of age, when Mother left home and went back to her family to live. Father remarried when I was in my twenties, to a nice old lady who made his life comfortable for him in his declining years. Mother never remarried.

"In later years, Mother was not as bitter toward my father as she had been. Age mellowed both of them, I suppose. Mother used to talk about Father in recent years, before his death, recalling his good qualities. Previously she couldn't stand him. This, of course, made my childhood rather unhappy. I graduated from the gymnasium at age sixteen, then spent a year going to school in Prague, and at eighteen years of age, I joined the army toward the end of the First World War. I was never on good terms or intimate with my father. You might say that since the age of ten, I had no family life. My mother was out of the picture, having taken my younger sister with her to her folks' home to live, and I remained, together with my brother, who was eight years older than I, with my father. Most of the time I went to the Maximilian Gymnasium in Munich, with the exception of the year in Prague and the short time in the army in 1918. I have few tender recollections of my early life. I really began to know my mother and realize what a fine woman she was after I had grown to adulthood and was independent. I was more or less independent all my life, at least from the age of ten, when my parents were divorced."

Frank then embarked on an idea that most of the family difficulties within Germany were a reflection of the unhappy life which was caused by a lack of living space and the large increase in city population as compared to rural from 1870 until 1933.

"I'm positive that the high divorce rate, the great incompatibility between married persons, the unsettled family life in Germany during those years was the result of crowded city conditions and lack of opportunities to develop. My own case is an example. When I was minister of justice I received thousands of letters asking for assistance in obtaining divorces.[9] Hitler was against making a divorce easy to obtain. I was in favor of it, but could do nothing about it. Hitler forbade me to divorce my own wife, with whom I was very unhappy, as I told you previously.

"I think that Hitler was abnormal in his sexual needs. That is, he needed too little from the opposite sex. He considered women as objects of beauty, and he often talked with affection about his own mother. I obtained the impression that he disliked his father, because he never mentioned him. But it is a bad thing if a man has too little Eros in him. It makes him insensitive, and probably leads to cruelty. Freud, Sigmund Freud, the last of the great German psychiatrists, who died in England, pointed out the relationship between frustrated love and cruelty. I believe it is what you psychiatrists term sadism. I'm convinced that a man who does not need the love of a woman, and thinks he can forgo it, or who does forgo it, can turn to cruelty and sadism as a substitute."

Had Frank ever read the works of Freud? "Not his works, no books of his, but I have read many articles about what he said and about his work. Have you ever seen the correspondence between Albert Einstein and Freud between the years 1928 and 1933? It is worth reading. Einstein probably has copies of that correspondence, which I was privileged to read. Freud predicted almost exactly what would happen in the future, and what actually did occur as far as the atrocities and mass murders. He was a great mind. He saw the inherent sadism and cruelty in Hitler and in Hitlerism. Both Einstein and Freud were clever in leaving Germany, because both of them would doubtlessly have been caught by Himmler and murdered."

Frank sighed. "What a horrible system we had. How blind we were."

# Wilhelm Frick
## 1877–1946

Wilhelm Frick was minister of the interior from 1933 to 1943. Found guilty at Nuremberg of crimes against peace, war crimes, and crimes against humanity, he was hanged on October 16, 1946.

## March 10, 1946

Wilhelm Frick is sixty-nine years old, with close-cropped gray hair. He is neither hostile nor friendly in attitude, speaks with a clipped, precise speech which has appropriate pauses, and rises and falls, but is apparently quite automatic, and practiced. He was interviewed this afternoon in his cell, Triest translating. He speaks little English. His German is easy to follow. He sounds consistently as if he were making an informal speech, whenever asked about anything regarding National Socialism, his role in it, and so forth. He does not look quite his age, is erect, not very wrinkled, and physically hardy. He is of slender build, medium height, moderate weight, inclined toward leanness rather than the opposite, but not thin.

Asked if he had any complaints, he said that his only complaint was the noise made by the guards at night, but that he realized it was difficult to keep young people quiet. His only physical ailment is an occasional sore throat "caused by the weather," which occurs two or three times a year at change of seasons.

**Previous Illnesses:** "Lung trouble" (probably mild bronchitis, from his description of the symptomatology) from ages six to twelve years. "Chronic bronchial catarrh" until the age of thirty. No other illnesses.

**Education:** Elementary school, four years, in Kaiserslautern, followed gymnasium from 1887 until 1896 in the same town. (He was born in Kaiserslautern on March 12, 1877.) He then attended the Universities of Göttingen, Berlin, and Munich, mainly the last, for three years. He received the degree of doctor of jurisprudence in 1901 from the University of Heidelberg.

**Career:** He practiced law in Kaiserslautern from 1900 to 1903. In 1903 he took a state examination and went to Munich as a state employee, working in the office of the district magistrate. From 1907 to 1917 he was in the administration of Pirmasens (Bavaria). From 1917 to 1919 he was in the police director's office in Munich, in charge of profiteers, "rackets," and so forth.

In 1919 he assumed charge of the political section of the police department, particularly against Communists. "After the signing of the peace, the kaiser was to abdicate and the Social Democrats were to take over. Then the government became more leftist. There was a Communist government for four weeks in April 1919, the Councils Republic." Frick helped to overthrow that. "That government was concentrated in Munich, where the Russian Jews were thick."[1] He remained in charge of the political section of police in Munich until 1923.

In November 1923, the Munich putsch occurred and Frick was arrested and imprisoned for four and a half months. He first met Hitler in 1923, "because every public gathering had to be applied for through my section of the police." He became a party member in 1923 soon after meeting Hitler. After the Nazi Party was banned, he rejoined as soon as the party was legalized again in 1925.

He was in prison from November 1923 until April 1924. On April 6, 1924, he became a representative at the German Reichstag. Until the end of the war, he remained the Reichstag representative of upper Bavaria, always on the National Socialist ticket. It was called, at times, the Völkischer Bloc. "I was in prison in Munich four and a half months, whereas Hitler was in Landsberg prison nine months," he observed casually. During his prison term, he spent his time writing about his experiences in the putsch for his defense. After his trial, he received a fifteen-month sentence, Hitler a five-year term, but both were released in the times stated above.

His career in the Reichstag was that of "party whip," or "fraction leader." There was a split in the northern and southern German parties. There was the so-called November Party, also called the Northern Liberation Movement. At first there were thirty National Socialists in the Reichstag, but in subsequent elections, they lost ground. By 1925, there were but seven Nazis in the Reichstag. The others went over to the Liberation Party.[2]

In 1928 the Liberation Party disappeared and the number of National Socialist Reichstag seats grew to twelve. There were four to five hundred seats in the Reichstag.

"In 1923 the party made the putsch instead of participating in the elections. After that failure, Hitler said we would have to choose parliamentary methods to gain a majority."

In January 1930 Frick became minister of interior and education for Thuringia, in Weimar. At that time, Thuringia had fifty-three seats in the Reichstag, only five or six of which were held by National Socialists. The Nazis "were between the Communists on one side and the bourgeois on the other side. We formed a coalition government with the bourgeois." In that way, Frick became minister of interior of Thuringia until April 1, 1931, at which time he was "urged to leave" the coalition government. He reverted to his old position of Reichstag representative.

"The years 1930 to 1931 in Thuringia meant a lot to us, because people always said that Nazis can talk but not govern. Hitler had appointed me to the position of minister of interior in Thuringia and people saw that I accomplished much good."

So in September 1930, "as a result of my work in Thuringia," the Nazi strength in the Reichstag jumped from a mere twelve seats to 107, making the National Socialists the second strongest party in the Reich. In 1930 there was actually a National Socialist vice president of the Reich, one Franz Stoehr, who has since died. "Stoehr retired from that position, however, because it didn't work out, in view of differences with other parties.

"Soon we made a coalition with German nationalist parties, and in a meeting at Harzburg in 1931, we took a stand against the Dawes Plan. A little later we came out against the Young Plan. We also wanted to make a people's election."[3]

From 1931 to 1933 Frick was "a most important leader" in the Reichstag. In July 1932 "we did away with Heinrich Bruening. I just wanted to mention how Hitler came to power."

In 1933, after President Hindenburg took Hitler into the government, Frick became minister of interior, a post he held until the collapse in 1945.

Asked whether he knew Harold Ickes, the American secretary of the interior, Frick replied that he never met him because he had never been in America.[4] He had heard of him, and said that Ickes had refused helium to the German zeppelin in 1932–33. That was the only comment he offered on Ickes.

"It was my job to transform the parliamentary way into the authoritarian way. One point in the prosecution in these trials is that the *Federal Law Gazette* has 234 documents bearing my signature, that is, charging me with changing the laws.[5] The parliamentary system itself broke down between 1930 and 1932; the banks failed.

"The Bruening government had emergency laws. The Weimar Republic's rules did not help, so we had to change to the authoritarian way.

"The basic law at that time was that not only the Reichstag but the Reich government itself could publish laws. Thus the whole parliamentary system was overthrown and in time all laws were taken out of the hands of the parliament and into the authoritarian control."

Asked if he had any comment to offer on the Reichstag fire, Frick replied: "It can be argued both ways. At the trial some Communists were convicted. There is the rumor that Goering and the SA started it. But I don't know." What is your own opinion? "The only thing I can say is based on the viewpoint of who gained what. If the Communists had done it, they were stupid because they were prohibited thereafter. If Goering and the SA did it, I'm unable to say. So far it has not come up in this trial." At the time, what was your opinion? "I had no reason to be suspicious, though rumors, of course, existed at that time, too."[6]

Among the duties of the minister of interior were "general powers over administrative processes; also ministerial counsel for defense of the Reich." On August 20, 1943, Frick became protector of Bohemia and Moravia in addition to his other duties. He maintained offices in Berlin and in Prague. "But I was in Prague for only about one week out of each month. It was merely a representative position. The real German statesman for Bohemia and Moravia was Karl Hermann Frank. The latter was directly under Hitler and held a rank equivalent to mine: *Reichsminister*." Frick was *Reichsprotektor* of Bohemia and Moravia, whereas Frank was *Reichsminister* for Bohemia and Moravia.

What is your opinion of Karl Hermann Frank in view of some of the atrocity charges against him? "He had his good side. For instance, after Reinhard Heydrich was murdered, Hitler ordered that fifty thousand

Czechs be murdered in reprisal.[7] But Frank said that these people had families, and suggested lesser measures." Isn't Frank accused of Lidice?[8] "Yes. But Hitler wanted more than that."

What is your opinion of Hitler? "He was too rash. Not enough self-control." Do you think another Führer might have been better? "Hitler was undoubtedly a genius but he lacked self-control. He recognized no limits. Otherwise the thousand-year Reich would have lasted more than twelve years." If you were Führer, would it have been different? "It all depends. Hitler had bad advisers, particularly Himmler, Bormann, and Goebbels. I lost Hitler's confidence in 1934. I worked closely and confidentially with him only until the Roehm putsch. After that, I was not really in the inner circle of Hitler's advisers. I'm convinced Roehm did not even want a putsch, but Himmler used it to gain power. From that time forth Himmler became more and more irreplaceable." Frick states that Himmler was "against" him since 1933, but gives no reason for this other than Himmler's "great desire for more power."

"Hitler's government, that is to say, the internal policy, worked well in 1933. It did away with unemployment. It worked smoothly as long as Hitler listened to his advisers. After the Roehm putsch in 1934, Hitler's chief advisers became Goering and Himmler." Were you ever friendly with Goering? "No.

"Hitler's lack of moderation was a fault. He was so stubborn he listened only to Bormann and Himmler, both of whom were criminals of the worst kind. His own ministers wouldn't be received anymore. I tried to resign because it was an impossible situation, but Hitler refused and said I had to remain. The last time I could see Hitler was in 1937. During the war I saw him only occasionally. I had a home next to Hitler's in Berlin because the living quarters of the Ministry of the Interior were located in the Foreign Office, which was next door to the Chancellery. Formerly the Foreign Office had been the Ministry of Interior. We retained only our living quarters there. It was Wilhelmstrasse, 74."

**Family History:** Father died in 1918 at age eighty as a result of falling from a wagon. He was a schoolteacher. He was a "good" father, a nationalist politically, and an admirer of Bismarck. He was never a soldier. Mother died in 1893 at the age of seventy-five of pneumonia. At the time Frick was sixteen years old. His father never remarried. The father's name is the same as the subject's, that is, Wilhelm. His grandparents on both sides were farmers who lived in the northern Palatinate. He has little comment to offer regarding his mother's or father's personality. He believes that he resembles his father in personality.

**Siblings:** He is the youngest of four children. (1) Brother, died at age thirty of tuberculosis, in the Canary Islands. His name was Hermann Frick, born 1870. He was a businessman. (2) Sister, died age seventy-two, in 1938 of a weak heart. She was single and kept house for Frick. (3) Sister, Emma, born in 1864, died in 1903 of tumor of the stomach. She was a teacher of English and Latin.

He did not see the sister who died in 1938 for the last five or six years of her life. She remained in Kaiserslautern, whereas he was in Berlin. He was on good terms with all members of his family, he says, but they were never very intimate.

**Marital:** First marriage was to a woman ten years his junior. They were divorced in 1934. The marriage was "satisfactory," but he wanted more children, "and she didn't want any more so we were divorced." They had three children. In the same year of his divorce, 1934, he remarried a woman nineteen years his junior. This marriage yielded two children.

**Children:** (1) Hans, born 1911, was a district magistrate in upper Bavaria. He committed suicide on May 3, 1945, together with his wife and children. (2) Walter, born 1913, was killed in action on the Russian front in 1941, at which time he was a first lieutenant. "I saw him on the banks of the Dnieper, wounded as a result of shell fragments. He had an abdominal wound. I had permission from the Führer to visit him. I flew there and next day flew back to Berlin. Later that day I found he had died." What was your emotional reaction? "It was sad. It's war. Many others died, too. It's war."

We discussed the business of war. "I am skeptical about preventing wars. I doubt if they can be prevented. There will always be wars. Judging by past experiences, working for peace now would be as ineffective as ever. It's a law of nature." That's a rather cynical, pessimistic philosophy. "No. I am just a realist. There's no use having wishful dreams."

Asked why his son committed suicide, he replied: "He had been a regional commander in Russia, and he was afraid that he would be handed over to the Russians. He was against that. He wrote his mother that he was going to commit suicide. I just heard about it in November."

(3) Anneliese, daughter, born 1920, is living and well, single; she writes often. She worked for the medical department of the air force. These first three children are of his first wife.

(4) Renate, a daughter, aged ten, born in 1935, and (5) Dieter, a son, born in 1937. The last three children are living and well as far as he is aware. His wife lives near Starnberg Lake. He has heard that his first wife is depressed because of the loss of her two sons. Personally, he is not particularly depressed, because of the "nature of life, the laws of nature, the ways of war."

# Hans Fritzsche

Hans Fritzsche (1900–1953) was a senior official in Joseph Goebbels's Ministry of Propaganda and head of the Radio Division from 1942. At Nuremberg, tried for war crimes, he was found not guilty.

## March 2, 1946

This pale, thin man, Hans Fritzsche, was at the end of the defendants' dock, and his defense would come last. He was forty-five years old, looked his age, but had a certain youthful, naïve, suggestively adolescent quality. I have had many interviews with him since January, when I came to Nuremberg. He appreciated the visits, and seemed to feel better after a talk. I pursued my usual attitude of asking him to say whatever came into his mind. Occasionally I directed a question, as today, when I asked him to give me an informal biographical sketch. He said he had written such an outline some time ago, and offered me a copy. I told him that I had access to that autobiographical account, but that I should prefer to have him talk to me personally about his life.

He said: "That is best. Those two written pages are at best a lifeless outline.

"I was born in Bochum, Westphalia, on April 21, 1900. Of course, I had the everyday childhood illnesses. From the age of twelve to fourteen, however, I suffered from a weak heart because I grew too fast. This necessitated my staying out of school for a year. It also prevented me from indulging in sports until I was almost twenty years old. The weak heart did not affect me after the age of twenty.

"In sports, I liked mountain climbing. In my middle twenties I was injured skiing, fracturing both my feet, a spinal process, and several ribs. But I was in bed only four weeks after the accident and recovered fully.

"I had one other serious illness, in 1936–37, when I required two operations for the removal of my appendix, which had ruptured. The first operation was an incision and drainage, the second was to actually remove the appendix."

I asked him about his education. "I went to school at Halle on the Saale for about three years. Then I attended the gymnasium at Breslau for five years. I never liked the rigid Prussian atmosphere of these schools. I was not a good student because I disliked the mechanical methods of teaching. My last four years of gymnasium were in Leipzig. I did well there because the school was more like a university, and the teachers were more liberal and modern. I graduated at the top of my class. For a graduation thesis I wrote something entitled 'Humanity, Our Eternal Desire,' and it was highly praised.

"Curiously enough, some of my best friends in the Breslau school were Jewish. These were the sons of Jewish emigrants from the East. There was always anti-Semitic feeling in the school, but I never participated in it.

"One of my closest friends was Lewisohn, about my own age, who was Jewish but later converted to Protestantism. Another dear friend was Lohse, also Jewish, who together with his mother and sister became Protestants under my influence. Lewisohn was killed in the First World War, but Lohse and his family, I believe, are still alive in Silesia."

Fritzsche said there were many things he learned aside from the actual studies in school. Among them was a great respect for individual rights. His schooling was interrupted for about a year or nine months in 1918 when he was drafted into the army and spent some time fighting in Flanders. In December 1919, after the war ended, he returned to gymnasium and finally graduated in 1920.

That same year he began his studies at the University of Greifswald, specializing in philosophy, but also taking courses in German literature, history, and economics. "Because of the difficulties of the times, the inflation, strikes, and conditions equivalent to civil war, I was naturally attracted to politics. I became president of the students' union at the university in my second year there. Then I transferred to the University of Berlin and was active among the students there."

He quit the university after three years, in 1923, for "financial reasons," and became at first an assistant, or secretary, of a new School for Geopolitics. Shortly thereafter he became historical-political editor of the *Prussian Yearbook* until sometime in 1924. He next became a reporter and editor for the Telegraph Union (similar to the United Press service), in charge of foreign news. He remained with this agency from 1924 until 1932, at which time he was editor in chief.

I asked him about his family background. He said that his father was born in the vicinity of Leipzig and his forefathers before him for many generations came from that territory. Most of his father's relatives were armorers or toolsmiths. His father was an "old postal official," who because he was disliked by his superiors, though respected by his inferiors, never achieved more than the directorate of a city post office. "My father's brother-in-law became a member of the Postal Ministry, but my father never achieved that because he was too independent. Father is now eighty-five. I last heard from him in April, when he was living in the Russian zone on an island near Pomerania, in the Baltic Sea. He retired from the postal service in 1925 or 1926. He rented rooms during the summer in his little home on the island.

"My father was completely apolitical. Whereas all his brothers and brothers-in-law entered the Postal Ministry, he chose not to play politics and stayed in the field. He was director of the post offices, at various times, in Halle, Breslau, and Leipzig." In general Fritzsche's father was rather stern and strict, but rarely used physical means of punishment toward the children. The relationship between father and son seems to have been a respectful but aloof one.

"My mother died in 1938 of arteriosclerotic heart disease. She was about five years younger than my father. I wrote about her in the short autobiography but I would much rather tell you in my own words. She did not have as much schooling as Father. She had what is termed in Germany the 'education of the eldest daughter,' that is, she spoke a little French, played the piano to a limited extent, and so forth. Mentally, however, she was much more alert than my father and had a shining personality.

"I had always been on exceptionally close terms with my mother. She was born a Catholic, but because the family was Lutheran and because there was no Catholic church in Linz, and since she believed that God would accept prayers in any form that they were offered, she became a

Protestant at the age of over sixty. A year later she became president of the Lutheran Women's Welfare of all Pomerania. Although she had little formal education, no ability to make speeches, and wore only the simplest of clothes, she actually had a very forceful personality."

I asked him what his feelings had been concerning his mother during the last few months. He replied that he often thought of her, particularly in dreams. "My mother was always my greatest sympathizer, and when I grew up, even as a man, I liked to put my head in her lap. That was a gesture which was so strong, that especially now I can visualize it again and again.

"My mother could be very sad about little things, but in a time of any great difficulty or crisis she was always brave. She always had a kind word in case of trouble. For example, when my brothers and sisters died, I shall always remember what she said. It was a religious sentence which I don't want to mention. I dream of those things often."

It seemed obvious that he wanted me to ask him about this religious sentence which he did not want to profane by mentioning. I did ask him why he was reluctant to mention something that was obviously good. "I hesitate because I consider the words so sacred because they were said by my beloved mother. But you are right, there is no harm in saying a good thing. The religious words my mother said were 'The soul is saved.'

"In my home there was little talk of religion but everything was based on it. I have a repeated dream in which my head is resting in my mother's lap and there is that gesture of hers, and that saying 'Now what is happening?' "

I asked Fritzsche what he felt was meant by that dream. He said he did not believe in the significance of dreams particularly, but that he supposed it had something to do with his innate innocence. "If I were a psychiatrist I should guess that that dream meant an unconscious feeling of innocence. Because when I'm awake there are two forces acting on me. One force demands to know, Why did you serve in this system — you saw things in 1932 and 1938 — why did you let yourself be talked into this system?

"The other force within me is a voice which always says, But how *could* you know of these atrocities, because you are innocent!

"Moreover, there is this completely false trial. I would participate wholeheartedly in a trial if it were to determine the guilt for 5 million murdered people[1] and the guilt for the atrocities. But I see in this trial endless other things brought out and I have the feeling that in the shadow of the guilt of these murders the German people shall be considered guilty of everything, and in the shadow of this guilt the Americans, English, French, and especially the Russians will want to get rid of their own dirty linen.

"I'm of the opinion that one must differentiate two things: First, the will of the German people to live and to wage a clean fight' for its existence — a fight which was conducted. Second, and on the other side, the guilt for the murders and the atrocities. These are two completely different things."

I remarked that it seemed hard to differentiate where one began and the other ended. "If we had a German judge he would sentence us more severely than any Allied judge, but he would draw a clean line between the two things I just mentioned. I cannot forgo the feeling that the German people had during the last war and during this one, namely, that they were on the right side. Now, for the first time, the German nation was abused of this right by Hitler through his ambition for war, which appeared to us as a war for defense, but which was sought after by Hitler as an aggressive war, and through mass murder and atrocities.

"That is the tragedy which I feel."

I asked him whether his mother had ever expressed any opinions about National Socialism. "She never did. She was completely unpolitical. Of course, she was very happy and very proud that I had become well known, but she had no conception of the party or of my actual function in it. For that matter I was left cold by the big party meetings and rallies, too.

"Mother had a great dislike for Goebbels. She met him only once, when she visited me at the office. I don't know why she disliked him so, because he was nice and polite to her, but she told me after meeting him that I should get away from Goebbels. She said that he was a *small* man and I was a *big* man, and that Goebbels wanted to misuse me."

### March 3, 1946

Fritzsche has been married for twenty years. His wife is six months older than he is. They have one child, born after twelve years of marriage, a girl of eight.

Much happiness from your child? "Very." Intelligent? "Very, and mature in her feelings. For instance, when my wife wrote a letter, she shed tears and the girl said, 'Don't cry, Mother. Tears won't help. I lost my pencil sharpener in school and tears won't bring it back.' "

Does she know where you are or why you are here? "She knows *where* I am, but *why* I am here, I think she will, for the time being . . . she will find out when older."

He met Hitler for the first time in the Rhineland in 1924 or 1925, in the house of a daughter of old Werner Siemens. "I heard Hitler speak. He had just come from prison and he spoke of a radical fight against Communism. That conversation ended with a remark by Hitler that he was not a politician but a propagandist. I was not impressed, did not join the party, because the propaganda Hitler introduced was too brutal and forcible." Did you converse with Hitler then? "Yes." Your impression? "An enthused dreamer. Something mystic about him. The only question was, how, out of a mix-up of thirty-six parties, could unity of the German people be found? That and the problem of Communism." Did he mention anti-Semitism? "Not in the speech. He spoke with the old lady, and I listened." Was she a friend of yours? "She was the aunt of a friend. I was invited there by chance."

**Brief Survey of Fritzsche's Activities in Propaganda Ministry:** Radio news reporter for the first five years. "No musical accompaniments, no speeches." In charge of German newspapers three and a half to four years. The last four years until the end, charged with everything on the radio. Were you the number two man in the Propaganda Ministry? "No, it's hard to say that. But I was charged with everything in radio and I was well known. But I formerly had many superiors between me and Goebbels. In the end there was only one superior between me and Goebbels. I was one of the twelve section chiefs. But I can say that I was the most independent person in the Propaganda Ministry. I commanded great respect. My official sphere of activity was not great, but my human influence was great."

For instance? "If I protected a man nobody did anything to him. There was an inspector for the party radio supposed to control me. In October 1944, I prohibited this party inspector entry into all radio stations in Germany." Why? "He behaved badly." What did he do? "He talked about me behind my back. Nobody but Fritzsche could do anything like that.

"Another example: The Gestapo sent agents into my department on three occasions. Each time I would fire them. Nobody but me would have dared to do that."

## March 9, 1946

"Mother's family came from the region around Münster. Her people were mostly tulip growers and gardeners. It must have been a peace-loving family. I never knew my grandparents, unfortunately.

"Being the youngest child, I was probably a little spoiled by Mother. I was always considered the most gifted of the children, and in a way that set me somewhat apart from the rest."

He virtually did not live with his wife after 1944. He had a younger woman as a lover and lived with her. Legally he remained married, but his intention was to obtain a divorce and wed the younger woman who had become his mistress. He heard from his young woman "indirectly" since his imprisonment, and still felt he would like to marry her, but because he heard regularly and devotedly from his wife, he was torn between emotions of "loyalty and devotion on the one side, and passion and love on the other.

"My wife is depressed but brave at present. She is prohibited from practicing dentistry, although she was Dr. Villiger's assistant, an excellent dental surgeon in her own right. When I was in the Propaganda Ministry we lived on my small income. Dr. Goebbels would not approve my wife's practicing, but I ignored his disapproval and she always practiced. Now she lives from hand to mouth in Hamburg, suffers because she is my wife — no doubt that is why the authorities won't let her practice — and she must earn a mark a day doing knitting."

## March 17, 1946

Today being Sunday, he was working in midafternoon on his typewriter upon questions for his own defense. "I don't think I will have a difficult time. My defense is that it was all pure idealism on my part. I can defend everything point by point. But I won't try to do that, because everything I did, I did before the world public.

"On the other side of the picture is the fact that on the basis of my work, 5 million people were murdered and untold atrocities took place. It is purely a question of judgment as to whether a connection can be established clearly between these two things.

"If it were merely my person that were involved, I could defend myself in one sentence — 'I did it as a German patriot' — because if all of the German people were betrayed, I was also betrayed; but it is a complex matter. It is not my person alone that is involved, but the whole German people, whom I for the biggest part informed."

Fritzsche smiled pensively and rolled a cigarette. His face suddenly clouded over with seriousness and he said: "Then because of the murder of 5 million people — and I am not excusing or minimizing such barbarity — it becomes now the question of the right for existence of 50 million German people who are pressed together in a space in which they cannot exist and on which they will probably starve."

There has been no indication from Allied policy that the intention is to starve 50 million Germans. "It is happening. By accident I received a letter from a Jewish landowner whom I once helped escape from a concentration camp. He writes that his family was arrested in Berlin after six months of flight from the East. This man describes dramatically the plight of millions of people, hundreds of thousands killed and starved to death."

Where? "In East Prussia and in Silesia. That is a tragedy."

From the foregoing it would almost seem as if you are implying that the present plight of the German people is the fault of the 5 million dead Jews. "No, no, no, a thousand times, the German people must now bear the accusation of these murders and rightfully. Everyone cries, 'Punishment! Punishment! Punishment!' The Russians say that they will take a tiny piece of East Prussia, but actually they moved Poland three or four kilometers to the west. And the Poles are deporting all Germans from that territory. It is the same in Yugoslavia and Bohemia.[2]

"Besides, I get a description of my daughter and wife starving or almost starving in Hamburg. She was given notice to give up her flat, which in itself was just shingles over one's head; and now she doesn't know where to move. I wrote to my wife, but what advice can I give? She is a brave woman and writes brave letters. She says that physically she is unable to move. She is probably very worn out and nervous. She has no permission to live in southern Germany.

"The worst thing is their taking away her permission to practice dentistry." Why? "I can understand, but really I don't understand. It is being investigated through Colonel Andrus and he says that she should be permitted to practice. Dr. Gilbert thinks so, too. Do you see any reason for such an order against her practicing?" None, as you have told the story. None. "She writes she had offers from twenty to thirty places in various dentists' offices in Hamburg, but it is forbidden."

Was your wife a member of the party? "No." I guess it is a matter of time and that eventually she will be permitted to practice. "Yes, time — but people have to live. I hope this man from Pomerania to whom I have just referred, and who wrote me the letter thanking me for helping him to escape from the concentration camp, will help her a bit." What is the story of your helping this Jewish man from Pomerania? "One day a woman came to my offices and waited in the foreroom. Her name was Karneka, and she was from Pomerania. She cried bitterly and I took her into my office and asked her what the trouble might be. She told me that her husband had been arrested and was in prison at Köslin. She said that both she and her husband had been declared Jews, but she didn't know upon whose orders the arrest took place. After that, I put in phone calls to the prison at Köslin and I requested to know who issued the orders for her husband's arrest. They answered that it was done on orders of the Gestapo.

"Then I called the Reich Security Main Office [RSHA] in Berlin, which replied that they knew nothing at all about the case and would investigate it. I called Köslin again and told them that I was investigating the case and that I was interested in it. The prison director told me then and there that the woman could come to the prison and visit her husband, who until then had been held incommunicado. This was followed by a fight of three or four months' duration. I will make it short. I involved the food minister, Herbert Backe; the party district administrator of Pomerania, Franz Schwede-Coburg; and also a man whose name I didn't know at that time — Adolf Eichmann of the Gestapo."[3] At this point, Fritzsche laughs rather sardonically and somewhat anxiously.

"I must have used up ten telegrams and thirty letters — it was a big fight, and finally I got the release after the man had already been in a concentration camp. I never met him personally and, having my own difficulties, had lost all track of him until last May. I was happy to hear from him. The letter was addressed to my lawyer. I also received a letter from my wife in which she said she too had received a letter from Karneka."

Was this family that you helped Jewish? "According to the law they were Jewish. He was part Jewish in his ancestry; he was the grandchild of Gaus, the founder of the IG Farben industry in Frankfurt. This man and his wife were about forty years of age."

Did you do things like that very often? Fritzsche smiles benignly, and says, "Frequently. I received many letters because I was a well-known man. I can't recall a single case where I refused help. It was only natural. I didn't think much about it."

Fritzsche asked me if I was familiar with what he had written while in this prison regarding himself and Goebbels. I told him that I had read that. He said, "What I wrote only goes up to the year 1925. If you write

two autobiographies, they turn out differently. If I should tell you a few
things today — I can tell you only the basic characteristics of my being —
but do you know, I might tell you something else."

I suppose that is true of all of us to a certain extent, but do you feel
that this susceptibility to change is more characteristic, is stronger in you
than in others? Fritzsche reflects and more or less assents. "I will tell you
something but only on one condition — that you don't make me blush,
because what I want to say now I want that you should believe. My
whole desire in life was not political or warlike — I wanted to be a gar-
dener. On my father's side for 350 years his family were always black-
smiths or such workers, until my grandfather founded a small arms
factory. On my mother's side for 250 years her family were gardeners
who grew Dutch tulips. Originally they were from Holland, but then
many generations ago they immigrated to Westphalia.

"As a boy of fourteen, we had no garden but lived in a big apartment
building. I had a large collection of cacti in 1914. As a matter of fact, I
was offered 250 gold marks for that collection. I also had an orchid collection. But I never had a garden until 1934, when I bought one. It was
located fifty kilometers outside of Berlin, was three thousand square
meters in size, and I worked it myself. On this homestead I made my own
garden with my own hands and I loved to work in it. My fundamental
desire in life was always gardening — to lead a contemplative existence,
not one of activity.

"I was also an editor, but even then more of the feature editor. I
edited fiction, novels, and human interest stories. I felt that by writing
these things I had more impact and influence on others. I entered politics only because of the misery of 1918, but even as a politician I cher-
ished the purely human side of my work. Because of this I had such
tremendous influence.

"Goebbels could make a speech and could bring a few thousand people to a tremendous crescendo of applause. When I spoke at times there
was no applause at all. I was not sensational, but I had developed a regular community of followers who were devoted to me. This community
of adherents was perhaps not as large as the group Dr. Goebbels commanded, but it was more lasting. The same is true in my work itself. My
official position was not as large or important as that of Goebbels, but
my human influence was greater.

"To be a coworker of mine — and I say this blushingly — was considered in our office to be a bigger honor than to be a coworker of Goebbels." Fritzsche smiles and blushes appropriately. "And if I should send a representative to some conference or other, that representative was far more respected and important than if Goebbels sent a representative. For example, it has been said often here at the trials that people were afraid of Himmler and of the Gestapo. I never had such fear and I didn't have to have such fear. Himmler once offered me a big position if I joined the SS. I declined and told him that I didn't fit into his organization, and nothing ever happened.

"In 1937, I made some kind of demand on Himmler — I don't remember what this demand was, but it was not fulfilled despite many reminders. Then I wrote him a letter and told him that if I received no satisfaction by, let us say, April 1, I would broadcast no more news of the SS and its meanings over the radio. Two days after I sent this note to Himmler, I was called into Goebbels's office. Goebbels was excited and said that Himmler had demanded my dismissal. Upon which I replied, 'I used to write friendly letters to small people because small people can't stand roughness, but to great people I have written tough letters because they don't react to friendliness.' I told Goebbels that if it is not the system within the state to do things in the opposite way, I would gladly accept dismissal. When he heard that, Goebbels excused himself, and a few days later I received a letter from Himmler in which he excused himself and fulfilled completely whatever demands I made on him." Can you recall what the demands were? "No, I really can't recall what it was all about.

"A third example of my independence is the following: I fired several of my employees after I found out that they were agents of the Gestapo. As a reason, I gave a written explanation that these employees had become members of the Gestapo without my knowledge. After that incident I was visited by the Gestapo, whose agents told me they had the right to investigate all state organizations. I replied that if they wanted to know anything, they could ask me, but I insisted that under no circumstances would I tolerate any illegal procedures. People that were dismissed by me are still alive, and I am sure they can testify to the veracity of these statements."

We went on to a discussion of Goebbels, which can be found elsewhere among my notes. There is a tract written by Fritzsche on the subject of Goebbels and propaganda, which is still at large. Fritzsche said that he had many fights with Max Amann, who was chief of newspaper publishers. Fritzsche called Amann a brutal businessman who persecuted many people and destroyed many existences. Fritzsche said that he often brought into his own department people who had been persecuted by Amann.

### April 6, 1946

Fritzsche was very glad to see Mr. Triest and myself again this week. He said that he had been feeling depressed because of a lack of news from his wife and child, and that his wife was still living in a garret room earning about a mark a day doing some knitting or sewing, and unable to practice dentistry because she had the misfortune to be married to him. He smiled as he said this, as if awaiting some reassurance that he wasn't such a bad fellow after all.

He said that he had been thinking over his future defense, which he figured would come in early June, and that he was torn between two conflicting ideas. First, he wanted to reveal to the court clearly that he was a tool of the Nazis, that he had been deceived by Hitler and Goebbels, and that he personally had no conscious part in the evils of the Nazi regime and the "terrible racial madness" which ensued. Second, he wanted to point out to the court clearly in his defense that the guilt lay not only with the Germans, but also with the Allies. He said that none of the defendants thus far had stressed this point sufficiently, because they had been so preoccupied with proving their own innocence. He said that in most cases the defendants, unlike himself, were not innocent but, like Kaltenbrunner, were creating a fiction in the courtroom. He felt that he alone was most notably an unconscious tool of the Nazis and that therefore he could devote less time to his personal proclamation of innocence and more time to showing how Allied propaganda should share, to an extent, in the guilt of the horrors of war. "I see the defendants justify themselves, but they cannot justify the Nazi movement. I have the feeling during this year of internment and half a year of trial that I have endured a spiritual suffering and depression more terrible than any death could be.

"I became guilty of the death of 5 million people — innocently; in any event, I participated in the guilt of this tragedy coming over the world. The role I played doesn't matter — but I did play a part in it. I have spoken with Dr. Gilbert about my suffering, but although he is personally very humane and nice, on the whole his attitude is one of hatred — I am very open with you, and he cannot understand or do anything because one must be objective in understanding me or the part I play in the Nazi movement. I feel that you are objective. I can talk to you and feel that you understand. Without being objective, my words would not serve the Germans or the Allies or the world.

"What I would like to express and which I cannot express in court is the following: I worked for ten years on German propaganda. I was not the only leader but I was one of the most important leaders. However, even ten years ago I made the remark that to make propaganda is the first step to hell. Propaganda is always done by bringing the attention of the people to one side and taking the attention from the other side. Thus, propaganda is always one-sided, be it for good or for bad. Now during the past year and a half I have been thinking of the propaganda I broadcasted. I can say that I did not try to bring the attention of people to something bad, but to something one-sided — and I did that during all those ten years of my activity. I painted only in black-and-white — no in-between colors. Your country and the other Allies did the same thing."

At this point, Fritzsche showed me a folder of matches on which was inscribed the slogan "Crush the Axis," with caricature drawings of Hitler, Mussolini, and Hirohito. Fritzsche smiled and said, "This, for example, is a tiny instance of the propaganda of hatred such as we never even dared to do in Germany. Now I can see, to my great disappointment, that in this trial, also, only a black-and-white painting is taking place. It may be necessary from a legal standpoint so that the trials should not take too long. A verdict of guilty does not matter. But I should like to see that this trial would advance humanity. Humanity must be advanced after the death of 5 million innocent people.

"And if this should be the case, Justice Jackson should not step up after Streicher said he was mistreated in Oberursel, and say emotionally that the Allies have tried to conduct the war within the limits of humanity. Those were exactly the feelings I had during the war. So the history of the world tends to repeat itself."

I told Fritzsche that I was in England consulting with some British psychiatrists at the time Streicher made the statement in court about having to kiss the feet of Negroes and other instances of his maltreatment when he was first taken prisoner. Just what was Fritzsche's reaction to Streicher's testimony? "Justice Jackson said that this should be removed from the official court record because it was not part of the trial. But I could give much larger examples of maltreatment and atrocities by the Russians. But I don't want to make propaganda here in prison and I shall desist. In short, I can see everything being painted in black-and-white all over again. This is just another step to hell. I can say honestly the following: After what I know today, the German people and myself were lied to and betrayed by Hitler, and Hitler did it in such a fashion that the German people believed it with an assurance stronger than any oath.

"During the last thousand years in Europe, many wars were fought for which the victors paid by sacrificing their own blood. That was the strongest assurance which Hitler could give to the people that he was against war, because the German people themselves were not for war. Every normal man is against war as much as he is opposed to tuberculosis. A few individual exceptions don't change that generalization.

"So if despite that, Hitler prepared war, he perpetrated the greatest lie and betrayal in the world. This trial clearly shows that Hitler did just that. I have no hesitation to state very clearly that Hitler was a liar and a betrayer on a mammoth scale. Even without the death of the 5 million extermination camp victims, Hitler would still go down in history as the greatest villain that ever lived." But the great decisive question here at this trial is how Hitler could keep up a betrayal like that. How could he manage to delude the people when hundreds of Allied radio stations were saying the truth or pretty close to the truth?

"Speaking for myself, I did not believe what the Allies said, though I had opportunity to always listen to Allied stations. The reasons for my not believing it was that it had been drummed into us that the Allies were telling lies in the form of propaganda. The tragedy of it all is that what these Allied broadcasting stations said was literally true. I must have said at least a hundred times during the war, whenever the Allied broadcasting stations talked about cruelties and atrocities, that the same type of Allied propaganda went on in the last war. I would say to my friends that in the last war the Allies talked about Germans chopping off the hands of Belgian children and that after the First World War it was admitted by the Allies that such allegations were false and merely propagandistic. I will say even today, that at the beginning of this war, hundreds of lies about Nazism were spread over the Allied stations. They even broadcast things about me personally — things that could be proven false. Therefore, that is what I mean by saying that the guilt lies on both sides, because propaganda, whether it be evil or good, tends to make one doubt it. If one refers to the many false statements made by Allied broadcasters at the beginning of the war, then one's belief in foreign broadcasts would necessarily be minimized.

"If you then refer to the Versailles Treaty,[4] to the theory of the necessity for living space, to the false propaganda that the Nazis spread about the persecution of Germans in the Sudetenland, and the border incidents which were supposed to have taken place before the attack on Poland or on Russia — then one can understand how we Germans, even we who were doing the propaganda, became affected and began to believe these things ourselves. You can see, too, how the effect of a sensational news broadcast from England or America, though it might have been true, would be as nothing. This is the satanic triumph of propaganda. It simply closes one's ears to what is right or what is wrong.

"My beliefs because of these facts are simple. I could dismiss as unimportant any discussion about what happens to the twenty men now here on trial as responsible for the horrors of the past war. But I should like to demand that an American Senate investigating committee, similarly created before this war, make an investigation of the conduct of the war by the Allies. Then the blame or guilt would clearly be shown as not being all Germany's but at least in part an Allied guilt. I don't mean that one can in any way justify Hitler's betrayal of the innocent German people by his aggression which led to war, or Hitler and Himmler's criminal extermination of innocent millions of men, women, and children. But if a United States Senate investigating committee would have the courage after these trials to try to ascertain honestly the guilt on both sides — then it would be proven that the Germans, disregarding for a moment the pure murders which were committed, did try to bring about a decent administration in conquered occupied countries. Such a Senate investigating committee, if it had the courage to acknowledge that, would be a great help to the present unfortunate plight of the German people. Such a committee would soon find that it was only after partisan warfare began in the occupied territories through the murder of German soldiers, et cetera, that German reprisals, shooting of hostages, and other crimes were set in motion, which brought about ever-increasing warfare and atrocities.[5]

"Then you will get to the result that in the German people there are also not only black-and-white colorations but also shades of guilt just as among the Allies. Then you will realize that the responsibility for the war, as seen by a sane man with two eyes, does not really exist. That it is the only way in which some advantage for all people can be gained from all these tragic events.

"I know that what I am saying is somewhat confusing, but I have a clear aim in mind. I mean that one cannot blame one man or one state for the war guilt. Other states and other men also bear a share of the guilt." I asked Fritzsche whether he meant any particular Allied nation was guilty along with Germany. He replied, "Almost all of the Allies. Hitler could not have waged this war if there had not been a constellation of guilt. The result is, of course, that the German people was betrayed and lied to by its own leader. But that this could be done is the fault, at least partly, of the rest of the world. I know. An understanding like this can only be brought out in a religious sense. But if you think of the possibilities for the advance of civilization, then at least one has to stand up and say so. In my defense, whether it be for my good or for my disadvantage, I shall make these statements in order to clarify the guilt of the world. I am not minimizing the guilt of the Nazi leaders. I am merely trying to show that the Allies bear their burden of guilt too and that in order for civilization to advance, mutual guilt must be recognized and errors corrected.

"Really, I come to this conclusion through personal suffering, such as no human being has ever suffered. It is the result of my thinking and brooding during the past year and a half, and that should not be mistaken for attempting to excuse myself or looking for some self-justification."

Was Fritzsche's view on this matter of Allied guilt and German guilt a philosophic one, or was it something concrete and based on examples which he knew? "It is not philosophic. It is a matter of ethics. The realization of a conviction like mine is impossible under the political status which exists today. I feel there is a religious demand — "Love thy neighbor as thyself" — a motto which has not been realized for two thousand years. What I would like to emanate from the darkness of this tragedy is one spark of life. I mean, the realization that crime does not begin when you murder people. Crime begins with propaganda, even if such propaganda is for a good cause. The moment propaganda turns against another nation or against any human being, evil starts. Whereas the Germans started propaganda toward the end of this tragedy, you Allies stand at the beginning of the tragedy."

Did Fritzsche mean the Versailles Treaty? "No, I mean now in 1946 you stand at the beginning of another tragedy." Did he mean that the Allies and the Germans continue to hate each other? "Exactly. We Germans carried our hatred from the First World War to the Second World War, and now you are about to carry the hatred about the murder of 5 million people on to another World War."

I asked Fritzsche whether he felt that it was unimportant to prosecute those responsible for the murder of 5 million people. "Without doubt. That has been my feeling for a year. I always complained when the lawyers spoke of petty things, such as whether Goering said this or that. It was unimportant — the only decisive question was not put to Goering. The prosecution should have asked him directly, 'You were the second man in the state where 5 million Jews were murdered, not to mention hundreds of thousands of innocent people, hostages, whole villages destroyed for no reason, et cetera. What about those Jews and the other innocent victims of murder?' It is completely unbelievable that Goering didn't know all about it. If I myself received letters regarding these atrocities, how many more letters did Goering really receive?

"And another question was also unfortunately not asked of Goering: 'The German people put faith in you even if they doubted Hitler because you were gentlemanly and more likable. What did you, Goering, do to justify this confidence? You have led a luxurious life and collected stolen art.' Such other questions should have been asked.

"Similarly, the defendant Frank was not asked decisive questions. For example, when Frank was asked what he knew of the Jewish murders, he said, 'You could smell it.' That is a complete lie and a dishonesty. Frank could not only smell it, he knew about it. There he was, the governor general of Poland — he couldn't just have smelled it, he must have known it. The rest of the trial is without any importance." I asked Fritzsche whether he did not think that Frank, during his defense, perhaps tried to be honest but, after so many years of deluding himself, was incapable of telling the truth. Fritzsche replied, "Yes, but that doesn't help the German people. At a moment like this the truth is the all-important issue. I have only one interest — that the fault of the other side, the Allies, be brought out, not as an excuse for us but for the future prevention of war and atrocities. An example of this is the case of the Bolsheviks. If they, in the face of their great cruelties committed in Germany, want to shed their dirty linen, then they should actually take it off. In Russia people just disappeared — in other words, became political prisoners. When I was a prisoner of the Russians after the war ended, I was in the same cell with a Russian general who had been there for four years without any communication or news from the outside. And I will not mention the millions of Germans evacuated from German territories in the East, most of whom were landowners and their families. One might say that they, too, were deported as 'night and fog' prisoners.[6] But I am not the man to go into actual politics."

I asked him what he thought of Schacht's defense. "Schacht is a disappointment because of another thing. If I would have had the terrible secrets of crimes committed by the Nazis in my hands, which Schacht said he possessed, then I would not have participated for ten years in a conspiracy. And I wouldn't participate in an *Attentat* solely in 1944, which incidentally was to be committed not by Schacht but by others — a cowardly *Attentat* at that, which meant placing a bomb under Hitler's table and then running off. If Schacht felt as nauseated by the Nazis as he now claims, he would have had to draw a pistol himself and shoot the man responsible for these dastardly actions, I mean Hitler himself. Anything else is unthinkable, with the knowledge that Schacht had."

## May 8, 1946

Fritzsche has been seen about once a week by me and we have talked of various matters, mainly about his early history and development. Today we spoke about his worldview, which has, of course, come up before. I asked him whether he believed in the basic principles of Nazism at this time. "I do not believe in the Führer principle. I always opposed that even while I was with the Propaganda Ministry during the height of the National Socialist regime. I was always of the opinion that the only form of government fit for human beings is a democratic one. I openly admitted that in a radio broadcast, but I said: The democracy which shows up in the United States and in England is not an ideal democracy, because the will of the people is under the pressure of property, which is in the hands of the wealthy capitalists.

"On the other side, democracy is overcome by dictatorship. So it appeared to me that a dictatorship was perfectly permissible for reasons of practicality for a limited time. I felt that there would be a slight differentiation from democratic lines in Germany for a certain time. I was convinced of this because the German people had had sad experience with the democratic parliamentarian form of government. But I want to say precisely after today, after the murder of 5 million people under a leadership state, that I am of the opinion that the Führer principle is not possible any longer, because under another form of government, even if it were not ideally democratic, such things could not possibly happen. I cannot agree with my own feeling during the time of my work for the Nazis any longer. There are other examples of the evils of the leadership principle, such as the bad examples set by district party leaders.

"I must say, however, that even today I see the tremendous idealism which came to life with National Socialism among the people. To express it very plainly, after one year of very intensive thinking on my part, all the years of National Socialist government were characterized by the fact that there were two groups: One, the mass of many millions of pure idealists who said that everyone had to forgo their individual rights, welfare, opinions, and wishes so that for once the state would be healthy. On the other side there was a smaller group, on top of which was the Führer, of which I can only say today that they broke their promises to the millions, and misused their power by breaking the faith which was put in them.

"And whatever bad things the millions of people who were idealists saw in this small group, they excused as revolutionary trends which would soon pass. In reality these were not just passing trends, but constituted the principle itself. That, in my analysis, was the tragedy of the German people and the German nation.

"I am under the impression that the prosecution does not try to bring out that point, and similarly none of the defendants bring it out. I feel that the prosecution is hindered by trying to paint a picture of black-and-white, and to paint the defendants black. I feel the necessity for finding out the real guilt once and for all, even if it occurred after this trial and after my death.

"Perhaps the first and foremost guilty ally is Bolshevik Russia. The gangster method in German politics was introduced in 1919 by the Communists. When the Nazis appeared in 1923 and 1924, the German people would have declined them because of their method if the Nazis had not used excuses: 'We could not deal differently with the Communists.'

"Secondly, all democratic governments of the Allies from 1919 to 1932 did not fulfill any of the peaceful, decent wishes of the German people. Then only when Hitler came to power did the Allies grant him and Germany everything they asked. Part of the Allied guilt no doubt was in granting to Hitler and his government his every last wish. Ah well, there is no use going into polemics here and now.

"But the prosecution does not see what a mistake it was to refuse the wishes of the German democratic government from 1919 until the advent of Hitler in 1933. Whenever Gustav Stresemann or Heinrich Bruening asked help from the Allies, nothing was forthcoming. But when Hitler with his gangster methods demanded anything, England and France handed it over on a silver platter and asked him if he didn't want even more.[7]

"The third point which I want to bring up when my defense starts concerns the fact that the prosecution pays no attention to the importance of the originally peaceful occupation of France by us Germans. This occupation only became harsh when the resistance movements were organized and Germans were murdered or sabotaged in France by partisans who were stirred up by the Allied radio propaganda."

I asked him whether what he was saying was a historical fact or was his own personal opinion and observation. "I can testify to it myself. I participated in the offensive against France for several days. I saw that that country was hardly destroyed. I could almost swear that not more than ten wristwatches were looted by our troops in the whole of France. I myself saw how tremendous masses of French refugees were taken care of by special German units, for example, the Bavarian Trucking Company, which had forty or forty-five trucks with built-in kitchens and supplies. I could give many such examples.

"In Russia, before I went to the front in November 1942, I drove all by myself through many villages near Kiev and Kharkov. I was in German military uniform, alone, unguarded, and yet slept peacefully in farmhouses and was fed by the population and I also observed that people were almost happy. Yet three-fourths of a year later, that whole country through which I had traveled was full of partisans — and that was how it came about that villages were burned, people shot, hostages taken, and general terror ensued."

I asked him to explain this transformation from a peaceful country to one which put up so much partisan resistance. He said with great certainty, "It was due to the propaganda which came from Moscow.[8] In my opinion, the partisan and resistance movements did not grow within the country itself but from the outside. From the time of the first shootings, because of partisans — at that moment the screw tightened automatically and continued to tighten with no help from the outside. I understand that these things are not mentioned in this trial. But I hope that at least after the trial they will be objective enough to investigate. I hope for it in the interest of my people, but God knows I hope for it in the interest of humanity.

"Because I want to make an end to all this tragedy. If one places the guilt of these tragic six years of war upon the wrong place, there will be always the germs of repetition, which will be kept alive, and perhaps another tragedy will befall mankind."

I asked him what the investigation would show, in his opinion. "That there was false propaganda on both sides. For example, I find it tragic now that I didn't believe various statements of the Allies that cruelties existed in Germany. The only reason for my not believing these statements was that I had heard so much false propaganda and lies from the very same broadcasting stations.

"I wrote down a sentence after our last conversation of a few days ago." Fritzsche smiled in his usual wan manner and took out a slip of paper upon which he had written in German one of his quasi-philosophic notations. The translation from German roughly was as follows: "The principle of bad has caused so much damage to the world that no excuse can be made for it. But the greatest catastrophe of humanity was the creation of hatred and the belief which a man has that he is right and his opponent wrong." I asked Fritzsche whether he would expound on this aphorism. He replied that what he meant was that fanaticism, whether it be for right or wrong, was ill-directed.

We went on to talk of the other defendants, a subject which always intrigued Fritzsche, because in a way it would appear that he felt somewhat distinguished by being included among cabinet ministers and other important persons, who during the war were mere names to him. "In the first place, there is the Hitler group, among whom are the most guilty of the defendants and about whom very little, if any, good can be spoken. By the Hitler group I include Goering, Ribbentrop, Kaltenbrunner, Keitel, Rosenberg, Frank, and Streicher. Then there is the group which one might call idealistic. Then there is yet another group which one might label as indifferent. Unfortunately, too many of us were indifferent. Not many belonged to the idealistic group, and I don't care to name them

because I think I would be stretching a point to call any of the defendants idealists. I feel that perhaps of all the defendants I was the only
idealist, although I suffered from blindness and indifference myself. In
this respect I am not like Speer, Schirach, and Funk. Schacht I consider
an opportunist.

"That is the tragedy in the case of Schirach. It is the old matter of a
feeling of dizziness which comes to a man when he stands at the height
of power. I always had a very open eye for these things. Because my
nature was completely strange to feelings of power, I always considered
it a burden to decide on the fate of people — even such little things as
whether they should be hired or discharged in my office.

"I, therefore, left those decisions in the hands of my deputies. On the
other hand, I had a quite different favorite hobby. The most pleasing
thing that I could do in my life was to 'catch a soul' — in other words, I
could think of nothing better than to convince people and outtalk them.
I never liked to speak in large public gatherings to simple, uneducated
people, but I did enjoy lecturing before a professional group of journalists. There was no more satisfying feeling in my life than to convince such
a group of people and have them say afterward, 'Yes, you are right.' I
guess I have something of the Pied Piper of Hamelin in me. My friends
always call me the soul catcher of Hamelin."

I asked him about radio broadcasters for the Nazis, and what he
thought of them. For example, did he know General Kurt Dittmar?[9]
"General Dittmar was a wonderful man who was purely a military commentator and could be relied on to broadcast nothing but the truth. I
know for a fact that for years Ribbentrop, Goering, and Goebbels
wanted to do away with General Dittmar. But that came in my department and I held on to him. He was a lieutenant general, a soldier who
had military staff duties, but in addition he was paid for the individual
broadcasts which he made under the German networks. General
Dittmar is now in English captivity and he said very recently during an
interrogation that I had defended him constantly. But I will not bring
that up in my defense. I will answer only the charges against me. I have
many letters from Jews I saved — but the prosecution would say it isn't a
matter of the Jews who were saved but of the Jews who were killed, and
the prosecution on that point is correct.

"I did one thing yesterday. I sent a cable to an English radio commentator. I had received a cable here in the prison from this commentator

and I asked him in my cable if he would give a statement about the nine hundred broadcasts I made during the war. I know an English commentator listened to my broadcasts constantly because he was sort of a personal opponent of mine over the radio. I want him to give a statement which I can use in court about the general line of his broadcasts. I don't know him personally but I used to listen to him from London and he used to listen to me from Berlin.

"For the rest, I must wait and see which of the nine hundred broadcasts I made the prosecution will select and criticize me for. At the beginning I used to make a daily broadcast, then it became three times a week, and finally once a week. In the first year I had fifty thousand fan mail letters. Ninety percent of them were favorable and ten percent critical. I received many letters and telegrams from the United States. All of these were favorable. Many of these letters were very funny. For example, a Mrs. Halifax wrote me that she was forbidden to listen but she heard me for the first time and she liked my voice. And she was of the opinion that things in Germany would go wrong. She said in her letter that she had a yacht and she asked that I give up my job in Germany and tour the Pacific Ocean with her in her yacht. I wrote to her, saying that I should be glad to consider such a trip after the war, but not at the time. There were many such amusing anecdotes."

**May 20, 1946**
"Sometimes I feel like screaming here in my cell. It isn't just my life that's ruined and frustrated. It's my guilt to my family and to the German people as a whole." He looks quite distraught as he says this, but there is also a patent element of pathos and bathos, and his words are always so well chosen, and neatly enunciated, with just the right amount of expressive dramatic quality.

Fritzsche said he wanted to continue to talk of the guilt for the war and the murder of the 5 million Jews. He mentioned that many Jewish journalists outside Germany made severe attacks on the Nazis, and that in a way caused new flare-ups of anti-Semitism within official Nazi circles. These men were not wrong, he pointed out, as history showed, but at the time they did utter false propaganda against Nazism, and this in a way caused the war and bitter anti-Jewish feeling. "But it is fully clear that it was not only the Jews who caused the war," Fritzsche said.

"I'm no anti-Semite like Streicher, but I resisted the Jewish influence in the press and theater. I was in favor of bringing Jewish influence to a percentage of strength, in accord with their relative numbers. I'm of the opposite theory today, since racial differences brought about 5 million murders. Therefore, any further racial policy is the intellectual ground-work for new murders."

I said that I shared his present views. I remarked that it seemed highly dangerous to human liberties and life itself to oppress minorities. Fritz-sche echoed these words and said: "In theory I had this as the basis of my life. Therefore I come back to a final conclusion — that nationalism must be fought. I don't mean that internationalism is the answer, but exces-sive nationalism is fanatic.

"I hope you come to some conviction about whether or not I'm guilty. If you can imagine that here I am, a human being who has suffered more than a human should suffer — and that I have discovered findings which should be passed on to others.

"I don't say these things to improve my chances in this trial. I know that my ideas are the only ones that must come out of these trials. I have a feeling I must stand up for misused German idealism."

For some reason or other, Fritzsche turned to his favorite subject of betrayal. Erich Raeder's case was on and perhaps that is what stimu-lated him again on this theme. "The *Athenia* sinking — when I broadcast that this was done not by our U-boats but by the British, I had Raeder's word for it.[10] It was Raeder's fault. He knew and Hitler knew it was a German submarine. Then Goering talked to me, telling me the same thing, and that is what I mean by misused German idealism. It was betrayal."

## May 24, 1946

He displayed his usual martyrish smile and said that he felt "down," but less depressed than previously because of Schirach's statement recently, which Fritzsche characterized as "the best thing that has come up yet in the trial."

"The main thing about my depression is that I have a feeling of regret — and if one feels regretful, one necessarily feels guilty. As far as the indictment is concerned, accusing me of murder and inhumanity, I do not feel guilty. I don't feel guilty because I was betrayed. But I feel depressed because this feeling of betrayal has no outlet. In other words, no one seems to understand that as my main tragedy — that I was used as a tool for evil by Goebbels and others, and whereas I never did anything wrong personally, my actions indirectly led to the crimes of which I am accused.

"I feel guilty because I trusted and believed Hitler and Goebbels and other people who did not warrant such a trust. Because of this I could almost kill myself in desperation for what I did. Please don't take me literally, because I would not commit suicide — it is just an expression which we Germans tend to use. But in reality, it is not a feeling of guilt but one of betrayal. It is a certain anger, so great you can't imagine it. I often said that never in the history of the world did one man receive so much faith and trust as Hitler. Similarly, no one has ever betrayed so many people and abused so much good faith as he did."

He was in a mood for discussing the other defendants, perhaps for the purpose of drawing a comparison between them and himself, although he did not directly compare them with himself. "All my comrades here I met for the first time, with the exception of Funk. Of course, I did see the others in public gatherings, but never really officially or personally.

"I can only say that I am recklessly frank and I've always made enemies because of this, even enemies now on the defendants' bench.

"For example, take Streicher. He is often classified with me because he was a journalist and propagandist. I always thought him very dumb and a sexual pervert. Therefore, I denounced *Der Stürmer* in public, although never on the radio, but frequently before classes of 200 to 250 journalists in the political propaganda courses which I gave at the university. I can state this quite frankly.

"In my defense, I want to touch the story of my relationship to Streicher with only a single sentence. On two occasions I attempted to prohibit *Der Stürmer* because of pornography. Regarding the *Protocols of the Elders of Zion,* I thought that to be a stupid invention.[11] Those are the only things that I will bring out in my defense in that regard.

"I think that in former years Streicher was a very cruel man, because I had several experiences with journalists who had been whipped by Streicher here in Nuremberg. They had been placed in concentration camps and I was able to liberate them only through the help of Hess at that time. I also believe that there was more than a little truth to the charges of embezzlement which were rumored at that time. Today I think a trifle better of him. I think he is mainly stupid. The crime does not lie in him but in the man who gave him power — the Führer.

"I think that Streicher's mind is slow but that he has a certain natural strength which causes him to be a fanatic. This type of dumb individual can often be used for fanatical purposes."

I asked Fritzsche how *Der Stürmer* happened to obtain such a large circulation. He replied, "That is actually the work of the party. The party leadership never gave any official recognition to *Der Stürmer*. The ownership was not in the hands of a party publishing house. It was a strange phenomenon. I think it was extremely shrewd and purposeful planning on the part of the party leadership. Imagine a party, which in 1933 has only about 100,000 members, and suddenly within a few months has millions of members. There were only 5 million members actually admitted, but if the party so desired, it could have had 30 million members. And all these people were trying to become good National Socialists. The party said, 'You can't just become a National Socialist — you must fight for it.' So the new ones looked for something which would prove that they were good National Socialists. They joined many organizations; as for example, the SA, the Women's Organization, and even the Air Defense League. And so whether people liked it or not, they supported *Der Stürmer* and purchased it because that would prove they were good National Socialists.

"And at that moment when so many people wanted to prove they were good National Socialists, the rise of *Der Stürmer* began. There was a showcase which displayed copies of it in front of every public building, business, hotel, et cetera. In this way the hotel keeper, for example, could advertise that he was a good National Socialist. That, in my opinion, is the basis for the sudden rise of *Der Stürmer*. It soared from an edition of ten thousand to almost one million. Actually, the contents of *Der Stürmer* were taken more seriously abroad than in Germany itself.

"I admit, however, that *Der Stürmer* had a tremendous influence on public opinion after all. I am simply trying to point out that this influence was not as great as it is estimated abroad. I can judge that because I was a leading journalist. You know that we German journalists would never even shake hands with Karl Holz, who was the chief editor of *Der Stürmer*. He was despised. I never saw him personally because he never dared come to a press conference."

I asked Fritzsche what Goebbels's attitude had been toward *Der Stürmer*. "Goebbels, strangely enough, helped me in my second attempt to ban *Der Stürmer*. I think he did so because I convinced him by a casual remark, in which I said, '*Der Stürmer* will do us much harm abroad because the only thing the enemy will have to do would be to photostat *Der Stürmer.*' Goebbels agreed immediately and the prohibition of *Der Stürmer* became a joint proposal of mine and Goebbels's. I am making no excuses or defense for Goebbels because he was a completely ruthless, conscienceless fanatic. I simply want to point out this interesting fact."

I remarked that in a recent conversation that I had with Goering, he called Goebbels more anti-Semitic than Himmler. Fritzsche said, "I believe that is true. Goebbels must have had a tremendous hatred for the Jews — but not more than Himmler. I have no doubt, at this date, that Goebbels knew of the murder of 5 million Jews, a fact which he kept hidden from me and others at that time."

I said then that it seemed that Goebbels's agreeing with him to suppress *Der Stürmer* was not idealism but something else. "That is correct. I didn't even think it was idealism at that time. It was for that reason that I selected only those arguments which I thought Goebbels would swallow. There were other things about which I argued with Goebbels. I would always think over carefully which argument would be most effective with Goebbels, and then I would use it."

The conversation turned then to the subject of Rosenberg. "Formerly I believed that Alfred Rosenberg was a pure theoretician who would fail if given any kind of practical job — even the most simple. As far as his writings, I personally only read the first chapter of *The Myth of the Twentieth Century.*" I remarked that Rosenberg had become rather disturbed when he heard Schirach remark that he, too, had read only the first chapter of that book. "That's too bad. I always had the impression that Rosenberg embodied German mysticism. I felt that he belonged to the Romantic era and that there was only a slight whiff of modernity about him. There was nothing unified or organized about the man. Now I want to say something terrible, which is not for the trial. This pure theoretician carries the main guilt of all those who sit here on the defendants' bench, although he carries that guilt to a certain extent innocently. In my opinion, he had a tremendous influence on Hitler, during the period when Hitler still did some thinking — later that stopped. I mean about between the years 1923 and 1928 Rosenberg influenced Hitler. Let me explain. Hitler was a man who lived in the present and was a tremendously active individual. Rosenberg's importance exists because his ideas, which were only theoretical, became in the hands of Hitler a reality and actually transpired.

"If Rosenberg would be honest and actually look through things, then he would see himself for what he really is. He is like a hen who has just given birth to a duck. The comparison is very mild. The same fate repeated itself for Rosenberg a second time. I have no doubt that in the case of Russia, Rosenberg provoked in Hitler's imagination the idea that wide spaces in the East could be used for colonizing. I think Rosenberg was put in charge of the activities in the East after the war was started without ever being consulted.

"But actually during the first few months of the war against Russia, Rosenberg still represented the colonial policy in the East. After three or four months he saw how wrong that policy was, but the locomotive sped forward on the wrong track. Rosenberg was minister for the occupied eastern territories and he did not have courage enough to refuse that position. In many regards Rosenberg is the most tragic figure, with the exception of myself, in this trial."

I probably looked doubtful although I actually said nothing. Fritzsche said, "As an American, you probably cannot understand. It is a question of a man who is basically peaceful, continually participating in this and that by way of compromise. It was always in the belief of choosing the better, perhaps the better of two evils, that he compromised. That is the tragedy. That is what I mean. It is not a question of my trying to defend Rosenberg, because his life or death in the big picture is of little consequence. My life or death in the big picture is of little consequence. That is my picture of Rosenberg."

I remarked that it seemed to me then that Hitler had some ideas about people, or at least how he could use people. Fritzsche said, "Yes, but Hitler had a limitless bad knowledge of humans. Either that or he is even a bigger criminal than I see him today, and I certainly consider him one of the greatest criminals in world history."

I asked him whether, in his opinion, *The Myth of the Twentieth Century* by Rosenberg had been widely read, because in spite of its large printings, everyone I had ever spoken to denied having read it beyond the first chapter.

"For myself, I can only say that I read parts of *The Myth of the Twentieth Century,* and I heard a few of Rosenberg's speeches, which incidentally were very boring and dull. I emphatically fought against

Rosenberg's ideas, especially in regard to the church question. I searched for an argument at that time which might be most effective in the surroundings I found myself in. Finally I used the argument that one doesn't destroy a religion until one has found a new one to replace the old. Because without religion, people cannot exist.

"Rosenberg was completely areligious. That was the deepest of his defects. Rosenberg has a one-track mind. He is a pedant. One gathers the impression certainly that he never obtained knowledge from his surroundings, which would be necessary in order to form new philosophic ideas, but he obtained his ideas from books and from his own mind, which was not subject to the influences of reality.

"Rosenberg had less influence among the old National Socialists than one would believe. But among the youth his ideas played a great part because they were utilized in every school. The tragic thing is that Rosenberg's fantastic theories were actually put into practice. Rosenberg's institute attempted to make speeches before my press conferences. They criticized articles which appeared in the press. In those regards I always had to fight Rosenberg."

I asked Fritzsche to tell me more about Rosenberg's institute. "It was in charge of the foreign policy education of the party. Rosenberg had an institute in Berlin, in the suburb of Dahlem. There was also the East Institute of Rosenberg and several other institutes.[12] He always mixed into those things. Rosenberg stemmed from Stewart Chamberlain. Chamberlain and Rosenberg had the same system and the same line, but the difference is that Chamberlain's theories were never put into practice. Furthermore, compared to Rosenberg, Chamberlain is mild. Really, there is no German philosopher after Hegel. He was a pure mental thinker. Hegel is the mental father of Karl Marx on one side and of Fichte on the other."

# Walther Funk
## 1890–1960

Walther Funk was minister of economics from 1937 to 1945. Found guilty at Nuremberg of crimes against peace, war crimes, and crimes against humanity, he was sentenced on October 1, 1946, to life imprisonment. He was released for health reasons from Spandau prison in 1957.

## March 31, 1946

Walther Funk is a fat little man, roly-poly in appearance, with an indeterminate air, given to sentimental phrases and platitudes, concerned mainly about his immediate comfort, and absorbed in his genitourinary complaints. I have seen him often in the past and he is always most ingratiating, eager to be visited, polite, and cooperative. When the question of his political activity is approached he becomes tearful or defensive or both, and reiterates in various ways his theme: "I was only a small man and I had no idea of what was going on."

We spoke at first of his genitourinary difficulties. He has had a urethral stricture for the past twenty-five years, and a slight hypertrophy of the prostate gland, requiring occasional catheterization. Later he corrected himself and said that his urinary problems began at the age of twenty-three, following a urethral discharge, so that he has had these symptoms and has taken genitourinary treatments for the past thirty-three years.

He was born on August 18, 1890, in Königsberg, East Prussia. He said that in view of his defense coming up soon, he would tell me the essential facts of his life because he might not be permitted to do so in court. I told him I thought he would be able to, but that he should relate whatever he pleased. He said that he noted that I am "very correct" because I take notes on my conversations with him. I assured him that these notes were for my own records and were not a concern of the prosecution. He looked slightly dubious but said agreeably that it was understood, since I was a doctor and a psychiatrist.

He recounted details of his early life in a broad manner, which seemed somehow rehearsed. He reminded me that he had written a short biographical sketch of his life some time ago, shortly after he came to the Nuremburg prison. He touched on his biography very briefly. "I come from a respectable bourgeois family in Königsberg. Most of my ancestors were businesspeople, but there were some relatives who were quite artistic."

Regarding his education, he said he attended the University of Berlin, taking courses in law, political science, art, and music. During the First World War he was in the infantry for a while, but then his genitourinary difficulties began and he was discharged in 1916. He then decided on becoming a newspaperman, although he toyed with the idea of devoting his talents to music. From 1916 until 1922 he was reporter, columnist, and editor of various newspapers. In 1922 he became editor of the *Berliner Börsenzeitung* and remained as editor in chief for the ensuing ten years. It was a commercial paper, mainly, although it carried regular news features.

In 1931 he retired from the editorship of the paper, "because I felt that the National Socialists were certain to assume power and I was drawn to the movement. Germany was in a crisis. Unemployment was great. Class struggles existed.

"The democratic parliamentary system was a failure. I had always spoken out publicly against the Versailles Treaty, which I felt was responsible for the bad conditions in Germany. I was always for private enterprise, and so was Gregor Strasser, who was a friend of mine, and a great follower of Hitler.[1] Private enterprise is important because without it there is Communism. Without it there would be no acknowledgment of the fundamental differences in talent and capacity between one human being and another. I was most interested, however, in preventing a class struggle, and National Socialism seemed to provide for a socialist nationalist state.

"Are you interested in hearing what the economic situation in Germany was before the National Socialists came to power?" Funk smiled weakly. I told him to tell me what he wanted to say. "Well, it's a sort of review for me of what I must tell the tribunal. Germany was in a financial mess due to reparations. We were sending out our money abroad to pay reparations without receiving anything in return. So there was inflation in Germany. We owed every foreign state more than we could repay. The middle class suffered most. And the middle class is the foundation of our German culture. Every third family was beset with unemployment. The government was ineffectual and weak. I agreed with Strasser that we required a strong authoritarian government and a unified political feeling among the people.

"At the same time, the National Socialists commanded a majority in the Reichstag.[2] The popularity of the party was tremendous, and Hitler's personal magnetism attracted millions. I, too, was attracted but I felt the economic program of Hitler needed practical support. I founded an information service for the purpose of issuing economic and political information to leading party circles.

"At that time I believed in the Führer principle because to me it meant that the best one should be the leader. If the leader is good and responsible, then the government is good. At any rate, through my friend Gregor Strasser, I first met Hitler in 1931 and I felt I could influence the economic program of Germany for its own good.

"When I met Hitler I was taken in by his unusual personality. He was very brilliant at speechmaking, at grasping a problem quickly. He agreed with my ideas about individual rights, the fine difference between individual capacities. He invited me to work with him. But I was never really close to Hitler. In 1933 and '34 when I was chief of the news service of the government, I saw Hitler regularly. He would often break off a conversation in the middle and have me play the piano for him. He had an ear for music, or at least so it seemed.

"But after I became minister of economics I did not see Hitler more than a few times. He rarely consulted me. I was really occupying a useless position because the direction of the economic program had been given to Goering. Afterward, as late as 1942, Speer, as head of armaments, became more or less chief of economy.

"I must go into the problems of the leadership principle, living space, and so forth before the tribunal. I was in favor of the leadership principle, because the leader was to be the voice of the people. Living space meant not the conquering of foreign territories, but colonies, trade pacts, other mechanics, but not war. I was interested in German economy on a world scale. To me, the concept of living space was that Germany could participate in world economy. We were hampered by the reparations and the trade barriers of other nations.

"I must reply to the prosecution's indictment that I helped manufacture the party program. That is nonsense. In 1921, when National Socialism was developed by Hitler, I had never even heard of it. It was in 1932 that I spoke with Strasser and told him some of my economic ideas, which he used in speeches. I favored lowering of interest rates and stabilization of currency, new credits for the Reichsbank. I also stressed the need for export trade. Among other things, I also stressed the importance of insuring investments, agriculture, industry. Oh, many things which would certainly be agreeable to you as an American.

"At first my ideas were respected. But later I was regarded as too much a liberal or democrat. I was against too much socialization of industry because that stifles individual effort and initiative. I succeeded in some of my aims. I succeeded in placing individual enterprise ahead of state enterprise.

"I want to tell the tribunal that I was against rearmament. That my ideas for solving unemployment were not rearmament. I wanted to foster building of new houses, new industries such as automobiles, and building of roads. I also wanted to put agriculture on a more advanced technical plane.

"I am not a politician. I never held a party job, even. Only for a couple of months I headed the Office for Private Business, in 1932–33. I was never a member of the corps of leaders. I never attended party functions such as the Munich festivities of November. I disliked rallies and big functions. I was never part of the inner circle of Hitler, despite what certain propaganda books claim. And the mention of me in Messersmith's court affidavit is false, too.[3] I was a member of the Reichstag for a brief time until it was dissolved. But to be painted as the economic adviser, the big man of the Nazi economics! Ridiculous! Schacht may be a financial genius, I don't know. Gottfried Feder was the leading economic philosopher of the party. And there was Wilhelm Keppler later on. These men were more important than me.

"I must tell them, I suppose — my lawyer says so — how I came to be chief of the press. Well, in January 1933 Hitler asked me to take the position because of my newspaper experience. Also I had friendly relations with von Hindenburg. So I became secretary in the Propaganda Ministry under Goebbels, but I didn't like it. Later Otto Dietrich became press chief.[4] But I had no power. All I did was deliver orders from Hitler to the press.

"I was present at cabinet meetings but I had no voice, was not a member of the cabinet.

"Am I boring you? I know that this sounds so dull. To me, also. But that is what I am charged with in this trial." Funk, who had been sitting like a Humpty Dumpty on the edge of the cot, arose and disposed of his cigarette in the toilet in the cell. He sat down again and awaited my reply. I was busy taking notes, and finally he asked whether he should continue. I said I had plenty of time and he should tell me whatever he pleased.

"They will certainly want to hear me talk about the Jews. Some of my closest friends were Jews. In the financial world when I was editor of the paper from 1922 to 1931, I had many Jewish friends, socially and in business. I never adhered to racial theory. I thought, as did so many others, at first that the anti-Semitism of the Nazis was a political point. It is true, though, and some of my Jewish friends agreed, that there was too high a percentage of Jews in the law, in the theater, and in the economic and cultural life of our Reich. Jewish influence in art and music were not true to German culture. How could it be? It was naturally Jewish. But I was not a radical. I did not foresee the mass murders or the extermination programs. Furthermore, I personally assisted many Jews who would have been excluded from economic or cultural life because of the Reich Chamber of Culture Law, which eliminated Jews from those fields. I had nothing to do with that law, because it was made by the cabinet and I was not a member of it. I helped Jewish editors, like the editor of the *Frankfurter Zeitung,* and many others. Richard Strauss wrote an opera based on a story by a Jew, Stefan Zweig, and he was criticized for it. Besides, he had some non-Aryan grandchildren, and I spoke up for him.

"I remained in the Propaganda Ministry until 1937. In November 1937 I took over Schacht's position as economics minister. It was a complete surprise to me. It was at the opera in Berlin, and Hitler said to me that Schacht and Goering could not get along, and I must take the position over from Schacht. He told me to see Goering. Really I did not become minister of economics until February 1938, because Goering himself was acting as minister of economics from the time Schacht left until he decided I should become a cabinet minister, in February. In any event, I was a minister but really not a minister because I was under Goering and the Four Year Plan.

"The prosecution accuses me of responsibility for rearmament. That is false. The armament program was headed at first by General Georg Thomas, then in 1940 by Fritz Todt, and from 1942 on by Albert Speer.

"In January 1939 I was called to Hitler. He was excited. He said Schacht had refused further Reichsbank credits and it was nonsense and he would not stand for it. He said he would assume responsibility as to Reichsbank credits, he alone. He told me that I should take charge of the Reichsbank. I said I would be glad to do so, provided the stabilization of the mark continued. There was no danger of inflation as long as the economy was regulated. I kept the mark stable until the very end. In all countries during a war, larger credits and debts are incurred. The amount of debt of the U.S.A. or England by comparison is larger than in Germany. But Schacht could control the credits from the Reichsbank; I could not, and it was Hitler himself who ran the Reichsbank.

"Concerning the war, I had nothing to do with it. Naturally when it came I did all I could to maintain the economy and transform the civilian economy into a war economy. But I personally did not expect the war. Before the war I did everything in my power to bring about better relations economically between foreign countries and Germany. Doesn't that prove I didn't want or expect a war? My God! In June 1939 I had a conference with bankers from your country, Sweden, England, France, and others. It was probably in August 1939, a few days before the war started, that I thought in terms of a war.

"I never worked for war, but rather to bring about international understanding and goodwill. I hoped for a diplomatic victory and that we would again have the old German city of Danzig, and the German provinces in the East, and that just as at Munich, Hitler would have a victory without a war. Furthermore, Hitler did not really need me; he was the real dictator of economics, and I was merely a title. To show how little confidence Hitler had in me, how little he regarded me, he never called me in on any conferences, especially in regard to war against Russia. It was through Hans Heinrich Lammers and Alfred Rosenberg that I learned that a war with Russia was inevitable. I was against it because the economic exchange was so satisfactory. We sent them manufactured products and in return received raw materials."

I said that I really was much more interested in Walther Funk the man than in his economic or political theories. Immediately he dropped his dress rehearsal, and smiled apologetically, saying: "Ach! I know. If I were to play the *Pathétique* or the *Moonlight Sonata* for the high judges, they would let me off. But my defense unfortunately will not be musical. They will accuse me, and with a certain degree of correctness, of being part of the criminal government. Already I've heard about a charge against me that gold from SS sources, concentration camp victims, was deposited in the Reichsbank. I know nothing about it. Of course I knew the Reichsbank had a deposit from the SS, but where the gold came from I never knew.

"But ignorance of the law is no excuse. A person is guilty even if he breaks the law unknowingly. I shall be perhaps the first of the defendants to get up on that stand and admit that I am at least partly guilty."

### April 7, 1946

"I have been working on my defense, such as it is," he said, pointing to the table on which were a number of notes and transcripts and the like. I told him to continue or not as he saw fit. Oh no, he was always delighted to have me, and it was indeed a respite from unpleasant labor. He does not enjoy working on his defense. "I'd rather play the piano — or the violin, or cello. Did you know I studied harmonics, was a concert pianist for a while?"

I asked him how his love of music was reconciled to the activities as economics minister and president of the Reichsbank. He said that he had done nothing personally of which he was ashamed. For example, "I know the prosecution will ask me about Otto Ohlendorf, who was manager of a committee on export trade when I met him. When the chief of export trade came in December 1943, he brought Ohlendorf with him. He was a good man, it seemed to me. People could not talk of atrocities, because they were under oath to keep secret. And if people were decent they would not tell me anyway because they would not want to involve me."

I asked him whether he therefore appreciated not having heard about the atrocities, because he had just said if people were decent, they would not tell him, because it would involve him. He dodged the issue by answering: "Well, such people might not know what I would do about it and might think I would go to the Führer and report.

"There may have been many individuals who knew about the cruelties and atrocities, but they knew better than to come to the ministers with such tales." I asked him again just what he meant and he said, "Can't you understand that a minister would be the least likely man to hear about atrocities or bad things, because people would be afraid of telling them for fear of being reported? That's what I meant when I said a moment ago that no decent person would report such things to me and so involve me.

"Now, the prosecution will probably bring up Ohlendorf, who worked for me and who admitted before his tribunal he killed ninety thousand Jews. I was quite upset when I heard Ohlendorf. I didn't know things like that existed. And secondly I didn't know Ohlendorf was involved.

"I assumed Ohlendorf had been at the front, but like Hitler, who had also been a soldier."

I asked Funk what sort of impression he had of Ohlendorf — what kind of personality and character did he seem to have in the associations Funk had with him? "Well, Ohlendorf was only in the ministry for a year. Now since I know of his being in charge of that *Einsatzgruppe* which killed ninety thousand Jews, I can explain something which up to now I just could not understand. I always had the feeling that Ohlendorf was spiritually depressed. I mentioned several times to my wife, when we had Ohlendorf to dinner, that he seemed like a man who just could not be happy. Ohlendorf must have been very depressed on account of that experience. He could not laugh heartily — and a man who cannot is either depressed, or sick, or bad. I thought he had something in his soul which bothered him."

This type of amateur psychologizing is one of his favorite pastimes. I asked him whether Ohlendorf was known to him as being very anti-Semitic. "The question never came up. I cannot recall that he ever spoke against the Jews. We never talked much politics. My friends are always famous authors, or scientists, artists, et cetera.

"But I thought Ohlendorf to be basically a very decent man. He had a happy family life, his wife and children — I knew them. She is a simple woman, comes from farmer stock, a very quiet type. I met her once at a concert. I can spot a musical type. I can tell by looking at a woman whether she is a contralto or a soprano.

"Schacht's witness Hans Bernd Gisevius will prove the worst witness for the defense and the best possible witness for the prosecution.[5] Gisevius was in the police under Goering, and Wilhelm Canaris, during the time when he was doing espionage work. As usual with such people, they work both sides of the fence at the same time. Gisevius was a member of the *Attentat* of July 20 against Hitler. Then he fled. Now he tries to sell his books. But don't forget Gisevius was and is a Nazi. And I predict he will try to say, like certain others, that he was against all Nazi politics."

For the first time I saw Funk become moderately incensed. He spoke coolly but with great contempt for Gisevius, who apparently will become a witness for Schacht.

I said nothing and was merely taking notes when Funk said with a quick return to his shallow good humor: "You know, psychiatrists interest me. My uncle was a great psychiatrist in Hamburg. My own psychology is very complicated."

I told him that I would be most interested in hearing his own view of himself.

"I'm a man who has suffered all his life from depressions. It's probably connected with my artistic tendencies. As a child I was a somnambulist until the age of five or six. During the time of the full moon I am easily upset. And strangely, after a depression was once over, I sometimes did my best work. It resulted in a strong manic reaction. In other words I had to be either up or down. This started in my childhood. Even as a child I had a tendency to melancholic feelings. It was probably inherited from my mother. She was very musical and melancholically inclined."

At that moment he was told that church services had begun and he reluctantly left the cell, after reassurance that I would return.

### April 14, 1946

Funk is again working on his defense. He is, as ever, eager for company and an audience reaction to his rationalizations. I asked him what point in his defense he was preparing as I walked in with Mr. Triest. He said he was addressing the issue of the elimination of Jews from economic life, which he says the prosecution wrongly charges to him. After we seated ourselves and lit cigarettes, he proceeded to enlighten me on the events of 1938.

"I became minister of economics in February 1938, and almost at once, Goebbels and Robert Ley demanded that Jews be eliminated from economic life and their stores shut. It led to difficulties because people were refusing to buy in Jewish shops. There had been a national labor law enacted before I entered the cabinet, which stated that the owner or manager of a business must have allegiance to the party. Therefore Jews could not own businesses. I was in favor of the program going slowly, and adequate payment should be given Jews whose businesses were to be sold. I even went so far as to believe that certain economic rights should be held by Jews.

"The events of November 9–10, 1938, were a complete surprise and frightful to me. It all began in Munich.[6] I tried to call Goering and Himmler, but both were away. I finally talked with Goebbels and said I disapproved of this measure and it hurt our economic prestige abroad and was a waste of goods. Goebbels told me it was my own fault because I should have eliminated Jews from business long ago. He told me that new Führer decrees were forthcoming.[7]

"The next day a meeting was scheduled for November 12, 1938. The minutes of that meeting are here and the prosecution has them. After that meeting, in which Goebbels was most radical, I saw that it was up to me to produce laws for the elimination of Jews from business for the protection of these Jews — to prevent plundering and exploitation.

"Thus I, as minister of economics, along with the finance minister and the minister of interior and justice, drew up the new laws. Jewish businesses were handed over to trustees and Jews were paid. These laws were necessary to protect the Jews from being robbed."

I asked Funk whether the Jews were paid the full value of the property and businesses which were taken away from them. He replied that it was done on a percentage basis, but that was all he could tell me on that score.

"But as far as extermination! I had no idea. True, at that meeting on November 12 it was mentioned that Jews should emigrate out of Germany. But to exterminate them! Never! As far as ghettos were concerned! That was Heydrich's idea. I told myself, if there are 3 million Jews among 70 million Germans, we can let them live without ghettos. But my only function anyway was to execute the directives of Goering's Four Year Plan. I do feel ashamed of having participated to the slightest even as a tool in those dark days. But I was obliged to serve the state to which I had taken an oath. It was a tragic fate."

He was absorbed in self-pity and a desire to shape arguments he felt he might have to use when he took the stand.

"There's one thing I must say. When the prosecution states that dispossessing the Jews economically was the first step in a planned extermination of the Jews, they are wrong. I just had nothing to do with exterminating a single Jew. Anyway, as Goering said, he was responsible for anything that came from my office as minister of economics and Reichsbank president."

I asked him whether that was to his defense, namely that anything which stemmed from his office was not his responsibility but Goering's. Funk looked shifty-eyed and helpless. "Well, but I had no direct authority except through the plenipotentiary of the Four Year Plan."

Funk looked over his notes and smiled. "What kind of a defense can one make, anyway? What difference does it make? I like to eat well, not a lot, but well, and here we get such food! Not that I'm complaining. The German people during the war, and I imagine now, eat a lot worse than we do. But I was always such a fussy eater.

"Do you know I have proof that I opposed inflation in the occupied countries, Denmark for instance?" No, I replied, I had not. "Yes. I did my best. Finally inflation came to occupied countries, but it was the doing of the Foreign Office, and the armed forces, not the Economics Ministry. I fought against black markets.

"My lawyer will ask me about slave labor. In some way or other the prosecution thinks I had something to do with that problem. Well, I did not. I was against it. For business as well as humane reasons. Labor should be where it is, because in the first place so many of our factories were being moved, because of bombings of Germany, to outlying lands. Besides, the French or Belgians were working adequately for the German nation in their own lands.

"What else can I say? If they ask, and my lawyer may, why I didn't clear out, leave my post until the end, I'll state that it was for patriotic reasons. I refused a Führer order that acceptance of invasion currency was high treason. I refused to encourage a scorched earth policy, so that after the Allies occupied, the Germans would not be in want. I saved the deposits of the Reichsbank."

Funk seemed to be reciting. He lacked any spark of enthusiasm or much affect of any sort. I asked him, when he paused after the last statement, whether or not he was not guilty of at least some misdeed, since he was denying everything. I said that it seemed to me that it was a matter of a sense of values being applied to the charges against him, and did he not consider that in some way or other he was guilty of something?

He hesitated, looked at the hard stone floor, shifted on his seat. "I am guilty of one thing — that I should have cleared out and not had any-thing to do with these criminals in the first place. Later it was too late. I was in up to my neck. But as for the atrocities, I had not a thing to do with them, did not know about them. And as for conspiring against peace, that is false, too. And that is my main line of defense.

"But I must make a statement to the court about my guilt. I will explain why I stayed on as minister of economics and president of the Reichsbank until the collapse. I did it to help the nation. I felt it was my responsibility to stay on and do everything I could so that conditions would be not too unbearable economically after the lost war. It was my duty to save as much as possible up to the very end. Especially in view of the proposed Morgenthau Plan,[8] which would destroy German industry, impoverish our people. Also Churchill made a speech in which he said the Germans will suffer from hunger."

I observed at this point that it would seem to me he was going to defend himself by patriotic raisons d'être. I wondered whether, actually, personal opportunity and power did not play a part in his being in his present fix. He said, with mechanical force, "Never. I've never been ambitious. I was never one of the big people, nor did I have a desire to become one."

## May 11, 1946

I saw Funk this afternoon. He looked somewhat relieved that his case was over, that Doenitz was now defending himself. He smiled wanly, and talked of his prostate, stricture, and so forth, with the usual complaints, which have been aggravated by the tension of the five days during which his defense was held, May 3 to 8.

I asked him how he felt about his defense and he said: "It's a relief anyway to have that over with. Of course, about the gold deposit from the SS in the vaults of the Reichsbank — I never knew anything about it. The movie was the first I ever heard of it."

I asked him what he thought of Mr. Dodd, who had cross-examined him for the American prosecution. "He's very nice. But when he asked me about whether I am guilty, self-declared, about Jewish persecutions, I think I didn't answer clearly. He asked whether I accepted being guilty. I said that I had conscience trouble at the time of the persecutions and afterward, but not because I signed those laws, which were for the pro-tection of the Jews themselves."

I said that, from what I heard in court and elsewhere, it seemed rather doubtful that anti-Semitic laws were for the protection of Jews. He said then that was exactly what he was afraid of, that he would be misunderstood. The laws were discriminatory against Jews, granted, but that was not his invention. He signed them and passed them on in order "that fresh spontaneous outbreaks against the Jews should not occur." I stated that I was sorry but I could not follow him. The logical thing, it seemed to me, was to suppress the outbreaks and punish the wrongdoers, not make anti-Jewish economic laws to dispossess Jews.

"Yes, of course," Funk said, "but all I could do was hand down what had been given to me from above. In that sense I am not guilty of crimes against humanity."

I had a copy of the transcript of Funk's testimony with me, in English, and I asked him a few questions in glancing through it. Now that these things are over, I said, you might care to comment on them.

I asked him about the business of his accepting some half a million marks as a birthday present from Hitler. "That I did not deny in court at all," said Funk. I said I knew that, but how did it happen? In our state, officials do not receive large gifts from our president, and if they did, an investigation and scandal would ensue, I added.

Funk seemed slightly depressed by this statement. "Ach! We all make mistakes. Besides, if the Führer wanted to give me a present on my fiftieth birthday, could I refuse? Besides, I gave this money to charity . . . to the families of men who died connected with the Reichsbank and Economics Ministry."

I asked him too how it was he knew nothing of the quarter million marks which were given to various other defendants — Alfred Rosenberg, Wilhelm Frick, Constantin von Neurath — and the 600,000 marks each given to Hans Heinrich Lammers and Wilhelm Keitel. He replied without facial expression and in a blank manner that his replies in court were accurate, that he himself did not dispense these funds, that they did not emanate from the Reichsbank, but were dispensed by Lammers on order of Hitler from other funds. I asked where these other funds were kept, and he replied that there was a special fund for gifts and he only knew it was not connected with his own activities.

I passed on to the part of the court record where Dodd obtained a statement from Funk that Schacht took up a collection from a group of industrialists who were gathered at a meeting to greet Hitler.[9] This was in contradistinction to Schacht's testimony on the stand, in which he stated he had not taken up the collection. I asked Funk for his opinion of Schacht and why he had made that statement.

"Schacht is now attempting to get out of an embarrassing situation. He founded the economic policies that I continued. Either he did not remember taking up that collection or he was lying. I know, and so do the others present at the time, that he did take up the collection. At least in my defense I don't try to make a hero out of myself. That's so disgusting."

Funk was quite heated in his remarks about Schacht. He said further that Schacht was a man who was personally ambitious, in contrast to himself, who was never ambitious. Schacht lacked loyalty and would be on any winning side, he said. As for Schacht's assertion in his testimony that had he, Schacht, been finance minister at the time of the great anti-Jewish actions of November 1938, they would not have taken place, Funk was scornful. "As I said on the stand the other day, if Schacht could have prevented those things, the anti-Jewish measures, he was more powerful in the party than I was. But the things which led up to those measures, and the necessity for my issuing such orders, which in a sense protected what little rights the Jews had, were they not born in the economic program which Schacht, not I, started?"

I asked him why, then, if he recognized the evil therein, did he accept, and continue until the very end, the wrongs that Schacht had conceived? "At that time there was no thought of atrocities and it is in retrospect only that I see — anyone can see — the beginning of these anti-Jewish economic measures were in Schacht's time."

I shuffled through the transcript pages of cross-examination by Mr. Dodd. I had marked certain passages about which I wanted Funk's comments. On one occasion Dodd asked Funk if he had been making economic plans for a war against Poland more than a year before war started. Funk had replied that he didn't know, and that he could not remember. Then the court presented a speech of Funk's in October 1939 saying that his ministry had been secretly planning Germany's economic preparation for war. Funk had answered it finally by admitting the statement, but said that it had not referred to a specific war against Poland, but any war. Funk now commented: "Well, what could I say? Naturally war was in everyone's mind. Preparations for a war were our main concern because of Hitler's driving such hard bargains. We wanted to be prepared. Because Hitler was relentless. He would go on and on, and we thought he would get away with it. But to be prepared for a possible war was only sensible. But that is not the same as saying I prepared secretly economically or otherwise for a war with Poland for a year before the war."

I remarked that actually what it amounted to was a statement to the effect that for a year he did prepare secretly for war. Again Funk repeated that he said a lot of things for public consumption which were for propaganda purposes. Actually he had made no preparations, and not against Poland at any rate. "It was not against any country in particular. It was to ensure our economic life in event of a war. That could be done by any minister of economics in any land. But I don't deny and haven't denied in court that the direction of our foreign policy was so strenuous, and false, that a war could be expected even a year before it occurred. So I had to be prepared."

We then went on to Dodd's important questions regarding the gold in the Reichsbank. Here Funk began to walk up and down the cell. I said that if he preferred, we should cut off this interview; that all I wanted was his psychological reactions to the matters, and my purpose was far from conducting a review of the cross-examination. "Surely go on, it is very nice to have company. I just feel better with my bladder if I walk a bit. If you don't mind. It also helps me to think clearly. That was one trouble on the stand. I had to sit there and answer important questions and half the time I had a feeling to urinate." Funk smiled.

I asked him for his feelings about Dodd's evidence that he knew about the SS deposits of gold dentures, eyeglass frames, personal property of Jews and other concentration camp victims who had been exterminated. Funk had a woebegone expression as he began. He stammered a bit, and he did not look at me directly but walked up and down the cell, preoccupied. "Quite as I said, and I was speaking the absolute truth, from the bottom of my heart. My God, if I had known such things!" I interrupted to ask, yes, if he had known such things, what would he have done? He did know of the actions against the Jews in 1938, felt they were criminal, but what had he done then? At that point Funk seemed crestfallen. "I am a German patriot," he began, "as I've said, and I think in time of war nobody should desert his post. Country right or wrong, that was not invented by the Germans but by the British. But if I connected the gold deposits of the SS with the extermination program, or even with robbing of Jews of their possessions unlawfully, I would have refused the deposit in the Reichsbank." I asked him if that were all he would have done, merely refused them a storage house? "I mean I would have gone to Hitler and protested in the strongest terms. But I had no idea where this SS gold was coming from." I asked him where in God's name he thought such merchandise could possibly come from. Surely people weren't donating their gold dentures or eyeglasses. "People might die naturally and it might come that way, or it might come from pawnshops or something. Extermination camps were not even in my mind."

I said that he had told the court that he was unaware of the nature of these deposits at all, but that from his present words, it would seem he was explaining how other possibilities for their presence might be conjured up. He replied that in fact he had never seen those SS deposits and only in retrospect was he explaining how, even if he had seen them, it was possible not to link them up with killing people. "I thought, when Oswald Pohl told me of the SS deposits, that they were gold coins seized from persons in concentration camps. Just as every citizen had to turn in his gold coins."

Regarding the actual deposits from the SS, as revealed in the short film shown in court last Tuesday, Funk said: "Believe me, I had no idea of those eyeglasses, watches, gold teeth. That affidavit of Pohl's accusing me of having said we should accept the deposits as confiscated property from the eastern territories is false in its implications. I may have had a conversation with him regarding SS deposits, but not of that nature."

I reminded him of Pohl's affidavit, in which it was stated that "with Funk's knowledge and consent these materials were accepted by the Reichsbank." I also reminded him that Pohl said he had inspected the vaults of the bank along with Funk. He repeated that he had never seen the gold teeth, watches, eyeglass frames, and so forth. He said: "Those deposits must have been sent to the Reichsbank by mistake. They should have gone to the finance minister." I asked him what difference that would make. He said, "All the difference. I was not finance minister. I had nothing to do with the Finance Ministry." And so Funk shifted the burden to someone else.

I persisted, however, and remarked that nevertheless the film showed these items in the Reichsbank, and Pohl substantiated their presence and said Funk had knowledge of it, and approved it. Again Funk agreed that such was the case, but he had not been informed of it. "The Reichs-bank presidency was a big job and I did not know everything that went on. If the bank did this, it was wrong."

I passed on to another facet of Dodd's cross-examination, namely the Roges Corporation and its being set up by Funk's ministry and its plun-dering the markets of France by black market means, using 100 million Reichsmarks in French francs. I asked him about his associate Friedrich Landfried's affidavit that 100 million was not enough because 30 million were used every ten days, and that 200 million was needed.

"That is so, as Dodd said. But the real thing is that in the Roges Cor-poration I had little to say either. I was told to go ahead, and a way was shown me. So I did. Later in 1943 I opposed black market dealings. The black market was encouraged by the plenipotentiary for the Four Year Plan, Goering. I had no say in the matter."

I remarked that his denial of previous interrogations was interesting to me, as, I daresay, to the tribunal. What did he have to say about them? "I was interrogated when I first came here and at the time everything looked black. Now I can review these things in my mind and separate the black from the not so black." Funk smiled. I asked him pleasantly but pointedly whether he did not find that with the passage of time and the attempt to justify his own actions, many black things became white. He weakly disagreed. "No. They become clearer." I asked whether that was the explanation for his having said, "I am guilty," during early inter-rogations here, and in court defended himself and denied practically all charges. He said, "In reality, I am guilty as every German who partici-pated in a regime that did cruel, inhuman things. But as to the specific charges, there are legal ways of proving that they are not accurate and I think I did well to repudiate these charges." He did not look as if he thought he had done too well, at that moment. He looked to me for agreement. I said I was of the opinion he had denied too much and had been too technical in his answers. He attributed that to his illness. "I told you, half the time I felt like my bladder was full."

I asked him what he thought of Counselor M. Y. Raginsky's cross-examination for the Russian prosecution. "Those Russians. They did worse things when they entered Pomerania than we ever did in Russia." I asked him if that was all he had to comment about the Russian cross-examination. "No. I told the court I was against economic plundering in Russia, but that I could do nothing about it. I was not in charge and it was not my responsibility but that of Rosenberg."

He went on to state that he was against low wages in occupied Russia, against forced labor, against not caring for the welfare of the Russian population. "I was against starvation because for one thing it destroys the production ability of the occupied territory, which was important practically for us. Another thing I was against was taking the labor and forcing it into Germany. I protested it."

## May 12, 1946

He is still somewhat absorbed in his recent defense before the tribunal, but today I wanted to ask him some questions on his development and family as well as on his marital situation.

**Family History:** "My father was an old Königsberg merchant and came from a family of businesspeople. My father himself was a construction engineer who built bridges, canals, sewers, streets, et cetera. At one time he held the title of state engineer. He was a university graduate."

In response to questions as to his father's personality and characteristics, Funk said, "Father was a very lively and spiritually alert man of impressive appearance. He was bigger and better proportioned than myself. He was greatly beloved, musically inclined, and had a wonderful baritone voice. One of my father's brothers was a famous actor of international reputation who had played at St. Petersburg and all over the world. This uncle of mine died early, at the age of forty-two, as the result of a heart attack. Father was sixty-four when he died, also of a heart attack."

Funk displayed no evidence of emotional disturbance in discussing his father's ailments or death. He said, "Father suffered for many years from bladder and kidney trouble, and in later years took cures at various spas. He died on his sixty-fourth birthday, when I was thirty-two years old. At that time I was chief editor of a large newspaper. As a matter of fact, just prior to his death I became chief editor, and do you know, it is a curious thing that on the very day my mother died, November 27, 1937, I became minister. My mother outlived my father by fifteen years. She died at the age of seventy-eight of an asthmatic heart attack."

I asked him whether he had any great emotional attachment to his father. Funk smiled and said, "I would say, 'Yes.' As a child, I was colossally spoiled, mainly because of my musical inclinations. At the age of seven I could repeat whole operas, to which my parents frequently took me. I remember after I was taken to see *The Gypsy Baron,* when I came home, my parents were astonished at my ability to reproduce the tunes from that operetta.

"My mother was also very musically inclined and played the piano. She was also well informed in the field of literature. She wrote well and her letters were like books."

I asked him whether he considered himself emotionally closer to his mother or to his father. "It is hard to say; I was close to both." In response to my question regarding the personality of his mother, he said, "She was very sensible but inclined to a melancholic disposition. Father was more sanguine but Mother was definitely temperamental. Father loved life, traveled much, enjoyed being with people. Mother desired more the quiet life and was more withdrawn, but they were happily married.

"They were happily married because their tempers were so different. Of course, they had their differences occasionally, and sometimes they would not speak to each other for a few days. But Father usually gave in easily, and was unable to carry a grudge."

In an attempt to obtain a clear picture of Funk's childhood, I had to be very specific in my questions. I had the feeling that he was somewhat evasive and was consciously generalizing in many respects. It soon became evident that Funk's childhood was a rather insecure one in that he lived at home with his parents only until he was nine years of age. "I was only home until my ninth year. After that I went to live in a boarding school. But until my ninth year, we lived in a nice house near the woods and close to a river. It was a rural environment and I grew up with horses and dogs and had no playmates except animals.

"I had an older brother who left home at the age of seven, when I was only four years old. Then I had a second brother, who was ten years younger than myself, and so he wasn't even born when I left home. Our home was secluded and that was the reason for my having no childhood companions."

Regarding the school which he attended, he said, "It was a humanistic gymnasium for children of the rich as well as those of the middle class. One had to have money to attend this school. I lived there full-time and visited my home only during vacation. I remained there for nine years, until I graduated at the age of eighteen."

**Education:** Gymnasium, ages nine to eighteen years. Funk gave as his reason for attending boarding school and not living at home the fact that his parents lived in the country and that there were no suitable schools in that part of East Prussia in which he lived. Regarding his life at the school itself, he said, "In school I was spoiled because of my musical talents. My comrades said that I never passed tests because of knowledge but by virtue of my musical ability. I think that they were a little jealous or resentful because I mingled a great deal with the finest families in town and with the professors in their homes. At the age of sixteen I appeared in public concerts as a pianist and organist."

**Siblings:** A brother age forty-six, ten years younger than himself, is at present in English captivity. He is married and has two sons. He was a reserve officer during the war, but later left the army to become a high administrative official. For this reason he is under arrest automatically. During the First World War this same brother was also in English captivity as a young officer. The brother is a party member and held the title of district magistrate.

Funk's oldest brother died in early childhood, before Funk was born. He has another brother who is three years older. He was an officer in the First World War and died at the age of forty-five as the result of the gas poisoning he had incurred years before, during that war. This brother has a son who is a soldier in British captivity.

Funk's only sister died at the age of three. She was slightly younger than Funk.

**Marital History:** His wife is two years younger than himself, will be fifty-five in a few months. They have no children. "We couldn't have children. In the early years of our marriage my wife had an operation because of fibroids, and her womb was removed." I asked him whether the marriage was disturbed in any way because of this occurrence. He said, "On the contrary, we have been very happy. Of course, we suffered because we could not have children. Recently my wife wrote me a letter asking whether I recalled that on Mother's Day poor women used to come to our home because they knew we couldn't have children of our own. They would bring their children with them. People were always good to us.

"My wife lives in a house in a wooded area in the neighborhood of my estate. One day an American officer called for her and brought her to the courthouse. He showed her the prison in which I am incarcerated, and told her that she could not see me. Then she was taken to the detention house on Novalis Street where Heinrich Hoffmann[10] and other people are staying. The American officer told her that my defense counsel would visit her there. She was nicely treated and four or five days later the American officer brought her back to her home. After that the American officer told my wife that when the trials were over she and I could live in another country. I guess the officer promised this out of courtesy and that it doesn't mean very much. It is funny, though. My wife was not called by the defense. Originally my defense counsel wanted to call her but I said it was nonsense and would only be a burden to my wife and to me. She did give an affidavit. You heard about that affidavit in court, the one in which she said that I called Dr. Goebbels on the telephone after the great acts against the Jews of November 9–10, 1938, and how I told Goebbels what an outrage I considered these acts. So, I think her being called here was a case of mistaken identity.

"You know about that conversation with Goebbels. It is funny, I didn't even remember it, or rather, I didn't remember that my wife was present when I spoke to Goebbels, because I was so distraught at the time. But my wife happened to be in the next room and clearly overheard my words on the phone."

I asked him about the personality of his wife, and he replied, "She is colossally lively. She comes from an old Rhineland family of manufacturers. She has traveled a great deal and as a young girl spent some time in Paris with friends. She is extraordinarily lively and skillful, with great ability as an interior decorator. Her favorite occupation is to furnish apartments, houses, et cetera, and she has talent and taste in decoration and in the selection of colors. Last year we would have been able to celebrate our silver wedding anniversary, but at that time I was already in the prison.

"My wife was never a member of the party, and inwardly was opposed to the party. When the persecution of the Jews started, my wife tried with all means to convince me to make a living as a journalist and to give up politics. Unfortunately, I paid no attention because I thought myself obligated to remain at my post and serve the state.

"Our home life was very quiet although we did enjoy good company. We hardly ever met with party people, and our guests were mainly artists, such as Richard Strauss, the conductor Wilhelm Furtwängler, and similar people of the artistic world, including authors, editors, and scientists. Of all the ministers, the only personal contact I had was with Lammers, and that was not very intimate. We always lived somewhat aside — we had a nice comfortable home which belonged to the Reichsbank, and I also had my personal estate in Bavaria. My wife was therefore fully occupied with these two large dwelling places. We always had at least eleven guests at my home in Wannsee. On weekends it had the appearance of a tourist hotel. Here in Bavaria in my estate we also had many guests. But what I said before, that we lived quietly and somewhat aside, is true in that we rarely visited other people and we selected guests who were artists and not party people. Occasionally my wife went alone to visit other people but it was hard to convince me to ever leave my home even on weekends. During the week I left home early in the morning to go to work and returned late at night. Saturdays and Sundays I spent at home, and since it was my only chance for relaxation and rest, I didn't care to leave. We had a wonderful cook who had formerly worked for a brother of the emperor Franz Josef. She was a marvelous baker. I liked to eat and drink well. I also appreciated good cigars. My wine cellar was distinguished for its rare Rhine and Moselle wines and we had some Chartreuse from the original cloisters where the stuff was made."

Funk spoke of these former luxuries with a nostalgic pride. He continued, "My house in Wannsee was looted by the Russians. I had a library of fourteen thousand books. Part of this was first editions. I had a great collection of musical biographies and a great library on economics and philosophy. I can still tell you where each book is placed. My house in Bad Tölz also had a nice library but was smaller. American officers live there now. The house was decorated by my wife. She furnished it with pieces from the Middle Ages, including a Baroque shrine from Würzburg. She remodeled this shrine for my library with figures of angels, and the like, in green and gold. My wife says that the Americans had left things intact but that Germans and Poles stole personal things such as linen and clothing. The library is in order and the furnishings are intact. My niece lives in this house and is in charge of my old domestic personnel. The American officers live there and she administers the home. My niece is thirty-five, married to a surgeon who is at present in Dachau. He was formerly an SS doctor. He has even gotten permission to visit her occasionally. He was originally in the air force and against his will was ordered to the SS."

At this point we turned to a discussion of music and his favorite composers. "As I said before, my favorite composer for the piano is Schumann. I also liked Schumann songs and I often listened to the great baritone Heinrich Schlusnus and often accompanied him on the piano when he sang Schumann songs. They say I am anti-Semitic and the prosecution accused me of issuing laws in the field of the economy as part of the program that led to the extermination of the Jews. To show you how false that is, the famous teacher for voice named Bacher, who was an American Jew, and who left Germany because he was Jewish, often came to my home and we were good friends. He was the first husband of Mrs. Schlusnus."

I asked Funk what he thought of the state of art, music, and the like under the Hitler regime. He replied, "Music was immensely furthered under Hitler. Concerts for the broad masses were given. For example, before 1933 the masses had no opportunity to watch a great conductor like Furtwängler. The art of sculpture was also promoted and some good work was done. When you go to Munich you should visit my good friend Josef Thorak, who continues to work there. The studio is sensational. Thorak is a small, longhaired man who makes figures as high as a house. If you go there be sure to visit my house in Bad Tölz.

"From my personal standpoint I did not like the type of painting or architecture that Hitler fostered, but the sculpture was good."

At this point Funk became spontaneously reminiscent and again spoke of his role in the Nazi state. He said, "If you follow a certain road for some time, it takes an enormous willpower to leave, although you might recognize that the road was not good. But in my case I believed and was convinced that I was serving and helping the people until the last. However, it is a terrible fate that has befallen me. If I had remained with my writing and my music I would be working now and not a criminal in the Nuremburg prison.

"I was not at all fit for being state minister. My own secretary Landfried said so in an affidavit." I asked him what he meant by this, or rather what his secretary meant. "My whole personality was against bureaucracy — it was strange to me. My talent is to give form to things which I, in my inner self, worked out. My strength is less productive and intuitional than responsive. I have a talent for taking things into myself, absorbing them mentally, and putting them out in a better and more artistic form for the consciousness of other people. I always had the urge to tell the other people what I think and feel.

"That is the valuable and precious thing of my personality — the ability to give to other people facts which I have gleaned from others in a higher and more intellectual form.

"One can learn a good deal by taking the works of such people as Kant and Goethe and rewriting them in his own personal way. I had the feeling before the court that the judges were extremely interested in what I said. No defendant was interrupted as little as I was. On only one occasion Judge Biddle said that I was making a speech about the relative merits of private enterprise and state subsidy. He was right — it had no place in the defense.

"Whenever, as Reich press chief, I gave a talk to the Führer, he would interrupt and say to me that I should go into his private chamber and play some Wagner or Puccini. The Führer did not like Brahms, and even Furtwängler couldn't convince Hitler about Brahms. I once succeeded in getting Hitler to attend a concert in which Furtwängler conducted the Fourth Symphony of Brahms — but Hitler didn't like it.

"I started out with great idealism, but the result is ruins, blood, and smoke. It is bad *Götterdämmerung* [*Twilight of the Gods*].[11] I think the Wagner ideology of *Götterdämmerung* had an influence on Hitler during the last few months, and everything had to go down in ruins with Hitler himself, as a sort of false *Götterdämmerung*. Hitler had thought that his leaders and all the people had to be exterminated with him, and when he gave his policy of scorched earth, even early in the war, or at least when the war was turning against us and there were advances on the east and west fronts on the part of the Allies, I was against it. It was the Wagner ideas. Nietzsche also had ideas like that. You will find this in old Germanic legends and fiction. Heroes and selected people who worked for a downfall in order to make room for a new uprising are part of the legend of Germany, and I disagree with it because it is destructive and senseless."

According to Funk, the German people now had to make sacrifices in order to obtain a government in which the leaders would not create war.

"Then all the historical happenings seen in this dreadful war might have some significance and might serve some useful purpose. This would be the only good thing to reconcile terrible happenings in the past or in the future. In world history we have other examples of frightful destruction. There was Alexander the Great and all of the destruction he caused. Napoleon, too, would have destroyed all of Europe. But unfortunately, the Nazi government, the government of which I unfortunately partook, had no Talleyrand, but we had a Ribbentrop. Through Talleyrand's policy France was saved from a catastrophe that Ribbentrop would have brought about.

"If the world is covered with too many rotten things and dirt, some power must remove it and some new instrument must be created. That is my view of the historical meaning of these terrible times.

"Mr. Dodd, the American prosecutor, should talk of these things with me and not the crap he put before me — for example, what the plenipotentiary for economics did and what he let befall him."

# Hermann Goering
## 1893–1946

Hermann Goering was commander in chief of the air force, president of the Reichstag, and prime minister of Prussia. Found guilty at Nuremberg of conspiracy to commit crimes, crimes against peace, war crimes, and crimes against humanity, he was sentenced to death by hanging. Two hours before his scheduled execution, on October 15, 1946, he committed suicide in his cell.

**Undated (March 15, 1946?)**
Hermann Goering is up and down — cheerful usually, on other occasions definitely glum, chin in hand — childlike in his attitudes, always playing to the public.

The uniform in his cell is quite dirty, and he is not too clean in his personal surroundings.

He can turn on a smile and turn it off like a faucet, almost at will or mechanically. But touch him on a tender spot — even a potentially tender one, such as his relations with his family members, wives, and so on — and he closes up and relates platitudes. *Sex Life:* "Oh, quite excellent." He is clearly not in favor of any such prying and it must be done, if at all, subtly and by his own methods.

Asked about his marriages — both women were "great" in different ways. "Each had her own type of beauty." He is apparently displeased by such personal questions.

A general question about the trial evokes a tempest of pettifoggery. "The damned court — the stupidity. Why don't they let me take the blame and dismiss these little fellows — Funk, Fritzsche, Kaltenbrunner? I never heard of most of them until I came to this prison! What do I care about danger? I've sent soldiers and airmen to death against the enemy — why should I be afraid? As I told the court, I am solely responsible — whenever it is a question of the government's official acts, not extermination programs. I was Hitler's successor and I stand as such to the German people. I did not dodge responsibility. We had many differences of judgment, Hitler and I. In the early days I could say what I pleased and freely, and he had a sense of humor. Later, less so, and finally, our conflicts were serious to the point of his final decree for my arrest and murder."

How did things turn out? I heard your defense, but what is the human angle?

"Do you think a man rises to the top of a great state without being a man? I was 'Hermann.' He was the 'Führer,' on a pedestal."

Yes, but on the question of your denying aggressive war intent — I really didn't quite understand it. Maybe it was the poor translation over the microphones. Or perhaps —

"Let me tell it to you briefly, without any court to-do. I tried to keep on best terms with England. I did things unbeknownst to Hitler — behind his back — to compromise with Halifax.[1] I thought we had enough after the Munich agreement in 1938 and the annexation of Austria because we had 10 million more — just what we lost in the last war. But it was the Czech question. And with some reason, Hitler felt it was a Russian base for planes. I warned against the march into the Sudetenland because England then would declare war should Germany demand Danzig."

Goering finally received a telegram that Hitler was going to march into Czechoslovakia. Goering was on vacation. "I told him to delay this action because England would be insulted. It was as much the fault of France and Russia as Germany." What do you mean? "They didn't keep their pacts with Czechoslovakia." The story I heard is that the Czechs refused Russian aid. "Ah, well."

What happened before Poland? "I told Hitler England would declare war and sooner or later the U.S.A. I advised the peace treaty with Russia. Hitler thought it was bad advice because he was afraid Stalin would refuse. But Stalin saw Ribbentrop and all was as I predicted."

Attack on Austria? "The agreement is well known. I arranged that."

Attack on Russia? "Hitler decided that. I thought it was stupid because I believed that first we had to defeat England. Also we had to take Gibraltar. Franco was afraid to let us have it but if we could have brought England to nothingness by bombing, Franco would have been agreeable. After that I had no objection — that is, after the defeat of England — to attacking Russia. I felt strongly the air force was not prepared. But Hitler felt the Russian campaign would be short and then we could finish the English campaign."

What were Hitler's reactions to your opposing him on Czech and Russian questions? "I don't say I opposed him. I tried to reason with him. But I lost ground with Hitler, and in 1943 already I was out of favor. In 1944 Hitler was not on speaking terms with me. Gradually it was worse. On April 22, I received a message to head the Reich. I was about to do so when Hitler changed his mind. Hitler then thought I was trying to succeed him so he ordered my arrest and execution. I was actually arrested by the SS at Berchtesgaden on an order signed by Bormann. Then one of my parachute groups rescued me very promptly."

Do you feel any resentment toward Hitler? "No. It was in the last hours and he was under pressure. If I could have seen him personally it would have been different."

**May 21, 1946**
This morning Goering asked to be excused from court because of "sciatica" in the right lower limb. He had some pain yesterday during the court session, he said, and it was worse this morning. He limped slightly, and straight leg bending was apparently somewhat painful. Erich Raeder's case, which obviously bored him, was closing yesterday, and Baldur von Schirach would begin his defense today or tomorrow. I had an idea that he had little interest in hearing Schirach, as it was well known among the defendants that Schirach was going to denounce many of the Nazi policies and probably Hitler himself.

We had been discussing his childhood for some weeks without getting anywhere particularly on that subject. He seemed in a mood for company as Mr. Triest and I walked into his cell. After my examination of his lower extremity, he invited us to sit down and "spend some time," as he expressed it. Had Goering thought of anything in connection with his childhood he might care to tell me? "I can't think much about it. I know you want to study me psychologically. That's reasonable and I appreciate it. At least you don't lecture to me and pry into my affairs. You have a good technique as a psychiatrist. Let the other fellow talk and stick his neck into the noose. I don't mean that the way it sounds. But you hardly say anything. Someday I'm going to ask you questions." Goering smiled broadly.

I admitted that his remarks were correct except that my desire was to get a picture of him as he really is and was, and not conduct a quiz or examination. I had no desire to trap him or anything of that sort. "Well, I feel freer to talk to you than to some other psychologists. I was only joking about the noose." I added that it was only natural for him to be curious about me, and that if he wanted to ask any questions he should feel free to do so. I would try to answer them as freely as possible.

"As far as my childhood, I don't see what importance that has on my adult personality. Maybe it has. That's your profession and I'm no expert on those matters. But I have been thinking about your repeatedly inquiring as to my boyhood days. I've come to the conclusion that there was no difference between myself as a boy and as a man — today even. I believe that the boy had all the markings which later on appeared in the man."

Was he more like his father, or mother, from a personality standpoint? "People who knew my parents and me often said that my mental abilities were from my father but my temperament and energy come from my mother. One explanation of their differences in personality might be that my father was a northerner and my mother a southerner. The north German is very quiet and constructive. The south German is more lively and artistic. All great statesmen were north German, whereas all the great artists came from the south.

"My father was minister in residence, which was a titled position in the Crown Council. He was formerly a governor of German colonies in Africa. Maybe I'm different from my brothers and sisters because I'm the only child not born in the colonies. Father died when I was twenty, and I was already away from home for many years. I was a young officer at the time. His death was not unexpected as he suffered from diabetes for a few years. He was seventy-four when he died. He was strict and stern but beloved by his subordinates. He was constantly planning and had a constructive, vital mind."

What about his mother? "She died at sixty-four, ten years after my father's death. I was more attached to my father for some reason. Mother was very good to the children, but I think I was out of the home so much I lost contact with her. Father never abided by his diet and drank wine and ate what he pleased right up until the end. My mother was father's second wife. My father's first wife came from western Germany."

His mother did not seem to be a subject he cared to dwell upon. He showed me a large monograph written by a professor at a university, which contained page after page of genealogy of the Goering family tree. The ancestors included princes, queens, and other nobility to as far back as the twelfth century. He said that this research had consumed an inordinate amount of time and that the work had not been solicited, but was a spontaneous production of the professor, who was a specialist in genealogy and heredity.

"I have always been interested in family history. Chromosomes are funny things, aren't they? They may skip a generation and you can find children who resemble the grandfather, rather than either parent. Heredity is more important than environment. Blood will tell. For example, a man is either musical by heredity or he is not. You can't make a man musical by the environment. You can find a person who is very musically inclined and be puzzled because neither parents nor grandparents had any ear for music. But if you trace it back, you will find that the great-grandfather was a musician.

"But the environment plays a great part in the development of a man. It is significant whether a man is brought up in the city or in the country, near a lake or on the shores of the ocean."

I remarked that modern psychologists felt that interpersonal relationships were also an important factor in shaping character. "Oh yes. Also whether you have sisters or brothers or are an only child is important. The human is a product of the environment and heredity."

This was not the same viewpoint as the Nazis had, was it? They stressed racialism, for example. "If one went along with National Socialism one didn't have to agree with the twenty-five points of their platform. Some of us were more interested in one point, others in another. Some National Socialists were members for political, others for social, still others for racial reasons."

Did he consider the race politics of the Nazis an intrinsic matter, or merely incidental? "Not basic at all. Completely irrelevant and incidental. It only became basic or important because a faction of Nazis who were fanatic racial exponents became politically powerful. Men like Rosenberg, Streicher, Himmler, and Goebbels. National Socialism could also have taken a much different course."

Would he have approved of another course? "Certainly. Many of us in the party were opposed to the sharp racial laws and politics but we were too busy. Political and economic strength are more important than all this racial propaganda. Furthermore, I was never so close to the party. I was more in the state section. Personally I would never have allowed the party to have so much influence on the state. There were two groups. One espoused the theory that the party should rule the state. The second felt that the state should govern the party. I was for the second idea."

What else had he been thinking concerning his childhood? "I never could paint or draw but from my earliest youth I was an emphatic lover of art. I liked bright colors, such as blue, red, and green. I always preferred strong bright colors. I like all kinds of art except for futuristic stuff, which I strongly dislike. I'm generally very skeptical about modern paintings. Picasso, for instance, nauseates me. Gothic art was my favorite. Perhaps that was the result of my childhood. I was reared in Gothic castles, one near Salzburg, and the family castle near Nuremberg. Fortunately both castles are still standing."

Did Goering have the same taste in art as Hitler had? "No. Hitler was an absolute opponent of Gothic art. He leaned toward the antique and classical-Romantic. Classic art is more Greek or Renaissance, such as was found in the beginning of the nineteenth century. Hitler liked the classic style with many pillars. He preferred in paintings the work of the nineteenth century, from 1800 to 1900, but he also favored Rembrandt. He disliked Dürer, who is one of my favorites. Whereas Hitler liked Michelangelo and the middle Renaissance artists, I preferred the German masters and the early Italians. Another example of our differences of opinion regarding art — Hitler didn't like wood carvings but was an enthusiast of bronze or stone. I prefer wood. Hitler was a south German — an Austrian, really — and I was more influenced by my northern German ancestry. In art I preferred the work of the Dutch masters, the Scandinavians, Dürer, and Holbein."

I remarked that I understood that both he and Hitler were musically inclined. Goering nodded, saying, "Hitler liked Wagner, Mozart, and Verdi as well as Beethoven. He was very musical." I asked him about his own musical preferences. "Well, I like Wagner too, perhaps because of his heroic themes but also because there are many beautiful lyric passages in his music. However, Hitler disliked the oratorios of Bach and Handel, which I love." I told him that someone spoke to me about

Hitler's intolerance of Brahms. "It must have been Funk. The only ones who know anything about music among the defendants are Funk, Schirach, or Frank. I know that Hitler disliked Brahms but personally I was never wild about his music either.

"In my theaters we played the music of all composers regardless of nationality. For example, Tchaikovsky was played in Germany all through the war. The same is true of the playwrights Shakespeare and Shaw. The Führer disliked Brahms, Bach, and Handel. My own favorite composers were first Wagner, because of the majesty of his themes, and next perhaps Mozart and Beethoven. Of course, I liked Haydn and Bach and the lighter music of the two Strausses." What about modern music? "Ach! I hate jazz, but I do appreciate a few of the modern things, for example, Meyerbeer, Offenbach, and others. I had my State Opera perform *L'Africaine* and *Tales of Hoffmann* for two years. I was in charge of the State Opera in Berlin and two other distinguished theaters. Goebbels was in charge of all other theaters in Germany. Although only one percent were mine, mine were the best."

I asked him to tell me about Goebbels and his taste in art or music. "He understood some music but I couldn't go so far as to say that he liked it. He was more interested in the theater. He was a journalist and was most interested in modern plays. It was Goebbels who put the ban on Jewish composers and playwrights in 1935. There was absolutely no sense to this ban and in my theaters I paid no attention to it. In the State Opera in Berlin I had three great conductors, Furtwängler, Leo Blech, who was Jewish, and Richard Strauss. I managed to hold Blech for three years, but then the pressure on me became so great that I had to let him go. I sent him to Stockholm, where he would be safe from the violent fanaticism of Goebbels. The whole situation was difficult because although I could keep such people in my theaters, Goebbels would not accept them as members of the Chamber of Culture. My artists did not have to belong to this organization, but on the other hand they could not play in other theaters or films if they didn't. According to the official theater laws of the country, my theaters were exempted from any general rules except those I made myself."

I remarked that I had often heard that the Germans resented the Jews because they had too much influence in business as well as the arts. Did Goering think likewise? "Yes, I guess so. In Berlin Jews controlled almost one hundred percent of the theaters and cinemas before the rise to power.[2] In the smaller towns throughout Germany this influence was less strongly felt. In America you have perhaps two permanent opera companies, whereas in Germany there were seventy-four opera companies and two hundred and sixty-two permanent theaters. Theatrical life in Germany was much stronger than in America. Each town had a state theater, opera, operetta, and playhouse. For example, right here in Nuremberg there is an opera house, and five kilometers away in Fürth there is another one. In other nearby cities such as Bayreuth and Ansbach there were similar theatrical and musical facilities. All of this cultural development took place in Germany between 1900 and 1930. Nuremberg brought many great players and operas before that pig Streicher became party district administrator of Franconia. If Schirach had been party district administrator, it would have been a different story."

Goering was obviously enjoying this type of nonobjective discussion which nevertheless omitted any reference to his activities as far as war or politics. He played the role of the savant and great patron of art, music, and the theater. I asked him what his preferences were in the field of literature. He said, "Oh, I like all sorts of good biographies, memoirs, and of course all classical literatures. As far as novels are concerned I don't have much time for them and I only read mystery stories when I am taking a train trip. It's interesting that the only mystery writers who achieved any circulation in Germany were English and American. Perhaps French, too. Germany is too orderly a state to produce good criminal literature." I asked him what happened in the field of literature after the Nazis came to power in 1933. "Hitler was not interested. More criminal stories were published, especially American fiction, than ever before. Even noncriminal fiction from America had a great sale, for example, *Gone with the Wind* and similar best sellers."

I asked him about his knowledge of philosophy. "I read them all including Kant, Schopenhauer, Nietzsche, Hegel, and Feuerbach. Of the modern philosophers I read H. S. Chamberlain's *Foundations of the Nineteenth Century*.[3] As far as philosophers are concerned I can't read much of their work at one sitting." Had he ever read Rosenberg? "I didn't read his books." I said that I had found no one who admitted having read Rosenberg, yet some of the latter books were circulated by the millions. Did Goering have an explanation for this? "It's hard to say. Rosenberg has a tremendous knowledge and has read much, but the title of his book is wrong. I told him that in regard to the twentieth century one can't write about a myth. *The Foundations of the Nineteenth Century* by Chamberlain might have influenced Rosenberg.

"The first chapter of Rosenberg is so difficult and I became tired of it so fast that I couldn't concentrate. Besides, Rosenberg never touched the real problem but ran around and skirted it." I asked whether he thought Rosenberg had much brains. "Rosenberg appears in the wrong light. He isn't a hard man — he's too soft — he's too damned much for a policy of conciliation. The same thing is true of me. You can't put every word spoken or written in the past twenty-five years on a golden scale such as is being done in this court, words which were spoken perhaps in a fit of temper or at a time of crisis. Rosenberg wanted things to turn out differently. He should have been harder in his policy."

We discussed the Ministry of the East headed by Rosenberg. Goering said, "In 1936 under Himmler, the whole policy was changed. This blew up the whole damned administration. For example, Rosenberg had the Ministry of the East but he had no executive power. The only one who could actually do anything was Himmler and the SS. All Rosenberg could do was sit back and write memoirs, which you heard in court. The Reich commissioner in the East was also under Rosenberg, but at the same time subject to direct orders from Hitler. Rosenberg could not dismiss his subordinates. They did what they wanted and not what Rosenberg wanted.

"You know Rosenberg. He's no official. He was an author. I don't know anybody who can say that he was a friend of Rosenberg's. He's the kind of a man who keeps to himself and is hard to understand, or get close to. I heard two cultural speeches he made in Nuremberg and both were excellent. But aside from that I never read anything by Rosenberg except the first chapter of *The Myth of the Twentieth Century,* which as I said put me to sleep. I also never read a work of Streicher or of that stupid journal *Der Stürmer.* I saw only one page of it and that sufficed. That paper was forbidden in my house. The whole administrative district here in Nuremberg was terrible under Streicher and I finally succeeded in dissolving it. The Goering Commission here in Nuremberg which investigated Streicher's activities was famous. Streicher was not a normal man.

"Of all the defendants the only ones I know well are Schirach and Funk. I never even heard of Fritzsche. Kaltenbrunner I saw once for ten minutes on official business. Keitel, Jodl, and Doenitz I knew only officially. Speer I knew a little better. I met Rosenberg about twice a year. I had no feeling toward him, I was completely neutral. Ribbentrop I never had any feeling about either. I saw him at the Führer's a couple of times and once I had breakfast at his house and once he came to mine. The only popular people in Germany were myself and Hitler — and in the end I was the only one."

## May 24, 1946

Goering tried going to court yesterday morning but requested to be sent back to his cell in the afternoon because of pains in his right lower limb. In court yesterday he made many facial grimaces and walked as if he were in great pain. There was no doubt that his sciatica was not as severe as he would give the impression, because later that afternoon in the courtyard and in his cell he walked easily. Examination of the right lower extremity yesterday and today revealed no objective evidence of sciatic neuritis; straight leg bending was normal, the ankle jerks were equal, and there were no sensory abnormalities. It seemed clear that he was utilizing his symptom to stay out of court for a while during the unpleasantness of Schirach's case.

He was friendly, eager to talk, and quite comfortable this afternoon. Concerning the Schirach defense he remarked offhandedly, "I know Schirach and I know what he is going to say. I don't want to comment on it, but personally, I think he is making a mistake. He is not any different now than he was, but he would have the world believe that he has become a Jew lover and that he was swindled by Hitler. Schirach did his independent share of Jewish persecution." Goering smiled as if he had expended the subject. It occurred to me that his attempt at solidifying the attitudes of the defendants having failed, he was turning on each of them as they deviated from his "line."

He asked me if I had spoken with Gerd von Rundstedt, since he had heard that the old field marshal recently came to this prison to testify for the general staff. I replied that Rundstedt told me that he was an anti-Nazi and that the so-called Rundstedt Offensive should have been called the Hitler Offensive.[4] Goering smiled and nodded. "That's correct. It was the Hitler Offensive. It was brilliantly planned by Hitler but poorly executed by the generals. It was not Rundstedt who was at fault so much as Dietrich and his Sixth Army, which was not capable. Dietrich was no army commander and should never have been made one. This

Sixth Army was an all-motorized panzer force. The offensive itself was planned by a genius. The Führer was himself a genius. The offensives against Poland and France were also his plans. The plan against Russia was also that of a genius, but its execution poor. The Russian campaign could have ended in 1941 — successfully."

I said that Rundstedt's attitude had been entirely different. He had told me that Hitler's plans for the offensive were "stupid" and that personally, Rundstedt had been in favor of merely holding the German lines defensively and making no attempt at an offensive. Goering frowned and said, "The army generals are all suddenly smarter than Hitler. But when he was running things they listened to what he said and were glad of his advice. For example, the army group of Fedor von Bock, which was the Army Group Middle, failed in its mission. The original plan was the encirclement of the northern and southern Russian armies. Instead, Bock drove on to Moscow and was cut off. The Russian southern army was later encircled but the northern army could not be defeated, which otherwise would have been the case if Bock had followed Hitler's advice.

"Hitler had the willpower of a demon and he needed it. If he didn't have such a strong willpower he couldn't have achieved anything. Don't forget, if Hitler had not lost the war, if he did not have to fight against the combination of big powers like England, America, and Russia — each one he could have conquered individually — these defendants and these generals would now be saying, 'Heil Hitler,' and would not be so damn critical."

I asked him when he first thought that Germany was defeated. He seemed thoughtful. I asked him if it was possibly at the time of D-Day in Normandy. Goering said emphatically, "No, that was far from the end. The situation was not bad at all until Ardennes. It was only then that things began to look dangerous. Field Marshal Guenther Hans von Kluge didn't do his duty. He could have closed up his tanks. He didn't do that and had to retreat. He poisoned himself later." I asked him why Kluge had not done his duty. "Well, it isn't settled yet. He wanted to meet a high English officer and betray Hitler. It's another example of the generals making an about-face and double-crossing Hitler."[5]

If Hitler had won the war, what would the new order be like? "After the victory of France, Hitler wanted very little indeed. From France he would have taken Alsace-Lorraine. He would also want the former German provinces in Poland. The English empire he never wanted. If we had won the war against Russia we would have done away with the colossal Soviet Russia that exists, and have instituted a federal system there. Hitler might have asked for several provinces in the region of the Baltic states, but certainly no more."

Did Hitler have any aims in South America? "Ach! What should he want there? Also in Africa — the only thing he was interested in was the former German colonies. Hitler was more of a continental man — not a colonial man. He wanted a union of European states under the leadership of Germany — just as the United States is now doing. It would have been a plan whereby the European continent would fit loosely together and work out harmoniously."

I remarked that in his court testimony, Goering had spoken very little of Hitler the man, although he had praised Hitler the leader. Could he tell me some more about this mysterious person about whom there was so much speculation? "To me there are two Hitlers: one who existed until the end of the French war; the other begins with the Russian campaign. In the beginning he was genial and pleasant. He would have extraordinary willpower and unheard-of influence on people. The important thing to remember is that the first Hitler, the man who I knew until the end of the French war, had much charm and goodwill. He was always frank. The second Hitler, who existed from the beginning of the Russian campaign until his suicide, was always suspicious, easily upset, and tense. He was distrustful to an extreme degree."

Was not Hitler always somewhat distrustful generally? "No. In political regards, of course, he liked to play all his cards, but personally he was not distrustful." I said that Dr. Karl Brandt, when he was here in this prison, told me that Hitler was quite nervous toward the end.[6] "Yes, Hitler's nerves were kaput. His left hand trembled and he was physically rocked. It took a tremendous willpower to keep him together."

We talked of the atrocities, a subject which Goering disliked but which was unavoidable whenever discussing Hitler. "I'm sure Hitler didn't know the details and that Himmler felt he could do what he wanted without having to fear reprisals. Previously Hitler was anything but cruel. That he became so in the last few years is obvious. Particularly in the last year of the war a human life was not worth much in his eyes."

Was your outlook different from Hitler's regarding the dignity and value of human life? "In the early years, Hitler pardoned many people who were sentenced to death.[7] Later he didn't do that. I myself was always strict in cases of treason and rape, but in other cases I pardoned people. Women I always pardoned and never sentenced to death." I asked him about his impression of Hoess, the commandant at Auschwitz, who had testified before the tribunal that he exterminated men, women, and children of all ages. "I didn't know anything about it. As Hoess said before the tribunal, it was kept secret. I can hardly believe it — the numbers were so great. I can't see it. I can't believe that Hitler knew it. Of course, it's sufficient what did happen — but that the numbers could be so large, I can't envisage. Of course, there were rumors at the time, but I never believed them. People like Hoess and Himmler and the smaller SS folk who carried out these orders must have known about them, but even so, I can't understand it. How they did such a thing is beyond me.

"The order to do away with certain groups of people was never discussed because if it had been discussed there would have been very much resistance against the idea. Himmler was undoubtedly a criminal and he should not have committed suicide. It was different with Hitler, whose suicide I condone. Himmler should not have left Kaltenbrunner and others to be responsible for his misdeeds. The only way Himmler got away with the atrocities he ordered was by either influencing Hitler in a wrong direction or by taking advantage of the great preoccupation Hitler had with the war and doing things on his own.

"I heard of a case once where the rumor said that a few thousand people had been killed. I thought it was enemy propaganda. When I asked about it I was told that it was only enemy propaganda. All of us knew that people were tried expeditiously in the concentration camps and were sentenced to death, but we didn't know of innocent people being exterminated. I heard the name Eichmann here for the first time.[8] That the Jews should be evacuated from Germany was clear. That the Jews should go to the general government in Poland was also clear. But not that they should be exterminated. After the war the Jews were to be brought to Palestine or elsewhere. The plan to evacuate them existed before the war. Such plans were made for the next ten years. For example, there was also a plan about how foreign exchange of money should be handled. I take all the responsibility for what happened in National Socialist Germany but not for the things I knew nothing about, such as the concentration camps and the atrocities."

Did not Goering introduce the first concentration camps in 1933 or 1934? "Yes, I frankly admit concentration camps for Communists and other enemies of National Socialism at that time, but certainly not with the idea of killing people or of using them as extermination camps."

Did you agree that the Jew was undesirable as a human being? "At the end of 1938 or 1939 it was not a question of whether they were desirable or not. The difference between Jew and German was so great that there was no chance for the existence of Jews in Germany. If the Jews had not been shut out of economic life by the vicious press and the economists, such as that great democrat Dr. Schacht, they would have been able to remain in Germany. At the beginning, in 1933, Hitler said that the Jews should be removed from economic life, but only from state positions. However, party pressure constantly increased. Then came the crisis of November 1938, which disturbed the entire economic existence of the Jews. After that, something had to happen. Either the Jews would have to be taken into economic life or something had to happen. Most of the Jews tried to get out of Germany themselves because they saw no way of living. So you see, it was not a question of whether they were desirable or not. The situation developed rapidly; it was not planned for. It was disturbing to the economic life because our relationships with foreign nations were cut. I believe it was the worst thing that Goebbels could bring about. Goebbels was a fanatic.

"Did I ever tell you about Goebbels? He incurred Hitler's disapproval after that incident with the movie actress for which he was beaten up. That clubfooted fanatic! He forced women to submit to him sexually because of his powerful position. He influenced Hitler to become anti-Semitic more than Hitler had been before. Hitler used to come to my house once in a while for a cup of coffee, and because I led a normal life, he would leave about nine o'clock. I was in the habit of retiring early. However, Hitler used to spend practically all of his nights, sometimes until four a.m., with Goebbels and his family. God knows what evil influence Goebbels had on him during those long visits."

What did Goebbels have in mind — what were his own reasons for anti-Semitism? "Goebbels was the strongest representative of anti-Semitism. He saw his big chance to become powerful by using the press for anti-Semitic reasons. Personally, I think Goebbels was using anti-Semitism merely as a means of achieving personal power. Whether he had any deep-seated hatred against the Jews is questionable. I think he was too much of a thief and dishonest opportunist to have any deep-seated feelings for or against anything. But for years Goebbels had been trying in vain to become a big power. At last he saw his chance. He had whipped up anti-Semitic feelings to such a point by his vicious propaganda that he now thought he could do anything. He probably didn't think about the consequences himself. He was a fanatic of an abnormal caliber. Streicher was a tame man compared to Goebbels, because Streicher is half crazy and stupid, whereas Goebbels was just unscrupulous, clever, and dangerous. You couldn't discuss anything with Goebbels. And for the same reason, you couldn't discuss anything with Himmler. Goebbels was so dishonest that it didn't pay to discuss anything with him."

Did you say that Goebbels was more anti-Semitic than Himmler? "Himmler might have done more in practice, but talked less about it. Himmler pretended to be much different than he was. For example, his speeches to the SS leaders in Posen, et cetera, were read here for the first time — they were very secret.[9] To the outside world, Himmler appeared as an ambiguous puzzle. He was always a psychological puzzle to me, too. I never understood how Himmler obtained so much influence with Hitler. He was a good organizer and an ambitious fellow, but not a man who could exert a strong psychological influence on the masses. The atrocities are, for me, the most horrible part of the accusation in this trial. They thought that I took it lightly or laughed about it or some such nonsense, in court. That is definitely a mistake. I am the type of person who is naturally against such things and my own psychological reaction is to laugh or smile in the face of adversity. Perhaps that explains my attitude in court. Besides, I was not to blame for these horrors. It's not just that I am a hard man because of my long experience in the army and in politics. It's true that I saw plenty in the First World War and during the air raids and at the front in this war. But I was always a person who felt the suffering of others. To paint me as an unfeeling ogre who laughs in court at the atrocities is stupid."

I remarked that some of his own anti-Semitic utterances had been read in court, and I wondered whether he considered them as indicative of political ideology or a personal anti-Semitic attitude of his own. He replied with serious demeanor, "I was very upset about it at the time when I made that speech which was brought out here in court. The speech was made after a conversation with Goebbels. There were only six or seven ministers present. I was very aroused because Goebbels had told Hitler that I was protecting the Jews. After that I was ordered to execute various plans. That was all my speech indicated. At that, the only passages which were read in court were those which are damaging to me. The good passages were omitted — for example, where I said that one can't let Jews starve. That was not read in court. The general anti-Semitic feeling had to be maintained by everyone. That was an order by Hitler.

"You must conceive, too, that the blame for the anti-Semitic reaction in Germany was not entirely due to Nazi propaganda or the Nazis themselves as a party, despite the fact that I blame Goebbels for the atrocities. Before 1933 there is some blame to be attached to the Jews themselves. They used rather impolite words against me personally, for example. Before 1933 there was a wild battle. My words are very tame compared to what the Jews said about us. They issued tremendous lies, nasty words, and slander."

Did Goering mean that the Jews brought on anti-Semitism and the subsequent extermination by their own actions? Goering said blandly, "No, but I mean it was a fight. At first I didn't take the anti-Nazi movement in the Jewish press seriously, but when we saw that the movement gained and became dangerous, we used other words. It was not my nature to torture or exterminate people. I am a practical man and I am hard enough to countenance things like reprisals if they are justified. But mass murder of innocent people such as the extermination of the Jews is unjustifiable."

I asked him whether in his early life he was anti-Semitic. "No, no. I was never anti-Semitic. Anti-Semitism played no part in my life. If it were on the basis of anti-Semitism I would never have been interested in the Nazi movement. The thing which attracted me to the party was the political program. I mean the creating of a greater Germany and the abolition of the Versailles Treaty. Of course, if one joined the Nazi Party one had to adopt all the points of the party more or less, including anti-Semitism.

"I suppose you will ask me why I didn't object to the atrocities or to anti-Semitism. The answer is complex. The feeling in Germany at the time was such that perhaps Hitler had to carry an anti-Semitic platform in order to be successful. I admit that if he had not handled the question so primitively, much of our foreign policy would have been more successful. I warned him frequently about this. I never had any feeling of hatred toward the Jews. I realize that it looks stupid — that it is hard to understand how a person like myself who made anti-Semitic speeches and who participated as number two man in a regime that exterminated 5 million Jews can say that he was not anti-Semitic. But it is true. I would never have made this policy. I would have gone in a much different direction and in a quieter way. I have two documents to prove this — but it is embarrassing to bring up these things now — I just wanted to mention it to you. There is no particular point in my bringing these two documents into court because there are so many other things in the hands of the prosecution which can be interpreted as anti-Semitic." He seemed to be waiting for me to ask him about these two documents and I did so. "Well, one of these documents was to the effect that the laws about mixed marriages should be toned down and postponed. You must see these documents in the light of the tense atmosphere which existed at the time. You can realize that they had a quieting influence on the violent anti-Semitism of Goebbels and the party in general. Of course, if you see it outside of this tense atmosphere, then this document, too, can be considered as a special law against the Jews."

I remarked that it was said that he had helped various Jews and prevented some individual persecutions. Could he tell me more about this? "Whenever Jews applied to me for help, I did so. Of course, these were people whom I knew before, and their friends and relatives." Do you think that Jewish people were just as loyal to their country as other Germans? "Yes. In all, the Jews were unified, but that they were loyal Germans, I believed to be true. I made a proposal, for example, that Jews who had received the Iron Cross in the First World War should be exempted from the anti-Semitic laws. I made other proposals, as for example that Jews who had been living in Germany for a hundred years or more should be exempted, but these proposals were all rejected."

What about Goebbels — what was his attitude? "Goebbels thought that the Jews were different, or at least that's what he claimed. I don't know what he really thought inside because he was such a liar. My contact with Hitler during those years was strong politically. But Goebbels had a strong personal contact. The difference in relationship with Hitler between Goebbels and myself was that I talked over things in conferences with Hitler. But Hitler would spend whole evenings with Goebbels and his family. His personal contact with Goebbels was great and he was probably more influenced by that clubfooted fanatic politically than I realized."

I remarked that it seemed to me that his attitude toward Hitler was quite different in reality, or at least in our private conversations, than it seemed to be from his testimony in court during his defense. Goering said, "The main line of my defense was that as a loyal German and a follower of Hitler, I accepted orders as orders. Secondly, as the most important figure in Germany next to the Führer, I had to assume responsibility, but I drew the line at accepting the blame for the ungentlemanly acts and the atrocities which I believe Goebbels and Himmler committed. Regarding orders, I am not a fanatic either. For example, if the subordinates of Himmler had come to me and told me of the dirty work that was going on, I might have been able to do something about it. Or they could have resigned and have asked to be sent to the front. But none of Himmler's subordinates ever came to me, and as far as I knew, atrocities did not exist. I am a man who is basically opposed to atrocities or ungentlemanly actions. In 1934 I promulgated a law against vivisection. You can see, therefore, that if I disapprove of the experimentation on animals, how could I possibly be in favor of torturing humans? The prosecution says that I had something to do with the freezing experiments which were performed in the concentration camps under the auspices of the air force. That is pure *Quatsch!* I was much too busy to know about these medical experiments, and if anybody had asked me, I would have disapproved violently. It must have been Himmler who thought up these stupid experiments, although I think he shirked his responsibility by committing suicide. I am not too unhappy about it because I would not particularly enjoy sitting on the same bench with him. The same is true of that drunken Robert Ley, who did us a favor by hanging himself before the trial started. He was not going to be any advantage for us defendants when he took the stand."

## May 27, 1946

Goering was in his cell all day today, suffering from a mild sciatica of the right lower extremity, which has kept him out of court for a few days. It was perhaps significant that this attack began simultaneously with the end of Raeder's case and the beginning of Schirach's defense. The sciatica itself seems minimal. Of his own complaints, Goering said: "It's worse because of this weather. Besides, the sitting upright in the court all day is so wearing." It was true that within the last few weeks Goering had suffered a distinct personality change in the sense of his being rather depressed, although not despondent or overtly brooding. Rather, he showed little interest in the proceedings in court, barely spoke to his neighbors; occasionally when Ribbentrop, who sat next to him, would say something, Goering did not answer.

He seemed glad to talk, but wary of saying too much or too little. His old technique, which he utilized effectively in the course of his cross-examination — to answer one question by averting it or scarcely paying attention to it, but speak at length on questions he believed favorable and to which he had a reasonable response — was still in evidence, but he was less alert or seemed to care less. His attitude was a combination of cheerfulness and indifference, particularly regarding some of the questions I put to him, which he found disagreeable last time I visited him for any length of time.

I said that I had read a biography of him, and also the short autobiography which he wrote when he first came to the prison, a copy of which existed in the prison safe. He smiled and shook his head, saying carelessly, "All *Quatsch*. Nobody knows the real Goering. I am a man of many parts, but the autobiography, what does that tell you? Nothing. And those books put out by the party press, they are less than useless." I replied that I should like to find the "real Goering" from a psychologically valid standpoint and that was the reason for my asking him questions which at some points might be disagreeable. I reminded him that his defense was over and that nothing which I wrote had any bearing on his case, nor was it accessible to the prosecution.

Goering scoffed, good-humoredly. "Like Gilbert, he is a psychologist, too. But the difference between a psychiatrist and a psychologist seems to be very marked." I asked him what he meant by this remark. He said that he meant there must be a great difference between the fields of psychology and psychiatry. The former, in Goering's opinion, had to do with "books" and the latter with "human beings." I told him that in my own view the differences were not great except that a psychiatrist has a medical degree and a psychologist a degree in psychology, but both were concerned with human reactions. He scoffed, laughed, and said, "You Americans must stick together, eh?" I knew that Gilbert, the psychologist, had been on rather strained terms with Goering for the past few weeks, so I said nothing except to remark that individual methods of understanding people varied.

We talked of many things. He liked to have free rein and not to be pinned down to any particular subject. In general I tried to steer him in an autobiographical direction. He said that he was born in Rosenheim in 1893 in a nursing home. His father's family came from the Rhineland and Westphalia. His mother's people stemmed from the Tirol and Bavaria. "I had a very happy childhood."

He spoke without sentimentality but with some affection for his old home and childhood associations. "My father was a high diplomatic official, very renowned, a lively-spirited man who loved hunting, fencing, and riding. He was mentally superior and a good conversationalist. When Father died, I was twenty. He had diabetes for two or three years. He refused to diet or take precautions — he loved to live actively and did so until the end. He did not have a gray hair in his head — he was as blond as a young man."

Goering's mother died when he was thirty. She was about twenty years her husband's junior, his second wife. "She was very clever, sparkling, but like all women, without any logic or reasoning power. I think that women are wonderful but I've never met one yet who didn't show more feeling than logic. Do you agree with that as a psychiatrist?" I remarked that there were differences of opinion on the subject, but that I should be interested in hearing more of his parents and childhood.

"Well, I don't like women who have strong wills and are too logical. Mother was all feeling and no reasoning. I don't mean she was unreasonable — far from it. But not like my father, who was cool and logical. My own energy and love of life I inherit from my mother, but my physical appearance and mental structure are from my father.

"Father was very ambitious, full of talent. He was governor general of German Southwest Africa for a while, as minister in residence."

His father married twice. His first wife died. Goering had three half brothers and one half sister. He had also two full brothers and two full sisters. He had little or no contact with his siblings, he said, because "the difference in ages was so great, and besides the children all lived outside the family when I was a child." He seemed loath to pursue the story of his siblings now, or of his relationship to them.

He mentioned that his father had a "great sense of humor." What about himself? "If I didn't have a sense of humor, how could I stand this trial now?" He smiled as if to prove it. I asked him about Hitler. Did he have a sense of humor? "I can't say about that after 1941 or 1942. I didn't see him often enough to know. He no longer did what I wanted him to do." But did Hitler have a sense of humor? "Oh, yes. In a way. I wouldn't call it overwhelming, but he made jokes and laughed at them. Seriously, he did appreciate a good story, but as time went on he told most of the stories himself and tended to repeat them too often." Goering seemed to resent his own statements deprecating the Führer. He added, slightly irritably, with the smile gone from his face, "But Hitler and his sense of humor is of little importance. He was a genius."

I remarked that I was much more interested in Goering than in Hitler at this time, and I agreed that Hitler's possessing a sense of humor or being devoid of one was of slight import. Goering continued to glare at his knees, sitting upright, his attention fixed for the moment on my words as Mr. Triest translated them literally. "Let me explain the difference between me and Hitler. In one word. The German people called him 'my Führer.' They addressed me as 'Hermann.' I was always closer to the hearts of the people than Hitler, but he was a great leader and I subscribe to his program completely. Naturally there are differences, which I am trying to get across to you and to the world, in that Hitler was a great man who was betrayed by some of his subordinates like Goebbels. Finally Hitler didn't know his real friends from his false ones. But it was a great betrayal. The National Socialist program, in which I played no mean part, was a great reform movement which would have benefited Germany if the enemies of Hitler had not betrayed him."

He continued listlessly to describe his family and siblings. His two half brothers, whom he rarely saw, were seventy-six and sixty-six years of age and still living. One half brother died at twenty-five of unknown causes. His two full brothers were two years older and two years younger than himself. His older brother died during the First World War at the front. His other brother, born in 1895, named Albert, was "never a party member." He was here in Nuremberg for a while, but is now interned at the camp in Hersbruck. "He lived in Austria and was opposed to the party until 1938. Then I had him appointed to become the foreign director of the Skoda Works in Prague. That was before the occupation of Czechoslovakia. In reality I had nothing to do with his appointment, merely recommended it. He remained in that position until the end of the war. His position was not affected by my station."

This brother, Albert, was married happily, but "always looked ten years older than I. Maybe it was because he took things too seriously. We never really got along well together. For twelve years we never spoke to each other because of Albert's attitude toward the party. Neither of us was angry at the other. It was a separation due to the situation." As children they had little in common, as far as Goering could recall. Albert was not the sport lover that Hermann had been. They would quarrel over small things, "like all children, but I can't remember any serious fights."

Goering's education in the early years was in the hands of a tutor and later in a private school. He attended a private gymnasium in Fürth until he was thirteen. He then was enrolled in the cadet school, at first in Karlsruhe and later in Berlin for five years until his graduation in 1911. He was bent on becoming an officer from his earliest recollection. "The cadet school had the same curriculum as the gymnasium. One could become a lawyer or doctor after attending the cadet school. But I stayed in the cadet corps and became an officer in 1912."

In 1912 he joined the infantry regiment of Prince Wilhelm in Mülhausen, where he remained during the years 1912 to 1914. He said that the regiment was named after the prince, but this was only an honorary title. It was the custom to name various regiments and corps after members of the nobility. "In our army it was changed. There were only two military units named after individuals. The Hitler Bodyguard, which was an SS unit, and the Hermann Goering Division, which was a varied outfit, mainly a panzer division but belonging to the air force. In the air force there was the Richthofen Squadron, which remained so named. I was Wolfram Freiherr von Richthofen's successor."

Goering seemed little interested in these details. I remarked that he seemed a bit depressed or at least thoughtful. "You know, what I'm thinking of is my brother Albert. You ask me about my own brother, and I can hardly tell you about him. It's strange but true of all human beings. It just occurred to me why we were estranged. He was always the antithesis of myself. He was not politically or militarily interested; I was. He was quiet, reclusive; I like crowds and company. He was melancholy and pessimistic, and I am an optimist. But he's not a bad fellow, Albert."

Goering felt as if he had acquitted himself well after this recital of the differences between himself and his younger brother. He launched into a description of his career from the time of the outbreak of the First World War. He was a lieutenant of infantry at the front and participated in the first few battles until October 1914. He then joined the air force. He was an aerial observer until June 1915, and then he became a pilot.

At first he flew a large bomber, and in the fall of 1915 became a fighter plane pilot. He was severely wounded in 1916 during an aerial battle. In the summer of 1918 he became commander of four squadrons, which was the largest single aerial formation in the last war. He remarked that toward the end of that war the English had the biggest air force, but the Americans had only a few poor planes, which entered into action only toward the end of the war. He said that his injury kept him out of active service for only three months of the entire war in 1916. For two months he was confined to a hospital bed, and another month he spent recuperating at a mountain resort.

"Ach," sputtered Goering, "I live in the present, not the past. All of this reminiscing is like so much dead fish." Obviously his recital of his past was so dispirited it was unenjoyable to him. He wanted to talk of more recent memories, of the glories that were his in the Third Reich, of the personalities among the defendants, of anything except himself and his personal life. There ensued a lively conversation about present affairs, which I found superficial and dull, but uttered by Goering as if he were a savant and philosopher.

At one point in the interview he commented on Ribbentrop. "He is a good fellow, but he always appears as if he will fall apart any minute. Sometimes I have a hard time when he bores me in his remarks in court. That he did the Führer's will and followed instructions is correct. He did more or less as I advised him during his defense, but he has no ability to spar with the prosecution. If I had been foreign minister I would be able to defend my actions, no matter what they had on me. But Ribbentrop is so weak and indecisive."

He enjoyed commenting on his fellow defendants. In the main he said nothing disparaging about their political ideas or actions, but his temptation to make an acrid observation often overcame his calculated desire to present the Nazi regime as a dignified body of high-minded statesmen. We spoke of Hess. I mentioned that Schirach had told me that Hess was always a peculiar fellow, who probably felt left out of things in 1941, and to show that he was important, flew to England. I repeated Schirach's analysis that Hess was a pilot in the First World War, just as Goering had been, but also became one at the end of the last war and was undistinguished. Schirach felt that perhaps unconsciously he flew to England to show the world that he, too, was a great flier.

Goering smiled. He obviously did not want to corroborate anything

Schirach might have said at this moment because the unexpressed tensions between the two men were running high. Goering knew that Schirach was going to abandon the "united front" policy which Goering strived so hard to maintain. He knew that Schirach had decided on admitting that Hitler was a murderer, for example, and this was certainly against Goering's tactics, which were all for putting the Nazis on a respectable basis, ignoring the atrocities, the warmongering, the general corruption of the regime. Nevertheless, Goering could not resist making a few remarks about Hess.

"Hess was slightly off balance for as long as I can recall. Why the Führer kept him on as head of the party was a mystery to most people, but to me I always felt it was Hitler's loyalty to his old friends. I remember Hess had a bright idea once in treating me for some neuralgia that I had at the time. It was in 1936 or so. Anyway, one day lots of pots and pans arrived of all different sizes. I didn't know what they were for. One was for soaking my arm, another my forearm, another size for my leg, my thing, and so on. I called him up and asked him what he had sent me so many pots for — did he think I wanted to start an aquarium? But Hess explained that I told him I had neuralgia and this was the treatment for it. I thanked him over the telephone and laughed for days."

I said that Schirach also told me that Hess was said to have had a pendulum in his office, which he used to detect whether the letters he received were worthy of answering or not — whether the writer was a friend or an enemy. If the pendulum swung in one direction, the letter was all right; if it swung another way, the letter was a bad one. Did Goering know anything as to the validity of this tale?

"Sure. I saw Hess's pendulum and he used it. I never paid any attention to his strange ideas. He was quiet and bothered nobody. I knew a great surgeon who believed in a similar pendulum, using it the same way Hess did. Apparently it's a common superstition." Goering went on to say that obviously it was not Hitler's idea that Hess fly to England, because it was too stupid. "There were many other means to negotiate a peace with England if Hitler wanted that. We could use our representatives in Sweden or Switzerland."

He returned to the subject of his attitude toward Ribbentrop. "Ribbentrop should say, 'This is my policy. I stand up for it. If a foreign tribunal tries me for what I did in a sovereign state as foreign minister, it's none of their business.' That's what I would have said if I were in his

situation when he took the stand. Instead he had many quibbling memoranda, legalistic notations, long explanations. I don't think much of that
kind of defense. A defense should be like mine was, clear, straight, no
quarter given to the prosecution. They can't force a foreigner to account
for his actions in his own country. It's none of the tribunal's business.
Personally I used the tribunal to give to history and the German people
a last statement about the National Socialist regime and my part in it. As
far as the cross-examination – I didn't give a damn for it. I was polite,
but firm. I answered questions intelligently.

"I never thought much of Ribbentrop's abilities. As a foreign minister
he was lacking in understanding and experience. I was against Hitler's
choosing Ribbentrop at the time he did. I wanted Neurath to remain. He
was not a strong man, and Hitler could tell him what to do, but he would
do it more intelligently and with more finesse than Ribbentrop."

I remarked that it seemed to me Hitler surrounded himself with odd,
weak characters, such as the two we were just discussing, Hess and
Ribbentrop. Goering did not reply at once, but finally said in a dry manner, "I have never pretended that in later years Hitler was one who
could stand for any disagreement. In the beginning I could speak my
mind with him, at least in private. I often disagreed with him. But later
on that was impossible, and he expected everyone, myself included, to
say 'yes' to his every word.

"Even in the early years of the war I had plenty of influence with
Hitler. I kept Sweden out of the war, when Hitler wanted to invade that
country. Through my friends in Sweden, I managed to get King Gustav
to write Hitler a note, to the effect that Sweden would resist invasion.
Hitler asked me about it and I said Gustav was entirely right. Besides,
what on earth did we have to gain by bothering a neutral nation that was
more help to us out of the war than in it? The Swedes know I spared
their country from war. Birger Dahlerus, my witness, knows that."[10]

We went on to talk about Hitler. It seemed obvious that Goering was
consciously trying to tell me breezily about people without in any way
insinuating their weaknesses, except unconsciously, because of his desire
to maintain his line of solidarity with all things Nazi, all "good Nazis,"
and produce a legend of betrayal by someone or other which accounted
for Germany's defeat and Hitler's change of personality. What about
Hitler's death? I asked. Did he really think Hitler committed suicide? If
so, was it not a cowardly thing to do? Goering assumed an air of loyal

disapproval of my effrontery in asking him if Hitler had done a cowardly action. "No, it was certainly not cowardly. Can you imagine that man in a cell like this? Hitler was the spirit and symbol of Germany. They did not put Kaiser Wilhelm on trial after the last war, they aren't trying Emperor Hirohito of Japan. But they would probably have tried Hitler. I am here to stand in for Hitler. It was not a matter of cowardice for him to allow others to assume the responsibility for his acts. It's a responsibility I gladly assume in Hitler's stead, as I told the court." There was little conviction in his voice as he said these gallant words. It was as if he had played a record that had gone stale and the music was off-key.

He said that he was certain Hitler had committed suicide because Speer had told him that on April 22, 1945, Eva Braun told Speer that she and the Führer intended to die together in Berlin. I asked him if he knew Eva Braun and what sort of woman she was. I said that Dr. Brandt, Hitler's personal physician, had mentioned to me that Hitler often said that the "greater the man, the smaller the woman he should have." Goering's cue for emphasizing the respectability of Hitler and Nazism had been given. He said loftily, "The Führer, like myself, had a great respect for women. He was satisfied with Eva. I never knew her well, saw her a couple of times. She was completely alive for Hitler, which is as it should be. She was no great beauty, but wasn't a bad figure. She had a sweet personality, I think. Hitler always disapproved of his party leaders divorcing wives and marrying younger ones. That is seen here among the defendants. Frick and Schacht, for example, married against the wish of Hitler. Do you realize that Schacht, in his late sixties, is married to a comparatively young woman? Schacht is now such a moral, upstanding man!"

Did Hitler really have much regard for the common people? Again, Goering appeared dignified and disdainful of the whole idea of questioning the motives of the man who "symbolized" Germany. "His whole life was dedicated to the German nation." He seemed to quit this subject abruptly. I continued for a moment, more or less ignoring his disdain. What about Hitler's last testament? Schirach, Speer, Fritzsche, and other defendants told me often that the last testament showed how megalomaniacal Hitler was, and how little he cared for the people. The whole tempo of his last testament, according to Schirach, I continued, was that of vitriolically blaming others for the defeat of Germany, scorning the existence of the German people, and so forth.

Goering stirred himself, and for the first time during today's interview seemed anxious and defensive. "In the first place I'm sure Hitler did not write that damned testament himself. Probably some swine like Bormann wrote it for him. But I don't see what is so terrible in the testament when you examine it, anyway. There was Berlin, bombed every minute. The noise of artillery from the lousy Russians, the American and British bombers overhead. Maybe Hitler was a trifle unbalanced by all that. If he wrote the testament at such a time, it was hysteria. But essentially, what difference does it make?"

I was silent for a moment and Goering fidgeted. "You probably think I'm jealous because Hitler named Doenitz his successor. Ridiculous. I was too important for him to name. I, too, was a symbol of Germany. Who was Doenitz? A little admiral who could negotiate a peace. Who could Hitler have named? Certainly not Ribbentrop, who was mistrusted abroad. Not me, his foremost contemporary!"

Was there anything about Hitler of which he disapproved? I asked. "Certainly in the course of the years I disapproved of much. But from 1941 onward, I was hardly with Hitler except on official occasions. There was the inner iron ring of Bormann, Himmler, and Ribbentrop. I think that the atrocities, if they existed — and mind you, I don't believe they were technically possible, or if they were, I don't believe Hitler ordered them — it must have been Goebbels or Himmler. Only one thing amuses me about Hitler's finale — his sentimental marriage to Eva Braun. That was a little too much drama and sentiment. He could have omitted that."

I said that a moment ago he had referred to Hitler as perhaps a trifle unbalanced. For example, in what way? "I don't think he was ever crazy. Not that. I meant the noise and bombing sounds in Berlin when he wrote the last testament. If he did lose his balance it was also because of the military defeats that could have been averted if he had not been betrayed by some of his generals and others. The *Attentat* of July 20, 1944, was an indication of the betrayal by some of the generals."

I said that we had wandered far afield but that the conversation had been interesting. Goering smiled and said, "It's been better than two APCs.[11] I forgot about my sciatica. Come back again tomorrow, or do you think I can go to court?" I replied that it would depend on how he felt. "Well, I think I'll stay down tomorrow. The court isn't so interesting these days." I remarked that Schirach was on the stand. "I'd rather be there for his cross-examination," he said, laughing. "Anyway, I know what he's going to say."

**May 28, 1946**

This evening Goering was in his cell smoking his long Bavarian hunting pipe and looking rather depressed when I entered with Mr. Triest. He smiled forcibly in an attempt to appear cheerful and invited us to sit down. I asked him how his sciatica was and he replied that it was much improved. He has been walking well and there were actually no signs of sciatic neuritis any longer.

I remarked that he appeared rather "down" and I wondered whether he was depressed about something. He looked at the far wall reflectively and said, "Well, this sciatica has got me down a little bit, but I must admit that in general I don't feel as cheerful as I might. I don't understand it myself. On the other hand, I am a prisoner on trial for my life, very much debased in position compared to the position I enjoyed for many years, and I suppose it is natural for me to feel occasionally low. You know, I spend a good deal of my time in fantasy. For example, when things get dull or unpleasant in the courtroom, I can close my eyes behind my dark glasses and I practically live in the past. I think of the many pleasant times that I had. For example, I think of the frequent large parties I had in Karin Hall or of my popularity among the German people, which gives me great pleasure and satisfaction. I am sure that I will go down in history as a man who did much for the German people. This trial is a political trial, not a criminal one. If there were criminal things perpetrated by the party, or the SS, or even the army, as is charged, I certainly had nothing to do with them. It is true that my position as second in command politically next to Hitler makes such a statement seem ridiculous. Maybe I closed my eyes to the real meaning of what was going on in Germany, but it was always for the benefit of the common people that I strived. I mentioned the big parties I had at Karin Hall, but they were few and far between. Mostly I had the highest ethics and the highest aims."

Would he tell me more about his art collection? Goering said, "I'm glad you asked me that question, because it is something I had little opportunity to answer comprehensively in court. They tried to paint a picture of me as a looter of art treasures. In the first place, during a war everybody loots a little bit. However, none of my so-called looting was illegal. I may have paid a small price — smaller than the articles were worth — for things, but I always paid for them or they were delivered to me by official channels through the Hermann Goering Division, which, together with the Rosenberg Commission, supplied me with my art collection. Perhaps one of my weaknesses has been that I love to be surrounded by luxury and that I am so artistic in temperament that masterpieces make me feel alive and glowing inside. But always my intention was to contribute these art treasures, paintings, pieces of sculpture, altarpieces, jewels, et cetera, to a state museum after I had died or before, for the greater glory of German culture. Looking at it from that standpoint I can't see that it was ethically wrong. It was not as if I accumulated art treasures in order to sell them or to become a rich man. I love art for art's sake and as I said, my personality demanded that I be surrounded with the best specimens of the world's art."[12]

I said that this seemed fairly clear and that my own interpretation of his art accumulations was that he felt happiest when in luxurious surroundings, that this was a facet of his personality, and that he never took it very seriously. I added, however, that in the eyes of the world he had taken art treasures which for centuries belonged to other countries and brought them to his home in great quantities, which in itself was not a laudable activity. Goering nodded and said, "You are the first one who seems to understand this. I admit all that you have said. Of all the charges which have been revealed against me, the so-called looting of art treasures by me has caused me the most anguish. But it was not done in the spirit of looting. I like nice things about me. I didn't want them for myself in the final analysis anyway. They would have gone to the museums of Germany for posterity. If I had not taken them they would be in the hands of those damn Russians for the most part." Goering smiled as if he had scored a point.

I asked him what his opinion about Russians was and why he constantly referred to them as "damn Russians" and why he seemed so antipathetic toward the Russian people. "The Russians are primitive folk. Besides, Bolshevism is something that stifles individualism and which is against my inner nature. Bolshevism is worse than National Socialism — in fact, it can't be compared to it. Bolshevism is against private property, and I am all in favor of private property. Bolshevism is barbaric and crude, and I am fully convinced that the atrocities committed by the Nazis, which incidentally I knew nothing about, were not nearly as great or as cruel as those committed by the Communists. I hate the Communists bitterly because I hate the system. The delusion that all men are equal is ridiculous. I feel that I am superior to most Russians, not only because I am a German but because my cultural and family background are superior. How ironic it is that crude Russian peasants who wear the uniforms of generals now sit in judgment on me. No matter how educated a Russian might be, he is still a barbaric Asiatic. Secondly, the Russian generals and the Russian government planned a war against Germany because we represented a threat to them ideologically.

"In the German state, I was the chief opponent of Communism. I admit freely and proudly that it was I who created the first concentration camps in order to put Communists in them. Did I ever tell you that funny story about how I sent to Spain a ship containing mainly bricks and stones, under which I put a single layer of ammunition which had been ordered by the Red government in Spain? The purpose of that ship was to supply the waning Red government with munitions. That was a good practical joke and I am proud of it because I wanted with all my heart to see Russian Communism in Spain defeated finally."

I said that there were many things about his worldview that I did not really understand. In the first place, what about his concept of the importance of the oath of loyalty and the matter of the all-importance of orders? "That is another thing I am glad you asked me about. We Germans consider an oath of fealty more important than anything. This tribunal fails to realize that accepting orders is a legitimate excuse for doing almost anything. The tribunal is wrong. Mind you, I said almost anything. I don't consider the extermination of women and children as proper even if an oath were taken. I myself can hardly believe that women and children were exterminated. It must have been that criminal Goebbels, or Himmler, who influenced Hitler to do such a dastardly thing. I am very cynical about these trials. The trials are being fought in the courtroom by the world press. Everyone knows that the Frenchmen and the Russians who are judges here have made up their minds that we are all guilty and they had their instructions from Paris and Moscow long before the trial even started to condemn us. It's all but planned and the trial is a farce. Maybe the American and English judges are trying to conduct a legitimate trial. But even in their case I have my doubts."

I asked him to give me further reflections or impressions about the trials as far as his opinion was concerned. Goering seemed wary and not too inclined to speak at length. He did say, however, "Frankly, it is my intention to make this trial a mockery. I feel that a foreign country has no right to try the government of a sovereign state. I have desisted from making any critical remarks about my codefendants. Yet they are a mixed-up, unrepresentative group. Some of them are so unimportant, I never even heard of them. I'll admit they are right in including me among the big Nazis who ran Germany. But why include Fritzsche? He was one of many section chiefs in the Propaganda Ministry. And then they try a man like Funk, who is guilty of nothing. He followed orders, and they were my orders. And then they try a fellow like Keitel, who, although he was called a field marshal, was a small person who did whatever Hitler instructed. Of all the defendants, the only ones who are big enough to merit being tried are me, Schacht, Ribbentrop perhaps, although he was a weak echo of Hitler, Frick, who proposed the Nuremberg Laws, and maybe a few others, like Rosenberg and Seyss-Inquart. The rest of them were followers and showed little initiative."[13]

"Then there is the farce of the case against the general staff. These military men were not a part of any conspiracy to wage war but simply accepted orders and obeyed them as any German soldier or officer would do. If there was a conspiracy, it lay among those who are dead or missing — I mean Himmler, Goebbels, Bormann, and naturally, Hitler. I always felt that Bormann was a primitive criminal type and I never trusted Himmler. I would have dismissed them." Goering smiled knowingly and added, "You know, you can get rid of a man in many subtle ways. For example, you can dismiss a man suddenly, but that is less effective if that individual has some power and backing than by slowly diminishing his power by giving him more and more meaningless titles. In the case of Himmler, I would have promoted him on paper and made him chief of this and chief of that, but in the end his power would be gone. I would have taken away from him the police power first, and later I would have assumed control of the SS myself. In this way there would have been no such thing as mass murders. For all that Hitler was a genius and a strong character, he nevertheless was suggestible, and Himmler and Goebbels or both must have influenced him to go ahead with such an idiotic scheme as gas chambers and crematoriums to eliminate millions of people.

"Even if one had no compunction about exterminating a race, common sense dictates that in our civilization this is barbaric and would be subject to so much criticism from abroad and within, that it would be condemned as the greatest criminal act in history. Understand that I am not a moralist, although I have my chivalric code. If I really felt that the killing of the Jews meant anything, such as that it meant the winning of the war, I would not be too much bothered by it. But it was so meaningless and did nobody any good whatever except to give Germany a bad name. I have a conscience and I feel that killing women and children simply because they happen to be the victims of Goebbels's hysterical propaganda is not the way of a gentleman. I don't believe that I will go to either heaven or hell when I die. I don't believe in the Bible or in a lot of things which religious people think. But I revere women and I think it unsportsmanlike to kill children. That is the main thing that bothers me about the extermination of the Jews. The second thing which I disapprove of is the unfavorable reaction politically which such a meaningless program of extermination of necessity brings with it. For myself I feel quite free of responsibility for the mass murders. Certainly as second man in the state under Hitler, I heard rumors about mass killings of Jews, but I could do nothing about it and I knew that it was useless to investigate these rumors and to find out about them accurately, which would not have been too hard, but I was busy with other things, and if I had found out what was going on regarding the mass murders, it would simply have made me feel bad and I could do very little to prevent it anyway."

I asked Goering about his attitude toward joining Hitler originally and why he had done so. "Well, I was against the Versailles Treaty and I was against the democratic state, which failed to solve the problem of unemployment and which instead of making Germany a powerful nation was turning it into a small, minor state. I am a German nationalist and have high ideals for Germany. I am convinced that German culture, even now with Germany in ruins, is the highest in the world because we had the greatest art, music, industrial capacity, and so forth. I have to laugh when the English claim that they are such a wonderful nation. Everyone knows that Englishmen are really Germans, that the English kings were German, and that in Russia the emperors were either of German origin or received their education in Germany. I met Hitler in 1922 at a meeting and was not too impressed with him at first. Like myself, he said very little at this first meeting. A few days afterward I heard Hitler give an address in a Munich beer hall where he spoke about a greater Germany, the abolition of the Versailles Treaty, arms for Germany, and a future glory of the German people. So I joined forces with him and became a member of the National Socialist Party. That was in the days when Hitler was a very minor politician, although his ideas were always big. He was honored to have me as a fellow worker because I had some fame as the successor of Richthofen. Hitler asked me to take charge of the SA, which at that time was in the process of being formed to become a military organization. I had great fun. At that time Hitler was open to suggestion, and if I say so myself, I played a vital role in his eventual rise to power. I am convinced that whether or not Hitler happened along, I would have been a leading statesman and military power in Germany and I would have succeeded in winning a war. In fact, if I had not been displaced in Hitler's confidence by such inferior people like Bormann and Himmler, I could have influenced Hitler further and perhaps averted a war.

"I said in court and I repeat to you that this war was not started by Hitler or Germany but by the Allies. Your country obliged England to go to war when we invaded Poland. England was all for appeasement and no war. I think that the duke of Windsor, who was king, resigned from his position not because he married an American lady, but because he was a friend of Germany and realized how right we were but foresaw that America was going to involve England in a war."[14]

I commented at this point that his views were markedly different from my own, but that I was interested in hearing them nevertheless. I asked him to tell me more about his feelings in reference to the war, the trials, Hitler, and so forth. Goering smiled wryly and said, "Yes, I suppose this is the last chance for me to tell the world, through you, all I know and what my worldview has always been. The strange part of it all is that I don't feel like a criminal and that if I had been in the United States or South America or anyplace else, I would probably be a leading figure in one of those countries. I am a capitalist and a cultured gentleman. That is why I can tolerate this prison where I am treated like a thief or a small criminal. I have to watch my step every moment. If I give vent to my spontaneous reactions — such as laughing at the Russians when they try to cross-examine, or, another example, when I laugh at evidence about the atrocities, which, as I explained before, is not meant because I think it is humorous but because it is my personality to laugh in the face of adversity — then Dr. Gilbert feels that I am making a mockery of the atrocities and they treat me like a naughty child. I am fully convinced that this trial is a mockery and that someday when you Americans have your hands full of Russian troublemaking, you will see me and my activities in a different light.

"The charge of conspiracy is a farce. It all goes back to the Versailles Treaty and the fact that Germany was forced to take steps to regain its dignity as a nation. The Weimar Republic was a failure, and I'd had enough of so-called democracy. That form of government may work in America, just as Communism may work in Russia, but it is not for us Germans. It is not a natural thing for me nor for my people. We Germans are apolitical and an election can be swung anyway one pleases because the people are so naïve. It is for that reason that I believed in the leadership principle. Germany will need a strong leader in the future just as it always required one."

# Rudolf Hess
## 1894–1987

Rudolf Hess was deputy leader of the Nazi Party. There is strong evidence that he was mentally incompetent at the time of the Nuremberg trials. Found guilty of conspiracy to commit crimes and of crimes against peace, he was sentenced to life imprisonment. Despite appeals for his release on humanitarian grounds, he remained in Spandau prison until his death, at age ninety-two.

**June 8, 1946**

Rudolf Hess was lying in bed, and although it was a warm day, he had on an overcoat and several blankets. He displayed the same pained, pinched facial expression, with a tightly drawn mouth and prominent masseter muscles. He said that he had unusually severe stomach cramps today. I asked him how his memory was and he said that it was "very bad." He seemed to be convinced today that the fat he was receiving in his food contained too much salt, and that salt was not good for his health. He requested a different type of fat, butter (if possible) which was unsalted. He also stated that he believed coffee in the morning made him weak and he wondered whether he could not have some other type of fluid because of this.

We discussed again his early life. I explained that I considered this type of discussion more advantageous as far as stimulating his memory than the formal memory tests. He said he agreed since such discussion had helped him in the past to a limited extent. Today he said that he could remember that his father had been a merchant in Egypt but he could not recall what the father sold or what business he engaged in. He could not remember either the personality of the father or what he looked like. He believed that his father was easy to get along with but this was merely an assumption, perhaps a result of my question as to whether he was easy or hard to get along with. He did not recall his mother's personality either. He says that he must have seen her sometime shortly before his trip to England because she was living in Germany at the time. He said that he had one brother and one sister, named Alfred and Margaret, both of whom were younger than himself. He could recall that Alfred was a merchant, just as was his father.

Alfred and the father left Egypt later than Hess but both of them came to Germany eventually. His sister, he believes, is single, but he doesn't know her occupation or what she looks like. He said that he probably saw his brother and sister before his flight to England, but he is not sure.

He said that he remembered what house he lived in in Alexandria, Egypt, before he left there. He seemed excessively agreeable and susceptible to suggestion, so that his answers were not particularly reliable.[1]

On his desk Hess had written certain words in German, which seemed to be rules for keeping in good health which he had probably jotted down in order to facilitate his memory. Mr. Triest took down the notes, which in translation are as follows:

> *Eat little. Don't take any sleeping pills.* They will only lose the effect in case that you should really need them. Also take little other *medicine* [analgesics]. Instead of egg, ask for *marmalade and bread. Don't eat or drink in the morning* in order not to get tired. Ask the doctor for *orange or lemon juice* every once in a while. Don't eat *salty food.* Otherwise the *cramps* may become more frequent.

# Alfred Jodl
1890–1946

Alfred Jodl was chief of the operations staff of the Supreme Command of the Armed Forces (OKW) from 1939 to 1945. Found guilty at Nuremberg of conspiracy to commit crimes, crimes against peace, war crimes, and crimes against humanity, he was hanged on October 16, 1946. On February 28, 1953, he was posthumously exonerated by a German de-Nazification court that found him not guilty of crimes under international law.

**March 17, 1946**

Seen for a short interview this afternoon, Alfred Jodl was his usual ruddy-complexioned, sharp-featured self. He is quite complacent, and almost the first thing he greeted me with was, "Ah, you come to see the others but rarely to see me." I replied, through Mr. Triest, that I was a psychiatrist, as Jodl knew, and therefore I have always looked on Jodl as not particularly requiring my services. I said this with humorous intent, and Triest so translated. It was taken quite seriously, however, by Jodl, who said: "Yes, I'm very normal, everything is okay, I won't become a psychiatric case."

I then told him that I was interested more in the personalities of the defendants, and therefore it was with no suspicion that he was in any way abnormal that I spoke to him. He said he realized that.

He seemed distant but not unfriendly. He said that his uncle Professor Jodl had been at the University of Munich and died in 1913, that he was a scholar and a professor of philosophy. He himself took after his uncle in many ways, he said — for example, his interest in philosophy and a philosophical inclination that allows him to accept these trials and present difficulties without becoming upset. He feels that is his uncle's influence.

He stressed his Bavarian birth, his Bavarian temperament, his old Bavarian lineage. He was born in 1890 in Würzburg, his father an artillery officer. He has five siblings and is the third in line.

**Education:** Elementary school in Landau, 1896–99. Munich, 1899–1900. High school to 1903. Cadet school in Munich, 1903–1910.

**Marital:** First marriage, to Countess Irma von Buillon. She died in April 1944 after an operation. He remarried in March 1945 to Luise von Benda. He showed me pictures of his former wife, now deceased, and of his present wife, a profile of her lying down in a bathing suit, an obviously much younger woman. His wife now assists his two defense counsels, he says, in the preparation of his case. He proudly points out that he alone, of the twenty-one defendants, has two professors of law as defense counsel. One of them, Professor Franz Exner, was formerly at Munich and knew his uncle Professor Jodl.

Regarding his present state of mind and attitude, he maintains that he spent the entire war in headquarters, in Berlin or elsewhere, with the Führer, from 1939 to 1945, so that he is not concerned with atrocities or other war brutalities. He feels an inner sense of innocence, he says, and therefore this incarceration does not bother him.

On his table behind the pictures of his two wives, he has a scenic view of Berchtesgaden. He described in detail just where his own house was, and where the Führer's home was in relation to the picture.

He is a colorless fellow who requires slow, careful study. He gives the impression of competence, coolness, and oxlike stubbornness and obsessiveness, which may be incorrect, but which is suggested by his bearing, detachment, and also the remark on my entering his cell concerning the infrequency of my visits as compared to my visiting some of the other defendants. He has apparently noted this.

# Ernst Kaltenbrunner
## 1903–1946

Ernst Kaltenbrunner was an Austrian police official who was an active supporter of the Nazi Party and Germany's 1938 annexation of Austria. He became chief of the Reich Security Main Office (RSHA) in 1943. Found guilty at Nuremberg of war crimes and crimes against humanity, he was hanged on October 16, 1946.

**22 March 1946**

This gaunt, scar-faced giant of a man, Ernst Kaltenbrunner, has had two episodes of subarachnoid hemorrhage within the period of his confinement here in jail, the last attack having occurred sometime in the past December. He has been comparatively well since then and has been returned from the American General Hospital, in which he had been treated.

He is busy today working on his documents, but welcomed the Sunday visit. He said it was a respite for him since he had been spending several hours perusing evidence. His manner is restrained, his voice well modulated and soft-spoken, and it seemed to me that he was striving to give the impression that he was not the ferocious police chief and successor of Himmler that he had been reputed to be in the press. Nevertheless, the meekness, calmness, and well-mannered attitudes seemed indicative of a capacity for harsh, ruthless action, if such would have been the possibility.

He was clearly reviewing his defense, and so, after making me comfortable on his chair and with Mr. Triest seated on the cot beside him, he began a very much self-directed recitation. He said, "I have talked to you in the past but we have always exchanged pleasantries. And it has always been assumed that I am Kaltenbrunner, the big bad man next to Himmler and the successor of Himmler. But I think you can see by this time, after having treated my brain hemorrhages, both in the hospital and here in my cell, that I am not the disagreeable, uncouth fellow the public probably thinks because of all the atrocities committed under Himmler's rule, and of which I am totally innocent."

Kaltenbrunner seemed inclined to give me a lecture on the structure and variability of the Reich Security Main Office.

"It was a very changeable organization and it was on a ministerial level from 1933 to 1945. If you don't understand the political situation in Germany, it is difficult to comprehend this structure. I entered Hitler's service in 1938. Do you realize that I learned most about what went on — the atrocities, the concentration camps, the mass murders, the gas chambers, the terrorization of the partisans, and the terrible methods of the police itself against the German people — I learned most about it here, because I only worked in Berlin as chief of the RSHA since 1943?

"In order to make you understand, I have to go from the time of the rise of power of Hitler in 1933. Let us deal only with the Gestapo at the beginning of 1933. Just as in any other state, there were original police organizations, and these policemen had enlisted and were civil servants.

"There were the Criminal Police and the Political Police in the Reich. They were called the Security Police, and these came together as one organization in 1936. Therefore, you must understand that the Security Police consisted of the Criminal Police and the Political Police.

"The second big body of police — but separate from the first party — was the Ordinary Police. This consisted of three parts:

"First, the Gendarmes, which were in every state and which also served the function of criminal police in the rural areas. If there was a robbing or shooting, we didn't send the Criminal Police from Berlin, but the Gendarmes took care of it.

"Second, the uniformed police in the big cities, who directed traffic, trade, et cetera.

"Third, the Fire Brigade Police, who were used in the city officially and who were a volunteer organization in the country and rural districts.

"After 1933 all the Criminal Police, officially all over the Reich, were put together in the Reich Criminal Police Office.[1]

"The Political Police, which existed before 1933, were put in the Geheime Staatspolizeiamt [Secret State Police Office]. Those words stand for the Gestapo. This abbreviation was used by the enemies of Germany and was patterned after the GPU in Russia. In Germany it was called, for short, 'the Stapo.' Now just to make this very clear to you in case there is as much doubt in your mind as in the tribunal's because of that ridiculous chart the tribunal had pasted on the wall of the court-room, understand: the Criminal Police and Gestapo were not uni-formed, the Ordinary Police were uniformed.

"Later on more and more Criminal Police and Gestapo people wore SS uniforms as they entered the SS from the ranks of the other police organizations. This was from 1935 onward.

"Before National Socialism came to power in 1933, people in the Political Police were opposed to Nazi ideas and naturally held stubborn beliefs in the old regime.

"The police, as in any other trade, had among their numbers a certain percentage of voters. So did the tailors or the bricklayers or any other group. For example, in 1928, five percent of the police voted for National Socialism; in 1929, ten percent; in 1930, thirty percent; in 1931, fifty per-cent; in 1932, seventy percent; and in 1933, eighty percent. In other words, it was the same with the police as with other groups. The police, as a whole, voted for National Socialism. And do you know, it is interesting that the percentage of National Socialist votes among the police even later than 1933 was slightly less than among the general population. For example, in the years after 1933 when there were elections, only seventy percent of the police voted for National Socialism, whereas a higher per-centage of the general population voted for it. Partly this was because of their own beliefs and because of a fear of reprisal without outward pres-sure. Just like your own de-Nazification program but less oppressive. This program existed when a new party came to power. After the Weimar Republic was overthrown, laws had to be created to do away with it and to find a legal way to put out of power those who were polit-ically democratic. After the Russian Revolution, Russia did away with everyone who was not a Communist. They did it much more openly by shooting any- and everyone."

Do you really believe this story of what seems to me fascist influence, which so many of your defendants are using as a basis for an excuse for your own defense — do you really believe that the Russians went around shooting 'any- and everybody'? "Well, in 1933 when the Nazis came to power, there was very little shooting by the police or anyone. In 1933, policemen were replaced in Bavaria; twenty-one percent were replaced in Berlin. It was a very mild action. You cannot speak of a Christian persecution."

I don't understand exactly what you mean about this exchange of policemen. "Well, what I mean is that some police people were replaced by Nazi policemen in Bavaria in 1933 and that in Berlin twenty-one percent of the old police department had to be replaced by Nazis, and that is why I say it was such a mild action.[2] Altogether perhaps in Bavaria there were forty policemen discharged. Can you call that an extermination of your opponent? And that is in cases where policemen had behaved badly, or had spoken insulting words or in an insulting manner against National Socialist ministers.

"In 1934 Heydrich arrived. It will be interesting for the prosecution — but they don't seem to care, and without knowing these details one can't get an adequate picture. You have to know the personal characteristics and aims of Heydrich. He was a terribly ambitious man with a great craving for power. This desire for power was measureless, and he was extraordinarily clever and cunning."

I asked Kaltenbrunner whether he knew Heydrich personally and he replied: "Yes. You see, Himmler at that time was still the leader of the SS, which was a party organization. I played a very subordinate part all that time. Because the SS consisted of the General SS, which was more than ninety percent of the total SS, together with the regiments of SS troops which carried arms — the Bodyguard, the General Service troops, the Death's Heads. The General Service troops were at the personal disposal of the Führer. The Bodyguard was a regiment of this latter organization; there were other regiments, called, for example, the Deutschland, et cetera. The Death's Heads consisted of three or four battalions. Himmler at that time was in charge of the SS when Heydrich came to power. In other words, the SS was a ridiculously small organization at that time.

"The army at that time opposed SS regiments carrying arms because the army felt that it should be the only defense of Germany. It also opposed the air force, and it is only thanks to Goering and his close connections with Hitler that the air force developed alongside the army."

I asked Kaltenbrunner whether he thought that this was a good thing. He replied: "I am not a military man and I don't know if it is more advisable to create a separate air force or make it a part of the army and navy. Experts all over the world were of varying opinions. The Japanese divided their air force between the army and navy, whereas in America, your air force was a new branch of the army. The education of the people will bring that with it. I believe there is a different feeling of comradeship in the air force as opposed to the infantry. For example, just think of the close comradeship of an air corps crew.

"I believe that because Himmler saw he could not form another branch equal to the army, he tried to develop or gain power through the police. And Heydrich, who was a clever organizer, brought together the Criminal and Political Police in the Security Police and later put it into the RSHA. And a third branch came into the RSHA when the SD was formed, which was not a police formation but only an information service."

At this point Kaltenbrunner took out a pencil and paper and charted the structure of the RSHA for me. He said that the chart used in the courtroom gave an inaccurate picture of the RSHA.[3]

"Every year things changed. There was Schellenberg, Ohlendorf, me, and others. It was a very confusing situation. The various offices were given different numbers. One can only describe how it appeared in a certain year. For example, let us take a man by the name of Meyer. He was in charge of anti-Communist activity in the Frankfurt branch. He must have a personal file, and there is also a personal file on him in Frankfurt. From the personnel division of the State Police Office in Frankfurt — it is their responsibility that Meyer should be promoted after four or five years in rank. Let us say he is to be promoted from administrative adviser to chief administrative adviser. Now Meyer's chief in Frankfurt will ask his personnel chief that an application be made for Meyer's promotion. This would be forwarded to Berlin. That is Office IV — the Gestapo. The personnel division chief of Office IV, if he has no objection to it, will approve it and give it to Heinrich Mueller, chief of Office IV, in order that Meyer be promoted.[4]

"Twice a year one could turn in names for promotion. Each time Mueller took eighty cases in file and went to Himmler with it. But, aside from that, a personnel division in the RSHA which was above the personnel division of Office IV existed. The RSHA personnel division was there to take care of general questions, such as finances, furloughs for all employees, et cetera. This personnel section in the RSHA was Office I —

for personnel and organization. The chief of Office I had no police functions.

"Now let us turn to Office II, which was administration. This can be seen as one big thing with a financial division for negotiations with the finance office and with the finance officer of the party, with the Reich's treasurer, et cetera, which was necessary because in the RSHA there were two categories of employees: one, state officials; and, two, party officials. The party officials worked in the SD. The state officials also worked in the Criminal Police and State Police. There were certain exceptions — like Offices I and II, which employed both categories of employees, such as accountants.

"That's only of importance as to who paid them — the party or the state. You will only understand it when I tell you the character of the SD, which consisted completely of party employees. When the party first came into power, it found a complete police organization and retained this organization. You have to think of the feelings and ideology of the party in those years. The party leaders thought that something was missing in the state, since they took theaters, press, cinema, et cetera, and steered them into their own way of thinking. There was no means of criticism and what was lacking was a way of obtaining a picture of the feeling of the cross section of the population, because the only information they received came from the district and local administrators, none of whom would say anything against the party, to which they were answerable. From a philosophical standpoint that is the weak part of every authoritarian state. This possibility of criticism is one point that I recognize and which I compliment in a democracy. Because after a period of years every authoritarian state will be informed in a one-sided manner if there is no freedom of criticism.

"And now Heydrich and Himmler got an idea which was, in my opinion, the cause of the beginning of the final downfall. By downfall I don't mean the catastrophe at the end but the destruction of the inner basis of confidence.

"This tribunal makes the SS one organization, and that is all false. If you talk to some officers who are interned in the SS camps, you will find that there are people who had about ten weeks of training and who were active in the front lines and never had anything to do with concentration camps or with Himmler.

"The Russians who fought against the armed SS must admit that the armed SS consisted of soldiers, and of course, there were bad ones among them just as in any army.

"To return to the SD. The party looked for an instrument which might bring information — aside from information through party channels. It had no police functions. The thought was correct from the standpoint of a single party within the Reich — but Himmler and Heydrich recognized they would thereby gain valuable leverage against the party itself.

"Now they had the opportunity to do bad things. There are bad people in any regime. You only have to check the statistics in 1918, 1928, and 1938 as to how many murders, et cetera, were committed. Now they [the SD] had the opportunity to observe the party and were the first to learn of any misstep by any district or local administrator. It didn't have to be a crime — for example, if the party district administrator had drunk too much. If any party district administrator had looked for material advantages, the SD would have reported it."

I asked Kaltenbrunner whether any examples of this had occurred. He said: "The Nazi Party consisted of sixty percent workers, ten percent farmers, and the rest, intellectuals and bourgeoisie. Through all those elections, a common workman could become a party district administrator, just like Fritz Sauckel, who was a common seaman, or August Eigruber in Austria, who used to be a mechanic. As a matter of fact, sixty percent of the party district administrators used to be laborers.[5]

"You can imagine what happened to a little laborer who suddenly finds himself a leader, builds himself a big estate, possesses not one car but perhaps four — and in a certain sense Hitler required that the party district administrators live up to their positions, with pictures in their homes, nice furnishings, et cetera. But Hitler did not want a great many nouveau riche developments.

"And now begins something interesting — Himmler and Heydrich had the opportunity of observing these weaknesses of the party district administrators and other officials through the SD. Himmler and Heydrich used to carry tales to Hitler and say, 'See what happened in your party' — and would use it as blackmail in the party. Heydrich played a still more devilish role. He would go to Bormann and the latter would say that he would take the matter up with Hitler. Bormann said, 'Give it to me.' And Himmler was told nothing. When Heydrich wanted something, he asked Bormann for a favor. Thereby Heydrich accumulated greater power — too great for Himmler."

I asked Kaltenbrunner whether he thought that Himmler had anything to do with the assassination of Heydrich. He replied, "No, but I am sure that it was welcomed by Himmler.

"Hess was an idealist, but the man who took his place, Bormann, was a definitely power-crazy, stingy man. Whereas Hess had the attitude of a worldly man, Bormann had the attitude of a newcomer. I believe that Bormann had no friends and that he was one of the most despised of men. The only reason he could hold the confidence of Hitler was that Hitler had been tremendously mistrusting during the last few years — a sickly mistrust. You realize these things can happen in any government, not only in the Nazi government — but in other governments they cannot handle these matters as they can in an authoritarian state, where everything pyramids to the top. There is no regime more in need of objectivity than the authoritarian state."

I asked him what he meant by this. He continued, "Well, for example, the colonel of the prison has under him, let us say, twelve officers. What I mean by objectivity is that these officers always inform him of what goes on and undoubtedly he allows these officers to see him at any time, et cetera. Or a better example — in England, every honest citizen who has been a lawyer becomes, at the age of fifty to fifty-five, a judge. Now, men who had only seen law from one side suddenly become judges. That, together with their experience of life, will allow them to see things from both sides.

"In other words, the authoritarian state would be good if the one on top is objective, but not if he is the type of man who becomes angry if something is said to him which he dislikes. Certainly it doesn't work if the leader mistrusts everyone, or if his wishes exceed his judgment, finally overwhelming him.

"For example, if Hitler tells himself that it is impossible to live peacefully with America and that the whole Communist system aims and works toward a war with Germany, and then someone says to Hitler that perhaps his conception is incorrect and that maybe America wants peace — then Hitler would not listen, would bang both fists on the table, and shut up his informant. It was not possible to talk to Hitler objectively.

"Hitler had an excellent memory for numbers and he knew exactly the tonnage of each warship any nation possessed. He knew this even better than the naval and finance experts. Hitler believed that America had to find a place to get rid of its investments in lend-lease, armaments, et cetera, and that it had to realize the money it had invested over here. That was Hitler's idea. Any attempt to talk peacefully or negotiate a peace with America was unsuccessful because Hitler felt that Germany could not offer America this financial settlement which it desired. Thus, Hitler thought that the war with the United States was not an ideological war but one that stemmed purely from economic reasons.

"I give this example to explain how objective reporting only has a point if it is to a man who is not possessed by a certain idea."

I asked Kaltenbrunner whether Hitler did realize finally toward the end of the war that it was in reality an ideological war. "No, Hitler always remarked that if America really fought for democracy, then America could have done away with the antidemocratic system in the Soviet Union twenty-five years ago."

I said that I could not see much sense in this reasoning since the Soviet Union had not declared war on us or committed any atrocities or breaches of international conduct. Kaltenbrunner replied: "But an ideo logical difference between the United States and the Soviet Union existed — and that was Hitler's viewpoint.

"As far as I know, Hitler did not completely condemn democratic principles — in fact, he favored a certain type of democracy. Because whereas you see the party now for the past ten years as completely authoritarian, Hitler's final aims were a completely parliamentarian system — well, not complete; there would always be the leadership principle, like the president in the United States, but that leader would use largely democratic principles."

We then went on to a discussion of the SD. "The way the SD was set up was correct for an authoritarian regime. Of course, the party soon recognized what a bad and dangerous instrument it would be for the party if it remained in the hands of Heydrich and Himmler, in view of the relationship with Bormann.

"Since Himmler couldn't get any financial contributions from the state for the SD, and because the SD was a party organization, therefore, Bormann could exercise a certain amount of control over the SD. This argument is a thing which can be found in any state, including democracies. If an information service becomes disagreeable in any country, there can be a cut-down on the finances. Corrupt personalities exist in any party.

"Now comes the important point. Heydrich took the SD and made it part of the RSHA. He took certain SD members and had them paid by the state, and placed them with the Criminal and Political Police. Heydrich did that to combat party power. Therefore the party had less and less to say about the SD. Heydrich could employ another thousand men by employing them in state positions. So Heydrich became more and more independent and the RSHA became a potent power. This was done with extraordinary skill. Heydrich faked friendship with Bormann, became friendly with all the ministers, et cetera. Heydrich and Bormann did not trust each other, but they had some advantages through each other.

"Himmler was a rival of Bormann, and Heydrich played both against each other. Heydrich pretended to be friendly with Bormann, but Bormann realized that Heydrich was a follower of Himmler. Bormann was trying to use Heydrich. Himmler saw what was happening. Between Himmler and Bormann, Heydrich grew bigger and bigger, until he was personally received by Hitler. But both Bormann and Himmler recognized Heydrich's threat.

"Bormann was born in 1900, Himmler in 1900, and Heydrich in 1904, so they were all within the same age group. They were all intensely competitive and jealous for power. Heydrich won the eye of Hitler at an early date through his organizational skill and his talent for exact reporting, in which Hitler was interested.

"The SD was founded by Himmler and organized by Heydrich. The idea might have originated with Bormann, but Heydrich organized it in 1934–35.

"There were many attempts on Heydrich's part to become a state secretary, with Bormann's help. The first step he achieved was the Police Ministry. On one side Heydrich supported Himmler; then he tried to push aside Himmler from the police section and he himself sought the Police Ministry. He would have succeeded if he had not had a very ambitious opponent, Kurt Daluege, who later became insane with dementia paralytica, I understand. Both Daluege and Heydrich wanted to achieve the same position. Daluege also wanted the Police Ministry. Both were dissatisfied with their ranks. Both stood on an equal level — Daluege was chief of the main office of the Ordinary Police and Heydrich chief of the Reich Security Main Office.

"Himmler used this rivalry between Heydrich and Daluege in not allowing either of them to come to power. That saved Himmler from these two power-crazy individuals, because Himmler was very much more primitive mentally than Daluege, who was still in good health at the time, and much more so than Heydrich, who was more shrewd.

"I knew Daluege in 1943. He had ideas of grandeur. He would say he had 3 million men if he had in reality 300,000. That was the reason Daluege had to be recalled.

"After Constantin von Neurath was recalled, Heydrich through Bormann's help was appointed as Neurath's successor to the Protectorate of Bohemia-Moravia. Thus Heydrich obtained the rank of minister. Himmler had not yet achieved so high a rank by the end of 1941.

"You can imagine the psychological reaction of Himmler when he found that Heydrich had achieved a ministerial rank above his own. And you can conceive the reaction of the progressively insane Daluege, who remained main office chief, but who until then had been on the same level as Heydrich.

"I believe from a medical standpoint, the sudden rise of Heydrich was the moment when Daluege's sickness became recognizable. Daluege was more stupid, more conceited, generally dumber than Heydrich. But Daluege was equally ambitious, although not in the same manner as Heydrich. Daluege was more personally conceited. Daluege was morally more decent than Heydrich, who drew no lines at using any methods to gain power. Daluege was more of an obedient officer."

Kaltenbrunner was speaking in slow, carefully enunciated words, as if he had been thinking of these things for a long time, and the effect was a studied one. He required no questions or comments from me to stimulate his talking. At this point, when Kaltenbrunner paused, I asked him whether Heydrich's nickname, "the Hangman," was appropriate in his opinion.

"Within Germany, Heydrich was of course not called that. But he was sadistic."

I asked Kaltenbrunner who, in his opinion, was more sadistic, Himmler or Heydrich. "Himmler was not sadistic — he was a stingy, small person. He was formerly a schoolteacher and he was always that kind of mentality. He obtained pleasure from punishing others, like a schoolteacher who hits a child with a cane more than necessary and derives pleasure from it. This is not truly sadistic; Himmler felt that he was responsible for the education and betterment of other people. The extermination of the Jews in concentration camps has no connection with this. I personally think this happened because of Himmler's slave-like obedience to the Führer."

**April 8, 1946**

"I am thought of as another Himmler." (Smiles.) "I'm not. The papers make me out as a criminal. I never killed anyone."

**June 6, 1946**

Kaltenbrunner was in his usual inhibited, frigid state. He was superficially polite and expressed pleasure at the visit of Mr. Triest and myself. He remarked that I had not been in to see him for a few weeks and, "I wondered whether you had become disgusted with us war criminals — particularly me, the so-called archcriminal of them all." Kaltenbrunner smiled periodically as he said this. It was apparent that he expected a polite response to the effect that I did not consider him the archcriminal. I explained that I had been in England for the week and that there had been a great influx of organization witnesses recently and that much time had been spent in interviewing them.

I asked him what he thought of Alfred Jodl's defense, which had terminated today. "Very good. The whole documentary evidence against Jodl proved that the war against Russia was not an aggressive war but rather a preventive one.[6] Naturally we all knew this before, but now the world will know it as a result of this trial and Jodl's defense."

I was somewhat surprised at this deduction since I had listened to Jodl's case carefully and found nothing in it which would justify Germany's attack on Russia as a preventive war. I asked Kaltenbrunner to explain what he meant, as it was rather mystifying to me. He replied in clipped sentences, with his usual precise manner of speaking, "If the Russians supplied their troops down to company level with maps and so forth and had so many divisions on the Romanian and Hungarian frontiers, then it is clear that our attack on Russia was not an offensive war but a preventive one. In other words, it is easily deduced that Russia intended to wage war against all of Europe." Did Kaltenbrunner really feel this to be true? "Beyond any doubt. Today you heard the testimony of General Winter, who was the chief of staff under Field Marshal Rundstedt and who is an excellent officer in charge of one of our best armies. General Winter confirmed the fact that the Russians had assembled their troops up to the Hungarian border prior to the outbreak of war against Russia. Why did the Russians march up to the Hungarian border?"

Kaltenbrunner drew a map of the situation at that time, showing the

Russian and Hungarian borders, and placed $X$ marks where Russian troops were said to have been assembled. "The Russians had troops on the Russian border of Hungary and Romania, which proves beyond any question of a doubt that the Russians intended an aggressive war in the Balkans. Thus, today the indictment was proven false — at least as far as Germany waging an aggressive war. One can't prove the intention of Germany to conquer Poland. At the time of the Russian-German war, a division of Poland had already taken place. One can speak of an aggressive war not only against Germany but against the whole of Europe.

"There is no human law or law of God or national law that states that any healthy being has to permit the snake to eat the mouse — but on the other hand it is perfectly justified to defend the mouse. In a modern war it is most difficult to determine whether it is an aggressive or preventive war. In the Hague Convention[7] it does not say at what time a war ceases to be defensive and becomes offensive.

"The Hague Convention does not mention a preventive war because owing to modern weapons, preventive war had not yet existed. The quicker humanity advances, the more important it is to be the one who deals the first blow. It was still possible in times of old-fashioned warfare to put up an ultimatum, but with all the new and modern weapons, tanks, and especially the atom bomb, this is impossible.

"That is, if by an espionage system or treason you learn of your opponent's intention to attack you, and then you attack first, you are still the defender and not the aggressor. That was the case with Germany against Russia. We just learned of Russia's intention in time. This question was decided in favor of the Reich today in court. As a matter of fact, it was brought out previously — although not as clearly as in the testimony of General Winter today — in the cases of Raeder, Keitel, Goering, and their witnesses, as well as in the case of Jodl. But the clearest proof and the establishment of this fact beyond any doubt came through Jodl's defense and I was very happy to hear it. Thus, the indictment of conspiracy for aggression is done away with completely."

Couldn't it mean that Russia deployed its troops because it felt there was danger of a German attack through Hungary and Romania, which were satellite states at that time? Kaltenbrunner coolly decided in the negative. "No. That is definitely not the case because our troops were tied up in the West. At that very moment the Reich had heard of Russia's plans. Russia expected that the Reich would lose still more blood in the West. And they thought, therefore, that the march of Russian troops to the West would be easier as time went on. For Russia the German Reich was only a part of Europe, and Russia was interested not only in conquering the Reich but in overcoming the whole of Europe and bringing Communism to the entire continent."

I asked Kaltenbrunner on what facts or deeds he based this rather far-fetched conclusion. He answered in more or less a non sequitur. "The prosecution conducts this trial for political reasons and has blinders on their eyes. That is necessary for them because of political reasons. But every sound American or Englishman must realize that the Russians don't care about Germany but want to get a hold of Trieste, the Dardanelles, and Spain, as had been proven. The western part of Russia was accessible to the warm European seas. Thus, they are endangering the British Suez Canal and the route from England to India."

I repeated my previous question, but Kaltenbrunner again ignored it and spoke of recent events such as Churchill's Fulton, Missouri, speech, which proved that both England and America were aware of the "Communist imperialist danger."[8]

I said that I would like to go back to another statement that Kaltenbrunner had made this evening and wondered whether he could clarify it. He had said that German troops were tied up in the West at the time of the attack on Russia by Germany in June 1941. Wasn't it true that France was defeated and that no western front had as yet been opened by the Allies and that, therefore, Germany was at the height of its power militarily at the very time he claimed that Germany had all its troops tied up in the West? Didn't this seem rather incongruous and didn't it place another light, perhaps, on the meaning of Russia's deploying divisions on the Hungarian-Romanian borders? "You just have to read what Churchill said. He said that those were the darkest hours for England. So that the war in the West could not be considered finished until we had defeated England. The Reich couldn't stop fighting a war against England because England had declared war on Germany, and not Germany on England as the prosecution is trying to say in this trial. Therefore, in June 1941, although it may seem as if Germany was at the height of its power because of a defeated continental Europe, we could never consider ourselves successful in the West until we had conquered England. Moreover, England had destroyed the French fleet, their own brothers in arms. England permitted the French government in exile to prepare war against Germany in Africa, which later brought about the American landing in Africa.

"Therefore, the Reich couldn't consider the war against England finished, inasmuch as aerial warfare against England had just started. One has to agree with Hitler in his feeling uneasy about the fact that on their eastern frontiers, which were not guarded, 150 Russian divisions marched up and were prepared to attack. As a matter of fact, I have information which proves that there were not only 150 Russian divisions in that area but more nearly 300.

"As soon as the demarcation line became stronger in Poland, our intelligence found that the Russians had built 120 airfields in Poland, each of which could accommodate squadrons of thirty planes. Originally the Polish had only twenty airfields in that part of Poland, and so it was obvious that the Russians intended to wage war because they built so many more airfields than already existed. It shows the mockery of the German-Russian Nonaggression Pact because a friend doesn't do that to another friend.

"Then you insist — I don't mean you personally, but the prosecution — that Germany declared war against America. That I consider true only technically because Americans shot first against us at sea without any declaration of war. If you recall, there was an order of Roosevelt's for American boats to carry arms and to shoot against German submarines. Because of all these things, the indictment of conspiracy for aggressive war against all these countries is repeatedly proven false. I myself, in this cell, must concentrate on these things without the aid of documents or history books but merely with my own mind. The prosecution must feel weak if it has to pass judgments like today, that the defense counsel would not be allowed to put any more questions to Jodl. In view of the fact that because of physical reasons, a human being can only be in one spot at a time, the whole thing is but a trick. It is similar to the actions of the tribunal which deny the defense other points every day. Every day another judgment is passed that damages and limits our defense.

"To the outside world the whole trial seems to be conducted according to English law and democratic principles. Your Dr. Gilbert goes around and praises American principles, saying that the court is justified in doing it the way they are, and on the other hand he personally acts in just the opposite fashion by torturing us. The defendants are not allowed to read an ordinary newspaper. They are prevented from being able to use for their defenses the common news items of the day. But Gilbert violates the rule of our not being able to see newspapers by showing us a copy of *Stars and Stripes* occasionally, but only if there is a picture in it of a man being hanged for war crimes at Landsberg, and similar things which he knows will make us boil. This is not the first time that Gilbert has done things like that, which make no sense and just show a cheap intention to create anxiety in those of us who are being tried here. I hope he doesn't do it intentionally because that would be without taste. I merely pointed this out because we see nothing of the newspapers except the sort of thing I have just mentioned.

"Now the Russians sit in the same court indicting us for a declaration of aggressive war when they really planned it." I asked Kaltenbrunner whether General Winter had any other proof that the Russians intended aggressive war beyond his knowledge of Russian divisions having been assembled on the Hungarian-Romanian borders. Kaltenbrunner replied smugly and with a tight smile, "Yes, of course. He had five different proofs of this intention, such as maps, et cetera." Could Kaltenbrunner be a little more specific about the proof of the Russian intention to wage war against Germany, the proofs he claimed General Winter had in his possession? Again, Kaltenbrunner ignored the details of an answer by saying, "I can't recall the exact proof, but I know that there were five pieces of evidence.

"I attribute the misinformation we had at the time to the inaccurate intelligence service, which at that time was still under Wilhelm Canaris. Canaris reported 135 divisions, among them 113 or 114 infantry divisions, and the rest armored divisions. He did not even report the occupation of Bessarabia by the Russians and was wrong about a few infantry divisions, which were really cavalry outfits. He was also inexact about the aerial strength of Russia. Therefore, the accusation of Hitler against Canaris later on was correct. Hitler accused Canaris of giving him an incorrect picture — in favor of Russia, not Germany.[9]

"But aggressive war against Germany by Russia was proven without any doubt. Another fact is that there were numerous violations of the treaty by the Russians against the Germans, that is, the Russian-German Nonaggression Pact. These violations consisted of illegal frontier crossings by the Russians, concealing the delivery of food and coal and so forth. There were also cases of deportation of German nationals by the

Russians. All of these things would point to Russia's planning an intensive aggressive war against us.

"It is highly interesting to listen and to watch, although unfortunately one does not quite understand the respective expressions or technical terms used — but it is interesting to see what points the various delegations try to bring out during this trial. For us the whole trial became very dull as a whole. It becomes more and more apparent as the trial goes on that the judges will find something against each defendant and routinely sentence him, whether it be to death or long-term imprisonment. But what really interests the various delegations can be seen from the individual questions put by the French, British, Americans, and Russians. For instance, the Russian prosecutor yesterday was very much interested in the happenings in Ankara. He would have been interested, although he didn't ask directly, about Turkish affairs. He wanted to know, I suppose, about Anglo-Turk relations, whether Germany knew of the English-Turkish relations and whether England knew of the negotiations between Russia and Turkey concerning future developments.

"Turkey was the guardian of the Dardanelles and Bosphorus. The neutrality of Turkey was guaranteed by several countries so that it could perform that job. Any historian will recognize that this is the same as the capture of the Russian fleet in the Black Sea. In other words, the English-Russian route through the Mediterranean is not being endangered by Russian boats. Therefore, the neutrality of Turkey, as seen by England, is only an armed neutrality which favors the British Empire.

"On the other hand, German foreign policy in Turkey was, of course, conditioned by these things. Turkey only in the first line had to be afraid of Russia. For its neutrality Turkey was paid by England, with money and armaments; and at the same time Turkey was paid by Germany through commercial treaties and armaments. At the very moment when Germany was weakest, Turkey turned to England. As long as Germany was strong, Turkish neutrality was tremendously friendly to Germany. Those are the basic principles of Turkish policy.

"One has to add that the Russian interests were exactly the opposite because Russia wanted free access to the Mediterranean either by having possession of the Bosphorus and Dardanelles or by having them opened by international agreement. Secondly, Turkey is the thinnest-populated country in Europe and western Asia, with only twelve inhabitants to the square kilometer. Therefore, it is an open invitation for southern Russia to spread and place its population. This can be seen by two demands of Russia for Turkish lands: one, Russia demanded southern Turkey, the Black Sea, which would mean the destruction of the whole Turkish commerce, and, two, Russia demanded Armenian territories, very cleverly using long-standing, bitter fights between Armenians and Turks.

"Armenia was always a minority nation. The Armenians were annihilated repeatedly by the Russians and then by the Turks. In reality the Soviet Union wants to prepare an attack through the Persian Gulf to the warm European sea and then reach England and recently American oil interests. You can imagine a German information service that wants to accumulate data about the potential resources of the enemy, not sending agents to Sweden but rather to Turkey. There are great political differences between the interests of Russia and England, and between the interests of Russia and America. Germany had nothing to look for in Turkey. Two generations ago, through Bismarck, Germany declared that the Dardanelles were not worth the blood of a single German grenadier. From the time of Bismarck, Germany always kept away from Turkey and gave many assurances to England that it should not be afraid, that it was English territory and would remain as such. The same neutrality was always promised by Hitler and respected by him constantly."

Kaltenbrunner became rather excited and absorbed in his own words by this time. His face was flushed and reddened, and his sentences and phrases were sharper and more clipped than ever. He continued, "As I said, you wouldn't send an agent to Sweden. I had been able to secure Turkish-English treaties from the English legation but one must also secure notes on Turkey drawn up by England for the USSR. I took photostats of all these treaties and notes and showed them to Hitler. For me that was the best barometer of the world political situation. Because of this and other similar happenings, I became the successor to Canaris and not, as the prosecution assumes, a proponent of the expansion of the SS against the army. I was appointed by Hitler to succeed Canaris because it was well known and proven that my abilities were greater than those of Canaris. Proof of Canaris's duplicity can be seen by the fact that he participated in the *Attentat* of July 20, 1944.

# Wilhelm Keitel
## 1882–1946

Wilhelm Keitel was general, field marshal, and chief of staff of the Supreme Command of the Armed Forces (OKW) from 1938 to 1945. Found guilty at Nuremberg of conspiracy to commit crimes, crimes against peace, war crimes, and crimes against humanity, he was hanged on October 16, 1946.

**March 27, 1946**

Keitel has complained frequently to me of pains in both lower limbs and varicosities. He receives occasional massages for this condition and feels it benefits him. However, he would prefer another type of massage and baths, treatments which he obtained at various spas in times gone by.

He was in a mood for talking, and he seemed quite keyed up, for him, regarding his coming defense, which would start in a few days as soon as Ribbentrop was finished.

He began with his military career. In 1901 he was officer's candidate. In 1914, at the outbreak of hostilities, he was a regimental adjutant. In September 1914 he was slightly wounded in action. In spring 1915 he served in general staff positions, and spent a short time in Flanders with the navy. After the war he voluntarily entered the army. In 1929 he was chief of a division in the Ministry of War. By October 1, 1935, he became chief of the armed forces department of the War Ministry. At the time he was a major general. On February 4, 1938, he was appointed chief of staff of the Supreme Command of the Armed Forces. On October 1, 1939, he became general of infantry, and after the defeat of France, field marshal.

In April 1939 Hitler presented him the golden party emblem, dated March 16 and 17—the Führer said it was a reward for the march into Czechoslovakia. Walter von Brauchitsch received the golden emblem at the same time.[1] Although in 1944 soldiers could become party members, he says he never became one insofar as he knows. However, he did send in a donation to the party at the time, and data for enrollment in the party.

He accompanied the Führer constantly and attended party functions. He denies attending secret conferences of the party leadership. In fact he was told by Hitler he was not to attend.

He received no decorations except the Iron Cross, in 1939–40.

His attitude is: "I am a soldier and I worked for the kaiser, under Ebert, Hindenburg, and Hitler, all the same way, for the past forty-four years."

Like Goering, he wants to assume "full responsibility." He intends to take responsibility if there was anything "wrong" done, rather than allow frontline commanders to take such responsibility. "I believe German soldiers are good and decent, and if they did anything wrong it was because of military necessity."

He admits that there are orders and directives bearing his name, and that they were not in accord with existing international law. Particularly regarding the group of directives before the attack on Russia, he feels they were justified from an ideological standpoint. Until February 1938 Werner von Blomberg was commander in chief of the army; when he resigned, Hitler took over this function. From then on Hitler gave orders directly to the army, navy, and air force. No one issued orders independently of Hitler. Of course "I signed them" is Keitel's attitude, but they originated with Hitler. "It was the wish and desire of Hitler to have all power and command reside in him. It was something he could not do with Blomberg."

### April 6, 1946

"I had no authority. I was field marshal in name only. I had no troops, no authority — only to carry out Hitler's orders. I was bound to him by oath. One of Hitler's prime ideas was that each minister and functionary was to mind his own business. That's why I learned about some of the business for the first time in court.

"I had no idea of Hitler's general plans. I was told to confine myself to military matters only.

"In 1938, when Blomberg was retired after his scandalous marriage, Hitler asked me to recommend a successor. He did not want Goering — now I see why. He had his own plans and did not want to confide in anyone.

"I was in it up to my neck by the time I realized the way things were going. What could I do? I could not resign in time of war; if I refused to obey I would be killed. Or I could commit suicide. On three different occasions I *thought* of resigning, but it was impossible.

"As for Jewish measures — I tried to keep the army clear of anti-Semitism. Hitler decreed that World War I veterans who were Jews would be safe. But even this went to pieces. What could I do?" How did you happen to become an officer? "I became an officer because in Prussia usually an officer was considered more highly than a businessman or other professions.

"I never knew of the linking of the army with atrocities. I see now how it all happened. We had too many connections with party organizations."

Hitler? "I understand him now. He must have known of these atrocities and to what purpose he was using me and the army. I was never really close to the Führer. He always had secretaries present when I saw him. It's true I represented the army at various festivals — such as placing wreaths on the monument of the fallen of the Munich putsch.

"There are three reasons for Hitler's failure: One, action against the church — every man must be religious according to his own fashion. Two, persecution of Jews. Three, the power of Himmler and the Gestapo."

Did you realize these three factors earlier? "Only since the end of 1944.

"I am no field marshal; I never commanded troops. A field marshal should be a tactician." Was Hitler a tactician? "I thought he was a genius. Many times he displayed brilliance. I often told him he should have a better tactician as chief of staff, but he said it was his responsibility as commander in chief.

"He changed plans — and correctly — for the Holland-Belgium campaign. He had a remarkable memory — knew the ships of every fleet in the world.

"Hitler's decision to attack Russia was because he feared the Russians might cut off his oil supply from Romania. We required 350,000 tons of oil a month for war. We got 150,000 from Romania. The air force needed 100,000 tons a month alone. The attack on Russia was an act of recklessness.

"Hitler was a smarter strategist than Goering or Ribbentrop." I didn't know Ribbentrop acted at all as a strategist. "No. He didn't. Neither do I. But I mean in the field of foreign policy.

"We could not march into England because we were not sufficiently prepared. We didn't have the ships. We could take Gibraltar, but General Francisco Franco would be afraid to allow that step. If we did nothing, England would tighten that ring around Germany and shove us out.

"Hitler proceeded as if the Russian campaign would certainly be a victory, but it would not be — I can see it now." Why not then? "Because I believed in Hitler and knew little of the facts myself. I'm not a tactician, nor did I know Russian military and economic strength. How could I?

"Hitler acted as if that war was inevitable. How could I know Chamberlain and Édouard Daladier and even Roosevelt were trying to avoid war?" What about Munich and Daladier? Keitel looked uncomprehendingly. "It all goes back to Versailles." I've heard that before — just how? "Everyone — all Germans — said, 'Down with the Treaty of Versailles.' They blamed the Treaty of Versailles for our unemployment and national difficulties.

"Hitler gave us orders — and we believed in him. Then he commits suicide and leaves us to bear the guilt. He should have remained alive to bear his share.

"If Hitler had not succeeded so well in the beginning — for instance, the Ruhr. We took the Ruhr — marched in with only three battalions. I said, how can we do it? But Blomberg said we could — we could rely on the lack of French resistance.

"Also, not only the Rhineland (1936), but the annexation (1938), without even our armies in action. And we were prepared to act or withdraw depending on the situation."

Keitel is the wooden soldier, the wooden ingratiating smile, yet suffering from the human woes of love of attention, desire for approval.

### May 17, 1946

Interviewed early this evening, an hour or so after court ended for the day, he said he felt tired out, but was very glad to see us (Triest and myself) and invited us to sit down. I told him to lie down and we brought another chair into the room. Keitel lay stretched out on his cot, puffing his pipe.

He said that the trials were wearing, but that it was mainly sitting in the upright position all day which tired him so. He felt very grateful, he said, for a personal visit, and hoped I would come more often. He has not had much of a chance to tell me all about himself as a person, and he knows that as a psychiatrist that is my main interest. He did not look too comfortable as he said that, but he did smile and attempt to be quite cordial.

"The last time you saw me was two weeks ago. I mean the last time we had a long talk. Where were we? Oh yes, I was telling you of my career and my relations to Hitler. What would you like to have me speak about today?"

I replied that it was of no consequence, and that I just wanted to pay a visit and see how he was getting along, physically and emotionally. Keitel puffed on his pipe, thoughtfully. He said, after a short pause: "I always wanted to be a country gentleman, a forester, and look what a muddle I got into merely because I was weak and let myself be talked into things. I am not cut out for a field marshal. The happiest time in my military life was when I commanded a division and was independent. In a division, it's your own little world and one can run it ideally, and without politics, as one desires. But I only had a division for a short time during maneuvers before the war." I told him to say anything that came into his mind. "I might as well start from the beginning. I didn't have the chance to say these things which are closest to me in court during my defense. The justices would have ruled it out as irrelevant, which is true. But to understand how I came to this criminal dock, it is important perhaps for a psychiatrist to know, just as it is important for myself.

"I was born in Braunschweig, September 22, 1882, in the country, near a city, but in the rural atmosphere of Lower Saxony. My family for over 150 years were farmers in Braunschweig and Hanover. My father, and grandfather, and great-grandfather were all farmers. At first they leased estates, but from the time of my grandfather they owned them. My great-grandfather had two large leases on two big estates in 1866 when Hanover became Prussian. My family immigrated because Braunschweig was not Prussian. It was the kingdom of Hanover, the county of Braunschweig at that time. Braunschweig was the last remaining part of the old English Hanover in Germany. Hanover used to belong to the English crown. Once there were kings of England who ruled Iceland, Braunschweig, and Hanover.

"In 1938 Hitler wanted for Europe what Bismarck wanted and

accomplished for Prussia in 1866. Bismarck actually succeeded with his union of Germany in 1871, and Germany became an imperial state. The king of Prussia became the emperor of Germany.

"Hitler on the other hand wanted to found a Middle Europe, to unite all those people who spoke German. This included the German part of Austria, German part of Czechoslovakia, and only the Prussian part of Poland, the part which became independent through the Versailles Treaty."

I asked Keitel whether or not he thought Hitler wanted too much. "At any rate he wanted too much too fast. It couldn't be done by force. It lacked the agreement of the smaller nations. But Austria in modern times could not live without an alliance with Germany. In these times of the radio, telegraph, and airplanes, those little countries couldn't live independently without a bigger country.

"I grew up in a small village in the country. I had nine years of gymnasium in Göttingen, graduated high school, and became a soldier. I became a soldier only because it was impossible for me to be independent in the agricultural field because of low family finances. My original youthful inclinations were farming and forestry. I'm still a man who hates life in the big city. I love the loneliness of the country. I'm very close to nature.

"Later I grew to like being a soldier, but I always nurtured the quiet hope and plan to become a farmer later on. That was always my aim — to become a farmer.

"Then came the First World War. My wife was also the daughter of farmers, but she was in good financial circumstances. I hoped that when my father became old I could take over his estates and buy out the shares of my brothers and sisters. But after the First World War my wife lost all her money in the inflation. And by that time we had five children and I had to bury all my hopes and plans. Therefore I remained in the army — because I had to earn a living for my five children.

"In 1934 my father died — he was over eighty years old — and he willed me his estate. In 1940 I succeeded in obtaining my sister's share, and then, through the will of my mother, to pay my brother for his share. I didn't have to live from the surplus of the estate but had my independent salary as a general. I used everything which the estate brought in to pay off the mortgages.

"So I decided to withdraw my application for retirement, and continued in the army in 1934. Werner Freiherr von Fritsch asked me to stay on. I agreed, under the conditions that I should be stationed near my home. Then I was advanced and advanced and we come to the time of Blomberg and later on Hitler.

"In 1938 I could not leave because it was by that time a matter of desertion because war was at hand. I couldn't pretend I was sick because I was in good health. That is just about the way it actually was. I had only one wish — that there should be no war — and that I should be able to return to my estates.

"In the seven years from 1938 until 1945 I saw my home only twice, and then for only a day or two. Once I returned in 1942 to bury my thirty-year-old daughter, who died of pneumonia after she caught cold during a bombing raid on Berlin. She had slight diabetes and that lowered her resistance."

I asked Keitel whether the death of this child affected him much. He said, with some feeling: "Yes. She was my favorite child. And it came on top of having lost my youngest son in 1941 on the Russian front, only six weeks after the Russian war began. He had been severely wounded during the French campaign but had recovered. When he died he was but twenty-one years old, and he was a lieutenant. He was killed before Smolensk in July 1941." I wondered if his son's death had made him bitter against the Russians. He replied: "Yes. It was quite unnecessary. He was shot by machine-gun fire from airplanes at the front."

Keitel went on to state that his second son is listed as missing in Russia. He has had no news from him since mid-1945. This son is twenty-nine, was wounded twice, was a major on the general staff of a division. "He was the best officer of all my sons. He was clever and strong. He was born in 1915 when I was in France during the last war. My son had been cut off in Russia three times and managed to escape. This last was the fourth time. The whole division at the front was lost. It was the 563rd Grenadier Division.

"I have lost everything. In Berlin my home and household goods were burned. I have nothing left but two suitcases. My wife lives in my former home in Braunschweig, with my eldest daughter, who is married to the administrator of my small estate there."

In all, Keitel had five children, two of whom are alive, his oldest son and daughter. The oldest son was a farmer and a reserve officer. After the war was on for two years, this son became an officer in a cavalry outfit. At the war's end, he was a major in charge of an SS cavalry division of ethnic Germans (Hungarians). He was ordered to the SS by the army. He participated in all the battles in Budapest. Shortly before the war ended he was again sent to the front, and is now in American captivity in the Darmstadt region, where he is in charge of a POW work battalion. He is married to the daughter of Field Marshal Blomberg.

I asked Keitel whether he was a close friend of Blomberg's. "Yes. I knew Blomberg when I was still a captain. We served together during the First World War, and that was one of the reasons I came to Blomberg in 1934–35. Blomberg was four years older than me. He became an officer in 1897 and I became one in 1901. I saw Blomberg here before he died. He had suddenly become very old."

I knew that the subject of Blomberg was a touchy one for Keitel. He disliked talking about his old friend because of the scandal connected with the latter's having married a woman of questionable morals many years his junior. However, I asked Keitel what sort of man Blomberg was, generally speaking. "He was a gentleman and a good man. I liked him very much. From a military standpoint he was good and efficient. I felt very sorry when he left the army in 1938. That was the beginning of my unhappy time as a soldier. I was not prepared for this position. I was suddenly called to take over without having had time to think things over.

"Prior to February 1938, when I became chief of the Supreme Command of the Armed Forces, Hitler didn't even know me. Blomberg recommended me for this position."

I asked Keitel for a brief description of his education. "I never attended military school. But I was transferred to the general staff in 1915 during the First World War and was with it from 1915 to 1934, with the exception of about four years. I was always concerned with organization. I therefore believed that in 1938 Hitler wanted to use my experience as an organizer of troops. Instead, six weeks later, the first military and warlike campaigns began, of which previously I actually knew nothing. My ideal to become a farmer always remained a dream.

"Before 1938 I saw Hitler but didn't ever really know him. I saw him on maneuvers in 1935, and a couple of times in 1938 with Blomberg, but I had never spoken to him. After 1938 I was with Hitler, and saw him at least once a week, when I was called over to sign my name to orders and directives. Most of the time Hitler was in Berchtesgaden and I was in Berlin.

"When the Austrian thing began, I saw him February 1, and he said not a word as to what he really wanted.[2] I was ordered there but I didn't know what for. It's almost impossible to imagine today how things really were."

Keitel seemed as dignified and composed as ever, but his hands were trembling. I said that something seemed to be bothering him, and I wondered what caused it. His hands had not shaken until he made the last remark about how inconceivable things were in Hitler's times.

"I realize that you talk with all the defendants and probably with the other generals here in the witness wing. The conditions under which the generals met Hitler one after the other were quite different and you will obtain a different picture from each. I can only tell you my experiences. I can see today that perhaps I was much too uncritical in my entire character. I had been in many adjutant and general staff positions, but of course always with professional soldiers, whose education was also my own. Therefore all the things which Hitler told me were, to my viewpoint, the orders of an officer. In 1938 I had been an officer for thirty-six years already. I would have led a division far better than that job.

"As chief of staff under Hitler, one had a position which was impossible. One had a superior officer who was a politician and not an officer — a man who had quite different basic viewpoints from mine. If I had had one year's time in which to get to know Hitler, things in many ways would have turned out far differently.

"But one has to recall that on February 4, 1938, I took over the job — a position which never even existed before. Really I was a chief of staff without responsibility and without knowing what Hitler really wanted, and without being told by him.

"I was to lead the staff more or less and do what Hitler wanted. In addition, Hitler was no officer, and lacked education, and was a revolutionary. In the army he wanted to change things constantly. And then, in the first few weeks, came the large political actions, the Austrian question, and at the end of April the Czech question. That was a bare eight weeks after the beginning of my activity.

"And so one fell from one event to another — like a man staggering from one thing to another without becoming fully conscious and without the ability to think things over. Developments followed too quickly. That was the way things proceeded.

"Five times I asked for my release. Each time I was refused with the sharpest words. And because of my inner feelings it was impossible for me to pretend to be sick."

I asked him what he thought, in general, from today's perspective, of Hitler. I remarked that if I recalled correctly, during his defense, Keitel called Hitler a genius.

He said with some deliberation: "Yes. He was a genius in my conception. To me a genius is a man with such extensive ability to look into the future, with a tremendous ability to feel things, with such extensive knowledge of historic and military matters — that I want to use the word in reference to Hitler. Besides, I'm a simple soldier, and nothing convinces a soldier more than success. All through the summer of 1938 I repeatedly told him that there should not be a war with Czechoslovakia for any price because it would be mischievous. Hitler told me always to calm down, that there would be no war. Hitler said he needed a stronger army as a means to success. This, too, was a success. There was no war. But during that time I asked for my release.

"After things had turned bad and there were reverses, I said to myself: Where I stand, I stand. One can only be killed in one spot.

"It isn't right to be obedient only when things go well; it is much harder to be a good, obedient soldier when things go badly and times are hard. Obedience and faith at such time is a virtue.

"But I often had the sharpest and harshest clashes with Hitler. But had I taken my life, I wouldn't have improved things, because this demon went ahead with whatever he wanted and succeeded."

Did he consider Hitler a demon? "Yes. He was a demonlike man, possessed of inordinate willpower, who, whenever he had something in his mind, had to accomplish it. Hitler had charm, loved children, charmed women. But in political respects he would stop at nothing. In other respects he had soft and touching emotions.

"Just as he could be terribly brutal in following up political ideas, so he could be humanely sensitive for the feelings of individuals, for the individual human life. At least that was my impression.

"However, I never heard of the brutality during the war. There was never a word of the Jewish persecutions or murders. Hitler was a great psychologist in that instance. He knew he could not ask such things of a gentleman and an officer — not even mention the ideas.

"No matter what Hitler said, he spoke with a fine feeling for the particular circle which he addressed. For example, he spoke quite differently to a group of officers than to a group of party leaders. And what he said to either of those two groups, he never said to the people or the Reichstag. His speeches were always timed and tuned to the feeling of the people to whom he spoke at the particular time.

"That was one of his greatest abilities — his power to convince others by speech. Before soldiers he always mentioned the noble traditions of the German soldier. In his study there were three pictures — Frederick the Great, Bismarck, and Helmut Karl Bernhard Graf von Moltke."

I said that Rundstedt had told me that Moltke would turn in his grave at Hitler's military tactics, particularly his tactics in the so-called Rundstedt Offensive, which Rundstedt said should be known as the Hitler Offensive.

Keitel replied: "It's true. It wasn't the Rundstedt Offensive, it was all Hitler's idea. I said that last September in an interrogation. Rundstedt did not want it — he disapproved of it. Hitler would have made Rundstedt high commissioner of the army if he had not been too old in 1938. Hitler respected Rundstedt highly. For example, when Rundstedt came to visit Hitler, Hitler actually went to the door to greet him, and escort him upstairs personally. He was the only general Hitler ever treated with so much respect. It was an honor paid only to Rundstedt, an outward politeness indicating the great respect Hitler had for Rundstedt's ability, although Hitler never considered Rundstedt a National Socialist. That was one thing he never demanded of any of us.

"Hitler always said that he selected generals because of their abilities, and not because of their political beliefs. Hitler said: 'I demand three things of my officers and generals. One, ability for their position; two, that they report the situation to me truthfully; and three, they must be obedient.' Those were Hitler's three demands.

"Originally there was a difference of opinion between Rundstedt and Brauchitsch. Hitler and Rundstedt had a conference and Rundstedt left for home in peace. The second time, Rundstedt became ill while serving on the western front. He wrote me a letter, asking that I inform Hitler that he was sick and could not bear the responsibility if something important happened. Both times Hitler asked him to take command again.

"Brauchitsch was active until December 9, 1941. He served as chief from February 4, 1938, until December 9, 1941. He was high commander of the army. Then Hitler assumed that title himself. A field marshal in

Germany is always active and cannot retire technically, but Brauchitsch, just like Blomberg, served no more after 1941. Brauchitsch had a bad heart, at least that is what he told me. In the winter of 1942–43 he was very ill. Every second day the state of his health had to be reported to Hitler. We thought he would die, but he must have a strong constitution because he recuperated."

# Constantin von Neurath
## 1873–1956

Constantin von Neurath was German foreign minister from 1932 to 1938, and appointed Reich protector of Bohemia and Moravia after Hitler's invasion of Czechoslovakia. Found guilty at Nuremberg of conspiracy to commit crimes, crimes against peace, war crimes, and crimes against humanity, he was sentenced to fifteen years' imprisonment. He served eight years in Spandau prison and was released in 1954 for reasons of health.

**July 21, 1946**

The old man, Constantin von Neurath, was sitting on his cot, wearing a plain black coat, dark trousers, and new shoes. The laces were removed (as with all defendants' clothes) but were tied by a small lace on the upper part. He spoke in a hesitant manner with a certain of degree of stuttering.

The interview with Neurath was carried out in English, which he spoke well, but not fluently. His German is not fluent either, for that matter — with frequent hesitation and phrasings. I showed him a copy of his biography, only a half page, which he had written on October 9, 1945, shortly after arriving at the Nuremberg prison. He recalled it and said, "Well, it's a brief version of life, isn't it?" I agreed.

What sort of town was Kleingladbach, his birthplace? "Not a town, just a tiny village with a population of four hundred in which my father and grandfather lived. My wife now lives there near it. It is close to

Stuttgart." He was born on February 2, 1873. He had no real grandchildren. His only son, age forty-four, married a widow and he has one stepchild, a daughter. "I often regret having no grandchildren."

He asked me what I thought of the trials — more or less reversing the usual questioning. I remarked that things seemed to be speeding up. "Yes, they should be over by Wednesday. All we can do is wait and see." He smiled anxiously.

What about the organizations? "Quite artificial — the case versus organizations — especially as far as general staff. You have a general staff in your country, too. The party organizations are a different story, but not every block leader in the party is guilty either. The same with the SS, SD, and SA. The Nazis had one great fault. They overorganized everything. In general, I think the indictment against organizations is poor."

He asked me whether I'd ever read Neville Henderson's *Failure of a Mission: Berlin, 1937–1939*. I said that I had. "It's a good book. It shows you really how conditions were in 1937–39. Not so good was the book by William Dodd, your ambassador.[1] He never did seem to understand reality. He was a professor of history at a university. And like most professors, didn't know politics and the world. He spoke fluent German and my English was sufficient. But I also asked that he bring his secretary with him — he often failed to understand what we were talking about. That is — he was like all — not a realist. I haven't read his diary, which was put out by his children after his death, but I can assure you it's not worth reading, from the excerpts I've seen from it at the trial."

Service in the government? "I left office in 1916 because I didn't agree. In 1918, President Friedrich Ebert, a socialist, called me back. I'm not a socialist, but more conservative. I was appointed by Ebert as ambassador in Copenhagen and later was ambassador in Rome. One party government after another. Chancellor Gustav Stresemann was liberal. Later, I followed my duty to my country, not to party. That was my line. When old Hindenburg came in 1925, I was then ambassador in Rome after the death of Stresemann. Hindenburg asked me to become foreign minister. I declined because I did not belong to a party and I could not become foreign minister for him without a party's support. I was sent to London for the second time as ambassador. London in 1930 had been my first post. In 1930 I was ambassador, and after two years, in 1932, Hindenburg called me to become foreign minister, so-called — the cabinet parties couldn't agree to form a government. I couldn't refuse. Papen was chancellor, but I didn't know him or the other ministers. When Papen's cabinet was replaced by Kurt von Schleicher's government, the Nazis had become very strong, with 230 seats in a short time in 1932, but I was there in the cabinet as the delegate of Hindenburg, not as a party member. At the end of January 1933, again there was a crisis. Hitler came to power as part of a coalition government.[2] I asked Hindenburg to let me go back to London, where the king of England asked for me to come back, but Hindenburg said no. It was my duty to stay. He made it a condition to Hitler that I remain for the time being. Already Hindenburg was ill, and he made me promise to stay there after his death as long as I could with my conscience.

"I didn't know any of the Nazis — none of them. I was absolutely not pro-Nazi on account of the methods they used in the election campaigning. Hindenburg died in August 1934. At that time one and a half years had passed, and Hindenburg had followed my advice in foreign policy. In interior policy I had nothing to do. It was only foreign policy. He followed my counsel, especially the peace line of the policy, as every German did against the paragraphs of the Versailles Treaty. I was in Geneva a month, at the League of Nations and the Disarmament Commission. As is known, it was without any effect. All our proposals were rejected at that time. Hitler was prepared to disarm totally if others disarmed, but the French especially refused. In 1935, I found the influence of some party members against my policy more and more. Ribbentrop was in the background as private counselor of Hitler.

"The first incident between Hitler and me was in 1935. I was against the nomination of Ribbentrop as ambassador at large in London. I had made Ribbentrop's acquaintance and said he was not the man to go to London. Ribbentrop was preceded by Leopold von Hoesch, an old colleague of mine. He died. More and more I was attacked by the party. But until 1937, with great difficulty, I could stand firm and Hitler followed. But in August 1937, he certainly turned and decided to follow his power politics. Until I objected that that would be foolish, we would have had war in January 1938. I asked him to relieve me of my office. I left office on February 4, 1938, and he nominated me secret state councillor — only a title. I had nothing to back me up, and he even refused to let me have any information anymore. Only a title. From March 1938 I left Berlin and stayed at home in my country estate near Stuttgart — a farm. In September 1938 one of my colleagues, Finance Minister Lutz Count Schwerin von Krosigk, called and told me Hitler intended to make war in Czechoslovakia. I should go to Berlin and try to stop him. The result was the Munich Conference.[3]

"At the conference, I assisted as observer — because I knew Mussolini, Daladier, and Chamberlain at the conference. Goering took me in his car to Munich. During the conference I acted as mediator. Next day I went to my home. Then I was without information, except what was in the newspaper and radio — which was little. I had also an apartment in Berlin, and from time to time went there on private matters. I stayed in Berlin at the beginning of March 1939 without any information beforehand. I saw that Czechoslovakian president Dr. Emil Hácha had come to Berlin and asked Hitler to take over the protection of his country. The next day, Hans Heinrich Lammers telegraphed me in the name of Hitler to come immediately to Vienna.[4] I flew there. To my great surprise, Hitler asked me to take over the post of protector of Bohemia and Moravia. I had told him in Vienna that I could not understand this — have you done this in agreement with France, England, and Italy? He said it was not necessary because Hácha had asked for Germany's protection. I myself was very upset. I was convinced that such a step must have been a great shock to England and France especially. I was further convinced that nothing must be done unless there was an acute danger of war. I refused therefore to accept. But Hitler insisted. He said it would be a great service to my country and I was needed because I was known as a moderate man and he would show them my name. He had nothing further to say. I told him that it was a difficult task, and it would be hard to prevent Sudeten Germans from taking revenge. He said he would proceed anyway. What power could prevent that? I was sixty-six years old already. I finally grudgingly accepted. I said I would try it — a patriotic duty.

"But the power Hitler gave to me was power against the Czechs. He gave me no power against Himmler and his cohorts. I complained sometimes to Hitler; sometimes he agreed. But it became worse and worse. Especially after he nominated a very bad man to become my secretary of state, my subordinate, Karl Frank. He was a representative of Himmler, and in powers of the police Himmler had executive power. I had nothing to say. All he did I only found out about afterward — either through Czech or private information. It was like being in a prison there.

After the war broke out in 1939, I asked Hitler to let me go. But he refused. Things were worse and worse. In September 1941, Hitler called me to the headquarters and told me I was too mild against the Czechs. And he had decided to take strong measures and to send Heydrich, and I said I would never agree. I would say good-bye. I knew Heydrich by name; he was called "Bloodhound." I refused to go back to Prague. I dissolved my household and decided I would never go back. That was September 1941. He did not give me my official dismissal until 1943. But I stayed at home. Heydrich arrived in Prague two hours after I left Prague by auto. He began his persecution of the Czechs."

## Franz von Papen
1879–1969

Franz von Papen was German chancellor in 1932, vice chancellor in 1933–1934, and appointed ambassador to Austria in 1936. Tried by the Nuremberg tribunal and found not guilty, in early 1947 he was reclassified as a major offender by a German de-Nazification court and sentenced to eight years in labor camp. He was released two years later, following appeal.

### February 7, 1946

Interview (with Gilbert present) with Franz von Papen. This gray-haired, somewhat deaf, but very alert, smiling man is polite, exerts a definite personality and "charm" of the "old school." Or what is associated with polite parlor behavior in my mind. He clears a place for us on his bed, offers his chair, a bit of matchbox for an ashtray. He gratefully and gracefully accepts and smokes the proffered cigarette.

Today was the Hess case to-do in court. The session had lasted until 5:45 p.m., which was half an hour later than usual. The defendants were most interested, and it was clear that to most of them the facts produced by the British prosecutor were as interesting as to the spectators. Hess alone of the defendants seemed unimpressed and untouched. He had maintained his usual frozen, apathetic face except for occasional glances toward the gallery, and once or twice smiling and whispering to Goering next to him, in what seemed a rather inappropriate manner. Also at times he leaned forward and seemed to be intent on what was being said, an evincing of interest beyond the usual as far as he is concerned.

Papen said that he believed the case against Hess was clear as far as his being one of the party founders and leaders, but that regarding conspiracy for war, it was Papen's opinion that the case was not strong. Papen himself said that Hess was a peaceful type of man, although he stated, too, that he knew him none too well as he had no contact with him aside from occasional cabinet meetings.

But Papen held his hand to his head and practically moaned at the stupidity of the Foreign Office's and Hess's ignorance of things outside Germany, which was illustrated by Hess's statements in England after his flight. Particularly his peace "offer," when he said the German government would not negotiate with the present English government (meaning Churchill) but would have to have some other government which was acceptable. Papen made disparaging remarks about Ribbentrop, and referred caustically to the latter's stupidity, blind following of Hitler, and his being a "whiskey salesman." He remarked about Hitler's saying that whenever he wanted to take a step forward, his advisers let him down, saying it was too dangerous, and that only one or two supported him, including Ribbentrop. And how Hitler had said that Ribbentrop was therefore a greater statesman than Bismarck.

"I have always stood for principles," said Papen, and that is why Himmler and the party kept watch on him all the time he was ambassador to Vienna and to Turkey. He told of his being summoned by Hitler in the middle of the night to go to Vienna on the evening after Engelbert Dollfuss was killed. Two SS men came up to the house he was staying at, late one night, in Silesia. His son and he thought the SS were coming to get them (as had been attempted once before, he said). His son said the SS were probably there for the purpose of killing them. They each took a pistol and approached the door. There were two SS men there. They said, "We have come to tell you Hitler wants you to telephone him at once." But Papen and his son were fearful of moving, lest they be shot. Finally Papen went to the phone and telephoned Hitler, who was in Bayreuth. "You must go to Vienna at once," said Hitler (Papen related), "after what has happened today." Papen said he replied that he had no idea of what had happened. Then Hitler told him that Dollfuss had been murdered in Vienna that day and things were in a turmoil in Vienna. "Well," said Papen, "I'll have to think it over." "I will send a plane for you in the morning," answered Hitler. In the morning, Hitler's plane arrived and took Papen to Bayreuth, where he saw Hitler, who told him that he needed someone who knew Austria and could handle the situation in Vienna at once. Papen left for Vienna immediately.

In Vienna, Papen was watched constantly by Himmler's agents of the Gestapo, he said, because he was not trusted on account of his friendliness with the Catholic Church. He remained in Vienna until sometime in February 1938, a few weeks before the annexation. Suddenly he was recalled to Germany. In March the annexation came. Of course, he had no idea there would be any annexation at that time, though he did favor, as did all Germans, he said, a union with Austria. Hitler did not want him in Vienna at the time of the annexation because he had gone to Austria only after extracting a promise from Hitler, when he saw him at Bayreuth, that there would be no "armed entry into Austria and no spilling of blood." He implied that he was removed from Austria because Hitler was about to break his "promise" to Papen. (At this point, Gilbert asked him, "I suppose you still believed in the word of Hitler then?" and Papen blandly sighed, and said, "Yes.")

His next assignment was to Turkey. Well, if you opposed Hitler, were followed by Gestapo, disapproved of his regime and treatment of Catholics (he mentioned nothing about Jews), why did you continue in Hitler's service? "It was because I felt that it was in the interest of peace," said Papen, "for me to go to Turkey and prevent the ring of encirclement being established around Germany."

Well, I said, that is puzzling, as it might have been better for the interest of peace if Germany had been encircled, would it not?

"Ah," sighed Papen, "you are looking at it from the viewpoint of history and what has happened. But at the time, it seemed to me that if Turkey joined the Allied ring around Germany, then Hitler would perhaps feel forced to strike out in some direction and war would ensue."

In Turkey he was not watched by the Gestapo as far as he knew, he said, "because I had made it a condition of my accepting the Turkish assignment that Himmler's men not follow me as they did in Vienna." Himmler had replied at that time, during an interview preceding Papen's going to Turkey, that Papen must agree to be less interested and friendly toward the Catholic Church. "At this I laughed," said Papen, "because as I said to Himmler, you must be quite unaware of the fact that Turkey is a country of Muslim religion, and there are practically no Catholics there." The situation in Turkey was "ticklish," said Papen. If he ever tried to even talk to another diplomat, let us say a Swedish or Swiss one, or any neutral, the result of this conversation, which "might come from the bottom of my heart," regarding his "desire for peace," would be picked up by the decoding experts on the cables, or overheard and reported to the Nazi government. He was under order on pain of death not to discuss peace with anyone.

When he was finally recalled from Turkey in 1944 he saw Hitler, who was a different man. It was after the *Attentat* of July 20, 1944, and Hitler shook all over, seemed to have lost his capacity for clear thinking. Did he ever really think clearly? I said. "Well," said Papen, "he was a most interesting man. You could talk to him about so many things. He was interested in art, architecture, politics, the military, music. He could have a thousand interests. Quite a remarkable man. But after the *Attentat* he was changed."

### March 30, 1946

Tonight, Papen was as usual in a receptive mood and eager to express his opinions. He asked me whether there was anything in particular I wanted to know, and I said that it was immaterial, and I would merely have an interview with him so that I could continue my acquaintance with him and further my attempt to understand his personality.

He began to talk about the history of Germany, and its pros and cons. "It is my opinion that the formation of federal states in Germany was a good one. There were centers of great cultural value. Each state had its court, which included a retinue of all sorts of people, including men of science. This gave Germany many cultural influences. Of all the variety of systems, federal states are as good as any. From another standpoint federal states that were not unified were bad, because there was no unity of foreign policy. For example, Bavaria, Baden, Prussia, in particular, had varying viewpoints. In 1871 Bismarck founded the Reich, and he overcame these differences of viewpoints by a magnificent conception. He made the prime minister of Prussia act as the chancellor of Germany so that the same policy in general would hold throughout Germany.

"After the breakdown in 1918 every state made its own policy. Each state had a president who was without influence in the general federation of states. This was a weak point. I felt that this should be corrected along Bismarckian lines. I felt, too, that the prime minister of Prussia should be the chancellor of Germany. At the time, Prussia had a socialist government, and the republic at various periods had mixed governments of bourgeois and socialists. You can see, therefore, of how many different stripes the government consisted.

"I had achieved a laudable aim in that I had made an arrangement with Hindenburg that if Hitler came to power, Hindenburg would appoint me prime minister of Prussia and at the same time vice chancellor.[1] Then came the election of March 5, 1933, and the Nazis were swept into power overwhelmingly.[2] Each state had its own parliament, and in the Prussian diet the Nazis were also predominant. It was clear that Goering would be elected prime minister. At that time Goering was minister of the interior of Prussia. There was no doubt that the majority of the Prussian parliament would choose Goering as their prime minister and in that event I would have to go. I therefore wrote a letter to Hindenburg and Hitler in which I said that I was glad that Goering was to be prime minister of Prussia since Goering was a close friend of Hitler's. By this, I meant that there would be agreement in the main points of national policy, which was so essential for Germany. It was in no sense an abdication of my former adopted policy such as the indictment states. It was understood that the federated state of Germany should preserve in its individual states separate finances, politics, et cetera. It must be difficult for an English or American judge who doesn't know German history to understand these things. The main charge against me is that I was an unscrupulous opportunist and that I changed my ideas as quickly as possible as soon as the Nazis came to power. That is not the case. I will prove to the court that in hundreds of speeches I made after the formation of the Hitler government, my political line differed immensely from the Nazi line not only in main points, but in most points."

I asked Papen what were the main points of disagreement between himself and the Nazis in 1933–34. "Since the time of Bruening we had tried to dissolve that Nazi Party several times. When I came to power, the Nazis had 230 seats, so I was unable to form a majority in the Reichstag without them. I was chancellor at that time. Now, for a chancellor to be effective in legislation, he must have the majority of the Reichstag. The problem was how to dispose of the Nazis.

"Now, when it finally came to actually building the Nazi government under these forceful circumstances, the main points which cropped up in the minds of all Germans were the 8 million unemployed, the 12.5 million who were not entirely employed, and the strikes which arose out of the class struggle. The main thing preoccupying all Germans was finding a solution for the social problems. Hitler always stressed the point that the solution of this social problem could not be found along the lines of

Marxism or Bolshevism, but rather along capitalistic lines mixed with a certain degree of socialism. This was not meant to be state socialism — but it was socialism insofar as private enterprise should not work for enormous dividends and profits. All profit made in every branch of the economy would be for the community and not strictly for private gain. That seemed to me to be sound.

"One of the slogans of the Nazi government was something to the effect that all profits went first to the community. The difference between the type of socialism espoused by the National Socialists and Communism was that the interests of private persons would not be suppressed as they were in the Communist state.

"As I said, that seemed to me to be a sound principle. The building of the government by the Nazis was not displeasing to the conservative group over which I presided. I came to the conclusion that the solution to Germany's problems would be based on a closer cooperation between private enterprise, management, and labor.

"I thought, being a Catholic as you know, that these lines were laid down by Pope Leo XIII in his well-known encyclical. Therefore, I stressed the point that basically there should be a general religious renewal. Hitler disagreed with that. I don't know much about churches, religion, and such things. For instance, I disagreed with him on his racial ideas, anti-Semitism, et cetera.

"In 1933 I made a speech in Gleiwitz in which I said that there was certainly some justice in stressing the good points of a certain race, but that we should never get to the point where a certain race should be fought on account of certain qualities and another race termed better. I said then that this was entirely wrong.

"I made a speech on June 17, 1934, which was a few days before the Roehm purge. That speech contains a great mass of my acknowledgments, of my political creed in opposition to Nazism. The speech was given before the University of Marburg. It aroused the bitter enmity of the Nazis. Goebbels gave orders that the speech should not be reprinted or published in the papers, and that was the reason that in the Roehm purge I was almost shot. Actually I was arrested for three days and on the death roll of Himmler. I was not shot because Goering, as far as I know, checked up on it, mainly because if I were shot there would be too much bad publicity outside Germany.

"I cited these examples to indicate what my real credo was, has been, is, and always shall be. As far as the Roehm affair — I had no connection whatever with it.[3] When that uproar started, I was summoned to see Goering in his office and he told me to consider myself arrested. Goering was excited but not angry with me. Himmler, however, who was with Goering at that moment, was angry with me and told Goering that I should be liquidated. Himmler has done every possible harm to me throughout my life.

"Himmler hated the church. He and Bormann were the two people who influenced Hitler most. When I spoke to Hitler in the beginning he agreed with me and said that no state could be governed without religion. In *Mein Kampf* he said that a man was a fool if he destroyed the religion of the people. Hitler also made the statement that a political reform should not be a religious reform.

"It was not my fault that Hitler went back on his word in this regard just as he has gone back on his word in so many other things. In the course of Hitler's evolution he changed his mind about many points. But at the time when he came to power, such was not the case. I really thought that it was his earnest desire to comply in matters of religion. In his speeches to the Reichstag in March 1933, he said that he respected Christian fundamentals and would do everything to uphold them. It was I who had asked Hitler to include this point in his speeches."

All of the previous reminiscence had been made by Papen in what sounded like a well-rehearsed, studied manner, without much emotional tone or feeling. I asked him whether he felt that anti-Semitism was compatible with religious freedom and tolerance. He replied, "Not at all. But Hitler didn't strive for the annihilation of the Jews — he stressed that fact in public life and in the newspapers. Hitler merely said at the beginning that Jewish influence was too great, that of all the lawyers in Berlin, eighty percent were Jewish. Hitler thought that a small percentage of the people, the Jews, should not be allowed to control the theater, cinema, radio, et cetera."

I said then that it would seem that he felt that a discrimination against individual rights on a religious basis was not incorrect. I further remarked that in effect he preached religious freedom and tolerance and practiced a form of anti-Semitism. Papen became somewhat excited and claimed with great charm and much smiling that I must have misunderstood him — that he merely meant that he was for allowing a certain percentage of Jews, Catholics, and Protestants to be present in certain professions and businesses but that he was not at all for disposing or dis-enfranchising the Jews. "I thought that a correction of what Hitler called the Jewish question could be done in a normal, smooth way. I don't think that at the beginning, Hitler had such radical ideas about the solution of the Jewish problem — or at any rate he never revealed it. When Hitler made the first law aimed at doing away with Jewish influence, I limited it so that all Jews who had been in Germany since 1914 could stay there. You see, after 1918, when the war was lost, we had an influx of Jews from the East. This overflow was absolutely abnormal in Germany and the only time it had happened was after the revolution in 1918. There was a considerable amount, that influx. We thought that this should be corrected."

# Joachim von Ribbentrop
## 1893–1946

Joachim von Ribbentrop was foreign minister from 1938 to 1945. Found guilty at Nuremberg of conspiracy to commit crimes, crimes against peace, war crimes, and crimes against humanity, he was hanged on October 16, 1946.

## January 27, 1946

It was Sunday. He was seated at his desk, apparently working on some papers connected with his defense (I assume). He was courteous, seemed pleased to see Gilbert and myself. We sat on his bed, which he cleared of papers, books, and so forth. He sat on the chair opposite, smoked an old pipe.

He is a handsome man who appears to be in his late forties or early fifties. There is an air of superficial depression about him, though he frequently smiles or grins agreeably. He speaks excellent English with a faint British accent, sometimes is stumped on vocabulary, but only when the German word he wishes to use is apparently more apropos for the idea than the English equivalent.

The dominant theme of his recital (it amounted to that — with certain questions asked by myself or Gilbert) was how puzzled and astounded he is by the turn of events. Just what he is puzzled about was unclear, probably is unclear to him. There were two leitmotifs: First, could Hitler have known of the atrocities, and if so, let them go on? No, it hardly seems possible. Hitler was such a good man, so ascetic, never ate meat, called Ribbentrop and his other close associates "eaters of dead flesh." It must have been Himmler, who perpetrated many things against the Führer's orders. Second, how could this whole disaster have happened to me? The latter was not expressed by Ribbentrop in words, but there were frequent exclamations of "It's amazing — I can't understand how it could have happened. It gets me."

His career began, insofar as politics are concerned, he said, in 1932, when Hitler and National Socialism were riding into power. Prior to that he had been a "businessman." He said that at the outbreak of World War I he had been in Canada, shipped out in a ship carrying coal ("coal bunker") in order to reach Germany and enlist in the army. Apparently he left the army at the end of the war with the rank of first lieutenant.

Just how he met Hitler for the first time is yet to be obtained from him. He met him first in 1932, he said. What Ribbentrop's first positions in the party or government were is also not mentioned. He does say that he assisted in "ways" (which he did not elaborate upon) to bring about the rise of National Socialism in the elections preceding Hitler's accession to power. I asked him about the episode which is widely known, the business of his having given a "Heil Hitler" salute at the Court of St. James's. He smiled wanly and said the English papers had taken it up badly, and extracted something out of it which wasn't there. He had given the straight-up Hitler salute to the king on being presented; but he had not said, "Heil Hitler," with the salute. In fact the king was very understanding and next day sent a note saying he understood, and that everything was quite all right. Besides, they gave that salute to many crowned heads, to the kings of Italy, Romania, and so forth. Gilbert remarked at that point that these were fascist states and that probably the fascist salute was appropriate there, but in England it was different perhaps. Ribbentrop said that Romania was not a fascist state, that it was the custom to give the salute of the country from which the ambassador comes.

There were many paradoxical statements in Ribbentrop's recital. Hitler's last testament was a bit disappointing, but once one recalled that he wrote it with shells exploding overhead, it could be understood. Hitler was ill during the last couple of years, became more unswayable, stubborn, became more anti-Semitic steadily. He never spoke of losing the war until late in April 1945. As short a time as six weeks before the end, Hitler spoke of winning the war by "a nose's length." At that time Ribbentrop first thought Hitler was not thinking clearly.

"I think the only way one can arrive at an understanding of his anti-Semitism growing all the time is because in America your Mr. Roosevelt had his brain trust which was made up of so many Jews, Felix Frankfurter, Claude Pepper — was it Pepper? I can't recall the other names. Oh yes, Morgenthau.[1] It made Hitler feel more and more that an international conspiracy had caused the war, with the Jews behind it."

Asked whether he didn't think Hitler knew he caused the war, Ribbentrop didn't reply.

### February 16, 1946

The former foreign minister was writing at his flimsy table (so constructed that the weight of a man would cause its collapse) with his back toward the door of the cell when I entered. He had on his horn-rimmed glasses, no tie, strings instead of shoelaces (all laces are removed when prisoners are brought back from court, as a suicide prevention measure). His cell is rather sloppy and littered with junk, in contrast with the spartan cleanliness of many of the other defendants' cells. Pieces of paper, boxes, matchboxes, coat strewn on bed, clothing not neatly hung up — certainly not the orderliness of the obsessive or the supposedly typical German.

He is quite an affected fellow, but his affectation is so practiced it is almost natural. He spoke of the work he was doing when I entered the cell. In large, sprawling letters he was writing several legal-size pages of material in pencil, telling of his impressions of the last few years, as he expressed it. He said it was hard to put down, because he could not recall many episodes, which would require his files. He has requested certain files through his attorneys, but as yet they haven't appeared. He read me part of what he was composing. It had to do with his impressions and attitudes toward Hitler. More and more I get the feeling that this is a calculated attitude on Ribbentrop's part: that he is assisting the building up of an already well-on-its-way myth of the magnetism of Hitler, the one-man rule, the self-enforced isolation of the man, his human qualities, at the same time the inability of any of his fellow workers to ever get to know the man.

He described his first meeting with Hitler. It was in 1932. He evades (it seemed to me) saying exactly where it was or under what circumstances. There were several others present. The impression one got was of a dark face, very blue eyes, a compelling facial expression which held you with a glance. Further, Hitler's personality was more strongly impressed on him when he met him the second time, in 1933. Then, he remarks, Hitler was becoming more powerful. He introduced Papen to Hitler at his (Ribbentrop's) house, and the latter already had a dictatorial air of great power and charm. "He knew how to handle people, especially men, and charmingly. He would speak for twenty-five minutes, then I would say two words; he would change the subject and talk for twenty-five more minutes on other matters. He had a wide knowledge of every subject. He dominated everyone. Once a 'prominent British' statesman was urged [by Ribbentrop] to meet Hitler. The former refused, saying, 'I can't talk to dictators.' By this he meant that normally he could sit down as you or I, have an exchange of ideas. With Hitler this was not possible. Hitler did the talking, you listened."

Ribbentrop has the air at times of a ham actor taking the part of the great statesman who has become a little foggy because of all he has undergone in the past few years. He has a serious face, at times illumined by his old, charming smile, which can be turned on and off at will. When at rest or repose, the face registers blankness and there is a dogged quality in the forced set of the lips. When observed or during conversation, he speaks constantly, with some moments of void in the conversation, but not moments in which he expects the listener to contribute any words. In fact, when I want to steer the conversation along certain lines, or ask a question which would perhaps open new channels in his thinking, he deliberately seems to have difficulty hearing, then asks for the question to be repeated, then usually answers evasively or in such broad terms as amount to an evasion.

The content of his monologue today was Hitler. What a great personality. How charming, diplomatic, magnetic he was. How he could hold the whole of Germany in his palm. "They were all like schoolboys in front of him, even Bormann." Yet it is so obvious from these trials that Hitler had his cruel side. But a man who brought Germany out of the dirt, didn't he have to be cruel at times in achieving his great purpose? But, of course, Ribbentrop never dreamt that Hitler or the Nazis were being cruel until the revelations of these trials. I asked about his reaction to the Russian case thus far. Terrible stuff they are saying, he said. Then he laughed and observed: "If you listen to them, every German is a monster." I queried, just how much did he think was true, how much exaggeration? He looked serious and blank for a moment. He admitted he

could not tell. Some must be true, he said. I then asked about his reaction
to Hans Frank's diary and the revelations which had been read. (Frank
confessed that if he had reported to Hitler he had killed 150,000 more
Poles, Hitler would have said, "Fine.")[2] Ribbentrop shook his head and
held the left temporal region. "That fellow, why did he write such stuff?"
he exclaimed.

I persisted in trying to get some reaction, good or bad, from him. If it
were true, was it not bad? Or was it justified in the sense that the Nazis
justified it? Ribbentrop said of course it was bad, but the feeling I got
was that he was really not concerned about the killings, brutalities, and
horrors of the German methods, but rather that such a fool like Frank
was injudicious enough to write it all down in a diary.

He then went on to describe his meeting with Stalin and Vyacheslav
Molotov in Moscow when he consummated the Nonaggression Pact.[3]
He was there but a day and a night, and later returned for a large ban-
quet, in which toasts were made. Molotov he considers very competent
and clever. Stalin rules Russia (using again the same cliché he applied to
Hitler) "holding the Russian people in the palm of his hand. That is the
way with dictatorial governments," he said. "In our government it was
Hitler's policy to have each minister or department head know only
what concerned his work. Therefore I didn't know of the invasion of
Norway, for instance, until twenty-four hours before it occurred. He kept
the Foreign Office out of the military. The same with the Russian war. I
never knew about it until twenty-four hours before it happened."

Personally, I believe this myth of Hitler's taking nobody into his confidence about his plans, methods, attitudes of state, and so forth is a means
of avoiding, in a rather obvious manner, the responsibilities of sharing in
guilt. Ribbentrop will state he knew nothing of anything until after it
happened. Goering says the same thing. So do all the other ministers and
members of the cabinet. Everything is now blamed on Hitler, Himmler,
and Bormann.

"I rather liked Stalin and Molotov, got along fine with them," Ribbentrop remarked in his bright, sophisticated, charming manner, so incongruous with the surroundings and the general atmosphere of Nazi
depravity that the trials have clearly indicated.

He also described that he had at times severe left-sided headaches
and once had slight weakness of the right upper and lower limbs. At the
time he was told it was a "cramp" of one of the blood vessels in the head.

I tapped his deep reflexes with my fingers but could not make out any large differences in responses. He does take sleeping pills at night, he says, and sometimes APCs during the day for the headache.

## June 23, 1946

Ribbentrop was seated in his cell, working on his notes. There were voluminous pages of court transcript, typewritten pages of his own notes, many large folders full of documents strewn all over the cell. On his table, he had some notes on the Czechoslovakian situation in the time of Hitler and said that he would give these notes to his lawyer.

He said that this morning he again experienced difficulty in opening his left eye and some buzzing sound of high-pitched quality in his left ear. I examined the left eye and found that there was some tendency to drooping of the left lid, which appeared to be on a nonorganic basis. It was interesting that during the course of the subsequent interview, which lasted for about an hour, his eye completely opened and there was no longer any ptosis.

He spoke again about his physical difficulties. He said that he wanted my frank opinion as to whether he had some disease of the brain or not. He repeated his oft-phrased opinion that there was something the matter with his vagus nerve and that probably the blood circulation to the left side of his head was defective. He said that this feeling came and went at certain periods, that he had been feeling fairly well and free of symptoms for about two weeks, but that today he felt worse. He said that the outstanding symptom he suffered was an inability to concentrate; for example, "I will read a page or a paragraph of my notes and not know what I have been reading at all." He gave other examples of a similar nature. He said that sometimes he could not remember what had transpired in court the previous day. Then suddenly he would recall such events and he would be startled because of his poor memory. He wondered at one time whether he was developing the same type of mental weakness that Hess had.

Ribbentrop went on to discuss his favorite topics, namely, Hitler and National Socialist foreign policy. He said, "I know that you don't like to hear about the Versailles Treaty, but you know and everyone knows that this treaty was a great injustice. Hitler sprang up as a result of this tremendous injustice that had been done to Germany. I have been thinking it all over these many months. I remember that in 1928, 1929, and 1930, before I became a National Socialist and before Hitler came into power, I told my French and English friends abroad that they must render assistance to the German government of Bruening, or they would have Hitler on their hands. But England and France refused to give Germany anything at all."

He said that the greatest mistake today was this trial. "I don't mean that it is important whether a few of us like Goering, myself, or the others are sentenced to death or hard labor or whatever, but to the German people we will always remain their leaders, right or wrong, and in a few years even you Americans and the rest of the world will see this trial as a mistake. The German people will learn to hate the Americans, distrust the British and French, and unfortunately, perhaps be taken in by the Russians. That will be the worst calamity of all. I hate to think of Moscow ruling Germany or Germany becoming a territorial possession of the Soviet Union. The Allies should take the attitude, now that the war is over, that mistakes have been made on both sides, that those of us here on trial are German patriots, and that though we may have been misled and gone too far with Hitler, we did it in good faith and as German citizens. Furthermore, the German people will always regard our condemnation by a foreign court as unjust and will consider us martyrs.

"Hitler has been the greatest riddle for me. He always was. We often commented in our private circle in the Foreign Office that Hitler had taken too literally the old Hapsburg slogan of 'Divide and conquer.' He went so far as to not allow his own ministers to achieve much power. He would not tell me of many things that were going on. The same is true of his other subordinates. As years went on, Hitler became more and more distrustful. In the end he appointed a new cabinet, with a new foreign minister. That was in his last testament. I can't understand it. I was one of his most faithful followers — perhaps *the* most faithful."

Ribbentrop brushed aside the Jewish extermination events. He said that in the long view, historically, the Jews' extermination would always be a blot on German history, but that it was in a way attributable to the fact that Hitler had lost his sense of proportion and, because he was losing the war, went "wild" on the subject of the Jews. But the big historical issue was not that Jews had been exterminated but that Germany had really been oppressed and never given a chance.

"In 1940 after the outbreak of the war I sent two Foreign Office representatives to America to contact several large Jewish banking houses, to try to get them to use their influence to keep America out of the war and influence England to make peace with Germany. Unfortunately, my representatives received a very cool reception. The American Jews and others obviously distrusted and hated the Nazi regime. They refused to cooperate in preventing President Roosevelt and his brain trust from lending assistance to England. Lend-lease continued and the whole American atmosphere toward Germany was hostile.[4] If only these American bankers had intervened and threatened England, forced her to accept Hitler's peace offers — and we were prepared to make a peace with England in 1940 — all these terrible exterminations of the Jews could have been prevented."

I remarked that it seemed to me he was still seeing things from a rather one-sided viewpoint. Did he really think, like Hitler, that it was the Jews in America who were opposed to Nazi Germany's aggression, or did he realize that all the democratic peoples in the world disliked Hitlerism and were opposed to it? Did he not realize that in the eyes of the world, Hitler and the Nazi government were seen as war makers and guilty of fascist terror and nationalism of such an abnormal sort, that any peace at that time would have meant the victory of Germany and the subsequent victory of Nazi ideology? Did he not see that no nation, other than Germany, wanted Hitler to rule the world?

Ribbentrop gestured with his hands. "I am sure that Hitler only wanted the Sudetenland, the Polish Corridor, a trade agreement with Austria, and perhaps a few colonies, that is all. I am sure that he would not have tried to pursue further aggressive actions. Hitler was not yet off balance and had not gone in the wrong direction, which he later did."

I remarked that in an interview that I had with Streicher, the latter told me that Jackson's real name was Jacobson, that the reason for all the difficulties Germany had was a "Jewish plot" by the rich Jews in America, England, and France, and the Bolshevik Jews in Russia. Furthermore, Streicher had told me yesterday that his opinion was that if all the Jews in the world, down to the last person with any Jewish blood in him, had been successfully exterminated, there would be no trials and the world would be better off. Did Hitler, in Ribbentrop's opinion, have more or less identical views? "I think he did. I think Hitler was off balance in regard to the Jewish question, too. He told me often that the Jews caused the war, and that there was a complicity between Jewish capitalism and Jewish Bolshevism. I never could understand this and I thought he was mistaken. In fact, I know he was mistaken. After I went to Russia and met Stalin, to conclude the German-Russian Nonaggression Pact, I came back to Berlin and told Hitler that I saw no Jews in the leading positions in Russia. The only Jew I met was Lazar Kaganovich, who impressed me as being a very nice old gentleman.[5] Hitler simply ignored my observation. I know for a fact that this idea of the Jews causing the war and the Jews being so all-important is nonsense. But that was Hitler's idea, and as time went on he became more and more obsessed with this idea. It was pure fantasy. As I say, Hitler is a riddle to me and will always remain so.

"Hitler had a brutal side to him as well as a decent side. It was the decent side that appealed to me. He was very nice to me. He was often very affectionate. Yet on the other hand, he would be most friendly and affectionate on one day, and the very next time I saw him he would criticize me and even accuse me of betraying him in some way or another. I was his most faithful follower and such accusations hurt me. Do you know that after the *Attentat* of July 20, 1944, Hitler said, in the presence of several generals, that it was I who sent emissaries to Sweden to sue for peace? It cut me to the quick. I said nothing. I clicked my heels and walked out of the room. It was another example of Hitler's mistrusting everyone." Ribbentrop went on at length to describe how Germany had had 7 million unemployed in 1932 and how Hitler came to power because the masses felt that they would be benefited by him. "Besides, they had no alternative — it was either Hitler and Nazism or Communism."

**July 15, 1946**
This morning Ribbentrop wanted to remain in his cell instead of going to court because he felt weak and had a headache. He localized the pain in his head as being in the left parietal region near the midline.

He spoke of the trials and of the past. He complained of inability to concentrate. "Maybe I can't concentrate because I work too steadily in my cell from the moment court is over until lights are turned low. Perhaps I work so hard because it prevents me from thinking."

He wanted to know what the general reaction to his attorney's court pleading the other day had been. I said that in general the other defendants seemed to have thought Dr. Horn, his defense counsel, had done a good job. I said there was one defendant who made a remark which was not flattering to Ribbentrop but complimentary to Horn. Ribbentrop insisted on knowing what this remark had been. I told him that Gilbert had mentioned the matter to me, that I had not heard the remark directly. According to Gilbert, the remark had been a jocular one, something to the effect that Dr. Horn would have made a better foreign minister than Ribbentrop.

He laughed in a halfhearted way. "Yes, they are always making digs at my expense. Nothing succeeds like success. While I was foreign minister nobody ever criticized a word I said or a deed I performed. Now, suddenly all these defendants feel they were smarter than I, that I was stupid as a foreign minister, and I have read that in the Allied press I'm referred to as the former champagne salesman who became foreign minister to the former corporal.

"I was truly under Hitler's spell, that cannot be denied. I was impressed with him from the moment I first met him, in 1932. He had terrific power, especially in his eyes. Now the tribunal accuses us of conspiracy. I say, how can one have a conspiracy in a dictatorship government? One man and one man only made all the crucial decisions. That was the Führer. In all my dealings with him I never discussed the exterminations or anything of that sort.

"What I shall never comprehend is that six weeks before the end of the war he assured me we'd win by a nose. I left his presence then and said that from that time forth I was completely at a loss — that I didn't understand a thing. Hitler always, until the end, and even now, had a strange fascination over me. Would you call it abnormal of me? Sometimes, in his presence, when he spoke of all his plans, the good things he would do for the *Volk,* vacations, highways, new buildings, cultural advantages and so forth, tears would come to my eyes. Would that be because I'm a hysterical weak man?

"I don't think I'm particularly weak as a man. Of course, you see me now, beset with illness, which may be functional, but it is nevertheless an illness I have had for at least four years. But until I met Hitler in 1932 or 1933 I was never a coward, or easily influenced. That is why I keep repeating what a magnetic, powerful personality he was."

The conversation, or monologue, lagged a bit. I asked him of what he was thinking. "Of you. Of your role here. It must be interesting to live with and speak to us defeated leaders of a foreign state. As a psychiatrist you probably know more about us than we ourselves know. Do you think perhaps I have a tumor up here?" He pointed to the spot on the head at the midparietal region. I said that it was doubtful and unlikely, since his eyegrounds were normal and there were no other neurological manifestations. "Yes, I hardly think it is a tumor either, because I never had any venereal disease. Tumors always come from venereal diseases like syphilis, don't they?"

I reiterated what I had told him several times in the past few months, that venereal disease was not usually the cause of tumor. He seemed quite obsessed with this concept, and unconsciously seemed to be defending himself from the charge that he might have a dread venereal disease. "Sometimes I think that my memory is going bad, like poor Hess. I know that is stupid and silly. Hess is quite without memory or logic at present. I can think all right, but only if I obtain enough sleep."

We talked for a bit on his early development. His memory had always been good, he felt, even as a child. Hence his aptitude for languages. He attended school in Kassel and in Metz. He is vague as to just how many years of school he achieved, but in all it was not beyond high school, if that far. He lived in Switzerland for a time and had some schooling there, and "private lessons in London and France." At the age of seventeen he went to Canada, "to visit some friends," and remained there from 1910 until the outbreak of the First World War, in 1914. He then went to New York, where he obtained work as a "freelance reporter" on several daily papers and lived for a time at the Hotel Vanderbilt, "which became too expensive and so I later moved to a boardinghouse." He spent six months in New York. Then war was declared, and he felt it his "patriotic duty" to return to the "Fatherland." He went aboard a Dutch steamer in New York harbor as a passenger. When the boat entered Falmouth, England, he was hidden by a German engineer in the coal bunker of the ship. An English officer came aboard and "was very decent but said I would have to be removed and interned in England along with several hundred other German nationals who were aboard." After this visit by the English officer he was hidden successfully in the coal bunker until the ship was cleared and came to Holland. He believed that the officer did not search very thoroughly for him aboard the ship because he had struck up an acquaintance with him and he was not too interested in apprehending him.

Thereafter he made his way from Holland to Germany, enlisted in the army, in which he served in a cavalry regiment until the end of the war.

In Canada he had a "very interesting and pleasant time." He met many wealthy people and had a position with a firm that built a thousand miles of the Canadian Pacific Railroad. He himself worked as a foreman and in other capacities, and helped build the cantilever bridge across the St. Lawrence River near Quebec. In Canada, a year or two after his arrival, he developed tuberculosis of the right kidney and it was removed in a hospital in Quebec. He was below standards for acceptance in the German army at the time he returned to Germany, but he managed to serve nevertheless. He had tuberculosis of the lungs for a short time during the First World War but was completely cured.

He feels that tuberculosis is a familial disease. His mother died in her early thirties of tuberculosis of lungs and kidneys, when he was eleven years of age. His brother, a year or so his senior, was in Canada with him, where he contracted tuberculosis and was hospitalized. He died in a sanatorium in Switzerland in 1918, at the age of twenty-six.

"Strange to say, my mother's death when I was ten or eleven was a great shock to me and my brother and sister. We loved her greatly, although for years we could not be with her much because of her ill health. I can see her lying dead in her bed just as clearly now as when it happened, forty-one years ago. But the second great shock of my life was even stranger for an adult to admit. That was in 1941, on New Year's Day, when my father, who was past eighty-two, died in my home in Berlin. I was depressed and shocked for weeks, and perhaps still am. He was my closest friend. He was a soldierly type of man, but very human and sympathetic with his children.

"Father resigned from the army in 1909 because of differences of opinion with Emperor Wilhelm II. But during World War I, my father again entered the army and fought bravely. He had an independent mind, always monarchist but also democratic in thinking. He approved of the National Socialist Party though he never joined until after 1933. He did so then in my interest and on my request. He opposed the anti-Jewish attitude of the party.

"I myself was always of the opinion that the Jewish question was a temporary political one that would find its own solution. I never conceived of the Jew as the great danger, such as Hitler later claimed, and which led to Himmler's atrocities. If I had known about them, even at the end of this war, I would have committed suicide. The first I ever heard of exterminations was late in 1944, when the Russians recaptured the region in which Camp Majdanek was installed. They spread the story of Jew exterminations after they captured Majdanek.[6] I went to Hitler and asked him. He said it was enemy propaganda."

Did Ribbentrop still feel he should have committed suicide? "I fully intended to commit suicide when I was captured. I had poison on my person. I wrote a letter to the British early in May after the capitulation, in which I strove for some sort of peace terms. But before I could mail the letter, British police arrived and arrested me. I handed them the letter. They searched me and I gave them the poison. I was sent at once to the prison in Mondorf."

Did he still feel he should have committed suicide? "No. I feel now that I must face the music, as you say in English. I must accept responsibility even though I had no power as foreign minister because it was a dictator state. That was what I meant when I said in my defense that I stand up for the foreign policy of Germany from 1938 to the end, but regarding the atrocities, the actions in domestic politics, or the actions in occupied territories I can take no responsibility. For example, Hitler often said, 'Wherever there is a German bayonet, we have no foreign policy but a military one.' Therefore the entire East, Poland and Russia, Norway, and so forth, were not in my jurisdiction. I probably had a liaison man there with the military authorities, that was all. My function as foreign minister during the war was with the neutral countries, the allied Axis countries, such as Romania, Hungary, Italy, and Japan, and with South America. In France we had an ambassador, Otto Abetz, but I had no control over him. In Denmark I had Werner Best of my office; for two years I tried to avert the Jewish deportations. Best can affirm that."[7]

I said: Werner Best, when I interviewed him a few weeks ago, had told me that he was of the opinion you were in favor of his policies in Denmark, but had sent several telegrams to you and had received no reply. Best interpreted that as an affirmation of his request that no Jew be deported, but he was unable to quote you or your attitudes, I said.

Ribbentrop sighed. "Ah, well. I should think Best would at least be loyal. I did a lot for him. I removed him from the Gestapo and placed him in the Foreign Office. Now to save their skins, all these fellows are apt to betray you." I replied that Best had said quite the opposite, had in fact attempted to support Ribbentrop but had done so in the fashion I just described. Had Ribbentrop sent any reply to the telegrams of Werner Best from Denmark? "I don't remember. I do know that it was through my efforts and those of Best that we averted Jewish deportations from Denmark for two years. Then finally Hitler gave Himmler the order, and it was done. But Best tipped off the Jews in Denmark and I think most of them escaped to Sweden or somewhere by small boats before Eichmann and his transports arrived."

We discussed his own attitude toward Jews again. He repeated the story of how he gave Hermann Neubacher of Vienna a job in his Foreign Office after the party wanted to remove him from office in Vienna because he had associated with Jews when he was mayor there. "I told Hitler that if Neubacher was to be prosecuted, I should be removed from office too, as I had many dealings with Jews before 1933. Hitler merely told me that he would arrange things, and I was able to take Neubacher into my office."

Ribbentrop's wife was the former Annelies Henkell, daughter of the German champagne manufacturer Henkell. "In Canada, I was engaged to marry the daughter of my boss, a millionaire, but the war interfered. I married in July 1920 in Wiesbaden. It was a love affair. I had completely gotten over my first love. My married life has been ideal. It's hard for me to talk about my marriage because it's so dear to me. Unfortunately, I could not spend as much time with my children as I should have liked because I was so busy with state affairs from 1933, and before that with international business. You met my daughter. What did you think of her? She's a sweet little girl, isn't she?"

I said she impressed me quite favorably, but she was not a little girl, rather a tall, well-built young lady. "Yes. She is tall. What worries me now is that she is expecting a baby in six weeks, and this is a terrible time for her to have a baby, isn't it? I don't give a darn for my own fate, but she will worry. The grandchild will be my first."

His daughter, the second oldest of his children, was twenty-two. She married last May while Ribbentrop was a prisoner in Mondorf. "Bettina has always been my favorite, though I love all of my five children. My oldest child, Rudolf Lothar, was born in 1921 in Wiesbaden. He was educated primarily in Berlin, then spent a year at a preparatory school in London when I was ambassador there, then the usual period in the Hitler Youth, labor duty, and the army. He was with an SS panzer division, and at the end of the war was a captain, sustained a few wounds, and was decorated for distinguished service. He is still a POW in an American camp. Bettina was born in 1922, Ursula in 1932, Adolf in 1935, and Barthold in 1940. All are in good health, with the exception of Adolf, who seems to have weak lungs."

Concerning his own childhood he said that his father never remarried and that for that reason they had housekeepers. Both of the housekeepers he recalled as unpleasant, domineering women. He thought that possibly the second housekeeper was the reason for his going to Canada in 1910, as she "made our lives miserable." However, his main reason for the trip to Canada was to "visit friends."

# Alfred Rosenberg
## 1893–1946

Alfred Rosenberg was an early
follower of Hitler, editor of the
anti-Semitic paper <u>Völkischer
Beobachter,</u> and appointed minister
of the occupied territories in 1941.
Found guilty at Nuremberg of conspiracy to commit crimes, crimes
against peace, war crimes, and
crimes against humanity, he was
hanged on October 16, 1946.

## February 3, 1946

Interview for over an hour with Alfred Rosenberg (Gilbert translating). The man appears about fifty years of age, states he has lost some
twenty pounds in weight, does not look particularly malnourished. On
the contrary he is a medium-sized fellow, with graying light brown
hair, in apparently good physical condition. He was dressed in an
American field jacket, tweed trousers, shoes without laces, colored
shirt without tie. He greeted us with superficial amiability, moved his
papers from the cot, and so forth, and invited us to sit down. He sat on
a chair opposite.

His face is a costume of sobriety and philosophic calm, smiling understanding, broad vision, and reflective of the true philosopher, who looks
on all that is transpiring with critical, but not bitter, detachment.

We discussed many things. It started out with Gilbert's asking him if
he had reread his own copy of the *Protocols of the Elders of Zion*,[1]
which Gilbert had given him a week ago. He was asked if on rereading it
he had changed his opinions any (the book was published in 1923), and
whether he still thought it reliable, since claims that it is fraudulent are
widely accepted. Rosenberg smiled enigmatically . . . and said he had

not had an opportunity to reread it all, but that he had not changed his mind. True, he was young and perhaps a bit one-sided when he read it, he said, but as for its authenticity or lack of it, that was still a "dark secret which might never be illuminated." Nor did he seem particularly interested in whether it was factual or not. His broad, philosophic concession that "it was a question" and a "dark secret" seemed to epitomize his liberalism. In this way he differed from Streicher's response to the same query on the *Protocols;* Streicher had said yes, it was probably not authentic, but everything it said was true anyway and could be found in various Jewish writings.

The Jewish question was one which required a knowledge of history, philosophy, the Greeks, a study of races, music, art, and so forth. This is not literal but a summation of the generalities and quasi-learned arguments he propounded. The cause of the Jewish question was, of course, the Jews themselves. The Jews are a nation, and like every nation, have a nationalistic spirit. That's all very well, but they should be in their own homeland. Now there were several places for Jews proposed in 1936 by the English (I believe he said the French and Germans, too — implying that a joint proposal was made that the Jews turned down). These places were Alaska, Guiana (didn't say which of the islands), Madagascar, and Uganda.[2]

Why couldn't the Jews be allowed to remain where they were, in other lands? That would have been all right if they didn't do bad things, but they did. What did the Jews do? They spat at German culture. How? They controlled the theater, publishing, the stores, and so on. Of course, Jews have a two-thousand-year-old culture, too, but it is not the German culture, which is so different.

He picked up a copy of his book *Blut und Ehre (Blood and Honor),* which I had beside me, and said something to the effect that he would show he was not a fanatic about Jews, that he once made a speech in which Jews were not mentioned. In that speech, contained in the book, he discussed nature and science.

Did Rosenberg consider himself a historian, or a philosopher, primarily? Well, both, because you can't separate the two things. Did he consider himself an authority on those subjects? Yes indeed, he had studied all kinds of history and philosophy since in his teens. What did he get his degree in, philosophy or history or what? In architecture, he said. But he never practiced it. He became a journalist soon after his student days were over, and he was a writer for a newspaper. In 1923 he was editor of the *Völkischer Beobachter* (Munich), which was the National Socialist Party organ. In 1924 it was banned (probably he meant it was banned from the time of the putsch in 1923 until a year and half later). In 1925 it resumed publication and he remained editor of it until 1936 or 1938 (I forget which year he mentioned), after which it continued to be edited by someone else (name given but not recalled by me).

It was not a paper like Streicher's. Yes, both were National Socialist, both anti-Semitic, but his was on a higher plane. There is always the mass of people who like pornography and cheap stuff such as *Der Stürmer* contained. There are analogies in every political party; some high-class stuff and some low-class stuff. Both serve their purpose.

Every doctor knows that there are different types of blood, various classes, Rosenberg said at one point, in discussing the differences between races. Would, for example, a blood transfusion from a Negro cause any character differences to ensue if given to an Aryan? Rosenberg said quite seriously, with his "philosophic" smile, he didn't know. That would be a brutal experiment such as was done in the concentration camps. He smiled as if he had scored a triumph of reasoning. We pressed the point though for his opinion; suppose a Nazi soldier were injured and given some Jewish blood, or Negro blood. Would character changes occur? It wasn't proven, he said. Negroes beget Negroes, Jews Jews, so it must be that blood will tell.

## June 8, 1946

What was Rosenberg's main objection to Bolshevism? He seemed surprised at that question, as if it were a subject which needed no explanation. After a few moments he said vehemently, "Bolshevism wants to destroy by power a very sensitive state culture without any consideration for the history of the nation. Secondly, Bolshevism wants to do this for the benefit of a single class of the population. Thirdly, Bolshevism fights principally against private property. It creates collectives among the farmers and destroys the agricultural system. It works against the principles upon which more or less all states are based.

"The Communist Party is under the control of a central office. This central office is in Moscow. Therefore, Communism in various countries is in the making of the individual state or an expression of nationalism. This international Communistic Bolshevism gathers its support from a strong state — Russia. Communism not only makes its policy in Russia but it prescribes the policy of Bolsheviks all over the world."

I asked him whether he would approve of the system of Communism if it existed in an individual country and gained power without the help of the Communist International or the Soviet Union itself. Rosenberg thought for a moment and then said, without conviction, "Every state can choose its own way of governing — that's a right which belongs to the nation. If, for example, on Russian territory, a Russian Communism existed, that would be no business of ours insofar as it would limit itself to that country."

I was taking notes as usual during this interview. Rosenberg turned to me and said with an ironic smile, "You always take notes when we talk. I don't care, in fact I am glad. But please take them accurately. Anyway, why do you take these notes?" I explained that I took notes in order to be as accurate as possible because I wanted to be able to refer to the interviews I had had with him and many other prominent political figures so that in the event of my ever writing something or being asked about such men as Rosenberg or Goering or the military people of Germany, I could base my remarks on their actual words, rather than on any vague impressions I may gather.

Rosenberg seemed satisfied with this explanation. He repeated, "As I said, I am grateful that you do take notes, but I do wish that you take them accurately and not misrepresent my rather complex theories and reasoning. After all, I am a philosopher and a student, and my thoughts may be complex. If at any time you don't follow me, please interrupt, and I will explain further. I have to smile when some of the defendants say in court that they never read my books or works, because it is a reflection on their inabilities to follow a philosophic trend of thought, which to the common man is much too deep and profound. It is difficult for one to express important opinions and theories scientifically and at the same time use simple construction. However, I have always tried to be as lucid as possible and I never strived to make my work or writings beyond the comprehension of the normally intelligent man."

We continued our discussion about political systems. "I am of the opinion that the seizing of power by the National Socialist Party by force would have been wrong. The National Socialists were elected legally in 1933 and there was no revolutionary movement such as in Bolshevik

Russia. I am also convinced that National Socialism achieved power because Germany in 1933 was poverty-stricken and close to civil war."

I asked Rosenberg whether he thought that if perchance Germany had become democratic in 1933, he might have adopted democratic ideas. He did not answer directly but it was obvious that as a fighter and writer for totalitarianism for many years before the Nazis came to power, he had no potential for democratic sympathy. But he did say, "For fourteen years Germany had a democratic administration. It failed. There are many party factions. The National Socialist Party was elected by the majority of the votes in what is called a democratic manner. As a matter of fact, if we had had the English or American election law system, the entire Reichstag would have consisted of National Socialist members and no others. In France and in Germany there is a law of proportion whereby members of rival parties achieve seats in the parliament if they receive the majority of votes in the particular section of the country from which they come. The National Socialist Party came to power in a legal way because it was the strongest party in the election.[3]

"In the preceding fourteen years, the democratic administration in Germany had left us 7 million unemployed, 6 million Communist votes, and firms which were in a bankrupt state — a total of firms bankrupt as big as the entire state of Württemberg.[4] In such a situation, the state had to place large and authoritative orders for the purpose of doing away with unemployment and to avoid civil war. In every state, laws must be made which cannot be voted upon if the situation of the state is critical. Even your President Truman recently had to threaten to take over the railroads because the workers threatened to strike. That's a small example, but if a general strike occurs, or a similar emergency, the government has to step in.

"There were many Americans who were prejudiced against National Socialism but who visited Germany and then returned to the United States fully convinced that Germany could not live under the Versailles Treaty. I can mention men like Averell Harriman and Curley, the mayor of Boston.[5] Similarly in England, members of the British Parliament made speeches in which they said that it was impossible to burden the German people by taking away our colonies and the other restrictions imposed upon us by the Versailles Treaty.

"The tribunal here and your American newspapers talk so much about our sharp Nazi methods, but do you realize that within the past year, since the defeat of Germany, 1 million Germans have been evicted from what was originally German territory and which has now been given to Poland? No League of Nations or other body intervened."[6]

Didn't Rosenberg know that it was understandable from a psychological standpoint that the Poles should evict Germans after the cruelties which had been inflicted upon them by the Germans during the war? Rosenberg evaded this question and, as was his custom, turned to another point of argument. "Do you remember the history of what happened from 1919 after the last war to 1932? During those years Germans also were evicted from territories given to Poland by the Versailles Treaty. These territories were taken away from Germany without legality and without fairness. Your representative General Tasker Bliss of the United States acknowledged this at the Versailles convention.[7] General J. C. Smuts of South Africa wrote to your President Wilson at the time that if the Versailles Treaty were carried out, it would abrogate the Wilson treaty. Smuts referred to the agreement between England, France, and America of November 1918, when Wilson's Fourteen Points were adopted. As a matter of fact, these Fourteen Points were thoroughly talked over and only twelve of them were approved.

"The Versailles Treaty was an international violation of Wilson's Fourteen Points. Even the very people who devised the Versailles Treaty later recognized the error of their ways. Prime Minister Georges Clemenceau of France was mainly responsible. Britain's Lloyd George was against the Versailles agreement. It is my impression that President Wilson, who was also present, likewise opposed it."

We talked of many other things. But I asked him about his own case, and what he thought of his defense. He seemed satisfied with it and apparently was under the impression that he had given a good account of himself in court. I said that I thought that his references to the inaccuracy of the Russian translation, a charge he made several times while on the witness stand, was rather puzzling psychologically since it seemed so far beside the point at the time. Rosenberg smiled wisely and said, "Anything I can say against the Russians I shall always say. I was listening with one ear to the German words and I had my earphones tuned to the Russian translation. They made many mistakes and although I knew that it did very little good to call attention to them, I did it nevertheless because I wanted those Russians to know that I understood their language and I wanted the American, British, and French judges to know that these Russians were trying to place the worst possible light on my words." I asked him to give me some specific examples of the inaccuracies which he heard in the Russian translation. He seemed uninterested and pushed the inquiry aside by saying, "I can't remember. It didn't make any difference anyway except that it showed up those Russians to the other translators in the courtroom."

# Fritz Sauckel
## 1894–1946

Fritz Sauckel was general plenipotentiary for labor mobilization from 1942 to 1945. Found guilty at Nuremberg of war crimes and crimes against humanity, he was hanged on October 16, 1946.

## February 9, 1946

I had a long interview today with this man, former minister of labor, with the aid of the interpreter, Triest. Sauckel spoke some English and seemed to comprehend more. He was a short man, probably five nine, stocky, with a bulldog-shaped head, closely cropped hair with some central baldness, and a thick neck. He wore a small Charlie Chaplin/Hitler–type mustache. He appeared tense but controlled, smiled often and nervously. His hands fluttered a bit toward the beginning of the interview, but this ceased once he began to talk freely. He had been a Nazi since 1925 or 1926. He considered himself a laboring man, a seaman, "with the workingman's point of view." Many of his utterances today seemed almost automatic responses, as if he had used the phrases, clauses, and sentences so often in the past, both in private and public speeches, that they came effortlessly to him. His clichés and platitudes were those heard again and again from the rationalizing postwar Nazis of the Nuremberg prison. The main stream of thought which he presented today consisted of the following currents:

- National Socialism did a good job in Germany until the latter years of the war, when too many enemies of Germany banded against her.

- The excesses, atrocities, exterminations within and without the concentration camps were unknown to honorable men like himself, and could be attributed to Himmler, who apparently was not a good man.
- The causes of the war lay in the Versailles Treaty and the economic depression within Germany ever since the end of the last war, augmented by the failure of other countries to buy German products in exchange for wheat, without which Germany would starve. There was a virtual boycott of Germany.
- Anti-Semitism was not Sauckel's department, and the specialists in that were Streicher and Rosenberg, who had devoted almost their entire lives to the subject; but he, Sauckel, believed it was brought on because there was too high a percentage of Jews in positions of prominence in Germany, in state offices, professions, the stage, radio, and so forth. Sauckel stated that the Jews were not really persecuted until late in the war, 1942 perhaps, and then it was a part of the general "war psychology" and not really known to him or other Germans, but again the work of Himmler. Sauckel's conscience was clear, and he would do anything he had done over again because it all had been honorable.

True, he had 5 million foreign workers under him in Germany — but 2 million of these were volunteers.[1] And France, which had its own government (Vichy), sent Frenchmen to work in Germany, though "some" were not volunteers. Of the 3 million nonvoluntary workers, "All were treated well, all had insurance benefits just as German workers, had good food and clothing." That will all be "proven with documentary evidence in court" when his defense arises. Besides, what would you do, he asked, if your country was at war and its welfare depended on the importation of foreign workers?

He was born in Hassfurt, near Schweinfurt, on October 27, 1894. His father was a postman of limited education and income. His mother had heart trouble as a result of his birth, and she was never well as long as he could recall. He described his father as "diligent and conscientious," his mother as "loving and kind." He said that despite his parents' poverty he was encouraged to attend school, but that after five years of schooling, he decided to go to sea because it would lighten the family financial burdens, especially in view of his mother's invalidism. His mother descended from a seafaring family, and he felt that his mother's blood influenced his decision. His father, on the other hand, was descended from a line of farmers.

At the age of fifteen, he shipped out of Hamburg, with his parents' permission, as cabin boy on a Norwegian three-masted schooner. He sailed to Montreal, Dublin, Oslo, Haiti, the West Indies, and Le Havre. Next he worked on a Swedish three-master, mostly in the Baltic and North Seas. In January 1912 he was shipwrecked off the Scottish coast. Soon after, he sailed on the largest German sailboat, from Hamburg to Philadelphia, thence to the Cape of Good Hope, Japan, and across the Pacific to Portland, Oregon. During a storm off Portland, he struck the top of his head and was treated in an American hospital in Portland by an American doctor. In 1914 he was seized with the rest of the crew from a ship en route to Australia. He was interned in France as a prisoner of war for five years, until 1919. He feels that this was tragic in that he had just saved sufficient money for furthering his nautical education, and had completed his seaman's apprenticeship. During his years in France he took certain courses in mathematics and national economy offered by a Swiss educational service set up for the POWs. He was treated poorly during the first three years, better the last two years of internment.

Upon returning to Germany in 1919 he found that there was no longer opportunity for German navigation and that his savings were worthless because of the monetary inflation. He became a laborer in a ball-bearing plant at Schweinfurt. In the factory there were "many divisions of thought, such as Communists, Social Democrats, Nationalists, Syndicalists." He felt "unhappy because of the poor conditions of the German people, and almost left Germany."

He married in 1923. He had known his wife since 1913, when he met her while on shore leave. He neither saw nor heard from her until his return from France in 1919. It was another four years before they married. There were religious differences, for one thing, in that she was Catholic and he was Lutheran. His family objected on those grounds, but his wife's "charm" finally overcame these objections. Her father, he found out sometime after he began courting her seriously, was a worker in the same factory as himself, and was "a confirmed Social Democrat." His wife, prior to their marriage, held a good position in a paint factory and assisted in the support of her parents and younger siblings. She was about a year his junior, and he depicted her as a very brave, faithful woman, who suffered much during her life, enduring poverty and the bearing of his ten children.

His oldest child, a son, would have been twenty-one this year. He was killed when shot down as a fighter pilot. His next oldest son, the third child, he believed was in an American POW compound in northern France, according to a report someone transmitted to his wife. He seemed anxious about this, and hoped for some definite information about that son. In all he had two daughters and eight sons. His youngest child was a boy of six. He had a picture of his ten progeny standing in line, each a little taller than the next, which he displayed on his table in the cell. There was also a picture of his wife surrounded by his four oldest children.

After laboring for two and a half years in the factory at Schweinfurt, he attended five semesters of an engineering school in Thuringia. Things in Germany were "very bad." There were many political parties, strikes, picket lines, and a lack of financial stability. "If someone had told me," he said, "while I was a prisoner in France, or before, that someday I would engage in political activity, I would have said he was crazy. But I felt forced into such activity because of the bad conditions within Germany."

His sister-in-law emigrated to America, as did many other Germans, but Sauckel felt this would have been "desertion." In his spare time he read Marx, Bakunin, and Hitler's speeches. He felt he must belong to some party. He rejected Marxism for three reasons, as follows: First, his personal religious upbringing and the fact that his wife had suffered because her father, a Social Democrat, was not religious. "And Marxism stated that religion is opium." Second, he could not agree that "property is theft," which is also a Marxian slogan. Third, mostly he objected to the idea of a class struggle, as it would lead to civil war. He decided finally to become a National Socialist because of Hitler's ideas of national unity, his promise of improving social standards and unifying intellectuals and workers.

"After my two and a half years in the ball-bearing plant, while I studied in engineering school, came a time of poverty for myself and my family." He had married in 1923, and although he was already a Nazi, he did not think in terms of holding a political position himself. He remained in Thuringia, which in 1922 had been known as Red Thuringia because of its leftist government. In 1923 Nationalists and National Socialists were elected in Thuringia for the first time, and soon it became a bulwark of National Socialism. In his spare time Sauckel did propaganda and organizational work. In 1925, when Hitler was released from prison and reorganized his party, Sauckel resumed his membership. He felt Hitler was "the man chosen by fate to unite Germany." Sauckel became district business leader of the Nazi Party that year at a salary of 150 marks monthly. He "never thought of war or the necessity for violence." Hitler had said that he wanted to achieve unity through nonviolent methods. In 1927 Sauckel became district leader of Thuringia, and in 1929 faction leader in the Landtag. In 1932 he was elected on a popular ticket as minister-president of Thuringia. At several points in the interview he inconsistently reiterated that he "never thought of a political career." He repeated this so often it became conspicuous: he admitted that he began to think of politics in 1920 or thereabouts and attended party meetings in 1923, after moments previously he had said that his thoughts turned to political action just when he returned to Germany from France.

This election in 1932 was his "only political activity," Sauckel insisted. He meant that it was the only time he was elected to office. He described that election campaign and its aftermath, his successful election, as "one of the most difficult mental and physical strains" he ever experienced. In other words, all his previous and following positions were appointments, whereas in 1932 he was elected. "The way was paved in 1932" with all parties in Thuringia behind his candidacy (he ran on a combined ticket) except for the Communists.

The economic conditions in Thuringia upon his election were "very bad." There were many closed factories and 500,000 unemployed; at another time he said one-third of the male population was unemployed. He inaugurated an emergency work program, financed a loan of 2 million marks from the Dresdner Bank through an old friend, who had been a fellow prisoner of his in France. He presented a report to Hindenburg on the needs of Thuringia.

While Sauckel did these things to help Thuringia, Hitler came to power a short time later, in 1933. In May 1933, Sauckel became governor of Thuringia through a document signed by Hindenburg (his calling attention to Hindenburg's signature was of interest as he admitted he was really appointed by Hitler). He repeated in oratorical yet simple style, with clipped German, that he desired only to bring about happiness and economic prosperity to Thuringia. He said it was his desire to "preserve the cultural, artistic, and traditional values of the greater Germany." During these efforts he "never thought of war," and he assumed that Hitler had the same aspirations. Sauckel disclaimed much contact with Berlin in those days or until much later. He did disagree with Himmler, Goebbels, and Bormann at times, but the nature or extent of the disagreements were vague, and apparently too unclear even in Sauckel's own mind at this time. Hitler himself he saw rarely, and he regretted this, because he was always "a devout follower and obedient."

He emphasized the same thing I've heard from Ribbentrop, Frank, and others, that he volunteered for army (in Sauckel's case he said navy) duty with the outbreak of war in 1939. But the request was denied. He was charged with caring for the economic and social well-being in Thuringia and on the borders of that province. Unexpectedly, then, in 1942 he received what he was again prone to call "the hardest assignment of my life" when he was called to Berlin to take charge of labor "deployment." He "had to obtain and place millions of laborers for German war leaders in various fields of the economy." The Führer told him he had "a soldier's job to do." He claimed that "both in written orders and oral commands he upheld the rights and protected the interests of not only German, but also foreign workers." He talked of "the solidarity of the European laboring man," and so forth.

I asked him what he knew of the reports of the mistreatment of slave labor, of families being cruelly separated in occupied countries and the able ones brought as workers to Germany, and of people having been seized in theaters and public places and shipped without notice as workers to Germany. His reply was evasive. "What would you do if your country's welfare depended on labor? When a ship is in a storm it requires one captain." These and other evasive non sequiturs were his stock in trade, and method of parrying vital moral and ethical points.

In 1935 Sauckel was appointed by Hitler as honorary member of the Gustloff Works, and while a member of this Sauckel tried to build a subterranean airplane factory in 1944 "according to my own engineering ideas."[2] Sauckel frequently referred to himself as a worker, a seaman, or an engineer.

What was his attitude toward the Jews? Was his family anti-Semitic? No, he recalled no particular anti-Semitism on his father's part. His father later became a party member, and so naturally shared the party ideas on the Jewish question. But in years gone by, when Sauckel was a child, he could recall no particular anti-Semitism. In general, however, he believed that the Jewish question "had to be handled," that even among Jews there were the Zionists who agreed that Jews are a race and should have their own land. As for extermination of the Jews, he was not in favor of it, and knew of no Jewish persecutions in Thuringia while he was there. What happened later, after he went to Berlin in 1942, he could not say. Indeed he knew the concentration camp Buchenwald had been there once in the early years, but that was "Himmler's territory" and not his. Although Buchenwald was in Thuringia he had no jurisdiction over it.

He attributed all his work to the highest of ideals, a devotion to Hitler, and the idea of unifying German life. He tried to glorify his own simple beginnings and use them as a raison d'être for his political convictions. He repeated proudly his not owning any property; having had no large sums in a bank; his wife's bearing their ten children almost without medical aid, at home; his avoidance of social functions; and his choice of a simple way of life.

His attitude toward Hitler was still that of the blindly loyal servant. Nothing that transpired at the trial thus far seemed to have changed his evaluation of Hitler. He did say that some of the "little things that have come out thus far in the trials are incomprehensible," but that did not seem to seriously affect his view of Hitler. As with so many of his followers, Hitler kept Sauckel at a distance, and was never intimate with him. At the times Hitler saw him it was to give him a direct order or policy, or to discuss literature, art, and music, things which were completely out of Sauckel's sphere of intellectual development, and thus probably made the Führer seem all the more wondrous. His attitude toward other Nazis was unoriginal and consisted of the same platitudes I had heard so often in the Nuremberg prison. "Himmler, Bormann, and Goebbels, they were probably bad fellows." Shifting the buck, especially to those who were dead or have disappeared, is as characteristic of Sauckel as of many of the others. He said that he never approved of these men or understood them, but on the other hand he had no occasion to negate their policies or object to their doings, because it wasn't his work. Asked if the slave labor which he controlled and Himmler's activities didn't in many ways relate to each other, he denied this vigorously. What about in the procuring of the laborers? "No." He considered the three men Himmler, Bormann, and Goebbels responsible for the isolation of Hitler. This last was a refrain I had heard before. He believed the "estrangement from Christianity" was the greatest error, and attributable to Bormann.

Sauckel admits he left the church, too, but that basically and within the confines of his family, he remained "deeply religious." Just what he means by that term I could not find out, and it was my impression that he was mouthing words that sounded nice and were part of the general picture he was trying to represent: a good, solid worker who was so busy doing good that he went along with the party, despite certain unsavory businesses which he sensed, because of his ideals.

Toward the end of the war, the fall of Thuringia was imminent and Sauckel saw Albert Kesselring. Even then he hoped some armistice or adjustment with the western powers was possible. It was again an instance of how little knowledge these men had of the overall picture of the war or of international events. On the eighth or ninth of May he was at Berchtesgaden and voluntarily gave himself up, through the Catholic parson there, to the Americans. He "returned to the arms of the church" then, he said. These statements were not made with much feeling, but rather in clipped sentences easy to understand, as if he were making a public address.

He was very unhappy and depressed at first over the war's loss. But now he felt better, and "secure in the knowledge" that he has "personally done nothing to be ashamed of." If he went "before God or the highest court" he could go with a "confident heart." Love had always been in his heart, not hate. Hate was too much present in the last few years, the war years, not before, among the Nazis. Then he uttered much platitudinous material that amounted to God is love, and without love nothing can be accomplished, and so on.

"I always tried to bring understanding between the Russians and the Germans and therefore I don't fear the Russian case which began yesterday. I can prove it. After I took office in 1942 as general plenipotentiary for labor, I tried to get billets and food for Russian POWs.

"I had nothing to do with concentration camps — Himmler's work. There was a labor minister, Ley, whose position is like your John Lewis in America.[3] My duties were to assign POW and foreign labor to factories or whatever work had to be done. I had nothing to do with punishment, criminals, and so forth. That's Himmler's work. If someone had told me as a seaman I should have engaged in politics I would have taken it as an insult. After my return from France, when I found the workers in the Schweinfurt factory all divided up into groups, many parties — I want to give you an honest reason — that's why I became a

National Socialist. In 1922–23 I knew, by fate, I must find a solution to the labor and social problem.

"I strove for socialism on a national basis without taking away private property.

"I knew Hitler well, since 1926, but although I had many talks with him, I did not have so much to do with him as others had. Hitler came to Weimar, the capital of Thuringia, and we discussed Goethe and culture.

"The Reichstag met less and less often after the Reichstag fire, but it was still semi-alive in 1933–34. Thereafter there was seldom a Reichstag meeting. The Führer always told me the authority he wielded and I wielded were necessary.

"I'm sure most of the Nazis wanted a parliament or some kind of institution of criticism or correction. Hitler always promised a big senate aside from the Reichstag, for the German people. He never kept that promise. That he never did depressed Hitler but he always brought up the excuse, namely, that during a war such an institution could not be established. I'm quite sure after the war some people including those like myself would have to manage such an institution.

"Up to 1940 I could still approach the Führer. But not afterward — particularly after Hess flew to England. Bormann, Goebbels, and Himmler kept him in isolation, which was bad for the German people.

"I'm convinced that Hess was a good influence on Hitler. I can only say what I heard myself. In a lot of things, like the occupation of Austria, he didn't know any more about it than I did.

"Everybody followed a rule, a very strict rule, to do his own work, and not interfere with or talk with others.

"I believe Hess was very just. I personally feel Hess wanted a peace treaty with England." I remarked that in the trial it was said that he wanted a treaty with the fascists in England and would not deal with the Churchill government. "I can't tell. I don't know what Hess thought of it. Personally I wanted to go to sea again but Hitler didn't let me." At this point Sauckel was close to tears. "Hitler told me I shouldn't go to sea because the sea was England's business, not Germany's.

"Hess always had a saying, 'National Socialism is not a thing for export,' so Hess didn't want to interfere with the affairs of other nations. I can't say much except I don't think Hess would want to sign a peace with a government other than the government the English people wanted. If Hess was wrong it was just an error. He was well intentioned.

Anyway in court at lunch the other day, Hess told me he did not demand this when he went to England. Hess is a clever man, was born in Egypt, and should know the English people, among whom he was reared."

I said that if Sauckel considered Hess such a good man, when he was associated with the Nuremberg Laws, persecution of Jews and other religious sects, and connected with fifth column activities, it indicated Sauckel approved these actions. "As far as the fifth column, I never heard of it. We had a union of Germans in other countries, a union of Germans in foreign countries — it's the perfect right of any nation to nationalize people in other lands if they are German citizens. This organization was headed by Ernst Wilhelm Bohle. It was an organization of party members in foreign lands. I see no reason why Germans can't do it, if there is a Communist International, and if England has people unified in all parts of the world. It is now clear that there was a fifth column but I never knew of it. And besides, it was just like England and America having intelligence services, so why can't Germany, too?" I said I thought that an intelligence service and a fifth column were not the same thing. "Well, there are Germans in all countries — you can't brand them all as fifth columnists." I replied that we don't — just those who worked against democracy.

He said, "There was no intention to go against democracy in other countries. I would have seen it as madness to try to force a German political belief on other people. I saw Fritz Kuhn's name in the papers at times.[4] His function was to make National Socialism popular in America. We National Socialists never had a remarkable organization, like the Communist International [Comintern]. Thuringia was Communist when I first went there in 1922. I *know*. I *lived* in Germany!" He became quite excited in a theatrical manner. I asked him if the large Communist vote in Thuringia meant the influence of the Comintern. "Sure. All the people had to do was read Marx or the *Communist Manifesto*."

I said that *Mein Kampf* and other Nazi books were available in America. Why didn't Nazis become stronger in America? Sauckel did not reply. I asked him, how did the Comintern influence the Communist vote in Thuringia? "With propaganda, gold, and agents. Whether documents to prove this exist or not is not important. It's fifteen years since then." I asked him what proof he had of the influence of the Comintern other than Goebbels's opinion. "Any opinion is honorable. I had many friends who were Communists and Social Democrats."

I said that Goering asserted he built concentration camps for Communists. Did Sauckel have any comment? "Only Communists and Social Democrats who acted against the state were incarcerated. Most of the Communists and Social Democrats I had known became Nazis later. Only those who were doing anything against the state were thrown in concentration camps.

"I have heard in the trials about the crimes against the churches. This is not so. In 1933 the church received 135 million marks from the Reich. In 1934 and 1935 this sum increased. In 1938 it was 580 million marks. The same year the colonies contributed 7 million marks, and communities 85 million marks. All this was a contribution from the state to the church. The National Socialist regime believed in complete freedom of church and belief." I asked him about the Jewish religion. "According to National Socialism the Jews were not looked on as a religious sect but as an enemy race. It's a big point — even the Jews don't agree. The Zionists say they are a nation; others say they should stay where they are. Bormann's and Hitler's policies were false, however."

I remarked that freedom of religion and burning of synagogues seemed inconsistent. "I never burned down synagogues. It was a revolution, and Russians burned churches during their revolution. If there are many different nationalities in a country, the leadership should be divided among people by percentages. In finance, press, radio — the Jews had taken over positions. That feeling existed before Hitler."

I asked if he had been anti-Semitic before his association with Hitler. "Don't ask me. Ask Rosenberg and Streicher, they are specialists in it. I was a prisoner in France for years. Since 1924–25 I was a Nazi. I followed anti-Semitism because of social feelings.

"For most of the people, workers like myself, National Socialism was to prevent class hatred between labor and the bourgeoisie. In Russia there are only forty people per square kilometer, in Germany there are one hundred and forty people per square kilometer. I don't know about the figures in England, but English workers can go to Africa, Canada, or Australia. I read a book by Jack London about conditions in London and Liverpool. It was about the same as in Germany.

"You must understand that the meaning of the word 'unemployed' in Germany is different than in America. In America, 'unemployed' means that a man may be unable to obtain work in his profession. In Germany it means he can't get work in any profession. In Thuringia there were 1.7

million people, of whom 500,000 men were unemployed in 1932 before Hitler came to power. In the whole of Germany there were 8 million unemployed and 7 million half-time workers.

"America is so big that it cries for work. In Germany, if you tried to find work, you couldn't. In America it was a strange economy which caused unemployment. German unemployment was due to the boycott of German goods. Not an official boycott. The world market refused to accept German goods. France, England, and America refused. Germany had no colonies and she had to export manufactured goods for grain. We had nothing to speak of. We managed to live during the war by rations. We all lived on a strict ration — even ministers in the government like myself — and we lived on things from the conquered countries, including Africa and Russia."

I noted that, as I understood it, for about fourteen years Sauckel was fairly well off. "I've always been a worker, with my ten children. I never became a rich man in my office. I lived on property owned by the state. I had no bank account. I possessed nothing, not even a garden."

I asked Sauckel what he thought of the evidence brought up in court in the last weeks about Goering and his art plundering. "Goering took these things for art galleries. Goering comes from a great family. I didn't know Goering and don't know his habits. If he took things for his own benefit, the German people will condemn him.

"The 5 million foreign laborers got the same treatment as Germans. You must differentiate between Himmler's treatment and my treatment of foreign labor. There were about 2 million voluntary workers; the other 3 million came to Germany by law." I inquired what he meant by "by law." "Well, the French had a government, for instance, and they made these people come to Germany." I asked whether in his opinion it was a good law. "If you were a German, and upon the execution of that law depended the welfare of a nation, wouldn't you do the same? We fought against Russia, and Russia is doing the same thing now. I know it from many sources." I said that he had been in prison and solitary confinement for a long while — since the war ended. How did he know or feel so sure of these things? "I know." I said that even if Russia were doing the same thing now, which I didn't know about myself, would that make it right? "No. But if we had not had foreign labor we would have had to capitulate to the Russians and the whole of Europe would be Sovietized."

I said I thought that Germany declared war on Russia. "Yes. But the psychology we were all under was that Russia had tremendous armies waiting to attack us, and it was only a question of who would strike first. Russia did the same thing with its attack on Bessarabia in 1940–41, and in Finland. And they took slave labor from those countries. And also many millions of Chinese laborers." I asked if it was forced labor. "That I don't know."

# Hjalmar Schacht
## 1877–1970

Hjalmar Schacht was president of the Reichsbank until 1939 and minister without portfolio until January 1943. Tried by the Nuremberg tribunal, he was found not guilty.

**January 27, 1946**

I saw Hjalmar Schacht again today. He was the same as ever — the hail-fellow-well-met, indignant at his being accused as a war criminal. He repeated the word "Frightful!" several times in the course of the interview, and reiterated that this is his tenth month in Allied prison and that before that he spent ten months in prison on orders of Hitler.

He spoke as if he were Hitler's archenemy, yet he was minister of economics and president of the Reichsbank for at least five or six years of Hitler's regime, and remained minister without portfolio until 1943. He explained this by saying that Hitler would not relieve him of that title. I asked him whether he requested to be relieved and he said, "Repeatedly, but Hitler wouldn't allow it. All I did was live on my little farm outside Berlin. Hitler retained me as minister without portfolio because of my international reputation and the prestige of my name abroad."

Schacht told me again of his meeting Roosevelt in 1934 and 1935, and how much he admired our president. For probably the fourth time Schacht told me that Roosevelt slapped his thigh, saying, "I appreciate your frankness in this meeting." At that time when he was in Washington, Schacht said, "at great personal risk I met with influential Jews and addressed them." Just what he said he did not mention, but he emphasized that it was "a risky business" for him to address Jews because of the nature of the Nazi government.

Schacht went on to expatiate on how he had met most of our American presidents, including Theodore Roosevelt, Calvin Coolidge, Franklin D. Roosevelt, and others. He regretted to say that he had never met Harding. He characterized Herbert Hoover as being "an honest man but a little cold and difficult to talk to because Hoover was socially shy. Coolidge was very nice." I asked Schacht whether he knew the late Ambassador Dodd, whose posthumous diary I had read some time ago. Schacht replied, "Oh, yes, indeed. Dodd died soon after he left Germany. Do you know perchance of what he died? Did he by any chance have a mental illness? Because Dodd, though undoubtedly an honest man, behaved queerly in Germany and never drew the right conclusions from what he saw. Besides, his children, William and Martha Dodd, were quite bad. They were full of Communist ideas." Schacht went on to state with a slight smile that Martha Dodd was constantly in the company of Louis Ferdinand, the son of the ex–crown prince of Germany. Schacht said that this companionship gave rise to some "ugly rumors." "Besides," said Schacht, "Ambassador Dodd's diary is questionable because it was issued after his death by his radical children."

Schacht repeated his indignation "that a man who has never been associated with anything but high finance for forty years, and who was never a soldier and never did anything to hurt anyone, should be locked up and tried as a common war criminal." Again he repeated that he did nothing but live on his farm since 1939, and besides, he was a party to the plot to assassinate Hitler on July 20, 1944.

It becomes obvious in talking to Schacht that he is attempting to devise two distinctly paradoxical pictures of himself: the one, that he was a harmless old man who had been inactive since 1939; the other, a picture of a great national German patriot who worked ceaselessly for Hitler's downfall and frustration, and was actively a participant in the assassination attempt of July 20, 1944. Clinically, it is obvious that Schacht has tremendous energy and vitality for a man of his years.

Regarding the Jewish question, Schacht said again that he never subscribed to race persecution. Of course, during his time as economics minister and Reichsbank president, from 1933 to 1938, Jews "were not hurt in any way economically or financially." Schacht said that he could not hold himself responsible for any Jewish persecution, looting, or whatever occurred during those years, because it was not within his province or jurisdiction. He repeated that he had many Jewish friends that he helped in one way or another, mostly by getting them out of Germany. "The Jewish problem was caused by several things. Of course, Hitler was always anti-Semitic, but immediately prior to his coming to power, many Jews were involved in large scandals of a financial nature in Germany. Moreover, many Jews were coming from the East to settle in Germany and doing business. Besides, there were so many Jews who were Communists."

Schacht said that he once told one of his assistants, a Jew, to take a message to the Central Union of Jews in Germany, which was the leading Jewish organization within Germany.[1] The message stated that the Central Union should adopt a resolution against Jews being Communists, and that they should forswear any connection with Communism. The man returned in a few days and said that he was sorry but the Central Union refused to consider action on Schacht's recommendation. "Well," said Schacht, "I said then that someday they would regret it." Schacht did not specify when this purported incident took place.

I remarked that it seemed to me a violation of civil liberties and individual rights for an organization to forbid its members freedom of political thought and that therefore I thought that Schacht's recommendation to the Central Union of Jews was rather fascistic. Schacht bridled at this and said that of course he believed in freedom of political belief as well as freedom of religion. He said that he did not, however, believe in Communism and that furthermore, all he was trying to do was to save the Jews from being found identified with Communism. As the interview ended, Schacht said, "One thing I fear, that you Americans will do the same thing that you did after the last war. I mean that you will pull out of here and leave Europe, then Russia will have her way. Private enterprise and individual rights will be lost just as much as under a Nazi government. Frightful!"

**March 10, 1946**
Schacht was cordial and as usual somewhat grandiose in his manner when I entered his cell this evening. He expresses confidence in his acquittal but is bitter against the "malevolent prosecution," as he calls it. His whole attitude of "These other criminals belong in the dock but not me" is unchanged and as adamant as ever.

Schacht said he would like to tell me the "whole story" of his connections and activities with the Nazi government. His speech was punctuated with the frequent "And now, Dr. Goldensohn, where is the crime?" — followed by a scornful, high-pitched laugh.

"I helped finance armaments," he began, "intending to bring them to a level where Germany would be on an equal footing with her neighbors, from 1934 to 1937. My reason for doing so was that the other powers would not disarm — I mean the twenty-seven powers who signed the Versailles Treaty. On the contrary, Czechoslovakia armed to the teeth although it was but a newly created state. Since I wanted Germany to be on an equal footing, either these other countries had to disarm or we had to rearm. The German government told these other countries that in March 1935."

I said that I had heard from other Germans that without Schacht's financial genius in putting Germany on a sound financial footing, Nazism would not have been possible. I asked Schacht what his opinion about that view might be. "Everyone can be replaced. The year after I stopped all financing, Hitler spent five and a quarter billion marks more than during the last year when I helped him. Now, who procured that five and a quarter billion marks? The financial genius was not operating. Hitler got the money by ruthless tactics and depriving people. I did my financing by maintaining the stability of currency value and without hurting economic life in any way. Hitler took money from sources which I would never have touched — but he got the money."

I asked Schacht whether he thought, therefore, that anyone could have done what he accomplished from 1934 to 1937. "Anyone. The only honor I claimed was that Hitler would have done it unreasonably and I did it reasonably. You see, the prosecution tries to accuse me, and I laugh at all that, and then when I found that Hitler wanted to arm more than was needed to get on an equal footing with other nations, I withdrew my credit to the Reich, would not furnish one penny more, and that led to my dismissal. The note circulation when I left my post was eight billion, and it is now seventy billion." I asked him what the significance of that was and he said at once, "Inflation. Hitler abused the Reichsbank. Funk succeeded me and he could not act individually as I could and did. The Reichsbank could give or deny credit under the rules at its own discretion while I was president of it. The very day I left the Reichsbank, Hitler issued a law which obliged the Reichsbank to give any credit he would ask for. It was under that law that Funk took office. Perhaps in that sense Funk was not responsible, but in another sense, of course, he was responsible because he was a willing tool. If he went so far as to take the post, he was willing to obey."

I said I had heard that one of the reasons for his leaving the Reichsbank was a personal struggle for power between himself and Goering. Schacht emphatically denied this. "I know that is said and I know that criminal Goering tries to say that repeatedly. The truth is that my difficulties with Goering were on quite another basis. From August 1934, I was minister of economics in addition to being president of the Reichsbank. I used the minister position to object and oppose any exaggerated rearmament. Hitler disliked that very much, and so he elaborated the so-called Four Year Plan and put Goering in charge of it, and Goering was, of course, in favor of tremendously exaggerated rearmament. That was in the fall of 1936. These diverging tendencies of his and mine brought us into permanent conflict with each other, in which, of course, Goering held the stronger position because he was backed by Hitler and I wasn't. In the fall of 1937 I resigned as minister of economics. I was dismissed from the Reichsbank in January 1939.

"Of course, in all of my difficulties which appear in letters and minutes you will never find any remark that I made saying that Hitler and Goering were driving toward war. I had no proof of it and if I had said so, they would have acted drastically against me. So, I could defend my position only by economic arguments. And now, these fools of prosecutors draw the following conclusions: 'Because we do not find in any document an indication that Schacht wanted to get out because he was against war, the conclusion is that he was not against war but that he merely had quarrels with Goering.' " Again Schacht laughs in a rather forced, scornful manner.

"I laid no stress on remaining minister of economics. Hitler had asked me to take on that position and I accepted it at the time because I thought I could thereby assist my financial policy."

I asked him why he allowed himself to be used by Hitler for four or five years until 1939 if he had such a low opinion of Hitler and the criminal Nazis, as he termed them. "It will be explained in the trial in the course of my defense. Germany could maintain her feeding and housing by export trade to some extent because we were short of food by about twenty percent, which we could not produce on our own soil. Therefore, we had to export and earn money outside of Germany in order to get food. This has been so since the 1880s. Furthermore, in order to maintain our export industries, we had not only to buy foodstuffs, but we also had to purchase raw materials.

"Now what did the Treaty of Versailles do to us? It took away from Germany all of the private assets of Germans. Do you realize what this means, Dr. Goldensohn? It liquidated the private assets of German citizens, a thing which has not been done since medieval times. By this, they destroyed one of the foundations of our life. For example, if we had an import or export house in Rio de Janeiro or New York, they took away our license and put us out of business. Such losses amounted to $11 billion, aside from reparations. By doing this the Allies destroyed not only a half-billion-dollar income, but also spoiled our whole sales organization. Then, furthermore, after Versailles, they imposed reparation payments on Germany, and as we had no foreign assets anymore, we could only pay by new exports. How could we pay the Allies otherwise? Therefore, the need for export trade became more urgent since we needed foreign money in order to pay for food and raw material, as well as reparations. The reparations amounted to $50 billion in cash! Can you imagine that? That means fifty thousand million dollars.

"Now, of course, Germany could not do that. An annual amount of money and reparation payment was fixed at about a billion dollars a year, and we could not afford that. And then, you must recall that after the First World War we had for the most part socialist governments, and these socialists followed a very lighthearted policy. They borrowed money from the outside, and with that money they paid for reparations. Mostly, the money came from America, and so Germany contracted many foreign debts. During the six years 1924–29, our foreign debts were not less than $8 billion. That is exactly as much as the United States borrowed before the First World War over a period of four decades. And then came the movement when foreign creditors said that they couldn't go on, and not only stopped lending but withdrew all short credits at maturity. This led to a financial crash of frightful proportions in the summer of 1931.[2]

"Immediately after these credits were stopped, the economic situation of Germany became worse and worse. The Bruening government of the middle-class parties, the so-called bourgeois government, followed a deflationary policy. They cut wages and salaries so much that many industries collapsed; and at the same time, the Allied countries had raised customs tariffs. Finally, we arrived at a situation of more than 6 million unemployed. Now if you take into consideration the fact that the farmer is never unemployed, but that only industrial folk are, it means that every third family suffered from unemployment. Therefore, people lost confidence in the socialists as well as in the middle-class parties and went to extremes.

"There was only the choice between Communism and Hitler, and I will tell you why Hitler won. People will not give up religion, rights, freedom of personality, the opportunity to develop by individual effort — which includes private property. And the other reason for Hitler's winning is that if a whole people is treated as the Germans were, everyone will say, 'Are we worse people than others? Are we of a minor race?' Just as every single individual needs and must have self-respect, just as every family is proud of decent traditions, so every nation wants to maintain her individual manner, culture, language, and customs. It was in these respects that Communism failed. The Communists said that God was nonsense and stupidity and preached internationalism without maintaining the natural national feelings of a nation.

"And now along came Hitler and he affirmed both things which Communism denied. He proposed to safeguard the national dignity and to maintain religion. It is in his program." I remarked that this was rather ironic since the German nation under Hitler lacked dignity and was the bloodiest regime in history, and since it persecuted religion of all types and even went so far as to exterminate entire religious sects, namely, the Jews. Schacht said, "Yes, today it is ironic, but then everyone believed him. Hitler betrayed everyone and he betrayed all his principles. He gave away religion and undid nationalism. But in July 1932, Hitler obtained forty percent of all the seats in the Reichstag.[3] It had never happened before in German history that one party received so many votes. Hitler obtained 230 seats and Bruening but 70 or 75. The Communists had about 70. There are about 600 seats in the Reichstag. It is evident therefore that Hitler alone had more than all other non-Communist parties put together.

"At that time, nobody knew what kind of a bad character Hitler was. No one expected that he would betray the nation."

I asked Schacht whether he thought that it was not a particularly bad trait that Hitler was always violently anti-Semitic. He replied, "Nobody took his anti-Semitism seriously. We thought it was a political propaganda issue and would be forgotten once he got into power. As for me, being a democratic man and accustomed to democratic methods, parliamentary procedure, I was left with no choice. Either all the other parties had to combine with the Communist Party, which neither the Communists nor the other parties desired, or the leadership had to be given to Hitler."

Was there no particular objection to Hitler at the time? "I met Hitler for the first time in January 1931 and I never spoke to him or voted for him. But in July 1932 there he was, and one had to make the best of it because he was legally elected." Who did he vote for? "I voted for a democratic party — the Bruening party was a Catholic one and I did not vote for that, but it was one of the parties that belonged to the Bruening coalition.

"Was there any other choice? What should I have done? I ask you, Dr. Goldensohn, where is the crime?" I replied that as an American, if he really wanted to know the honest answer to his questions, my opinion was that if he really disapproved of Hitler, he could have refused to enter the government; and in fact, since it was no mystery as to the type of fascist Hitler was, even as far back as 1925 after *Mein Kampf* was published, one could have told him to go to H. Schacht disagreed. "Yes, and if I told him to go to hell, I would have to retire to the position of a private citizen. I wanted to work for my country." I said that I didn't follow his argument because was it in the interest of Germany to have Hitler as its leader? "It turned out that it was not in Germany's interest, but I did not know that at the time." I proceeded along this theme and asked, if Hitler had succeeded in winning the war and in building a powerful fascist Germany, whether he would say that therefore Hitler was a desirable leader for the German nation. "You are implying that I am a fascist, but my dear doctor, there was only one way out, and that was to establish a military, nondemocratic type of government, and we tried that. You would be surprised. In December 1932, Hindenburg made General Schleicher chancellor after Papen was overthrown. And mind you, Papen was overthrown by the Reichstag and the Communists and by Hitler. But when Schleicher assumed the Chancellery, he found that to rule without parliament — that is, a government by military force — would lead to civil war. The Schleicher government lasted not quite two months. When they saw that rule by such methods would lead to civil war, they abandoned it and changed their minds.

"Then Hindenburg was obliged to accept Hitler in order to remain within parliamentary lines. In order not to let him reign alone, small parties of the right made a coalition with him, in order to participate with Hitler in the government, and to influence him thereby. In the elections of March 5, 1933, the National Socialists alone obtained 280 seats, which was very near the absolute majority, even if you include the Communists.[4]

"All of this was done within the lines of the Weimar constitution — along democratic parliamentary lines." I said that I was very much interested in Schacht's observations and opinions. But was he sure of his facts? It seemed to me that Hitler already had some strong-arm organizations, such as the SA and SS, by that time. I asked him whether there were not some elements of coercion about the elections. Schacht replied, "If so, am I to blame for that?" I said that I had not implied that he was to blame for it, but he had made the statement that everything "had been done along democratic parliamentary lines." Schacht said, "I believe there was an SA and SS operating, but I mean that the elections themselves were seemingly fair."

I said it was puzzling to me that Schacht seemed to ignore the fact that Hitler had written *Mein Kampf* and that in it were contained the Führer principles and the concept of the *Volk,* and anti-Semitism, and national superiority, and inferiority ideas, and similar fascistic matters. Schacht said, "Yes, you can blame me for going into it in the first place, but don't forget that political activities and actions are complex. People said that once Hitler achieved power, he would find himself up against so many hindrances he would never be able to accomplish his fascistic ideas.

"There is another consideration. Can you check him better by retiring and living as a private citizen and leaving him with sole power? Or isn't it much wiser to get involved and try to check him? I mean, to see how far you can influence him. That is what all of the men who remained in the cabinet did. By the way, I was not in the cabinet. But there were Papen, Neurath, and others who remained. I myself never entered the government previously because I never wanted anything to do with party politics.

"I was offered a seat in the Reichstag when I was about twenty-six years of age, and I declined. And a good many times later I declined also." I asked Schacht from what district he had been offered this seat in the Reichstag, and he replied, "Oh, several. Elections were not by districts but by lists. Once I was to be from Westphalia, another time from Schleswig-Holstein. Residency made no difference.

"So I took the post as president of the Reichsbank because it was an independent position, as I told you. Then Hitler managed, within the cabinet of which I was not a member, to establish his totalitarian state." I remarked that it was then, after Hitler managed to establish a totalitarian state, that Schacht accepted a cabinet ministry. Schacht hastened to explain. "Yes, I became minister of economics in August 1934 after Hitler had been given the two powers of the chancellery and the presidency after Hindenburg's death. But strange to say, my nomination was signed by Hindenburg and it was the last official document that Hindenburg signed." Was that document still available? "I once had it, but it is now in Russian hands, I think. It was handed to me two days after Hindenburg's death." Why did he think or how did he know it was in Russian hands? "I don't know."

Was it not true that Hitler's ruthlessness was apparent before 1937? "His amoral policy was apparent and my suspicions began in 1935 or thereabouts. I have taken every opportunity to oppose him in all of these unlawful matters, such as his persecution of the churches, the Gestapo, the Jewish question, and everything else that was against common human decency. I opposed him on these points, publicly and privately and personally to his face. Believe me or not, I was the only man who did it. No clergyman, no politician, scientist, or businessman would have dared to say to him what I publicly and privately said.

"What is the crime? Where is it?

"When I felt that he was aiming at war, I retired from the ministry. He insisted that he would accept my resignation only on the condition that I should remain minister without portfolio. His aim was to show the world that there was not any conflict between his criminal government and a responsible economist and banker who had great influence abroad — myself. Otherwise, he would not accept my resignation. And further, I stopped credits on the Reichsbank. What else could I do? Where is the crime?

"They accuse me only of planning aggressive war. In 1938 Hitler dismissed his chief of the army, General Fritsch, one of the best characters we had in the army. And he dismissed Neurath, which means he dismissed the chiefs of foreign policy and of the army.[5] Now, when I noticed that, I was sure that this man did not want to avoid war, although I knew nothing about his various communications, which were revealed later to leading military figures, that he was actually aiming and preparing for war.

"Hitler at that time was at the height of his successes in foreign policy. The foreigners had added to his success and glory to such an extent that considering the sentiments of the whole people and the younger military circles, the generals were afraid not to find the proper support. So it was Neville Chamberlain and Édouard Daladier who saved Hitler and Nazism. That is what you might call the irony of history. Now, where is the crime? And the prosecution knows all of that. They know it. I don't think they are fooled, but they are malevolent.

"I tried to do something during the war several times, and again with Field Marshal Erwin von Witzleben, the last attempt being July 20, 1944.[6] I was imprisoned two days later. Hitler arrested six thousand people in connection with that attempt. You can see that not all of these six thousand knew about the *Attentat*. Now, where is the charge of aggressive war against me?"

I asked him why, if he thought so badly of Hitler and Nazism, he did not leave the country just as many self-respecting Germans who disagreed with Hitler for what he had done. I mentioned for example, the writer Thomas Mann. Schacht replied, "Thomas Mann is a very unhappy man. I often thought of it. What good do emigrants do? Thomas Mann served no good. Before the war, but after Hitler came to power, my Jewish friends in Switzerland told me that they would come back to Germany if they could, even if forced to do so creeping on all fours. But that was before the war. Now I would advise none of these Jews to return, because Germany is an atrocious place to be. It is a great pity for Germany. German culture and the German people have lost tremendously by the fact that the great German Jewish families are no longer in Germany. They were a great contribution to our knowledge and culture. By the way, the prosecution does not accuse me of anti-Jewish behavior, so there is no need for me to defend myself in that regard."

I said I had heard from other defendants that some definitely anti-Semitic laws had been promulgated by the Ministry of Economics under Schacht, and that many people considered these anti-Jewish rulings, which dispossessed the Jews economically, to be the beginning of the persecution that eventually led to extermination, mass murder, and the rest. Schacht was indignant. "Who told you that?" I said that I had no reason to withhold the name of the man who made that comment since he had not asked me to keep it secret, and that actually I had heard it from two persons now in this prison. One of them was the defendant Funk, Schacht's successor, and the other was Hemmen, who had been an ambassador of the Foreign Office.[7] Schacht said, "Funk is trying to put the blame on me. Hemmen I have heard of, but he is unreliable." I asked Schacht whether he recalled any anti-Semitic economic laws which he had promulgated. "I did not call any of the laws I promulgated anti-Semitic. I did promulgate a law preventing Jews from holding civil service jobs, and limiting the number of Jews in certain business fields. I had to promote that law because I was ordered to do so. But this was not unreasonable, and I do not call that persecution."[8]

I remarked somewhat pointedly that at any rate one could hardly describe him as an ardent proponent of equal rights for all peoples. Schacht did not reply, but he went on to say, "The prosecution says that I am innocent." I asked him whether he did ever come out against anti-Semitism in any public utterance or any publication; he said with conviction, "Often." Were there any documents or other proof of that fact? He replied, "I don't know of documents. Proof of such things is difficult to obtain. But I ask you, is there any argument that shows I favor anti-Semitism?" I stated that I did not want to indulge in questioning his statements but that it seemed to me that he was not very much bothered by anti-Semitic policy, in view of the fact that he served in the Hitler government for so many years. "I stayed in the Hitler government, as I told you before, because I felt that at least one honest man in that government might serve as a check on Hitler."

I smiled at this, and Schacht asked me in a puzzled tone what I was smiling about. I replied that I was sure it was just a coincidence, but I had just recalled that the notorious SS general Erich von dem Bach-Zelewski had told me in almost the very same words that that was the reason he was in the SS. Schacht bridled. "Bach-Zelewski is a liar and a criminal — a terrible man. I repeat, he is a liar, a criminal, and a killer. I have proof of what I am saying about myself, but I know that Bach-Zelewski is a frightful liar."

Schacht was not at all pleased by my last remark. He was coldly polite when I left his cell shortly thereafter. He seems unable to brook any criticism or challenging of his stories or statements. My comments from time to time, my obvious failure to be convinced of his complete innocence and lack of guile were irritating to him, and his voice reached heights of shrillness at times. As ever, his is still the pose of outraged innocence, and the honest banker indignant.

## May 18, 1946

This afternoon we discussed some personal history, particularly regarding Schacht's family. He said, "For centuries my ancestors came from Schleswig-Holstein. Originally they were peasants and farmers, but my paternal grandfather was a physician. My grandfather was a Danish official district physician, who had eight sons and one daughter. My father was the fourth or fifth child. Three of my father's elder brothers emigrated to the U.S. and their families are still living there. Two remained here in Germany. My own father emigrated to America, became an American citizen, but after six years in the U.S. returned to Germany. Two of my older brothers were born in America. One of them is still alive, a physician in general practice in Baden-Baden. I myself was born in Schleswig-Holstein.

"My maternal grandfather was also a Danish official, by the name of Baron Eggers. He was president of police in Schleswig. His father was a famous man — a Danish minister for Schleswig-Holstein, also a baron.

"All of my mother's brothers and sisters, with the exception of one, remained in Denmark after 1864. Their families are still living there. My mother had six brothers and three sisters. One of them emigrated to the U.S. and is still there. On one of my trips to America, I met a cousin, but I don't know if he is still alive.

"My maternal great-grandfather was a great Danish financier and, like myself, was a Freemason. Ironically enough, he stabilized Danish currency. His masterpiece was the liberation of Slav farmers, in Schleswig-Holstein, with the help of a count who was another Danish minister.

"Another granduncle of mine was the discoverer and inventor of many important things in the field of electricity. One of my mother's sisters married his son. He was also a Dane. So, you can see that Denmark is my second fatherland. I have another cousin who was married to a physician in Denmark, and my other Danish relations include a pharmacist, judge, lawyer, and colonel in the Danish army."

Regarding his father, Schacht said, "My father died as a young man at the age of eighty-three in 1930. I say he was a young man because my grandfather, who always smoked a long pipe, died at the age of eighty-five. I began smoking at the age of sixteen — also a long pipe." I remarked that Goering had a long hunter's pipe which he smoked in the prison here. Schacht deprecated the length of Goering's pipe and said, "Ach! That is only a half pipe. The pipe I smoked at the age of sixteen was a really long pipe which came down to my knees. That man Goering . . . is a frightful man. It is surprising that he came from a good family, I believe, whereas Hitler didn't. But on the other hand, I don't know. I have heard that Goering spent lots of money having his family tree investigated and written up, but that it was a hard job because although his father comes from good stock, his mother was a waitress. This waitress was Goering's father's second wife. But Goering's father himself seems to have been an orderly man.

"Physically, I resemble my father rather completely, in fact, exactly. He was not quite as tall as I am. Mentally, I resemble both my father and my mother. The Schachts are witty and intelligent and so are the Eggerses. My feelings and temper are more like my mother's. My mother was cheerful, easily touched — which is my own greatest fault. She was also sentimental to some extent, and that too is something I inherited from her.

"My father, on the other hand, was industrious and orderly — and so am I. Wherever he would be placed he would find his way about; so would I. My father was very honest from his head to toe, and so am I. My father had a great feeling for right and justice and was a Freemason — and so am I."

I asked him whether he had inherited or acquired any features of either his father or mother that might be considered weaknesses. He reflected for a moment and said, "Just the tendency to softheartedness and sentimentality which were my mother's. But in all, I think I represent the best traits of both my father and my mother. As a psychiatrist, have you found it to be true that the middle child is usually the best?" I replied that I had not done sufficient research on that point to be able to answer him. At this point the guard handed Schacht some writing paper and envelopes, for which Schacht was made to sign a receipt. When the operation was concluded, Schacht said, "This man, your commanding officer, the colonel, must come from Lithuania — some of the best sergeants of the German army came from there. These men automatically make excellent soldiers, without any imagination; they were bound by the rules, they thought in uniform, and were very orderly and correct. Can you imagine making us sign a receipt that we received a piece of paper to write a letter on?" I did not reply to these cutting remarks but merely observed that Schacht seemed to take out his hostility on the commandant of the prison. I said that I thought there was probably some reason for having the defendants sign a receipt that they had received certain articles such as writing material, because of the large number of persons in the prison at the present time and to make sure that every prisoner received his allotted materials. Schacht grunted. "My watch and money were robbed here in this jail. I reported it to your colonel and he is still investigating it. It was robbed the first night I came here, I think — probably by one of your lieutenants who has since gone back to America. They never gave me a receipt for that watch or for the money. I shall demand to be repaid for this."

We returned to the subject of his father. "My father was a trained teacher but later became a businessman and was employed by the Equitable Life Insurance Company for thirty years. When he returned to Germany he gave up teaching, which he detested — and I can understand that — and obtained a job with the Equitable. The last ten years of his life were on a pension from that company. He was a man of moderate means and had built a little home which he called the Villa Equitable in Berlin. Before that, we had lived in Hamburg for a while."

Regarding his mother, Schacht said, "She died in 1938 at the age of eighty-five. She died praying, 'Our Father,' in Danish. It was interesting that her last words were in the language of her childhood. Whereas my father was very active, pushing, ingenious, always trying to find something new, my mother was more sentimental, gay, and full of feeling. She was a very faithful wife and devoted mother who concerned herself mainly with providing us with a good home and food. It was Father who always had the ideas and was constantly planning."

Schacht went on to talk of the other members of his family. He is one of six brothers. There were no sisters. Two of his brothers died in infancy. Two more died during this war. Schacht is the third child. His only living brother is the physician in Baden-Baden, now seventy-four years old but still vigorous and with a great international clientele. Years ago, he practiced in Egypt during the winters and in Baden-Baden during the summer. He is absolutely an international man, speaks seven or eight languages including Arabic, Swedish, Dutch, French, and English.

"I said before that I thought the second or third child was usually superior to the others. I believe that is true, but in my own family it does not hold because my first wife's oldest child, my oldest daughter, is the most intelligent of my children. She is married to a Bavarian official in the Ministry of Justice. I saw my son-in-law in Nuremberg early in the trial. Now I am unable to see anyone — although it has been proved in my defense that I am absolutely not guilty. My son-in-law was born in Holland. My second wife was born in Hungary but of German parents. My son speaks French and English well. He lived in Chicago for over a year because I wanted him to get American banking experience."

The rest of the interview was spent discussing the cruelness of war, with particular emphasis on the fact that Schacht disapproves of war because two of his brothers died in the war. "I was never in the army — I never had a uniform — I was never a soldier. I detest uniforms because they make one unfree. There is an old quotation that goes something like this: 'Your mind will be trained well, but confined to Spanish boots.' That quotation is very apt. It signifies how narrow the military mind becomes."

### June 9, 1946

This Sunday, Schacht was in a fairly depressed mood at the beginning of the interview, but he became more grandiose and boastful as we talked. He remarked that he always felt better after speaking with me and that he was glad that I had dropped in. He said that the meals were monotonous but the food was sufficient. He wished that he could have some jam or other sweet such as marmalade in the mornings because he needed the energy. He was pessimistic about the date for the end of the trial, which he placed at mid-September at the earliest. Previously he had been even more pessimistic, at one time saying that he believed the trials would go on until December. He felt depressed today particularly because he had just received a letter from his wife, who lives in Hollenstedt. She complained of having no money because his bank accounts are frozen, and of the very poor food situation. He said, "My wife is forty years old, a resourceful, charming woman, and it is a pity. You might be interested in knowing that the village in which she lives is a famous one, having been built in 800 by Charles the Great as a fortress against the Vikings. My poor wife lives in two small garret rooms." Whenever Schacht referred to his wife, he always added that she was forty years old.

I asked him how he thought the trials were progressing and he said, "Not badly. I think Jodl was quite dignified and put up a good defense. The English assistant prosecutor, Roberts, didn't get very far with him in the cross-examination."

I said I had recently been interviewing Oswald Pohl of the SS, who said he knew about these Reichsbank deposits from the concentration camps but that nevertheless he claimed personal innocence because he did not order the executions. "That is being foolish. Ask him his position and that is enough. I never met him. I heard his name for the first time in this court here. He was in charge of the administration of the concentration camps and had the feeding and housing of internees in his power. He must have known what happened."

I said that Pohl admitted he knew but that he simply denied having given the order and therefore disclaimed any guilt. Schacht replied in a disgusted tone, "Ach! If Hitler had given me an immoral order I would have refused. Think of it! To break teeth out of a dead body! Think of it! Why, if I had been only a simple soldier, I would not have obeyed. I would have said that it was against my religious conviction. That dog Pohl knew all about it."

Schacht asked me what I intended to do with all of the notes I had taken in the course of our conversations. He was obviously curious. I told him that I was simply trying to obtain a more or less well-rounded psychological study of him and the other important people in the prison and that that was about the extent of it. Schacht discussed the subject of psychiatry, saying he felt that it was extremely interesting. He said that for some time he had been bothered when he thought about a twenty-year-old man he once saved from a death sentence for having spoken against Hitler while this man was in a manic insane state. However, although Schacht had managed to save his life, he could not prevent the man from being sterilized. Schacht asked me whether I thought he had done the right thing — should he have intervened to save this young man's life, or was it better to die than to be sterilized? It was the type of question that required no answer. As usual, Schacht was talking for effect. He went on to expand on this little story. He said that the twenty-year-old's father had been a manic-depressive individual, and that the boy's sister had committed suicide.

"All of those laws about sterilization that Hitler introduced — I told him he shouldn't.[9] These laws were supposed to be based on popular opinion. I told him that he would have to establish a court to determine the people's opinion. Popular opinion varies. For example, the opinion of the poor is quite different from that of the rich. Another example is as follows: In Bavaria among the peasants, nobody would marry a girl until he knows that she can bear children, and the man tries before marriage. In other parts of German society that is not so." Schacht laughed in a cackling, strident manner at the described Bavarian peasant customs. "I want to add, however, that this is not a slander against Bavarians. It is considered extremely dishonorable if the man does not marry her afterward."

I asked him whether he thought in general that the morals of Germans had suffered as the result of fourteen years of National Socialism. "I doubt it. People as a whole had little to do with atrocities, except for fanatics like Bormann and the SS. Bormann was absolutely criminal. But as for the threat to morals, I think Bolshevism is much more dangerous than Nazism. I know that the Bolsheviks have never exterminated 5 million people, but aside from that single incidence, the Red idea is immoral because of its contempt for private enterprise."

I asked Schacht in what way he connected immorality with a contempt for private property. He said, "In the Russian occupation zone, laws have already been introduced to seize property without payment. In Saxony five thousand manufacturers have been deprived of property and their industries taken over by the state without any consideration. If you do away with the institution of private property, the fundamental element of social life is undermined. I am in favor of allowing everyone to become wealthy. But to take the property of another man is criminal. This was introduced by the Bolsheviks and by the Versailles Treaty. It is the greatest mistake. My feelings, Doctor, are that the only big power which tried to build up a foreign policy based on morals has been the Americans for the past thirty years.

"I was rather surprised when Justice Jackson said to me in court that I 'misled Hitler by joining his cabinet.' I replied, 'Leading, not misleading.' Justice Jackson replied ironically, 'I am glad I know your philosophy.' You know, I think Jackson is an excellent prosecutor but I doubt if he will make a good judge.

"Some remarks of Jackson's astonished me. He said, 'I have never pretended to be impartial.' Now, with us Germans, that could never happen.

A German prosecutor must try to be impartial. The judge does the questioning but it is also the case that a prosecutor must be as impartial as the judge.

"Here in this trial the judges sit back and listen and weigh the evidence. With us Germans the judges try to find the truth. The defendant's counsel as well as the prosecutor are also bound to find the truth. Here, the prosecutor conceals evidence if it is favorable for the defendant, and does not bring it before the court.

"But the judges here are favorable. The best is Francis Beverly Biddle — an excellent man." I asked Schacht what he thought of Biddle's questioning of Sauckel when the latter was on the witness stand. Schacht replied, "Excellent. Biddle was obviously so well-meaning. He was trying to find the slightest thing in favor of Sauckel, and believe me, that was hard to find with the judges and evidence they have against that man. I don't mean that Sauckel himself is bad exactly — he is a poorly educated man of poor descent. I am sure his parents never went to school, even.

"Of course, I can't form an impression of the other judges because they hardly speak. This is especially true for the Russian judges, since they never say a word. The Russian prosecution is poor. General G. A. Rudenko, the chief Russian prosecutor, is very poor. Colonel J. W. Pokrowsky is somewhat better, but the best and most intelligent prosecutor is Robert H. Jackson, with his very quick, subtle mind. The Englishman Sir David Maxwell Fyfe is an excellent jurist, extremely well instructed and with great knowledge. His assistant, Roberts, I don't think much of. Mr. Dodd, the assistant American prosecutor, is good. One can see intelligence, clear thinking in his every word and manner. By the way, is he any relation to the former ambassador, Dodd? I knew Ambassador Dodd very well. He had a clean, sober, excellent character. He was frightfully against the Nazis. I sympathized at that time with his attitude. He was an obstinate man who stuck to his opinions — but I don't mean that in the bad sense. He was an absolutely fine character, moderate in his behavior and decent in his life. I appreciated him greatly. He invited me to come to the United States and once he warned me of an attack against me.

"This tribunal is principally concerned with judging deeds of the past. But I hope that from this trial some hope for the future will spring forth. That means a better understanding for the problems in Europe.

"The problem of Europe is how to feed the mass of people living here. There are, of course, constructive ideas and I have some myself, but they can't be carried out without great changes and without great courage. The only hope I have is that President Truman will have the courage to approach this problem. The people in Europe can't live without something being done. It is worse now after the Russians have taken possession of one-third of Germany and of the agricultural districts. Millions of Germans have been driven out of the East from Poland and Czechoslovakia."

I asked Schacht what direction Truman should take, in his opinion. He replied, "President Truman is the only man with power because his people have power. To discuss my ideas on what he should do is not worthwhile without talking directly to Truman or the secretary of state, Byrnes, or even to Mr. Bevin of England. There is some truth to the words of the late Georges Clemenceau that there are 20 million Germans too many.[10] Either these Germans have to perish or you have to find some way out, without hurting any other people, of course."

I remarked that these words of Clemenceau always seemed rash to me. "I can be more precise than that. When I am a free man I will talk of it perhaps. When previously I tried to convince Hitler of something, I was not listened to. With more patience on our side, maybe I would have succeeded, but what happened was that Hitler managed to get into power with an awful propaganda program. Hitler had neither patience nor understanding. I tried very hard to bring those qualities to his policy, but I failed. That is my tragic life — I can't help it. It is the great tragedy of my life.

"I have never believed in war. It is a crime against humanity whether you win or lose. I just read an article in this magazine I have in my hands that one day the moon will fall on the earth, but it is my feeling that until then, we should try to make the world a better place to live in."

# Baldur von Schirach
## 1907–1974

Baldur von Schirach, leader of the Hitler Youth, was appointed governor of Vienna in 1940. Found guilty by the Nuremberg tribunal of crimes against humanity, he was sentenced to twenty years' imprisonment, and released from Spandau prison on September 30, 1966.

**March 10, 1946**

I spent several hours with Baldur von Schirach this Sunday afternoon. He is his usual bright, self-effacing self, very courteous and friendly. He takes himself rather seriously, as is obvious and can be gleaned from his general demeanor and words.

We began today discussing the problem of the case against the organizations. Schirach is very much against the indictment of any or all of the organizations for the same reason that so many of the defendants have given. "If you outlaw half a million people you make martyrs of them. For example, if you outlaw Robin Hood it is all very well, but if you outlaw a whole group of people around Robin Hood, then Robin Hood and his merry men become legends."

"There is something in the German nature that tends toward aggression. That is why the German press today goes further than the American military government." Why? "Perhaps it is idealism. The German wants to make everything better and better. I mean if the American military government system is to de-Nazify Germany, the German government would say we have to do more than that — not halfway — more labor camps. It must be something in our nature." Do you really mean that this is idealism? "What I mean really is an attempt to reach perfection. It is perfectionism more than idealism, I suppose."

Do you think that this perfectionism in the German people might explain Bach-Zelewski's statement that Himmler wanted the extermination of 30 million Slavs, as well as the already realized extermination of 5 to 6 million Jews? "Yes, yes, indeed. However, that would be an idea that the German people could not stand because many Slavs lived with Germans for years. Many Austrians had Slavic grandmothers, grandfathers, uncles, et cetera. It was an entirely ridiculous idea, but Himmler always exaggerated.

"In the beginning there was no exaggeration. It is true there was some anti-Semitism, also the propaganda that the Slavic nations and all other nations were to be considered inferior. It started as a policy that the Jews should not have power. But the Germans went too far — like Streicher. Even Streicher didn't say ten years before what he said ten years later. Finally Himmler and Hitler say we must extinguish the Jews, and with the German tendencies to perfectionism and exaggeration, it is taken literally.

"It could happen in any country, provided the conditions were as they were in Germany; namely, a lost war, a harsh treaty like Versailles, the unemployment situation, poor housing, and food shortages.

"For example, in the French nation there is the tendency for 'la gloire.' That alone would not make Napoleon — but that, with other circumstances, explains sixty percent of his great achievements. Between Napoleon and Hitler there is a fundamental difference. Napoleon may have looted — he stole treasures from all of Europe — he was not kindly or soft in his treatment of other nations, but he did have an idea of a united Europe and a wonderful collection of laws, which are known as the Napoleonic Code. The German state would not have been forced together if it had not been for Napoleon. Napoleon knew the world because he had sound military and scientific training in his youth. He lived in Paris and he had contact with people belonging to other nations. Hitler never had that. He had no facility to conduct a simple conversation with anyone, much less with any foreigners.

"You probably notice that Germans try to talk about philosophical problems. It is difficult to get them to talk of simple things. The *idea* was always more essential than bread and butter for our nation. Had we thought more of bread and butter we would have realized that Russia

and Germany must live together. But Bolshevism and National Socialism were two worldviews that the German people could not accept."

Do you think the Bolsheviks are as bad as Nazi propaganda claimed
them to be? "I know from talking to many young men who were in Russia that the standard of living there was far below the German standard.
Moreover, the form of government in Russia was as undemocratic and
as totalitarian as can be."

What were some of the Nazi propaganda slogans against the Russians? " 'Reign of Terror.' 'No Culture.' 'No Individual Rights.' 'The
Stakhanovite System.'[1] Our workmen always criticized this system. I
suppose you know about it? If a Russian workman comes late to work
once, he receives not a warning but punishment. And if he comes late
three times in a row, he is sent to Siberia without an investigation. That is
a fact because I have talked to young German engineers. It is a fact. I
heard it from engineers who worked in Russia."

Were they German engineers? "Yes, yes, German engineers.

"An Allied-Russian war would be the end of Germany. Germany
would be the battleground. Anyone hoping for a revival of Nazism
through such a war is an idiot.

"But what I would like to know is whether Europe is going to be Bol-
shevistic or European." Just what do you mean by European? "By European I mean western culture and the western standard of living."

Did you do much reading as a young man? "Yes, I had access to large
libraries. I always read for two or three hours daily — it was a habit. During the last five years of my life in Vienna I had hardly a spare minute,
but I acquired the custom of reading between two a.m. and four a.m.,
and then I would go back to sleep again. This was to keep up my spiritual
well-being." What type of reading did you do? "In the last two years, I
read several books by Churchill. I also read English and German classical literature. Goethe and Shakespeare were always my favorites." Did
you ever read any French literature — Zola, for instance? "I read world
literature and I read French romances in the originals. I had quite a profound knowledge — no, that sounds conceited, but I did have a profound
interest in everything spiritual.

"My idea of leading youth can be seen in two ways. People can say, if
they choose, that the Hitler Youth was just a form of Nazi ideology in a
form to be understood by youth. But I developed a special idea of education which others before me had been working on for years.

"The idea of self-leadership, of self-responsibility, the idea of a state of youth within a larger state is not my own. It began with the schools of Hermann Lietz. Lietz founded a new type of school system in 1898, consisting of ten or twelve schools. They were what you might call country boarding schools. The first school was founded in Ilsenburg.

"Lietz was a student of Friedrich Froebel, as well as Jean-Jacques Rousseau and Johann Heinrich Pestalozzi. His idea was to overcome dangers which he saw in the industrial centers, such as large cities, by uniting youth, not only in school tasks but in other things. So, for example, we did work together with boys, built homes, carpenter shops, plumbing shops, and the like. The schools were located on estates which had their own gardens, cattle, et cetera. And so the school itself was a picture in miniature of a state. Every boy had his function within this miniature state. But they also had their lessons to learn. The important thing was that they were working for the community. You can call it Communist or socialist or democratic in the modern sense of the term. It was developed from Pestalozzi, Rousseau, and Froebel eight years before Lietz. But Lietz developed and formulated and put into practice these theories.

"I myself as a young boy attended a school of that type. It was not a Lietz school, but it was directed by a man who was associated with Lietz. I learned many things which other boys didn't know. I always thought of self-education and self-leadership of youth, and then along came the Nazi Party, which gave me the opportunity of putting my ideas into practice at home. I developed this idea of the youth state.

"The main drawback of the Lietz schools was that cities and industries had dangerous influences on youth — well, Lietz just let that problem lie untouched. The boys and girls he had in school — it was a coeducational system, which I believe in firmly — were all children of wealthy parents. And the schools themselves were expensive to attend, so that the drawback was that these were all children of one class, the children of wealthy people.

"So I tried to build up something which brought together all classes of youth. It was a youth state which included boys of the working classes as well as children from aristocratic families: youth would be discovered by youth itself. Therefore, at the top leadership it would be possible to have a representative in every ministry who was concerned about the life of young people.

"Our fight for a holiday of eighteen days per year for every young man was successful. We could only reach these things by the power of young people, in every legislative community where a man working on youth problems always came from the community of youth itself. These things will not be seen accurately in these times when Nazis and Nazism are criticized and the Hitler Youth is merely looked at as just a part of Nazism. But in a few years when the world has quieted down, the positive features of my program will be recognized. My program will not survive just as Nazism has not survived, and I recognize that the latter is quite dead, but some things will be recognized in my youth program.

"A realization of my program in some ways means perfect democracy. That is strange, isn't it?" Schirach smiled charmingly as he asked me this paradoxical question. How about racial and national chauvinism? "There is nationalism connected to my program because it is a youth movement of its time. National Socialism was the only possibility for this movement to develop. But if you want to understand the amazing development of the youth movement in the past ten years, you must see and notice the effect on a boy of ten or twelve years of age. Such a boy is not interested in politics. One must give him something useful. The idea of self-leadership and self-government — the responsibility of every boy for himself and his little job — the youth state that was constructed — all of these ideas were half developed, but essential. One must not say that the Nazi youth movement was just an appendage of the Nazi Party.

"Because if you say that, they will never believe it. I mean the people. They got something, especially the working classes, or they would not have accepted my program so enthusiastically. The working classes realized that they had a possibility to move up." It seems to me paradoxical. "Yes, it is paradoxical that in a totalitarian state something is invented with characteristically democratic features."

Do you think that if Germany had won the war, your youth movement would have made Nazism more democratic? "The idea of Germany winning the world war is absurd. I did think that the utmost we could achieve would be a peace with acknowledgment through Great Britain and America. And as for the Polish question, we would have had to draw back and permit an international solution of the Polish question. I thought at the time that the German-Russian pact was very dubious. The world should not have been outmaneuvered by Nazism. At any rate, for

ten years after such a war or such a peace, there would have been a quieter time."

And your movement — the Hitler Youth — would that serve to temper Nazism? "Yes, many features in the youth movement were critical of
National Socialism. I spoke with the youths who were in Russia and they
told me that the way we treated the Russians in the occupied areas was
wrong. They said we cannot say that the Russians are inferior to the Germans. I remember how many German boys told me how clean the Russian girls were both physically and in their mental attitudes. I remember
some of my German boys showing me many schoolbooks from the
Russian schools which were printed in the Russian language; they even
contained poems.[2]

"In Nazism as a whole there was no opportunity to express our opinions on a parliamentarian basis. Boys accustomed to the youth movement could not become accustomed to this severe form of National
Socialism. Youth was accustomed to live in camps, to hike together, and
it was natural for things to be discussed among the young which in the
older generation would simply have been obeyed. Of course, boys and
girls obeyed but they could tell their young leader what was wrong. We
grew up as a generation of leaders. I started my work in the youth movement in 1930, just sixteen years ago. I am thirty-eight now, and I was
twenty-two then. The boys I worked with were twenty. There were a few
thousand girls and we were accustomed to talking about everything that
concerned us. I never gave an order except where it was needed for the
functioning of the organization. It was similar to a board of directors in a
plant. We would sit down and have a chat, opinions would be offered,
but finally the general director announces that we will do it in such and
such a way."

### June 16, 1946

Schirach's defense ended recently. Today was Sunday and we had our
usual afternoon conversation. He obviously wanted to get away from
discussing his defense, with which he was not completely satisfied, and
significantly he asked me whether I had yet interviewed Oswald Pohl,
the chief of the concentration camps, who was recently imprisoned and
interned in the Nuremberg prison.

I said I had interviewed Pohl on several occasions. Schirach asked me
for my opinion of the man and I said I would rather not indulge in char-

acterizations of persons who might subsequently be defendants and that fundamentally my opinion of Pohl was not as yet tested. Schirach realized that I was evading his question, incidentally a not unusual type of question-in-reverse which he employs. He obviously wanted me to ask him what he thought about Pohl. I did so. "Pohl I did not know at all except, of course, that I had heard of him and perhaps I did see him occasionally at the Führer's headquarters or at large meetings. But that a man could be in charge of all the concentration camps in Germany, Himmler's right-hand man without a doubt, making him one of the great criminals of our age — what sort of a man is he? Does he talk? Does he proclaim innocence like Kaltenbrunner? I really can't understand such people."

I told him that Pohl was adopting the usual attitude, namely, that he did not deny knowledge of exterminations and atrocities within the camps, but explained them on the basis of his merely obeying the orders of Himmler, and excusing himself by stating that he was not personally responsible for the extermination program, which was executed by one of his deputies, Richard Gluecks.[3] Schirach made a wry face and said, "Horrible."

That seemed to take care of Pohl as far as Schirach was concerned. He had apparently wanted to impress me with the fact that he disapproved of such people as Pohl, Kaltenbrunner, and the other agents and deputies of Himmler. He did not want to continue discussing the matter and I asked him to tell me anything that came into his head.

We talked of various things thereafter, mostly about the termination of the cases against the defendants and their individual defenses of them. I asked him for his opinion about Bormann, who was being tried in absentia, whose defense lay in the hands of the court-appointed lawyer Dr. Friedrich Bergold. "I am firmly convinced that Bormann will show up — that either the Americans or the Russians have him in custody and will try to create a sensation, for news effect, when his case comes up, and suddenly produce him. I once heard that Bormann had given himself up to the Russians. Bormann is being treated in absentia just as if he were sitting in the dock. He left Berlin in a tank. His secretary made a statement that she saw this tank struck by shells and that Bormann was killed. I doubt if one could take Bormann's secretary's word for what was happening."

He went on to describe Bormann insofar as he knew him. "It is difficult to describe such a character. He was not highly educated but he was able and extremely industrious in technical office work. He was also extremely unscrupulous and very practical. His practicality was obvious even in his speech and appearance. He was a short, stocky man, quite fat, with an oxlike character. He had been a schoolteacher early in his career just as Streicher had been a schoolteacher, so you can see that being a schoolteacher is no sign of education.

"Technically and officially Bormann was the head of the party. Besides that, however, he was in reality the prime minister because all of Hitler's orders went through his hands. Bormann's real period of power began in 1941, although long before that, as far back as 1937, he had had a strong personal influence on Hitler. It was very strange. You know he was the chief of staff under Hess, but even while Hess was his superior, Bormann was much closer to Hitler in the hierarchy than was Hess. I think that Hess lost all his power because Bormann took it away from him, despite the fact that Hess was Bormann's superior. Bormann virtually became Hess's boss.

"Bormann entered party history in 1929 when he came to Munich. Before that he lived in my hometown of Weimar and used to chauffeur Sauckel, when the latter made propaganda and campaign speeches in Thuringia. Bormann at that time worked for Sauckel, and in a very minor, subordinate position. In 1929 he began doing financial work within the party. He continued with this task until 1933, when Hess made him his chief of staff."

We talked about his recent defense. I asked him what he thought of the cross-examination, which was mainly performed by the American prosecutor Dodd. Schirach smiled and said, "I am not good at cross-examination. As far as youth education is concerned, I thought that putting all the songs that were sung before me was a little apart from the essential matter. For example, they put a song before me entitled 'Put the Red Hand on the Roof of the Cloister.' That is a song from the sixteenth century and was originally sung by Lutheran peasants fighting against cloisters and the Catholic bishops. It's a story of the Lutherans who were fighting for their rise against the princes and was written in 1525. It will be sung as long as the German language continues.

"Dodd is the most skillful of the prosecuting attorneys. He really does research and works, whereas Justice Jackson is more of a supervisor and doesn't know the details as does Dodd. That was one of the reasons why the cross-examination of Goering by Jackson didn't work.

"After I made the statement in court about Hitler being a million-times murderer and my other statements about the fallacy and complete wrongness of anti-Semitism, I have rethought all the ideas which directed me during the last fifteen or twenty years of my life. Having come to the conclusion that racial policy as a whole is one of the greatest menaces to mankind, I now also try to see in what way all these different men were wrong in what they said, not only as far as Jewish influence but regarding other matters. I am still thinking about it. I must deliberate and try to get a real understanding of the errors of our ways.

"What I was working for was the socialist idea, which I still hold. But I understand socialism in a different form than the older generation did. In fact, I think I don't have to understand so many of my social ideas in that direction. What is necessary is to solve the problems of the working class and to work toward the welfare of those who have difficulty and struggle for a living. There is the everlasting question of how to educate youth so that the poor boy may have the chance to get into government or other positions — and I think it's worth fighting for.

"Now as you have often asked me and as I have been thinking about many months, I want to talk about the leadership principle in the youth movement. We had something quite different than in the state. We discussed problems freely and only then were orders given, which were considered correct by the leaders on down to the lowest member of the Hitler Youth. Such was not the fashion in the party or in the state. But in retrospect, and realizing where we have come to, I am absolutely sure that a real system of government must prevent one man or twenty or thirty men from getting all the power of the state into their hands. Power is what spoils people. Yes, it seems to me that the seeking after power is the great danger and the great corrupter of mankind.

"Some of the defendants say that dictatorship can be good if there is a good dictator. But I say that a man cannot stay good if he becomes a dictator. Authoritarianism is a system that destroys man's morality. If you take a saint and give him power, he will change into a Hitler or a devil." Did Schirach think that perhaps in his own case this psychological phenomenon held true? "In my own life, my way of living was so different that it didn't affect me. I know what happened in other districts — something must have been different in my way of living. Probably my friends saved me from that. I lived with people who had varied opinions, some of whom did not accept my Nazi views. I encouraged this. If a man said something that was critical of me or my ideas, I wouldn't consider him an enemy."

I asked him about the somewhat touchy subject of his removal of Jews from Vienna. Schirach was as smooth and rationalizing as ever. "In the case of Seyss-Inquart the correspondence between him and Himmler about the sending away of Jews was brought up in court. This occurred long before I went there. Once there were 190,000 Jews in Vienna, but when I went there, there were only 60,000. These are plain facts. Hitler told me that he wanted to send all the Jews away. I admit that I committed what might be called a crime because under my aegis 60,000 Jews were sent away, but it must be stressed that this occurred after 130,000 had been removed from Vienna.

"The trouble was that my thinking and reasoning were not deep enough. Since 1938 I thought that it was best to have all the Jews of Europe out of the reach of Dr. Goebbels and his sudden attacks. I thought that if the Jews were brought to Poland, where they could live like any other human beings, it would be quite a good idea — at least better than having them in Germany, where you never knew what might happen. Goebbels would make a new speech and the shops of the Jews would be smashed, Jews would be rushed off to concentration camps, many would be killed, and so forth. The removal of Jews from Vienna, one must recall, was done by the special office of Heydrich, who had his representative in Vienna. I think that this representative, whose name was Alois Brunner, was put to death a few weeks ago after trial by an Austrian court.[4]

"And now I come to my great guilt. I made that stupid speech once where I said, 'I have sent these Jews away to the East,' which seems to be a confession made in public that I was doing this. It is so hard to explain. However, it was part of a big action initiated by Himmler, but that doesn't make it any better. It doesn't throw a good light on the party, if I claim that by doing this I kept my opponents quiet. That happens to be the truth. Kaltenbrunner said that the western Nazis were less radical, but my opinion is that the Nazis of Austria were more radical. I always had to meet criticism from below in Austria, charges that I was not being active enough and not putting through National Socialist ideas.

"I am just telling the whole story as it is. If in later years you have the opportunity to talk to some decent people from Vienna who were once in party work, they will confirm it. I was in a difficult position. I went to Austria when great difficulties existed between Austrians and Germans. I had to calm people who had been insulted and hurt by Josef Buerckel, and at the same time I had to calm the violent Center Group of the Austrian Nazi Party. They assassinated Austrian chancellor Engelbert Dollfuss in 1934. They were radicals and anarchists, and the thing they always pointed at was my weak stand on the Jewish question.

"For that reason I always thought that the idea of Hitler's sending the Jews away from Vienna was reasonable because the violent group would always cause conflicts. And so with this speech to which I referred a moment ago, I put in that bad sentence which is now held against me, in order to take the wind out of the sails of people over all these shoutings about my not going against the Jews. If you read all of my books and speeches, there is nothing of that connection in them. In the preceding twenty years prior to that speech, I never made such statements. Unfortunately, during my cross-examination I couldn't make that point. The only thing I could do was to state that it was true that some songs, like the 'Horst Wessel,' were sung by SA men and not primarily by the Hitler Youth.

"I tried to be quite truthful about this because it bothered me. The idea that people probably died as a result of my evacuation of fifty or sixty thousand Jews from Vienna is something terrible for me to think about. Actually I have no feeling of guilt about sending them away, but the speech identified myself with such a dirty criminal step. Now I would say that the deportation of people anyhow, in any way, for any reason, is something terrible and criminal. But you must remember that my reaction to the events of November 9 and 10, 1938, was a good one. I claim that it is to my credit that I kept the Youth out of any of that dirty work. I think it is something positive in my favor. I forbade them from participating in those actions. My idea always was that the critical things were laws against the Jews, and that there was no possibility left for the Jews to live securely in Germany after those laws were passed."

Were there not other opponents to Nazism than the Jews? "Undoubtedly. Most of them who were politically opposed to Nazism were called Communists and were confined to concentration camps indefinitely at the very beginning, in 1933 and 1934. It is interesting that I personally could walk through factories where laborers worked, and although they may have hated my politics, they never assaulted me because I think that they realized I was essentially a socialist and they knew after a while that I always saw to it that the workingpeople had what they needed. Probably now the Austrian people are talking about their resistance movements or their underground opposition to the Nazis. Such talk is all fibs and fantasy. I had no difficulties in Vienna. I don't know what difficulties the Gestapo men encountered in individual cases of anarchists or Communists, although such individuals were probably arrested and tried legally before a court. But in a political way these opposition groups were hardly noticeable in Vienna. The great mass of Viennese and Austrians were heartily in favor of the Nazis and our policies.

"There is one exception to my last remark in that when I first went to Vienna in 1940, there did exist a strong political feeling against the Reich. I think I was partly successful in overcoming this opposition. I got on quite well with the Viennese and had lots of friends there. The whole story would have been different if Hitler had sent me to Vienna in the very beginning, instead of first sending Odilo Globocnik and Josef Buerckel and other awful people like them.[5]

"At first, Buerckel had no difficulties because he was the first man appointed and the people welcomed him as a representative of Nazism, which they approved. Soon he began to hurt the feelings of the Viennese. There is a certain way many Germans had of talking about Austrians — especially in Prussia — which made an Austrian boil and which even I myself would become enraged about. The German is too much in the habit of saying, 'He is just an Austrian,' in a derogatory fashion.

"Buerckel's followers and officials talked in this way and were generally always tactless. Then came Buerckel's action against Cardinal Theodor Innitzer, which was idiotic. Innitzer's palace was stoned and stormed and many of his fine ecclesiastical pictures and books were ruined. When I arrived, I stopped all that nonsense. The feeling among the radical group of the party in Austria was strong against Catholicism. I broke down the idea of demonstrations, and I forbade speeches against the church and other actions which might violate the feelings of the Austrian people.

"Vienna is the most complicated political place and it is not easy to work there. I soon felt entirely at home in that environment nevertheless. In fact, I identified myself so much with the Austrian people that my feelings toward Germany became very different. Austria was divided into various administrative districts, which was one of the great political mistakes made by Hitler. Hitler wanted to break the supposed danger that might derive from a single administrative district in Austria. He was always afraid of having any single entity become too strong. My district, for instance, stopped immediately outside of Vienna. Hitler cooperated with August Eigruber, who was the party district administrator of the upper Danube, and Hitler tried to make Linz the principal city of Austria. That was ridiculous, too, because Linz was just a provincial town. Hitler spent millions on buildings, and on the Hermann Goering Works in Linz.

"Eigruber was here in this prison in Nuremberg, but he has been transferred and brought to trial somewhere else. He was very fanatical, especially toward the end, when he turned against people and hanged them right and left for very little cause. The notorious concentration camp of Mauthausen was in his district. Eigruber is probably dead by now. He was only thirty-nine, but he looked about fifty-five. He was of the Globocnik-Bormann type."[6]

Schirach married in 1932 the daughter of Hitler's favorite photographer, Heinrich Hoffmann. His wife, six years his junior, was eighteen years of age at the time of their marriage. "I'd known her since she was sixteen. It was entirely a love affair. I met her first and then met her father, who introduced us formally. Professor Hoffmann was astonished when I asked him for his daughter's hand. I don't think he was aware that I was in love with her. My parents met her prior to our marriage when I took her to Weimar to introduce her to them. That was two years before we married. In the beginning my mother didn't like her very much, but later, when our children began coming, the old grandmotherly feeling arose and later my mother got to know my wife better and to like her very much."

There were four children: a daughter, thirteen years of age, and three boys, eleven, eight, and four.

"My mother was a very rich woman, but nevertheless I always stood on my own feet and never accepted a penny from my family. As a student I worked for a newspaper and earned money. In 1932 I was already leader of the Hitler Youth. That same year, before my marriage, I was the youngest member of the Reichstag. After 1933 the Reichstag had no importance. Of course, it met at times to accept laws unanimously, but its real function was negligible. I had one year of being a member of a republican parliament, from 1932 to 1933. It was a terrible period. Members of the Reichstag threw ink at each other and there were heated arguments and debates. You can't imagine what things went on. It was a time of violent antagonism in political life."

He said that in 1943, when his wife and he spent a few days at Hitler's home in Berchtesgaden, life was so unbearable because of the peculiarity of Hitler's living schedule that both he and his wife had to leave prematurely, utilizing some excuse that they had to go home to their children. He said that at that time his wife had remarked to him that she was certain Hitler was insane. Schirach described the visit as a combination social and political one. There were many other guests present. The visitors had to follow the schedule of Hitler insofar as meals were concerned, and this was very erratic. For example, Hitler would have breakfast sometimes at three o'clock in the afternoon, lunch at eight o'clock in the evening, and dinner sometime around midnight. On the following day, the schedule of meals might be quite different, depending on Hitler's whim.

At that same visit to Berchtesgaden, Schirach noted that Hitler was impervious to outside influence, even during a conversation. The Führer would either remain completely silent during a meal or hold forth at great length, soliloquizing, and brooking no comment or opinion from his guests. Sometimes between courses Hitler would speak for forty-five minutes or an hour, as if he were making a public address. Schirach said that the entire performance during the two or three days' visit was difficult and intolerable.

He said that his wife was quite uninhibited and would usually express her opinions about anyone quite freely, but that it was impossible for even her to tell Hitler anything. He did credit his wife with having recognized Hitler's abnormality and cruel nature years before he himself recognized it.

# Albert Speer
## 1905–1981

Albert Speer was Hitler's architect from 1937, and minister for armaments and war production from 1942 to 1945. Tried at Nuremberg and found guilty of war crimes and crimes against humanity, he was sentenced on September 30, 1946, to twenty years' imprisonment, and released from Spandau prison in 1966.

**Undated (April 14, 1946?)**

"I felt this war coming. I tried unsuccessfully to assassinate Hitler in 1945. I am not concerned with jurisdiction of the court as Hess or others are." (Laughs.) "History will show the trials to be necessary." He feels he is less guilty than some, but that anyone who accepted a position of responsibility in that government was guilty. "In that sense I am guilty. That Hitler's government was criminal is a fact. Also I was made party to the use of forced labor, although Sauckel is the one who supplied it. I was an architect, but less interested in architecture than arms production after 1942, when Hitler made me production chief." He fell from Hitler's good graces, he feels, a month or two before the end, because he advised surrender two months before Hitler's suicide. Hitler wanted to fight to the last German.[1]

# Julius Streicher
## 1885–1946

Julius Streicher was founder and
editor of the anti-Semitic journal
<u>Der</u> <u>Stürmer</u>. Found guilty by the
Nuremberg tribunal of crimes
against humanity, he was hanged on
October 16, 1946.

**January 24, 1946**

I interviewed Julius Streicher with the aid of Gilbert, who translated.
Streicher's German is easy to comprehend. Streicher had developed a
tachycardia (flutter rate) in court Wednesday at 2 p.m. I saw him Thursday morning with Captain Horowitz, at which time he had a pulse of one
hundred; he said he felt fine, and looked his usual self. Streicher wanted
very much to go to court that day, but both Horowitz and myself agreed
he should not. Meanwhile we arranged for a portable EKG to be taken
on Streicher. That was done Thursday morning. In the afternoon, the
results of the EKG were reported as normal.

Streicher is a short, almost bald, hook-nosed figure of sixty-one years.
He appears about his given age. He smiles constantly, the smile something between a grimace and a leer, twisting his large, thin-lipped mouth,
screwing up his froggy eyes, a caricature of a lecher posing as a man of
wisdom. He requires no stimulation to embark on his unique and
favorite topic, anti-Semitism, which has been and remains his raison
d'être. "I know more about the Jews than the Jews do themselves. I've
known all along you are Jewish [referring to Dr. Gilbert] by your voice.
At first I wasn't sure. But then one of the others [apparently another

defendant] told me. Then I listened and I could tell by your voice." All this in a friendly fashion.

He said he had no personal feelings in the matter. He was a student of the Jews for the past twenty years. He is a "scientific and psychological" observer. The Jews were always a small group, and in a way he admires them, in that such a small group should have always gotten into a position where they dominate the world. For example, Christ. A Jew. And now that Germany is defeated, Jewish Bolshevism reigns in Russia. Stalin is just a figurehead. The Jews are behind him. And in North America we have Jewish democracy. All this with automatic enthusiasm and fluency, as with a well-rehearsed speech.

He has a frequent mannerism of looking at his hands, first the right and then the left, as if examining the fingernails. Asked why he does so, he dismissed the question by stating it was "a little nervousness."

He is really a Zionist, he continued. He knows such men as Chaim Weizmann and other Zionists and shares their opinions. The Jews should be in their own country, not allowed elsewhere. Asked about the *Protocols of the Elders of Zion*,[1] he replied that they were not "exact" but that every word stated in them was true, and could be found elsewhere in Jewish works as in the Talmud. He poses as a scholar and researcher into Jewish writings, of which he has accumulated, in fact, a library.

He seems to me to be a man of probably limited normal intelligence, generally ignorant, obsessed with maniacal anti-Semitism, which serves as an outlet for his sexual conflicts, as evidenced by his preoccupation with pornography. Circumcision is a diabolical Jewish plot, and a clever one, he said, to preserve the purity of the racial Jewish stock. Christ, a Jew, was born of a mother who was a Jewish whore. Who could believe the story of the immaculate conception? he said, smiling or leering. Of course, he couldn't write that in *Der Stürmer,* and he only mentions it to show how deep-rooted is the Jewish problem.

He denies any personal animosity toward the Jews. He considers himself merely a beacon of truth and has dedicated his life to that end. He can prove in court, he said, that he knew nothing about the anti-Jewish riots that occurred in Nuremberg in 1938;[2] in fact he was just returning from somewhere, and was told about the riots starting on the night he returned, which proves he didn't order them. His chauffeur could testify to it.

Streicher impresses me as an old psychopathic personality with sexual and other conflicts, whose inadequacy found expression in an obsessive preoccupation which for the past twenty years has filled the narrow stream of his life. He says he suddenly came upon anti-Semitism one evening years ago, and in the morning he realized that his life work was to become an authority on anti-Semitism. When Hitler appeared, Streicher fitted a ready-made niche.

### April 6, 1946

For the past few days Streicher has been ill with a slight upper respiratory infection and displayed some cardiac arrhythmia, which was probably a combination of fibrillation and flutter. Several EKG records were taken and confirmed this clinical impression. There was, however, no cardiac failure.

Today he was completely asymptomatic and was his "old self." He constantly asked for small favors, such as longer walks, more sweets or chocolate in his diet, less noise from the guards, which he has asked for in the past on many occasions. I have always had the impression that he is really not too concerned about obtaining these requests but that it is part of his obsessive-compulsive nature and that he tried to avoid any serious discussion about his childhood or development or about his actual activities or worldview by so doing.

We did discuss Streicher's favorite subject, the "Jewish problem." He had very little new to say about it but repeated his old line more or less as follows: "The Jewish problem is historical. I stumbled across it and chanced to become an authority on it through having read the Talmud, which the Jews call a Christianlike book. That is false. The racial laws emanate from the Talmud itself. I consider myself a leading scholar and student of Jewish writings, particularly of the Talmud." A characteristic smirk or leer passed over Streicher's face and he smiled thinly and leaned forward, and said in a confidential manner, "Have you ever thought about circumcision?" I replied that as a doctor I had performed many circumcisions of babies, both Jewish and gentile children, and that I had not thought about it very much. I certainly knew of it and considered it a surgical procedure. Streicher looked at his fingers a few times while I said these words and glanced at me incredulously. He said that circumcision was a Jewish mischief and its only aim was to preserve racial purity among Jews. "I have no objection to that as long as the Jews don't interfere with our pure Aryan bloodlines because we must preserve our racial purity, too, then. As far as what you say about circumcision being practiced on gentiles as well as on Jews, I know that to be the case, and don't you see how devilish that is?" He smiled again in the manner of a wise man instructing a young student.

I said I did not see the point, and just what was devilish about it? As usual, Streicher had no rational explanation for what he called this devilish procedure, but made some inconsequential remarks about how, if circumcision was Jewish, it should not be inflicted on non-Jews. It was clear that he considered circumcision as something which had no medical or surgical import, but merely a racial custom. I asked him whether he did not know that in certain instances circumcision was a necessary operation to prevent various infections and mechanical difficulties due to phimosis. I explained to him what I meant by the term "phimosis." Streicher replied, "Well, if an operation like that must be done, it should be done on Jews and not on gentiles. I have never heard of an Aryan whose bloodline was pure requiring such an operation." He spoke with vehemence and a repetitive clicking tap of staccato speech. His remarks and speech were interjected with squinting of the eyes, peering at his fingertips, and frequently wetting his lips with his tongue.

Pinning Streicher down to any particular subject was most difficult because his ability to discuss anything logically was quite limited. We talked for a while about this and that, but in general, I gave him free rein to discuss what he wished. He asked me whether I had interviewed Ernst Hiemer, who was here in this prison as a witness for Streicher. Hiemer was Streicher's chief editor of *Der Stürmer* after the removal of Holz. I replied that I had interviewed Hiemer. I asked Streicher what he thought of that man. Streicher said, "Hiemer is a schoolteacher, an honorable man, who could put into writing anti-Semitic articles and make them clear and simple so that the common man could read them and believe them. He was a very valuable, faithful worker and I chose him because of his simple but useful abilities."

We continued to talk about *Der Stürmer.* "My publication was for a fine purpose. Certain snobs may now look down on it and call it common or even pornographic, but until the end of the war I had Hitler's greatest respect, and *Der Stürmer* had the party's complete support. At our height we had a circulation of 1.5 million. Everybody read *Der Stürmer,* and they must have liked it or they wouldn't have bought it. The aim of *Der Stürmer* was to unite Germans and to awaken them against Jewish influence which might ruin our noble culture."

I said he had mentioned a few moments ago that although he was in disfavor with certain party elements since 1940, he nevertheless regularly received greetings from Hitler and party support. I asked him what had happened in 1940 and why he was in disfavor and banned from Nuremberg at that time. "I had a trial then and it took place right here in this same prison. I was supposed to have said something about Goering's child — that it was artificially conceived or something. But really, the trial was a farce. Goering was angry with me and he had his so-called Goering Commission investigate my activities as party district administrator of Franconia. There were some charges, which were never substantiated, that I had purchased stocks or bonds illegally — stock which had been seized from Jewish holders. It was true that I had certain stocks from Jews in my possession for a short time, but I had returned them to the state after I found out that I had been wrongly informed about my right to take them.

"As a result of the trial in 1940, I was forced to leave Nuremberg and to live in Fürth on my estate. I continued to publish *Der Stürmer*. I never ceased my editorial supervision of that publication, and Holz or Hiemer and my other associates held daily or weekly conferences with me so that I vetted everything that was printed in *Der Stürmer*. Hitler promised me protection after I had participated in the Munich putsch in 1923. I am very proud that I marched alongside Hitler in that affair. Hitler was never forgetful of that fact, and his faith and confidence in me was unshaken until the end. I, in turn, never broke my oath of loyalty to him."

We discussed next the problem of religion. I said that I had heard that he was areligious. Could Streicher tell me what his real attitude toward religion might be? "It's hard to say. Christ was a Jew and God, he is supposed to have made the universe. That's a little far-fetched because if God made the world, who made God?" He smiled complaisantly as if he had scored quite a point. I asked him whether he had any other thoughts on the subject of religion. "Well, in my mind I have many things to say but I can't tell them to you because who knows but that you might tell them to the newspapers. For example, if I were to tell you that my idea of the Virgin Mary and the immaculate conception was that both of these ideas were ridiculous, and that in my own opinion, Mary must have had relations with somebody in order to give birth to Jesus, you might think that was an insult to the church. Personally, I don't care if the church is insulted or not, but I didn't want the newspapers to get hold of such things because that might hurt me more than any of my anti-Semitic statements, which are well known and which were published regularly in the press."

We seemed to have expended the subject temporarily and Streicher suddenly abandoned it and turned to the subject of his personal hygiene. "I was sick yesterday and the day before as you know, but nevertheless I had a terrific urge today to take a bath. I know that you doctors would probably say I should take it easy because of my heart, so I just went ahead and got as much water as I could and washed myself all over from this basin." He pointed to a galvanized water basin which lay on the floor next to the toilet.

"I also scrubbed myself from top to bottom with cold water and soap. I used this piece of rag. It's good for me. I think that it is important for me to bathe with cold water and to have myself scrubbed down regularly. I did that at home, too. Sometimes in the middle of the night I would have an impulse to take a cold sponge bath and I would do so."

I said it was my professional medical opinion that he should limit these cold baths and avoid strenuous activity during the next few weeks because of his recent heart attack. I had also noticed his fast walk during the exercise period in the prison yard and felt it would be more beneficial if he walked slowly. One of Streicher's habits is to literally walk around the courtyard rapidly in a half run, half walk, passing the other defendants three or four times while so doing. Streicher smiled and smote his breast, saying, "No, my heart is strong. My pulse goes fast sometimes and has done so for years now, but it is nothing. Just a little nervousness perhaps. I don't mean that I am nervous because of this trial or because of my imprisonment. I have been in prison before and I've been tried before. It's just that I am a high-spirited man, and though my nerves are very steady I have a tendency to do things fast, and that is probably the explanation for my fast heart at times." I asked him whether he had any feeling of guilt in connection with the extermination of the Jews. He replied, almost laughingly, "Why, I had nothing to do with it! Since 1940 I lived as a gentleman farmer in Fürth. Hitler must have decided to exterminate the Jews in 1941, because I knew nothing about it. Hitler probably felt that 'they caused the war, now I will exterminate them.' I am not saying that Hitler was right. I think that it was the wrong policy. I was all for setting up a separate Jewish state in Madagascar or Palestine or someplace, but not to exterminate them. Besides, by exterminating 4 million Jews — they say 5 or 6 million at this trial, but that is all propaganda, I am sure it wasn't more than 4.5 million — they have made martyrs out of those Jews. For example, because of the extermination of these Jews, anti-Semitism has been set back many years in certain foreign countries where it had been making good progress."

He said, commenting further on the trial, that most of the Russian and British prosecution were Jewish, and that applied as well to the American staff. I asked him whether he thought Justice Jackson, the chief American prosecutor, was Jewish. Streicher grinned leeringly. "Do you mean Jacobson?" For the moment I really thought Streicher was referring to someone else. I repeated that I meant Justice Jackson, the American prosecutor. Again Streicher leered and said, "That's Jacobson. He may call himself Jackson, but to me he is Jacobson and a Jew. Besides, you can very easily tell by looking at him. I thought for a while that he was not Jewish because the others among the defendants assured me that he was not. But within the last few months I have watched him walk, I have watched his face, and he is a Jacobson, probably of German Jewish ancestry." What about Mr. Dodd? Streicher replied, "Von Papen said that Dodd is a good Catholic and I really haven't paid much attention to him. Besides, it would be a good idea for Jacobson to have a Catholic assistant because the prosecution claims that the National Socialists persecuted Catholics as well as Jews."

As I was leaving his cell I asked him how he felt generally and whether his sleeping had improved any. "Major, it is indicative of the fact that you are a gentleman that you ask me such questions. If everyone had as clear a conscience as I have, nobody in the world would have to take sleeping pills or visit doctors. My conscience is as clear as a baby's. If you read through the volumes of *Der Stürmer* or any of the other publications put out by Der Stürmer Publishing Company, of which I was president, you will find not a word regarding the extermination of Jews. I'll prove all that. You'll see."

### June 15, 1946

Streicher was, as usual, in a talkative mood today when Mr. Triest and I entered his cell. He said he had been feeling very well and had not been bothered recently by the fast pulse or palpitation to which he had been subject on several occasions in the past. He said he had no complaints except that his sleep was interfered with at times because of the lack of consideration displayed by the guards who stand outside his cell.

"I don't want to complain about these young people, of course, because I might have done the same thing when I was their age. They are all youngsters, in their twenties, or even younger. Some of them knock with their fingers on the door and when I wake up during the night because of this, they laugh. Four weeks ago one of these guards hung a figure in my room through the window in the door and he thought it was a good joke. This has happened twice and it was not the same guard each time. It really doesn't matter to me — I'm not the type who is sensitive or easily upset. In general the guards are courteous and decent, but some of them are annoying. For example, this week I was awakened twice during the night by the noise of the changing of the guard. I wrote a note to the prison officer to complain about it but I am sure that the guard just tore up the note or kept it and didn't pass it on."

Streicher said he had one favor to ask of me and whether I would be so kind as to try to grant it. "Could we have more marmalade or some fresh carrots, onions, or other vegetables in our diet?" I said I had very little to do with the diet or rations beyond ascertaining that there were sufficient nutritive elements in it. I explained that the POW ration was prescribed by the American headquarters in Frankfurt and that it was the same throughout the theater. I told Streicher that the diet for the defendants was, as a matter of fact, the working prisoner-of-war ration and was better than existed in most camps and prisons. Streicher replied, "Oh yes, I am not complaining. We get plenty to eat. I just thought that if you could get us some marmalade, carrots, or onions, it would be very good for my system."

Streicher again asked me for a favor. "I would be grateful if you could get me my wife's address. I know she is in an American internment camp in Ludwigsburg near Stuttgart. I haven't received any letters from her because she can write only once every four weeks, I think. Of course, she has been away from here more than four weeks but I guess the American authorities won't let her write to me. That is all right but I would like to write to her. I am permitted to write as often as I please from this prison." I said I would try to find out where his wife resided at present.

I asked Streicher what he thought of the events of the trial during the past few weeks. "It's very hard for the individual defendants. After all, we've just lost the war and we can't do much. I think Jodl did well in his defense. As far as Seyss-Inquart is concerned, he defended himself well but he had a very hard case because of so many accusations against him. He has to answer for a great deal of responsibility."

I asked him about his own defense and what his reactions to his taking the stand had been. "The main thing I tried to stress was how badly I was treated in the American camp at Freising, but the American prosecutor and the judges ruled that my comments on my poor treatment there had to be expunged from the record because it was irrelevant. I don't think it is irrelevant when we National Socialists are accused of war crimes and of murdering 5 million Jews and millions of other innocent people such as partisans, hostages, war prisoners. Therefore, I should have been allowed to insert into the record of this trial how badly I was treated personally as a prisoner of war, after the war was over, mind you, in Freising."

Streicher thought the trials would end sometime in August. He said he was not surprised at the tentative ruling by the tribunal that only two weeks would be allowed for summation by the defense lawyers. "It has always been my viewpoint that a long defense would serve no purpose. My conviction is and always has been, since the beginning of this trial, that in the final analysis it doesn't matter what defense arguments are given because the minds of the judges were made up in advance and nothing the defense lawyers or the defendants and their witnesses can say could possibly change anything. This is not a normal trial. It's an international political trial and as such is highly irregular.

"It is a trial within a nation but a trial of victors against the vanquished. Even before the trials started, the victors who are our judges were quite convinced that we were guilty and that we should all pay the price."

Did Streicher feel that the trial as such was conducted in a fair manner? "Well, I can't express my innermost thoughts on this subject at this time. There is a superficial attempt at fairness. It is difficult to say or to express what one thinks or feels inside. I am convinced that some of the judges, as human beings, have the intention to be just, but that they are dependent on their home nations and the feelings that exist in those nations."

Did Streicher feel that any of the defendants were guilty? Did he feel that any of them merited punishment? "From a German viewpoint, any good German would say that none of us is guilty. On one side there are the mass murders and it is quite clear that whoever performed them in particular is guilty. But I don't know anyone among us twenty-one defendants who can be accused properly of having participated in the mass murders. Hitler admitted that in his last testament. He said quite clearly that he had ordered these mass murders. I am absolutely convinced that no one sits on the defendants' bench who wanted these mass murders. The charge that I have something to do with having stirred up the populace by propaganda or by my speeches to commit such atrocities is false. Then there is the question of Kaltenbrunner's responsibility. I never knew Kaltenbrunner until I met him here, but I think that Hitler gave his order about the exterminations directly to Himmler. I heard the name Kaltenbrunner for the first time here in this prison. I think that Himmler and Heydrich were the chief exterminators."

Did Streicher believe that Himmler influenced Hitler to make the decision about the racial exterminations? "I don't know. I didn't see Hitler after 1938. I was in the country for five years during the war." He seemed quite unconcerned about the matter and rather bored with it. I asked him for his opinion about the other defendants. Streicher grinned broadly and enjoyed his role as savant and commentator. "Well, let me begin with Ribbentrop. I must insist that Ribbentrop is wrongly judged. Ribbentrop didn't want such far-reaching responsibility as he was forced into taking. As far as the Jewish question, Ribbentrop had nothing to do with it. Ribbentrop always talked of the great difficulties he experienced abroad in foreign political circles, and was, therefore, opposed to radical methods. I never heard one remark by Ribbentrop concerning the Jews. He is wrongly judged in my opinion.

"Now as far as Goering is concerned, you know that for many years he was my enemy. The Goering Commission investigated my actions here in Nuremberg and even caused me to be put on trial and exiled from Nuremberg so that I had to live on my estate in Fürth from 1940 until the end of the war. But what Goering says in this court is very true and I must agree with it. He was the representative of Hitler, deputy leader of the state, and as such he assumed responsibility for whatever the Führer ordered. Of course, he does not accept the responsibility for the mass murders because he had nothing to do with them. But he does accept responsibility for everything else. Everything Goering says is very true. Of course, as far as the pictures and art collections — it's hard to judge. It was his hobby. As he said himself, there is no other excuse for it and it was just a weakness."

Streicher next turned to the subject of Sauckel. "Sauckel is an honest, honorable man who had the bad luck of being given the task of bringing foreign workers to Germany. He did not have bad intentions and he tried to take good care of these workers. The fact that it wasn't done everywhere is not really Sauckel's fault." What did Streicher think of the policy of bringing slave labor into Germany? "If a people is engaged in a fight for life or death and if the leaders think that they can win the war by importing slave labor — then it was correct. On the other hand, things did happen which were not absolutely necessary. I mean things done by the Allies. For example, old historical towns like Rothenburg and many other towns where no armaments were made were bombed mercilessly. In Dresden thousands of the civilian population were killed during bombing raids. Then when the Russians approached Dresden, 120,000 refugees fled. I remember reports that the American and English newspapers were very happy about the fact that so many were killed in Dresden. There are many instances of barbarity and cruelty on the part of the Allies which I could tell you.

"As far as Keitel and Jodl and other military leaders, they have nothing to do with the mass murders and other atrocities. As a matter of fact, no one knew about it or believed it in Germany, and that is true among the defendants as well as among the population in general. I did not hear about Auschwitz until now — I never knew of it before this trial. It's perfectly understandable and proper for one to be an anti-Semite, but to exterminate women and children is so extraordinary, it's hard to believe. No defendant here wanted that."

PART TWO

# WITNESSES

# Erich von dem Bach-Zelewski
## 1899–1972

Erich von dem Bach-Zelewski, Higher SS police leader, SS general, and police general from 1941, was appointed chief of antipartisan units in Russia in 1943. Sentenced by a Munich de-Nazification court to ten years' "special labor," he was retried in 1962 in Nuremberg and sentenced to life imprisonment.

**February 14, 1946**

This forty-seven-year-old man, Erich von dem Bach-Zelewski, was born in Berlin on March 1, 1899. He is rather stout, tall, with regular features and blue-gray eyes. His manner is ingratiating but pompous, and his attitude is of wanting to be sincere, a fact which he repeats so often during the interview that it begins to lose its conviction.

**Previous Illnesses:** He states that he had the usual childhood illnesses, but has always been constipated, even as a child; however, his constipation was aggravated in 1918 when he was gassed in the First World War. In 1942, he had "paralysis of the intestines" while serving in Russia, which he attributes to the cold climate. He spent four months in the hospital at that time and required six months of convalescence thereafter.

He has been wounded slightly in the head and right shoulder; both wounds were incurred during the First World War and were slight. He received a life pension after that war because of the gas poisoning in 1918, as well as because of the paralysis of the intestines at that time. He is quite interested in this intestinal complaint and goes into great detail about it, although he stresses that he has no such difficulties at the present time and has never felt better in his life than he does now in prison.

He states that he has had several rectal operations because of small ulcerations. He estimates that he has had minor rectal surgical operations on at least twelve different occasions. The last operation took place in January 1942. (Apparently, it was the removal of an impacted stool.) He frequently went to spas, particularly Karlsbad, where he received massages, baths, drank mineral water, and took colonic irrigations. It has been a life habit for him to take self-administered enemas quite frequently, perhaps more than once a week. Since his captivity, however, he has not required these ministrations.

**Education:** He attended elementary school for four years and gymnasium for six years. That was the extent of his formal education. He states that he was a good student, but never had any desires for further study.

**Occupation:** "At the age of fifteen, I became a soldier, and I was the youngest volunteer in the whole German army. I became an officer in 1917. After the war, I stayed on in the 100,000-man army.[1] In 1924, I left the 100,000-man army because two of my sisters married Jews and things became unbearable for me. At the time, I was first lieutenant. I became a social outcast because the sentiment in the 100,000-man army was anti-Semitic."

Did you oppose your sisters' marriages? "No, on the contrary. I helped both sisters and their husbands to go to Rio de Janeiro in 1934. My older brother also emigrated to Rio."

Please tell me of your career and life after 1924. "I worked for a firm in Landsberg, near the Oder, buying land and converting it to farms. I worked for that concern for ten years until 1934."

What happened? "The owner also went to Rio de Janeiro in 1933. I remained in the concern until that time."

And after 1933? "I was in the SS, and starting in 1934, I became a full-time member. In 1934, I was appointed lieutenant general in East Prussia." How do you explain that you achieved such a high position in the SS in so short a time? Bach-Zelewski smiles benignly and answers, "It was because I was such a good soldier," with apparent pride.

"I testified in court that in 1934, my headquarters was in Königsberg and that one of my first assignments, which I took on myself, was to bring an indictment against Erich Koch, district party boss and senior administrative official in East Prussia, on charges of corruption.[2] I was later reprimanded by Goering in 1936 for filing charges again Koch. And Koch remained. The case went up to Hitler and because Koch was a friend of

Goering's, the whole thing was forgotten. Instead, in 1936, I myself was transferred to Silesia.

"Koch brought suit against me because I helped the Jews in Königsberg. Koch ordered everybody photographed who bought in Jewish stores and I personally countermanded these orders." What were your duties in Königsberg? "I was in charge of the SS cavalry and training." And in Silesia? "That was my best time. At that time Josef Wagner was party district administrator. At the outbreak of war, Wagner was shot because of an order from Hitler.[3] And that was because Wagner and I developed our own political ideology, so that until the outbreak of the Russian war, no Jews were shot or placed in ghettos.

"As my successor, there came a man named Ernst Schmauser in 1941.

"Since 1941, I participated in the Russian campaign."

Do you know Rudolf Mildner? "No, he must have been after my time. I left Breslau in April 1941."

Did you know anything about the camp at Auschwitz? "No, it didn't exist at that time.

"I was in charge of the Jewish problem. At the time of Wagner, there were no concentration camps. General Blaskowitz protested because my predecessor had shot Jews, et cetera. But when I took over command, I ordered that there be no persecution of the Jews, no ghettos. My predecessor was a man named Udo von Woyrsch. He is a nephew of the famous Marshal von Woyrsch of the First World War, who has died long since. The great marshal would be ashamed of the deeds of his nephew. It was criminal. But when I came, I established justice and order." At this point, Bach-Zelewski looks like a man who has thoroughly convinced himself as to his faithfulness and is quite willing to condemn and lay the blame on others.

"Auschwitz was a troop training center. There was the factory of the Goering Works and maybe the workers in that factory were from concentration camps. There might have been barracks around the factory, but it was not a concentration camp at that time, because if it had been a concentration camp, it would have been an extermination camp." Do you mean to imply that all concentration camps were extermination camps? "No, but I know that Auschwitz became an extermination camp and so did many others. But during my time in that region, this was not the case."[4]

What were your duties on the Russian front? "At first, I was chief of police and SS general on the staff of General Max von Schlenckendorff in the middle regions of Russia. Schlenckendorff was the commander of forces in the rear areas. I founded all of the police stations."

What was the nature of your testimony in the court here in Nuremberg? "Yes, let me tell you about that. There were instances where I refused to obey Himmler's orders. I testified about Warsaw and Himmler's orders to shoot all of the women and children. I counteracted Himmler's orders and even had a brigade leader and staff shot because they were carrying out these orders."

Where were you during the burning of the Warsaw Ghetto?[5] "Oh, I was nowhere near there at the time. I was in Kovel, a commander there. I was a kind of division commander. It was in the Polish uprising in 1944 that I made the Polish war minister sign the capitulation. Your newspaper, the *Stars and Stripes,* carried an article about my humane activity. By 1944, there were no longer any Jews in Warsaw. But I saved the Polish women and children who would have been killed according to Himmler's orders. A short time ago, I was interrogated by the Poles, and I was not charged with any crimes." Have you been interrogated by the Russians? "Yes indeed, and I became a witness for the Russians. My attitude can only be seen from the diaries of Sauckel and Frank, which tell of my disobeying orders of Himmler."

How can you be of such a sterling character and still have been an SS general until the end of the war? "Psychologically speaking, it is an interesting case. Himmler was a most cunning man. He is not exactly as he is being branded today. He undoubtedly felt that it was wise to have a man like myself who was by ancestry half Polish and by character incorruptible — I guess Himmler felt that I could be useful because of these qualities."

Bach-Zelewski showed me three newspaper articles, one in English and two in German, which reported his evidence at the present trials. "You know that Goering was punished later on because he loudly called me a traitor and a pig in full view of the court. That was because I said to the tribunal that the war against Russia was planned by Keitel, Goering, and others. The cruel misdeeds against civilians were intentional, and I said that too. I also told how different it was in my territories when I was in charge anywhere. Whenever I took a town, I would summon the man in charge of the synagogue and assure him that no harm would come to him or to the other Jews. I figure that I saved ten thousand lives of Jews by telling them to hide in the Pripet Marshes. Those marshes are not exactly as the word implies. They are mostly woods and canals. I told the Jews that from the marshes, they could find their way to the Russian lines.

"I was the only SS leader in Russia who was not assassinated or upon whom an assassination was never attempted. I could walk anywhere without a bodyguard.

"My best witness is General Bor-Komorowski,[6] and the bishop I had taken care of." Why didn't you do something to prevent the burning of the ghetto in Warsaw? "Himmler had specialists for ghettos. I was a specialist only in the fighting against partisans." Did you execute partisans or order their execution? "No, I was against that policy. Frank mentions it in his diary. I made a speech in 1943 which criticized the policy already set against the partisans, and that is a policy that will now cost Frank his head. I said at that time that one cannot fight partisans with arms. My advice was to give them enough to eat, et cetera."

Since you are opposed to everything that was accepted in the SS, how did it happen that Himmler kept you on as a leading SS general? "You have to look at Himmler's policy from a broad viewpoint. Himmler wanted to take Hitler's place. My name, the name Bach-Zelewski, was popular with the German people. I was very well known, respected, and beloved. If Himmler had arrested me, the German people would get suspicious and would wonder how it happened."

At that point, Bach-Zelewski seemed to be taking stock of the effect of his words on me. I was smoking a cigarette and taking notes and made no comment. I believe he felt that it was important to explain further, and that prompted his next statement, which was more revealing. "I myself always played things very tricky. I played two different cards. I told Himmler that Hitler was plotting against him, and I told Hitler that Himmler was against him. Finally, in 1943, I had my family moved near the Swiss border, because I expected at any time to be arrested.

"I was very much opposed to the assassination attempt on Hitler's life of July 20, 1944, because the wrong people were in it. For example, the most famous Jew killer in Russia, the notorious SS general Arthur Nebe, was part of that conspiracy.[7] I believe that Himmler himself had a hand in it. In my eyes, Himmler was worse than Hitler. The assassination attempt should have been directed against Himmler in the first place.

"In January and February 1945, I was near Stettin on the Oder. At the time, I was suffering from food poisoning and was being treated in a hospital. When the war came to an end, I had been transferred from one hospital to another and was recuperating. At the beginning of May 1945, I recovered. I was not arrested. From May until August, I went on a search for Himmler. Finally, I gave myself up voluntarily in August 1945. I went from one village to another looking for Himmler in order to kill him. I also wanted to find my family, whose whereabouts I did not know. I didn't know what the future held in store for me. At that time, I thought it was certain that since I was an SS general, I would be taken prisoner and executed at once.

"It took me two months to walk on foot through the Lüneburg heath, which is between Hanover and Hamburg, and then down to the Swiss border, where my family resided." Why did you give yourself up? "Because I had a clear conscience and had nothing to hide." Then why didn't you give yourself up in May? "Everything was a big mix-up and all was confusion. I didn't know what would happen to war criminals. To be honest, the first newspaper accounts I read about concentration camps I thought were propaganda. I didn't realize until after the war that all of the Jews were dead. I don't want to say I didn't know Jews were being exterminated, because I did know that a long time ago — many years before the end of the war. But I didn't know that it was being done on the scale — I didn't realize it was being done in such great numbers."

Have you yourself ever seen Jews executed? "Yes, I saw executions, however not only of Jews, but others. I remember that Himmler was once personally present when 120 were executed. On another occasion in 1941, in Minsk, Himmler ordered me to go there to witness the execution of twenty Jews."

How were the 120 people you refer to executed? "They were shot in regular military fashion, three men shot at once. The whole group of 120 men were shot by an entire battalion. I made a detailed description in my report because it afforded an interesting view of Himmler's character.

"At the time of the shooting of these 120, there was a young Jewish boy of twenty who had a Nordic appearance, with blue eyes and blond hair. Himmler called that boy aside from the pit where he was to be shot and asked him if he were Jewish, whether his grandparents were all Jewish. The boy replied that as far as he knew, his entire family was Jewish. Then Himmler said that he couldn't help the boy, and the boy was executed along with the others. You could see how Himmler tried to save the boy's life."

Are you giving me this example as an instance of the nobleness of Himmler? "No, but I just want to show that Himmler was not as he is branded today. He was not a man who was hard-hearted in the sight of blood. He was hard-hearted by reason of a fanatic ideology. But he was undoubtedly soft and cowardly.

"After the execution, we went to look over an insane asylum for very sick inmates. It was a very nauseating sight. Himmler, Nebe, and I went through that institution, and I was present when Himmler talked with Nebe about liquidating the inmates of that institution. I think that the reason for this was that Himmler wanted to give me a sign, a hint, that is, that my younger brother, Victor, who was mentally sick, would be liquidated in the same way if I didn't stay in line.

"After my Warsaw accomplishment, I became the SS commander of Budapest, but I was relieved after five days because I refused to liquidate the Jews there."

Why did you join the SS in the first place? "I don't want to say I joined because of idealistic motives. Firstly, I believed in the 'stab in the back' legend.[8] The generals said that after the last war, Germany had been sold out from the inside. Now, of course, I don't believe it anymore, but as a young lieutenant, I believed that Germany was not beaten actually on the battlefield in the first war, but had been sold out from the inside.

"There were other things. The Poles had the corridor. Parts of my family lived in Poland.

"Another factor is that the Ludendorff movement was more anti-Semitic than the Hitler movement. I thought that Hitler would drop most of his anti-Semitic ideas. I was impressed by the Nazi election victory in 1930. I lost a job with a Jewish firm. I liked the profession of soldier and I talked with my Jewish brothers-in-law, and both of them agreed that it would be best for me to drift with the stream instead of opposing it, and thus get more out of it by joining the party rather than opposing it.

"My wife's cousin was married to a Jewish banker in Berlin. He was a member of the National Union of Jewish Students, and in the last war, he was a captain of the reserve. We were very intimate friends. This man financed the Baltic undertaking against Riga by General von Goltz. In other words, the Jewish banker had nationalistic feelings. He told me to join up with the Nazis and that after a few years, things would quiet down and there would be good times among the ruling classes.

"After that, my career was fast and my rise was rapid — too rapid — so that I could not quit without endangering my family.

"Even today, looking back, when I ask myself what I should have done, I must answer that it was for the best that a few decent fellows like myself were influential in the SS and thus staved off bad things."

Bach-Zelewski looks particularly smug and hypocritical as he makes this latter statement. I asked him quite directly what he had ever "staved off." He said, "In Warsaw alone I saved a thousand people at least in 1944. And I told you about at least ten thousand Jews that I saved by sending them to the Pripet Marshes."

I have heard from many people here in this prison that you were one of the most severe and influential SS generals and that many mass executions took place under your direct supervision. "I know some of these people whom I have spoken against will say that, but all I can do is testify to the truth. I saved a thousand lives in Warsaw — known Jews, I mean — in 1944, and ten thousand Jews by sending them to the marshes." And therefore, you feel that it was worthwhile for you to be a member of the SS, of which Himmler was chief, because you saved, or claimed that you saved, ten thousand Jews, when the SS has admittedly exterminated between 5 and 6 million Jews? "Yes, but I was just a small man, and ten thousand Jews saved is ten thousand. What more could one man do?" Well, you seem to blame one man, namely Himmler, for the death of the remaining 5 million Jews and the murder of many innocent Poles and Russians. "Yes, but Himmler was a man who had much more power than I did. Besides, I didn't say that Himmler alone was responsible. The whole crowd — Hitler, Himmler, Goering, Frank, Rosenberg, just to mention those who were responsible in the East alone — have blood on their hands. But I have none.

"The reason Goering calls me a traitor is that I have said these things in interrogations and before the tribunal. And I say again that I know personally that Himmler planned the systematic extermination — the cold-blooded murder — of 30 million Slavs. That is the reason Goering calls me a traitor. If I had stayed in Silesia, the Jews there would still be alive." Why didn't you stay in Silesia? "I was ordered out." Well, what good did you do when you were there? "I have told you repeatedly that I saved a thousand women and children who were ordered to be shot in

Warsaw, that I saved many Jews in Russia, and I could give you other examples, for example, how I saved Bialystok."

Therefore, you feel justified in becoming a Nazi SS man? "No. I must be responsible for everything I did in my life. This doesn't excuse my deep guilt for joining the party." Yes, but a moment ago you said that in retrospect you thought it was a good idea for a few decent fellows like yourself to be in the party and in the SS. "No, what I meant is that one can't compare me with the rest of them. What I mean is that in retrospect — in trying to look backward over the past — fate and the act of God made me join the SS and the party."

Do you think it was fate and the act of God, or do you think that it was your own decision, which, as you told me a few minutes ago, was carefully thought out and discussed with your brothers-in-law at the time you decided to "drift with the stream"? "God is over all. I don't mean to say that it was not my own free will. But all the free will of people is influenced by God."

Do you mean that anything that happens in this world, good or evil, can be excused on the basis that God so wanted it? "Yes, yes, I believe so much in God." Then you believe that God wanted 5 or 6 million Jews killed in gas chambers and in pits? "No, that I don't believe God wanted. That I believe was the devil, who was fighting against God and who temporarily got the upper hand, using such people as Himmler and Hitler and the SS — including such good influences as myself and a few others within the SS. I believe so much in God — and it is proven by the way in which the war ended. If Germany had won, it would have been the victory of the will of the devil.

"If I ever get out of here, and I want to help people, I will write a book about my experiences as an SS leader and the name of the book will be *Lucifer's Angel.*" Do you mean in your book that you are an angel? "No, only by comparison. Hitler and Himmler were fallen angels, that is, they were devils. Lucifer's angel would be the SS. In the Catholic religion, Lucifer's angel wanted to be like God and was cursed by God.

"Looking at it from a religious viewpoint and summing up all of the lives that this war lost — Jews, Germans, Allies — if this is the last war, if the Allies now succeed in bringing about eternal peace, then it is worthwhile. But if it is not the last war, it is not worthwhile."

During all of this time Bach-Zelewski has the pious, pompous bearing of a preacher or well-fed schoolteacher who has a rather platitudinous idea which he believes to be of great depth.

Do you think that this has been the last war? "I believe it is the last war because if it isn't, it means the end of humanity. If this has not been the last war, I would just as soon have seen Himmler gas me and my family some time ago.

"I have regretted my step a hundred times. I have seen my children gassed and done away with in my imagination, and I have lived through horrible times. Right now, I feel almost in Paradise because I know that the kind Americans won't hurt my family. In the Bible, there is only one man who is ready to give his son to God, and that was Abraham."

**Family History:** Father died at fifty-two of rheumatism when the subject was ten years of age. The father was an insurance agent who had a small income of about a hundred marks a month. He was always in poor circumstances.

**Mother:** Died in 1935 at the age of seventy-one after her daughter had emigrated to South America. She died of cancer.

**Siblings:** The subject is the fifth of seven children. He has four sisters and two brothers: (1) Carola, who is married to a teacher in East Prussia; (2) sister in Rio de Janeiro, married to a Jew; (3) another sister, also in Rio for the same reason; (4) brother Kurt, also in Rio; (5) the subject; (6) Eva, married in Leipzig, where her husband is a barber (How did it happen that your sister should make such a lowly marriage? "We were always very poor, and the 'von' in front of my name doesn't mean that we are rich"); (7) Victor, the youngest brother, whose fate was mentioned above.

After your father's death, how did your mother earn a living? "She was supported by my older sisters and later by me. Our home was in Berlin, where my mother lived until her death."

Can you tell me something about your early family life and your childhood? "Well I was brought up by another family from the age of six to ten years. After that, from the age of ten to fifteen, I lived in the gymnasium that I attended. I never really had a family life. It was only after I married that I found a home with my wife and children." Why were you brought up by another family and why did you spend so little time with your own people as a child? On this point, Bach-Zelewski was definitely evasive and answered in generalizations, which seemed to be evasions. "We were poor and my father died when I was ten, and the other family that brought me up took a liking to me."

**Marital History:** He states that he was married at the age of twenty-two, at which time he was a lieutenant, to a girl one year his junior. He states that his marriage has been happy, although of necessity during the last six years of war he has not had as much time with his wife and children as he would have liked. He has six children. The oldest is a girl of twenty, who recently married in Vienna. The other children are a girl of seventeen, another of twelve, another of seven, and two boys, ages eight and six years. Regarding his wife's personality, he resorts to the cliché that she was always quiet, good-natured, a faithful wife and devoted mother.

**Religion and Religious Education:** In view of the subject's frequent references to God and his pious attitude, I inquired as to his religion and religious education. He said, "Of course, during the time of my being in the SS, from 1930 or thereabouts, until the end of the war in 1945, I could not practice my religion. I have to admit I did a thing which was morally not very good. What I did was write a certificate and present it to the SS when I joined, which stated that I had left the Lutheran Church. My wife is a Lutheran, but you see it was a trick because I was a Catholic, and although I did not practice my religion for several years before, I had actually never left the church."

Did you become religious here, or before coming here? "As an SS leader I had to deny religion. If I went to mass, I could go only secretly, that is, anonymously, and in civilian clothes. It was absolutely impossible for me to attend church in my SS uniform, which I had to wear on all occasions because I was an active general. For example, when I was stationed in Breslau, I could not go to church. I have found out here in this prison from the Catholic chaplain that I am still a Catholic and have always been a Catholic officially. The Catholic Church only recognizes leaving the church if one requests it of his priest. And I have never requested it. This is confidential, and I only tell it to you. I don't want to bring it up to the court — as far as the church is concerned, the Catholic chaplain tells me that I am a good Catholic. In the eyes of the state, I had left the church. In the eyes of the Catholic Church, I find I had not left it." If Germany had won the war, would you be back in the Catholic Church now? "That goes much deeper. Germany could not win this war because it was in league with the devil. This war would not have ended without revolution."

# Kurt Daluege
1897–1946

Kurt Daluege was SS colonel general and colonel general of the police. In 1942 he succeeded Reinhard Heydrich as Reich protector of Bohemia and Moravia. Brought to trial in Czechoslovakia and condemned to death, he was hanged in 1946.

### January 26, 1946

Kurt Daluege, who was chief of the regular uniformed police of Germany, is in solitary.[1] He is a big fellow, with hooked nose, beady eyes, somber, piqued facial expression, in his forties. He is polite in a restrained way, talks easily, but says little of anything revelatory of emotional or factual content. He is apparently fastidious, keeps his cell in barren order, a description that might apply as well to his face. When I knocked the ashes from my pipe several times into his cardboard ashtray, inadvertently spilling a few flecks on the table, he invariably, and automatically it seemed, blew the ashes from the table. He is composing some kind of autobiographical account of his early years for Colonel Schroeder, who he says asked him to do so. The sheets containing this material lay neatly on his writing table. They superficially gave the impression of having been turned out by a printing machine. He is doing it by hand, each letter printed, marvelously uniform and neat. The context of his early life, he said, is as follows: He was brought up to live in the outdoors, was a member of an organization of nature lovers called the Wandervogel, which taught him to hike, rely on himself in the woods, build fires for cooking in the open, and in general have manly objectives.

That fine, neat printing, he said, was done because his longhand script is "not so good." He was born in Upper Silesia (1897). His father was a small government official, having something to do with land assessments.

He said everything with a minimum of emotionality, an affectless quality to both vocal and facial expression.

Yes, he said, he was an SS general during the war, but that was an automatic affair, because as chief of the Ordinary Police, he received the title. Well, then, I asked (through Dr. Gilbert, who was translating), was the police part of the SS? No, his police were nonmilitary, not part of the SS. However, Himmler was his superior. Was his police force related to the Gestapo? No, nothing to do with the Gestapo. Yes, Himmler was chief of Gestapo, and he was subject to Himmler. Asked pointedly if his police protected Jews and their property when attacks were occurring all over Germany, he said he knew nothing about these attacks, nobody ever told him. Once, just once, he recalled, now that it was mentioned, he witnessed the burning of a synagogue in Munich, but it happened so quickly, what could he do?

His relationship to Himmler? They didn't get along well, because he was considered by Himmler to be a rival. He even heard at one time that Himmler was going to have him arrested. This never happened, however. What does he think of Himmler? Well, they just didn't care for each other because they were rivals. But Daluege remained chief of the Ordinary Police all the time, and had frequent business conferences with Himmler. He could not, or would not, give any estimate of Himmler, seemed to lack either the desire or willingness (probably both) even to comment on Himmler as a human being, or to remark on any criticisms of, or for that matter agreements with, Himmler's activities and policies.

Did he feel guilty of anything? "No." He was in charge of the police force of Germany, and everything had gone all right as far as he knew.

The general impression he leaves is that he is insensitive, hard-boiled, capable of great ruthlessness, amoral, conscienceless.

He said that he inherited syphilis from his father, but it was not discovered until he was thirty-six. He has taken yearly treatments for the past ten years. His father lived to be seventy-three, had syphilis for years, but it never affected his health. Daluege was told that his syphilis was inherited, and that it was not unusual for the type of syphilis he had to go undiscovered for many years without symptoms. During the first ten years of his marriage, he was childless, and thought that the syphilis caused him to be sterile. However, after a few years of treatment, he was able to have children. He has a picture on his writing table of his wife and four (perhaps five, I forget) small children.

Asked if there was anything I could do for him, he said he would like a blood test again, as it was about a year since he had his last, which was negative. However, a few years ago he was given malaria treatment for syphilis, which might indicate that spinal fluid was indicative of central nervous system involvement at the time.

I examined his pupils, which seemed to react well in accommodation, but not adequately to light.

There is no indication of organic mental affection. Sensorium, etc., intact, no evidence of mental dysfunction in any sphere. Emotionally, he seems callous, affectless, unimaginative, and there is evidence of obsessive character (namely the disturbance at ashes on his table, and the neat, printlike writing). He presents himself as being just an officeholder, the son of an officeholder; knows nothing about atrocities and so forth. It is clear that he would be the kind of executive who would neatly and obsessively be well informed about everything his forces did, and in fact exert a rigid control over them.

That it is fairly improbable to get much emotional response out of this man, I am convinced. There is a long-conditioned hardness, an outer shell which has been worn and used so long, probably nothing exists beneath it. Having dealt with force, violence, and easy dispositions of the lives of others, it is questionable as to how much value he puts on life in general, including his own in particular. This was not discussed with him, though it would be interesting to get some information on that point. Getting a sincere or emotionally meaningful answer from him is like trying to bail water from a long-dry well.

# Sepp Dietrich
## 1892–1966

Josef "Sepp" Dietrich, an early supporter of Hitler, was head of the Hitler Bodyguard regiment, SS general, commander of the Sixth Panzer Army from 1944 to 1945, and appointed SS colonel general in 1944. Captured by the Americans and sentenced to life imprisonment, he was released from the American war crimes prison in Landsberg in 1955. Tried in Munich in 1957 for crimes committed in the Third Reich, he was sentenced to eighteen months' imprisonment.

**February 28, 1946**

Sepp Dietrich is a fifty-four-year-old, stockily built fellow with a wry, humorous smile, a somewhat rough-and-ready attitude, quite friendly, and eager for the companionship that an interview affords. His general manner of speech and his mannerisms are not consistent with any notion of a German general, in the Prussian sense of the term. He gives the impression of competence, an easygoing manner, a minimum of military bearing, and a hard-boiled, rough, accepting attitude toward the facts of his present life in prison.

He has no particular physical complaints other than rheumatic pains in the left shoulder, which have been present since the winter of 1941, when he was at the Russian front.

In the First World War, he was injured twice. He spent three years in active service prior to that war, then spent four years' service during the war. He was twenty-two when war began.

He was injured by a spear in the left supraorbital region in World War

I, when he fell from a horse. This became infected and he was four months in a hospital for that injury. He was wounded the second time by shrapnel in the right leg. He became a noncommissioned officer first, and finally an officer in 1921. He had been in the army steadily since the age of nineteen. After the last war, he remained in the 100,000-man army.

He never attended military academies. In 1917–18 he was with the panzers, and in the last war was exclusively a panzer commander.

He knew Field Marshal Erwin Rommel very well.[1] "He too was about my age. He was not exclusively a panzer general." Was he a good panzer general? "So-so." Dietrich is obviously very cool toward Rommel. "It's hard to change over from another branch of service. Rommel was really an infantry general.

"Rommel was jumpy, wanted to do everything at once, then lost interest. Rommel was my superior in command in Normandy. I cannot say Rommel wasn't a good general. When successful, he was good; during reverses, he became depressed."

Asked further about his own previous illnesses, he said, "I'm iron," and laughed. "I lasted through ten years of war, and now I can last through this. It's true, it's not good for the nerves." Is there enough to eat? "Yes. But we are never spoiled here. But I come from a workman's family and was never spoiled as a child."

Dietrich has been a POW for the past ten months, since May 10, 1945. On that date, he surrendered his army, along the Danube. They covered a front line of 220 kilometers, partly on the Danube, partly off it. His army consisted of two corps of SS and two army corps. He had under him two SS generals and two army generals.

He spent three years in Russia and one and a half years on the western front. In 1940 he was in France, Greece, Russia, and back to France.

"General Patch of your Seventh Army was a fast Rommel — faster than Rommel. I spoke with Patch."

**Marital:** First marriage was at age thirty, for ten years, terminating in divorce. "We didn't get along." They had no children. His present marriage occurred seven years ago, his wife now thirty-three; has three children with her, all boys. He has a picture of his wife and the youngsters nearby and shows them to me. He is loath to talk much about his marital life or sexual adjustment, and the matter was not pressed.

**Family:** Father and mother, ages seventy-six and seventy, respectively, died in 1942. Father was a storehouse keeper who worked for a cheese factory. He never made much of a living, but it was adequate for immediate needs. There were six children; two brothers were killed in the last war.

**Mother:** Always well until she suffered a heart attack in 1942 and died. They were "very good parents," but Sepp had to start to work early because of financial conditions.

**Siblings:** He is the oldest child — five others. His two sisters are healthy, married.

Before the father died, he did not have political ideas or convictions. "Father was more of a Catholic — nonpolitical." Do you feel yourself nonpolitical? "I never actively engaged in politics, never made speeches. Politics is a whore. It's too high for me. Just as I don't understand American politics, so I don't understand German politics. The only interest in politics is to get to know how to lead a life under the most favorable circumstances.

"I observed a lot of suffering — in all the countries of Europe except Norway. People suffered before, during, and now after the war — it is worse. I know we lost the war, but if Europe is destroyed . . ."

What's the point you want to make? "I understand by politics the whole life of people, misery, wealth, intelligence, nonintelligence, a whole setup of people. This is my opinion. I could notice it best because I was in all countries. I didn't have fifteen people carrying my bags. I lived in farms, even ditches, and had plenty of opportunity to observe and get acquainted with the intelligence and manners of people. Also, in Russia. A man who doesn't know Russia shouldn't even talk about it." What do you think of the Russians? "They have a wealth of children, are diligent, healthy, have fertile ground. Their industrial and business economy just fits Russia and has no application for anyone else. You can't do it in the United States or Germany. There might be a democracy after a time in Germany, but not Communism. But in Russia, it fits one hundred percent."

What about the character of Russian soldiers? "All Asiatics are cruel dogs. All they captured of my soldiers, they beat to death. The Russian soldiers are very brave, stable, tough." Do you feel the Russian soldier is basically more cruel than the German soldier? "In the way of his fighting, yes. They are a different kind of people — can't compare them with Europeans. Americans are for the most part Europeans. On the other hand, White Russians and Ukrainians are more similar to our own."

Did more cruel things happen on the eastern than western front? "Yes. You can't find these cruelties in the West or southwest. Down to the lower Balkans."

Do you think it might be because the Russians lost land and people? "No. It was a racial factor." Do you believe in the Nazi philosophy of racism and the master race? "You can find masters all over the world, not only in Germany, so I don't believe in it. In all races, you can find good, intelligent folk. You can see the German people as they are now." Yes, and we saw it before. "Yes, we did too. We fellows in the army didn't fall for that." But weren't you a member of the party and working with it? "I agreed with the economic aims of the party since the last war, but I didn't work politically with the party. Weimar had a political leadership that accomplished nothing. There were forty-six different parties; it wasn't like in your country, with two parties. The Weimar Republic had a lot of good ideas, but never could get them together. If we had had strong, unified movements, we might have accomplished something."

When did you become a Nazi? "I joined the party in 1928." Why? "I was interested because I saw the Social Democrats and Communists were not for me. All my relatives were unemployed. The German people are hard to lead — they need an iron rule. They are square-heads." Why? "Because intellectually, culturally, practically, they are stubborn." Then why, if stubborn and hard to lead, did they suddenly follow Hitler? "He was not stupid. They actually ran after him. He must have been the best of our leaders at the time, or he would not have had such a following. Most of the party people had belonged to other parties, such as Homeowners' Party, or Union, Trade Unions, Social Democrats, or Communist."

Did you know Hitler personally very much? "Almost only on official business." What did you, or do you, think of him? "Some people say he was crazy. Most of such people are non-Germans who are trying to get something out of it. You couldn't get close to Hitler as far as private conversations are concerned. Not even Goering." Always, or just during the war? "Always. He stood above anyone else. As soon as he became Reich chancellor, he became more and more distant, et cetera." I've also heard the reverse, that Hitler could be seen if someone had a problem. "No. He was like a stern father. No, Hitler never even told Goebbels about his own problems." Could you go to Hitler with your problems? "For quite a while. Then suddenly, in 1942 or 1943, one couldn't go to Hitler.

Or one could go up to him, but not achieve anything. When things got bad, as in Stalingrad, Hitler became stubborn, and one could not reason with him.

"We tried to see things from a more human side. Hitler didn't see it. We fought against an enemy six times as large as us." When was the last time you saw Hitler? "On February 25, 1945." How did he look? "Sick. Almost completely finished. After the assassination attempt, he went down and down. First of all, he must have suffered some kind of injury and strain of the last twenty years. Even the strongest bull couldn't stand it. He never went to bed before four or five a.m. He was a typical night worker. Maybe four to five hours' sleep per day. You can do it for a month, not for years. We weren't so dumb we couldn't see it. We just couldn't help ourselves." Did you think Hitler made any big mistakes before 1940? "Yes. Starting the war. Whenever people lose a war, the losers look foolish. We had a poor foreign policy, even before Hitler's time." What do you mean? "Take a map. See where Germany lies — look at the countries surrounding Germany, count her enemies and her friends, and see what I mean." Do you mean German foreign policy should have created more friends? "A friendlier economy should be some way of bringing people of the world together. It's not the way of doing it now."

What do you mean? Afraid I don't follow you completely. "Look at the whole setup. I don't know the American or English people. Look at the East — a force that can't be beat, if the Russians and Chinese face us. A few little nations in Europe. Take a look at the Balkans and Greece and other little countries — it's the same all over.

"If the U.S. and England had given us a little help, Hitler wouldn't have been needed." Do you recall that the U.S. was in a depression? "Yes, but before that. Giving the Saar region to France, the Polish Corridor, southern Tirol to Austria, et cetera. How can there be peace with people pressed together for want of land? Hitler took the bad points of the Versailles Treaty and used them to his own advantage. People were hungry, would run after anyone who promised food and clothing."

Dietrich says he was in the army until 1927, when he was obliged to leave and enter the tobacco business. He remained in that business until 1930. He was a customs official with an Austrian tobacco monopoly. He handled 1.5 to 2 million pounds of tobacco and made six hundred marks per month.

In 1930 he returned to Nazi Party politics, as Nazi representative to the Reichstag from Schwabia. He had no "political mandate" until 1933, when he was given the organization of the SS Bodyguard regiment. He received a salary of 780 marks or 1,100 marks per month, with taxes taken off the former figure. He laughs wryly at this Dietrich humor.

He was Hitler's personal choice to lead the Bodyguard regiment. "Originally, it was seven hundred men. At the end, it was twenty-one thousand men. Of these, in 1942, about thirty-two were still alive. What came after that is just a name — not the real thing. I gave up command of the Bodyguard regiment in March 1943." He was with the SS from the beginning — in Poland, France, Greece, the western front, Russia, and again the western front. He became army commander in September 1944. Did you know General Anton Dostler?[2] "No." Hear about him? "Yes." What do you think of his trial? "A prisoner is a prisoner and shouldn't be shot. As far as I know, Dostler's orders came from other orders by the Supreme Command of the Armed Forces. For example, from Normandy, where seven Canadians were shot. Colonel General Kurt Meyer was convicted for the shooting.[3] He claimed he did not know who gave the orders. In my own army at Malmédy, I heard, after I was captured, that 164 people were shot. I was general of the Sixth Panzer Army, but nobody had reported anything about it to me.[4]

"In all the armies in the West, we observed the Geneva Convention." How about in the East? "No. There was no Geneva Convention. But we didn't shoot Russians either.[5] Where would we get 3 million prisoners if we shot all the Russians? Propaganda! You can't open your mouth, even in the biggest democracy. Do you think it's so nice to sit in prison after ten years of war for the Fatherland? If I would be God, I would do it differently!"

What are your views on religion? "I never left the church." Do you know the Catholic chaplain? "Yes, a very decent fellow." What do you think of the crimes against the Jews? "The biggest nonsense they could do. They could have told the Jews, if they didn't want them, they could get out. The Germans could have given them three to four hundred millions and let them go somewhere. Personally, I was never anti-Semitic. In childhood, I lived next door to some Jewish people and never even knew it." Did you believe Streicher, Rosenberg, et al.? "I never read Streicher! Rosenberg I never could understand — too complicated." Hitler was also against the Jews. "He seldom spoke about it. In 1943, I read a letter from my wife [in Greece] that the Jews were all brought together. I went up to Himmler and asked him. Himmler said it was not true. Himmler said he would bring them together to work because they weren't too good to work. But that was at a time when the Jewish people didn't live anymore. I never learned as much as here in prison now. You should talk to Wilhelm Hoettl and Schellenberg; they were Himmler's second men."

## Franz Halder
### 1884–1972

Franz Halder, colonel general, was chief of the army general staff from 1938 to 1942, and dismissed on September 24, 1942, because of a dispute with Hitler over the German offensive against Stalingrad. After the attempt on Hitler's life in 1944, he was sent to a concentration camp, and liberated by the Americans at the end of the war.

**April 5, 1946**

There was a short interview with Franz Halder today, devoted to discussion of his family life and experience in the concentration camp after the July 20, 1944, assassination attempt on Hitler's life.

"I lived a simple soldier's life from my youth on. I was married very young, at the age of twenty-three. I was twenty-one when I became engaged. I had the good luck to marry the woman I loved. I can say now at the close of my life that my home and family was the foundation of my strength. My wife was not wealthy; we lived simply and very happy. We did not participate in social functions, which neither of us cared for. We have three daughters and fourteen grandchildren. Each daughter has one daughter herself, and the rest sons."

Halder is completely shook up emotionally at this point and is frankly weeping. After several moments he said, "To see daughters grow up is one of the most beautiful things in life. For a father to have daughters is the finest experience. A scientist who wrote about heredity science claimed that daughters resemble the father and sons the mother." I believe that depends on the situation and the parents. "Yes, of course." General Halder's daughters were born in 1909, 1913, and 1914. They married in the order of their ages, each when she was between nineteen and twenty.

We discussed the personalities of his daughters. "They vary quite a bit. The oldest one doesn't show much similarity to either me or my wife — but you find that frequently in the firstborn. In my middle daughter and youngest daughter there is a greater resemblance to my side of the family. The middle one has taken the best from my wife's family and from mine. The youngest resembles my family almost exclusively."

Which is your favorite daughter? Halder smiled and again becomes emotionally labile. "I love all of them and they love me, too. The oldest lives with my wife, the youngest lives in upper Bavaria, the middle one lives in Schleswig. I hear from the oldest and the youngest frequently because the postal service is good, but the service from Schleswig is poor. My greatest aggravation here is that I cannot write a decent letter to my loved ones. This telegram style of letter on these POW blanks, that is the worst that I have to experience. I cannot give any of myself in these letters. In Hitler's prison I could write to my family as much as I wanted, although I couldn't write to my wife or to my oldest daughter, who were also imprisoned. They did that to make me suffer. I was not even supposed to know that she was in prison.

"My wife was in Ravensbrück concentration camp during two months of my stay there. I was not supposed to know that she was there." Did they treat your wife fairly in Ravensbrück? "She was not mistreated, but that is the best one can say for it." What was the routine in Ravensbrück? "It was a prison. I was allowed to go outside once a day in the air alone for a half hour. I was in solitary and the door was locked. It was not open like here, where I am allowed to walk about at least inside. After I had been at Ravensbrück for some time they asked me if I wanted to do some work, such as making lists, et cetera, to just pass the time away. There were no other advantages. During the day one could hear the yelling of people who were being clubbed. At night one could hear shots, people being shot. When the window of my cell was open, the cell would be filled with smoke from the crematory. There was contact between internees from window to window, and I heard in a short time what was happening."

How far was the crematory from your billet? "It was a distance about twice as long as this room; then there was a wall, and just beyond it the crematory. When the wind blew in at the south I got smoke in my cell. It was a fat smoke, big flakes of smoke — human smoke. I don't know who invented the crematory, Hitler, Himmler, or some other criminal, but I know that they stink."

Halder went on to describe how he remained in Ravensbrück for two months, then he was sent to RSHA prison in Berlin, where he was in solitary custody and never given any fresh air. "That was the worst. There was no real light in the room, and day and night they had light-bulbs burning. I only left the cell for interrogations and whenever I had to go to the toilet. There was no toilet in the room. In this way they could torture you because sometimes they didn't open the door for twenty-four hours, so that you suffered greatly if you had to go to the toilet. This they did consciously, but otherwise I was not tortured."

Who interrogated you there? "I wrote it all out so that I could remember it all. I was interrogated once by Heinrich Mueller, the chief of the Gestapo, and another time by some representative of Mueller's. That whole black bank of Kaltenbrunner and Schellenberg I had never heard of at that time."[1]

What sort of person was Mueller? "He lacked personality, made no impression."

Halder went on to describe how in the beginning of February 1945 the RSHA buildings were bombed out and for a few days he and other internees sat in the basement ruins. Then he was brought along with several others to Flossenbürg, in Upper Palatinate, near the Bohemian border. This was a concentration camp similar to Ravensbrück. Halder said that Ravensbrück seemed to be a women's camp generally, whereas Flossenbürg was a camp for men. He remained at the latter place through February and March and was liberated by the American troops on April 9, 1945.

"In Flossenbürg you noticed things more; you had to notice every day so many people hanged in the courtyard. People were brought to their execution completely naked. They were driven into the courtyard and I could hear the noise of naked feet on the court ground right outside my window. Stretchers with corpses were carried past the doors of our cells. If by chance the peek holes were open, one could see them going by. In the courtyard where you took a walk, they had gallows arranged in such a way that you were obliged to look at them.

"About half the group that were brought with me from Berlin were hanged. This included Admiral Wilhelm Canaris and General Hans

Oster.[2] They were hanged at Flossenbürg. I learned about it when I was transported away. I went to Flossenbürg with Canaris and Oster, and when I left they were absent."[3]

At this point, Mr. Triest, the interpreter, mentioned that a letter had been received that was addressed to General Halder from an officer named Oster. I recalled that it was a pamphlet entitled, more or less, *In Memoriam to the German Army*. Halder said that this must have been a communication from the son of General Oster, who as far as Halder knows was a major in the army.

What kind of man was Canaris? "Extremely hard to describe. He was very clever and it was difficult to see through him. He came from a Greek family and he possessed many characteristics which were strange to one who had grown up in German schools. I had no real close connection with him; it was only through our mutual enmity to Hitler that we came closer together. I knew him during my whole fight with Hitler. Canaris worked with my predecessor, Ludwig Beck, and then with me. He was a lively man, an admiral.

"I knew General Oster better than Canaris. Oster and I grew up together. He was very lively, clever, temperamental, but in my opinion, somewhat superficial. But he was a decent man and opposed to Hitler."

Why did they hang Canaris and Oster? "They must have had something definite on them. I know the Gestapo found a diary written by Canaris. Canaris was absolutely unpolitical, just like Oster and myself, and he fought against Hitler only because of his idealistic ideas. None of the officers who fought with me against Hitler had any political aims. It was a matter of possessing a different worldview. It was to liberate the German people from the Hitler regime, and then the German people could find a new government themselves.

"There was nobody in Germany who could liberate the German people except the military. In the later years we had the aid of some nonmilitary persons, such as the German ambassador to Rome and the finance minister, Schacht, although neither of them was very active. As a matter of fact, I myself could not participate actively in 1943 and 1944 because I was closely guarded by the Gestapo. I warned everyone not to get in touch with me but I always heard indirectly what was going on."

Did you know of July 20 prior to its occurrence? "No. I felt that something like this would happen. I disapproved of the idea of an assassination. I don't think political murder is a good basis for reform. Because things were becoming increasingly difficult in 1943–44, civilian members took up connections with the SD, and the trade unions, and resistance groups all over the country. Several of these people were in Ravensbrück with me and they were all hanged."

## April 12, 1946

It was a beautiful sunny day as we sat in Halder's open cell, discussing his recent grippy feeling, "as if I am going to catch a cold for the past few days." He said that he wished his cell could be changed from the north side of the prison to the south side, where there was better exposure. He said, "It was like this in Hitler's prison. I had a cell on the north side."

We went on to discuss his family history and the relationships therein.

**Siblings:** Halder had one sister, a year older than himself, who died of grippal influenza in 1918, at which time she was thirty-five years old. She was married and had two sons, one of whom was killed as the result of a fall from his horse many years ago; the other is a major in the German army, a prisoner in an American POW camp. Halder says that he always had contact with these nephews, whom he regarded affectionately. His older sister, until her death, was his "closest friend." Regarding her personality he seemed very vague and said, "It is such a long time ago; she had characteristics of both parents."

**Father:** He was an artillery officer who died of diabetes at the age of sixty in 1912. There was no other diabetes in the family. The father suffered from this illness for about twenty years prior to his death. "The doctors said that my father was in good physical health and that diabetes came because of overwork. I don't know whether that is medically true or not." Halder went on to say that his father became a major general in the War Ministry. "It might be interesting for you to note, because it is often said that generals in Hitler's time were promoted so rapidly, that I followed my father's career almost exactly. I became a general exactly at my father's age, there being thirty years' difference between us."

I suppose these quick promotions were mainly in the SS? "Yes, in the SS, but also during the last years of the war in all branches, especially after Brauchitsch and myself were thrown out; then the whole nonsense started.[4] You can see now all of the crimes were after Brauchitsch and my own time. Hitler was in charge of the army and could do as he pleased."

We went on with the discussion of the family history. His father was chief of artillery in the Bavarian War Ministry, at a time when artillery was being developed greatly. Halder states with pride that his father was one of the pioneers in the use of modern artillery weapons.

Asked about his father's personality, he said: "He was a very tall, big, imposing man, two meters tall, whose disposition was cheerful and pleasant, but who had a very strict conception of right and justice. He was a man who never did anything wrong. Like myself, he never had any sense for making money and was devoted only to his soldierly duties." Was he devoted to the children? "Yes, but he was strict toward the children as well as toward himself. However, he did have understanding and tolerance for the joy of childhood. We had the greatest respect and love for him and he never oppressed us in any way."

What was the relationship between your father and mother? Halder weeps and his voice breaks. After a few moments he replies, "As nice as I could think."

**Paternal Grandfather:** "He was also a soldier but I didn't know him. He was in an accident, falling from a horse when he was a captain, and died as a young man. My grandmother had three sons, of whom my father was the middle child. Conditions were very modest, one might even say poor. My family never owned any land. My parents' home was always as simple as possible, but despite that it was warm — and I must still thank God for my childhood." Halder is again tearful and has diffi-culty speaking because of being shook up with emotion. These emotionally labile states are quick to pass.

**Mother:** "She died on the same day I was brought here to Nuremberg, on October 12, 1945. She was almost ninety. Just before she died she was told that I was still alive. She thought I had died in Hitler's camp. That made her last year difficult. By the time I was permitted to write to her here, she had died.

"In 1944, during the big raid on Munich, my mother went to a cousin's home in upper Bavaria. This cousin was married to an Englishwoman and had been in America. The cousin is now seventy years old. He allowed my mother to have a room in his apartment. I couldn't take her with me because I had only a small apartment and no room. She died at my cousin's home in upper Bavaria."

When was the last time you saw your mother? "It was July 1944, just two weeks before I was taken prisoner by Hitler."

Do you have much interest in poetry or music? "I like both, but I never played any instrument myself. But in school and later I came to prefer scientific subjects. My wife is very musically inclined and the children also love music. My wife filled the house with joyful music and the laughter of children. My wife also participated in many sports, including tennis, for which I never had sufficient time. However, I participated in mountain climbing and I was always in the saddle. Even when I was chief of the general staff I would arise at 4:30 a.m., go horseback riding at 5 a.m., and later have breakfast. Perhaps that is why I am in good health. I became accustomed to missing so many meals because I was so busy.

"Life in the general staff since 1915 was difficult. It became even worse when war started in 1939. During my last year, in 1942, I averaged three or four hours' sleep per night and once or twice a week I worked through the night without any sleep. The reason for this was that during the day we received all troop information from the front. After that came conferences with the various fourteen section chiefs. Then I had to have a few hours daily to work by myself — this could only be done about midnight. In between times the telephone rang continuously. You had to know how to work in a place like that without wearing yourself out completely."

When Hitler marched into Poland, did you advise against it? "We had no right to do so. In the first place, I was under Brauchitsch. I spoke with the latter several times. That was the reason for Brauchitsch speaking very seriously with Hitler in the summer of 1939 just before the outbreak of war." But what did you think yourself personally? "I honestly don't think Hitler wanted war. The same with Brauchitsch — he didn't think so either. Of course, when I tell you that now it seems as if I just want to say it because of present circumstances. But some time ago I received a letter from a former secretary of mine, in which she writes that my subordinates made a remark to the effect that 'General Halder was not seriously considering war at that time.'

"You might not understand Brauchitsch's and my opinions if you do not know Hitler personally. He was a man, as I told you the other day, who saved decisions for the last minute. When Hitler said you should be ready for an attack, it in no way had to be understood literally — it might mean he wanted to threaten someone with an attack.

"Before that, there was the Sudeten matter. During that time military preparations were bad. After the Sudetan crisis [1938] was passed, people talked about such things as the poor military preparations.[5] Hitler heard about it, and urged war preparations so that in the future people would not doubt Germany's war potential again. During the Sudeten crisis the army had not been ready. Do I make that clear? People who knew Hitler never took his threats seriously. For instance, in the Sudeten crisis, Hitler published a written decision that he intended to solve the Sudeten problem with force of arms. That he did not do this is well known.

"In November 1939, Hitler expressed three times, once in outspoken form, that he had decided to overthrow Belgium and the Netherlands by force of arms. Despite that, two days before the march into the Netherlands in 1940, a special ambassadorial envoy stood by with bags packed, ready to go to the court of Queen Wilhelmina of the Netherlands to settle matters peacefully.

"On August 22, 1939, in a conference at the Berghof, Hitler said that negotiations with Poland were still under way. Therefore, we thought that it was just another bluff, this Polish question, like the Czech question. On August 26, 1939, Hitler issued a first order for an alert. Several hours later the order was rescinded and again it was said that negotiations with Poland were under way.

"Therefore, the reasons for Brauchitsch and myself believing as we did, namely, that Hitler was engaging in a game of extreme political blackmailing, became obvious. That there had been negotiations with Russia to occupy half of Poland we didn't know until the present trials here in Nuremberg. Brauchitsch and I had no contact with the political situation. What we learned, we learned from Hitler. We knew we were lied to in the press, we recognized Goebbels's lies, et cetera. It was impossible!

"I did have personal connections with a member of the Foreign Office, one of the chief state secretaries, by the name of Ernst von Weizsaecker. The latter had been prohibited by Ribbentrop to have any contact with Brauchitsch or me. But we did anyway. Weizsaecker didn't know many things either. All of these things were done by Ribbentrop. So we had no clear picture except that we knew just what kind of game Hitler was playing and we knew it was a dangerous one. Therefore, I spoke to Brauchitsch, and he in turn with Hitler, but to no avail.

"On December 10, 1941, Brauchitsch retired, presumably because of serious illness. It is true that he did have several heart attacks, but he was glad to use that as an excuse to retire, because the differences between Hitler and Brauchitsch were wider than ever. I can well imagine that the continual excitement and arguments against Hitler contributed to Brauchitsch's heart ailment. He was not retired, because once one is a field marshal, there is no retirement; but he had no more duties.

"About half a year later, on September 24, 1942, I left my post, just as Brauchitsch did, except that I was not ill and it would have been most unlikely that I could get anyone to believe that a person in perfect health would suddenly become sick. I could do nothing else because my request for retirement was not accepted. As for playing sick, I couldn't — I was well, nobody would believe me. If I wanted to break with Hitler I would have to behave badly."

Were there any particular arguments with Hitler? "There were daily quarrels all summer. The point upon which we had our final disagreement was the decision of an offensive on the Caucasus and Stalingrad — a mistake, and Hitler didn't want to see it. I told him the Russians would put in another million men in 1942 and get another million in 1943. Hitler told me that I was an idiot — that the Russians were practically dead already. When I told Hitler about Russian armament potentials, especially for tank materials, Hitler flew into a rage of fury and threatened me with his fists.

"Hitler issued several orders to the eastern front, contrary to military advice. This caused the setback. Then he blamed the army group for the defeat and claimed that they were purposely at fault. At that point I became furious, struck my fists on the table, made scenes, et cetera. When we finally parted, Hitler mentioned those scenes, and said that my nerves were bad and that his nerves were bad and that they would get worse if we worked together any longer. But between us, Doctor, those arguments were provoked by me because in twenty years of general staff work I have served with many superior officers and have not had arguments and I have always gotten along."

# Rudolf Hoess
1900–1947

Rudolf Hoess, SS lieutenant colonel from 1942, commandant of the concentration camp in Auschwitz from 1940 to 1943, was arrested by the British in 1946 and passed on to Poland. Tried by a Polish military tribunal, he was hanged at Auschwitz on April 7, 1947.

## April 8, 1946

A forty-six-year-old man, Rudolf Hoess, in the C wing in isolation. He sat with both feet in a tub of cold water, his hands clasped in his lap, rubbing them together. He said he had had frostbite for two weeks and that soaking his feet in the cold water relieved the aching.

I remarked that it hadn't been cold here, how did they get frostbite? "I was in Schleswig-Holstein, barefooted in a cell. When the British captured me I was naked and they just threw a couple of blankets around me and took me to prison. They didn't give me any shoes or socks." I asked when he was arrested. "On March 11, 1946." Tell me about it, I said. "I was hiding after I had been discharged under a false name as a navy sailor. I worked on a farm in Schleswig-Holstein."[1]

I asked how the authorities found out who he was. He said, "As far as I know, they questioned my family, who live in Schleswig, and my oldest son, age sixteen, must have given them my address." Why didn't you give yourself up before? I queried. "I thought I could get away with it." What was your official position? I asked. "As of November 1943 I was head of a branch of the Economics and Administrative Main Office in Berlin. Our office was actually in Oranienburg. This office was formerly called the Inspection Division for concentration camps. We had charge of the inspection of all concentration camps, including Silesia. The only camps which were not under our supervision were those in Russia and in the Ukraine, which were under the higher SS police. The General Government of Poland was under my supervision, but concentration camps farther on in Russia itself came under the aegis of SS generals.

"I was commandant at Auschwitz for four years, from May 1940 until the first of December, 1943." I asked how many people were executed at Auschwitz during his time. "The exact number cannot be determined. I estimate about 2.5 million Jews." Only Jews? "Yes." Women and children as well? "Yes."[2]

What do you think of it? Hoess looked blank and apathetic. I repeated my question and asked him whether he approved of what went on at Auschwitz. "I had my personal orders from Himmler." Did you ever protest? "I couldn't do that. The reasons Himmler gave me I had to accept." In other words, you think it was justified to kill 2.5 million men, women, and children? "Not justified — but Himmler told me that if the Jews were not exterminated at that time, then the German people would be exterminated for all time by the Jews."

How could the Jews exterminate the Germans? "I don't know, that is what Himmler said. Himmler didn't explain." Don't you have a mind or opinion of your own? "Yes, but when Himmler told us something, it was so correct and so natural we just blindly obeyed it." Do you have any feelings of guilt for this? "Yes, now naturally it makes me think that it was not right."

**Health History:** Hoess stated that he was born at Baden-Baden on November 25, 1900. His birth was normal and he was a full-term baby. He knows nothing about his developmental history. His general health as a child was good and the only specific illness he recalls was measles at an early age.

**Education:** He attended elementary school for three years and the gymnasium for five years. He is vague as to his accomplishments or achievements in school.

**Career:** At the age of sixteen, in 1916, he volunteered as a soldier. He spent two years in Iraq and Palestine at the front, fighting against the English. In 1918, at the cessation of hostilities, he was a sergeant of infantry.

From 1918 until 1921 he was a member of a Freikorps, called the

Rossbach Freikorps, which was stationed in the Baltic states, the Ruhr, and in Upper Silesia. "Officially the Freikorps was not paid for by the government, but unofficially it was financed by the government and by industry. The Rossbach Freikorps consisted of three thousand men. There were innumerable Freikorps, from company to regimental strengths."

After 1921 he became an apprentice agriculturalist on an estate in Silesia and Schleswig-Holstein. He worked there until 1923, when he was imprisoned, "because of the murder of a man who had given Leo Schlageter to the French; Schlageter was one of the leaders of the active resistance against the French in 1923." You murdered the man who gave up Schlageter? "Yes, I was one of four men who clubbed him to death." Why? "This man had been a member of the Rossbach Freikorps and then stole some money and made illegal dealings and took off. Then in May 1923 he reappeared in Mecklenburg in order to get some people in my school to work for the French. His name was Walter Kadow. He was an unemployed German teacher about twenty-five years old."

How long were you in prison? "I was sentenced to ten years' hard labor, but was released after five years." How is it that you didn't receive a longer sentence since it was murder? "It was not seen as murder by the court, at least not as a plain murder. It was considered death as a result of an argument. It happened in a restaurant where we met. The other three men received twelve-, ten-, and eight-year prison terms. I was in prison in Brandenburg on the Havel near Berlin. I was released from prison in 1928. There was a political amnesty when all people who were Communists or belonged to the rightist parties were released. It was the so-called Hindenburg amnesty. My crime was called a political murder." What is the difference to you between a political murder and any other murder? "There is a difference. If you kill to take money or rob, it is plain murder, but if you kill because of political reasons, that is a political murder." Do you mean that it is all right to kill your political opponents? "No, I only mean the emotions which lead to such things are different, that is, the causes vary." But in both cases, it is murder? "Yes."

From 1928 to 1934 he returned to work on various farms and estates in Mecklenburg, Brandenburg, and so forth. He described his duties as being mainly "inspector of estates."

Concerning his political activity, he said that he had been a National Socialist since 1922, but participated in no political activity between

1928 and 1934. He had attended party meetings but never held any office. In 1934 he joined the SS because the owner of the estate for which he worked wanted to establish an SS horse stable, and "I was an ex-cavalryman." Once while on an inspection tour in Stettin, "Himmler met me and asked me if I wanted to take the position of supervisor of a concentration camp. I agreed." How did you happen to be in Stettin? "There was a general inspection of the SS there and I was leading an SS cavalry group."

Hoess said that while he was commandant of Auschwitz, soap was not manufactured from human fat. "We cut the hair from women after they had been exterminated in the gas chambers. The hair was then sent to factories, where it was woven into special fittings for gaskets." Was this hair also from men and children? "No, in 1943 I received the first orders to do it. We cut the hair only from women and only after they were dead." Did you supervise gas chamber murders? "Yes, I had the whole supervision of that business. I was often, but not always, present when the gas chambers were being used." You must be a hard man. "You become hard when you carry out such orders." It seems to me you must be hard to begin with. "Well, you certainly can't have soft feelings, whether it is shooting of people or killing them in gas chambers."

People were shot at Auschwitz also? "Not Jews, but Poles of the resistance movement were shot. This was done under orders of Rudolf Mildner." Were you a friend of Mildner? "He often came to Auschwitz." Did he have his court at Auschwitz? "After the Poles were sentenced, after the party district administrator signed the death sentences, then they came to Auschwitz to Mildner's court and were told that they were sentenced to death. This amounted to about sixty or seventy men per month." How many months was Mildner there? "Mildner came in 1941 and left in 1943. I would estimate about 1,500 men were sentenced to death by Mildner's court."

**April 9, 1946**
Hoess was sitting on his bed when I entered with Mr. Triest, the interpreter. He came to stiff attention and kept standing until I invited him to sit down. He said that his aching feet were somewhat relieved but that he still occasionally put them in a tub of cold water for temporary relief.

"I am going to court tomorrow or the next day, I was told this morning. I am going to be a witness for Kaltenbrunner." He has a somber but apprehensive and vacuous facial expression. He said: "Did I give you a report of the actual proceedings?" I told him to tell me whatever came to his mind. He said, "Auschwitz was originally thought of as a quarantine camp for Poles from the General Government. Poles were originally scheduled to come to a concentration camp in the Reich itself, and Auschwitz was originally meant to be only a transient quarantine station where prisoners would be held for a few weeks to determine whether they had illnesses which were contagious, such as typhus or fleck fever.

"The actual spot where the camp was is near a little city near Auschwitz. Originally it was the site of artillery barracks for the Polish army. I had the order to cultivate and work the surrounding farms with internees. This was a hard job because all of the surrounding territory was often flooded and quite run-down.

"Until 1918 Auschwitz was part of Austria and Silesia. Then it became Polish. It was on the Galician border. It is sixty kilometers from Krakow. But Auschwitz was not part of the General Government, it was considered part of the newly created province of Upper Silesia.

"I arrived at Auschwitz in May 1940 and I brought with me a cadre of thirty internees from the Sachsenhausen concentration camp, where I had been the first adjutant and then camp commandant. Auschwitz was just an empty couple of barracks when I arrived.

"Then Polish concentration camp inmates began arriving from the General Government and other Polish territory. Auschwitz at that time became a camp for people who had participated in the Polish resistance movement. Very few were executed during the first year — only those that were sentenced to death by the Gestapo and SS corps." About how many would you say were executed? "I don't know. A few hundred or maybe more." How were they executed? "By shooting.

"The camp was run-down and I supervised the rebuilding of houses and barracks and prepared it for twenty thousand internees, but in the first few months we received only two thousand to three thousand men.

"In the spring of 1941, Himmler arrived on an inspection tour. He ordered me to enlarge the camp to the greatest possible extent, and party district administrator Fritz Bracht, who was present and who was responsible for the area, was ordered to put at my disposal the entire territory, which was about twenty thousand morgen, or five thousand hectares. In the camp itself I was ordered to erect several large workshops such as carpentry and machine shops.

"Then I was ordered to dry out the swamps and erect model farms and build up agriculture as much as possible. I was ordered to construct a prisoner-of-war camp to accommodate 100,000 in a neighborhood three kilometers from the original camp, called Birkenau. The population in that territory, consisting of about seven villages, was evacuated and sent to the town of Auschwitz. Those that could be employed in factories or the railroad stayed in Auschwitz, but the others, who were only farmers, went to work for the General Government elsewhere.

"The 100,000 prisoners of war for the camp at Birkenau, the POW camp, never arrived, and that project was later discarded.

"In the summer of 1941, I was called to Berlin to see Himmler.[3] I was given the order to erect extermination camps. I can almost give you Himmler's actual words, which were to the effect: 'The Führer has ordered the final solution to the Jewish problem. Those of us in the SS must execute these plans. This is a hard job, but if the act is not carried out at once, instead of us exterminating the Jews, the Jews will exterminate the Germans at a later date.'

"That was Himmler's explanation. Then he explained to me why he selected Auschwitz. There were extermination camps already in the East but they were incapable of carrying out a large-scale action of extermination. Himmler could not give me the exact number, but he said that at the proper time Eichmann would get in touch with me and tell me more about it. He would keep me informed about incoming transports and like matters.

"I was ordered by Himmler to submit precise plans as to my ideas on how the extermination program should be executed in Auschwitz. I was supposed to inspect a camp in the East, namely Treblinka, and to learn from the mistakes committed there.

"A few weeks later, Eichmann visited me in Auschwitz and told me that the first transports from the General Government and Slovakia were to be expected. He added that this action should not be delayed in any way so that no technical difficulties would arise and that the schedules of transports should be maintained at all costs.

"Meanwhile, I had inspected the extermination camp of Treblinka in the General Government, which was located on the Bug River. Treblinka was a few barracks and a railroad line side track, which had formerly been a sand quarry. I inspected the extermination chambers there. These chambers were built of wood and cement; each was about the size of this cell [approximately eight feet by eleven feet], but the ceilings were lower than in this cell. Along the side of the extermination chambers, motors from old tanks or trucks were set up, and the gases of the motors, the exhaust, was directed into the cells, and this is how the people were exterminated."

How many people at a time? "I couldn't tell you exactly but I estimated that in each chamber, which was about the size of this cell, but not as high, about two hundred people were shoved in at one time — pressed into the cell very close together."

Men, women and children? "Yes, but they were brought into the cells separately, that is, the men were exterminated in the same chambers but at different intervals." You have this cell to yourself and it is not very large, therefore, two hundred people would have to be packed like sardines. "Yes, the door had to be jammed shut and the people pressed very close together, standing up." How many chambers were there at Treblinka? "There were ten such chambers, each made of stone and cement. There were no peek holes, just big doors covered with metal sheeting. The authorities at Treblinka would leave the people to be exterminated in these chambers with the motors running for one hour after they had started the motors, and then they opened the doors again. By that time all were dead. I don't know how long it really took for the gas to kill them." How did they remove the bodies? "They were removed by other internees. At first they were placed in mass graves in the sand quarries, and later when I inspected they had just started burning the corpses in open sand quarries or ditches and had begun to excavate the mass graves and burn those that had been buried." How long did you stay in Treblinka? "Only a few hours, then I went back to Auschwitz.

"Then the first transports arrived in Auschwitz.

"I had two old farmhouses somewhat removed from the camp which I had converted into gas chambers. I had the walls between the rooms removed and the outer walls cemented to make them leakproof. The first transport that arrived from the General Government was brought there. They were killed with Zyklon B gas."

How many people at a time were exterminated in each farmhouse? Hoess stared at the floor and thought for several moments. He shifted his eyes from me to the floor to Mr. Triest, and finally after about thirty seconds of silence, said: "In each farmhouse eighteen hundred to two thousand persons could be gassed at one time. The two farmhouses were separated by a distance of six hundred to eight hundred meters. They were completely closed off from the outside by woods and fences."

How often were these buildings used? "Well, it was like this. These transports didn't come daily; sometimes two or three trains arrived on a single day, every train containing two thousand people, but there were periods when no transports arrived for three to six weeks." How long were these people kept at Auschwitz? "No time at all. A side track went to Birkenau and unloaded, and there the selection was made. Those who were able to work were sifted from those unable to work." What criteria for selection were used? "Well, we had two SS doctors and they sat at tables, and the people from the transports got off the train and walked by these doctors. These people were fully clothed; they just walked by and the doctors judged by their looks, age, and strength."

Out of the transport of two thousand, approximately how many were saved for work? "In all of those years, I figured an average of twenty to thirty percent of the people were able to work." And then what happened? "Those not able to work were marched to the farmhouses. These were a good kilometer from the side track. There they were made to undress. At first they had to undress in the open, where we had erected walls made of straw and branches of trees that kept them from onlookers. After a while we built barracks. We had big signs, all of which read 'To Disinfection' or 'Baths.' That was in order to give the people the impression that they would merely receive a bath or be disinfected, in order not to have any technical difficulty in the extermination processes.

"And the internees whom we used as interpreters and general helpers in those stations instructed the people that they should take care of their clothing when they laid it on the ground in neat piles so that they should be able to find their clothes when they came out of the bath or disinfecting room. These internees helped quiet all of the people by answering their questions in a reassuring manner and telling them they would only be bathed in those houses.

"Then the people were brought to the chambers and the internees who accompanied them went along with the people into the extermination chambers so that the people would be quiet, since they saw the attendants go inside themselves. It was so done that all of the chambers were filled up at the same time. At the last moment, when the chambers were filled, the internees who worked for us slipped out, the doors were jammed shut, and the Zyklon B gas was thrown through small openings." Was there any panic among the people prior to their murder? "Yes, sometimes, but we worked it smoothly, more smoothly as time went on. The men were always exterminated in a separate chamber, and the women and children together in the same chamber." At what age, for example, did you distinguish between a child and a grown-up, that is, between a boy and a man? "I can't say. We judged by the looks of the boys — you know, some are grown-up at fifteen years, others at seventeen. We judged mainly by stature."

Do you mean that all of those executed were unfit to work? "Not exactly, but one can assume that the majority of those exterminated were not able to work." Why? "Well, the doctors who checked on the people fully clothed when they filed out of the transports also were present when the people whom they had selected for extermination were undressed, and they often remarked that their quick selection at the railroad siding was accurate because with few exceptions the people who had been selected for extermination were not capable of much work." I don't understand. You said that the doctors who made the selections sat at the railroad siding and the people filed past fully clothed? "Yes, but what I mean is that the doctors said such things later, when they were present at the undressing, right next to the gas chambers, out in the open. They would say that their selection generally had been accurate."

How long did it take for Zyklon B to work? "After all of the observations done all of those years, I feel that it depended upon the weather, the wind, the temperature; and as a matter of fact, the effectiveness of the gas itself was not always the same. Usually it took from three to fifteen minutes to extinguish all these people, that is, for no sign of life anymore. In the farmhouses we had no peek holes so that sometimes when we opened the doors after a considerable period of time had elapsed, there were still some signs of life. Later on, in the newly erected crematory and gas chambers, which I designed, we had peek holes so that we could ascertain when these people were all dead.

"After a half hour, the farmhouse doors were opened. There were two doors, one on each end, and the room was aired. The workers were equipped with gas masks and they dragged the corpses out of the rooms and placed them at first in large mass graves.

"I believed that crematoriums could be erected fast and so wanted to burn the corpses in the mass graves in the crematory, but when I saw that the crematory could not be erected fast enough to keep up with the ever-increasing numbers exterminated, we started to burn the corpses in open ditches like in Treblinka. A layer of wood, then a layer of corpses, another layer of corpses, et cetera. To start the fire we used a bundle of straw dipped in gasoline. The fire was usually started with about five layers of wood and five layers of corpses. When the fire was going strong, the fresh corpses which came from the gas chambers could merely be thrown on the fire and would burn by themselves.

"In 1942 the great crematoriums were completed and the whole process was then done in the new buildings. New railroad tracks led to the crematorium. The people were selected as before, with the only exception that the ones unable to work went to the crematory instead of being marched to the farmhouses. It was a large, modern building; there were undressing rooms and gas chambers underground, and crematory above ground, but all in the same building. There were four gas chambers underground; two large ones each accommodating two thousand people and two smaller ones each accommodating sixteen hundred people. The gas chambers were built like a shower installation, with shower outlets, water pipes, a few plumbing fixtures, and a modern electrical ventilation system so that after the gassing, the room could be aired by means of the electrical ventilation apparatus. The corpses were brought by elevators to the crematory above. There were five double stoves.

"Burning two thousand people took about twenty-four hours in the five stoves. Usually we could manage to cremate only about seventeen hundred to eighteen hundred. We were thus always behind in our cremating because as you can see it was much easier to exterminate by gas than to cremate, which took so much more time and labor.

"When the act was in progress, two or three transports came daily, each with about two thousand people. Those were the times that were hardest because we had to exterminate them at once and the facilities for burning even with the new crematories could not keep up with the extermination."

How many were killed in this way? "I can't give the exact number. In the first place, all files on these people had been destroyed. There was no record or names, and even numbers were only roughly estimated. In about 1945 Eichmann had to submit a report to Himmler, because Eichmann was the only one who had to save the numbers for Himmler. Eichmann told me before he went to Himmler that in Auschwitz alone 2.5 million people were killed by gassing. It is quite impossible to give an exact figure." Do you think the figure might have been higher, perhaps as high as 3 million or 4 million? "No, I think 2.5 million is too high, but I have no proof. None of the people exterminated were registered, only those who went to work were registered in the camp." Were those who were selected to work, instead of being killed, exterminated later if they were Jews? "No, only there were some who died a natural death, like an illness, for example." Did many die of sickness? "Yes, there were constant epidemics of typhus as a result of the crowded camps and the lack of sanitary installations, which could not be built as fast as people came in.

"I reckon in all of those years in all of the epidemics, approximately half a million people died as a result of sickness."

How many people went through Auschwitz? "That is impossible to say. I have no idea how many went through the camp. I know that in the years 1943–44 we had 144,000 internees in the camp who worked there. Most of the newly arrived people able to work were transported away from Auschwitz, and I don't know what happened to them."

I have heard that the gold was taken out of the teeth of those exterminated. "Yes, after the bodies were taken from the gas chambers, since early in 1942, orders were received from higher headquarters to remove all gold from the teeth and send it to the Finance Department. From there it was sent to the treasurer, I believe." Who did this removal of gold from the teeth of the dead? "Internees, mostly dentists who worked there. We usually saved doctors, dentists, and nurses from the gas chambers in order to use them in technical positions."

How many Germans were there in Auschwitz on your staff? "Do you mean including the guards?" Yes. "Well, in 1943, about December, when I left, there were 3,500 guards and about 500 men on the administrative staff, and that included those who supervised the agriculture section, the testing laboratories, the supervision of the extermination chambers, crematories, et cetera."

How could the Germans not know of these affairs if at Auschwitz alone 3,500 Germans worked at it? "I can't answer that because there is no doubt that it was widely known among many people, but certain precautions were taken. For instance, it was not carried in the newspapers; we used the same train crews for the transportation; and almost everyone who worked in Auschwitz had to make a sworn statement not to talk." Can you explain more about these 3,500 Germans who worked at

Auschwitz? "Until 1939, that is until the outbreak of the war, concentration camps were staffed by the SS Death's Heads units. When war broke out, Eichmann, who was inspector of concentration camps, took them in one division for combat. The guards were replaced by older people from the General SS. In the later years, that is from 1941 on, we used many so-called ethnic Germans, from Hungary, Galicia, for example, who had to serve there.

"In 1943 and 1944 the large units of the army, navy, and air corps were transferred to the SS to supervise work in war factories, armament production, and the like. For example, in an armament factory that worked for the navy and that used internees for labor — in such a case, the navy had to supply its own guard personnel. The same was true for the army and air force, because there were not enough guard units in the SS. The army, navy, or air force personnel that were used as guards later on were transferred to the SS."

What happened to you after December 1943, when you left Auschwitz? "I went to the headquarters in Oranienburg to work for the inspector of concentration camps. Auschwitz had become so big it had to be divided into three camps, called Auschwitz 1, 2, and 3. Or they could be labeled 'Auschwitz' itself; 'Birkenau,' which would be Auschwitz 2; and 'Monowitz,' which would be Auschwitz 3. In Monowitz were all of the work labor camps that belonged to Auschwitz. The figure 140,000 which I gave you before takes into consideration only those who worked in Auschwitz and not the transient internees, who were either liquidated or sent on to other places.

"I went to Oranienburg in December 1943. My immediate supervisor was Lieutenant General Richard Gluecks. My job was chief of Office I, the so-called political section. My work included the complete supervision of all concentration camps, the administrations, releases, punishments, exterminations, all dealings with the RSHA, all files of internees — in short, everything that went on in the concentration camps."

From the time you left Auschwitz until the end of the war, how many people were exterminated there? "The figure 2.5 million takes care of 1944." Were there any exterminated in 1945? "No, at the end of 1944 the whole thing stopped. It was forbidden by Himmler." What happened to the transports that arrived in 1945? "Hardly any transports arrived in 1945, and the only people who came were those able to work." Why did the exterminations stop? Was it because there were no more Jews to exterminate? "In November 1944 I was with Eichmann in Budapest and he told me that there were negotiations going on between Himmler and representatives of the Jews in Switzerland through various middlemen and that from then on exterminations would have to stop immediately."[4]

When do you figure the last exterminations occurred? Hoess thinks and rubs his hands together. He finally says: "I am not sure, but I think in October 1944."

What sort of man in your estimation was Eichmann? "Eichmann is thirty-four or thirty-five years old, a very active, adventurous man. He felt that this act against the Jews was necessary and was fully convinced of its necessity and correctness, as I was."

Do you know Bach-Zelewski? "Yes, not officially, but in 1940 and 1941 Bach-Zelewski was the Higher SS and police chief in Austria. He was succeeded by Ernst Heinrich Schmauser.[5] From then on I had nothing more to do with Bach-Zelewski." Did Bach-Zelewski know of the extermination of the Jews? "At the time he left Silesia the extermination program in Auschwitz had not begun, but in Russia there were *Einsatzkommandos* [action commandos] of Security Police in every district. There it surely happened, too. Because we never received any Jews from occupied Russia and I know for a fact that the Jews were rounded up and exterminated in Russia by these commandos."

**Marital History:** Hoess was married in 1929. His wife is now thirty-eight. They have five children, ranging from ages two and a half to sixteen years. He states that he was happily married during his four years in Auschwitz. His wife and children lived nearby in the city itself. He had no marital difficulties as a result of his work.

About the time of VE Day, Hoess was with Lieutenant General Gluecks in Flensburg. Himmler was also in Flensburg. "Himmler ordered us to go into hiding with the army or navy. I made some connection with a navy commander, a well-known submarine commander. He gave us navy papers and we were dressed as sailors and later discharged as navy men by the British in Schleswig-Holstein."

What happened to Gluecks? "I never saw him since Flensburg. He was quite sick and went to a navy hospital; I think he died there. The last time I saw Eichmann was in April 1945 in Oranienberg, when he told me that he was ordered to go to Prague. That was in the last days of the war. I never heard from him again. His family was in Prague." Did you work near your family? "I was seven kilometers away from my family in the navy camp until my discharge, then I went to a farm near the Danish border. I secured this job through the labor office. I worked there eight months before I was arrested." Did you see your family during that eight months? "No, my wife and oldest son knew where I was and communicated with me but I did not see them."

During the time you commanded Auschwitz, where did your family live? "In Auschwitz." What did your wife say or think about what went on under your command? "My wife only learned about it in 1942. Whenever an SS man or guard talked to her or there was mention of these things, she declined to believe it. I myself didn't tell her when she asked me; I answered something else. In 1942 she heard a remark made by party district administrator Bracht of Upper Silesia, who referred to the extermination program, and then she believed it. After that she asked me about it and I told her." What was her reaction? "She was very upset and thought it cruel and terrible. I explained it to her the same way Himmler explained it to me. Because of this explanation she was satisfied and we didn't talk about it anymore. However, from that time forth she frequently remarked that it would be better if I obtained another position and we left Auschwitz."

Hoess's children are as follows: boy age sixteen; girl age thirteen; girl age twelve; boy age eight; girl age two and a half. All are living and well.

Didn't it bother you to kill children of the same ages as your own? "It was not easy for me or other military SS men but we were convinced by the orders and the necessity of these orders.

"If I had not had direct orders plus reasons for the orders, I would have been unable to carry them through on my own initiative — to send thousands, millions of people to death." Do you feel guilty, or merely a soldier who has done his duty? "Up until the capitulation of Germany I believed I carried out orders correctly and acted in the right manner. But after the capitulation, when I read newspaper reports of the trials, et cetera, I came to the conclusion that the necessity for extermination of the Jews was not as they told me — now I am guilty, as are all of the others, and I have to take the consequences." What do you think your punishment should be? "To be hanged." Do you really, or do you think that there are others more guilty than you? "There are others more guilty than me, particularly those who gave me the orders, which were wrong. But as I saw it in the trial in Belsen where SS men worked under the same orders as I had, I will have to face the same punishment."

Do you know Josef Kramer?[6] "Yes, I know him well. He was my first adjutant at Auschwitz, then he was in other camps. For a time he was commander of Birkenau, which is Auschwitz 2. His last job was commandant of Belsen." What sort of man was Kramer? "He was a quiet, practical man but he lacked wide horizons, had no perspective or outlook, was not very active or elastic, and therefore I couldn't use him as adjutant. He could not conceive of things easily or use his own initiative. Even later when he was camp leader in Birkenau, he executed orders very precisely but he was not able to adapt himself to new situations or to change orders to fit existing conditions. He had to be led at all times and to be told precisely how to do things."

Was Kramer a sadist in your opinion? "No." In your own opinion, are you a sadist? "No, I never struck any internee in the entire time I was commandant. Whenever I found guards who were guilty of treating internees too harshly, I tried to exchange them for other guards."

Who invented gas chambers? "They developed out of the situation. The courts brought in a lot of people who had to be shot. I always objected to having to use the same men for firing squadrons over and over again. During that period one day my camp leader, Karl Fritzsch, came to me and asked me whether I could try to execute people with Zyklon B gas. Until that time Zyklon B was used only to disinfect barracks which were full of insects, fleas, et cetera. I tried it out on some people sentenced to death in the cell prison and that is how it developed. I didn't want any more shootings, so we used gas chambers instead."

How many concentration camps in Germany or outside of it had gas chambers? "Mauthausen, Dachau, Auschwitz, and in the east, Treblinka; in Russia, they used gas wagons." What about Majdanek? "They had temporary gas chambers but that camp came under the Security Police — the *Einsatzkommando* and Security Police. In Lublin there was a concentration camp which came under our inspection and supervision but it was not an extermination camp. Majdanek was near the city of Lublin and was an extermination camp under the direction of Lieutenant General Globocnik, who was the SS and political leader of Lublin."

**April 11, 1946**
Hoess was sitting on his cot rather transfixed in facial expression with his hands clasped together, cracking his knuckles; he wore shoes today. I

asked him how he felt and he said, "Good." He then went on to say that his feet still ached at times, which he attributed to frostbite incurred three weeks ago. Asked to describe this pain or discomfort in detail, he seemed unable to do so except to state that it was an aching beneath the skin. He took his shoes off and I examined his feet, which were not abnormal, of good color, and with no particular sensory disturbances as far as pinprick, light touch, or deep pressure are concerned.

I asked him today what he had been thinking about, and he had the usual puzzled, apathetic expression and gazed from me to the wall and back to Mr. Triest, the translator, in a doleful manner, and then answered, "I haven't been thinking of anything particular. The prison psychologist, Dr. Gilbert, asked me to write a short biography of my early life, and I have done so." He had beside him a few sheets of pencil-written material which he had just composed. He asked whether I would like to see this composition which he had almost completed. I did so and I hastily glanced over it. I asked him to tell me in his own words what he had written. "Just what I told you in the last few days and also something we began yesterday about my father and mother and sisters. It is hard to remember one's early life, and my life was a very good, happy childhood, only I wanted to be a soldier very early and I kept trying to run away from home to join the army. Many times I was taken off the transports on which I had hidden myself and returned to my mother."

**Family History:** "I come from a comfortable home. My father had been an army officer and later a merchant. I have two sisters, four and six years younger than myself. My father died in 1914 and my mother in 1917."

**Father:** He died at the age of forty-two of a heart attack when the subject was fourteen years of age. As an officer in Africa, he had been shot with a poisoned arrow in the upper abdominal region, insofar as Hoess can recall, and he never completely recovered from that wound. He also had recurrent attacks of blackwater fever, also contracted in Africa. He was retired from the army as a major after these illnesses and thereafter he engaged in business enterprises. Just exactly what business he worked at was vague but apparently he was an agent of some sort. At one time his father had been a teacher in the military school in Metz.

**Mother:** Died in 1917 at the age of thirty-nine. "I was in the field at the front at the time. When I returned my sisters told me that she had died of general sickness. She had always been sickly, never healthy." He was completely unable to depict the personalities of his mother and father except to say, "Both were very quiet, self-contained, very religious Catholic people. I can't remember any more, just that they lived well together and dedicated all of their love to the children. My parents wanted me to become a Catholic priest. Because of this I studied at the gymnasium."

Did you yourself ever want to become a priest? "No, I always wanted to become a soldier. In my childhood I might have been talked into becoming a missionary in Africa because my father told me much about the life of these missionaries there."

**Siblings:** Sister born in 1904; sister born in 1906. Both are married. The older has one child, the other has two children. The older sister is married to a carpenter, the younger one to a cement worker. Both brothers-in-law own their own businesses. Neither, so far as Hoess knows, was a Nazi Party member, nor were his sisters. The husband of the older sister was never in the army, but the younger sister's husband was drafted, wounded soon thereafter, and retired to civilian life.

When was the last time you saw your sisters, and how often do you see them? "Since I left home at the age of sixteen, I have seen my sisters very few times and have had little contact with them. Sometimes there is correspondence between us; once a year at birthdays, but nothing regularly. I saw my younger sister for the last time in 1937 and the older sister for the last time in 1941. The older one lives in Ludwigshaven and the younger one in Mannheim.

"I inspected the IG Farben factory in Ludwigshaven at that time, 1941, and so I dropped in and visited my sister." Did either of your sisters know of your occupation? "Yes, they knew I was in the SS and in charge of concentration camps, but of course they had no conception of the details of my work. Moreover, neither of them, being good house-wives, had any idea of concentration camps, and I didn't talk much about them."

**Adolescence:** "I had little patience for school and was only an average student because I always had it in mind to quit school and join the army. In 1914 when the war broke out I had a very strong impulse to be a soldier but I was too young. I tried to smuggle myself to the front with troop transports but I was always caught and brought home. In 1916 when I was working as a helper in a hospital — all schoolboys were used in army hospitals part-time — I met a cavalry captain in the hospital who knew my father. He had served in the same regiment as my father. I talked him into taking me with him into his squadron.

"At the end of the school term in early summer, I pretended to be going to visit my grandparents in the Black Forest. That was the usual thing for me to do during the summer vacations, and so my parents did not become suspicious. But that year, instead of visiting my grandparents, I actually went to the garrison of the captain of cavalry. He was organizing a unit to be sent to Turkey — the Asiatic Corps. I was trained hurriedly and two weeks later left for Turkey. It was only after my departure that I wrote my mother of my whereabouts, because I was afraid if they knew where I was in Germany, they would have me returned."

Why did you want to leave home so urgently? "I had a good life at home but I wanted to become a soldier, that is the only reason." Was your father a companion to you as a child? "A companion? What do you mean?" A friend — that is, was he easily approachable and very friendly to you? "Now that you mention it, I can hardly answer that question because it is so long ago and he died when I was fourteen. Most of the time he was away from home. No, I shouldn't say most of the time, but a good deal of it, and when he was at home he was a good father, but he was, like myself, so busy. He did not have much time to play games or other things with us, if that is what you mean."

Further attempts to get a picture of his father or of his mother were fruitless. It would seem, however, that the mother was a chronic invalid, sufferer from illnesses which are either unknown to the subject or were possibly psychosomatic. This is all so vague that a conclusion about it cannot be made. The only certain thing that can be said in regard to Hoess's relationship to his mother is that it was not an intimate one and that at her death he was left quite unaffected and not at all surprised, since she had always been, as Hoess says, "sickly and unhealthy."

"Then I served in the field in the Freikorps after my army career. Is there anything else you want me to tell you?"

Of your five children, who is your favorite? "There is no difference, all five are alike." Do you love them? "Of course, my only concern now is not my own fate, because I know I shall hang, but the welfare of my wife and children." The latter expression of concern was made with the same apathetic appearance and lack of expression as previously.

Regarding the disciplining of your children, what did you do? "I hardly did it, my wife took care of it. Only rarely did I take care of disciplining, and that was with the older children. Maybe I hit them lightly two or three times if they were bad. There was never any occasion for punishing the children; they were never bad and always well behaved. My wife is a very energetic mother in bringing up the children." What do you mean by energetic? "Well, she treated them with love, but in their whole education and upbringing they were taught to obey immediately."

How many servants did you have in your home at Auschwitz? "Until 1940, I had just one girl servant, whom I obtained from the Labor Service. These girls had to serve a year of compulsory service in a home plus a half year with a family with children. It was part of the labor movement. After 1940 when I lived in Auschwitz, I had two women internees who worked for us. These women belonged to a religious sect, the Jehovah's Witnesses. Whenever they circulated pamphlets or participated in active ways in that sect, they were placed in concentration camps. The two women who worked for me in my home were over fifty. These women from the Jehovah's Witnesses, when physically fit, were put into families with children in order to make them forget their religious sects. They lived in my house, were free to go shopping, wore civilian clothes. Of course, they had to remain in the house at night and could not go around visiting."

How did you meet your wife? "When I was released from prison in 1928 I went to an organization which was called the Union of Young People, people who wanted to be sent from the city to the country in order to learn farming and eventually become farmers themselves. My wife was also a member of this union and I met her on an estate where she was a helper in the household of the estate owner. But she was never a servant girl." How old was she and how long did you court her? "She was twenty years old when I met her and I knew her three months before we married."

Have you ever had any difficulties sexually? "None. Such things were always very good. As a young man they were always very good, too. When I was seventeen I had my first sexual experience with a nurse in a hospital in Damascus. She was in her twenties, slightly older than myself. Everything went fine." Have you had any sexual experience since May 1945? "No." Any sexual desires? "Well, no, first of all there was the hard work on the farm, and further the knowledge that I was sought after by the police."

Have you ever had any nervousness at any time? "Yes, for example, in

Auschwitz during my last year there, 1942, 1943, I had much to do. The exterminations were just a small part of my work. Every night the telephone would ring and I would be summoned somewhere. I was rundown not only because of the exterminations but because of the other work, too. My wife often complained that I spent too little time with my family and that I lived completely for my job. Only in 1943, after I went to Berlin, my doctors reported to my superiors that I had worked too hard and that I was run-down. I then had a six-week vacation toward the end of 1943. I spent that time alone in a hunting lodge in the mountains. My wife did not come along because she was in her last months of pregnancy with our last child and so she remained in our house in Auschwitz."

How did your nervousness manifest itself? "I don't know, except that my efficiency suffered a little and I found that I was a little jumpy and more irritable than usual. Usually I am very calm and self-possessed." How do you feel at the present time — nervous, or self-composed? Hoess seems to think for quite a while, stares at the floor, looks at me and then at the wall with his unblinking, wide, flat eyes. "I feel less nervous now than I did then."

What kind of house did you have in Auschwitz? "I had a house which was located just before the gates of the camp. It originally belonged to the administrator of the Polish artillery. When I arrived in Auschwitz, the house was not quite finished. I had it fixed up, put in a garden around it. I had ten rooms, not considering the baths and kitchens. But they were small rooms, nothing very large or fancy."

I asked him whether he subscribed to any religious belief. "I left the church in 1922 and my wife left it in 1935." Why did you leave the church? "During my experiences at the front in Iraq and Palestine I thought that there was a lot of humbug connected with the so-called holy places and that things were not done right, especially by the Catholic Church, of which I was a member. And that diverted me from my formerly rigid, strict Catholicism." Just what humbug did you see and what in particular was wrong with the Catholic religion as you found it in Palestine and Iraq? "I don't know, it is a long time ago and I was so busy since then I have had no time for thinking about religion, but all of this money that went to the church, well, it seemed to me that it was humbug." Has there been any change in your religious attitude since your arrest? "I wouldn't say a change, but for the first time I desire to see a Bible because I want to see what religion teaches a person. When I left home and was no longer under religious influence I was too young and inexperienced to really understand it."

Do you attend the Catholic services here? "No." Have you any desire to do so? You know that you can if you want to. "That would be saying too much that I have a desire for religion. But now since I know that my life is over, I want to find an inner peace. Now I should like to find out whether what I have done in my life, not only at Auschwitz but before that, was not wrong. Maybe what I did and what I always considered to be the right thing was wrong, because I see, since the defeat in Germany in May 1945, that in the eyes of the church and in the eyes of the world culture and ideology these things were wrong." What do you think of your activities yourself? You mentioned you wanted to find inner peace. Do you feel some emotional disturbance? "Just that my feet ache and that I am more concerned with my family's welfare than with my own."

Does the fact that you put the phenomenal number of 2.5 million men, women, and children to death, not to mention your supervision of exterminations and excursions in all of the other camps that you supervised since 1943—does that fact not upset you a little at times? "I thought I was doing the right thing, I was obeying orders, and now, of course, I see that it was unnecessary and wrong. But I don't know what you mean by being upset about these things because I didn't personally murder anybody. I was just the director of the extermination program in Auschwitz. It was Hitler who ordered it through Himmler and it was Eichmann who gave me the order regarding transports." Do you ever have any thoughts of these executions, gassings, or burning of corpses — in other words, do such thoughts come upon you at times and in any way haunt you? "No. I have no such fantasies."

What newspapers did you read during the last ten years? "There were only the party papers, for instance, *Das Reich,* the weekly political paper published by Goebbels. I also read information circulars and magazines given out by the SS." Did you ever read *Der Stürmer*? "Occasionally I got hold of one, but I myself disapproved of it because it was too superficial, pornographic, and had too much propaganda in it. I don't think it was completely truthful, either." That is an interesting observation: you murdered 2.5 million Jews but you disapprove of *Der Stürmer.* "Oh yes, all people with any sense disapproved of *Der Stürmer.*" Did you ever read the *Völkischer Beobachter?* "Yes, I got it too, but I paid less attention to it than to the other periodicals. I don't care much for daily newspapers."

Do you have any dreams of any sort? "No, once in a while I dream but I can never remember the next morning what they are." Do you ever have any nightmares? "Never."

Is your wife a good cook? Do you have any preference in regard to the different types of food? "No, I paid little attention to food — to the sorrow of my wife, who is a good cook. Food always played a minor role in my life."

Was your wife ever a party member? "No, she was a member of the Women's Organization but was never active, had too much work to do in the home, bringing up the children."

Did you ever have any secretaries? "No, in concentration camps we had no secretaries, only adjutants and military clerks." What was the highest rank in the SS you ever achieved? "Lieutenant colonel."

Do you have any favorite sports or hobbies? "Riding and hunting, to a certain extent, but I had little time for the latter because I was always so busy and tired out from my work."

# Albert Kesselring
## 1885–1960

Albert Kesselring was general field marshal of the air force and later supreme commander of the German armed forces in Italy. In 1947 he was tried by a British military court in Venice and sentenced to death, but the sentence was later commuted to life imprisonment. He was released from prison in 1952.

**February 4, 1946**

Interview this morning and afternoon with Albert Kesselring, a gray-haired, smiling man of sixty, whose erect posture and undecorated uniform are the only overt evidence of the former field marshal. He was pleasant and cooperative in a mild, restrained manner. His smile is broad, teeth somewhat discolored. There is a tortuous superficial temporal vein over the right temple.

He was asked if he had any physical or other complaints. He replied that his teeth were loose, but that he was being attended by the prison dentist. A year ago he had a fractured skull with paralysis of the left side of the face. Questioned about this paralysis (the word he used), it would appear that he suffered no motor impairment of the facial musculature, but that there was some dysesthesia (hyperesthesia possibly) of the left face and neck.

Since then he has had transitory periods of dizziness or "amnesia," wherein his thinking becomes momentarily clouded. This occurs particularly when he is emotionally upset, and lasts for about thirty seconds. When he turns his head to the back or to the left or right sides, some dizziness, very slight, occurs. He can lie only on his right side; if he lies on the left side the sensitivity of the facial skin causes him discomfort. The injury occurred in Italy near Bologna when he drove his car near a large gun. His head struck the barrel of the gun and he lost consciousness for twenty-four hours. There was a delay of eight hours before he reached a hospital. He recalls considerable vomiting thereafter and some bleeding orally. The only skin damage was a small laceration of the left eyelid. This accident occurred in late October 1944. By January 15, 1945, he was declared fit for active service again.

He was born in Marktsheft near Würzburg on November 20, 1885. He was a "normal" baby, a "sunny child," of normal weight. His development regarding walking, talking, feeding himself is unknown to him but he assumes it was not remarkable. He is the sixth and youngest child of his parents.

**Education:** He attended elementary school in Wunsiedel for four years, and the gymnasium in Bayreuth for nine years. He then attended the military academy in Munich for a year, after which he was enrolled in the artillery school at Munich for eighteen months. While in the military academy he took courses in mathematics, history, chemistry, and military history. During his artillery school period he attended lectures on history and national economy.

He said that the military schools he attended were not similar to the American West Point military academy. Almost every corps had its own military school. He believes that the military schools in Bavaria had a more extensive curriculum. There the military course was three years, whereas in Prussia it was only one year. One of the requirements of the Bavarian schools was graduation from the gymnasium. After the First World War the northern schools adopted the Bavarian pattern. There were schools in Dresden, Berlin, Munich, and other large cities, as well as aviation military schools after 1933.

Kesselring was originally an artillery officer, he said, then a general staff officer, commander of artillery, and pilot; he then assumed a major role in the air force, becoming a field marshal. At the war's end he had been commander in the West for four weeks. Prior to that he had been commander of the German forces in Italy until March 1945. He had been in the Mediterranean theater until the end of November 1941, in Italy, Greece, and Africa at various times.

I asked him if he considered himself a Hitler general or more of the old school of generals. He replied that he did *not* consider himself a Hitler general. He mentioned various men whom he called "Hitler generals" but did not include himself. He was noncommittal about Erhard Milch, saying he was a good technical administrator, and did not name Jodl or Keitel. Field Marshal Walther Model he said was a "Hitler general." In 1919 Kesselring was a captain and in 1923 a major. He was never wounded in the First World War. He was never a member of the Nazi Party.

"The mixing of northern German and southern German characters make excellent results." I asked him what the differences were between north and south Germans. The northern type has broader horizons, a bigger viewpoint, because the land is flatter and he can see greater distances. He is better at organizing things than the southern German. The Bavarian is more narrow-minded, tends to be melancholy; perhaps the mountains and isolation have something to do with it. The flatter the country, the wider the horizons. In Schwabia the people are inclined to be artistic and ambitious, and poetic.

Does he feel more a Prussian, or a Bavarian, general? I asked. He feels, he replied, a German general. He feels that Germany as a state is too small for Europe. He believes that, as in America, there can be a united Europe. "The time of the horse-drawn carriage is over." Airplanes now substitute for the carriage. Does he feel that Germany must lead Europe? "Not at present. The time has passed."

I pursued that by asking if he thought eventually, or philosophically speaking, that were so. "Well, geographically and mentally Germans are representative of a culture that originally represented Europe. But it is most important that these countries should get together." Would you be in favor of a U.S. of Europe, a democracy? "Oh, yes. It might be better to call it the United People of Europe, rather than states. The character of the people is most important. It is very important that Bavarians remain Bavarians, Prussians Prussians." No mixing at all? "No. I mean the character should be preserved. Rhineland is different from Pomerania."

Do you think it possible to do away with war? "Yes. War is possible only if you have a lot of enemies. If all the enemies get together and form one front — if you cut down the number of enemies — there would be no war."

I asked him to elaborate on this curious panacea for war. "Well, if England, France, Germany, Spain, and Italy and Greece make a united front, they would face only one front — the eastern front. That would make only one enemy."

Do you feel, therefore, a war with Russia is inevitable? "I have been in

jail for months, but I have the conviction that Russia desires to dominate." What, for instance — Europe, Germany, the world? "It is impossible to dominate the world, but Communism could spread through the
world. I can imagine a domination of Europe by Russians who would
gain a bloc of Europe and add it to the Asiatic bloc."

He did not speak easily or elaborately on these questions. I obtained
the impression that he was rather vague and ill-informed about world
affairs but opinionated, and pretty conservatively, along well-known
Nazi lines.

**Habits:** He says he stopped smoking in 1925 because of severe
headaches, which he attributed to smoke. During the First World War he
had smoked as much as twenty cigars a day. One day he stopped smoking and has never resumed it. He drinks very little at any time. There was
never any alcoholism in his family, though there were no religious or
other scruples exercised within the family against smoking or drinking.
"I don't smoke anymore myself but I enjoy having other people
smoke — it is a manly thing to do."

He is certain that his opinion about war would be the same as other
generals', namely that the common soldier is least enthusiastic about
war because he knows the cruelties of war. His opinions about the
impossibility of having many small states in Europe is based, he said, on
his experiences in piloting planes. In air travel you are over a foreign
state's borders in a few minutes. "In the present day you are over someone else's borders in a plane before you realize it." Besides, small states
would not be self-sufficient.

He last piloted a plane in March 1945. He went through all flying exer-
cises at the age of fifty-five years. Since 1934 he averaged three to four
days' flying a week. He has flown A and B planes (two-motor fighters)
and has flown the C type (heavy bombers) as second in command. He
believes he has the record for the largest number of air kilometers
flown.

Was there any connection between you and Milch in your work? Until
1933 Kesselring was an artillery officer with the air force. Milch at the
time was a state secretary. Three years later they parted and Milch
stayed in Berlin while Kesselring went to the front. "Milch was in Norway for a short time to get some medals, but he was not a combat commander." They were originally good friends and comrades, but then
some differences arose. Just what these differences were, he did not

state. But they were still good friends. What differences did you have with Milch? He eluded this by replying that they were personal reasons, but that it led to Kesselring's being taken out of the Air Ministry and sent to the front, something that Kesselring appreciated. Was there any feeling of personal rivalry between you? "Well, General Stumpf, Weber, and a whole group of others of which I was part were enjoying privileges, whereas Milch at the time was still a colonel, and it might have been the case that Milch was jealous. Milch was always older in rank than they, but when he was made field marshal he was younger than the rest. Milch is a good administrator."

Kesselring has been a field marshal since 1940. There are twenty field marshals in the German armed forces, including the navy. It is the highest rank except for Reich marshal, a position held by Goering.

Kesselring said that his general health has always been excellent, that his energies were so great he frightened his staff, who were younger men. He laughed and said literally: "I would destroy others around me." By this he meant he worked harder and longer than his associates and wore them out.

Did you know Rommel? "Yes. He was the best leader of fast-moving troops but only up to army level. Above that level it was too much for him. Rommel was given too much responsibility. He was a good commander for a corps of army but he was too moody, too changeable. One moment he would be enthusiastic, next moment depressed." Was Rommel ever so depressed he had to be hospitalized? "Yes. Rommel had a nervous breakdown in Africa and was hospitalized. He was depressed mainly. At El Alamein he was not the Rommel he had been anymore. From then on it was too much for him." Is there any truth to the story Rommel was ordered executed by Hitler? "I believe it to be 99 percent true. I heard that Rommel was given the choice of suicide. I heard that his son said so, too. He was supposed to have been implicated in the *Attentat* of July 20."[1]

At the time of capitulation Kesselring gave his word that none of his officers would commit suicide, "and my word and honor is worth more than any guard." The entire treatment of higher officers by the Americans is bad, he said, because it gives the American guards the impression that the same thing might happen to their leaders. "It is bad for the American soldiers.

"I have always had plenty of friends, and now at age sixty, I face four walls as a common prisoner." There was no anger in his voice, but considerable bitterness. "A military leader often faces a situation he has to deal with, but because it is his duty, no court can try him."

I asked him about the kaiser's rule about not violating human rights, namely that a soldier should not obey an order which is against human rights. I had heard this from Halder. He answered: "A soldier's first duty is to obey, otherwise you might as well do away with soldiering." He handed me a book by Thomas Carlyle in which it was stated that a soldier's duty is to obey body and soul. He also read a quotation from Polish head of state Marshal Pilsudski stating that the institution of militarism was a history of obedience. A soldier without obedience is no soldier.

"In the military code," continued Kesselring, "no soldier should commit a crime. But during war, with blood in the air, a soldier might do it. But if an officer, knowing it wrong, countenanced this, he would be wrong. Sometimes," he said, "strict orders are necessary to do away with things which threaten to overcome one. The mass executions are impossible to discuss." Well, what do you think about them, or have you thought of them? "I don't know about them. Of course, they are wrong. Things which come up against human rights and had bad consequences, however, couldn't necessarily be called crimes. Wars should be fought by soldiers." I don't see that your two statements have much relationship; that is, affairs against human rights and that wars should be fought by soldiers. Do you mean that crimes were committed by civilians? "Yes. No soldier under my command committed crimes." I have been told by several other generals that the army had detachments of SS troops with them, also Gestapo detachments. "Maybe — yes — not Gestapo but SS." Did they come under your general command? "Not exactly." What do you mean? This system of command is very complicated, it seems. In other words you had SS troops in your armies but their command was autonomous. "No, they were responsible to me at the front." The SS are reputed to have committed crimes. "Not the SS under my armies.

"Furthermore," he said, "many cruelties could have been avoided if there was no war behind the front." Do you mean if the partisans, guerrillas, and so forth had not operated? "Yes. Often a car would be stopped by civilians and soldiers shot. In other cases soldiers were induced to come to a village and murdered. It is impossible for any military commander to sit idly by while his soldiers are being killed in other ways than in battle."

Any reprisals in Italy therefrom? "After my soldiers were in retreat, I had to issue strict orders to prevent my soldiers from helping themselves and thereby creating a chaotic situation. If human rights are broken by one side they can be broken by the other." Yes, but were there any actual reprisals for partisan activity either before or after the retreat of your soldiers? "Yes. A few."[2]

**Family History:** His father died in 1934, at eighty-nine, almost blind but alert mentally. He had been a schoolteacher, appointed superintendent of schools in Bayreuth. He stopped working at seventy-three, but did calisthenics. Kesselring feels that he resembles his father, though his father was somewhat stouter. Did your father approve of your going to military school? "Yes. It was with my father's permission." Can you describe your father's personality? "Introspective, very strict, at least the children thought he was, even when we were grown up. He was the president of clubs, unions, et cetera. In 1880 he was a Freemason. He was assistant headmaster of a great lodge. He was very religious, a Lutheran. Politically he was a national-liberal, which today might be called a mixture of democratic and nationalistic ideas." Do you think your father would approve of National Socialism? "I think that as a Freemason, he would have opposed it. But aside from his own Freemasonry, everyone to his own liking, I don't think he would have opposed it. Father was an absolute German man, and his belonging to the Freemasons was not against that." What was Hitler's objection to Freemasonry? "Because it was international. A cousin of mine was a member of a lodge in Bayreuth and was looked on askance. Understanding of other nations does not mean a feeling against your own country. That's the whole trouble with Germans. They can see only their own country, the local church steeples only. If only German youth could go abroad, and youth from other countries come to Germany. You always have to have criticism if you wish to become better."

When your father died, were you particularly upset emotionally? "The death of my father was felt keenly, because we were a very closely knit family." But he was quite old — eighty-nine is a ripe old age. "Nevertheless, you know how it is." Yes. "One of the troubles with the Nazis was that at too early an age children were taken away from their families. Especially girls. One of the first things to do is give children back to their families. Particularly the fifteen- to sixteen-year-old ones. It was not so much, or not only the influence of the Labor Service, but the taking of the children on Sundays and evenings, instead of having children educated by parents.

What do you think of Schirach's idea of youth education? "It had a lot of good points, but for one thing the educators were too young. I don't agree with at least one of their slogans, 'Youth must be educated by youth.' "

**Mother:** "She died of kidney disease at fifty-five, when I was twenty-eight. She had been ill several years. There is no hereditary tendency to kidney trouble in the family." Personality of mother? "An ideal woman and mother. She lived only for the family. You might call her a sunny figure of light." Was she the dominant one in the household, or would you say your father seemed to have more power? Kesselring laughed. "You might say it was a united front against the children. Discipline was Father's task — and he believed in beating us if we deserved it. Which was not too often."

As youngest in the family, would you say you were in any way the favorite? "My brother and sister say it was like that, but it was not really so."

At the time of the death of his mother, Kesselring was already married and living in Metz. Mother was sickly, death expected, and he was not at her deathbed. He was in the habit of returning once or twice yearly to visit her. When he was stationed in nearby Grafenberg he would go home on weekends.

**Marital:** Married at age twenty-five. Wife now fifty-seven, living and well. She lives with her eighty-nine-year-old mother, near Telz. Most of his money was confiscated and he lost many personal belongings while in the camp in Braunschweig. His wife lives on money he gave her. "She is poor as a church mouse." Wife is very religious and comes from a family of priests. No children. In 1912 a vaginal operation was performed on his wife without benefit. The menopause was artificially induced in 1926 by electrical means (she was about forty at the time). She had leukemia and was receiving electrical treatments for it, and that accounted for the artificially induced menopause, he said. Asked about his marriage from a sexual standpoint he says it was successful. "Yes," he said, casually.

## March 12, 1946

Kesselring testified that he had some German soldiers shot "on the spot" for looting.[3] Did he consider shooting the proper penalty for looting? Well, he could not "quite admit that," but if an army gets into the habit of doing misdeeds, then the severest type of measures were justified. That was in the best interests of the civilian population and the army. He had "a pretty bad quarrel" at headquarters because of this problem. Otherwise, paradoxically, Kesselring believed in educational methods, and that explained some of the milder penalties.

He knew nothing about the removal of art treasures from the Abbey of Monte Cassino in Italy.[4] On the contrary he protected artistic treasures by cooperating with SS general Karl Wolff in having these treasures removed to secure spots.[5] He tried to exclude art treasures from areas of combat, avoided using cultural towns as places which might cause the enemy to bomb them. Later, after he was captured, he heard that art treasures were removed from Monte Cassino. As far as he knew they were in the Vatican. Did he know that art treasures from Monte Cassino were delivered to Goering? Well, he heard something about a holy statue but nothing else. Besides, the Hermann Goering Division was stationed in this sector, and Kesselring was not sure just how far their activities went.

At the trial, Sir David Maxwell Fyfe brought out the point that Kesselring had admitted in a previous interrogation that the real purpose in bombing Rotterdam was "to present a firm attitude and secure an immediate peace." He admitted this but denied that it was to terrorize the people of Rotterdam. He denied the interrogation's accuracy by saying that he never used the expression "firm attitude." Finally Kesselring settled on having said "severe measures" were indicated. Furthermore he said he was a soldier and not a politician and was merely complying with General Kurt Student's request for the bombing.

Then Admiral Raeder's statement was read to him, to the effect that "whereas it was desirable to base all military measures on existing international law, nevertheless if a decisive victory could be obtained and success achieved, measures beyond existing international law should be executed."

Kesselring said he did not completely agree with that point of view. As far as Rotterdam was concerned it did not apply. It was then shown that negotiations for the capitulation of Rotterdam had begun at ten-thirty in the morning and Kesselring's bombing began at one-thirty or two. Kesselring said that General Student called for the attack, and the capitulation was unknown to him at the time. Maxwell Fyfe pointed out that the communication between Student's ground forces and Kesselring's air bombers was excellent and that the attack could have been called off by radio or flares if a terrorization attack, not a tactical one, were in mind. Kesselring admitted that the conditions were such that an attack could have been called off, but still clung, rather unreasonably, to the idea that it was tactically indicated because he had been ordered to do so, and he was not a politician but a soldier.

Later it was pointed out that General Student apologized to the Dutch for the attack, since it had occurred after the war was over. Maxwell Fyfe proceeded to ask Kesselring about the attack on Poland. He said that Kesselring had claimed yesterday that Warsaw was a military objective. If so, he asked, what about the fact that fourteen other towns and cities in Poland had been bombed simultaneously? They must have been military objectives, too, said Kesselring. This attack began at 5 a.m., September 1, 1939, and thus there was no time for a single reconnaissance plane to fly over Poland, Maxwell Fyfe observed. True, answered Kesselring, but we had sufficient agents who furnished intelligence beforehand. In fact, said Maxwell Fyfe, had not the whole plan for the attack on Poland been worked out in April 1939?[6] Kesselring said that in April 1939 he knew nothing about it. He admitted that it was quite possible that Goering had been at his secret headquarters for a week before the attack on Poland began. Maxwell Fyfe said that the general attack on Polish towns was a well-planned scheme to break down Polish resistance.

Kesselring became rather indignant and said that if his statements as a field marshal and soldier under oath were disregarded and not believed, as obviously Maxwell Fyfe did not believe them, there was no purpose in his making any more statements. He repeated that his attack was not on Polish towns but on military targets, and that as a soldier he should be believed.

The examination turned to the subject of the partisans in Italy during the time of Kesselring's command. Keitel's order of December 16, 1942, was read, a copy of it having been found in Kesselring's headquarters in Italy. It stated:

The Führer has ordered that the enemy employs in partisan warfare Communist-trained fanatics who do not hesitate to commit any atrocity. It is more than ever a question of life and death. This fight has nothing to do with soldierly gallantry or principles of the Geneva Convention. If the fight against the partisans in the East, as well as in the Balkans, is not waged with the most brutal means, we will shortly reach the point where the available forces are insufficient to control the area. It is therefore not only justified, but it is the duty of the troops to use all means without restriction, even against women and children, so long as it ensures success. Any consideration for the partisans is a crime against the German people.

Kesselring remembered the order. He was then confronted with his own order of June 17, 1944, which read:

The partisan situation in the Italian theater, particularly central Italy, has deteriorated to such an extent that it constitutes a serious danger to troops, supply lines, war industry and economic potential. The fight against the partisans must be carried out with all means at our disposal and with utmost severity. I will protect any commander who exceeds our usual restraint in the choice of severity of methods he adopts against partisans. In this connection the old principle applies that a mistake in the choice of methods in executing one's orders is better than failure or neglect to act.

Kesselring admitted having issued that order. Furthermore, three days later he issued another "top secret" order saying:

It is the duty of all troops and police in my command to adopt the severest measures. Every act of violence committed by partisans must be punished immediately. Reports submitted must also give details of countermeasures taken. Wherever there is evidence of a considerable number of partisan groups a proportion of the male population of the area will be arrested, and in the event of an act of violence being committed these men will be shot.

Kesselring was reminded of two instances of how his words were carried out. A Colonel von Gablentz was captured by bandits. The entire male population of the villages on the stretch of road concerned were arrested. As reprisal for the capture of this colonel, 560 persons, including 250 men, were arrested. Maxwell Fyfe asked him if taking 410 women and children into custody was what was meant by his order of "steps necessary to deal with partisan warfare." Kesselring answered equivocally that it was unnecessary.

The other example was what happened to the village of Civitella, on

June 18, 1944. Two German soldiers were killed and a third was wounded in a fight with partisans in the village of Civitella. Fearing reprisals, the inhabitants evacuated the village, but when the Germans discovered this, punitive action was disposed. On June 29, when the inhabitants returned and were feeling secure, the Germans carried out a well-organized reprisal. Inhabitants were shot. Two hundred and twelve men, women, and children were killed that day. Some of the dead women were found naked. The ages of the dead ranged from one year to eighty-four years. Approximately one hundred houses were destroyed by fire. Some of the victims were burned alive in their houses.

Maxwell Fyfe asked Kesselring if military necessity demanded the killing of babies of one year and people of eighty-four years of age. Kesselring said, "No."

# Ewald von Kleist
## 1881–1954

Ewald von Kleist, general field marshal, tank commander in the 1940 invasion of France, led the First Panzer Army against the Soviet Union in 1941. Captured by the Allied forces in 1945, he was tried for war crimes in Yugoslavia and sentenced to fifteen years' imprisonment. Later released and turned over to the Soviet Union, he died in 1954 in a camp near Moscow.

**June 12, 1946**

This sixty-four-year-old man, Ewald von Kleist, was born on August 8, 1881, in Braunfels, Hessen. He said that he lived in the town of his birth for only four weeks, after which he lived in Hanover.

In general, he was healthy as a child. He had measles and scarlet fever and a few other minor childhood illnesses. On three occasions he suffered a concussion of the brain as a result of falling from horses. The first concussion occurred at the age of twenty-seven. At that time he was unconscious for two hours and had to spend six weeks in bed in a darkened room. The last concussion occurred in 1924, and Kleist told the following story about it.

"Hindenburg was about to become president of Germany. I happened to be in bed and Admiral Alfred von Tirpitz came to my house and asked me to join him in a visit to Hindenburg. Admiral Tirpitz was refused admission because Hindenburg's son did not want his father to become president. I didn't want Hindenburg to become president either. I told Hindenburg that he was a famous soldier but that if he became a politician he might lose face both as a statesman and as a human being.

"Hindenburg for the first time took part in the candidacy for president during Easter 1924. Stresemann visited Hindenburg in Hanover and brought him a draft of an Easter message that he wanted Hindenburg to sign and deliver. I just want to tell you about this anecdote to show you what sort of a man old Hindenburg was. He took the message, read it through, and tore it up, throwing it in the wastebasket. Hindenburg sat down at his desk and wrote his own Easter message. He told Stresemann that if he were president, he would not be a puppet but would do things in his own way.

"Well, this is getting a long way from my concussion of the brain which I suffered that year. It was an ordinary concussion — I fell from a horse, and the horse landed on top of me. I think I was unconscious for a few minutes and was kept in bed for several weeks. I never had any bad results from any of my concussions."

I asked Kleist to tell me more about himself and his early career. "I was a captain in the First World War and I knew Hindenburg slightly while stationed in Magdeburg. After the war I knew Hindenburg better because he lived in the same city as I did, Hanover."

Kleist went to elementary school for three years, then spent nine years in a gymnasium. He then entered the army as the equivalent of an officer candidate and attended military school. "Our system of becoming an officer was quite democratic. I was more or less elected on democratic principles from the corps to become an officer. At the next occasion, which was usually on August 18 or on the emperor's birthday, we would be appointed to the status of officer in groups. I was officially commissioned on August 18, 1901.

"On February 5, 1938, I retired from the service along with General Fritsch. Then I was called back when the war broke out." Why had Kleist been retired in 1938? "I was inactive for one and a half years, from February 1938 until September 1939, when the war with Poland began. I withdrew from the army because of the attitude of the National Socialist Party toward the church and other religious questions and because I spoke up for religion too much."

He said that he was a Lutheran, "but I stood up for all religions and all churches. The Catholic bishops in Breslau know how I fought for religious freedom." Had Kleist ever discussed this subject with Hitler? "Not personally, but I was an outspoken advocate of religion and I issued a directive in my command that the young soldier must attend church services and be religious. I received an order from the OKW that I should retract such an order. I declared that I would not do so."

Who was the leader of the OKW at that time? "It was in the summer of 1937 and Wilhelm Keitel was the leader. Of course, Keitel is not to blame — he did it because of pressure from the party."

Kleist described how he was ordered back to duty in 1939 in the beginning of the war. "I was awakened in the middle of the night in my house by the mayor of the small village in which I lived. He told me that mobilization for war had begun and that I must report for duty at once. I reported to Field Marshal Gerd von Rundstedt in Silesia. Our formations against Poland were in readiness at that time, which was toward the end of August 1939."

Kleist said that he married in 1910. His wife was fifty-six on her last birthday and was well when he last heard from her. He had two sons, aged twenty-nine and twenty-five. The older one was in a Russian POW camp, the younger was with his wife. The twenty-five year old son had been drafted as a soldier for a short time but became ill with asthma and was discharged before the end of the war. The older son was a professional cavalry soldier who held the rank of captain until the end of the war. Kleist said that he had received one postcard from this son, dated March 1, 1946, saying that he was alive and well and that his address was care of the Red Cross, Moscow, USSR.

He described his marriage as a very happy one. His wife's father was a wealthy industrialist in Hanover. "Women are wonderful — they never complain. For example, my wife has backaches but she does not trouble others about her own difficulties. She always tries to cheer me up. Our own family is generally healthy except for my younger son's severe asthma."

I mentioned to Kleist the fact that I had read that the Kleists were among the richest landowning families in Germany. I wanted to know whether this was correct. Kleist smiled and denied this categorically. "No, on the contrary. My immediate family was very poor. In general, the Kleists are very numerous as a family and it may be that in aggregate we own a considerable amount of land. There are no Kleists who are millionaires, however. There are no industrialists among us, no large factory owners or other rich people. I have always been interested in family history as so many other people are, and I have traced the family name of Kleist to the year 1175. Since then we have spread out a great deal. I suppose that this is the reason that my name is included among the richest landowners in Germany. It is true that all of the Kleists have the same ancestry and we always treated each other as relatives and if one member of the family was poorly off, he was assisted financially.

"The bulk of the Kleists were poor and owned small farms in Pomerania. If you count all those farms together, there were about thirty or forty. But you can see how ridiculous such reasoning is. It would be the same as if you said in America that all the Smiths were rich. However, because they stuck to the soil in Pomerania and were very industrious people and were thrifty, they maintained their farms and bought up adjacent land and so became landowners. I would like to express it succinctly that the Kleists are a thrifty and industrious group, proud but poor, whose common pride held us together through the loose bonds of blood. There is only one millionaire in my family that I know of. He is a Swiss citizen who married a Kleist and so cannot be said to be really a member of our family by blood. But in our family we have two poets of international fame as well as a great physicist."

We discussed his family history. "My father was an old philosopher, philologist, and student of ancient languages. He died at the age of seventy-five, in 1923 or 1924. He served as a soldier for one year voluntarily in the War of 1870, but developed pneumonia and was released. My father was very unhappy when I became a soldier. For some reason he didn't like it. I don't know why. He probably believed that I wasn't inclined to be a soldier. I joined the field artillery, although at that time it was very difficult to be accepted because too many people wanted to join."

Kleist smiled and reminisced. "My father had to apply for me to be accepted. He did so unwillingly, and wrote, 'My son wants to be an officer but I don't think he would be satisfactory as a soldier and officer.' Then came an unexpected answer, to the effect, 'Please send your son immediately.'

"My father was a philosopher. He was a wonderful man, an idealist and against war. He was a bookworm with no conception of politics or economics. He lived a life apart. I suppose that if he did express any political view, it would have been National Liberal — that is the party of Stresemann." What would Kleist's father think of National Socialism if he had been alive in January 1933? "There was no National Socialism then." I said that I realized this, but nevertheless in retrospect and theoretically, what did he think his father's opinion would have been? "My father was like a Greek philosopher. He often said in Greek, 'One man should be our kind, one should be our leader.' But this was not meant in the sense of what happened in Germany under Hitler. The Greeks also had the term 'tyranny.' It was recognized that there were good tyrants as well as bad ones, but in general, most tyrants were hated by the Greeks. There is also the verse by Schiller, 'To Dionysius, the tyrant, came the man with a dagger in his pocket.' It's very difficult for me to say what my father would have thought, but since he loved the Greeks and their philosophy, he would without doubt, therefore, have disapproved of Nazism. He would have understood that if one man is given special powers in an emergency, it might be all right; but he would not have approved of what Hitler became later, namely a tyrant."

Was I correct, then, in my assumption that Kleist considered Hitler a tyrant? "Yes. Hitler developed into a tyrant. He became chancellor by democratic means but he then developed into a dictator. He was a tyrant in the sense of the old Greeks."

Did Kleist agree with the American viewpoint, or perhaps any civilized viewpoint, that Hitler was a murderer? "One cannot deny that." When did Kleist first come to that realization? "I knew nothing about the mass murders, the atrocities, the violations of military code, and so forth, or anything about Hitler's murderous activities and orders until after the war, when I was imprisoned."

Had not Kleist received orders from the chief of the OKW, Keitel — which were presented here in court as evidence against him — that were contrary to the international military code of ethics? Kleist gazed at the floor and pondered the question. "That is something rather complicated. I know what you are referring to. It is very complicated. I agree that Keitel was wrong in many of his directives, but I personally followed nothing but an honorable method of fighting and disregarded any directives that might violate human decency. I did this even when I fought in Russia, where the campaign was most violent. Furthermore, I am here as a witness for the general staff and army, and that is almost the crucial point of our defense. It is something that the prosecution will, without doubt, dwell on, and I must think this over rather carefully and talk to Manstein before I express any official opinion on Keitel's orders."

I said that I understood his position, but since this interview was quite unofficial, as far as the tribunal was concerned, and was not accessible to the prosecution at any rate, could he tell me what he thought about the problem according to his own standard of values? Kleist dodged this question by saying, "I really can't go into much detail about orders which might be construed as criminal because I am not a lawyer, and I can't find the legal loopholes that a lawyer might be able to detect. If you want my own plain opinion about Keitel's orders, I will tell you. They were the orders of a stupid follower of Hitler. I myself paid very little attention to them and I think any attempt to justify his orders would be a mistake on the part of those of us who are steeped in military tradition and good conduct. I trust you will not quote me on these observations. I knew Keitel fairly well and I think that he is a decent person. It was simply that Hitler wanted a weak general in that powerful position in order to be able to have complete control of him. If I had held Keitel's position under Hitler, I wouldn't have lasted two weeks."

We returned to the subject of Kleist's family history. He went on to describe his father in greater detail. "Father was quite an affectionate man but was always sick as a result of the lung infection incurred in the War of 1870. He lived a lonely life aside from his contact with the immediate family, and as I said before, he was a bookworm whose mind dealt not with reality but with books, the works of the old Greeks, and his family. Frankly, he was more absorbed in his books than in his children. We children only saw him at mealtimes, and occasionally he would take a walk with us."

Did his father's lung trouble make him irritable? "Not exactly, but he was always very careful of his health, and being with his children too much would tire his nerves. He was a man of extremely moderate habits, who drank one small glass of beer a day, did not smoke in the time I remember him, although I recall he told me that as a young man he smoked one or two cigars a day." Did he consider that his father had a quite different personality from his own? "Oh, yes, indeed. I am more like my mother. My mother is still alive, although she is ninety.

"It's a remarkable thing, but at ninety Mother is still a good housekeeper, active, lively, and possessed of all her faculties. Unfortunately, I haven't seen Mother in five years. She lived in a small town near Hamburg, whereas my wife lived in Silesia. During the war, if I did take a short furlough, I naturally went to visit my wife. My mother unfortunately broke her hipbone in 1942. It was placed in a cast and a nail inserted, and she is now able to get around well, even to walk up and down stairs. She doesn't look her age except for a shrunken mouth because she has lost all her teeth. Her memory is perfect."

Kleist himself was a man of medium height, reddish brown complexion, thin auburn hair, stocky build, and an alert, ingratiating, smiling manner. He did not appear to be sixty-four but looked more like a man in his early fifties. He said that it interested him greatly about this "legend" that I mentioned to him earlier that his family was among the richest landowners in Germany. "All my immediate relatives, I must repeat, were poor. For the most part, my relatives were officers and officials. In earlier generations they were mostly farmers. I did get a letter recently from someone who said that there was a woman by the name of Kleist in Washington, D.C., and he wanted me to write to her to find out if we were related. I heard that she was extremely wealthy. Perhaps the author of that book you mentioned met the Kleist in Washington. I know that she talked about me since I have been in captivity and so we must be related. I want to send her the family files, which would be better in America than over here, in view of the fact that all of us have lost our homes and houses and are in a state of bankruptcy."

Kleist had one sister, aged fifty-seven, married, and whose husband was alive. This sister had one son, aged twenty-four, who was at present in Russian captivity. "I was always on the best of terms with my sister. My mother lived with this sister for many years, ever since the death of my father. My brother-in-law has been a district magistrate since 1917. He joined the Nazi Party soon after 1933, not because of conviction but because it was the only way for him to retain his official position. After the war he was arrested automatically but immediately released.

"My sister is more like my father. She is less active than my mother and more of a recluse. Father had a greater liking for his daughter, whereas Mother was more fond of me. My sister could never keep house because ever since Mother came to live with her, Mother did everything. Mother still does everything in my sister's household." Did his sister's husband get along well with his mother-in-law? "Oh, yes, I think so. I saw them every few years for a short visit and there was no particular discord. I think that it is my sister's way to let others run her life, and therefore, it is no fault of my mother's that she does everything in my sister's home." Kleist smiled as if he had thought of something humorous. "Besides, my mother would be a little difficult to repress if she once made up her mind that she was going to make dinner."

We discussed Kleist's own children and family. I asked him which of his children he felt closest to, and so forth. "My older boy is strangely closed up, almost impolite at times, and therefore has had it more difficult in life. For that reason my older son has given me more aggravation than the younger one. Nevertheless, I love both my sons, the older as much as the younger one.

"My two sons have two quite different personalities. The older son developed at a later age and had to overcome many of his own fears. I believe that in his inner self my older son was against leaders or authority in general. He has an independent streak. He refused to be led and he never wanted to listen to the experiences of his elders." Was his son a good soldier? "In a way he was a very good soldier, not in time of peace but during combat. He was certainly not cut out to be a peacetime soldier and would not have remained with the army after the war was over. His education and training was that of a professional soldier, but he would have quit this military career, I am sure." Why did his son become a career soldier? "We lived among soldiers because I was a professional officer and so it seemed natural that he become one also. I think that he always had the idea of using the army as a means of touring the world. I know, because he told me frequently that he wanted to become attached to the secret service, or be a military attaché in order to travel and see the world. At the time he joined the army, of course, such things didn't exist."

Would Kleist consider himself a strict father? What were his ideas on rearing children? Kleist smiled and said, "Unfortunately, I was never very strict. My wife often told me that if I had given my older boy a beating once in a while he would have been better off. I myself never used physical punishment on either of my two sons. My wife always said to me that my heart would break if I struck them. But they are not ungrateful, and we are a very close family.

"I always said if my children are ever pushed out into the world because they lost their parents, they should have something to reflect upon and to look back on happily — that is, good parents and a good home." Did Kleist feel that he would like to be a grandfather? "Yes. I have wanted grandchildren for a long time. But unfortunately it did not take place, because of the war and because neither of my sons had the opportunity to marry."

I asked him why he was here in the Nuremberg prison — had he been

arrested automatically, was he charged with war crimes, or had he volunteered or been requested as a witness for the general staff? "I was in a
POW camp in England and I came to the Nuremberg prison voluntarily
as a witness for the army. Recently I was discharged from the German
army while in this prison and was informed that I am on the so-called
war criminal list number seven. I haven't the faintest idea of what war
crime I could have committed. The main thing is that I have a clear conscience. It was my understanding that I was to return to England at once.
I know that the English authorities wrote a letter to the Nuremberg tribunal that Rundstedt and others including myself should be returned to
England when our usefulness here was terminated. That letter arrived
from England after we had been here for three or four days. Dr. Hans
Laternser, the counsel for the general staff, received a letter from the
general secretary of the tribunal in which it stated that if we were not
needed here, we should be returned to England. I don't know what's the
matter with that fellow Laternser! Manstein has assigned us each sections upon which we were to work, and each of us has completed his section and more. All of this material was given to Manstein, who, in turn,
delivered it to Dr. Laternser, and it has been in his hands for weeks. Now
we sit around doing nothing, except for Manstein, who has in a way
assumed the responsibility for the defense of the general staff and the
army. I know that the general secretary of the tribunal warned Laternser
twice that he was keeping us here too long and that we should be
returned to England. It seems to me that Laternser can't make up his
mind whether I should remain here to testify personally or whether an
affidavit of mine will suffice."

I asked Kleist what he thought of Laternser. "He's not a very superior
counsel. In the beginning I thought he was a real dummy. After yesterday's conversation with him, however, I feel that he is catching on and is
improving. I never did understand lawyers anyway, and I suppose, in
view of his reputation as a well-known German defense counsel, he is
competent." Did Kleist feel that Laternser was very intelligent? "It's not
for me to say whether he is intelligent or not. I have often thought about
the meaning of intelligence. Frankly, I believe intelligence is not an
entity but a composite of various adaptabilities. I think that lawyers in
general are sharp but not extraordinarily intelligent because they think
in certain prescribed lines, and are, therefore, not very adaptable. It
would be a great advantage if we had a German soldier as defense coun-

sel for the general staff — a man who in addition to being acquainted with military matters was also a legal expert. Of course, offhand, I can't think of any particular individual who would meet those requirements, since most of our military judges were also dummies, who had failed as officers in the field and who were, therefore, assigned to the legal department of the army. I can name a dozen of them, some of them with the rank of general. To return to Laternser, however, I would say that in view of the fact that he was so ignorant of military matters, at first he swam and almost drowned in all the material which Manstein and the rest of us here in Nuremberg submitted. Laternser didn't know the difference between the high command and a sergeant. It was as strange as if I were to be called to give a talk about the atom bomb."

I cautiously asked Kleist what Manstein had assigned to him and in general what the nature of his testimony in defense of the general staff would be. Kleist smiled craftily, and replied with an attitude as if to say, "Wouldn't you like to know?" He did say, however, "I am answering certain questions that Manstein is devising and we divided these questions among us. Certain of us, like Halder, Brauchitsch, Westphal, Wilhelm List, Wilhelm Ritter von Leeb, Rundstedt, Guenther Blumentritt, and so on, will each take the responsibility for answering certain charges and explaining certain aspects of a military situation."

Again Kleist smiled whimsically and remarked, "It's interesting to me because you know not all of us generals and field marshals present here were of the same military and political faiths. On the question, however, of the preservation of the general staff, we are all united. It is an interesting phenomenon and indicative of the real unity of the German national spirit to observe how we stick together in this hour of crisis despite our differences of opinion previously. I think it is a noble thing. Our main effort is to disprove that a conspiracy existed. I personally am a frank and straightforward man and I will tell you that a conspiracy is so much *Quatsch*. As to whether a conspiracy existed among the politicians, that's another matter. I have no opinion about that except to state that I personally hardly believe it.

"You see, the ridiculous aspect of the conspiracy charge is most clearly brought forward when you consider that there were officers in 1939 who were simple colonels or even lieutenant colonels and by 1945 they ended up as generals. How could any of these small officers have been involved in a conspiracy to make aggressive war? I have the viewpoint that no party dictatorship would suffer another organization rivaling it, such as the general staff. For example, take Mussolini with his Black Shirts and the purge he found necessary among his army people. Or another example is Stalin, who shot Tukhachevsky and so many other generals just to prevent their becoming too strong and turning on him. So the indictment is ridiculous."

Did Kleist feel that the indictments against the other organizations, such as the SS, SD, and SA, were likewise unwarranted? "That's a different thing. In the first place, I am not particularly interested in those other organizations. It is the army and the general staff — the tradition and backbone of Germany — which must be preserved. But if you ask me about the SS and SA and so forth, I must say, too, that I don't think the indictments are completely fair since there must have been some harmless people within those organizations. My impression of the SS and SA is that they were like unions, and that people were forced to join them, or did so voluntarily, because of expediency." I remarked that I was sure that there was some truth in what he said but that the indictment was aimed at the leadership and not directed toward prosecuting a stenographer, for example, who happened to be a member of one of the organizations. Furthermore, I said, Justice Jackson had emphasized in his opening address on the subject of the organizations that it was not the intention of the Allies to prosecute every member of such an organization, but rather to try cases individually, utilizing the criteria of whether the individual involved had committed or had been a party to a war crime. "Then I must admit that the indictment against the SS, the SD, the SA, the Gestapo is correct — that the leaders of these organizations were criminal and not of the same high gentlemanly character as the leaders of the general staff, is well known. I would rather not say anything about this, however, and I wish you wouldn't quote me. As a German, I feel that I could say this to a German court but not to a foreign tribunal. You can take my answer as a hint. You are a psychiatrist and I don't have to say too much for you to understand what my feelings are. You can take a hint. I was always an opponent of Himmler and Heydrich."

Would Kleist tell me more about Himmler and Heydrich? "I believe that Heydrich was the worst criminal of them all. I myself saw him and he looked with such a glance of hatred that I shall never forget it. In Silesia I had a hard battle against the SS and SA. We called it, jokingly, the 'Fourth Silesia War.' Three of the Silesian Wars were led by Frederick the Great and the other one was led by me against the SS and the SA.

My main battle was against the methods used by such party organizations by which they tried to get control and power."

Did Kleist have any relatives or close friends who belonged to the Nazi Party? "No, just a brother-in-law and a small nephew."

I asked him about his career and position in 1933 at the time of the Nazi accession to power. "I was a division commander in Silesia. At that time I was against the Nazi Party. In fact, all of us old army generals were against the party except for one or two, like General Walter von Reichenau, who was for it. On the other hand, Hitler came to power quite constitutionally because his was the strongest party. Yet in retrospect it wasn't quite constitutional, because Hitler was unable to select his own ministers because of the fact that Hindenburg appointed many of the early ministers who served under Hitler at the beginning. For example, from the old Hindenburg cabinet came Schleicher, Neurath, and Papen."

## June 25, 1946

The interviewing of Kleist continued today. I had seen him a few times in the interim between June 12 and today, but never for any prolonged period. He has remained a hearty, youngish-appearing man despite his chronological age, and life in prison has not particularly affected him.

We began to talk in greater detail about his military career. He said that he joined an artillery-cavalry unit in 1900. He liked to ride horses and the military life in general was most agreeable to him. "I liked to command men and to have them obey orders." In 1907 he attended the military riding institute at Hanover. There he participated in horse racing, tournaments of various sorts, and high fence jumping with horses. "Horses were my whole life at that time — my entire passion was horses." He stayed at this institute for riding for three years. In 1910, he became a senior lieutenant, after having been a first lieutenant since 1901. From 1910 to 1913 he attended the War Academy, after which he went to join a regiment of hussars in Danzig. In 1914 he became a captain of cavalry and a squadron leader.

During the First World War, until 1917 he served at the front, as captain of his squadron. In 1917 he was ordered to the general staff with a division of guard cavalry in the field. In 1918 when the war ended, he served in the Ruhr, at Münster, in Westphalia, until May 1920. "I helped quell the revolution which took place in 1918 and 1919."[1]

In 1922 he was promoted to major and returned to Hanover, where he commanded a squadron in the 100,000-man army. In 1924 he was transferred to the cavalry school as an instructor. In 1924 he became chief of the general staff of the Second Cavalry Division in Silesia. In 1927 or 1928 he was promoted to lieutenant colonel. In 1931 he commanded Infantry Regiment Number Nine in Potsdam. "I became an infantry commander at that time and have been an infantrist more or less ever since. I prefer horses." On January 1, 1932, he was promoted to colonel and assumed command of the Second Cavalry Division in Breslau as the successor of Rundstedt.

In October 1932 he was promoted to major general, and in 1934 became lieutenant general. In 1936 he became the commanding general of all forces in Silesia and was promoted to the rank of general of cavalry.

I asked him whether he considered his promotions and rise in rank as quite rapid or not unusual. "I was a competent soldier and I would not say that my promotions in rank were unusual. I deserved to be promoted, in my own estimation. Furthermore, I have been a soldier since 1900 and have thus been an officer for over forty-five years." I asked him why he had been called to the general staff. Had he been particularly outstanding in any military field? "It's hard to say. I was a good frontline soldier and a practical man. Perhaps that accounts for my success in military life. There are too many shrewd politicians among us military folk and too few plain, practical soldiers with a knowledge of how to fight. For example, I never wrote any military books. I once wrote three lines in a cavalry newspaper about something or other. Essentially I was a frontline general and my interests were in achieving a military victory and not in writing theoretical tracts."

I mentioned to Kleist that Field Marshal Leeb had told me about having written a book on the art of defense. Kleist said that he had never heard of Leeb's book and that it was the first time he had ever heard it mentioned. I said that Leeb claimed that his book ranks with the military classic of Clausewitz. Kleist said smilingly, "Is that so? To tell you the truth, I never read Clausewitz either. I don't know enough about Clausewitz to be able to tell you what his theories are. I know that the Russians must have read Clausewitz a good deal and perhaps it's too bad I didn't read it."[2]

As he had told me the other day, on February 5, 1938, he retired from active duty along with Colonel General Fritsch, but was recalled to active duty at the end of August 1939, to serve in the war against Poland. He then led a panzer army corps, which consisted of about two divisions and attached troops, in the blitz against Poland. "I was very successful in this operation because I was able to use cavalry tactics. I was in Poland for only sixteen days in all. Then I left Poland and got together with the Russians for the first time, on friendly terms. That was the time of the Russo-German Nonaggression Pact, and there was a division of Poland between Germany and Russia. My impression of the Russians then was that they were exceedingly good troops, advanced in military technique, motorized to a surprising extent, and very correct in their behavior."

He then assumed command of three panzer corps which were known as Kleist groups. "This was in May 1940, and I began organizing this small army, which bore my name, in the territory behind Düsseldorf. We then went to the West and if I say so myself, it was my army which is largely responsible for the rapid victory in France. I broke through the Sedan and Maginot Lines and I reached the coast of France within seven days, near Abbeville. In the course of my victories I took the towns of Bastogne and Calais and it was the Kleist groups that attacked Dunkirk from the west. This was during the tremendous British disaster which occurred there.

"I must say that the English managed to escape that trap in Dunkirk, which I had so carefully laid, only with the personal help of Hitler. There was a channel from Arras to Dunkirk. I had already crossed this channel and my troops occupied the heights which jutted out over Flanders. Therefore, my panzer group had complete control of Dunkirk and the area in which the British were trapped. The fact of the matter is that the English would have been unable to get into Dunkirk because I had them covered. Then Hitler personally ordered that I should withdraw my troops from these heights."[3]

Why had Hitler ordered this? "Hitler thought it was too risky. It was nonsense — those orders of Hitler's in those days. We could have wiped out the British army completely or taken the whole army as captive if it weren't for the stupid order of Hitler. The proof of it is that three days later the English occupied the heights and I was obliged to attack them again to take them back. The masses of English troops, however, had already reached Dunkirk and were escaping in small boats. The sad part of it is that I could have captured the whole English army, or such a great part of it, at any rate, that an invasion of England would have been a simple affair. I did capture many French soldiers, including General Henri Giraud.

"Altogether I captured 1 million prisoners of war on all fronts. I think I did pretty well. Giraud's capture was very amusing. An intelligence officer conveyed an English radio message that the French front had been torn open through tank attacks. My intelligence officer said that the English radio had broadcasted, 'The French general, the beloved General Giraud, would take over command of the French front and restore the situation.' Now the amusing thing about it is that as I was reading this intelligence report, the door opened and in walked a good-looking French general who turned out to be Giraud. He had been very brave but was a little mistaken about the situation. He had taken a reconnaissance car and driven into our territory searching for his troops but instead he found mine, and had been taken prisoner by a couple of enlisted men." Kleist chuckled.

"I told General Giraud that I was worried to have to greet a famous French general in such a commonplace way. We were on very good terms and I can assure you that I treated him with as much respect as I would any German general.

"In the second part of the French campaign I crossed the front near Amiens, and broke through the so-called Weygand position across the Oise River. Again I was successful and took an enormous number of prisoners, traversing a large area. In the third part of the French campaign I crossed the Marne at Château-Thierry and pressed my way down to Lyons and the Swiss border. In the last part of the French campaign I occupied the Atlantic coast from the English Channel down to the Pyrenees."[4]

I remarked that it seemed to me that he must have been one of the most active army commanders in France. Kleist agreed eagerly. "Without being unduly modest I can assert that I was *the* most active army commander in France and that I shortened the French campaign by many months by my panzer actions. You know there is a great deal said about the French soldiers lacking fighting spirit. I think that is exaggerated. They fought quite bravely until the situation was made hopeless by our powerful German elements, and the French were completely surrounded. Perhaps there is a difference between a French and a German soldier: as soon as a Frenchman is surrounded he gives up. Later on in this war we German soldiers were in much worse and more hopeless situations and we continued to fight with our true German spirit.

"The same thing can be said in a different sense about the Russian fighting spirit. The Russians are so primitive that they won't give up even when they are surrounded by a dozen machine guns. I would say it is a difference between German bravery and Russian bravery in the sense that the former is logical and the latter brutal. The French, on the other hand, lack push. Probably one of the reasons for this French weakness was that they did not have anyone in whom they believed at that time. At least I gathered such an impression because during my months in France whenever I entered a French house, I never found pictures of leading French statesmen or generals or even of Napoleon. In other words, the French did not think of their leaders as important. Anyway, that was my impression at the time, and whether it was correct or not, I don't know."

Was it true that the French in general greeted the Germans enthusiastically? "No. I can't say that. I know there were many propaganda stories, including newsreels, showing Frenchmen greeting German soldiers and waving their hands. I would characterize all that as untrue propaganda. The French were very correct — just as I would behave if I were invaded by a gentlemanly opponent. The French were cool but polite. In the mountains, of course, there were partisans, but I never had much trouble from them. I think they became active much later, when the Normandy invasion got a good start.

"I drove around France constantly during my stay there and discovered that although the French people in a certain town might be cool for the first two or three days, they later adopted a friendly attitude, which one might expect would exist between one civilized nation and another. In their favor I would say that in general, the French were never subordinate or ingratiating in their attitude."

After he had completed his mission in the war against France and in the occupation of the French coast, he was transferred to Romania on January 1, 1941, where he began training Romanian soldiers for the war against Russia. I remarked that it would seem obvious, therefore, that he knew that the war against Russia had been planned that early. Did Kleist train these Romanian soldiers for a war against Russia? "I meant to say in case of a war against Russia because there were so many Russian divisions deployed along the Romanian border." For the first time in the interview Kleist seemed to be nettled and from that point on he appeared to choose his words more carefully and to be less free-spoken.

I asked him to continue the story of his military career. "Certainly, certainly. I have nothing to hide. I stayed in Romania until the beginning of March 1941, after which I went to Bulgaria because of the news that the British had landed in Greece. There was no fighting in Bulgaria — everything was on very friendly terms. Then on April 6, 1941, I was in charge of the march into Greece and Yugoslavia. In this war against Yugoslavia I commanded two corps. One of these corps was in Romania and consisted largely of ethnic Germans, and the other of similar composition from Bulgaria. On April 8 I assembled my army, and on April 12 took Belgrade. A serious battle occurred on the road near Sofia, and another fairly severe encounter against Yugoslav troops on the road near Belgrade.

"The actual march into Belgrade was peaceful and I had a fairly good time. On the way in I shot a few deer with Yugoslav hunters who were sympathetic to the German army because they were so opposed to the threat of the Reds. I left the country soon afterward to assume a more active command.

"I was then stationed in Silesia and had my own staff and my own army group until the middle of June. I was then attached to Army Group South under Field Marshal Rundstedt in his campaign in Russia. I was Rundstedt's panzer expert and in charge of several corps of panzer units. In that year, among my other successes, was the capture of Rostov, which is near the big bend of the Dnieper, which is slightly north of the Crimea.

"In 1942 I had progressed farther than any other troops into Russia. I was actually in the Caucasus and closer to China than to Berlin. Then I reached the Caspian Sea and Stalingrad very well on my way back. The Russians came to within sixty kilometers of Rostov and there came a time when my only communication with the rear was in Rostov. My headquarters were located at that time six hundred and fifty kilometers within reach of Rostov. In January or February 1943, I received an order to retreat. I was in charge of the army group as the successor of Field Marshal List. Rundstedt was no longer in Russia but was commanding the battle in France again.

"The Russians were five times superior to us poor but brave Germans, both in numbers and in the superiority of their equipment. My immediate commander was Hitler himself. Unfortunately, Hitler's advice in those critical periods was invariably lousy."

Had Kleist succeeded in retreating with most of his army? "I really had two armies at that time when the order for the retreat came. One of my armies I managed to bring back to the rear via Rostov. The other army, which I left in command of one of my leading generals, held the line until late in the summer of 1943 and then retreated with heavy casualties but without decimation. This was possible because the Russians stood at their back, north of the Crimea. The Russians advanced north of Crimea against the army group of Manstein, who was obliged to retreat. It was therefore necessary for me to follow Manstein's withdrawal. Then the Crimea was cut off because Hitler refused to agree to a withdrawal of our troops in time from that region. In the winter and spring of 1943 and 1944 I slowly withdrew to the river which marked the boundary of Bessarabia and Romania. The Crimea was cut off behind our front and was in a state of siege by the Russians. On April 1, 1944, I went home."

I asked Kleist what occasioned his retirement at that time. "Well, on December 1, 1943, I told Hitler to give up his supreme command. On March 29, 1944, I again had a very severe argument with Hitler and I had the impression that it was more the people around Hitler than Hitler himself who said that I was an inconvenient subordinate. Hitler himself told me when I said good-bye to him that he could find no fault with me as a soldier. Hitler said many friendly things to me. He said that he had very few people who were capable of leading an operational war. He advised me to take a rest because I had worked so hard and he implied that I would be asked to serve again. I really think that the reason for my going home at that time was that I always told Hitler my frank opinions."

What did Kleist think of Hitler during the last few years? "I think that Hitler was more of a problem for a psychiatrist than for a general."

Had Kleist himself, in his own contacts with Hitler, recognized any abnormalities? "No. I knew his loud manner, his habit of striking a table with his fist, his temper tantrums, and all that. I'm just a plain soldier and not given to analyzing temperaments. He was the chief of state and I accepted that as enough. I thought that the features I just mentioned were part of Hitler's temperament and therefore not remarkable. I have a good deal of temperament myself — in fact, twice as much as Hitler.

When Hitler shouted to me, I shouted twice as loud. I am no psychiatrist and I couldn't understand that Hitler really was an abnormal character. If you nailed him down, Hitler became quiet or even silent. If you talked for two hours and you thought that finally you had convinced him of something, he began where you had started just as if you had never said a word.

"It is interesting but it was tragic. If you receive a military order you must obey. That is where the big difference between a military and a political order comes in. One can sabotage a political order but to disobey a military command is treason."

I asked Kleist who were the guilty ones for the trouble the Nazis created. "I can't really tell because whatever I say is only an assumption. For example, from June 1942 until the end of 1944, I was at the front every single day. I flew back to visit Hitler for an hour perhaps on many occasions but I never stayed long enough to apprise myself of the great picture of what was going on. Today if I should make a judgment, I would declare the guilty ones to be Hitler, Heydrich, Himmler, and as I have heard here, Bormann. Hitler was always suspicious of the generals from the very first, and this suspicion increased as time went on."

Did Kleist feel that political leaders such as Goering, Goebbels, Ribbentrop, and others were also guilty? "In my opinion, Ribbentrop had nothing to say and very little influence. As far as Goering is concerned, he is now on the defendants' bench and it is hard for me to say anything against a man who is being tried for his life. Secondly, Goering was completely under the suggestive, hypnotic power of Hitler, so Goering, too, had little influence. Goebbels was the cleverest of the lot, but unfortunately his bad influence became clear to me only after the end of the war."

I asked Kleist of his opinion concerning the persecution of churches, the extermination of Jews, the killing of partisans, and the other atrocities committed by the Nazis. "I feel strongest about the persecution of the churches. In fact, when I went away for the first time, on February 5, 1938, it was partly because I fought for the churches and was opposed to the National Socialist attitude toward them. As far as the Jews — I can only say that some of my best friends were Jews. I think that expresses in a nutshell my feelings about the matter. I grew up in a small city in north Friesland, where we lived in a small two-family house. It was a sort of duplex home. Our neighbors were a Jewish family of a very respectable and honorable type. The father of this family was an old Jewish teacher and was either a rabbi or a preacher. He had two children who were about the same ages as my sister and myself. During my whole childhood I played with these children and we were like members of the same family. When the Jewish Eastertime came, we visited our Jewish neighbors and ate matzos and sugar.

"Our other neighbor was a Jewish cattle dealer. I used to ride his horses across the meadows. I first learned to ride horseback that way. I could go on with endless examples of Jewish friends and neighbors.

"The neighbors of my in-laws in Hanover were Jewish bankers by the name of Meyer. There was constant contact between my in-laws and the Meyer family. Until 1928 I always kept up a friendly, intimate, neighborly contact with the Meyers. After 1928 I left Hanover and so my contact with them came to a natural end.

"What I have told you characterizes my attitude toward the churches and the Jews. There are bad Christians and bad Jews. When I was brought to this prison, I told Rundstedt that Nuremberg gives me the second great humiliation of my life. The first time was when the Nuremberg Laws were proclaimed and I was forced to listen to them."[5]

Had Kleist ever taken any public stand against the Nuremberg Laws? "There was no opportunity. I was invited to Nuremberg at that time because of a military exhibition. The military guests, myself included, were ordered to attend a Reichstag session in a theater in Nuremberg during a party day. I sat there with my mouth open and heard the Nuremberg Laws proclaimed. I couldn't speak against these laws because I was just a part of the audience.

"In Silesia when someone asked me for help, especially Jews, I always did as much as I could. In Breslau a lawyer who was the representative of the Jews in that city often came to me and asked me for help."

Did Kleist know of the mass murder of Jews that took place from the year 1941 until the end of the war? "No. I have stated under oath that I knew nothing about it. In the winter of 1941 to 1942 I heard rumors at the front that Jews were being deported in order to be assembled somewhere. Then I heard of a pogrom in Lemberg, which was eight hundred kilometers behind my front. It was reported at that time to me that the Poles or Russians were responsible for it. Then I heard that Jews were being shot in masses in Bessarabia, which was one thousand kilometers away. I had never been there. We were told that the Romanians did it, and I thought this was the case until I came here.

"In the year 1944 there was the massacre of Jews in Kishinev, and again I was told that the Romanians had done it. I noticed that a certain part of the city of Kishinev was destroyed. I asked the Romanians what had happened and they told me that this destroyed section of the city had consisted of Jewish homes which the Jews themselves burned down. I must confess that I didn't believe it because it was too ridiculous. But I never knew any reliable facts about Germans being responsible for these atrocities.

"In January 1943, when I took over the army group, I heard that Jews were to be murdered in my territory. I immediately called for the Higher SS and police chief, whose name was Gerret Korsemann, who incidentally was not under my command.[6] I told him what I had heard. I told him that I would not tolerate any actions against the Jews. He assured me that he had not taken steps against the Jews, nor did he have orders to do so."

And was this so? "At that time I heard nothing more about it. Now in the Russian documents it is said that Jews were murdered in an area that would have been under Korsemann and in my territory. But these documents are undated. I don't think, since that time, that any Jews were murdered anymore in my area."

Had Kleist been emotionally upset about these things at the time he heard the rumors? "How could I be? I just learned of these things now. To me at that time they were just rumors. Of course, when I heard such rumors I was outraged, but when I was assured that they were only rumors, or that non-Germans had done these beastly things, I was pacified."

Had he ever heard of Auschwitz? "No. I heard of it only after the war. Of all the concentration camps, I knew only about Dachau and Oranienburg. Perhaps it sounds as if I wanted to hide something, but I can say it under oath. There were friends and relatives of mine in concentration camps." Why? "For political reasons. I don't know exactly. Some of them might have made critical remarks about the regime, and had been sentenced to periods of six weeks' internment. Two cousins of mine were shot later on because of complicity with the *Attentat* of July 20, 1944." We discussed many other things, among them his personal worldview. "I am a religious Christian. I believe that I am an upstanding, decent man, and I think I tried never to do any injustice to anyone in my life. I feel that one has to think the best of every man until the contrary is proven."

What did Kleist think of the leadership principle? "I spoke to you about it the other day. By education and tradition I am a constitutional monarchist. I mean I would prefer a monarchy as it exists in England. My main reason for this belief is that in case of the death of the leader, there is no unrest and the oldest son or other relative takes the throne.

"I am also in favor of the leadership principle whereby a leader is elected by the people — but not a dictatorship. Hitler had the favor of the people to the last but he had destroyed the people and all of us, and had done away with every form of freedom of speech, press, radio, and life in general. Actually, it was just the workmen who believed in Hitler. The so-called bourgeois were always hated by Hitler and the Nazi press and were distrusted by the workers. On July 20, 1944, I was in my home. I saw how the workers assembled to defend Hitler and how they threw suspicion on all bourgeois people including persons like myself.

"The social program of the NSDAP had its good points and was honestly intended. On December 1, 1943, Hitler said that after the war was won, the position of the German workers in the state would be elevated for the first time. I remember Hitler's own words: 'The German worker made no mistake in relying on me.' It is clear to me that my class — the middle class — would have disappeared whether Hitler won or lost.

"Planned economy is used in Germany at present by the occupying powers. It is done in all countries with the exception of the United States, and sooner or later your country will get around to it. For example, there are the questions of wheat, gold, silver. If the U.S.A. wants to sell two hundred pounds of wheat for five marks, and Russia will sell the same amount of wheat for three marks, then you can easily see that free economies cannot exist. It would take only a few such instances and the entire stock exchange would break down."

# Erich von Manstein
## 1887–1973

Erich von Manstein, general field marshal, was a professional soldier and skillful strategist. A dispute with Hitler over war strategy on the eastern front and over his own command led to his dismissal in March 1944. He was sentenced in 1949 by a British military court to eighteen years' imprisonment; that was commuted to twelve years. He was released in May 1953.

**June 14, 1946**

This fifty-eight-year-old man, Erich von Manstein, has been interviewed several times in the past. He was born November 24, 1887, in Berlin. He stated that he had not grown up there because his father was an officer and his family moved to various parts of Germany. He was reared in various garrisons, wherever his father happened to be stationed.

He is a tall man, about six feet in height, well developed and well nourished. He wears a black patch over the right eye, which had been operated upon for a cataract several years ago. He has been the main organizer of the defense of the general staff and the driving spirit behind the other field marshals and generals imprisoned in Nuremberg. It was Manstein who delegated various roles to these officers in the preparation of the defense of the general staff.

His past history was uneventful. As a child he had frequent sore throats and attacks of tonsillitis. His tonsils were removed for the first time three years ago, although they had been "clipped" previously. As a young child he had measles, and at the age of nineteen a severe attack of scarlet fever without sequelae.

At the age of forty-five, about thirteen years ago, he began to develop fogginess of vision in both eyes. The right eye was worse than the left and in 1944 the right lens was removed by an ophthalmologist in Breslau. He could no longer read with the right eye, except with strong glasses. The left eye is better than the right, but also foggy. He was advised by his ophthalmologist that the left eye should not be operated upon because if it were, he would have to wear glasses constantly.

About twelve years ago he began to suffer from neuralgia of the neck. This has become worse and more frequent as time has gone on, especially in bad weather or following a sore throat. In general, he said that even today he considered himself to be in good health.

He began his education at the age of six years in Strasbourg, in Alsace. His father was stationed there at that time in the German garrison. He attended the gymnasium from 1896 until 1900, when he joined the cadet corps in Lübeck. He eventually transferred to Lichterfelde, near Berlin, from which he graduated in 1906 at the age of nineteen. He entered the army as a cadet.

In 1907 he became a lieutenant of the Third Guard Regiment. In 1914 he was at the front with the same unit and was severely wounded in the left shoulder and left knee. The sciatic nerve in the left knee was nicked but except for some slight weakness of the left leg, it healed satisfactorily. The left shoulder was not permanently affected. As a result of these wounds, he was in the hospital for six months. In 1915 he was transferred to an army corps. In 1916 he entered the general staff as a captain in the field, serving in Poland, Serbia, and France. He became the first general staff officer in the border guard against Poland. He served with troops in the 100,000-man army. In 1928 he became a major in the War Ministry in Berlin, where he remained until 1932.

In the fall of 1932 he was stationed in Pomerania. In 1934 he returned to Berlin as chief of staff of Military District III (Third Division). The commander of that unit was Field Marshal Erwin von Witzleben, who was later connected to the *Attentat* of July 20, 1944. "Witzleben was a friend of mine — a perfect gentleman. He had good judgment, that is, not for the masses but for officers. He was a very polite and kind man, clever, but not ambitious and not particularly diligent. One should not go so far as to call him lazy but he was not particularly fond of hard work. He was a competent military man as far as his abilities and character were concerned."

I asked Manstein whether he was surprised at Witzleben's complicity in the July 20, 1944, affair. "I didn't approve of the *Attentat* because when one is in a war one can't take the responsibility for a revolution in the interior. However, in July 1944, Witzleben had no command. He was sick and had been retired. He was about sixty years old. He had been chief commander in the West during the campaign against France and had served well. He had to leave the army in 1942 or '43 because of his health."

Manstein's next position was chief of the operational section of the general staff in 1935. Werner von Fritsch was commander in chief, and General Ludwig Beck was in command of the general staff itself. "The cleverer of the two men was Beck; the stronger personality was Fritsch. These two men were the best officers we had. They were the best of my superiors. I can't say how they would have been in a war, but in time of peace they were certainly the best."

Manstein related how Beck was retired in 1938 because he did not favor the attack on Czechoslovakia. Fritsch was removed from his post in February 1938, also because of ideological differences with Hitler, and he participated in the war against Poland voluntarily. Manstein had no comment as to whether Fritsch's death in Poland was accidental, suicidal, or otherwise.

"Fritsch, Beck, and myself had to leave our positions in the high command in February 1938."

In 1932 Manstein had become a colonel. Later he achieved the rank of major general, and on April 1, 1938, he became lieutenant general. When the war started in 1939 he was in command of a division in Silesia. At the time, Manstein was chief of the general staff of Rundstedt, who commanded Army Group South in Poland. After the war in Poland was over, the high command of this army group was transferred to the West and Rundstedt commanded the forces on the frontiers of Belgium and Luxembourg. Manstein was Rundstedt's chief of staff until February 1940.

In 1940 Manstein commanded an army corps. In June, he was promoted to general of infantry. He was in France until March 1941, after which he commanded a panzer corps which had been newly formed in Germany. Although Manstein was not an authority on panzer warfare, he considers that he later became one during the Russian campaign.

At the start of the war against Russia he was at the north front in charge of the aforementioned panzer corps. It was his outfit which began the attack in East Prussia. He remained in that position until September 1941, when he took command of the Eleventh Army in Ukraine, replacing that army's former commander in chief, Schobert, who had been killed in action. Manstein stayed in this position until November 1942, at which time his staff was changed automatically to that of Army Group Don. "I had command of Army Group Don. In February 1942, I was again promoted, to colonel general, after I had conquered Crimea. On the first of July, 1942, I became field marshal after I led the forces that conquered Sebastopol. That was a very difficult battle because of the tremendous resistance offered by the Russians and because of the rocky terrain of the natural fortress of Sebastopol."

In November, the Army Group Don underwent changes and became known as Army Group South. This reshuffling was done after the German Sixth Army under Friedrich Paulus had been encircled in the battle against Stalingrad. "I was the officer with the highest command in Russia. My new army, known as Army Group South, consisted of the Sixth Army of Paulus, which was already partly encircled, plus two Romanian armies and a small panzer army. Paulus was my subordinate but I had little if any contact with him. In reality Paulus received orders from Hitler, who advised him not to withdraw."

I asked Manstein whether it was possible at that time for Paulus's army to withdraw. He replied, "In the first days it was possible. However, after the encirclement there was too much risk, especially in winter, to attempt to withdraw." Did Manstein believe that Hitler's order to Paulus to fight to the last was a reckless, foolish order? Manstein's face hardened and he glared with his one uncovered eye, but answered in a steady, monotonous voice, "No. If Paulus's army had capitulated before the end, the Russians would have had the advantage of withdrawing forces against Paulus and against the southern front, where I had only two Romanian armies. Therefore, the resistance of the Sixth German Army, even to the death of the last man, was necessary."

Did Manstein mean that it was necessary despite the fact that it would cost so many lives, as Paulus had testified before this tribunal a few months ago? He replied with the same cold monotony, "Yes. Lives would have been lost anyway. And the breakthrough of the Russians at that time would have meant the loss of the war and the complete defeat of Germany.

"I tried at that time to relieve the Sixth Army, of which I was supreme commander, above Paulus, by counterattacks — but it was not possible. I gave the order finally for the Sixth Army to break out, but then Paulus said it was too late and not possible. Hitler did not want the Sixth Army to break out at any time, but to fight to the last man. I believe that Hitler said if the Sixth Army tried to break out, it would be their death."

Did you agree? "Well, perhaps a part of the Sixth Army personnel would have been able to escape, but of course, without weapons — therefore, I wanted to do this in order to save some lives. However, it might have also occurred that they would perish in the cold even if they had escaped the trap."

What kind of a man was Paulus, in your opinion? "A very clever man though perhaps not a very strong character." Did you always think that of him? "Yes. It would have been his duty at the time he saw the danger ahead to take the responsibility on his own shoulders and try to break through to the rear." Did Paulus give up instead? "No. Instead, he went to Hitler and asked if he could be permitted to try to break through to the rear, and Hitler said he should remain at Stalingrad and be annihilated. My criticism of Paulus is that he should not have asked Hitler. He should have done it on his own hook. That is why I say Paulus was not a very strong character, because to make a decision like that during war takes a strong personality."

I thought that Manstein was more or less contradicting himself. Didn't he state a moment ago that Paulus should stay to the end and fight? Now he seemed to be saying that Paulus should have broken through to the rear without asking any questions of his superiors. Just what did Manstein mean? "What I meant to say was that Paulus should have broken out to the rear before he was encircled. I mean that once Paulus was encircled, he should not capitulate but should fight to the end. In that sense I agreed with Hitler."

Did Paulus finally capitulate? "No. His army was conquered in the course of battle. About 90,000 men were captured, and in our estimation only 20,000 or 25,000 of these men remained alive." Paulus said in court that because of Hitler's order, about 100,000 men were killed due to freezing and battle, because of fighting to the last. "In my estimation there were about 200,000 men in total in Paulus's army. I figure that 100,000 probably died as a result of wounds or freezing."[1]

Did this tremendous loss of lives depress you at the time? "Of course. For myself, as a leader with the responsibility for 100,000 people, the spiritual burden was very great. But I blame Paulus to a certain extent for not taking some responsibility himself and breaking out to the rear before he was encircled, despite Hitler's wishes. On the other hand, I agree with Hitler that once Paulus was encircled, he should stand ground and fight as he did, despite the loss of life, because if he capitulated it would have meant the defeat of Germany then and there."

Manstein said that in March 1944, he was recalled and retired to his home in Silesia. I asked him what the reason for this had been. He replied enigmatically, "Officially I don't know. I assume it was the controversy concerning leadership between myself and Hitler. I was in a constant feud with Hitler about leadership ever since I took command of the army group until the end. The chief of the general staff, General Kurt Zeitzler, told me that the orders at that time were dictated mainly by Himmler and Goering."

I remarked that it was my understanding that Hitler himself had given most of the orders regarding army strategy at that time. Manstein said, "Yes, but I had many military controversies with Hitler and it was my impression that he was undoubtedly influenced by Goering and Himmler against me."

What was Manstein's general feeling about Hitler? "He was an extraordinary personality. He had a tremendously high intelligence and an exceptional willpower." Was this willpower directed toward good, or evil? "It's hard to say. He always put through his will. I suppose at the time it can be said that his willpower served both bad and good purposes."

At the present time, what did Manstein think about Hitler? "Apparently as time went on Hitler lost all moral scruples. However, this is a recognition I have made in retrospect, but which I did not have at the time." When did Manstein first believe that Hitler had no moral scruples? "After the war was over. After I heard about all the things that had happened. The first sight of Hitler's lack of morality was his behavior after July 20, 1944, with the subsequent trials, hangings, et cetera. And later when I heard all about the annihilation of the Jews."

These annihilations of the Jews began earlier. Did Manstein mean that he previously had no inkling of such events? "I know that it began much earlier, probably in 1940 or 1941, but I didn't know about it. I was a soldier and occupied with winning a war." Did Manstein not know about the great actions against the Jews of November 1938? He replied without much feeling, "Yes, naturally. We all considered it an unfortunate thing but we looked on it as part of a revolutionary movement."

Did Manstein have no idea of the many concentration camps within Germany? "In peacetime I heard of Oranienburg and Dachau. I remember that a younger general staff officer once visited Oranienburg and he later told me that there were two or three thousand men interned there, but that for the most part these internees were professional criminals with a small sprinkling of political prisoners. This officer of mine also told me that the internees there were treated correctly. That was in 1939—or maybe before that. During the war, however, I was on the front all the time, and I never heard any more about concentration camps, atrocities, or other things that didn't concern me."

I remarked that he must have heard of the *Einsatzkommandos* (action commandos) and the *Einsatzgruppen* (action groups) in the Crimea. Manstein looked slightly uncomfortable but remained cool and indifferent. "Ohlendorf's *Einsatzgruppe* was in my district. I heard that here for the first time. As field marshal in charge of all activities in that district, I naturally heard that there were such commandos operating in the area. But we were told that these SS formations had purely police functions. What they did, I never knew. They were active in the territories of other army groups, too."

Then, if I understood him correctly, Manstein must have known about them. Manstein replied, "Well, there might have been somebody occasionally who told me that something was happening which was bad, around September, when I first arrived, but I was sent as a military commander and most of my time I spent at the front. I never personally saw or reliably heard of the shooting of Jews en masse by these *Einsatzkommandos*. Such installations were not under my command and in reality I could not do anything about them."

# Erhard Milch
1892–1972

Erhard Milch, general field marshal and armaments chief of the air force, was tried in 1947 by the military tribunal at Nuremberg and sentenced to life imprisonment. In 1951 his sentence was commuted to fifteen years' imprisonment. Later amnestied, he was released from prison on June 4, 1954.

## January 22, 1946

Lengthy conversation with Erhard Milch, field marshal of the air force, next to Goering as power behind the building of that machine. He is a shrewd, Napoleonic, short man, who is very affable, but as poisonous as hell with his affability. There will naturally be a war between Russia and the U.S.A. England is no longer a major power. Allied atrocities are just as bad as German ones. When captured, he himself was beaten up by an English general. It was inconceivable, he said, that a field marshal could be beaten. Why was he beaten up? I asked. Because the English had just captured a German concentration camp and he was made to ride through it and see the horrors. Then he was accused of saying, "The Russians are not human beings." He denies ever saying a word. He knew nothing of all that. He had heard of concentration camps but was never interested in them, never saw one before.

He never read accounts of atrocities in foreign papers, nor did he listen to foreign broadcasts. This was against German law, as listening to foreign stations was forbidden. He, being field marshal, had to set an example for his men, so he never violated that law.

Mistreatment of Jews? He knew nothing about it until after the war. It was the "nonsense" on top, namely Hitler and Himmler, and some others who are conveniently dead now, who must have given the orders. Did Goering, after all, next in command to Hitler, know of these things? Milch couldn't say except that he rarely spoke to Goering, as they did not get along well. But Goering is the kind of man who "lives and lets live," and has no racial prejudices, judges men by his own methods.

He and the German general staff had nothing to do with it. Besides, aren't Allied war crimes just as bad? For instance, his own case, the beating up of a field marshal! It's against the Geneva Convention. And he just read in the paper that Robert Patterson, our assistant secretary of war, came to Europe and said all German POWs are being treated in accord with the Geneva Convention. Not in one case is that so, not in a single instance. Milch became quite vociferous about it. He'd heard that German soldiers, noncommissioned officers, and officers, were being sent to Belgium and France and auctioned off for three, four, and five marks apiece for slave labor. It was indisputable; he heard it from an American officer himself. And in the reeducation camp for Nazis at Garmisch-Partenkirchen, a camp run by the American army, the methods of reeducating the Nazis is by beating and starvation. He knows because he asked an American officer if it were true and the American officer said it was so, and that he was ashamed of it himself.

Milch feels that he has done no wrong. Quite the contrary, he fancies himself a pioneer in aviation and a benefactor of mankind. He is fifty-four years old, has two children alive, and two grandchildren by a married daughter. This daughter's husband was an air corps officer who is a POW in Canada. Milch appears forty, hale and hearty. He has been a flier for thirty-one years, he says. He was the head of Lufthansa and also of the air force. He hopes after these trials are over to become German representative for Pan American Airways, because someone in that concern is an old buddy of his.

Wasn't Milch a Nazi? Sure, but so what? You had to be a Nazi. Persecution of Nazis would have to stop because it's the same as persecuting Republicans, Democrats, socialists, or Catholics. He had heard of persecution of Jews but it was not his work, he said.

**February 28, 1946**
Today Milch was working on some notes when I entered the cell. He smiled pleasantly and invited me to have a seat at the table. I sat on the cot and told him to keep his seat.

I remarked that I had heard from others in the prison here that were it not for him, Milch, Germany's air force would not have developed so greatly. Milch replied noncommittally, "I don't know. I wouldn't say that. Not exactly." He went on to elaborate on how through his years of experience he knew all about air transportation mainly, having been a civilian director of aviation for years before the war.

In the First World War he was a captain in the air force, although originally he had been an artillery commander. From 1920, when he retired from the air force, he occupied himself with civil aeronautic and commercial flying. In 1933, at the beginning of the Hitler regime, he became general inspector for the air force. I asked him concerning his relationship to Goering. "I had little to do with him. He was more in contact with Hitler than I was. I am essentially a businessman. I did not agree with many of Goering's ideas. But essentially, Goering was the leading figure, and if the building of the air force can be credited to any single individual, it is Goering, not me."

I asked him what he was working on. "I shall probably testify early in Goering's case. I don't know what about, but whatever I am asked."

He said that the essence of his testimony was to break down the accusation that he or Goering had planned an aggressive war by building a large air force. "That is not in accord with the facts. After Germany left the Disarmament Convention in 1933 we decided to rearm to be on an equal footing with our neighbor states. As far as the air force was concerned, my responsibility was to build, from nothing, a defense in the air. Our activities were known to the English, French, Belgians, and Swedes because they visited Germany and I personally visited their air industries. There were no secrets."

I said that I thought there were many secrets in Germany during Hitler's time, since nobody seemed to know what the other fellow was doing or had done. For example, I said, nobody but Himmler and Ohlendorf seemed to know about the mass murders of Jews. Milch looked serious but composed. "That is true. And it applies to me also. There was a policy by Hitler that nobody should inquire into anyone else's business and each should limit himself to his own field of activity."

I asked Milch what the main line of his testimony might be, if he had no objections to telling me. "Not at all. The main thing I shall say is that I did not expect or want war. As far as Goering is concerned, I can give only my impressions. That is true for the Polish war as well as for the Russian war. One thing I will say, I tried to dissuade Hitler from a two-front war. I believe Goering did, too. But I failed."

He was looking through some notes, obviously trying to locate something. I asked him what he was looking for. "There is another thing which I should like to explain before the tribunal, and that is my signature on a letter to the SS regarding medical experiments. The prosecution has a letter from SS general Wolff addressed to me, regarding medical experiments conducted for the air force. There is evidence that these experiments were criminal. I want to point out that I knew nothing about these things and merely signed a polite note to Wolff, Himmler's adjutant, in which I expressed approval because the medical inspector had assured me there was nothing to these experiments. Goering was advised of the matter by me, but he knew no more about it than I did. Goering was no more fond of Himmler than I was, but we had to be polite about it. To this day I don't know what happened as a result of those experiments, but I have heard that criminal things were perpetrated."

In speaking of this last business, Milch seemed personally concerned. He refused to elaborate on the experiments or anything else connected with them, except that he and Goering had no knowledge of them, other than to have received a letter from Himmler's adjutant Wolff regarding such experiments. He knew they were to be done on "criminals" he said, but had been assured by his own medical inspector that everything was "in order."

We dropped this line of discussion. I asked him whether in his official function as field marshal of the air force he had anything to do with any of the other defendants. "Yes, but only slightly. With Speer, the armaments minister, of course, in the last years of the war, I had greater contact."

What did he think of Speer? "Personally I know little about him. I think he was honest. I know he told me in late 1944 that we should not follow Hitler's ideas of scorched earth policy. Speer, as well as myself, was interested in saving as much as possible for the German people so that after defeat there would be something to fall back on. By this I mean food stores, housing, and prevention of destruction of factories that might produce goods for the German people."

I asked him what he thought of the Führer principle. "False." That was his total answer. And what about the concept of "living space"? "Well, the German people did need more room. But Hitler exaggerated as he always did." What about the ideology of master race, in his opinion? "Ridiculous. I have never subscribed to racial theory." I asked him if he ever did anything to prevent its practice in Nazi Germany. "What could one do? Nothing." Did Hitler or National Socialism have any real concern for the people, despite slogans about the *Volk,* in his opinion? "I thought originally when Hitler came to power that he was thoughtful about the people's welfare and wanted a greater Germany for nationalistic reasons with which I agreed. But soon it became obvious that Hitler cared about nothing except more and more personal victories."

I asked him the usual question concerning why he did not resign if he saw Hitler for what he was. His response was the stereotyped "One could not resign in wartime, and before that I did not know he was aiming at war."

What about concentration camps? I asked him. "I told you when we first met that I was beaten up by a British general because I denied knowledge of a small camp he took me through. I repeat that I knew of only two camps, Oranienburg and Dachau, and no others. The SD knew about these things. They were kept from the average German and certainly from a person like myself who had nothing to do with such affairs.[1] Once I visited Dachau just to see what sort of things were happening because I had heard rumors — it was 1935, I believe, but everything I saw was in order."

I asked him what he thought of Hitler personally. "I knew him but slightly. He was always correct when I saw him. But later on he became impossible, and could not be approached. I think personally he was the greatest tragedy for Germany."

As far as National Socialism is concerned, Milch said, "I never voted for it and never approved it. I was invited to build up the air force for defensive purposes and I did so. I never approved of the racial theories or other trappings of Nazism. There was no personal liberty. Everyone felt spied on. One could not listen to enemy radio broadcasts. There was no free press. No wonder things could go on as they did and only a small group of people knew anything about it."

I tried to draw him out more on Goering's personality and his relationship to him. "Not everything he did I approved of," was all I could get.

**March 13, 1946**
Milch has been on the stand in Goering's behalf for two days. He presented a picture of Germany as being unprepared for a war in 1939 from

the air force standpoint. He actually said little about Goering personally during his testimony. His cross-examination by Justice Jackson had yielded little except that he had received a gift from Hitler of 250,000 marks in 1940 on the occasion of his fiftieth birthday.

I asked Milch about that gift. He treated it with equanimity. "What was wrong with such a gift? It was a birthday present. It was not a bribe." He went on to say that others received similar gifts, some larger than his own, and that in a way it was unfair for Jackson to have brought it up because it might give the German people the wrong impression about him — that he was personally growing rich on the war. "That is not the truth. In private enterprise, which I gave up when I entered the army in 1933, I could have earned a thousand times as much as I did. The impression that might leave on the German people is false."

I asked him what he meant by trying to convince the court that Germany was unprepared for war in 1939. I reminded him of Jackson's asking him how long it took Germany to conquer Poland, to drive English troops off the continent, to conquer France. The answers Milch had given were eighteen days, six weeks, and two months, respectively. Later, when Jackson pinned Milch down to how an unprepared nation could conduct blitzkriegs, Milch had amended what he said to a statement about Germany being prepared for a war against Poland but not against the world.

Milch said to me, with eyes slightly narrowed, "Justice Jackson was very clever. But I never disagreed with a word he said. I said Germany was rearming. The only point of disagreement was in the extent." I remarked that this was a crucial point.

What about Milch's statement that Poland and France were better prepared for war than Germany, because Germany had only five years in which to prepare? "The facts speak for themselves. By that I meant exactly what I said. That Germany beat these countries was due to better planning and not better preparedness."

In the course of his cross-examination, Jackson had mentioned an interrogation by Milch in which he had said he warned Hitler to get rid of Ribbentrop or there would be trouble with England. I asked him if he had any comments to make on Ribbentrop. "Need one comment on that fool? He is not a foreign minister but a blind adherent of Hitler. He is also personally disagreeable and vain."

What about the statement Jackson extracted regarding everyone's fear of Himmler and the SS, from the Reich marshal on down? I inquired. "As I said in court, it is true. And I could say much more. Himmler was the most feared man in Germany by everyone, including the most loyal German. It was a bad system and I am the first to admit it. But what could I do about it?"

In the course of his cross-examination by Jackson, Milch had been reminded that he considered Hitler "abnormal" after March 1943. As a psychiatrist I was interested in this, I said; did he have anything more to add? "Hitler was progressively self-centered as time went on. That he was mentally abnormal there is no doubt. If the court received the impression, as Jackson cleverly pointed out, that Goering as number two man was continuing his fidelity to a mentally abnormal Hitler, he is correct. I didn't disagree in court." Milch almost chuckled.

"It's surprising how little I disagreed with your Mr. Jackson. I wanted those things that I thought about Hitler to come out, but there was no place for it until Mr. Jackson produced them from previous interrogations."

I asked Milch why it was that he was testifying for Goering if he was really quite opposed to him, as seemed obvious. "In the first place, I am not opposed to Goering, except in certain details. Goering was an early and fanatic Nazi. That I did not agree with. I only joined the party after its rise to power, as Jackson brought out, in 1933. Then I soon became in charge of the aviation end of things. My intentions were to build an industrial air force, not a war machine. I was convinced that we needed aerial parity with other nations in the matter of bombers, fighters, and so on. By 1938 I could see the direction Hitler was taking, and as was brought out in court, that was well known. It was impossible to quit by then."

Jackson had hinted that Milch's father, or at least his mother's husband, was Jewish. Goering had steps taken to "Aryanize" Milch in some way. Jackson had referred to Milch's "alleged father" as having been Jewish. Milch had said that was a matter that had been cleared up in 1933. In court it had been rather mysterious. Just what is the truth? I asked Milch. "I had applied for admission to the National Socialist Party in March 1933, I believe. There was some question about my father's father because his papers could not be found. So I had to make an affidavit, which Goering signed, that I was fully German. My father was, as far as I know, not Jewish, as Jackson mentioned. It is possible he was partially Jewish, but of that I am not ashamed."

I said that I had heard a rumor he had declared that he was born out of wedlock and that his mother's husband was not really his father. "That is not true. Definitely."

When I asked him for details about his family history he was evasive and I did not pursue the subject. I was more interested at this time in obtaining his views on the cross-examination.

I passed on to Jackson's question about Milch's having taken measures to accelerate the procuring of Russian POWs from the camps for laboring purposes. I also asked him about his statements obtained from records of minutes of meetings of the Central Planning Board, of which he was a member, that Russian labor should be supplied to work the mines and that Russian women should be enlisted in agricultural work. Milch was as evasive as he was in court. He looked more uncomfortable than he had managed to appear in court two days ago, however, and said that "many things were said in the heat of a war, and not all were calculated to be read back to you later."

I asked Milch whether he felt that he was morally or ethically wrong in his suggestions for the use of Russian labor. "No. If we had lost territory to the Russians they would have done the same thing. Besides, the Russians had plenty of manpower and we were short."

I said that was begging the question, from a moral standpoint, but I was merely interested in his attitudes and that it was clear he had no regrets regarding his actions. He said again that the British general had struck him over the head shortly after he was captured and taken through the concentration camp for an inspection of it; as a result his memory was faulty and he could not really tell whether some of the things he was accused of having said were true or not.

I inquired: What about the statement you are reported to have made regarding the draining off of French young men to work in Germany, so that in the event of an attack of the mainland by the Allies, these Frenchmen could not act as partisans? Milch said he gathered that the interpretation put on his words regarding clearing France, and Italy for that matter, of partisans or possible partisans was that he was in favor of forced labor. "Nothing could be farther from the truth! But our Fatherland was threatened by defeat from these bands of Maquis and other wild groups, and what else could be done by a loyal German anxious to achieve a victory for his Fatherland?"

I did not reply to this rhetorical and cynical question. I asked him if he had anything further to say regarding his part in fostering slave labor. "It was not fostering slave labor. Not at all. It was strategic economic policy. Besides, not all of what I am purported to have said can be interpreted literally. Much was never put into practice. Perhaps if it had been, it would have been a different story and I would not be sitting here in a cell."

I went on to rehash Jackson's quoting Milch that he, Milch, would personally see to it that German foremen physically assaulted foreign slave workers who protested. Milch had reportedly replied that he would not tolerate any foreigner saying to a German foreman, "I will cut your throat." I went on with the Jackson quotations about Milch saying he had personally ordered two Russian airmen who had attempted to escape to be hanged or shot and that this was done by the SS the very next day. It was done in the factory, where others could see it. Milch had denied it. He still denied it but quite feebly, as he had done in court. I said that it seemed unlikely that such stuff should appear in minutes of a German meeting if it were untrue. Milch said that minutes could be false.

Milch looked washed out. It was curious because he had not seemed that way in court the other day. I remarked on this.

"I did not want to take the stand. Goering insisted on it. I thought I would be able to testify about Goering and that would be the end of it. But instead they drag in all these things I am reported to have said. It's probably all groundless. Things taken out of context sound so much worse. Besides, we were at war."

But Milch looked worried and harried. It was the first time I had seen this little compact man, who looks younger than his fifty-six years, in any way ruffled. I said in parting that his testimony for Goering had incriminated him, in my opinion. He replied, "No. Let them try me. I shall have plenty to say about the Allies. I have some very good friends among the Americans and English, and the French industrialists, too. I have done nothing of which I am ashamed."

It was true enough, he did not appear ashamed — merely worried about his own immunity from trial as a war criminal.

## Rudolf Mildner
(1902– 1951)

Rudolf Mildner was a senior official of the Gestapo, including head of the Gestapo in Chemnitz and later in Kattowitz, Poland, and thus responsible for sending thousands of Jews to their deaths in Auschwitz, which was in Kattowitz. In September 1943 Mildner became commander of the Sipo and SD in Denmark, just before the Nazis began an "action" to deport the Jews in that country. He testified for the prosecution at Nuremberg and remained in custody until 1949.

**January 24, 1946**

Interviewed Rudolf Mildner with the aid of Gilbert, who translated. Mildner was chief of police in Kattowitz.[1] A couple of days ago he was officially interrogated, and broke down and was depressed thereafter when some of his underlings testified as to how many Poles he had ordered to be executed. He would not eat, vomited occasionally, wept, and showed other evidences of agitated reactive depression. The interrogation was on the business of Mildner's part in the executions at Auschwitz while he was a presiding member of the court that sentenced to death, he says, between five hundred and six hundred Poles.

Last night he was amiable, friendly, mild-mannered, ingratiating. He told us that he was police chief and a puppet in Silesia; that though he sat in the court and handed the sentences to the convicted Poles, the trials were formalities; and that the sentences and convictions were pre-arranged without his being consulted by the party district administrator. He and other officials just had to obey orders.

He is a big-boned, forty-three-year-old man, with beginning baldness. He could be a policeman anywhere.

He said the number of Poles he had executed for minor misdeeds, like stealing, was not more than five or six hundred. He absolves himself from any blame in the matter, saying the order came from party district administrator Fritz Bracht. Furthermore, he said, "Suppose you Americans were in Germany fighting Russia, and some Germans sabotaged you, or shot your soldiers, or stole. You'd hang them. And rightly so. So to preserve order and prevent sabotage, the Germans in Poland and Silesia had to do that, too."

Seen today, he was red-eyed, had a pleading facial expression, said he had always been healthy, liked sports, and could not understand his present symptoms. Asked if he thought they might be the result of some emotional disturbance, he agreed. He also attributed it to the interrogation, which he said was brief but seemed aimed only at getting him to state the dates and numbers of persons executed and not the reasons, not the circumstances.

He was born July 10, 1902, in Silesia. He lived there until the age of fourteen years. As far as he knows his birth was normal; he walked, talked, and so forth at appropriate ages. The only childhood illnesses he recalls are measles and an occasional cold. His appetite up to a day ago was excellent. During his childhood the family financial conditions were always satisfactory and he had a good home and enough food, clothing, and the like. He never had any food fads or similar difficulties.

He attended elementary school until nine years of age. He wanted to become a physician but read *Robinson Crusoe* at about that age and decided to become a sailor. In 1914, when he was twelve, the First World War began and he wanted to enlist in the navy at once. Actually he enlisted in the Austrian navy when he was fourteen years old, and served until November 1, 1918, when the war ended, a period of two years. He was stationed in the Adriatic and did not participate in any battles, because the Adriatic was mainly occupied by German and Austrian submarines. The usual age was seventeen for enlistment in the navy, "but I was big and tall, and appeared older." He was accepted though it was known he was but fourteen.

He attended a school for noncommissioned officers for a short while (Austrian navy), but in 1918, when the war ended, he abandoned his original plans, which were to stay for ten years in the Austrian navy and then to go to the Austrian Lloyd Lines and take an examination as a seaman.

In 1918 he went to Hamburg and Bremen to seek employment. However, there were at that time over sixty thousand unemployed seamen in those cities, and he found no job. He joined some friends and enlisted in a German infantry regiment until July 19, 1919. In August 1919 he went to Berlin, met some friends, and went to Latvia. There were anti-Bolshevik armies stationed in Latvia — German, Russian, and Latvian. He became a member of a Russian anti-Bolshevik army. "We were supposed to settle down and each man get sixty acres of land. We wore part Russian and part German uniforms, but the insignia were Russian." He remained until December 1919. There were no battles, little to do other than regimental training.

"All Russian and German troops were required to leave Latvia and go back to Germany at that time." In 1920 he held several short-time jobs in Czechoslovakia. He took private tutoring lessons in English and French and other high school subjects while working as a laborer or factory hand.

He then went back to Germany and joined up to go to sea again, because by then Germany had a small merchant fleet. He signed on a boat as a fisherman until September 1921, then signed as a seaman and went to Norway and South America, Valparaiso, and so forth. He was never seasick, enjoyed the work.

He went from Norfolk, Virginia, to Antwerp on an 8,500-ton steamer, and the trip took nineteen days. "On that trip all the other seamen were seasick but not me. I was never airsick either and I've traveled a lot by air.

"In 1922 I saw clearly that I could never become an officer because I would have to go on a three-masted training sailboat for twelve months, and Germany had only two such boats. On these sailboats only sons or nephews of captains went — or other people who had influence — not the average person like myself.

"I therefore went to Salzburg, where I had relatives, and on July 1, 1923, I joined the Austrian police force." He spent two years in police school in Salzburg and Vienna, after eight months' practical work. He says he studied penal law, criminal law, state law, history of the Austrian constitution, all trade and traffic laws. After these two years he was hired as a regular employee for life, and stationed in Salzburg until 1935. He spent short periods, too, in Vienna.

"Meanwhile I took a nine-month course for higher police officials. I had private lessons in high school subjects, and in 1927 I studied most of the things one gets in a gymnasium." In 1930 he graduated high school by examination, and proceeded to study law at the University of Innsbruck. In 1934 he graduated with the degree of doctor of jurisprudence. He became an instructor in the police force. He worked hard, at night, during the day. He took no time off, learned easily, slept little, but ate well, and lost no weight.

In the fall of 1934 he became a member of the Criminal Police. Then he became a member of "the higher administration of law." What is that? "The Austrian police had several departments — State Police, Criminal Police, et cetera. I was in the Department of Traffic and Administrative Law."

He had a good friend whose career followed his closely. Both were in Department 6 of the police force. They wanted Department 8 to take over Department 6. The police director promised to have 6 taken over by 8. It seems that Department 6 was a "plain police officers group" whereas Department 8 was "an academic group." Both Mildner and his friend would have studied medicine, he says, if they had not been promised positions in Department 8. When he had broached the subject of studying medicine years before to the police chiefs, the chiefs said that he should stay with the police — that it was cheaper and besides he would be given a permanent place in Department 8. By the time he and his friend were to be transferred to Department 8, the political life in Austria had changed. Until 1933, said Mildner, Austria was a free democratic country. After 1933 the National Socialists and Communists were banned and the dictatorship of the Christian Socialist Party under Dollfuss took place.[2] In February 1934 there was a home guard uprising. In June or July 1934 there was a Nazi insurrection.

People who had promised Mildner and his friend that they would be taken into Department 8 had by then been retired or transferred. "In Salzburg the police director hated us and wanted nothing to do with part-time students like my friend and myself."

After an exceptionally disagreeable quarrel, Mildner and his friend quit the police force and went to Bavaria. "I didn't know what I wanted to do. I intended either to start a business or go to my brother-in-law in Potsdam. But in Bavaria we were both arrested on suspicion of being espionage agents of Schuschnigg."[3]

After three days of arrest they were released on the approval of Heydrich, who was chief of the Security Police in Berlin. The friends proceeded to Munich. At the time there were forty-five thousand Austrians in Germany — Nazi refugees from Austria. There was a special department in Munich to handle these people. Most of them, said Mildner, were really murderers and thieves who stayed in Germany under the guise of being Nazi refugees. Heydrich ordered that Mildner and his friend be hired as employees of this agency in Munich for the sorting out of these Austrians. Were you a member of the Nazi Party at the time? "Not yet. My friend and I were members of the Austrian home guard. That was June 21, 1935."

Their duties were to screen all Austrian refugees and check whether they had criminal records. The criminals were to be arrested and turned over to the courts. "My friend [Pifrader][4] went to Berlin in 1936 to take over a similar department. I stayed on in Munich until March 13, 1938." Mildner was assigned to Vienna by Heydrich at the time of Austria's occupation. In May, Mildner received a document that stated that as of January 1938, he was administrative adviser of internal administration.

In March 1939 he was sent to Prague. He received the orders while he was vacationing at an Austrian-Swiss border resort. He did not like the idea of having to serve on the Security Police there, because he knew Prague and liked the city.

"While I was in Munich I tried to get away from the police job. I tried to take an examination as an assessor. I didn't want to stay with the police. I appealed to the Ministry of Justice in Berlin but I was refused. I wanted to become a legal adviser to industries. But according to German law, I would have had to pass an assessor examination before I could do that."

He learned later that his petitions to Heydrich for release had been refused and he was ordered to remain with the State Police. He stayed only two days in Prague. He knew the Czech people from his navy experiences. He knew there would be terrible battles because the Czechs were a freedom-loving people. He managed to get reassigned to Linz.

"On August 1, 1939, my wife was ill after bearing our second child. I took my other child, my daughter, who was twenty-six months old then, and went by car and canoe for a vacation. We spent four weeks together while my wife was in a hospital. On August 25 I was called to Salzburg as representative of the chief of State Police."

He remained in Salzburg until December 10, when he became chief of the State Police in Chemnitz, Saxony. At the outbreak of the war, he says, he wrote two petitions to Heydrich asking that he be allowed to join the navy. He says he hoped Heydrich would release him. He never met Heydrich personally, and had never requested assignment to the State Police but was "forced into it." Heydrich refused to allow him to leave. In Chemnitz he was supposed to get a detachment of Security Police, for Schleswig-Holstein. He learned of that "just in time to get out of it." Once he was supposed to go to Oslo, Norway, as commander of the Security Police there. That he could prevent through friends in Berlin. Later he was slated to go to northern Norway, but he thwarted that, too.

In February 1941 he and a friend had some business in Berlin. There he received the news that he was transferred to Kattowitz. "I didn't know the region, but the East as a whole was unwelcome as an assignment." Why? "Nobody wanted to go east. The nature of the duties, the paucity of culture, the coal dust, general conditions." When he received the news he became "very excited, even my friends told me that they had never seen me so excited and upset before." He immediately decided to go to Heydrich though his friends warned him against the idea. His friends said that Heydrich would imprison him if he refused Kattowitz. Mildner reported to Heinrich Mueller, who was his immediate chief, and told him of his dislike of the East. However, there was nothing to be done about it because Heydrich had signed the order.

"I was in Kattowitz from March 1941 until September 10, 1943. From there I went to Denmark as chief of SD and Security Police. I spent only three months in Denmark. After I left I believe conditions in Denmark became worse." In December 1943 he left Denmark to become inspector of the SD and Security Police in Kassel. He was there for forty-eight hours when he received a written order from Berlin telling him that the chief of SD in Berlin had found another use for him and he should stop his inspection tour. His successor took a long time getting to Kassel, however, so that he remained there until March 1944. For the next three months he was in Berlin, in the RSHA. Then he went to Vienna as representative of the Security Police and SD. That was on December 1, 1944. His superior was Huber.[5]

The difference between the Security Police and the SD, according to Mildner:

1.  Security Police — employers of Criminal Police and Gestapo
2.  SD — part of the party organization

However, at the top, in Berlin, was Himmler, chief of all police, and Kaltenbrunner, who had succeeded Heydrich as chief of Security Police and SD. Mildner knew Kaltenbrunner from Linz. He does not know Kaltenbrunner well, but he knows that people thought highly of him in Austria. "I know that Kaltenbrunner was unhappy in Berlin because he is a typical Austrian. I'm sure Kaltenbrunner would not misuse the SD or Gestapo as Himmler and Heydrich did. Kaltenbrunner loves women, wine. He does not like police activity any more than I do.

"After the war Kaltenbrunner would have reorganized the Security Police, but not as a tool of Heydrich or Himmler. Eighty to eighty-five percent of the Gestapo people were not volunteers, but when Hitler came to power in 1933 he took the best experts from the Criminal Police and made them Gestapo agents. The same was true in Austria. Nobody could refuse."

Mildner remained in Vienna until the Russians arrived. Hitler gave the order through Schirach, the party district administrator, to defend the city. This meant Mildner would have to stay in Vienna. He had six thousand people under his command, including nineteen hundred mail censors and customs officials. "I had responsibility for all these men — it was a difficult time." About eight days before the encirclement of Vienna, Schirach left, so Mildner released his men. He stayed on until the bridges were blown across the Danube. Then he retreated to territory that was not occupied by the Russians.

"I would have taken all the police, put them together under my command, and prevented all the blowing up of bridges. I would have surrendered the city to the Americans. I went to Salzburg to Kaltenbrunner, who gave me permission to go to the mountains because he knew what we had to expect and I didn't want to stay in Russian territory."

From May 1 until May 28 he went skiing in upper Austria. He used his true name, and had his chauffeur with him. He was taken prisoner on May 28. When he returned to his hut that evening there were five Americans who took Mildner and his chauffeur prisoner. His captors were polite and courteous, he says.

**Marital:** Married 1928, wife aged forty. He has known her since 1923. Three children, ages three, six, and eight years, all girls. Wife had diphtheria in 1943 and it had a bad effect on her heart. His children are well. Two of them had mild attacks of scarlet fever. His married life has been a happy one except that the unrest caused by his numerous shifts in position and the war caused many separations that otherwise would not have occurred. He became tearful discussing his wife and children, and this subject was not stressed during the interview at this time.

**Family:** Mother died in 1924, at fifty-six, of pneumonia, father died in 1933, at age sixty-one, following a fall from a construction platform on which he was working as carpenter. **No Siblings:** Family history not obtained at this interview beyond a statement that his parents were "very good."

**February 12, 1946**
He has improved somewhat insofar as his depression and appetite but is still rather morose. Today he asked to tell me all about Denmark as he has been thinking about it and feels if I listened to him it "might take my mind off the subject."

On September 10, 1943, he received a phone call from Office I of the RSHA, in Berlin, to establish a Security Police office in Denmark. He was called to Berlin for instructions. He went to Hamburg to get seventy-five Gestapo men.

On April 9, 1940, Denmark had been occupied by the Germans. The former German ambassador had a conference with the Danish king, who was assured that there would be no launchings from Danish soil by air or sea against England. Germany was not to attack Denmark. The army commander was put in office for all of Denmark, for civilian and economic affairs. Werner Best had a big conflict with Heydrich and Mueller and that was the reason he was assigned to a foreign post.[6]

Such was the situation until June or August 1943. Meanwhile certain sabotage was being done by the Danes. The punishment of these Danes was in the hands of Danish officials and at the same time the German military police.

In the summer of 1943 sabotage was great, and strikes broke out. Martial law was dictated by the military commander of Denmark. The reason for calling in the German Security Police, said Mildner, was to combat underground organizations, strikes, and sabotage by illegal groups.

Mildner seemed quite content on that score. I asked him if he didn't feel the Danes were to be admired for such resistance to Nazism, but he seemed confused by the question. "No. It was wrong. If they didn't do those things I wouldn't have had to arrest people, and the later mass arrests, hostages, et cetera, wouldn't have occurred." This business of his "blocking" on such questions of values when on the other hand he tried to get out of going to Prague because the Czechs were "a freedom-loving people and would fight" is something to follow up at a later date.

"On September 17, 1943, I got to Denmark. I carried an order with me from Mueller, to arrest Niels Bohr, a famous atomic physicist. He was a Jew or half Jew. That was the reason for the order." Mildner said he imagined his work was to be different because he had known many Danes in the past fifteen years, including Danish girls. He didn't know actual Danish conditions, he said. "I knew there might be some resistance but I didn't want to mix into Danish affairs any more than I had to. Bohr was a Danish citizen and I didn't like the order Mueller gave me. I was not in Denmark long, but during that time I received an order from Himmler through Best. I had already established a central office of the Security Police in Denmark in the five larger cities. The telegram said that "the evacuation of Danish Jews was to start at once. There were six thousand Jews in Denmark."

These Jews, said Mildner, were people who had fled Portugal in the fifteenth and sixteenth centuries and lived in Denmark for hundreds of years. "I was very distressed. I went to Best and asked why the Jews should be evacuated. They kept quiet and did no harm. They were Danish citizens and Denmark was a sovereign state. Best explained that Ribbentrop had spoken to Hitler and said he thought it was best to have the Jews evacuated from Denmark. Ribbentrop was afraid he might be called on the carpet for not having taken any action against the Jews in Denmark." In other words, Ribbentrop anticipated Hitler's wishes in this regard. "Yes. That was what Best said. I can say that the reason for the deportation of Jews from Denmark is Ribbentrop. Whether it would have been ordered later by Hitler, I don't know." Do you know of any documents in that regard? "No. Best told me. All of us were distressed, Best as well as my coworkers.

"I immediately sent a telegram to Mueller with recommendations that the deportation of Jews of Denmark would cause many misgivings. First because the Jews were quiet politically, and did not appear in any way disturbing. Second, the deportation would have serious conse-

quences for the German-Danish relationship, because Danish agriculture sent food to Germany and Danish industry also worked for Germany. Then there were the repercussions it would have on the
Scandinavians and in North America. I added that all the Danish people
object to it. I said in the telegram, too, that it would result in more sabotage and unrest. I requested that the order for deportation be canceled."

In a few days the order came from Himmler to Best, informing him to
proceed with the given order. "Desperate about it, I went to the airport
and flew to Berlin. I wanted to see Kaltenbrunner. I actually saw Mueller. I again told Mueller all the misgivings, although I had to omit the
humane reasons — I had to use other arguments." Mueller called his secretary, in Mildner's presence, and dictated a telegram to Himmler. He
wrote all that Mildner told him. "I flew back although Mueller said the
cable wouldn't do much good. I still had some hope. Paul Kanstein was
assigned for liaison between Best and the Danish government. Kanstein
knew Denmark well. He was very friendly with all the Danish ministers.
A meeting was called with Kanstein, Best, and myself present and we
decided that all Jews should be warned. If the order had to be carried
out, I had no interest that any Jews should fall into our hands. A few days
later another cable came from Himmler — to deport the Jews at once. A
representative of Eichmann came with two ships and a detachment from
Oslo consisting of a battalion of Ordinary Police. One night, October 1,
I think, the action began. I spent that evening with Kanstein. In all they
seized four to five hundred Jews. They were put on a ship, and I believe
went via Oslo to Stettin to Theresienstadt [Czechoslovakia]. The other
Jews, who were warned, were hidden by Danes and by night fled to Sweden. There was very lively traffic. One could go by rowboat — the distance was only three kilometers. That was the whole action.[7]

"There was big excitement in the Führer's headquarters. Hitler and
Himmler were furious and issued orders that all Jewish capital should be
confiscated." Did they blame it on you? "I don't know. But Himmler was
furious at me, and Eichmann was also angry at me and Best. They
assumed correctly that the Jews had been warned. Therefore the whole
action fell through." Do you consider it insignificant that four hundred
to five hundred Jews were shipped away from their homes? "No. But
think of what it could have been.

"In addition, I didn't arrest Niels Bohr because I didn't want to arrest
Danish scientists. Bohr fled to Sweden. That was long after the Jewish

deportation. From Sweden Bohr went to England, was received by Churchill, and Radio London announced that Bohr decided to give his work to the Allies.

"Then came a cable from Himmler, after Bohr's visit to Churchill, that the official responsible for Bohr's escape was to be made accountable at once. Mueller in Berlin gave the order to confiscate the Institute of Physics in Copenhagen. I wrote back that they should send experts from Berlin. This they later did.

"I was about to sign an agreement with the Danish police regarding the increasing Danish sabotage and murder of Germans by Danes. Trains were being derailed. German officers and enlisted men were shot in the back even during the daytime. Dynamite exploded in factories working for Germany. There were wounded and dead. Time bombs went off in restaurants frequented by Germans and Danish girls. Thirty died that way. Every day there were explosions in factories.

"The Danish police did not participate in the prosecution of these people. It was in the hands of the military commission. The prosecution was up to the German military and secret police. People caught were turned over to the army and tried by court-martial.

"I made a pact with the Danish police that they assist in the prosecution of these saboteurs. Everybody then caught by the Danish police could be tried by the Danes themselves. Various parties were intact — not forbidden in Denmark as they were in Norway — and the police agreed to my proposal. If Germany won the war, then amnesty would be given the political prisoners — they would still be prisoners because there is no death penalty in Denmark. If the Allies won the war, people would be released and made heroes."

General Hermann von Hannekan, army commander in Denmark, had to be consulted about this pact, Mildner continued. His court-martial would have to relinquish the trying of saboteurs caught by the Danish police. "I received permission from Hannekan but I needed Himmler's approval. That was still in doubt but something else entered the picture in between. Up to that time there was no higher SS or police leader in Denmark. I was under Best. After the Jewish deportation and the increasing sabotage, a cable arrived from Himmler to Best saying: "In order to prevent sabotage and murder by Danes, act immediately with countersabotage." Best called me, gave me the cable, was upset, feared we might have to take hostages and shoot them as they did in

Norway and France. By doing that Himmler would destroy all of my plans of being friendly with the Danes. My plans included capture of saboteurs and getting them away from the public. Himmler would destroy the cooperation of the Danish police. I immediately sent a cable to Mueller telling him of Himmler's cable.

"I added to that cable that it was impossible to execute the order with the staff I had, that the cooperation between the German and Danish police would be an illusion, and furthermore be very bad for the name of the German Secret Police in Denmark. The cooperation between my people and the Danish officials was excellent at the time.

"I told Mueller that it would be useless to use countersabotage — that it was just murder." What did countersabotage mean? "That I shall explain in a moment. It's very interesting. Whenever a Danish or German businessman who did business with the Germans was murdered, an important Dane should be murdered — at first unofficially; later it became quite official. Or if a Danish factory working for Germany was blown up by sabotage, another factory working only for the Danes should be destroyed." A crazy idea. "Yes. It was Hitler's idea, not Himmler's, I can prove it. And if such was the case, the work of the Security Police in Denmark was finished because there would be continuous murderous activity, blowing up of businesses, and giving the Reich a bad name.

"Mueller agreed that we could not use the Danish officials for countersabotage and agreed to send a detachment from Berlin. I believe it was just one of those spontaneous thoughts of Himmler's; he gave an order and it had to be executed at once. I thought Himmler might forget all about it." I understood you to say it was Hitler's orders. "No. The basic idea of countersabotage was Hitler's. That is what I meant.

"I didn't do anything. I knew Guenther Pancke was to come to Copenhagen to be my immediate superior. I decided to wait until Pancke came, and then ask him to go to headquarters and try to talk Himmler out of it. I did nothing. Pancke came in mid-October. He became the highest SS and police chief in Denmark.

"I advised him of the situation. Best was afraid because we had not done anything as yet about countersabotage. I asked Pancke to go to Himmler and he agreed and went in the middle of November. They met in East Prussia, in Rastenburg. Pancke said that Himmler was furious with me and demanded immediate countersabotage with his own staff. I postponed the whole thing. There was still slight hope something might change.

"An SS and police court had been established for crimes committed in Denmark by Germans. But Pancke opposed my plan of turning over Danish sabotage to Danish police because he was eager to extend the court's powers to the SS and police courts. While in Berlin, Kaltenbrunner and Mueller agreed to my plan; Pancke, an agent of Himmler, canceled it and induced Himmler to be against it too. The police and SS court was enforced only after I left Denmark in January 1944.

"I just want to add something about Jewish persecution. Every day letters were received from the Danish people protesting the action against Jews, against strikes. One day a telegram came to Pancke that the Danish minister of economics was to be arrested together with his family. I did not even know who this man was or where he was. I wrote back to Himmler via Mueller, which resulted in another cable from Himmler to Best that orders must be executed in Denmark. I learned the Dane was in the Ministry of Economics and had declared that if the Jews were deported, there would be a general strike. I sent back a cable that if we were to arrest this man we must arrest the whole Danish people, because as he thinks, so think the whole Danish people. These things happen like that quite frequently.

"One day I received an order that the Italian consul in Copenhagen should be arrested because he was against Mussolini. By the time I got around to it the consul was in Sweden with everything he owned." Mildner laughs a bit at this.

"Hitler had a great dislike for the Danes for the following reason: the Danish king had been congratulated by Hitler on his birthday, and the king answered cryptically with 'Many thanks.' Hitler was said to have had an attack of rage. And ever since then Hitler hated Denmark."

The Danish king was never arrested during Mildner's time there. Also, listening to foreign radio broadcasts was not forbidden, nor was Jewish capital confiscated, until January 1944.

What happened to the property of the four hundred to five hundred Jews deported during your time? "I don't know." In other words, actual laws regarding confiscation of Jewish property were not existent during your time? "That's what it amounts to."

At the time of declaration of martial law in Denmark, Mildner continued, the Danish army of three thousand men was interned by the Germans in Denmark. Best and Mildner, he said, tried to have the army released. "Then Himmler had the crazy idea to take the Danish army and force them into the armed SS. Best spoke against the plan.

"Sabotage became more frequent and more German army personnel were shot in the back. The army reported all these daily happenings to headquarters, so Hitler, Ribbentrop, Jodl, Keitel, and the rest must have known about it.

"Countersabotage was still not employed. One night a German officer was shot in the back and the army asked for reprisals, but Best tried to impose money fines. Pancke became afraid of Himmler and ordered me to shoot several Danes at once. I told him I didn't know who, we just could not go on the street and shoot Danes. He ordered me to take political prisoners. Three internees, Communists, should be brought before a court-martial and shot while escaping. It was to be prearranged. Himmler was to be informed that three Danes were shot while escaping." What do you think about Himmler's personality or character? "I didn't know him personally. I know that in upper Austria fifteen German girls had sexual intercourse with workers from the East. Himmler ordered eight-and-a-half-year concentration camp terms for the girls." What happened to the workers? "I presume that they were executed.

"In Krakow a Criminal Police officer, over fifty years of age, shook hands with a Jew. Himmler was informed and ordered a two-year term in Dachau for this employee. This was at the time of the battle of Stalingrad. It shows that Himmler had time to think of these ridiculous things.

"Pancke did the execution of the three Danes in order to quiet Hitler and Himmler, when they read of the fatal shooting of the German officer. The three were shot. It was in the papers the next day. Himmler was informed about it.

"Himmler realized they wanted to fool him. 'How did you do it?' he cabled. Next day Pancke received an order from Himmler that he was personally responsible for a countersabotage program that must be carried out at once. And Pancke must submit a death list.

"When the next act of sabotage occurred, Pancke chose two names from a list. That contained names and professions of people. There were no Communists on it. The first selected by Pancke was an author and priest. The second was another author. These two were to be murdered immediately. From Berlin came four men, with possibly a fifth. They were from the armed SS."

Personality of Pancke? "He was a powerless tool in the hands of Himmler, of whom he was afraid, and by whom he was treated poorly. Himmler insulted Pancke like a schoolboy. Pancke was about forty-eight to fifty years old, came from northern Germany.

"Pancke gave me orders to blow up a museum in Copenhagen, where students gathered, and some other places. I declined and said I needed a written order by Himmler. Pancke was angry, but it was not done. Another example: The State Police were billeted. These billets included the offices of Best, my own, Pancke, and staff, and commissioner of the Ordinary Police and his staff. Near it was a big tourist hotel. Pancke ordered that property blown up as an act of countersabotage. I asked why. The reason was that once in that hotel Pancke's secretary couldn't get a meal served after 7 p.m. There was also a strict police order that restaurants were not allowed to sell after 7 p.m.

"In Copenhagen there was an associate of Best, Paul Barandon. Pancke asked that I put an explosive in Barandon's desk or house. Barandon was a German. Pancke and Barandon had served in the same regiment in the last war; they had had an old quarrel years before, and that was enough for Pancke. It wasn't done.

"Sabotage became more frequent. On December 18, I went on a furlough and was supposed to return on January 5. When I arrived home I got a wire to be back in Copenhagen on December 29. It came from Pancke through his deputy. I later learned the reason through the deputy. Best, Pancke, Hannekan, and Kaltenbrunner were all called to Hitler's headquarters on December 30 for lunch. I went to Berlin, reported to Mueller on December 28 and 29, and told him that because I didn't execute countersabotage orders these people were to be scolded by Hitler. Mueller said: 'Comrade Mildner, watch yourself. Himmler is angry with you.'

"I flew back to Copenhagen with some idea of what was in store for me. On January 1, Best called me to his house, and after dinner, with just Best, his wife, and myself in the smoking room, he told me of the trip to Hitler's headquarters. Best and Pancke were received in Rastenburg, terribly bawled out, told they would get a good spanking from Hitler if they didn't carry out the countersabotage program. At the same time Kaltenbrunner, Best, and Pancke were told that Mildner had to disappear immediately. Best and Kaltenbrunner tried to stand up for me, but not Pancke. Mueller told me that later. In Heydrich's time I would surely have been brought before an SS court. Pancke was seriously repri-manded by Himmler, who placed him on three months' probation. If orders were not carried out in that time, Himmler promised Pancke there would be disciplinary action.

"Present at the lunch with Hitler were Hannekan, Best, Pancke, Jodl, Kaltenbrunner, Keitel, and Himmler. Ribbentrop was ill at the time. The lunch took three hours and not because it was an elaborate meal. Hitler explained his plans for Denmark and said it could only be made peace-ful through intensive countersabotage. In other words, murder and explosion. It shouldn't be kept at all secret. If a Dane who worked for the Nazis was murdered or a Danish factory working for Germany dam-aged, on the very same day a Danish factory or prominent person should be murdered, and the papers should carry the story prominently the next day. A prominent Danish scientist was murdered by unknown men, or a factory blown up, the papers should read, with satire and irony. In other words it was not to be made secret anymore. The Danes were to know." Plain terrorism? "Yes. Hitler explained quietly that he wanted these things done. It is of interest that no one objected or talked back. It was law and it was genius speaking.

"I was relieved as of December 31, and my successor was Otto Boven-siepen, who took over my duties on January 5. I went on to Kassel."

**February 14, 1946**
Mildner finished his story of Denmark the day before yesterday after a lengthy session, and he continued today. He seemed less inclined to talk-ing, but once the subject of Kattowitz was broached, he went on like a phonograph machine, and I barely interrupted him but let him tell his story in his own way, as he willed it. His depression and poor appetite, with some morning vomiting, has improved. He seemed brighter and more cheerful, also more reserved than on Tuesday.

"I was in Kassel only a short time, as inspector for the SD and SS. What happened there is unimportant." What about Kattowitz? "I am leading up to that. I stayed in Berlin for three months. In mid-June 1944, I came to Vienna and stayed there until the end of the war. I want to give you some background about Silesia.

"After the war in Poland, Silesia was divided into two districts: one, Lower Silesia, whose capital was Breslau, and, two, Upper Silesia, whose capital was Kattowitz. Parts of Silesia and of Poland were taken into the

Reich. The whole district had a population of 4.5 million. Upper Silesia before 1918 was partly German, a smaller part Russian, and the greatest part Austrian. The inhabitants were mainly German or of German ancestry, as well as Polish-German, and pure Polish. There were two groups: a Polish minority with German citizenship before 1939, who lived in the territory of the Reich, and a second group that was mainly German before 1921, but became Polish after 1921.

"In the district itself there were tremendous supplies of coal, very valuable hard coal, worth millions and millions. Coal there was more plentiful than in all the Ruhr, Rhineland, and Westphalia. During the war it outproduced the entire western coal region. Wherever there is coal, there is other industry. There were tremendous war industries, private industries; and an additional factor was that it was never bombed. Due to aerial bombardments in the West, much industry moved to this territory. Gigantic factories were built by IG Farben at Auschwitz. Manufacturing of synthetic rubber, fuel, and other allied chemical products was done. There were refineries for Romanian oil. Zinc, iron, and steel works. Factories for panzers, U-boats.

"Thus, since Upper Silesia was not endangered by aerial attack it was the most important industrial region of the Reich. On the east it was bordered by Poland. On the south by Slovakia. In the southwest by the Protectorate of Moravia. In the west, Lower Silesia and the Sudetenland.

"In this territory there had been a high rate of political and criminal crimes before 1914. In the first place, it was tremendously overpopulated, and secondly there was an unusual mixture of peoples. And there were the three borders of Russia, Austria, and Germany. Just seven and a half kilometers east of Kattowitz were three borders. Entire segments of the population lived on smuggling, and fights ensued. There was the easy possibility of switching to another country to escape prosecution for deeds done in one country. Anyone committing a crime in Austria could go to Russia or Germany and vice versa. Crime spread. High treason was widespread, Russians against the Russian government, Germans against Germany, Austrians against Austria. In 1920 or 1921 there were three Polish uprisings against the government. It was mostly German territory. Many thousands of Germans were murdered by Poles. In 1939 when the territory was occupied by German troops, there began underground and resistance movements and political activity by mixed language groups. A great part of the Polish people were illegally organized to procure weapons and explosives. There were many assassinations.

"Such was the situation when I arrived in Kattowitz on the first of March 1941." His highest superior was party district administrator Bracht of Upper Silesia. The latter had all the party powers "in his hands." As far as the Security Police, he had two superiors, both stationed in Breslau. Bach-Zelewski was chief of SS and police in Upper and Lower Silesia. He replaced Schmauser in May or June 1941.[8]

Mildner reported to Bracht explaining he did not know the territory because he had never been there before. "He told me of the situation, that Upper Silesia was the most important province of the Reich, on which might depend victory or defeat in war. Bracht said he was willing to rule with an iron hand in order to keep security.

"He told me he was afraid the Poles might have an uprising. The Poles worked by all means and organizations, with time bombs, reaching up to Breslau and Berlin. Poles started a fire in a railway station in Berlin. They maintained spy rings in the whole Reich. Time bombs. Blown-up tracks. Water poisoned. German police killed. Army men shot. Bands of eighty bandits fought with pistols, grenades, in the woods. At the same time there arose criminal bands that robbed farms and homes. Robbery was a daily occurrence. Poles who were made mayors were murdered, too. The police suffered over a hundred dead in my time there. In Krakow and Warsaw it was even more hectic. Trains were attacked by daylight, all Germans shot. Open uprisings in Polish territory. Uprisings in Warsaw and other districts.

"There were no military personnel in Upper Silesia. Only the Ordinary Police, which were divided among the towns and the State Police, numbering 250 for the entire area of Kattowitz. There was a constant fear of riots spreading, and the population could not be counted on to help at all. The Polish population gave no Polish criminals into German hands. The German population feared reprisals because the criminals were so well organized.

"Then there was the fear that Germany might lose the war, the territory might again become Polish, and the Poles would take terrible reprisals as they did in 1920–21.

"On June 1, 1942, the party district administrator decreed martial law. The minister of justice, Otto Thierack, and Minister of Interior Frick, with Himmler and Heydrich, agreed to set up a court-martial at the disposal of Bracht. For the court-martial, the president of the court was to be the chief of the State Police, which was myself. The second member of the court-martial board was chief of the Criminal Police. And there was to be one other member. Before this court came all the political and criminal crimes committed against the interests of Germany."

# Otto Ohlendorf
## 1907–1951

Otto Ohlendorf was a member of the National Socialist Party from 1925, head of the security services of the Reich Security Main Office during World War II, commander of <u>Einsatzgruppe</u> D on the eastern front, and SS lieutenant general from November 1944. Sentenced to death in April 1948 at a Nuremberg hearing, he was hanged on June 8, 1951.

**March 1, 1946**

Otto Ohlendorf was born in Hanover in February 1907. Actually, he said he was born in Hoheneggelsen, near Hanover. He lived there until 1927. He looks older than his thirty-nine years, and has a washed-out, ghoulish appearance, short, slumped forward, affectless. He tends to speak precisely, but his manner is of a man who is expected to be insulted at any moment and is being defensive about it.

He attended elementary school three years; gymnasium at Hildesheim — nine years of gymnasium, repeated two years. One year he could not graduate, the other year he purposely did not graduate because of political activities. That was in 1925.

When did you first become a member of the Nazi Party? "Nineteen twenty-five." Why didn't you graduate? "Because I talked in many gatherings to the public, in villages." He was eighteen years old, and spoke publicly of questions pertaining to the SD and especially against a Hanover splinter party called Guelphs. There were two parts to the Guelphs, a monarchist and a republican. Ohlendorf was against both, because he was "against the destruction and dividing of Prussia." Did you meet Hitler in 1925? "No." Did you discuss anti-Semitism at age eighteen? "They were general political questions. Anti-Semitism was among them."

When you were eighteen, what were your views on the Jewish questions? "General views — mostly I was interested in doing away with class fights and social questions. I was formerly in the Bismarck Youth — all these parties were represented in a class of people. The NSDAP represented all of the people, regardless of classes." And Jews? "They were members of other parties." Then how do you figure the NSDAP represented all of the people? "I meant it represented all classes."

When did you first have anti-Semitic feelings? "It goes back to the time with the German National People's Party. It was anti-Semitic. The leader was Alfred Hugenberg, later minister of economics and agriculture in 1933."[1]

Was Hugenberg's the same type of anti-Semitism as Hitler's? "I can't say." Did Hugenberg advocate annihilation of the Jews? "I doubt it. It wasn't in Hitler's program until 1942." 1942? "By that time, Hitler gave the orders." Did you follow the orders? "I didn't know of the general order at that time. I found it out here. I'm convinced Hitler could not have found support of the people or even party members for that idea."

"Later, after 1925, to go back, anti-Semitism was dropped, and just differences between nationalities were stressed." When was anti-Semitism revived? "In 1942–43." Are you not the man who testified concerning ninety thousand Jews killed? "Yes." And there was no anti-Semitism in Nazi Germany before 1942–43? "In 1938 those persecutions were not anti-Semitism. There were a large number of Jews who held more favorable positions than they should have, according to their percentage of the population. Germans should have held those positions. This accounted for the 1938 action of Goebbels against the Jews." Therefore, all Jews were dispossessed? "No. That was the November 1938 action of Goebbels against the Jews without the consent of Hitler. That was in reprisal for the murder of a Paris Nazi official by the Jew Herschel Grynszpan." Do you believe that? "No. Goebbels was just looking for an excuse."[2] Did you know Goebbels personally? "Yes." What sort of person was he? "I met him several times. He was clever, fanatic; having a clubfoot he might have suffered a minority inferiority complex, knowing that because of his physical appearance, he knew he never could reach leadership. He was unscrupulous in his propaganda. I always opposed Goebbels. I always tried to have people educated on a broad basis, while Goebbels tried to supply them with knowledge for the moment. Goebbels considered humans as objects to be used for political purposes — for the moment."

Did you do anything concretely against Goebbels? "My reports in the SD always referred to these facts." Anything else about Goebbels? "I always had the feeling that Goebbels didn't respect people as a whole. He was reckless in his contacts in his own office. He had no consideration for anyone. He was only concerned about governing. He took his way of governing from the Catholic hierarchy. As far as I know, Goebbels attended a Catholic school and was brought up in a cloister." He seems to have turned against the Catholics. "Yes. But it did not hinder him from agreeing with authoritarian methods of governing. Goebbels kept faith only with himself."

**Education:** Ohlendorf graduated from gymnasium finally and then studied jurisprudence and economics at the Universities of Leipzig and Göttingen. He spent one year in Italy and studied fascism — in 1931. It was an academic exchange service. "I returned as a fanatic antifascist. Then I went to the courts in October 1933 and became an assistant in the Institute of World Economy at the University of Kiel."

Were you still in the NSDAP? "Yes." How could you be in a fascist party and be a fanatic antifascist? "It's regrettable that you think they are the same. There is much difference. Fascism is a purely stately principle. Mussolini said in 1932, 'The first thing is the state — and from the state are derived the rights and fate of the people. Humans come second.' In National Socialism, it was the opposite. People and humans come first, and the state is secondary."

Do you believe that? "I did. The bad thing was that Hitler hated the state so much, the government never functioned." Do you think Hitler really liked people? "Oh, yes. The fault I see in Hitler is that he left his original base, his liking of the people, and sought the recognition of other nations by waging wars." Do you think Hitler really liked people if he ordered millions of Jews destroyed? "In this was Hitler's downfall." But do you think Hitler liked people? "In 1933–1939, Hitler did tremendous things for the German people." Do you think Hitler liked people in general, or only a concept known as the *Volk*? "I can't answer it generally." Be as specific as you care to be. "Well, he liked the German people." Any other people? "I don't know." Do you think Hitler liked people when he ordered men, women, and children killed regardless of race, color, or creed, in cold blood, not in battle against a town, or air raids, but in files near ditches, as you know the process better than I do? "I can't answer the questions generally or specifically. I don't know the psychological reasons which brought Hitler to do this."

What do you think of it yourself? "One can't generalize, looking at it from a German point of view. Just how many people were shot because of race or creed, I don't know. Not many Germans were shot. Hitler believed in having it done for the good of the German people." How could Hitler love people and shoot others? "Hitler did it for his people. Hitler didn't believe it would end this way." What do you think? "Hitler didn't expect world war." The whole world seemed to expect war. "I don't think such questions can be answered simply." What is your own idea? "I didn't say he was a wonderful man — we started out with a discussion on the definition of fascism and Nazism." As it worked out, was there any difference? "The chief of state in Germany adopted imperialistic beliefs. The extermination of the Jews goes back to the campaigns of Streicher, Goebbels, and Ley, who continually stressed the fact that Jews were enemies of the German people." How did you figure a six-month-old Jewish infant must be killed — was it an enemy? "In the child we see the grown-up. I see the problem differently." How? "I saw the Jewish question in 1933–34 in this way: Give the Jews a region where they would have a base and they could have minorities in other countries. Nothing particular happened — and then came the Goebbels action in 1938. Until 1938 there was no plan to exclude Jews from economic life. The economic experts never agreed with it."

What was your testimony in court? "I described how an *Einsatzgruppe* received an order to liquidate Jews in Russia. This was not an anti-Semitic order; rather the Jews in Russia were said to be the main carrier of Bolshevism there. It was against my will that I was ordered to an *Einsatzgruppe* in Russia. There were five hundred men. Mostly Ordinary Police and armed SS. The region included Odessa and from Nikolaiev to Rostov and Crimea." Did you know what your function was to be? "Yes. I knew the orders. *Einsatzkommandos* in the charge of colonels general executed the orders." And you were a lieutenant general in charge of the *Einsatzgruppe?* "No. I was only a brigadier general at the time. It was 1941–42." What did your *Einsatzgruppe* do? "The Jews were shot in a military manner in a cordon. There were fifteen-men firing squads. One bullet per Jew. In other words, one firing squad of fifteen executed fifteen Jews at a time." Did you supervise or witness? "I was there twice, for short periods." Were the victims men, women, and children? "Yes." Were the children shot? "Yes." Was Uman in your territory? "No. Uman is in Ukraine."[3] How many Jews were killed by your group? "Ninety thousand reported. I figure actually only sixty to seventy thousand were shot." Any records kept? "Not individual names." Where did these Jews who were shot come from? "From Russian towns."

Did you feel you were doing the right thing? "I myself didn't have to do it." Didn't you direct it? "Yes. But orders were given to the *Einsatzkommando* leaders. All I had to do was see to it that it was done as humanely as possible." Would you do it again? "I didn't do anything." Would you direct it again or obey such an order again? "I don't think such a question is right. I think you can save that question. I suffered enough for years. Many people had to carry out orders they disapproved of. I rejected the order twice, but had to obey it the third time. The order came from Heydrich." Was your appetite or sleep disturbed? "Of course. And I had to relieve people who had nervous breakdowns." Many? "A few." Any sadists among the executioners or on your staff? "No. These people were ordered to do it — they were not selected. They were ordered to do it, and so they did it."

At this point, Ohlendorf is glumly reminiscent. He has shifted the burden of the mass murder onto Heydrich. He feels no remorse now except nominally. He looks like a burned-out ghoul, and his conscience, if it can be called such, is clean as a whistle and as empty. There is a dearth of affect, but nothing clinically remarkable. His attitude is "Why blame me? I didn't do anything."

"Those Jews stood up, were lined up, and were shot in true military fashion. I saw to it that no atrocities or brutalities occurred." Was there an age limit? "There was no age limit." He thought for a moment then said flatly, "Thank God, very few children were shot." How many? "I don't know. Hardly a thousand." And ninety thousand reported exterminated, yet only a thousand children? "The treatment of the Germans by the Allies was at least as bad as the shooting of those Jews. The bombing of cities with men, women, and children burning with phosphorus — these things were done by the Allies." Did you ever hear of Coventry? "They were done on both sides. I don't want to bring up any excuses, just state the facts."

The Nazi racial laws — what do you think of them? "They are correct.

The same as the Zionists think — to differentiate the German from the Jewish people. Absolutely correct." And the Nuremberg Laws — what do you think of them? "I don't remember the Nuremberg Laws." At the time of the issuance of the Nuremberg Laws, did you have any objections? "No."

What is your opinion of the Führer principle? "I oppose any Führer principle if it leads to a dictatorship. But the Führer principle could also allow someone with a good character to make himself leader, and that would be good." In general, do you approve of the Führer principle, or do you not? "First, I must understand what is meant by the Führer principle. As handled in the Reich, I oppose it."

What is your opinion regarding the principle of the *Volk* and of the idea of a master race? "The individual peoples are differentiated — it speaks against the national principle." I don't follow you. "The national principle is based on individual nationalities and abilities that these nationalities have." For example? "I mean that each nationality has some abilities peculiar to it."

Then why did you shoot ninety thousand Jews? "First, I didn't shoot them. Firing squads did that. Secondly, I didn't approve of it."

Then why did you go through with it? "What else could I do?" If you disapproved of it, you could have protested and refused, it seems to me. "Where could I desert to? I was under oath to Hitler." Under oath to commit mass murder? "Under oath." For what? What did the oath state? "I could not have prevented it if I had killed myself. It would still have gone off according to schedule. These orders were given to the *Einsatzkommandos* in Berlin before they joined my group." Does the commando leader have more power than the group leader — is that what you mean? "No. I too received orders from Berlin."

And after this small episode of the *Einsatzkommando* in 1941–42, you rose to become a lieutenant general from the rank of brigadier general? "Yes." So that your career was not damaged in any way by the emotional disturbance of the shooting of the Jews? "I told you I was upset. But it did not interfere with my efficiency and I went on in other fields."

How long were you in Russia? "One year." How long did it take to kill ninety thousand? "A year." What was the maximum on one day? "Four or five thousand in one day." Did Jews who were to be killed know it? "About ten minutes prior to the shooting." Was there any disorder?

"No." How were little children who could not stand up to be shot executed? "I don't know. I didn't see any." No reports? "Only numbers."

"I told you how I spent sleepless nights, how it upset my inner self." But you went right on working for the Nazis and reached the rank of lieutenant general? Ohlendorf does not answer this, just sits tight-lipped and rather hostile. None of the questions were expressed in a hostile manner.

Did your wife know of this business of the *Einsatzgruppe?* "No." Have you seen her since 1941–42? "I saw her, but never talked to her about those things. I didn't think it was good conversation for a woman."

But it's all right to shoot women, not all right to talk to them about shootings? "In the first place, I didn't shoot women. I merely supervised."

In general, would you describe yourself as emotional, or cold? "Emotional." Did you ever think of your own children in that position? "That was my first reaction." But it didn't stop you? "I couldn't stop it." You could not get sick or run away? "It would not matter. By my being there, I thought I could prevent inhuman acts." What do you mean? "If you talk to people present at Uman and other such places, you will agree it's best to have good people present to prevent bad executions."

Who is responsible for these crimes? "The Führer and Himmler."

**Father:** Died of old age, in 1943, at the age of eighty-four. A farmer.

**Mother:** Age seventy-two, in good health.

"My father was a very emotional, frank, and honest man. Politically he belonged to the German People's Party — a liberal." Was he anti-Semitic? "No." Do you think your father would have carried out these orders? "I don't know." Was he a strong character? "Yes." Do you think you have a strong character? "Yes." Then you must really hate Jews. "No. We grew up under strict discipline and were used to carrying out orders. My human emotions were the same as those of the others."

How did you get along with your father? "For many years, we didn't get along well. But in the last few years, good. My political activities as a youth were in conflict with my father's ideas."

What sort of personality is your mother? "She is a good housewife and straightforward." Whom do you resemble most, from a personality standpoint? "My father." In what way? "Scientific inclinations. I wanted to become a teacher of philosophy, sociology, and national economy." How much education did your parents have? "Little. But Father read a great deal."

**Siblings:** He is youngest of four children. Brother, age fifty, a chemist, not in the war, is married, has three children, is opposed to the Nazi Party. He is "liberal and theosophical." He ascribes to a religion "after Steiner." He is not anti-Semitic, has an "anthroposophic religion."[4]

As children, did you have any Jewish friends? "No. There was no opportunity. There were no Jews in my hometown." When did you first meet a Jew? "I don't recall. Some Jewish merchants came through my town." Was your father against the Jews? "No." Your mother? "No."

Brother, forty-nine, farmer, attended public and agricultural school. He was a private in the first war. He was not politically interested, but he did join the Nazi Party after 1933. He is single. His mother keeps house for him. He "had bad luck with some women and never got around to marrying."

Sister, forty-seven, single, has a textile business, retail, never married. "She might have been a party member after 1933, but she was never politically active."

Which sibling are you closest to emotionally? "Most of my contact has been with my oldest brother. I had intellectual talks with him regarding anthroposophy. We have a good family feeling." Any reason why the sister is unmarried? "You can say it was because it was a war generation."

Ohlendorf is loath to talk much of his family or siblings, but we did manage a few more minutes on the subject. I believe it adds up to a minimal emotional relationship between himself and any member of his family and a good deal of hostility between himself and his father. There seems no particularly warm relationship between Ohlendorf and his mother, though the hostility seems less in evidence toward her. He did say that the mother favored the oldest son.

**Marital:** Married twelve years. Wife, age thirty-nine. Knew each other seven years prior to marriage. States they are happily married, never separated.

**Children:** Five. Nine-year-old girl; seven-year-old boy; five-year-old boy; two-and-a-half-year-old boy; and a girl born in May 1945.

**Religion:** Protestant. He left the church in 1942. His family, wife also left the church that year. They have all gone back to the church since May 1945. Why did you leave the church? "Because I didn't agree with the dogma of the church." For example? "I felt it was in conflict with the state."

Do you know Bach-Zelewski? "I knew him twice in Berlin and since I'm here in the prison." What do you think of him? "I hardly recognize him here. He was very egocentric, tried to get ahead without considering others." That was as much as Ohlendorf would say about Bach-Zelewski.

What about plans for the future of Germany? "I would depoliticalize Germany. Intensify agriculture. Create 2 million laboring jobs. Two to three million agricultural jobs. Bring together voluntary groups of people with shared interests. Youth itself is opposed to the whole militaristic style of education. I opposed the politicalizing and I saw Ley and Goebbels as opponents of National Socialism."

# Oswald Pohl
## 1892–1951

Oswald Pohl, head of the SS Economic and Administrative Main Office, was tried by a U.S. military tribunal in 1947 and hanged on June 8, 1951.

## June 4, 1946

This fifty-four-year-old man was seized by the British authorities on May 27, 1946, after having hidden in northern Germany since the end of the war. He was a large, stocky fellow, disheveled, with a two or three days' growth of beard, and raggedly clothed. There were slight superficial abrasions of the left face. He said these were incurred when he was beaten up by British soldiers — "about twelve of them" — in the prison to which he was taken after captivity.

He was a soft-spoken, passive-appearing man who said, "I don't hold it against the men who beat me because undoubtedly there are some ruffians of every nationality and the English are not exceptions." He remarked that undoubtedly, because of his high position under Himmler, people would consider him guilty even before trial. He asked if he would be permitted a defense counsel because he intended to prove his innocence and establish the fact that he had never acted dishonorably. His manner was courteous, deferential, and ingratiating.

He said that he was in charge of all administrative and economic problems of the SS. He was chief of the WVHA (Economic and Administrative Main Office) of the concentration camps, and their factories which worked for war production. There were about thirty factories under the SS, he explained, for example the German Equipment Works at Dachau and Oranienburg, and the German Stone and Earth Works at Oranienburg. These plants manufactured armaments.[1]

Pohl was born in Duisburg in the Rhineland on June 30, 1892. As far as he knew, his birth was not remarkable and he developed normally. He had no serious illnesses except for uncomplicated diphtheria as a child, and occasional painful sore throats.

I asked him whether he had much direct contact with Himmler. He replied, "Yes. In the beginning, I saw him constantly, but later, when I achieved my very important office, I saw him about once every three months. I only spoke to Himmler about economic affairs, such as supplies, clothing, and problems which arose about the factories, concentration camp labor, and so forth."

Had he ever met Dr. Emil Puhl, the vice president of the Reichsbank, in order to arrange for the deposit of gold from the concentration camps in the Reichsbank? "I had occasional meetings with Puhl on official business regarding the depositing of gold in the Reichsbank. More important was when Puhl helped me to secure foreign funds to buy land in the East."

Pohl attended elementary school for seven years and gymnasium for another seven years. He was a "fair student" and graduated at the age of twenty. He enlisted at once in the navy, to become a paymaster. He stayed in the navy until January 31, 1934.

He left the navy after twenty-three years of service, to enter the SS. He was charged with organizing the SS administrative and economic section. He remained at this increasingly important post until the end of the war.

He was married twice. The first union ended in divorce in 1936, after eighteen years of marriage, "because of incompatibility." He had three children with his first wife, who was three years younger than himself. In 1942, he married a young widow, fourteen years his junior, who had three children of her own and, since their marriage, has had one child with him.

### June 5, 1946

Today Pohl's appearance was neat and well groomed. He wore the same ragged clothes, but he was shaved and the facial abrasion marks noted yesterday were barely visible. He had a square, heavy face with large regular features, sparse gray hair with some central baldness, and a slight frontal dental malocclusion.

I asked him how his interrogation had fared yesterday. He replied that it had lasted for three hours and was somewhat tiring, but that he had been treated courteously by the numerous interrogators. They had confronted him with various documents and asked him many detailed questions, which were difficult to answer promptly "because after twelve years in the SS, one can't remember everything." He said that he had made up his mind to tell the truth and to withhold nothing.

We continued with his personal history. During his hiding in the past year, he was in contact with his two daughters and his daughter-in-law. He lived with the latter periodically, but most of the time worked as a hired hand on a farm owned by an old friend of Pohl's present wife.

When the war ended in May 1945, Pohl was with his family in Halfing, near Rosenheim in Bavaria. "I used a false name and had forged papers, which I obtained from friends in a small village in northern Germany. On my way up from Bavaria to the north, I traveled on foot from village to village. Whenever I entered a new town, I would report to the local police, and thus acquired several papers bearing my assumed name. It was fairly easy for me to get through in this way."

Had anyone recognized him during the past year? "My children and my daughter-in-law. I lived with my daughter-in-law and her parents, who are named Westphal. I don't know whether they are arrested. My son was a captain in the SS and is now interned in a French POW camp."

How had he managed to avoid arrest during this period of more than a year? "The authorities repeatedly searched my daughter-in-law's house, but I received advance tips, and would not be present at such times. Besides, I had hired out to work on a farm and stayed there much of the time. It must be that in searching my daughter-in-law's home, the authorities found some clue, perhaps some article I left behind, and traced me to the farm."

He said his wife lived in Halfing and that he had not seen her since May 13, 1945. About four weeks before he was captured, he wrote to her for the first time. He doubted that the letter led to his arrest because he used a false name and a fake address.

He outlined his activities in the navy. "I was an administrative officer, or paymaster, in units ashore and at sea from April 1, 1912, until

January 31, 1934. I began my career as a paymaster candidate, which was equivalent to an ordinary seaman, except that to become a paymaster candidate, one had to have reached at least the final year of gymnasium. In 1920 and 1921, in my spare time, I attended some lectures on commercial subjects at the University of Kiel. When I left the navy in 1934, I held the rank of captain."

I asked him for a brief sketch of his career in the SS. "I was administrative chief of the SS. I was in charge of the WVHA." Had he begun as chief of this section, or had he worked up to the position? "I started in as chief. I was invited by Himmler specifically to build up the administration and economy of the SS."

How did he happen to become acquainted with Himmler? "In May 1933, Hitler paid a visit to the navy in Kiel and Himmler accompanied him. It is quite a story. You see, about six months prior to that visit, I had written a letter to Hitler regarding First Lieutenant Heydrich, who later became chief of the RSHA. I told Hitler in my letter that there were rumors rampant in navy circles that Heydrich had been ousted from the navy because of affairs with women and other bad characteristics. I mentioned that it caused me considerable discomfort because naval personnel poked fun at me by saying that only those who couldn't get along in the navy joined the party or SS. At the time I wrote the letter, Heydrich was already becoming prominent in the SS. In that way, Hitler's and Himmler's attention was drawn to me."

In what way did navy personnel poke fun at him? "Well, they teased me by saying that if a man couldn't amount to anything in the navy, he would join the Nazis. I wrote to Hitler that if all the things rumored about Heydrich were true, then I couldn't understand why he was permitted to wear the SS uniform." Had Pohl's letter been a character recommendation of Heydrich? "No. I had not known him at all. I only came to know him later after I joined the SS." What were these rumors that existed in the navy about Heydrich? "They were ordinary rumors, that he had been forced to resign from the navy because of bad character, that he had affairs with women that ended immorally, and numerous other stories which I don't recall anymore."

I remarked that it was still unclear to me — just why had he written such a letter to Hitler? "I wrote that if all the things being said about Heydrich were true, then he should not be permitted to wear the SS uniform, because according to the rumors, he had been dishonorably dismissed from the navy. I said in my letter that in my opinion the SS was as honorable and important an organization as the navy, and therefore, if a man were unfit to wear a navy uniform, he was unfit to wear the SS uniform."

What happened as the result of this letter? "Because of my letter, Himmler addressed me at Kiel and told me that what was said in the navy about Heydrich was untrue, because he had personally investigated the rumors. Himmler dismissed these rumors as the usual accusation that if one couldn't get along in the navy, one joins the party."

Was it true that Heydrich had been retired from the navy? "Yes, but I personally don't know whether it was of his own free will or if he was forced to leave." What was his opinion of Heydrich? He replied evasively, "I never knew him at all in the navy. In the SS later on, he was one of the leaders, and I had frequent contact with him officially, but of his personal nature or behavior, I don't know. I think that everything he did was ordered from above."

Pohl joined the Nazi Party in August 1926, while he was in the navy. He said that he would not have been permitted to join a political party as an officer, but that his position as paymaster was classified as "navy civil servant" rather than officer. "Therefore, I could join the party. Later on, in 1933, paymasters became administrative officers and could not engage in political activity. But at the time, I was a civil servant, and not an officer, and could become a party member." Did he then relinquish his membership in the party when he became an officer? "No. The whole thing came up just about the time I went over to the SS. If I had stayed another half year in the navy, I would have been obliged to resign from the party.

"After Himmler talked to me about my letter and his investigation of Heydrich, I told him that I agreed with him. Himmler then advised me to join his ranks as an administrator, and told me to think it over. That was in May 1933. Himmler became very insistent and wrote me one letter after another urging that I take over the administrative organization of the SS. In December 1933 and January 1934, he invited me to Berlin and Munich, and showed me the whole SS administrative setup and the many complex problems that were involved. It was only in February 1934, after I saw what a big job was in store for me, that I finally accepted."

What had Himmler shown him? "Mainly, he showed me the SS headquarters in Berlin and Munich and outlined my job." Did Himmler also show him any concentration camps at the time? "No, no. We didn't even speak of them." Did he know of the existence of concentration camps at the time? He hesitated, looked at the floor blankly for several moments, asked me to repeat the question, and finally said, "No."[2]

In February 1934, he began to "organize and build up" the SS. "When I took over my office, the SS was a comparatively small organization, like a union, with a group here and there in various towns and cities. I started by installing administrative commands in various key cities, and I selected personnel who would be fit for their jobs. I inaugurated schools that taught these administrative officials for a few weeks before they were dispatched to take over my branch offices all over Germany. I achieved a sound administration in the SS, with orderly bookkeeping and financial sections."

I asked Pohl to tell me, if he would, the high points in his career since 1934.

"When I came to the SS in 1934, there was only the general SS. The armed SS didn't even exist. The office to which I was appointed was not independent, or rather, not as independent as it became later. At first, my office was part of the SS main office and was simply known as the administrative office. In 1935–36, things changed when the SS general service troops was created. This was the predecessor of the armed SS and consisted of two small units, each of company strength, located mainly in Stuttgart and Munich. These were financed by the Reich. It was then that my work broadened and my office became more independent. Of course, in my administrative directives, I had to respect the leaders of the Reich because the budgets of those SS companies were covered by the government. It did not end with those two companies — it was to grow by leaps and bounds.

"Between 1934 and 1936, the administrative office under my jurisdiction was removed from the SS main office and became an independent organization under the name of the Office for Budget and Building."

"From those units of the SS general service troops, the armed SS was finally created in 1939. From 1934 to 1939, the whole business was embodied in the Reich budget and removed from the party, so that by 1939 the entire armed SS was paid for by the Reich. The general SS continued to be financed by the party and always remained a party organization."[3]

"Until 1939, I had been only a lieutenant in the general SS. In 1939, I was promoted to the rank of general in the armed SS. I began to receive my pay from the Reich instead of from the party. Also, in about the year 1939, the Office for Budget and Building was revised and became known as the Economic and Administrative Main Office, and I remained chief of it until the capitulation."

He continued with his description of the intricacies of the SS organization over which he presided. His only superior in the SS was Himmler himself.

"In my office, I kept two budgets, one for the party and one for the Reich. Naturally, as time went on, the Reich budget was overwhelmingly the larger.

"My principal business relationships outside of the SS were with Treasury Minister Schwarz and Finance Minister Lutz Count Schwerin von Krosigk. I had very little to do with the Economic Ministry. During a period of ten years, I saw Funk but twice, and I saw Puhl, Funk's Reichsbank representative, only two or three times."

I inquired about the nature of his business with Funk and Puhl. He replied cryptically, "With Funk, I discussed general economic questions about the eastern region. As for Puhl, I arranged with him to deposit valuables from the concentration camps in the Reichsbank. As I mentioned yesterday, Puhl also helped me to secure funds from foreign countries to buy land in the East, food in Hungary and Romania, and so forth."

Whence came these funds of foreign countries that Puhl had helped secure for the SS? Pohl seemed surprised at my question. "Naturally from the Reichsbank. That was the only organization that would have Austrian schillings, French francs, Hungarian pengös, and other foreign currencies."

What sort of valuables had Pohl arranged to deposit in the Reichsbank in his conferences with Puhl? "Mostly valuables from the Jews," he answered breezily. "There were rings and other gold things that were sent from the concentration camps to my office in Berlin. It was then my responsibility to deliver them to the Reichsbank." Did these gold articles contain anything besides rings? "Oh, everything a man has on him that might be made of gold, such as money, watches, rings, and sometimes little bars of gold." Were there any other types of gold articles taken from the concentration camp victims and deposited in the Reichsbank by the SS? "Nothing."

I said that I had heard other stories, and in fact, had seen a film in court a short time ago, during the case of the defendant Funk, which showed other items of gold as well as those he mentioned. Were these articles taken from Jews who were exterminated in the gas chambers and shooting pits of the concentration camps? He replied simply, "Yes." Were there any gold teeth or dental bridgework among the articles he had deposited? Pohl's oxen facial expression did not change as he said, "I assumed that some of the gold bars which I received were melted gold teeth."[4]

I remarked that this subject did not seem to disturb him very much. He probably felt it incumbent on him to display some emotion, and he made an attempt at righteous disapproval of such gold items. He spoke in a slightly louder tone of voice and with some gesticulation, which seemed theatrical. "What could I do? I never ordered those things to be taken. It was not my responsibility. I didn't ask for them to be sent to my office. There they were, and I was supposed to bring them to the Reichsbank, and so I did. I never inspected the gold teeth or bridgework personally because I was too busy with other duties. Do you think I went downstairs myself to unload the trucks and open the sacks to look inside? I was a very busy executive! I had an expert in charge of those gold articles — several experts who changed from time to time. Usually the expert was a man from Office Group A or B, which was part of the SS main office."

Had his office given directives about the securing of this gold from concentration camp victims? "None whatever. In fact, I was surprised the first time those gold articles arrived. The whole business was discussed by Funk, Himmler, and Schwerin von Krosigk, and they arranged for the articles to be sent first to my office for accounting before depositing them in the Reichsbank. I found out about it later. As far as I was concerned, it was a surprise."

Once these sacks of gold articles arrived, had he ever inquired whence they came or upon whose orders? Pohl thought for a while and replied blandly, as if he were talking about stocks and bonds, "I really can't remember the first time they arrived. I assume that the first shipment was accompanied by a man from the concentration camp itself, but I personally didn't bother with details like that because I had more important things to do than unload a truck or inspect the contents of the sacks. I had my experts do that for me. It is also possible that the fellow who brought the gold articles never saw me personally. I had 1,400 to 1,500 people employed in my office in Berlin. Throughout the Reich, I had over three hundred branch offices. Whenever gold shipments from the concentration camps arrived, an officer of the day reported it to me. You must conceive the whole picture as it really was. I had five or six generals working under me. I never brought the gold articles to the Reichsbank personally."

I persisted: Had it ever occurred to him that this was gold with human blood on it? "That it came from exterminated Jews I knew and everyone knew. But I didn't touch it. It was merely sent through my office by Himmler, with the arrangement and agreement of Funk and Schwerin von Krosigk, on the way to the Reichsbank."

Had he ever objected to the whole business? "No. Nobody asked for my opinion. It would have done no good to protest anyway. For example, I protested against the entire concentration camp responsibility, when the camps were placed under my authority in 1942. I said that I was just an administrative officer and had no desire to be in charge of all the concentration camps. My protest was ignored, and I was saddled with the concentration camps because I had so efficiently handled the labor and factories within the camps. I accept responsibility for the camps, but as far as measures against the Jews, I had nothing to do with them. Those orders came from the RSHA. Himmler sent orders to Kaltenbrunner, who transmitted them to Mueller of the Gestapo, and the latter had the entire extermination program under him. That was the way all of Himmler's orders went. I did not participate in the murder of the Jews."

I remarked that nevertheless, he did run all the concentration camps. "Yes, but the camps had nothing to do with it. Himmler chose certain camps and, together with Kaltenbrunner and Mueller, ordered the commandants of these camps to carry out the extermination program. This was done in the chain of command as I have just told you. I emphasize that it was Himmler to Kaltenbrunner to Mueller to Gluecks, who was also one of my subordinate generals, to the individual concentration camp commandants, who had been selected by Himmler to perform the exterminations. Otherwise, Himmler would have had to give the orders to me because I was technically in charge of the concentration camps. What I am trying to bring out is that although I am responsible for the camps, and the extermination program took place within these camps, I am not responsible for the extermination program itself, because these orders did not go through me, but went through the chain of individuals I have just mentioned.

"I had eleven main concentration camps under my command.[5] From these eleven camps, internees were sent to other so-called labor camps. That was my job. I had nothing to do with the final solution of the Jews. That was an act done by camp personnel such as the commandants. Of course, the center of all those orders for the extermination of the Jews was Mueller of the Gestapo, who received his orders from Kaltenbrunner, who carried out the plans of Himmler.

"Mueller was the successor of Theodor Eicke, who had been in charge of concentration camps for ten years.[6] Gluecks continued in charge of Office Group D, which was part of my office but was specifically the office for concentration camps. All of those exterminations were talked over by Gluecks and Mueller, who had very secret conferences every week."

Was not Gluecks's concentration camp office a part of the large administrative office headed by Pohl himself? "Yes, but as I told you, Gluecks did not take orders in regard to the extermination program from me, but directly from Mueller."

I commented that it seemed to me that as Gluecks's chief, Pohl was responsible for what Gluecks did. "Well, those were special duties Himmler gave to Gluecks. The same thing is true with Hans Kammler, also one of my subordinates, but at the same time he was in charge of reprisal weapons, and in that special job was in direct connection with Speer, the munitions minister. Those were the V-1 and V-2 bombs and other reprisal weapons.[7] That too had nothing to do with me, although Kammler was under me.

"I can give you another example. First Lieutenant August Frank was also one of my subordinates, but in his special job he would go to Hitler personally.[8] He was in charge of remodeling the entire armed forces — a tremendous job that included the army, navy, air force, and Labor Service. I had nothing to do with it. Incidentally, for the past year, I have had so little contact with the world, I don't know whether Frank is alive or dead, captured or not. So you can see that Gluecks, Kammler, and Frank, who were all subordinate generals in my office, each had special jobs in which I had nothing to say."

Did Pohl know Eichmann, one of the foremost organizers of the extermination program? "Only by sight. He was under Mueller in the Gestapo — not a member of my office."

As a human being, did Pohl approve of the extermination program practiced by the Nazis? He replied without too much feeling, but some attempt at righteousness, "I always felt it would be nauseating — as a man."

Did he have any other comment on his attitude toward the extermination program? "What can I say? If I knew in 1934 what I know now, I would have remained in the navy. I didn't know that this was going to happen and I didn't know that Germany was going to lose the war and be in ruins."

I remarked that Hoess, the commandant of Auschwitz, told me he "personally despised" the extermination program which he executed by gassing and then cremating 2.5 million Jewish men, women, and children. Hoess told me he could not allow human feeling to enter into the matter, because he had been convinced by Himmler of the necessity of exterminating the Jews, and moreover had been given an order by a superior, which made his actions quite in order. I asked Pohl if he felt that was more or less his own position. He replied, "No. That is one of the reasons why I did not participate in the Jewish pogroms of November 1938. I was not convinced that it was necessary. I felt that there were quite different and legal ways to solve the Jewish question.

"I know many Jewish mixed marriages. Many of these people were friends of mine. My wife, prior to our marriage, worked for the famous Berlin banking house Jacob Goldschmidt, a Jewish firm. Some of my present wife's best friends were Jewish. That is proof enough of how I feel. In fact, my wife's best friend is either half or fully Jewish. I believe she is now living in England."

I interjected that it seemed of minor importance that some of his best friends were Jews, since I had heard that from many Nazis in Germany, who nevertheless lent their support to the economic and finally the physical destruction of Jews. Pohl seemed unimpressed. "If I were really an anti-Semite, I would have hated Jews — but I never hated them. All I did was follow orders. My conscience is clear. I never ordered the death of a Jew or personally killed one. I have explained how the extermination program was not part of my command, but skipped me."

What about this half or fully Jewish friend of his wife's who now lives in England? "I never met her. She left for England shortly after Hitler's rise to power. It was before I met my wife. My wife had another girlfriend whose father was Jewish, and as far as I know, she was still in Hamburg in 1944." Had Pohl personally saved this girl from extermination? "Excuse me, it was not her father who was Jewish, but her grandfather. Yes, I stood up for her. I saw that nothing would happen to her."

Therefore, if a girl had a Jewish grandfather, she was likely to be executed, was that correct? "Well, I wouldn't go so far as to say execution — that would depend on other factors. Such people with Jewish blood were persecuted, lost their apartments, couldn't work in civil service positions, and were labeled as Jews." Were such persons required to wear the yellow patch of the Star of David over their hearts? "All Jews had to do that for identification purposes after a certain year."

Would he tell me more about his wife's girlfriend with the Jewish grandfather? "Her parents were supposed to be evacuated to a concentration camp, where I presume they would have been exterminated. They were very decent people and I took care of the matter and I arranged for them to remain in Hamburg. I arranged false papers for them. Now, does that look as if I were an anti-Semite? Why, on another occasion, I wrote to Himmler to obtain permission for a mixed person to marry a German girl." He seemed to drop this subject abruptly. Had he succeeded in getting Himmler's assent for this "mixed" man to marry the Aryan girl? "No. I tried for almost a year, but didn't succeed. I was told that I should wait until after the war. I can bring witnesses to prove it, and I didn't even know the man personally, yet I did it. Doesn't that prove that my personal beliefs never agreed with the official or party ideas?"

Earlier in the interview, Pohl had alluded to his "legal and different" solution to the racial question. What would this have been? Pohl smiled and said, "Simple. So simple it hardly needs explaining. I would have left all the Jews in Germany, but put them on an alien status, under alien law, and naturally closed them out of jobs like doctor or lawyer. But why execute them? In that way, strong Jewish influence would have been cast aside and there would be no need for atrocities. Whenever we had discussions in our own circle, I would mention my solution, whereupon Himmler would say to me, 'Pohl, you are too soft.' Therefore, I did my best to keep out of the whole final solution of the Jewish problem."

Until what date had he held office? "Until the end — until the capitulation." Then what did he mean by saying he did his best to keep out of the final solution of the Jewish problem? Was he not in it up to his neck? "I could have participated in the thing actively if I so desired. I could have taken Gluecks's job, for example. When I sent Gluecks to Himmler in 1942, because he asked me for a man who would carry through the final solution of the Jewish question, I demanded of Himmler that I not have to do it. I agreed to send him one of my subordinates, who was Gluecks. I stipulated that I should have to do only with the administration of the concentration camps themselves, and the internee labor, and nothing to do with the extermination program."

I observed that perhaps he did not take Gluecks's place because he had a higher position than Gluecks, who was one of his subordinates. Pohl hesitated, but was not stymied. "By taking Gluecks's place, I mean I could have asked Himmler to let me take care of the extermination program myself. Then Gluecks would have been spared. But I personally sent Gluecks to Himmler for this purpose, and he did the job, and I did the same as I always did."

I asked Pohl if he considered himself in any way responsible or guilty, as an accomplice or a direct participant, in the murder of the 5 million Jews in the concentration camps, and the countless other thousands of internees who perished through disease, neglect, starvation, beatings, hangings, and shootings. By this time, Pohl looked anxious and no longer the composed practical businessman talking about stocks and bonds. That he could still not visualize his own importance in the criminal world of the Nazis was clear, but he was beginning to get an inkling at least of one individual's view of his activities. He replied, "In no way am I responsible or guilty for the murder of the 5 million Jews or the deaths of others in the concentration camps.[9] About the murder of the 5 million Jews, I had nothing whatever to do with it. The fact that I was in charge of all the concentration camps in Germany from 1942 until the end is beside the point. I have explained and explained again that I sent Gluecks, one of my subordinates, to take charge of this program, and that I stayed out of it. Now, as far as the others who died in concentration camps or who were punished because of bad behavior or who might have been executed because of the hostage system — the reprisal system — that too is not my responsibility, but was ordered by the local party district administrator, or police functionary, or Himmler and the Gestapo, and it was a bad policy. I was just an administrator.

"Now, I am beginning to think that the whole thing was done by

Himmler and the Gestapo. I admit that I occupied an extremely important job in the SS, but I was just one of thirteen main office chiefs, and
besides me there were men like Daluege, Kaltenbrunner, who was Heydrich's successor, and Hans Juettner, who had the leadership main office
and were in charge of the guards in the concentration camps. Those
guards, for example, were under my command, but Juettner had the
power to replace them. Then there was Gottlob Berger, who was in
charge of recruiting for the SS. His office was even bigger than mine.
And then there was the personnel chief, Maximilian von Herff." I said
that I would not quibble and that if he were not number two or three
man under Himmler, the least he could be would be number thirteen,
since there were only thirteen main office chiefs. However, my question,
I said, was whether he felt responsible in some way for the murder of the
5 million Jews, and the other atrocities that had taken place over so
many years in the concentration camps of which he was in charge. "I can
only be responsible for my orders. I cannot be responsible for all the acts
of Himmler."

I asked him whether he knew of the murder of Jews. He replied,
"Much later, probably in 1942, and it began before that." I asked him
what was the earliest time he might have learned of it. "About that time
or a few months earlier. I had nothing to do with it. Before that time, I
had nothing to do with it." I said that from 1942 to 1945, a period of at
least three years, he had been in charge of concentration camps in which
mass exterminations of millions of men, women, and children had taken
place — and he did not have time enough to think about it during those
three or more years? "Well, it was war — I could not have carried on as
an administrative officer if I had let myself be swayed emotionally by my
feelings."

Did he think that a responsible, normal person such as the average
American, Frenchman, or Russian, or German for that matter perhaps,
would have carried out his business? He replied, with typical evasiveness, "Those are questions which are very hard to answer. What is decent
is a very hard thing to put your finger on. I often asked myself. After
all — the extermination program was no secret of Himmler's. Funk and
Schwerin von Krosigk knew of it. Why didn't they try to stop it?" I
replied that they had little actual connection with Pohl himself, but that
nevertheless Funk was on trial for his life. "Yes, those men like Funk
were the government — they were people who could have prevented it. I

always asked a man who was close to Himmler why those close to Himmler didn't prevent it. But, do you think that things would have taken a different course if I would have resigned? The main job was the administration of the armed SS." I added that it seemed to be also the direction of the concentration camps. He replied, "No, that was under Gluecks. Although he was my subordinate and had to report to me like all subordinates do, I specialized in labor in concentration camps." I said that I thought he had told me that after 1942, the concentration camps came under his jurisdiction. "Yes, but Gluecks did it. He was my subordinate and he did the inspection of the camps." I rejoined that this was the very point — that Gluecks was his inferior in the office and that everything Gluecks did, he had to report to Pohl. "In certain things he was my subordinate, but Himmler and Gluecks had private conversations." I said that that did not impress me very much because every large organization had conferences between the chief and some subordinate. "I could not talk things over with Gluecks — therefore, I only talked questions of policy with Himmler. I mean policies of labor."

I asked him whether the labor situation in the concentration camps was strictly honorable. "It was important for the conduct of the war. It was important and not a bloody affair to make sure that the internees of the concentration camps were not split up but used systematically in armament industries."

I asked him whether these workers were not more or less slaves. Pohl's face appeared as blank as usual and he said indifferently, "No." I said it was my understanding from my conversations with other prisoners here, as well as from evidence produced in court by the tribunal, that if the internees did not work hard enough, they were starved, beaten, or exterminated. Pohl said with no assurance in his voice, "Well, in general, as far as I know — and mind you, I don't know everything because the individual concentration camp commandants were responsible for conditions within their own camps, and in the case of factories where concentration camp labor was supplied, the plant owner or manager was responsible — but as far as I know, these workers had the same working conditions as every German, including premiums."[10]

What were these premiums? "Every worker in Germany received coupons that were premiums to reward him for hard or extraordinary labor. These coupons were good for cigarettes, bread, butter, tea, et cetera. The concentration camp internees received these premiums just like other German workers. That was something I am responsible for. I instituted it over the protest of many who did not agree with this system."

Tell me more about the ideal working conditions of the concentration camp labor, since I found it to be interesting and at great variance with anything else I had ever heard about it. Pohl said, "Of course, I must repeat that there were cases where the responsibility for the handling of these people was in the hands of the factories themselves. These plants or factories themselves were responsible for handling these people. It worked out that there were plants that did not abide by the rules I laid down. But all of the thirty or more plants which I had directly under me abided by my rules."

I said I had visited a camp near Landsberg a few days after the end of the war last year in which were housed some four hundred Russian workers. The place had been evacuated immediately upon liberation, but it was miserable beyond description. Workers slept on long wooden shelves without bedding, and the lice and fleas were so apparent that one could not enter the dugout itself because of the danger of contracting typhus. I had spoken to several of the former inmates of that camp, and they told me that it had existed for years, that its death rate was tremendous, that the food rations were below starvation level, and that each night after the workers returned from the factory, they would be locked up in dugouts until the next morning, when those who remained alive had to report for a roll call before being sent to work. One of the rules in that camp was that internees had to remove those who had died during the night and bring them to roll call in the morning, after which the bodies were disposed of. I asked him whether he had anything to do with these labor camps, of which there were several in the vicinity of Landsberg. Pohl seemed not in the least upset by my description and said, "Yes, you see what I mean, what a hard job I had and how disagreeable it was. I had nothing to do with those camps around Landsberg, but such places existed. In most instances when I came across such a camp in my travels, I tried to correct things. But in many instances I had no jurisdiction because it was the responsibility of the factory or plant itself, and in the second place, I was just one man and what could I do?"

I said that it seemed to me that he was becoming very technical in his answers and that when he was confronted with facts, he merely dodged them by presenting an illusory picture of the delightful and ideal conditions of concentration camp workers. Pohl looked at the floor and said, "I am not trying to be technical about this. I know conditions were not ideal. It was war and one can't be too softhearted in such a time. Whatever I tried to do to help conditions, even when I presented it as something which was economically sound, rather than for human reasons, Himmler would say that I was too soft. But I think you should know that there were several groups, for example, the armament factories, which were under Speer.

"Whenever those factories needed labor, they received it through Sauckel or Speer, and I had very little to say about it except to supply it. Every week clerks would take those applications from Sauckel and Speer and submit them to me. There was nothing I could do about it except to approve them and refer them to my subordinate Gluecks, who had his headquarters in Oranienburg. I often had conferences with Gluecks, Sauckel, Speer, and others and we discussed whether we could possibly furnish the large number of concentration camp workers these people requested. Whenever we had enough people on hand in the concentration camps, I would approve the applications, but it was Gluecks who picked out the camp which was to furnish the labor. Furthermore, before any internees were given to a factory, a camp representative visited the factories in order to determine that the following conditions could be met: One, that the quarters must be sufficient. Now as far as the quarters for the camp workers in Landsberg that you referred to, that was a bad one obviously, and there were several bad ones. Two, food had to be adequate. Three, there had to be medical care.

"These questions were always arising and had to be talked over by the camp representative and the factory representative. The rule was that only after the things I mentioned were secured could the concentration camp commandant hand over the workers to the plant.

"The same thing was applicable to the guard situation. In the last few years, the camp commandants utilized only skeleton guards because of insufficient personnel. The factories themselves had to provide the other guards. These were regulations that I inaugurated. If these regulations would have been kept and the procedure worked according to my directives, the mishaps and bad conditions that were found later on would not have occurred."

Had he himself ever seen these mishaps and bad conditions? He replied, "Yes, unfortunately I saw them. For example, in Württemberg, I found a tremendous labor camp consisting of thousands of internees whose condition was completely deplorable. There was a complete lack of sanitary provisions. I was very upset and when I returned to Berlin after that trip, I ordered that all such internees should be returned to their respective concentration camps for medical care. I insisted that only after the factories installed better conditions could the internees be sent there.

"Whenever I traveled and passed by a camp, I visited it. I did this whenever I was able to do so. But there were several hundred labor camps, and I could not see them all. I can tell you about the airplane factory located north of Oranienburg, and I know personally that everything was in order there. Another factory in Silesia had three or four hundred workers from concentration camps, and everything was in order there. The only thing I found to criticize in that camp was the canteen, and I ordered it improved so that prisoners could buy cigarettes, et cetera, which up to the time of my visit, they had been deprived of."

What happened to the internee who did not work hard enough? "He did not get additional rations. The good worker received premiums and the poor ones did not." Were internees ever beaten to death? He replied automatically, "No, that was forbidden. Whenever I found out about a case where an internee was beaten to death — and it did happen, I don't deny it — but if I caught such a thing I would take steps to bring those who did the beating into the other world.

"I hope that later on my legal adviser will help, and I will be able to prove how I treated such violators. I even investigated anonymous reports from internees. I remember a particular case where a thing like that happened. I received a report from a camp in Stutthof — a concentration camp near Danzig in East Prussia, where an internee was tied up and beaten to death. At first, I didn't believe it. Previously, when the concentration camps were under the direction of Eicke, we knew of things like that happening all of the time because Eicke was a hard and ruthless man. Therefore, I sent my legal adviser to Stutthof to investigate personally for me. He returned and told me that it actually did happen. I was outraged. I brought the guilty man to trial.

"In all cases where I heard of such things, I proceeded sharply against them. But you have to consider that in many of the labor camps there were no longer SS guards, but civilian guards, and I could not punish civilians."

I asked him whether he meant then that SS guards were better and kinder than the civilian guards. Pohl said emphatically, "Ach, yes! I don't mean the SS guards were perfect, especially since you must understand that those SS guards who were left were not the best. The original SS guards had been drafted for frontline duty a long time before.

"For example, in 1944, I issued a directive concerning premiums and additional things which were to be given to internees — that is, to good workers. I printed a booklet about special premiums for prisoners. That never existed before."

I supposed that this was what he had previously referred to as good business rather than a humane act. Pohl disagreed. "No, that was a humane deed. I was inwardly convinced that these internees had to be treated decently. I had internees — not too many, but several — whom I took from the concentration camps because they were good men and good workers. Later on these men became my employees. I was the only one who ever did anything like that. The manager of a plant for making wooden parts for airplanes was a former concentration camp internee whom I liberated, and whom I later paid a salary of a thousand marks a month. I didn't have to give him a thousand marks — I could have paid him a hundred marks. Also in Dachau, there were other former internees to whom I gave such positions. I did it of my own free will. All of these facts I can prove. I can prove how I thought on the question of internees. Personally, I was humane. Whether the camps themselves were humane is another story, but not my fault.

"There was an excellent foreman in an iron foundry near Oranien-burg. I spoke with him and told him I would get him out of the concentration camp. He is still around, and you can check with him about this story. I personally wrote to Kaltenbrunner to get approval for his release. Kaltenbrunner answered that it was impossible to release this man because he was a former Communist. That illustrates how hard it was to do anything. I can cite several cases."

I asked him whether the man he tried to help was ever released from the concentration camp. "No, because Kaltenbrunner prevented it. I helped many internees out for humane reasons, and I didn't personally profit by doing so.

"I had in my household five internees. I was the one who took up the question of Jehovah's Witnesses with Himmler. I was instrumental in making the ruling that members of this sect, all of whom were in concentration camps because they were pacifists, were to be employed in various households as servants. I employed five in my household. There were four women and one man. Now, would I do that if I thought there were no good people? Why, my wife even gave our own children into the care of these internees. They were middle-aged or elderly women who were Jehovah's Witnesses and who would otherwise probably have died in the concentration camps. In my home, they received a regular salary, and up until the capitulation, they remained there.

"A better example of my feelings towards these internees cannot be given. You can ask them how they were treated by Pohl! Surely you can't think that I murdered internees on the one hand and kept internees in my house and treated them well on the other hand!" I replied that unfortunately, I could very well imagine this because the notorious Hoess, the commandant at Auschwitz, who had exterminated 2.5 million Jews and others, told me that he too had several Jehovah's Witnesses as servants in his house. Therefore, Hoess had murdered on the one hand and had internees working for him on the other hand. I remarked that it seemed to prove nothing. Pohl replied, "It is frightful! I could never have done what Hoess did." I remarked that it was interesting to hear him label Hoess's actions as frightful at this late date; he obviously knew all about it because Auschwitz was merely one of the many concentration camps of which Pohl was in charge. He replied lamely, "In 1942, after the extermination program at Auschwitz had started, was when I first knew of it." I asked him whether he ever did anything about it. "What could I do? If I had seen any means of preventing it, I would have done so."

# Walter Schellenberg
## 1910–1952

Walter Schellenberg was chief of Office Group IVE (counterespionage services) from 1939, chief of Office VI (secret intelligence services) of the RSHA from 1942, and appointed head of the united SS and army military intelligence in 1944. After the war Schellenberg was brought before the American military tribunal at a follow-up trial at Nuremberg. He was found guilty of complicity to murder Russian prisoners of war. Sentenced on April 2, 1949, to six years' imprisonment, he was released from prison in December 1950.

**March 12, 1946**

Walter Schellenberg is thirty-six years old, with a thin, asthenic build, medium stature, reserved manner, thin smile, some slight facial scarring near the chin.

**Occupation:** "At first I was in charge of counterespionage and later of the secret intelligence service, Office VI and Office Military (military intelligence). The latter two organizations were part of the RSHA. The counterespionage department was part of the police systems."[1]

He is uncertain as to whether he is a prisoner of war or a witness. As a member of the RSHA, he believes, he is subject to automatic arrest. He also states that he thinks, because of the "special tasks" of Office VI and Office Military, those organizations might not be counted by the trials as part of the RSHA.

What was your work in the RSHA? "Practically, our function was collecting news — military, economic, and technical — from foreign countries. We had nothing to do with the Gestapo, headed by Mueller."

Did you have anything to do with Himmler? "I had to take orders from Kaltenbrunner, as chief of the RSHA, but I had the right in certain important cases to request a conference with Himmler directly without having to go through Kaltenbrunner.

"That right was always attacked, but I maintained the privilege. I saw Himmler every five to six weeks for a report on my work."

**Early Development:** Born in Saarbrücken January 16, 1910. He lived there until graduating from the gymnasium in 1928. He then attended the Universities of Marburg and Bonn, where he studied jurisprudence until his graduation in 1933. He then took his law examinations but practiced law for only about three months, toward the end of 1936.

When were you first associated with the Nazi Party? "In 1933. I was short of money from home, and that year there was a law passed that one could get support financially only if one belonged to a Nazi organization. I needed support from the state."

For what? "For my activity on the court — I had to bring a certificate every two months, and if I were lazy or indifferent I might not get this support. I was learning law by apprenticeship at the time."

**Previous Illnesses:** Measles for short period, at age six. Two attacks of pleurisy at eight or nine years. "I was always sickly as a child, with infections, head colds, and diarrheas. In general I was weak and sickly, until the age of fourteen or fifteen, when my health improved. In 1940 I was ill in Africa, got 'poisoning of the liver' and spent four months in a hospital."

Although very sickly as a child, he still made progress in school because of his capacity for learning quickly. He always stood first or second in his class, he says. As at present, he was always thin for his age, though of medium height.

How did you happen to get into such an occupation as espionage? "It was all a matter of chance and accident as I view it retrospectively." He threw up his hands and smiled as he said that.

"In May 1933 I became a member of the general SS, because I had to be a member of an active organization — I had to bring a certificate that activity was being undertaken."

How much did you devote to the SS at the time? "Tuesday and Thursday afternoons, and the weekends. We stayed in SS camps. It was difficult, and I always tried to get away with as little work in the SS as possible. I tried to work in the office, things like that. I applied for a job as a teacher of history to the SS boys."

Could you not have chosen an organization less noxious than the SS? "Retrospectively yes, but at that time I was completely unpolitical. The choice was between the SS, SA, and so on. There were five in my crowd and we had to decide what organization to choose. We decided to join the SS, because the SA might have entailed more work. Later we discovered that the reverse was true, that the SS had more of a working schedule."

Did you enjoy the work at all? "No. That's why I turned to more intellectual things like giving history lectures.

"One evening, while I lectured, two professors from the University of Bonn attended. They were members of the same SS group as I was. They advised that there was no sense in my lecturing to the SS, and that I really belonged to the SD. I made an appointment with these professors, who were also members of the SD. The professors were probably in the SS for the purpose of finding people for the SD.

"The professors told me that the SD was in charge of controlling all information pertaining to economic and social life and political developments in Germany. By my belonging to the SS and SD, I would be able to avoid all work for the SS, and for the SD all I would have to do was write an article every few weeks." What sort of article? "About new regulations and civil laws — the results of the heredity health laws — a new set of laws that stated that such illnesses as schizophrenia should be curtailed by having such people sterilized or castrated."

What do you think about those laws? "I had nothing to do with them except I was charged with conducting nationwide propaganda to determine the reaction of the people to these laws. Opinion was split into two groups.

"The first group had stricken relatives, and the other group was merely interested in the laws. In the first group, some thought it was a good idea — it would relieve them of worry. Others, particularly in the Rhineland, were against it for religious reasons."[2]

What was your own opinion? "I had no opinion. I had little interest in it. One day I had the opinion of one group, next day of the other group. I wrote articles that were neither favorable nor unfavorable because they were all objective articles."

To this day don't you know what you think of it? "Today I consider it too deep a violation of human rights." You did not think so then? "At that time I had no opinion." How about castration and sterilization of political enemies? "That was not the question. It was only to judge public reactions through work in trials."

We know that political enemies and Jews were castrated? "At that time there were no such cases. It was not debated then."

You know now. "Yes. In April 1945 I found out about it, in Stockholm, during a conversation."

Schellenberg made the preceding statement with a smiling smoothness, which might well be considered an attitude of "I don't expect you to believe that but that's my answer." I remarked that it was difficult to believe in view of his intimacy with the goings-on in Himmler's inner circle. He replied that he was sorry I was of that opinion. I said that from a psychological observation standpoint he didn't seem sorry. He further said that he was naturally against such measures, that is, castration and sterilization. However, it was said without much concern or affective reaction.

I repeated that it was hard to believe in view of his close association with Himmler and Kaltenbrunner and the rest. He said, "My work was so different it was quite understandable. If you knew my personal feelings about Himmler and Kaltenbrunner, or rather the feelings between us, you would know that I was glad to be through with my own work with them." What were your feelings about them? "I didn't trust them and they didn't trust me, except that Himmler began to feel I was siding with him rather than Kaltenbrunner and especially after my using horoscopic means to convince him."

He explained about his telling Himmler of his horoscope and predicting certain events. Himmler was inclined to believe this horoscope business because he was "a weak character and superstitious."[3]

But people over the whole world heard reports of castrations and sterilizations and similar practices in camps before the end of the war — much before, in fact. "I purposely didn't listen to news from abroad — if you did listen it would influence your work." What would your reaction be if you were a psychiatrist and heard such an answer to your question? "It is difficult if the psychiatrist is prejudiced." What prejudice do you mean? "Well, you are an American, and have been subject to certain propaganda yourself." That's true, but can you elucidate? "In my case, though I had an idea of what was going on — I purposely didn't see it." I can believe that more easily. "You have to think of yourself in the place of a German, where hundreds of jealous people, other Germans and foreigners, and foreign news too, were threatening them. That was one of the reasons why anything that would have cost me more work was just — well I just shunted it to one side. I had no more to do with it, no more than I had to.

"I felt at a very early date that many things in the system were bypassing human rights. That is why I tried to do my job in such a way as to get Germany out of it." What do you mean? "I wanted a quick finish of the war and a reforming of the regime." When? "From 1940 onward. My first great disappointment was that Germany did not sign a peace with France in 1940 after France fell. What we signed was only an armistice — the Vichy regime." What do you mean? "A true peace with France should have been signed, and then with the whole West. A peace with the Vichy government."

What did you do about making a quick finish to the war as you just mentioned? "I tried to get the political secret service into my hands." German secret service in other lands? "Yes. To get reports so that I could show the government objectively that things couldn't go on like this."

The *Einsatzgruppen* — to what office were they responsible? "To Offices III and IV. I had nothing to do with it."

To what office if any was Colonel Skorzeny accountable? "To Office VI, but I had little to do with him because he occupied an independent position following the Mussolini incident."[4]

Did Office VI have anything to do with atrocities? "No. In the early days we started to make contact with the English and American people, and the Vatican too. I tried repeatedly to bring about political talks and conferences, grounds for establishing peaceful relationships." But always with the idea of furthering Nazi Germany? "It was still my idea in 1941. But not in 1942. It was so hard to do anything with Hitler, I gave up the idea." But you continued to work for Hitler and the Nazi regime until the end of the war. "Yes. But I conspired. Several people know about it, Swedish and Swiss people." Nazis? "On the contrary. No."

In the summer of 1942, Schellenberg attempted to "get Himmler on my side." He tried to convince Himmler of his contacts, and the advisability of overthrowing Hitler and having Himmler take over.[5]

So that you were really a Himmler man and not a Hitler man? "No, one can't say that exactly. I had to work with reality.

"My plan was to work with Himmler against Hitler as a means to an end." Did you or do you believe Himmler would be an improvement on Hitler? "I believe that under my influence, Himmler would have changed the foreign policy." Did you have, therefore, such a great influence on Himmler? "At one time no, but from 1943 onward, my influence on Himmler in the area of foreign policy grew steadily.

"The only difficulty with Himmler was that he was of a sneaky nature. I never knew whether I would be alive or imprisoned the next day. But I gained new strength from my firm idea that Germany — that I must save Germany from chaos.

"That was the reason for my contacting the Americans in Stockholm in 1943, against strict orders from Hitler. Abraham Steven Hewitt was a Roosevelt adviser in Stockholm. Hewitt was married to a Vanderbilt."[6] What was the nature of your contact with Hewitt? "To open up boundaries to the West, and for the time being to have Himmler take over Germany, and for the creation of a western alliance against Russia."

What were the results of your conference with Hewitt in November 1943? "I reported to Himmler about this, and he conferred with Kaltenbrunner, who influenced him to decide the opposite. From then on I had a difficult time." Were you convinced that the western allies would link up with Germany against Russia? "I did. Hewitt had left the question open, said he must confer with Roosevelt." Do you think the U.S.A. would conspire against her ally Russia, when they had been allied and were in the middle of a successful war? "There was that chance. It would bring a change in government in Germany and peace in the West." What do you mean? "Germany would then have had to carry the main burden of a fight against Russia and have to pull back to its borders." Yes, but you asked for an alliance against Russia? "Not an active alliance — just passive. Just stopping the fight in the West."

So that Germany could defeat Russia? "Well, not defeat Russia necessarily, but with a change of political governing in Germany — a stop in the fighting." With Himmler at the helm of the new German government — was he favorably disposed toward Germany withdrawing to its own boundaries and stopping the war with Russia too? "Himmler hated Russia but I had him convinced that Russia could not be defeated." Was Himmler convinced? "At first Himmler hated me for it but then he began to think about it because of my documentary evidence." It's fantastic. "Yes, but I did it. In 1943 I began to use astrology with Himmler. I needed it as an instrument to get more influence with Himmler because he believed in astrology. In my horoscope of Hitler I predicted the *Attentat* against Hitler in February 1944; as you know it actually took place on July 20, 1944. When the *Attentat* began, Himmler was very much convinced. Although Himmler himself played a small part in the *Attentat,* he was convinced. I also predicted Hitler would not survive April 1945. When Hitler did kill himself, Himmler was more than ever convinced."

That was rather late in the game, was it not? "But not too late. I purposely told Himmler that he was supposed to be the successor to Hitler — to be a reformer, and that then he himself must step down."

Himmler a reformer, the man who ordered 5 million Jews murdered, and who according to Bach-Zelewski wanted 30 million Slavs exterminated? "Himmler believed there would be chaos, and I strengthened in him that belief — I used him as a political tool for my own political purposes. I told him that he had to make good all the bad things — that he had to release all political prisoners. Jews were to be released." What Jews? Hoettl said that in August 1944 Eichmann told him between 4 and 5 million of them had been killed to that time. "I didn't know that. In October 1944 I had a conference with Jean-Marie Musy, former president of Switzerland, with Himmler present, and later Himmler and Musy had a conference alone.[7] I learned at a later date that Himmler gave positive orders on the treatment of the Jews, showing that my ideas had taken root in him."

Peculiar, because when Allied troops moved into Germany, concentration camps were burned and the inmates burned alive or shot. "I know. I was allowed to take 1,200 Jews into Switzerland. That began in January 1945. Every two weeks a train with 1,200 Jews could leave Germany for Switzerland. It only happened once because Kaltenbrunner went up to Hitler and had the whole thing stopped."[8]

Was Kaltenbrunner then, in your opinion, worse than Himmler? "Yes. Especially during the last phase of the war. Kaltenbrunner had more influence with Hitler — in practice Kaltenbrunner was worse than Himmler.

"The same with the evacuation of camps — they should have been handed over to the Allies as they were. I talked with Musy about it. Himmler agreed with that. These instructions were subverted by Kaltenbrunner's influence on Hitler.

"Musy sent a cablegram from Switzerland to Washington that these camps would be handed over intact when captured. Kaltenbrunner gave orders to the contrary, with Hitler's backing." Kaltenbrunner says he had nothing to do with it. "I testified under oath about it in court.

"Further evidence that these facts are true is that Himmler, while Hitler was yet alive, called for capitulation to the western powers." Is that rumor, or fact? "Those are facts. I delivered the offer from Himmler to Count Folke Bernadotte in Stockholm, and President Roosevelt declined the offer."[9] Would it have meant unconditional surrender? "Toward the western powers but not toward Russia. That was my influence." But Russia was an Ally. "That was as much as I could influence Himmler. Himmler was such a coward he refused or was afraid to act because of Kaltenbrunner and Hitler. It was not my fault.

"You can see how far I had Himmler under my influence, when Himmler, of all people, declared he was ready to receive the Zionist representative from Sweden." After the liquidation of the Jews? "I always thought the Jews were for the main part still alive." Until when? "Until April 20, 1945." By that time 5 million Jews were dead. "I had nothing to do with those things." It's a mystery story. "I thought the Jews were alive in concentration camps."

But you knew they were in concentration camps. "I knew — and therefore I worked for the release of Jews from concentration camps."

Sounds like something out of Grimms' fairy tales. "I proved it to you." Have you? "Yes, well I know I haven't convinced you and I don't care, but I'm telling you the truth." Yes, I'm interested in it psychologically and as a story. Does it sound logical to you? "The only way I can explain it is that Himmler had two or three souls. I see that from the trials." You saw only the good side of Himmler at that time? "No, not a good side only, but I saw the chance to use that side to have Himmler follow along the lines that I wanted. I never valued Himmler. Personally. I steadily felt Himmler's unbalanced character. I myself was in danger for my life. More than once I thought of leaving Germany before 1944. But I was convinced I would have to remain in my post and do what I could."

I don't exactly see how you helped, with such atrocities being committed while you were so close to Himmler, and all the Nazis now say it was Himmler who ordered the butchery and atrocities. "I managed to do many humanitarian things." I should like to hear about these things.

"For instance, against the tremendous resistance of Hitler and Kaltenbrunner, and at first Himmler too, I managed to save nine thousand Norwegians and Danes, whom I had released from concentration camps."

It occurs to me that this act might have been a diplomatic thing to do to please Bernadotte when Germany was already losing the war. "No. If so I wouldn't have had so much difficulty. And I had many cases released from concentration camps."

Then you had great influence on the concentration camps? "I had no power over the concentration camps — it was another department. But I always found a reason to go there with demands — pretending it had something to do with the secret service."

Aside from the Norwegians and Danes just mentioned, about how many people did you have released from concentration camps? "About one hundred, with their families." Innocent or guilty people? "Innocent." Then you knew that innocent people were in concentration camps? "I knew it only from those cases. I didn't pay much attention to other cases."

You didn't care very much, perhaps? "I have to agree that I didn't care because I was from day to day actively engaged in my work. I cannot be accused of having anything to do with it.

"Knowing and believing are two different things. I knew many innocent people were in concentration camps and used for forced labor, but I saw in the thing only another bad point in the whole system, and another reason to fight against the system."

What do you think of Bach-Zelewski? "He is a complicated character. Many of my personal enemies picture me as a cold type — a person who acts according to a certain line, a calculating type." And you feel you are not? "Not as my enemies mean it. My enemies don't know my inner emotional life. But to go back to Bach-Zelewski — I think Bach-Zelewski has the kind of personality that can't differentiate between the truth and lies. He gets himself so much into the whole thing he can't differentiate. He convinces himself and believes he has gone so far that he has to die for the cause. Originally it was not the truth, but he so convinces himself — he's ready to die for it."

He's trying not to die but to live, I guess. "Yes. I'm telling you this in confidence."

**March 13, 1946**
Schellenberg greeted me with his usual aplomb this afternoon, seemed quite pleased to have another interview.

**Family. Father:** "Yesterday I received the first news that he is alive. It was more than a year since I heard." He is eighty. He was a piano manufacturer. The firm was founded by subject's great-grandfather. A musical aptitude runs in the family. "I played the cello. Father plays the piano and violin. Grandfather plays the organ and violin. I began taking cello lessons at the age of eight."

He went on to say that his favorite composer was Edvard Grieg. He ceased playing cello after he fell from a horse at age twenty-three and fractured bones on both hands. He displayed scars and deformities of both hands to me. He said that when he plays the cello for five or ten minutes he gets cramps in the hands, so that it was impossible for him to continue playing. He said that other favorite compositions were Beethoven's Third and Ninth Symphonies, and some of Mozart, though he feels that the latter is "harder to appreciate and understand than Beethoven. My sister always says that the only real music is Mozart."

Asked if he cared for any of the Russian composers, he said he did not know much about them, but liked *The Sleigh Ride* by Mussorgsky. He wanted to know whether Tchaikovsky was a Pole or Russian. He was puzzled. Anyway, he did not know any of his compositions. "I heard of a new Russian composer — read about him since I've been in prison." He could not recall the name, but when I mentioned Dmitry Shostakovich, said it was he.

He also mentioned Paul Hindemith, who was, he said, a pupil of Tchaikovsky, he believed. Hindemith was "hard to appreciate" because he was "atonal." He has never heard any Stravinsky because it was banned during the Hitler regime. Aleksandr Borodin he believes he heard prior to 1933, but not during Hitler's time. "My sister plays Rach-maninoff, but he too was not played during the war." How about before the war? "I don't recall hearing his work in concerts." I asked why Hindemith left Germany and he said he did not know.

What is your opinion of suppressing music because of political or national or racial reasons? "I think it is a sign of weakness." Yet you were a part of Himmler's organization that suppressed it. "Yes. But in the early days I lacked political mental development. Later I tried to develop. I wanted to use my own power in my job and develop along new lines." What sort of lines? "A full end of the regime. I went so far as to talk with Himmler about the murder of Hitler." Was Himmler liberal, or more liberal than Hitler? "I believe Himmler knew he was not liberal but saw himself as a facilitator of a temporary system." What was your idea of the ultimate system that should prevail in Germany? "I realized at an early date that our system was nothing but a latent living appearance of inner revolution that had been suffocated at its beginning. And because of this, they wanted war. In my opinion a war between England and Germany was a war between brothers. In my inner self I admired the English government and political system.

"I must say today that — after all I saw — I'm glad England won the war, because Germany with its corrupt system and false selection of people in the government would never have been able to give the continent what the continent needed. I told this to a Swedish friend in 1944, who told it to the English ambassador in Sweden." What were you doing in Sweden in 1944? "I tried to seek peace on my own responsibility." Did Himmler know? "I could not tell Himmler everything because he was too false and two-faced.

"The English ambassador said that negotiations with the German system at that time were impossible" and suggested that Schellenberg "do away with Hitler.

"But I didn't dare take this last step because of my family, which was still in Germany, and I didn't dare move them out. Therefore, I tried to stir up Himmler against Hitler by astrology.

"It's interesting that in March 1945 Kaltenbrunner informed Himmler that I had brought my wife to Switzerland. This was untrue, of course, but Himmler had it investigated."

Did Himmler trust anyone? "No one. That was the difficulty of my position. Any day something might happen to me. Himmler told me at the end of April 1945, after I had held a conference with the Zionist leader in Sweden, that he felt sorry for what he had done in his life, regretted his sneakiness toward other people, and excused himself for that. He said, to quote Himmler from my memory: 'If I had only listened to you, Schellenberg, in 1943, there still would have been time to do something for the German people.' I always had the impression that Himmler was under the influence of Hitler. Himmler was suggestible — could easily have been under the influence of Hitler. Himmler conspired with me too much for it to be true that Hitler was under Himmler's influence. Himmler and I plotted against Hitler too much for that. Toward the end of 1943 Himmler actually talked with me about killing Hitler. That was the danger in my position. Should someone change his mind, it would be the end of me. It became even more obvious after the *Attentat* of July 20, 1944, when Kaltenbrunner worked more and more closely with Hitler. Kaltenbrunner conspired against Himmler."

Asked about Himmler's personality, Schellenberg replied: "He was a schoolmaster type outwardly, and that was as far as his foreign political horizon went. Therefore, in the field of foreign affairs I had an easy time convincing him. As far as other things are concerned, Himmler was a sphinx, hard to understand. He was a coward, not a brave man." For instance? "He tried to evade all difficulties. When I had difficulties with Ribbentrop, Himmler wouldn't stand up for me.

"This cowardice was the reason Himmler agreed to everything the powerful, suggestive Hitler said to him."

Whose idea was it to execute the 5 million Jews? "It must have been Hitler's, because Himmler did not have the courage of a soldier, the ability to make a courageous decision."

So the decision to kill 5 million Jews, exterminate that race, was a courageous one in your opinion? "I'm not saying it was right. I was against it. But what I mean is not so much courage as decisiveness." As a psychiatrist, it seems to me to require more sadism than courage or decisiveness. "Himmler may have been a sadist, but Hitler was more so. Hitler was the devil of the whole thing — more sadistic than Himmler." A sadist is not only the man who breaks the bones of babies and enjoys the work, but the one who orders it, or knows about it and is undisturbed. "If you define a sadist so, yes, Himmler was a sadist." Do you feel you have any sadistic tendencies? "I was deeply moved when Himmler had a conference with the Zionist leader from Sweden, in 1945. Up to that time I thought that Jews were only in concentration camps and industrial camps."

Did you hear of any sadism within the concentration camps? "No." Ever in a concentration camp? "I inspected one camp once — but it was all right. Whether they showed me everything I don't know, but what I saw was good." What camp? "Oranienburg." What did you observe there? "I saw medical installations there that were certainly better than charity institutions. That was in 1943."

How did you happen to visit Oranienburg? "I was asked to go by another high official." How many people in Oranienburg? "When I visited, I was told there were eight thousand." Rather small compared to Dachau. "I don't know how many were in those camps, later or even then. That's the figure I was told.

"To return for a moment to sadistic tendencies, doesn't each war have sadistic tendencies?" Yes. But for instance? "For instance, in one night, didn't Dresden have sixty thousand people burned?[10] I also know a case of a relative of mine who was pregnant and was fleeing down a road when she was strafed by low-flying aircraft." What nation did this aircraft come from? "I don't know." Could it have been German? "Hardly."

"I know from my own experience on country roads, English and American planes would swoop down and shoot every farmer and refugee on the road." I guess there were irresponsible pilots on either side. "Yes." He smiled broadly.

But we had no people on the Allied side who killed and lined up in trenches, gas chambers, and crematoria, infants, children, women, and men — in an organized manner. "I understood the whole aerial warfare to be sadistic."

And is the point you are making, that this accounts for German atrocities, the murder of 5 million Jews, the gassing of people and shooting of hostages, the other things that have been brought out in court? "No. But what could I do? What could the German people do? Sure, they knew bad things were going on in those camps. If they lived nearby, they couldn't help knowing, just as I knew. But what of it? We despised those happenings, but what could we do about it? I could have gone abroad as I told you yesterday, but I thought it best to stay at my job and try to change the government. In view of today's political situation I think my work was more correct than going abroad and writing articles about it from abroad. I mention this because of all the people who come back to Germany now, and say they worked against Hitler. Of those who left Germany, how many can say they liberated a Jew from a concentration camp? Not one."

Did you ever do so? "Many." For instance? "A family Notebaum. And a family Rosenbaum in 1944." In what way did you help? "I always pretended that they were political people, and that for political reasons they should be released." What did you do with them? "Sent them to Switzerland."

"Toward the end, about April 28, 1945, I saved Ravensbrück camp and two thousand French, two thousand Polish, and two thousand Jewish women from death. I evacuated them to Sweden by the Red Cross toward the last of April 1945. There was an order in the camp that all inmates of the camp were to be shot when the front broke." Whose order? "Kaltenbrunner.[11]

"And the decision to send Swedish cars there for evacuation of these women of Ravensbrück was on my own instigation and responsibility." Any proof of that? "It's all in the court."

**Father:** "Free from political beliefs, always made a good living. Prior to World War I was a very rich man. His factories in Saarbrücken were closed but he still had branches operating in Luxembourg and Trier (on the Moselle).

During the last few years he lived in Luxembourg, but since the end of the war has been evacuated to Germany." Father now lives with one of his daughters.

**Mother:** Died in 1941 at age sixty-one from liver cancer, had been ill two years. Died following second operation. Personality of mother? "A very good, beloved person. Perhaps too good a mother." What do you mean? "She always stood up for the children, whereas Father was very strict. She worried excessively perhaps about us. I was the favorite child of my mother's — and the youngest. Possibly it was caused by the fact that my brother was six years older, so that the span of difference in our ages made my mother favor me." Why? "Well, I suppose six years is a long span between children.

"Maybe that was the reason I was the favorite [laughs], and also my father always told me I wasn't expected." Were you also your father's favorite? "Yes, although he didn't expect another child when I was born."

Personality of the father? "A very strict and stern man. Father was a very emotional man who lived only for the music and his profession." For example? "He was an idealistic man — therefore a poor business-man. He didn't know how to speculate. He had too much confidence in people." Do you think confidence in people is one of your weaknesses? "No. I have a realistic approach."

What did your father think of your activities? "At first I wanted to study medicine, but Father didn't want that. He wanted me to become a lawyer. But of my activities in the party, he had no idea or conception as to what they were." Think he had a concept today? "He knows I was employed by the secret service but no details.

"Father felt he had given me a professional education and that now I was old enough to get along in life." When was the last time you saw your father? "When mother died, in 1941." Why not since? "Couldn't get away from Berlin because I was so busy."

How often did you see your mother before she died? "Once in 1937, 1938, and 1940. In 1940 I spent two weeks in Luxembourg."

**Siblings:** Three brothers and three sisters. 1. Sister fifty, married, has twins, age eleven years. "She married late, at twenty-eight. She had children several years later. Her husband is very ill, a heart ailment. He was a bank director and then employed by the city of Saarbrücken. He has been unable to work for the past two years." She has been evacuated to a smaller town. He has recently heard through his wife that she is in contact with this sister.

Personality of the fifty-year-old sister? "Very sensible. Inclined to art. Many headaches until her children were born. Since then she has been better. I got along best with her, was her favorite brother. I got along all right with my brother-in-law too."

2. Brother, forty-eight, was in World War I, gassed, and has had stomach troubles since then. He married two or three years ago, no children. He was employed in his father's business. Personality of brother? "A quiet, content, introverted type of man. I got along well with him. He always protected me because I was little, and he was strong. He is two heads taller than me and stronger. He is a good sportsman."

This brother was never a member of the Nazi Party, Schellenberg made a point of saying. But he was inducted into the armed SS toward the end of the war. He was at the western front. There is no news of him as yet.

3. Sister, forty-six, in good health, single, lives with father. At the end of 1941 she was in America, where she had been for fourteen years. She was deported as a German national. She had worked as a governess in a millionaire's home for six years, helping to rear children. She plays piano perfectly and speaks English fluently.

She quit the governess job because the children had grown up. Thereafter she worked in the German consulate in New York until the outbreak of the war. She was a chief secretary.

He was reluctant to give much information as to his sister's personality, except to say she was competent and cheerful. He does not know whether she was a member of the Nazi Party.

4. Brother, forty-four, living, in poor health. "We think he might have inherited some liver ailment from his mother. He is married, has four children.

"He was in charge of father's business in Saarbrücken." He was inducted into the air force for the extent of the war. He returned home a few weeks ago, according to the latest letters from home. He was "a mere private" in the air corps. He was a high school graduate — "he hated soldiering, never cared for it." Schellenberg never saw his brother since the start of the war. He believes he was in the ground crew of the air force. "I never had much to do with him — he was a very stubborn man. He always wanted to have his own way." He was not a member of the party insofar as subject knows.

5. Sister, forty-one, good health, married, four children, husband just returned from war service. She married at a young age. "She had a lot of fantasy and temperament, a very alert and awake person." He never saw her during the war. She was evacuated from Saarbrücken at the outbreak of hostilities.

How is it that you never saw members of your family during the war? "The only leave I could get from the office was to see my mother, and I had to fight for that. Besides, I had my young wife and children, and after my mother died I cared only for my own family."

6. Brother, forty-one, good health, single, "was always a sort of adventurer who didn't want to tie himself down." He was in the U.S. for twelve years until 1939. He is an agriculturist and ran a hothouse for roses in Providence, Rhode Island. Why did he return to Germany? "He earned less and less, he wanted to change." What did he do after he returned to Germany? "He was representative for Coca-Cola for part of Germany. Then he was inducted into the army. I only saw him once. He was in motor transportation, possibly in the air force. He is home now."

**Marital:** Married 1940. Four children: a boy of five years, and three girls, ages four, three, and seven months. The boy suffered from headaches as an infant but is now cured. All are living and well. Wife is a Catholic, as is the subject. He knew her six months prior to marriage. She is a high school graduate, and later attended an art academy, but never painted professionally. She does some portrait painting as a hobby. At the time of his marriage he was chief of Office IV in the RSHA (counterespionage).

His wife's picture is on his table in the cell. She is a pretty blond girl, the photograph a regular studio portrait. Alongside it is a snapshot of his wife and the children, in which she looks quite unlike the larger studio portrait. He apologized more or less for her "bedraggled" appearance on the snapshot, saying she had just had their fourth child at the time that picture was taken, and she was "run-down." He fails to give much emotionally laden material regarding his marriage, except to state he is happily married.

Asked for a brief outline of his career, he gave the following:

1936—Took his state examination as a lawyer.
1937—Came to Berlin and worked in finance and personnel section of the SD.
1939—Began to work in counterespionage, Office IV, as senior administrative adviser. He was a state employee.
1941—About July, became chief of the SD (Office IV). Schellenberg's last rank in the SS was major general, but when he first took over, he was a colonel.

"I always wanted to be promoted in the civil ranks but they promoted me in the SS." Mainly he wore civilian clothes in his work.

"Wilhelm Hoettl was an employee in Office VI under my leadership. He represented southeastern Europe, was chief of that department."

Asked of his impressions of Hoettl, he replied: "Hoettl is a very intelligent man, and very industrious in his work. I'm sure in due time he would have made the Foreign Office."

Were there any differences of opinion between you and Hoettl? "In official business or personal contact, none. But Hoettl was too easy with his money, spent too much, legally and illegally. I always had to keep a strict watch and hold on Hoettl."

Is Hoettl a man to be trusted, in your opinion? Schellenberg thought for a while before replying. "Yes, but you must always have him under supervision."

What does that mean? Schellenberg smiled and raised both hands in gesticulation. It was as if to say, "Who knows?"

Going back to his marriage, Schellenberg said that his wife's mother was Polish. On that basis Himmler disapproved of the marriage. Her family came from and lived in Silesia. Schellenberg met his wife in Berlin at a party. Finally Himmler consented to the marriage, under Schellenberg's insistence.

He saw his wife last in March 1945, when he left for Sweden. He made several trips back and forth between Sweden and Germany. "It was my idea to make an agreement with the Swedish government to prevent any more actions in Denmark and Norway.

"I succeeded with my mission. After that, Denmark was occupied by the British and I could not return to Germany." He therefore contacted a U.S. military attaché in Sweden and was brought to Frankfurt in the company of Count Bernadotte.

The latter stayed two days in Frankfurt, just long enough to turn Schellenberg over to the authorities, and then returned to Sweden. That was June 1945. Schellenberg's last trip to Sweden began May 2, 1945.

# Paul O. Schmidt

born 1899, year of death unknown

Paul O. Schmidt was Hitler's interpreter.

**March 13, 1946**

Hitler's interpreter, Paul O. Schmidt, was present at most international conferences and the like as Hitler's personal aide, with rank of ambassador in the Foreign Office. He is middle-aged, has some puffiness under the eyes, but is otherwise in a state of good nutrition and a cheerful, talkative mood.

He came to the Nuremberg prison a week ago, having been in a hospital until then, suffering from nephritis. He showed me a copy of a request, which he wrote, asking for his release from detention and dated February 1946, Alaska House, Oberursel Interrogation Center.

He was in hospital in Frankfurt for three months with nephritis. Of that period, he was confined to bed for one month. He was interned. "I gave myself up to American troops at Salzburg on May 22, 1945."

**Previous Illness:** Nephritis — started November 1945 and is still not completely cured. He never had an attack of nephritis prior to that time.

**Past History:** He said that for twenty-two years, from 1923 until 1945, he was employed in the Foreign Office as an interpreter for international conference work.

He was a Nazi Party member since 1943. He never wanted to join the party, he says, but did so under pressure. "I was expected to join, and the director of personnel in the Foreign Office had asked me several times. I intended to keep out of the party until 1940, so that I could tell my son, who is now eighteen, about it. So you can see what my opinions regarding the Nazis were."

Did you disapprove of the Nazis? "Yes. My whole education and background was anything but National Socialist. I was a liberal. My first chief in the Foreign Office was Stresemann. I first began conference work in 1924."

I remarked that I had often seen pictures of him alongside Hitler. He replied that such pictures were frequent and numerous. Were you a friend of Hitler's? "At first he thought I was no good because someone said I had been at Geneva. I began working with Hitler in 1935, and he liked my work." Any rewards for it? "No, I naturally received normal promotions. I was a secretary of the legation, then promoted to councilor. I received another promotion after the Munich Conference. Another promotion came after the armistice with France."

He states that he speaks French as fluently as English, and Spanish not quite so well, but well enough. "I translated once in Spanish for Serrano Suñer. Once I translated for Sumner Welles too; he knew some German but wanted a translator to make sure.

"I'm called as a defense witness for Ribbentrop, so his lawyer told me. I shall probably have to give evidence this coming week. My presence is not necessary, in my opinion. It was my duty to write minutes of all conferences. All those documents are in American hands, certainly all the minutes of meetings held during the war. On one occasion I was translator at a conference between King Leopold III of Belgium and Hitler. I was interrogated on that by American and Belgian authorities. This conference report had been in American hands, and was used in the Belgian government's controversy with Leopold."

Regarding his attitude toward the Nazis, for whom he worked from the rise to power until the end of the war, he says, "I was of a fundamentally different opinion. I was a member of the Foreign Office, as were most of us — not Ribbentrop, I mean the old bunch. We knew that compromise was something Hitler didn't have in his vocabulary.

"Almost anything — the racial business, the blood and soil business — I couldn't agree with it. It would have made life easier to have agreed. As it was, these people stole your own country from you. I said to an English friend in 1933, 'It's funny, I'm a stranger in my own country.' Now I don't think that's funny anymore."

Why didn't you leave Germany? "Well, I was in the Foreign Office until Ribbentrop came. Neurath was there before Ribbentrop. I needed to work, had no other means of income. I now wish I had left in time."

I asked whether that point of view could not apply to Ribbentrop or even Goering at this time. He said, "Well, Goering was a pilot in Sweden, Ribbentrop had been in the liquor business. They could more easily have left Germany if they wanted to. I was really dependent for my livelihood on my job."

I've had several interviews with this former ambassador of the Foreign Office who was the official interpreter for Hitler and other leading Nazis in the government from 1933. He speaks good English, has an excellent Anglo-American accent, although his vocabulary is not extraordinary. He is bright but not impressively intellectual, and is given to making platitudes and aphorisms which are unremarkable but which he obviously feels mark him as a man of wisdom.

His general attitude is that he was an ideological opponent of Nazism from the very start, but since he was a public servant and "merely an interpreter," stayed on in the Foreign Office after Hitler's rise to power. The fact that he advanced in his position, finally becoming ambassador, is more or less neglected by him, and he depreciates this by saying that by chance he happened to be well liked by Hitler and thus received promotions which might ordinarily have occurred anyway in the course of his many years of service.

He is forty-seven years old, born on June 23, 1899, in Berlin, where he grew up and studied. He attended elementary school for four years and then went to a school where he could specialize in modern foreign languages, instead of going to a gymnasium with a more classical curriculum.

In 1917 he was drafted into the army as an infantry soldier. In November 1918, he was wounded by an American shell splinter, which penetrated the flesh of his right thigh. This occurred about ten days before the armistice. He was hospitalized until January 1919. He made a full recovery.

Thereafter he attended the University of Berlin from 1919 until 1923. He majored in English and French and also studied Spanish and philosophy. He received a Ph.D. in 1923. He wrote a thesis on the reading and literary criticism of the English author Oliver Goldsmith.

Immediately after his graduation from the university, in 1923, he entered the Foreign Office. "They invited a number of students and I was selected from fifteen or twenty young men. I was sent on trial trips to The Hague as an interpreter." He then went from one conference to another as an interpreter. In 1924 he attended the London Conference on Reparations and on the subject of the Ruhr and the Dawes Plan. In 1925 he served at the Locarno Conference. From 1926 until 1933 he was a member of the German delegation at the League of Nations in Geneva and interpreted at general assemblies, special council meetings, sessions of the Economics Committee. He also was the official German interpreter at the World Economic Conference in Geneva in 1927 and again in 1933 in London.

He was present also at the Disarmament Conference in Geneva in 1929 to 1933, which, he said, "began but never ended." Germany withdrew from this conference because, he said, "We obtained the equality of rights on paper but Hitler decided we did not really obtain equal rights and so in 1933 we withdrew completely."

At that point he smiled. "When we withdrew from the League of Nations in 1933, I made the remark that we were throwing overboard our instruments, our diplomatic navigation, and had installed a few brass bands in the passenger cabins. Strangely enough, the passengers seemed to like it. They played and sang patriotic hymns to these brass bands without seeming to realize the danger to the ships." Schmidt seemed quite pleased with this allegorical remark.

He served as the interpreter for Hjalmar Schacht in 1929 at a meeting of the Young Committee, among other meetings. At that time Schacht was president of the Reichsbank and was employed as a government financial and economic expert. This led to the 1929 Hague Conference and its subsequent meeting of January 1930. In the latter conference the evacuation of occupied German territory was decided upon. "My former chief, Stresemann, set what I consider a minister's record in that he succeeded in removing a foreign army without using an army of his own. The reverse is true of Hitler and Ribbentrop, who used armies of their own and ended by having Germany occupied by Allied armies.

"There were many conferences with Chancellor Bruening at the time of the 1931 crisis and the subsequent depression in America and Europe. Prime Minister Ramsay MacDonald of England presided over a six-power meeting in 1931. It was there that I met Andrew Mellon, your former secretary of the Treasury, who impressed me as being a fine man. I especially liked his head, which was finely chiseled and impressive."

Schmidt continued his recollections and mentioned that he met Cordell Hull for the first time at the World Economic Conference in 1933. "Hull impressed me as being singularly inelastic for a foreign minister — rather stubborn. I agree with Sumner Welles on that account."

We discussed his family history. His father died in 1930 at the age of seventy of a ruptured appendix. He was a railway official in Berlin, having begun his career as a clerk and having ended it as the deputy head of the district railway administration in Berlin. "All his life my father was a man of principles. He had started his career in the army, in which he served twelve years as a sergeant — a not unusual beginning in Germany — and then he was given a job in the civil administration. Thus began his railway career.

"Some of the principles my father had I didn't like. For example, he was too strict with me until I reached the age of about sixteen, when he became softer. I don't know why he gave me a pipe on my sixteenth birthday. That day my uncle came and also gave me a pipe, admonishing me to keep it a secret from my father. But I told my uncle that Father had just given me one himself. My father was strict about obeying orders, which was more or less the military influence. I never discussed politics with him but he was a Conservative and subscribed to the *Berliner Lokal-Anzeiger*."

I asked him whether his father used corporal punishment. "He used to spank me whenever I deserved it but he never went to extremes."

Schmidt's mother was seventy, lived as a refugee in the American zone after her house in Berlin was bombed. She was considerably younger than her husband and always enjoyed fairly good health. She now lived with a former nurse who had been a governess for Schmidt's baby. This nurse had invited Schmidt or his mother to live with her if they ever needed to do so.

"My mother is completely uninterested in politics and is only concerned with her family." Neither parent had any particular ability as far as speaking other languages. His father could speak Polish because he came from the eastern German region near Posen. Schmidt said, however, that he had no Polish or Slavic relations.

I asked him what he thought of Bach-Zelewski's statement before the tribunal that Himmler wanted to exterminate 30 million Slavs. Schmidt replied promptly and with conviction, "I think it is a fact. Himmler hated Poles and Slavs and was quite capable of not only making such a statement but of putting it into practice if given the opportunity."

He described his mother's personality in general terms. "A typical housewife and good cook whose interest concentrated on me because I was the only child." I asked him whether he thought that his mother might have been possessive in her attitude toward him. He replied, "I don't think so because I would have felt that when I married at the age of twenty-four. I imagine that a possessive mother would have raised some objection to her son's marrying."

Schmidt married in 1925, at the age of twenty-four. His wife was about the same age. Their only child, a boy, was born in 1926. Schmidt believed that this boy was serving as an interpreter in a British POW camp. "I think he's free because he draws a salary. It's quite surprising to me that he can be an interpreter. It may be he was gifted for languages. I remember that as a young child he had an extraordinary ability to reproduce the sounds of American and English phonograph records, which we always had in abundance in our home. For example, there was a tune called 'Hallelujah,' and my son, even as a small boy, could pronounce the word perfectly. That word is extremely difficult for a German to pronounce because we have no such sounds in our language."

Schmidt's wife, when he last heard from her, was in Berlin in good health, and living with her sister because her own home had been destroyed by bombs. "I met my wife when we were both students at the University of Berlin. She specialized in English and German literature. During the First World War she was a teacher of languages in an elementary school." He described his marriage as "happy."

His previous illnesses were not remarkable. About ten years ago he suffered a mild cerebral concussion as result of an automobile accident, which incapacitated him for eight weeks. The only other illness of importance was the case of nephritis that began in November 1945 while he was a prisoner at Oberursel. This started after a severe cold or "maybe because I hate the heavily spiced food to which I was not accustomed." In general, his health was good. Recently, urinalyses here revealed no albumen, casts, or other signs of nephritis.

He described his wife's personality in glowing, chivalrous terms. "She has the best of all qualities you can think of. She is very intelligent, has high moral standards in the real sense of the word. That is why she objected to National Socialism from the very beginning, and strongly. She didn't like my contacts with National Socialism, which were, of course, necessary for my job. When the bombing of Berlin began, she decided that she would rather remain in Berlin than accept favors from the party or Foreign Office. Most of the wives and families of members of the Foreign Office were evacuated to Lake Constance on the Swiss border."

His son was drafted into the air force in October 1944. He wanted to become a pilot and actually succeeded in becoming a glider pilot. Then suddenly many members of the air force were transferred to the infantry. "One day in 1945 my son turned up in Berlin on his way to the Russian front. He was an auxiliary antiaircraft man. He served on the Russian front near Stettin. The last time I heard from him was at Christmas, when he wrote from the British POW camp. I think my wife hears from him more regularly. Apparently he is not allowed to return to Berlin."

We discussed his career after 1933. "At first I did nothing but remain in the Foreign Office as a secretary of a legation. I first started working for Hitler personally in 1935. Before that, from 1933 to 1935, I worked in the Foreign Office relative to private industry, cartels, for instance, the chemical and pharmaceutical industries.

"In 1935 when Sir John Simon and Anthony Eden visited Berlin, I was called in by Neurath to act as interpreter. I was told that Hitler inquired where I had worked previously. When he was told that I had worked at Geneva in the League of Nations, Hitler said, 'He can't be any good, then.'

"After the morning conference in 1935 with Simon and Eden, Hitler was softened and very complimentary to me. He said he liked what I had done and that he wanted me to work for him personally. From that time forward I was present at every one of his conferences or contact with foreigners. Hitler never spoke English or French. Eventually, Hitler's example was followed by Goering and Ribbentrop. The latter took me to London in 1935 for negotiations about the naval agreement. Britain and Germany were negotiating. They at that time agreed on a naval ratio: one hundred for the British to thirty-five for the Germans. We had been convicted of violating the Treaty of Versailles only six weeks before and it was remarkable that Britain agreed to sit at the conference table with us. It was one of the encouragements Hitler received from the appeasers.

"At that time the Stanley Baldwin government was in power in Great Britain and Sir Samuel Hoare was foreign minister. The German naval expert present was Admiral Schuster. He is now in American custody. That conference was one of the most outspoken steps in the policy of appeasement. It was definitely encouraging to Hitler because the conference occurred such a short time after the disarmament violation of Versailles on the part of Germany."

I asked Schmidt for his own opinions or views of these events. "I was not in favor of rearmament or of treaty breaking. I felt that with a little more patience we could have achieved equality of armaments. Under Bruening, with Neurath, we had received assurances of 'equal rights in a system of security.' That was the French idea — security. The French wanted real assurances from Great Britain and the United States that they would be supported in case of any trouble with Germany.

"Therefore, I was opposed to these treaty-breaking methods. I was in opposition both privately and personally. I had a taste of the darker aspects of militarism when I was a corporal in the First World War. I don't believe in the educational value of military training. I felt that military training as practiced in Germany or elsewhere was bad. I disliked the caste system, and bullies. From this general point of view, I was against the reintroduction of compulsory military service. Compulsory military service began again in Germany in 1936. It was a decision taken by Germany in violation of the terms of the Versailles Treaty."

The conversation turned to some of his impressions of various leading international personalities whom he had met. "I knew Anthony Eden fairly well at Geneva. Although he may not carry the weight of a first-class statesman, he is an excellent foreign minister. I always admired the way he succeeded in bringing together forty-two nations in the sanctions meeting at the time of the Abyssinian war.[1] It was a masterpiece of statesmanship because it was difficult to unite members of the League. Yugoslavia had to sacrifice the whole of her foreign trade. I hoped Eden would succeed in bringing Italy to her knees. Of course, I felt that such an example would serve as a useful warning to my own nation.

"Eden and the League were within an inch of success. If oral sanctions had gone through, the Abyssinian war would not have lasted another week. Mussolini told us as much in Munich. He stated definitely that if the oil sanctions had been applied, the Abyssinian war could not have succeeded. But Eden was stopped by the Frenchman Pierre Laval, who had fascist leanings. So ironically enough, France was the country which did not agree to the oil sanctions.

"The League was not the failure it is often called. It was within an inch of success — it all depended on oil. If that one thing had succeeded, war would have been averted. The oil sanctions would have served peace and would have been a warning to the people who later made trouble.

"Sir John Simon, who was the international expert on law, was engaged as counsel for the German concern Siemens, in a private arbitration case. Between that company and the American International Telephone and Telegraph Company it was a matter of international business concerning automatic telephone distribution of the world market between the two concerns. A private arbitration committee was set up. Simon, as counsel for Siemens, received a fee of ten thousand guineas.

"It was a private agreement and had nothing to do with politics. Simon was brilliant but not on that occasion. He lost the case for Siemens because he was busy with politics at the time. That was my first impression of Anglo-Saxon procedure, with cross-examination, et cetera.

"I interpreted for Hitler, Goering, Goebbels, and many others. I once interpreted for Goebbels at the League of Nations. He held a press meeting where he answered questions. He also made a speech as to the aims of Germany. It was a typical League of Nations speech. He used the old clichés.

"I was present at several interviews with Goebbels. Superficially he appeared intelligent, clever, and refined. He might have been a literary man or a professor of history. That was the astonishing thing when one met him privately. Even Hitler himself impressed many of his foreign visitors. Hitler was a charming host, very considerate, and so was Goebbels. Goebbels behaved and spoke as though he was a cabinet minister in any western democratic country. I disliked Goebbels's public speeches and never listened to them. For that matter I disliked both Hitler and Goebbels in their loud public speeches, with the shouting of the multitude. I just turned the radio off when those speeches were on. I never went to any of the large mass meetings. I often remarked that a man who is employed as a stagehand for a show does not go to witness another show. It is too awful.

"That made me realize the difference all the more between public performances and private talks. Now, for example, Goering made an excellent impression. I must say I rather liked him. The fashion was for 'strong men.' Goering had his weaknesses — he was like a child in many respects — but he was a human being. Hitler could not be classed as a human. He was too aloof from the very beginning and he never changed."

Schmidt said that he saw Hitler for the last time in February 1945, when the Hungarian puppet government visited him. "I served as secretary at that meeting and wrote up the notes. Salasay was the Hungarian representative. Hitler appeared a little shaken after the explosion of July 20, 1944, and his right arm was stiff. Otherwise, he was the same as ever. The purpose of the meeting was to encourage the new Hungarian government — to give them backing and instructions on what they were to do. At that time the situation of Hungary was desperate. The better part of Hungary had been occupied by the Russians. At the time Hitler said we would start a new offensive and liberate Hungary from the Russians. It was fantastic but it was just about the only thing that we could have said.

"I used to analyze Hitler's speeches. I always asked myself, What could Hitler have said? In most cases the only alternative was silence. What else could he have said? So a great many of his speeches were meaningless. If he wanted to make a speech at all, he was forced to say what he did say."

I asked Schmidt whether he had any contact with Himmler and what his impression of the man had been. "I met him officially only once, at which time I translated for him. He had a meeting with Marshal Antonescu and we discussed police methods. I had no personal impression of Himmler. He was just a background figure as far as I was concerned. I was in the front group."

Had he ever met Bormann? "Yes, he was a sinister-looking fellow. I believe he was the evil spirit behind the scenes, but I have no personal knowledge of his activities. Bormann was Hess's successor. He was really the deputy leader, though he was not called that. He was the head of the party secretariat. Bormann was the first man in the party after Hitler.

"In September 1938, there was a meeting at Berchtesgaden between Hitler and Chamberlain. Hitler put forth Germany's claim to the Sudeten territories. Chamberlain did not agree. There were no Czech representatives. The Czechs were not even invited and were hardly informed. One ally quietly signed away territory belonging to another ally. It was a terrible encouragement to Hitler, who saw the weakness of the Allied situation. France was an ally of Czechoslovakia but also ceded Czech territory through the French prime minister, Daladier.

"There was a meeting at Bad Godesberg seven to ten days after the one at Berchtesgaden. Chamberlain and Hitler met without any other parties present, except myself. The famous Munich Conference of September 29–30, 1938, took place two weeks after Bad Godesberg. The parties met on the basis of the proposition put forth by Mussolini to the French. Mussolini made the initial Munich draft. He saw things more realistically than my own people. That was always so. The Mediterraneans are always greater realists than the people of the north. The fact that war was avoided in 1938 was as much due to Mussolini as to Chamberlain. We Germans had no part in it. Hitler was quite prepared to go to war.

"At Berchtesgaden feelings were strained. The atmosphere improved a little at the Godesberg meeting. At Munich the personal relationships were again strained. But once the agreement had been reached and the famous 'no more war' agreement was arranged between Britain and Germany, the atmosphere was better. I thought Chamberlain was very happy to have Hitler sign the paper he had typed and brought along with him from England. Chamberlain was warmly welcomed at Munich. He was the hero of the German people on that occasion. It was definitely Chamberlain who was the idol of the German people in Munich — not Hitler. The German masses gave flowers to Chamberlain. One could see on their faces that they thanked Chamberlain for saving the peace of Europe despite Hitler.

"Hitler didn't like this show at all. He feared that it would give the impression that the German people were pacifists, which, of course, would be unpardonable in the eyes of the Nazis. Therefore, the Nazis didn't like this Munich show at all."

On points of detail when Chamberlain repeatedly raised the issue of Czech property and the proper financial settlements that should be agreed on, Hitler became nervous. But these were comparatively rare occurrences. The Munich agreement as such was certain before it took place. It was practically a certainty as to what would transpire. There was no reason for Hitler to become excited. Hitler always became excited on slight points of detail and not of fundamental points. This time he was exercised about the question of the Sudetenland.

"In January 1939, there was an interview with Colonel Beck, the Polish foreign minister. Hitler hinted that something would have to be done about Danzig. Beck cold-shouldered the proposals of Hitler regarding the return of Danzig to Germany. Beck did not see eye to eye with us. He said that Danzig was always a part of Poland and that it would be difficult to influence Polish public opinion to agree to changes.

"Beck and the whole Polish government were fascists. They were supposed to be on friendly terms with us for ideological reasons. Pilsudski was held in high esteem in Germany. Certainly Hitler could easily have been made an ally of Poland for ideological reasons.

"Hitler's idea was to regain German territory and to reincorporate the city of Danzig into the Reich. He resented Poland's unwillingness to surrender these territories to him. Despite fascist leanings, Beck refused to contemplate a solution of that kind."

I asked him what sort of a man Beck appeared to be. "He was a sinister-looking chap about forty-five years of age. He was also held in high esteem in Nazi circles. He believed in the 'strong-hand policy,' and that was much appreciated in Germany."

I asked him about Spain's dictator, Francisco Franco; had he ever met the man? "There was a meeting with Hitler at Hendaye, France, in October 1940. Franco and Hitler talked together for a long time. Between the lines of the conversation Gibraltar was discussed. It was our idea to conquer Gibraltar. Special troops were being trained in fortress warfare. Specialists in taking fortified places were trained near Liège in Belgium. There were new methods of approach and attack, studied with a view to an assault on Gibraltar. Of course, it was necessary to obtain Franco's consent. As I said, this was one of the subjects of discussion between the lines. The meeting didn't go well at all.

"In the first place, Franco was hesitating, uncertain; he is of weak character. He obviously played for time. We wanted to precipitate matters as usual. We thought that getting Franco's consent for the attack on Gibraltar would be a matter of one afternoon and that would be enough — but it wasn't. Hitler and Franco separated without achieving anything. Hitler was disappointed and so was Franco."

I asked Schmidt in what way Franco played for time. "He was too cautious. He thought the end of things hadn't yet come. Franco didn't want to get too involved with the British. In fact, he said that because of the long Spanish coastline, he might be in a very awkward spot.

"Franco's brother-in-law came to Berlin. That was, of course, Ramón Serrano Suñer. We offered him large slices of the British colonial empire. But Franco wanted a written guarantee. On the way to Hendaye, we met Laval. On our way back from Hendaye we met Marshal Pétain. Hitler said that if these deals became known, the French colonial empire and the French fleet would, without doubt, join de Gaulle. So it was resented by Franco. We separated in disappointment and mutual distrust, particularly about the cession of French colonial empire in Africa. Serrano Suñer helped himself to large slices of the French colonies in Africa. In exchange we wanted submarine bases in Fernando Póo and in central Africa. Serrano Suñer also cold-shouldered us, saying that these were old Spanish territories."

What sort of man was Serrano Suñer? "He was extremely intelligent, a thoroughly fascist man. I heard that he had been minister of police in Spain. He was not very popular in Germany. He was far more intelligent than our foreign minister, Ribbentrop. Serrano Suñer had trouble with his brother-in-law, Franco, and he subsequently resigned his office because he had backed the extremist wing of the Falangist Party, at a time when Franco made some concessions to western powers. Serrano Suñer was too pro-German at that time, which was 1943 to 1944. That was just about the period when Franco sent General Beigbeder to the United States, saying that it was a private trip. Franco wanted to be on good terms with Britain. He sent the duke of Alba as ambassador to England. There was an obvious strain in Spanish-German relations, supposedly on the basis of religious persecution within Germany. However, until it appeared that the Allies were winning and Germany was slipping, Franco was on excellent terms with Hitler and the religious persecutions in Germany didn't seem to bother him."

I asked Schmidt to tell me something more about his ex-boss Ribbentrop. "That man always made it a point to speak German, although he spoke English well enough. That was because he imitated Hitler to the last degree. He would say that his reason for speaking German instead of English during conferences with English-speaking representatives was that he wanted to concentrate on the subject in hand, and not on the language. Ribbentrop was a complete imitator of Hitler — even to the design of his cap. Originally he had a nice cap, but then he imitated the stationmaster type of cap preferred by Hitler. Ribbentrop invariably wore a uniform. He invented a special Foreign Office uniform, which was black and double-breasted. Those of us in the Foreign Office looked like admirals. Whenever we went to Italy, they would call us the *ammiragli,* which means 'admirals' in Italian. I have a friend on the tribunal prosecution staff who is a German, formerly in the Foreign Office. He had quarreled with Ribbentrop and was sent to Japan. He was always on friendly terms with the other side. He's now here in Nuremberg with the British delegation. He has been out of Germany since before the Russian war. We knew several months prior to its occurrence that a war with Russia was planned by Hitler and was imminent."

How long before the outbreak of the Russian war did you know about it? "About three or four months. We did not know officially because Ribbentrop never told us. In fact, Ribbentrop and Hitler supposed that we didn't know. But we had our informants."

I remarked that Ribbentrop claimed that he never knew of the atrocities and of the extermination camps. Did Schmidt think this was so? "To a certain extent it might be true. If he had known, he might have raised objections for international reasons. But that he heard rumors about the exterminations and atrocities is unquestionable. The fact is Ribbentrop was not interested in those things. He was interested mainly, I might say, solely in his personal standing with Hitler. He spent hours and days drafting letters of protest about Goebbels's interference in his affairs — merely because he was jealous of maintaining his prestige. Ribbentrop had an abnormal desire for rank and position. He wanted personal influence and good standing with Hitler. He did not want anybody to be closer to Hitler than himself. In this way he was unlike Himmler, who, I am convinced, wanted military power. Ribbentrop wanted to satisfy his own vanity. He is a very superficial man."

I asked Schmidt about his impression of Ribbentrop's wife. "She played a large part in pushing him. I always avoided her. She suspected everyone of not being respectful enough to her husband. She was socially ambitious. She came from the Henkell champagne family. She was more intelligent than her husband. For example, she expressed more intelligent views on how the English would resist invasion. On that subject she had much more sense than her husband. She said that the English would fight to the last ditch. Ribbentrop on the other hand always described how England was on the brink of collapse. His desire to please Hitler led him to say these things unconsciously even when Hitler was not present."

Had Schmidt any contact with the economic minister, Funk? "I had a little contact through some economic talks with foreigners. Furthermore, Funk is a reasonable fellow, as quiet and sleepy as he appears in court. Whereas he doesn't have any principles, he is not the criminal type. He is a sort of intelligent middle-class man without much principle. Of course, I never knew him when he was at the Propaganda Ministry. It is not difficult to imagine him as the editor of the right-wing *Börsen-Zeitung.* We knew comparatively little of things, which have come out since the beginning of the trial, so I don't know too much about what has happened in court. I know that Funk plays the piano well, is a type of man who wakes up after midnight, and is the life of any party he attends."

Had Schmidt any impression of Sauckel? "That man who is responsible for slave labor in Germany does not have my sympathy. I did not like the whole idea of what he did. After all, there are limits to what one can do with foreign populations in the forced labor business. In the first place, the whole idea is completely unproductive. One needs three or four men to watch one compulsory worker. Sauckel deserves the severest punishment. You can see that there were no strong characters surrounding Hitler. There were only weaklings like Ribbentrop, Funk, and so forth. Hitler wanted a silent audience. Even Goering, who superficially gives the appearance of a strong man, was in reality a childlike, weak character who was known as a dope addict in the inner circles.

"I remember one time at Goering's place, Karin Hall, I happened to be sitting next to the Japanese representative, Yosuke Matsuoka.[2] He said to me, 'Do you know that Goering is crazy?' He added that Goering had been in an asylum in Sweden for dope addiction. Matsuoka said, 'But never mind; they also say that I am crazy.' Matsuoka was a highly intelligent fellow. He represented Japan in the Manchurian conflict. When I congratulated him on it at the time, he said shrewdly, 'I was not entirely successful at Geneva because Japan had to leave the League.'

"I happened to be at Geneva at the time when Japan walked out. It was not an impressive exit, as had been calculated. The Japanese walkout from the League took place at the lunch hour and it was a trickle and sort of fell flat."

I asked him about his feelings toward Russia. Schmidt replied, "I am naturally anti-Russian just as most Germans are. I admire their achievements in industrial fields. I was in Moscow personally. I would not be in favor of the Russian system in the western nations. I don't condemn the system — I recognize the good results that it has produced in its proper setting. But in order to be Communist, one must be a fanatic. I am very suspicious of all systems requiring fanaticism. I am convinced that the world would be a better place if people were satisfied with enough to eat and a job to keep them occupied.

"If that problem were solved, there would be no isms. Therefore, the economic problem is the fundamental issue. If the economic problem were solved, the extremists would be unable to disturb the world. Extremism arises only as a result of economic depression. The Russian system requires such a different type of man. It just isn't dear to my heart. I consider myself a capitalist. Communism and National Socialism are not the same by any means — but they spring from the same sources. If one respects the individual, everything is all right. On the other hand, if the individual is considered but a grain of sand, the system is no good. I am not in favor of such a system. In that respect I am an individualist.

"I met Molotov when I was in Russia. He reminded me of my old teacher of mathematics. He's the type of man who makes sure to cross his *t*'s and dot his *i*'s. He likes meticulousness. He is a legal expert, a hard worker, and rather stubborn. But I don't know if he has much imagination. Like all Russians he will obey Stalin's orders unwaveringly. He wasn't present at that particular meeting, but our people in Moscow reported that Molotov did not say a word to Ribbentrop at the conference. On the contrary, Stalin, like Hitler, did all the talking. But don't misunderstand me — Stalin was infinitely wiser and more balanced than Hitler.

"I met the Soviet representative Maksim Litvinov at Geneva. He was a very clever ambassador.[3] I think he had been an insurance agent in London before he took up diplomacy. He was the businessman type of diplomat. He spoke English well, but with a heavy Russian accent. He has an English wife. He is an excellent debater at the council table.

"In 1927 we were on excellent terms with the Soviet delegations because, like ourselves, they were opposed to the Treaty of Versailles. There was a silent understanding that we would work together. I was called in once to interpret but there was little need for it because English and French were the official languages of the League."

We went on to a discussion of Schacht. "He's a very intelligent fellow, but a man who is after short-term effects. If you consider his financial policy, in which he banned foreign loans — he forgot that the money that would have flowed into Germany came as short-term loans. His chief fault was a lack of foresight. He thought that foreign loans were bad and forgot the disadvantages of short-term loans. Schacht was a man of expedience. He was not an outstanding person who could carry weight and take a reasoned line of policy for a long time to come.

"But Schacht was infinitely more reasonable than the Nazis. He was fundamentally a dynamic, changeable person. In the beginning, there-fore, it was quite logical that he should be attracted by the dynamic, dra-matic, short-term ideas of the Nazis. As I said, Schacht has intelligence, but is not particularly a man of principle, although I think he believes he is. But it is reasonable to assume that later on he differed with the Nazis. He was too intelligent to go along to the extremes, which they pursued in their folly.

"Our foreign policy was an improvisation. Like Schacht's financial policy, it lacked foresight. The Nazis kept talking about a thousand-year Reich, but they couldn't think ahead for five minutes!"

# GLOSSARY

*Einsatzgruppe:* Action group

Gestapo: Geheime Staatspolizei (Secret State Police, also called Staatspolizei or Stapo)

Kripo: Kriminalpolizei (Criminal Police, plainclothes detectives)

*Luftwaffe:* Air force

Nazi: Nationalsozialist, or National Socialist

NSDAP: National Socialist German Workers Party, or Nazi Party

OKW: Oberkommando der Wehrmacht (Supreme Command of the Armed Forces)

RSHA: Reichssicherheitshauptamt (Reich Security Main Office, founded in 1939 as the umbrella organization for the Gestapo, Kripo, SD, and other police groups)

SA: Sturmabteilung (the Nazi "Brown Shirts," or Storm Troopers)

SD: Sicherheitsdienst (Security Service of the Nazi Party)

Sipo: Sicherheitspolizei (Security Police, founded in 1936 as the umbrella organization of the Gestapo and Kripo)

SS: Schutzstaffel, Himmler's "Black Shirts"

*Wehrmacht:* Armed forces

WVHA: Wirtschafts- und Verwaltungshauptamt (Economic and Administrative Main Office, a branch of the SS created as the umbrella organization to administer the concentration camps)

# NOTES

## INTRODUCTION: NUREMBERG — VOICES FROM THE PAST

1. Quoted in the excellent study by Arieh J. Kochavi, *Prelude to Nuremberg: Allied War Crimes Policy and the Question of Punishment* (Chapel Hill, 1998), 36. See also Richard Overy, *Interrogations: The Nazi Elite in Allied Hands, 1945* (New York, 2001), 8–9.
2. This document, along with many others, is reprinted in the very useful book by Michael R. Marrus, *The Nuremberg Trial, 1945–46: A Documentary History* (Boston, 1997), 20–22.
3. Kochavi, *Prelude to Nuremberg,* 73–74.
4. See Winston S. Churchill, *The Second World War: Closing the Ring* (Cambridge, Mass., 1951), 373–74.
5. According to Elliott Roosevelt, FDR had used the figure of 49,500 that evening; cited in Michael Beschloss, *The Conquerors: Roosevelt, Truman and the Destruction of Hitler's Germany, 1941–1945* (New York, 2002), 27.
6. Churchill, *Closing the Ring,* 374.
7. Sections from Morgenthau's and Stimson's memoranda are conveniently reprinted in Marrus, *Nuremberg Trial,* 24–27.
8. Quoted in full in Kochavi, *Prelude to Nuremberg,* 88.
9. Kochavi, *Prelude to Nuremberg,* 91.
10. Kochavi, *Prelude to Nuremberg,* 65.
11. See Gerd R. Ueberschär, "Die sowjetischen Prozesse gegen deutsche Kriegsgefangene 1943–1952," in Gerd R. Ueberschär, ed., *Der Nationalsozialismus vor Gericht: Die alliierten Prozesse gegen Kriegsverbrecher und Soldaten 1943–1952* (Frankfurt am Main, 2000), 245.
12. The American position on the criminality of Nazi organizations was presented to the tribunal on February 28, 1946, and was later published separately. See Robert H. Jackson, *The Nürnberg Case* (New York, 1947), 95–119.
13. See Bradley F. Smith, *Reaching Judgment at Nuremberg* (New York, 1977), 27.
14. Overy, *Interrogations,* 8.
15. See Beschloss, *The Conquerors,* 246.
16. For the draft memorandum of Cordell Hull, Henry Stimson, and James Forrestal (November 11, 1944) and the memorandum of Henry Stimson, new secretary of state Edward R. Stettinius Jr., and U.S. attorney general Francis Biddle (January 22, 1945), see Marrus, *Nuremberg Trial,* 28–32.
17. Copies of the agreement and charter are published in *Nazi Conspiracy and Aggression* (Washington, 1946), 1:1–12.
18. See the useful account and especially Table 3, which charts the various estimates of the death toll, in Richard Overy, *Russia's War* (New York, 1998), 288.
19. Soviet judge Major Iona T. Nikitchenko, quoted in Overy, *Interrogations,* 18.
20. See Telford Taylor, *Anatomy of the Nuremberg Trials: A Personal Memoir* (Boston, 1992), 64. Taylor was a member of the prosecution staff at the trials.

21. The full indictment and many other important documents are reprinted in the series *Nazi Conspiracy and Aggression* (Washington, 1946); here see 1:15.

22. For an excellent account of the origins of the concept "genocide" and the role of Raphael Lemkin, in particular, who both invented the word and worked tirelessly to have it adopted by the United Nations after 1945, see Samantha Power, *A Problem from Hell: America and the Age of Genocide* (New York, 2002), 1–60.

23. For a useful analysis of the terms, see Omer Bartov, "Antisemitism, the Holocaust, and Reinterpretations of National Socialism," in Michael Berenbaum and Abraham J. Peck, eds., *The Holocaust and History: The Known, the Unknown, the Disputed, and the Reexamined* (Bloomington, 1998), 75–98. This volume contains many other useful essays.

24. Interestingly enough, historians tended to adopt one or the other of these two positions, which later became known in the field, by the 1960s and beyond, as the debate between the "intentionalists" and the "functionalists" or "structuralists." This point is made by Michael Biddiss, "Nuremberg Trials," in I. C. B. Dear, ed., *The Oxford Companion to World War II* (Oxford, 1995), 824–28.

25. Marrus, *Nuremberg Trial*, v.

26. Most libraries have copies of these volumes. I have used the German edition, which is generally more accurate. It is also still in print and available in a paperback reprint. A photo reproduction of the original volumes is published as a *Sonderausgabe* by KOMET MA-Service und Verlagsgesellschaft GmbH, Frechen, as *Der Prozess gegen die Hauptkriegsverbrecher vor dem internationalen Militärgerichtshof* (Nuremberg, 1946–47). Most libraries have copies of these volumes. The English edition publishes the testimony and cross-examinations in the first half of its series in English. Unfortunately, however, the important documentary half of the series remains available only in the original German. Nevertheless, a selection of some of these documents is published in a separate series of volumes, as *Nazi Conspiracy and Aggression* (Washington, 1946). Eight volumes of the latter series, as well as the English-language edition of the trial at Nuremberg — that is, the testimony and cross-examinations of the major war criminals — can now be found on the Internet. The transcripts of the trial can be located by searching for "The Avalon Project at the Yale Law School." These transcripts can also be found by searching the Internet for "The Nizkor Project." Both sites have many other useful documents and provide numerous additional links.

27. See Robert E. Conot, *Justice in Nuremberg* (New York, 1983), 19.

28. Overy, *Interrogations,* 16–17.

29. See Overy, *Interrogations,* which also provides a useful account of the general conditions in which prisoners were held. For a more complete account, see Ulrich Schlie, ed., *Albert Speer: "Alles, was ich weiss": Aus unbekannten Geheimdienstprotokollen vom Sommer 1945* (Munich, 1999). This volume also includes a report by Dr. Karl Brandt about "women around Hitler." For the general background see Joseph E. Persico, *Nuremberg: Infamy on Trial* (New York, 1994). Although this book is generally well researched, it does not mention Dr. Leon Goldensohn and it is unlikely the author was aware of Goldensohn's interviews.

30. The phrase is recalled by Dr. G. M. Gilbert in the introduction to Florence R.

Miale and Michael Selzer, *The Nuremberg Mind: The Psychology of the Nazi Leaders* (New York, 1975), xii. The authors study the results of the Rorschach tests administered to the Nazis by Dr. Gilbert.

31. Persico, *Nuremberg*, 91.

32. Persico, *Nuremberg*, 103.

33. See the article by Soviet journalist Arkadi Poltorak reprinted in Steffen Radlmaier, *Der Nürnberger Lernprozess: Von Kriegsverbrechern und Starreportern* (Frankfurt am Main, 2001), 125–26.

34. Douglas M. Kelley, *22 Cells in Nuremberg: A Psychiatrist Examines the Nazi Criminals* (New York, 1947).

35. G. M. Gilbert, *Nuremberg Diary* (New York, 1947).

36. A medical doctor assigned to Nuremberg recently published an interesting memoir of the trial. It provides new details, particularly about the executions that followed. See Roy A. Martin, *Inside Nürnberg: Military Justice for Nazi War Criminals* (Shippensburg, Pa., 2000).

37. See Gitta Sereny, *Albert Speer: His Battle with Truth* (New York, 1995).

38. Albert Speer, *Spandau: The Secret Diaries* (New York, 1977), 2–3.

39. I used a wide array of references and sources, but found the following to be especially helpful: Robert Wistrich, ed., *Who's Who in Nazi Germany* (New York, 1982); Israel Gutman et al., eds., *Enzyklopädie des Holocaust*, 4 vols. (Munich, 1995). A parallel edition of this encyclopedia was also published in English. Also useful is Erich Stockhorst, ed., *5000 Köpfe: Wer war was im 3. Reich* (*Sonderausgabe*, Kiel, 2000).

40. The opening address and many more important documents are published in Jackson, *Nürnberg;* see 54 for the exact statistics and 97 for the figure of 5 million.

41. Wilhelm Hoettl Affidavit (November 26, 1945), Document PS-2738. See *Der Prozess gegen die Hauptkriegsverbrecher vor dem internationalen Militärgerichtshof* (Nuremberg, 1946–47), 31:85–87.

42. I have calculated the figures based on the difference between the 1939 and 1945 Jewish populations in each state involved in the Holocaust. The figure is based on Raul Hilberg, *The Destruction of the European Jews*, rev. ed., 3 vols. (New York, 1985); here see 3:1048, Table 11-1, "Jewish Population Loss."

43. Hilberg, *Destruction of the European Jews*, 3:894, shows that approximately 1 million Jews lost their lives at Auschwitz. He estimates that another 250,000 people, mostly Poles, also died there, as well as many Gypsies. There is general agreement in Franciszek Piper, "Auschwitz Concentration Camp: How It Was Used in the Nazi System of Terror and Genocide and in the Economy of the Third Reich," in Berenbaum and Peck, eds., *Holocaust and History*, 327–86. Piper estimates about 1 million Jews lost their lives in the camp; 140,000 to 150,000 Poles; 20,000 Gypsies; 15,000 Soviet prisoners of war; and between 10,000 and 25,000 people of other nationalities.

44. See the account of a member of the British War Crimes Executive Team, who was assigned (among other things) to hear what was very contradictory evidence concerning the criminality of various organizations, including the Gestapo, in Airey Neave, *On Trial at Nuremberg* (Boston, 1978).

45. For an introduction, see Robert Gellately, "The Third Reich, the Holocaust, and Visions of Serial Genocide," in Robert Gellately and Ben Kiernan, eds., *The*

*Specter of Genocide: Mass Murder in Historical Perspective* (Cambridge, 2003), 241–64.

46. See Conot, *Nuremberg,* 233.

47. The *Einsatzgruppen* were originally created in 1938 at the time of the annexation of Austria as special police units. Six such units, each comprising smaller commandos (of 120 to 150 members), were used during the invasion of Poland in September 1939. The members of the *Einsatzgruppen* were drawn from the SS, the SD or the Sipo (Security Police, that is, the Gestapo and Criminal Police). However, it was during the invasion of the Soviet Union (beginning June 22, 1941) that the *Einsatzgruppen* were most active and became full-blown death squads. There were four such groups (A to D), drawn from similar personnel, particularly from the RSHA, but with the addition of men from other police forces, with each *Einsatzgruppe* divided into various "special commandos." The *Einsatzgruppen* varied in size between 600 and 1,000 men, and each of them was initially led by highly educated officers. One estimate suggests that as many at 6,000 people served at one time or another in these *Einsatzgruppen,* but the groups and commandos were generally small. They operated behind the lines of the advancing German forces into the USSR, from the north (initially led by Franz Walter Stahlecker, in Lithuania, Estonia, and Latvia), to the center (led by Arthur Nebe in White Russia), to the south (led by Otto Rasch in Ukraine), and into the southeast (led by Otto Ohlendorf in southern Ukraine and the Caucasus). Leaders of the *Einsatzgruppen* were tried in case nine of the follow-up trials at Nuremberg in 1949; four of them were sentenced to death. The main tasks of the *Einsatzgruppen* had been to murder Jews and others who were defined as enemies and "security threats" behind the lines. The *Einsatzgruppen* also deported Jews to the death camps.

It is most difficult to estimate the total number of murders committed by the *Einsatzgruppen.* Many (not all) of their written activity reports survive. These documents show that at a minimum, and not even for the entire period of their operation, these groups — overwhelmingly the victims were Jews — operated as follows: Einsatzgruppe A shot 240,410; Einsatzgruppe B shot 71,555; Einsatzgruppe C shot 105,988; Einsatzgruppe D shot 91,678.

For a complete account, see Helmut Krausnick and Hans-Heinrich Wilhelm, *Die Truppe des Weltanschauungskrieges: die Einsatzgruppen der Sicherheitspolizei und des SD 1938–1942* (Stuttgart, 1981); here see 618–19.

48. For the role of many battalions of the regular, uniformed police, many of them composed of non-Nazi Germans, see the chilling accounts of Christopher R. Browning, *Ordinary Men: Reserve Police Battalion 101 and the Final Solution in Poland* (New York, 1992), and Daniel Jonah Goldhagen, *Hitler's Willing Executioners: Ordinary Germans and the Holocaust* (New York, 1996).

49. This account is in Conot, *Nuremberg,* 233.

50. The test was carried out by Dr. Gilbert and can be found in Gilbert, *Diary,* 34.

51. Albert Speer, *Inside the Third Reich: Memoirs* (New York, 1970), 509.

52. For useful information and a convenient list of the defendants, charges, and verdicts in the twelve follow-up trials, see Whitney R. Harris, *Tyranny on Trial: The Trial of the Major German War Criminals at the End of World War II at Nuremberg, Germany, 1945–1946,* rev. ed. (Dallas, 1999), 550–58.

53. For a general overview, including the statistics on the number and type of all the

postwar trials, see Adalbert Rückerl, *The Investigation of Nazi Crimes 1945–1978: A Documentation* (Hamden, Conn., 1980).

54. For an interesting account, see Norbert Frei, *Adenauer's Germany and the Nazi Past: The Politics of Amnesty and Integration* (New York, 2002).

55. In the American zone from October 1945 to August 1946, seven surveys of public opinion found that 79 percent of the people considered the trials were "conducted fairly," and only 4 percent unfairly. A clear majority (75 percent in surveys from December 1945 to March 1946) considered those on trial were guilty, but that figure fell off to 52 percent by August 1946. See Anna J. Merritt and Richard L. Merritt, eds., *Public Opinion in Occupied Germany: The OMGUS Surveys, 1945–1949* (Chicago, 1970), 33–35.

56. For a brief introduction, see Harris, *Tyranny on Trial,* 571–94. For current information on the ICC— which changes almost daily — and how it differs from U.N. courts, simply search the Internet for "International Criminal Court."

57. For a clear account of the legal-philosophical positions and the attitude of the American government, see William J. Bosch, *Judgment on Nuremberg: American Attitudes Toward the Major German War-Crime Trials* (Chapel Hill, 1970).


KARL DOENITZ

1. Francis Beverly Biddle (1886–1968) was U.S. attorney general from 1941 to 1945, and President Harry S. Truman appointed him a judge of the Nuremberg trial.

2. Gen. Lucius Clay (1897–1978) was Gen. Dwight Eisenhower's deputy and the American member of the Allied Control Commission. After the Allied victory he was appointed military governor of the U.S. zone of occupied Germany.

3. The prosecution said that certain organizations (such as the Nazi Party, the Gestapo, and the SS) could be indicted, not just a few individual leaders. Such organizations would also be charged with being part of a criminal conspiracy, so that it would be necessary only to charge "representative individuals," not every single person. Once the organization was tried and convicted, each member could be judged as a criminal coconspirator, and given a summary trial by the Allies. It is important to note, however, that contrary to what some of the defendants said, Article 10 of what became the charter of the International Military Tribunal did not simply declare certain Nazi organizations criminal; that decision was left to the tribunal to determine. Moreover, every member of those organizations that the tribunal eventually found to be criminal was not automatically deemed to be criminal, but had the right to a trial. The American position on the criminality of Nazi organizations was presented to the tribunal on February 28, 1946, and was later published separately. See Robert H. Jackson, *The Nürnberg Case* (New York, 1947), 95–119.

4. Heinrich Himmler (1900–1945) was head of the SS, creator of the concentration camp system, and one of the key leaders who pushed for and carried out the mass murder of the Jews. He was captured by the British in May 1945 and committed suicide. For a good general introduction to Himmler and for a collective portrait of the Nazi leaders, including most of those tried at Nuremberg, see the

still useful Joachim C. Fest, *The Face of the Third Reich: Portraits of the Nazi Leadership* (New York, 1970); here, see 111–24.

5.  Grand Adm. Erich Raeder (1876–1960) was commander in chief of the German navy until 1943, when he was replaced by Doenitz. Raeder was tried as a major war criminal at Nuremberg and found guilty on the first three counts in the indictment, but not crimes against humanity. He was sentenced to life, but released for health reasons in 1955.

6.  Hitler's "last testament" consisted of statements he dictated the night of April 29, 1945, in advance of his death the following day. See Adolf Hitler, "My Private Will and Testament" and "My Political Testament," in Jeremy Noakes, ed., *Nazism 1919–1945* (Exeter, 1998), 4:667–71.

7.  Martin Bormann (1900–1945) was head of the Party Chancellery after Hess's flight to Britain in 1941. Historians suggest that behind the scenes and more or less anonymously, Bormann became the second most powerful man in the Third Reich after Hitler.

8.  Block leaders were the neighborhood party watchdogs who reported up the line. For a full examination, see Michael H. Kater, *The Nazi Party: A Social Profile of Members and Leaders, 1919–1945* (Cambridge, Mass., 1983). For a recent account of the social basis of the party, see Carl-Wilhelm Reibel, *Das Fundament der Diktatur: Die NSDAP-Ortsgruppen 1932–1945* (Paderborn, 2002).

9.  Doenitz refers to what happened in Germany on November 9, 1938, often called "the night of broken glass." For a brief account and the literature, see Robert Gellately, *Backing Hitler: Consent and Coercion in Nazi Germany* (Oxford, 2001), 121–50.

10.  For a brief account of the camps, including the statistics, see Gellately, *Backing Hitler,* 51–69. The last census (January 15, 1945) of the German concentration camps revealed 511,537 male and 202,674 female prisoners; see 243.

11.  Ernest Bevin (1881–1951) was a British Labor leader and in 1945 became secretary of state for foreign affairs in the new Labor cabinet of Prime Minister Clement Attlee (1883–1967).

12.  W. Rogge is described in the court documents in one place as a navy captain who was in charge of a postwar camp for marine officers. However, in the index to the trial he is described as a retired vice admiral.

13.  Doenitz is referring to the internment camp run by the Americans at Mondorf-les-Bains, in Luxembourg.

14.  Doenitz scored 138, well above average, on the IQ test administered by Gilbert. For the results of the test given to Doenitz and the other defendants, see G. M. Gilbert, *Nuremberg Diary* (New York, 1947), 34.

15.  Clement Attlee defeated Winston Churchill in 1945 and, as prime minister, formed the first Labor government.

### HANS FRANK

1.  Among other things, in lectures at several universities in summer 1942, Frank called for a return to some kind of constitutional law. Hitler soon took away all his Nazi Party offices and forbade him from speaking in public in Germany. Frank kept his position as governor general of Poland.

2. It is likely this book is Frank's *Im Angesicht des Galgens: Deutung Hitlers und seiner Zeit auf Grund eigener Erlebnisse und Erkenntnisse* (Munich, 1953).

3. These figures are hardly exaggerations for the great inflation in Germany, particularly during 1923. The standard work on the subject is Gerald D. Feldman, *The Great Disorder: Politics, Economics, and Society in the German Inflation of 1914–1924* (New York, 1993).

4. The full names of those mentioned by Frank include Towia Axelrod, Eugene Leviné, and Max Levien. According to historians, none of these men helped Kurt Eisner in the November revolt. For details see Allan Mitchell, *Revolution in Bavaria 1918–1919: The Eisner Regime and the Soviet Republic* (Princeton, 1965), especially 193 n. 80.

5. Anton Drexler (1884–1942) was one of the cofounders of the Nazi Party.

6. Joseph Goebbels (1897–1945) attained infamy as the Reich minister for popular enlightenment and propaganda. He played a key role in the Third Reich and, after a period out of favor, had a comeback during the latter part of the war. He was with Hitler to the end and committed suicide on May 1, 1945. He was a compulsive diarist, and the final diary, much of it found in Moscow only in the last several years, is being published. It represents an important source for the history of the Third Reich. At present twenty-two large (German) volumes have appeared, edited by Elke Fröhlich, with more to come. For a brief introduction to Goebbels, see Fest, *Face of the Third Reich,* 83–97.

7. See Feldman, *Great Disorder.*

8. Oswald Spengler (1880–1936) was a well-known cultural historian, most famous for his book *The Decline of the West* (1918–22).

9. Frank must mean his appointment as the minister of justice in Bavaria in 1933.

## WILHELM FRICK

1. Some prominent figures in the Bavarian revolution were Jewish, but the involvement of the Jews as a whole has been vastly exaggerated. For more on this, see Mitchell, *Revolution in Bavaria.*

2. For a thorough account of the National Socialist Party, see Kater, *The Nazi Party.* For discussion of all the parties mentioned, see Thomas Childers, *The Nazi Voter: The Social Foundations of Fascism in Germany, 1919–1933* (Chapel Hill, 1983).

3. American bankers Charles C. Dawes (in 1924) and Owen D. Young (in 1929) each put forward plans to make it possible for Germany to pay the reparations established at the peace conferences ending the First World War.

4. Harold L. Ickes (1874–1952) served as secretary of the interior in the United States for the period 1933–46.

5. This gazette was the *Reichsgesetzblatt.*

6. On the Reichstag fire of February 27, 1933, and its consequences, see Gellately, *Backing Hitler,* 12–13.

7. Reinhard Heydrich (1904–1942) was the influential founder of the SD and one of the key leaders in the establishment of the Gestapo and of the rest of the Nazi police system. He was assassinated in Czechoslovakia and died on June 4, 1942. For a brief introduction, see Fest, *Face of the Third Reich,* 98–110.

8. Karl Hermann Frank (1898–1946) managed to reverse Hitler's reprisal orders in response to the assassination (May 27, 1942) of Reinhard Heydrich. However, the village of Lidice was targeted. It was leveled to the ground and its inhabitants were either killed immediately (192 men, 71 women) or sent to concentration camps (another 198 women); the children (98) were sent away to "special schools."

## HANS FRITZSCHE

1. See my general introduction to this volume. Compare Raul Hilberg, *The Destruction of the European Jews,* rev. ed. (New York, 1985), 3:1048. A general account by Yehuda Bauer, *A History of the Holocaust* (New York, 1982), 335, shows a "total of Jewish losses" to be 5,820,960. Franciszek Piper, "Auschwitz Concentration Camp: How It Was Used in the Nazi System of Terror and Genocide and in the Economy of the Third Reich," in Michael Berenbaum and Abraham J. Peck, eds., *The Holocaust and History: The Known, the Unknown, the Disputed, and the Reexamined* (Bloomington, 1998), 327–86 (here, 376), estimates about 1 million Jews lost their lives in the camp; 140,000–150,000 Poles; 20,000 Gypsies; 15,000 Soviet prisoners of war; and between 10,000 and 25,000 people of other nationalities.
2. For a brief account of the postwar era and the various transfers of population, see Philipp Ther and Ana Siljak, eds., *Redrawing Nations: Ethnic Cleansing in East-Central Europe, 1944–1948* (Lanham, Md., 2001).
3. Adolf Eichmann (1906–1962) is often considered the architect of the "final solution." His infamous position was to be in charge of Office IV B4 in the RSHA, whereby he had control over the "resettlement" of the Jews. After the war he escaped to South America, and was captured by the Israeli secret service in Argentina in 1960. He was tried in Jerusalem and executed in 1962. The best account of Eichmann and of the process as a whole remains Hilberg, *Destruction of the European Jews.*
4. For a recent examination of Versailles, see Manfred F. Boemeke, Gerald D. Feldman, and Elisabeth Glaser, eds., *The Treaty of Versailles: A Reassessment After 75 Years* (Cambridge, 1998). See also Margaret MacMillan, *Paris 1919: Six Months that Changed the World* (New York, 2001).
5. In fact, the brutality was planned beforehand. Hitler made it clear in July 1940 and again in March 1941 that in the forthcoming war in the East, Russia would be "utterly destroyed." He insisted that the war would be a life-and-death struggle in which Germany would reject the idea of the foe as a comrade in arms. "We do not go to war to preserve our enemies." For an introduction to the criminal orders given for the treatment of POWs in the East, see Hans-Adolf Jacobson, "The *Kommissarbefehl* and Mass Execution of Soviet Russian Prisoners of War," in Helmut Krausnick et al., *Anatomy of the SS State* (London, 1968), 505–35.
6. For a short account of "night and fog," see Gellately, *Backing Hitler,* 225–26. Special courts began in February 1942 to sentence foreign nationals, but though many went to their deaths, on Hitler's orders their fates were concealed from friends and relatives.
7. Often regarded as the Weimar Republic's most brilliant politician during the

great inflation of 1923, Gustav Stresemann (1878–1929) was chancellor from August 13 until November 28, 1923, and Heinrich Bruening (1885–1970) was chancellor from March 29, 1930, until May 30, 1932, the immediate predecessor in office to Papen.

8. For a recent account of why and how Russia won, see Richard Overy, *Russia's War* (Harmondsworth, 1998).

9. Kurt Dittmar (1891–1959) was a well-known German radio commentator on military affairs.

10. A German submarine sank a British passenger liner, *Athenia*, on the first day of the war in 1939. Many lives were lost, including a hundred or so Americans. The event reminded many of the sinking of the *Lusitania* in the First World War. The Germans denied sinking the *Athenia*, with Goebbels going so far as to claim the British did it to bring the United States into the war. For a brief account and the context, see Robert E. Conot, *Justice in Nuremberg* (New York, 1983), 418–19.

11. These "protocols" were a well-known forgery going back in Europe well into the nineteenth century. For a brief account and excellent background, see George L. Mosse, *Toward the Final Solution: A History of European Racism* (New York, 1978), 117–20.

12. For an excellent account of the many and varied research institutes on Eastern Europe in Nazi Germany, see Michael Burleigh, *Germany Turns Eastward: A Study of Ostforschung in the Third Reich* (Cambridge, 1988).

## WALTHER FUNK

1. Gregor Strasser (1892–1934) was a leader of the early Nazi Party. He eventually split with Hitler and was murdered on June 30, 1934, as part of the so-called "night of the long knives."

2. In the elections of March 5, 1933, to the German parliament, the Nazis obtained 43.9 percent of the vote and 288 seats out of a total of 647 seats. Their coalition partners, the German National People's Party (DNVP), won 8 percent of the vote and another 52 seats, thus giving Hitler "command" of a majority in the house. Altogether, more than 20.3 million people voted for these two parties out of a total of 39.3 million who cast their ballot in the elections.

3. George S. Messersmith was U.S. Consul General in Berlin, 1930–34. He was then sent to Vienna, where he remained until 1937.

4. Otto Dietrich (1897–1952), was Reich press chief for most of the Nazi era. On the press in Nazi Germany, an older but reliable study in English is Oron J. Hale, *The Captive Press in the Third Reich* (Princeton, 1964).

5. Hans Bernd Gisevius (1904–1974) happily rushed to join the Gestapo in 1933, but eventually distanced himself from the regime and became involved in the resistance.

6. For a compelling account of the prewar persecutions and also of the "night of broken glass," see Saul Friedländer, *Nazi Germany and the Jews,* vol. 1, *The Years of Persecution, 1933–1939* (New York, 1997).

7. The meeting of November 12, chaired by Hermann Goering, was called to deal with the pogrom of November 9, 1938. For an introduction and reference to the literature, see Gellately, *Backing Hitler,* 126–32.

8. U.S. secretary of the Treasury Henry Morgenthau Jr. put forward a plan in the autumn of 1944 that aimed at preventing Germany from starting another war. The nation was to be returned to a premodern pastoral condition, with the country divided and its economy destroyed. The plan was opposed by U.S. secretary of war Henry Stimson, as well as by President Franklin Roosevelt and Prime Minister Winston Churchill.

9. The meeting was likely a gathering of wealthy industrialists on February 20, 1933. For a full account, also of the broader issues, see Henry Ashby Turner Jr., *German Big Business and the Rise of Hitler* (New York, 1985); here, see 328–33.

10. Heinrich Hoffmann (1885–1957) was Hitler's official photographer.

11. *Twilight of the Gods* is the fourth of four operas constituting Richard Wagner's *The Ring.*

## HERMANN GOERING

1. Edward Frederick Lindley Wood, first earl of Halifax (1881–1959), was British ambassador to the United States 1941–46.

2. Although many German Jews belonged to the middle-class elite in society and culture until 1933, Goering exaggerates their role. For a more differentiated account, also with useful references to further literature, see Friedländer, *Nazi Germany and the Jews.*

3. For a still useful account of Chamberlain and his role in the intellectual background to the rise of the Third Reich, see Mosse, *Toward the Final Solution.*

4. The "Rundstedt Offensive"— sometimes referred to as the Ardennes Offensive (December 1944–January 1945)— is commonly known as the Battle of the Bulge. The German attack was commanded by General Field Marshall Rundstedt, but it was Hitler's plan and he was involved at every stage. He hoped to break the Allies will, but failed disastrously. The battle cost both sides dearly, with each suffering around 80,000 casualties.

5. Field Marshal Hans Guenther von Kluge (1882–1944) is said by one historian to have "displayed his zeal for carrying out Hitler's commands to the letter" in the attack on the Soviet Union in 1941. See Barry A. Leach, *German Strategy Against Russia 1939–1941* (Oxford, 1973), 226. On the other hand, Kluge was ambivalent about the later military resistance to Hitler, and opposed assassination, much as did Rommel. For the full details, see Peter Hoffmann, *The History of the German Resistance 1933–1945* (Cambridge, Mass., 1977).

6. Karl Brandt (1904–1948) was a physician to Hitler and became directly involved in fostering the notorious euthanasia program that began in 1939. At the "euthanasia" trial in Nuremberg he was sentenced to death, and executed. For details and reference to the vast literature on the topic, see Michael Burleigh, *Death and Deliverance: "Euthanasia" in Germany 1900–1945* (Cambridge, 1994).

7. On Hitler's use of amnesties, see Gellately, *Backing Hitler,* 39, 88, 196.

8. The reference here is to Adolf Eichmann (1906–1962), whose importance was realized fully only later, particularly at his trial in Jerusalem in 1961.

9. The notorious Posen speech (October 4, 1943) is reprinted in J. Noakes and G. Pridham, *Nazism: A Documentary Reader* (Exeter, 1988), 3:1199–200.

10. Birger Dahlerus was a friend of Goering. He is described in the court docu-

Goering tried to use Dahlerus in late September 1939 to get the British to accept that Germany have a free hand in Poland and be able to resolve the "Jewish question" as Germany saw fit. Dahlerus thought initially he was being used to broker a peace, but finally realized he had been duped by Goering and to some extent also by Hitler. For this matter, see Richard Overy, *Goering: The "Iron Man"* (London, 1984), 93.

11. APC is a pharmaceutical compound of aspirin, caffeine, and phenacetin.

12. See the in-depth discussion of art and politics under Hitler in Jonathan Petropoulos, *Art as Politics in the Third Reich* (Chapel Hill, 1996).

13. For the precise background to the decision-making process and these laws, see Ian Kershaw, *Hitler 1889–1936: Hubris* (London, 1998), 568–69.

14. Edward, duke of Windsor (1894–1972), abdicated the British throne in 1936 in order to marry Wallis Simpson. They went initially to Paris, left for Madrid when France fell in 1940, and sailed to the Bahamas on August 1, 1940, quite unaware that the Germans were plotting around them. Rumors continue to circulate of the duke's positive feelings toward Hitler and the Third Reich.

## RUDOLF HESS

1. For the context and Hitler's highly emotional response to Hess's flight to Scotland on May 10, 1941, see Ian Kershaw, *Hitler 1936–45: Nemesis* (New York, 2000), 369–81. Kershaw shows convincingly that "there is not a shred of compelling evidence" that Hitler had any prior knowledge of the Hess "mission." The deputy führer evidently got it into his head that he might be able to arrange an Anglo-German agreement of some kind before the Germans launched Operation Barbarossa, the attack on the Soviet Union that had been planned just shortly before, for June 22, 1941.

## ERNST KALTENBRUNNER

1. For details on the Criminal Police (Kripo), which was finally centralized in 1936 in the Reich Criminal Police Office (RKPA), see Gellately, *Backing Hitler*, 34–50.

2. On the mythical "purge" of the police in 1933 and the creation of the Gestapo, see Robert Gellately, *The Gestapo and German Society: Enforcing Racial Policy, 1933–1945* (Oxford, 1990), especially 50–57. See also George C. Browder, *Foundations of the Nazi Police State: The Formation of the Sipo and SD* (Lexington, Ky., 1990).

3. For an excellent account of the RSHA (with full organizational charts) and a biography, see Peter R. Black, *Ernst Kaltenbrunner: Ideological Soldier of the Third Reich* (Princeton, 1984). For a detailed account of the RSHA, see the detailed study of Michael Wildt, *Generation des Unbedingten: Das Führungskorps des Reichssicherheitshauptamtes* (Hamburg, 2002).

4. Heinrich Mueller (born 1901) was the notorious head of the Gestapo and what became known inside the RSHA as Office IV. He played a key part in the cre-

ation and operation of the Gestapo, and disappeared in 1945. For an introduction to his career, see Gellately, *Gestapo and German Society,* 55–56.

5. For a social analysis of the party, see Kater, *Nazi Party.*

6. The claim continues to be made that Hitler and Nazi Germany had carried out a "preventive war" to parry an attack that Stalin and the Soviets were about to launch. For a solid rebuttal, see Gabriel Gorodetsky, *Grand Delusion: Stalin and the German Invasion of Russia* (New Haven, Conn., 1999). For a precise account of the military preparations and dispositions of both sides, see Overy, *Russia's War.*

7. The Hague Conventions (1899 and 1907), as well as other international treaties such as the Geneva Convention (1929), had attempted to work out the rules of war.

8. In a seminal speech in the evolution of the Cold War, Churchill warned — on March 5, 1946, at Westminster College in Fulton, Missouri — that "an iron curtain has descended across the Continent" of Europe. He was referring to how the Soviet Union had extended its control over what became the Eastern Bloc countries.

9. Wilhelm Canaris (1887–1945) had been head of the German military intelligence (*Abwehr*). His reservations and doubts about Hitler eventually led him to participate in some resistance activities; he was arrested and tortured in the wake of the *Attentat* of July 1944, and finally hanged on April 9, 1945. For the details and general account, see Hoffmann, *History of the German Resistance.*


### WILHELM KEITEL

1. Walter von Brauchitsch (1881–1948) was commander in chief of the German army 1938–41. He was appointed by Hitler to replace Werner von Fritsch (1880–1939). Brauchitsch was dismissed by Hitler on December 19, 1941. Hitler demonstrated who was boss with the ousters of military leaders like Brauchitsch and Fritsch, as well as Field Marshal Werner von Blomberg (1878–1946). Blomberg was commander in chief of the army until 1938 and minister of war 1935–38. He was forced from office through an orchestrated scandal in 1938.

2. The German annexation of Austria took place on March 12, 1938. Most Austrians responded with enthusiasm and euphoria. See Evan Burr Bukey, *Hitler's Austria: Popular Sentiment in the Nazi Era* (Chapel Hill, 2000), 33.


### CONSTANTIN VON NEURATH

1. The reference is to William E. Dodd and Martha Dodd, eds., *Ambassador Dodd's Diary, 1933–1938* (London, 1941).

2. On the subsequent elections of March 5, 1933, to the German parliament, see above, chapter on Funk, note 2.

3. The Munich Conference (September 29–30, 1938) was the high point of British and French appeasement policies toward Germany. Czechoslovakia was in effect given up in return for keeping the peace. In the end this policy failed to appease Hitler, who was determined upon war.

4. Hans Heinrich Lammers (1872–1962) was chief of the Reich Chancellery throughout the period of the Third Reich. At one of the follow-up trials at Nuremberg (the Wilhelmstrasse case in 1949), he was held to account and sentenced to twenty years, but was released from prison in 1954.

### FRANZ VON PAPEN

1. For Papen's role in helping Hitler into power, see Turner, *German Big Business,* 322–29.
2. Hitler came to power as part of a coalition government. See chapter on Funk, note 2, above.
3. This refers to the murder of Ernst Roehm (1887–1934) among others on the "night of the long knives," June 30, 1934. For a brief introduction and literature, see Gellately, *Backing Hitler,* 38–39.

### JOACHIM VON RIBBENTROP

1. For an analysis of how the Nazis portrayed Jewish influence in the United States during the Roosevelt era, see Dan Diner, *America in the Eyes of the Germans: An Essay on Anti-Americanism* (Princeton, 1996), especially 79–103, "Uncle Sam as Uncle Shylock."
2. The revealing and massive diary is published: Werner Präg and Wolfgang Jacobmeyer, eds., *Das Diensttagebuch des deutschen Generalgouverneurs in Polen 1939–1945* (Stuttgart, 1975).
3. The Nazi-Soviet pact was signed on August 23, 1939.
4. Lend-lease was an American military and economic program introduced by FDR in 1941 to aid nations warring against the Axis powers. By August 1945, when the war ended, the United States had sent a total of $48 billion in material aid. Most of the money lent countries such as Britain was eventually repaid. The Soviet Union also repaid some of what it owed — perhaps less than one-third of the total.
5. Lazar Kaganovich was Jewish, a loyal Stalin supporter, and at one time member of the Politburo and Central Committee. For a recent Russian account see Dmitri Volkogonov, *Stalin, Triumph and Tragedy* (New York, 1991).
6. For a general account of Majdanek (Lublin) — created in 1941 — and of all the other camps, see Hilberg, *Destruction of the European Jews.*
7. Werner Best (1903–1989) was one of the most influential leaders of the Gestapo and was head of the office in charge of administration and law from 1935. From September 1939 he was leader of Office II of the RSHA, but in 1940 he was appointed to a major position in the administration of occupied France. From November 1942 he became the Reich plenipotentiary in Denmark, and played a role in saving the Danish Jews. Nevertheless, he was sentenced to death in 1949 in Copenhagen, but amnestied and released in 1951. He testified at Nuremberg, but was not put on trial there.

## ALFRED ROSENBERG

1. See chapter on Fritzsche, note 11.
2. In the literature on the persecution of the Jews, there is no evidence of such an English proposal in 1936. Some of the destinations mentioned in the text have been verified by research, particularly Madagascar, but others, such as Alaska, Uganda, and Guiana, may have been mentioned from time to time among leading Nazi officials but do not seem to have been seriously entertained. The standard account of the persecutions, including the policy of forced emigration to specified areas within and outside of Europe, is Hilberg, *Destruction of the European Jews.*
3. Proportional representation was used in the elections of the Weimar Republic, but the Nazis, the strongest party, did not win a majority. See above, chapter on Funk, note 2.
4. On the crisis and collapse of the Weimar Republic and how this made Hitler possible, see Gellately, *Backing Hitler,* 9–33.
5. William Averell Harriman (1891–1986) was closely associated with the New Deal. He was the American ambassador to the USSR (1943–46) and also administrator of lend-lease. James Michael Curley was the colorful Irish-American mayor of Boston and served on and off, between 1914 and 1950.
6. On the postwar forced population transfers and the "ethnic cleansing" of Germans from Poland, Czechoslovakia, and other newly liberated areas in Eastern Europe, see Philipp Ther and Ana Siljak, eds., *Redrawing Nations: Ethnic Cleansing in East-Central Europe, 1944–1948* (Lanham, Md., 2001), 2. Some 1.5 million people lost their lives when an estimated 12 million ethnic Germans were driven from this area.
7. In 1919 Gen. Tasker Bliss (1853–1930) was in Europe as the American military representative on the Supreme War Council. He became one of President Woodrow Wilson's representatives to the Paris Peace Conference. Jan Smuts (1870–1950), an Afrikaner in Britain's imperial war cabinet (1917–18), helped plan the League of Nations. For a recent account, see MacMillan, *Paris 1919.*

## FRITZ SAUCKEL

1. For the background and precise statistics, see Ulrich Herbert, *Hitler's Foreign Workers: Enforced Foreign Labor in Germany Under the Third Reich* (Cambridge, 1997).
2. The Gustloff Works (Gustloffwerke) were factories that produced various kinds of weapons for the German military. At a number of sites, such as one located near the Buchenwald concentration camp, the factories used slave and camp labor.
3. Presumably this refers to John Llewellyn Lewis (1880–1969), the American labor leader who, among other things, once headed the United Mine Workers and the American Federation of Labor.
4. On Kuhn, see Sander A. Diamond, *The Nazi Movement in the United States, 1924–1941* (Ithaca, N.Y., 1974).

## HJALMAR SCHACHT

1. On Jewish attempts at self-protection in Nazi Germany, see Friedländer, *Nazi Germany and the Jews.*
2. The stock market crash in the United States began in October 1929 and ushered in the Great Depression. The effects were reflected almost immediately in Germany, where stocks also fell and unemployment rose dramatically. For the crisis at the end of Germany's Weimar Republic, see Gellately, *Backing Hitler,* 9–33.
3. On July 31, 1932, the Nazi Party won 37.4 percent of the votes cast and 230 out of a total of 608 seats in the Reichstag elections. In the November 6, 1932, elections, they won 33.1 percent of the votes and 196 seats out of a total of 584.
4. In the March 5, 1933, elections the Nazis gained 43.9 percent of the votes cast, and 288 seats out of a total of 647 in the Reichstag.
5. Neurath was ousted on February 4, 1938. On the same day, there were announcements of the "retirement" of commander in chief of the army Gen. Werner von Fritsch and his colleague Minister of War Werner von Blomberg. An additional sixteen high-ranking generals were retired at that time and forty-four were moved about in order to remove any potentially unreliable elements. For a brief account and introduction to the larger problem, see Gordon A. Craig, *Germany 1866–1945* (Oxford, 1978), 700.
6. For a brief account of the postassassination crackdown in Operation Thunderstorm, see Gellately, *Backing Hitler,* 225–26. Germans generally disapproved of the attempt to assassinate Hitler. Field Marshal Erwin von Witzleben (1911–1944) was executed for his part in the attempted putsch.
7. Ambassador Hemmen had been in charge of the Economic Department of the Armistice Commission dealing with France after its defeat in 1940.
8. For the importance of the Law for the Restoration of the Professional Civil Service (April 7, 1933) see especially Friedländer, *Nazi Germany and the Jews.*
9. For an excellent account of sterilization and euthanasia programs, see Henry Friedländer, *The Origins of Genocide: From Euthanasia to the Final Solution* (Chapel Hill, 1995).
10. Georges Clemenceau (1841–1929) was a veteran French statesman and known for his role in forging the Treaty of Versailles (1919).

## BALDUR VON SCHIRACH

1. For an innovative account, see Lewis H. Siegelbaum, *Stakhanovism and the Politics of Productivity in the USSR, 1935–1941* (Cambridge, 1988).
2. The reference appears to be to texts used in German schools, which the German boys were surprised to find in the Russian language.
3. Richard Gluecks (1889–1945) was one of Theodor Eicke's (1892–1943) staff leaders in 1936, and succeeded Eicke as inspector of the concentration camps after the outbreak of the Second World War. Gluecks contributed to the creation of the concentration camp system, including Auschwitz, working under Oswald Pohl. It appears that he committed suicide in 1945.
4. In fact Alois Brunner (born 1912)—who was one of Eichmann's close col-

leagues — managed to escape justice and, according to a recent investigation, as of 2000, continued to live in Syria. See Georg M. Hafner and Esther Schapira, *Die Akte Alois Brunner* (Frankfurt am Main, 2000).

5. Josef Buerckel (1894–1944) was Nazi Party boss (*Gauleiter*) of Austria for a time after its union with Germany in 1938. Odilo Globocnik (1904–1945) was, among other things, the organizer of the notorious Action Reinhard death camps. On the latter see especially Yitzhak Arad, *Belzec, Sobibor, Treblinka: The Operation Reinhard Death Camps* (Bloomingdale, 1987).

6. For the background see Gordon J. Horwitz, *In the Shadow of Death: Living Outside the Gates of Mauthausen* (New York, 1990).


## ALBERT SPEER

1. Speer was evidently reluctant to be interviewed by Goldensohn, but in the end Hitler's former architect proved to be the most talkative of all those tried at Nuremberg. He published two lengthy and important books, which are cited in my introduction to this volume. He has been the subject of many studies. For the latest and most thorough, see Gitta Sereny, *Albert Speer: His Battle with Truth* (New York, 1995).


## JULIUS STREICHER

1. See above, chapter on Fritzsche, note 11.
2. For the November 9, 1938, pogrom, see above, chapter on Doenitz, note 9.


## ERICH VON DEM BACH-ZELEWSKI

1. The limited size of the army was imposed by the Versailles Treaty; see Boemeke, Feldman, and Glaser, eds., *Treaty of Versailles*.

2. Erich Koch (1896–1986) was tried in Poland after the war and in 1959 sentenced to death, but the sentence was commuted to life imprisonment.

3. Josef Wagner was at one point district Nazi Party leader in Westphalia South, to which he added Silesia in 1934. He was dismissed in 1940 for pro-Catholic sympathies, but that resulted less from Hitler's own appreciation of the situation than from inner-party intrigues and power struggles. See Dietrich Orlow, *The History of the Nazi Party, 1933–1945* (Pittsburgh, 1973), 270. Hitler had Wagner's case sent to the highest party court, which, much to Hitler's consternation, acquitted Wagner and reinstated him as a member of the party. See Donald M. McKale, *The Nazi Party Courts: Hitler's Management of Conflict in His Movement, 1921–1945* (Lawrence, 1974), 178–79.

4. On Auschwitz, see Franciszek Piper, "Auschwitz Concentration Camp: How It Was Used in the Nazi System of Terror and Genocide and in the Economy of the Third Reich," in Berenbaum and Peck, eds., *Holocaust and History*, 327–86. For an account of specific issues, see Yisrael Gutman and Michael Benenbaum, eds., *The Anatomy of the Auschwitz Death Camp* (Washington, 1994).

5. The Jews of the Warsaw Ghetto began an uprising on April 19, 1943, and ultimately cost the lives of an estimated 14,000; another 7,000 were transported to Treblinka or Majdanek. The Germans suffered an estimated 400 dead and 1,000 wounded. For a brief, general, and reliable account, see Doris L. Bergen, *War and Genocide: A Concise History of the Holocaust* (New York, 2003).

6. General Bor-Komorowski is mentioned in the trial documents in the context of the Warsaw rebellion of July 1944, which Bach-Zelewski was ordered to repress. For a brief account of what happened, including the deaths of an estimated 225,000 civilians in the failed rebellion, see Overy, *Russia's War,* 246–47.

7. Arthur Nebe (1894–1945) was an SS general and head of the Criminal Police. He attained infamy as the leader of Einsatzgruppe B. He is also said to have become involved in the plot to assassinate Hitler on July 20, 1944, but then disappeared. The complete story is told in Hoffmann, *The History of the German Resistance.*

8. For discussion of the significance of the "stab in the back of 1918," see Michael Burleigh, *The Third Reich: A New History* (London, 2000), 27–101.

## KURT DALUEGE

1. For a brief account of Daluege, the uniformed police, and references to further literature, see Gellately, *Backing Hitler.*

## SEPP DIETRICH

1. Erwin Rommel (1891–1944), field marshal in the German army, won fame at the head of the Afrika Korps, and became known as the Desert Fox. He was not directly involved in the plot to assassinate Hitler (July 20, 1944) but was thought to be implicated, and took the choice offered him of suicide, instead of arrest and trial before the people's court.

2. Gen. Anton Dostler was one of the commanders of the 63rd Army Corps in Italy. In March 1945 he ordered the execution of fifteen captured American soldiers. He was tried and found guilty by a postwar court and was sentenced to be shot to death. Dostler evidently became used to using brutal methods in the eastern war, as for example, following a raid in Kharkov on November 15, 1941, when his division took 500 hostages. Of these at least seventy were hanged in public soon after in reprisal for Soviet sabotage. For the latter story see Bernd Boll and Hans Safrian, "On the Way to Stalingrad: The 6th Army in 1941–42," in Hannes Heer and Klaus Naumann, eds., *War of Extermination: The German Military in World War II, 1941–1944* (New York, 2000), 237–71; here, see 262.

3. Kurt Meyer was a general of the Waffen-SS who was sentenced to death before a Canadian court in 1945 for ordering the execution of some twenty Canadian prisoners of war after the beginning of the Allied invasion. By the end of 1951 he was turned over by Canada to Britain, and after special pleading by Chancellor Konrad Adenauer, he was eventually released. For this case and the con-

text, see Norbert Frei, *Adenauer's Germany and the Nazi Past: The Politics of Amnesty and Integration* (New York, 2002), 223, 387.

4. The Malmédy massacre took place at nearby Baugnez, in Belgium, on December 17, 1944. The Sixth SS Panzer Division, on the orders of Dietrich, carried out a mass execution of American prisoners of war in which eighty-six were killed and forty-three survived. This was the largest such incident, but not the only one. Although the German perpetrators were caught, tried, and sentenced to death, none of the death sentences were ever carried out. See I. C. B. Dear, ed., *The Oxford Companion to World War II* (Oxford, 1995), 713.

5. Based on German records, at least 3.3 million Soviet prisoners of war died in captivity, many of them shot out of hand or starved to death. For details, see Gellately, *Backing Hitler,* 225.

### FRANZ HALDER

1. Halder had considered participating in a coup against Hitler as early as 1938. For these plans and later developments, see Hoffmann, *History of the German Resistance.*

2. Admiral Wilhelm Canaris (1887–1945) was head of military intelligence, and Hans Oster (1888–1945) was his chief of staff. Both were involved in the attempted assassination of Hitler and both were executed. For details, see Hoffmann, *History of the German Resistance.*

3. For an overview of the resistance in general and these executions in particular, see Hoffmann, *History of the German Resistance.*

4. Walter von Brauchitsch (1881–1948) was commander in chief of the German army 1938–41, appointed by Hitler to replace Werner von Fritsch (1880–1939). Brauchitsch was dismissed by Hitler on December 19, 1941. Hitler demonstrated who was boss with the ousters of military leaders like Brauchitsch and Fritsch, as well as Field Marshal Werner von Blomberg (1878–1946). The latter was Reichswehr minister and (from 1935) minister of war and commander in chief of the *Wehrmacht* until 1938. He was forced from office through an orchestrated scandal in 1938. Halder was dismissed on September 24, 1942.

5. The crisis that almost led to war in 1938 concerned the Sudeten area of Czechoslovakia. The crisis ended with British and French appeasement at the Munich Conference, September 29–30, 1938.

### RUDOLF HOESS

1. For his recently translated autobiography, see Rudolf Hoess, *Death Dealer: The Memories of the SS Kommandant at Auschwitz,* edited by Steven Paskuly (New York, 1996). The editor provides numerous corrections to the autobiography and especially on technical details in the construction and operation of Auschwitz.

2. The exact number killed has been much disputed. According to the standard work in the field, Hilberg, *Destruction of the European Jews,* 3:894, approximately 1 million Jews lost their lives at Auschwitz. He estimates that another 250,000 people, mostly Poles, also died there, as well as many Gypsies. There is

general agreement in Piper, "Auschwitz," who estimates about 1 million Jews lost their lives in the camp; 140,000 to 150,000 Poles; 20,000 Gypsies; 15,000 Soviet prisoners of war; and between 10,000 and 25,000 people of other nationalities.

3. Recent historians have concluded that the meeting with Himmler took place in June 1942. See Karin Orth, "Rudolf Hoess und die 'Endlösung der Judenfrage': Drei Argumente gegen deren Datierung auf den Sommer 1941," in *Werkstatt-Geschichte* (1997), 45–57.

4. For the complex history of attempts of Nazi leaders to hold Jews in Europe for ransom, see Yehuda Bauer, *Jews for Sale?* (New Haven, 1994).

5. Ernst Heinrich Schmauser (born 1890) was Higher SS and police leader of Upper Silesia from May 1, 1941, to 1945. Auschwitz was in his jurisdiction. For brief remarks see Hilberg, *Destruction of the European Jews,* 2:524.

6. Josef Kramer (1907–1945) was an infamous *Kommandant* of Auschwitz-Birkenau and later the horror that was Bergen-Belsen. He was tried and executed by a British military court in 1945. For a good overview of Kramer and other camp leaders, see Tom Segev, *Soldiers of Evil: The Commandants of the Nazi Concentration Camps* (New York, 1987).

## ALBERT KESSELRING

1. The place of Field Marshal Erwin Rommel in the general context of the attempt to overthrow Hitler is told in Hoffmann, *History of the German Resistance.*

2. For a recent account, including of specific atrocities committed against civilians in Italy and elsewhere, see Hannes Heer and Klaus Naumann, eds., *War of Extermination: The German Military in World War II, 1941–1944* (New York, 2000).

3. German military discipline was brutal in the Second World War. In those years, military courts sentenced more than 30,000 German soldiers to death, and about 15,000 of the verdicts were carried out. See Wolfram Wette, *Die Wehrmacht* (Frankfurt am Main, 2002), p. 165.

4. For discussion of the looting of the Abbey of Monte Cassino, including Kesselring's part in it, see Lynn H. Nicholas, *The Rape of Europa* (New York, 1994), 238 ff.

5. Karl Wolff (born 1900), key SS leader and from 1933 to 1943 Himmler's adjutant, played an important role in Italy as Mussolini's power declined from 1943 onward.

6. For a readable and reliable account of these events and of the military history of the Second World War, see Gerhard L. Weinberg, *A World at Arms: A Global History of World War II* (Cambridge, 1994).

## EWALD VON KLEIST

1. For the revolution, see Craig, *Germany,* 396–433.

2. Karl von Clausewitz (1780–1831) was a world-famous Prussian soldier and writer of the treatise *On War* (1833).

3. The decision to hold back the attack of the tanks at Dunkirk on May 24, 1940, was taken by Hitler, but expressly on the advice of Rundstedt. According to Ian

Kershaw, there was a military mistake, but it was Rundstedt's and not Hitler's. The latter did not to wish to let the British save face, and so the decision to hold back the tanks and let the British escape was not taken because of Hitler's magnanimity. On the contrary, Hitler wanted to deliver a "knockout blow" and thus force the British to accept peace terms, but he listened to Rundstedt, his trusted general. See Kershaw, *Hitler,* 2:295–96.

4. For a complete account, see Ernest R. May, *Strange Victory: Hitler's Conquest of France* (New York, 2001).

5. The laws proclaimed at the Nazi Party rally at Nuremberg in September 1935 were infamous in that they essentially created an apartheid system for all Jews in Germany, and represented an important step in their persecution. For an account, see Gellately, *Gestapo and German Society.*

6. Higher SS and police leaders like Gerret Korsemann (1895–1958) can be studied in Ruth Bettina Birn, *Die Höheren SS- und Polizeiführer: Himmlers Vertreter im Reich und in den besetzten Gebieten* (Düsseldorf, 1986).

## ERICH VON MANSTEIN

1. A recent estimate puts the total loss of the Axis armies at Stalingrad, including Manstein's failed attempt at rescue, at "over half a million" lives. For the harrowing story, see Antony Beevor, *Stalingrad: The Fateful Siege, 1942–1943* (New York, 1999), 398.

## ERHARD MILCH

1. For an account of extensive and generally supportive public knowledge of the concentration camps in Nazi Germany at the time, see Gellately, *Backing Hitler,* 51–69.

## RUDOLF MILDNER

1. According to Mildner's own testimony at Nuremberg, he worked for the Gestapo for ten years. He arrived in Denmark to serve as head of the "Security Police and SD" (from September 20, 1943) just as an "action" was planned to deport the Danish Jews. He regarded the plan as impossible on technical grounds, as did Reich plenipotentiary in Denmark Werner Best. At the same time, Ribbentrop felt the action might cause domestic "unrest" in Denmark. Nevertheless, Hitler expressly insisted on the deportations. However, Best and others made it obvious that the deportations were about to take place. The Jews grew alarmed and tried to flee; they were helped by some Danes and thus were saved.

2. In February 1934 there was civil unrest by the socialists (not the Nazis) against Austrian chancellor Engelbert Dollfuss. The Nazis did attempt to seize power in Vienna in July 1934, shot Dollfuss, but failed in their attempt to take over. See Bukey, *Hitler's Austria,* 14.

3. Chancellor Kurt von Schuschnigg succeeded Dollfuss, but was soon isolated and pushed aside when Hitler moved to take over Austria in March 1938.
4. It is likely that this refers to another Austrian member of the SS, Dr. Humbert Achamer-Pifrader (1900–1945), a man who later became one of the leaders of Einsatzgruppe A. He was killed in action in 1945. For a complete history, see Helmut Krausnick and Hans Heinrich Wilhelm, *Die Truppe des Weltanschauungskrieges: Die Einsatzgruppen der Sicherheitspolizei und des SD, 1938–1942* (Stuttgart, 1981).
5. Franz Josef Huber (born 1902) was a career policeman in the Weimar Republic, like Heinrich Mueller, and also like Mueller stayed on to serve in the new Gestapo and rose in the ranks. Huber eventually became the head of the Gestapo in Vienna. For a brief account, see Gellately, *Gestapo and German Society*, 56–57.
6. Werner Best had the conflict with Heydrich in early summer 1939, mainly because Heydrich did not agree with Best's ideas on personnel and organizational questions inside the SD. Contrary to what is often supposed, when Heydrich essentially fired Best, he did not thereby get rid of the "last hindrances" to policies of "mass destruction" of the Jews, for Best was far from such an obstacle; indeed he not only agreed with such policies, but formulated many of them and justified them ideologically. See Ulrich Herbert, *Best: Biographische Studien über Radikalismus, Weltanschauung und Vernunft 1903–1989* (Berlin, 1996), 228–29.
7. It should be noted that the Germans in charge in Denmark, particularly Werner Best, did not have a "change of heart," but had been and remained true to their idea to remove all the Jews from Europe, either through mass murder or deportation. When they recognized in September 1943 that Hitler's order to deport the Jews from Denmark was not feasible, they contented themselves with making the upcoming action obvious, in the expectation that the Jews would rush to leave and Danes would willingly help. The net effect, from the Nazi point of view, was that Denmark was "free of Jews." Best was not the slightest bit interested in "rescuing" the Jews as such, but took the only politically workable approach open to him at that moment. For a convincing account of the rescue of approximately 7,900 people, including the Jews and several hundred of their non-Jewish relatives, see Herbert, *Best*, 366–73.
8. Ernst Heinrich Schmauser (born 1890) was an SS leader, and from May 1, 1941, to 1945 he was the Higher SS and police leader in Breslau. Auschwitz camp was in his jurisdiction.

## OTTO OHLENDORF

1. Alfred Hugenberg (1865–1951) was a press tycoon, head of the German National People's Party (DNVP), and Hitler's coalition partner after the March 1933 elections. Hugenberg was quickly pushed aside, with his party dissolved by June 1933.
2. The event was the pogrom of November 9, 1938.
3. Uman was in Ohlendorf's area of operation. An estimated 24,000 were murdered there.

4. Reference here is to the Austrian scientist, philosopher, and educator Rudolf Steiner (1861–1925), founder of a spiritual movement called anthroposophy.

## OSWALD POHL

1. On the economic side of the concentration camps and for literature in the field, see the recent study of Michael Thad Allen, *The Business of Genocide: The SS, Slave Labor, and the Concentration Camps* (Chapel Hill, 2002).
2. For the extensive publicity surrounding the concentration camps in Germany, see Gellately, *Backing Hitler.*
3. For a brief account of the SS, see especially George H. Stein, *The Waffen SS: Hitler's Elite Guard at War* (Ithaca, 1966).
4. For the story of this gold and its role in the war, including especially the successful recent attempt to gain compensation from the German government, see the remarkable account of Stuart E. Eizenstat, *Imperfect Justice: Looted Assets, Slave Labor, and the Unfinished Business of World War II* (New York, 2003).
5. For an overview of the camp system in the war years and the development of many hundreds of camps inside Nazi Germany, see Gellately, *Backing Hitler,* 204–23.
6. Theodor Eicke (1892–1943) is known in history for his key role in the creation of the Nazi concentration camp system from the moment he was made *Kommandant* at Dachau in 1933. He rose to be the inspector of concentration camps. For an account of the internal functioning of the camps and Eicke's role, see Eugen Kogon, *The Theory and Practice of Hell* (numerous editions; originally published in German in 1945).
7. Allen, *Business of Genocide,* deals at length with Kammler and these programs.
8. August Frank (1898–1984) became head of the administrative office of the SS in 1939. By 1942 he was one of the leaders of the armed SS WVHA. He served eventually as Oswald Pohl's deputy in the WVHA, but is mentioned only briefly in the Nuremberg documents. At one of the follow-up trials in Nuremberg (case four), however, he was given a life term, but that was changed to fifteen years in 1951. He was released from prison in 1954.
9. For the exact figures on the number of Jews killed, see my introduction to this volume and the most important literature, as cited above in the chapter on Fritzsche, note 1.
10. Allen, *Business of Genocide,* and Gellately, *Backing Hitler,* show in detail that Pohl's claim was a complete lie.

## WALTER SCHELLENBERG

1. For an office chart of the RSHA in 1944, with its ten branches, see Black, *Kaltenbrunner,* 297–99. Schellenberg was in charge of Office VI, foreign intelligence or SD-Ausland, as well as military intelligence, or Office Military.
2. For reactions and background to the sterilization program, introduced in 1933 and eventually leading to the compulsory sterilization of 400,000 people, see Gellately, *Backing Hitler,* 93.

3. Much useful information on Himmler can be found in Richard Breitman, *The Architect of Genocide: Himmler and the Final Solution* (Hanover, 1991).

4. Otto Skorzeny (1908–1975) worked for Office VI of the RSHA (under Schellenberg) and was in charge of Department S, or sabotage. Among other things, Skorzeny became almost a folk hero in Germany for leading the daring and successful raid to rescue captured Italian dictator Benito Mussolini in September 1943. During the Ardennes offensive in 1944, Skorzeny led a brigade of 2,000 troops disguised as American soldiers, and helped to sow chaos behind the lines. He was acquitted of charges brought by a postwar American court in 1947. See Black, *Kaltenbrunner*, 210–11.

5. On Schellenberg's peace efforts, see Black, *Kaltenbrunner*, 220–21.

6. Abraham Steven Hewitt was an OSS agent in Stockholm, and had contact with various people around Himmler, including Schellenberg. The latter seemed to believe that Hewitt was on special assignment from President Roosevelt. Schellenberg somewhat cautiously invited Hewitt — who informed OSS chief Gen. William J. Donovan of these peace feelers — to visit Germany, but nothing came of the whole thing. Hewitt made wide-ranging demands for what the Germans would have to do in order to win U.S. support for peace, and these never would have been accepted. For a detailed account see Yehuda Bauer, *Jews for Sale?: Nazi-Jewish Negotiations, 1933–1945* (New Haven, Conn., 1994), 104–5. See also Wildt, *Generation des Unbedingten*, 718–19.

7. Schellenberg apparently arranged a meeting between Himmler and Jean-Marie Musy, who is described by a historian of this event as a "Swiss conservative statesman." See Black, *Kaltenbrunner*, 228–29.

8. Musy met with Himmler on November 3, 1944, and January 1, 1945, and tried to negotiate a ransom, whereby the Germans would be paid so much for each individual Jew or shipment of Jews who were released from the camps. Musy (former Swiss president and former Nazi sympathizer) agreed to pay $1,000 for each of 1,200 Jews who were released, but Himmler hinted that many more could be rescued. The release of these 1,200 Jews was reported in the press. Kaltenbrunner did not agree with this deal, and to stop it, he presented information about it to Hitler in early 1945. Hitler ordered the program halted. See Black, *Kaltenbrunner*, 229–30, and Bauer, *Jews for Sale*, 225–30.

9. Count Folke Bernadotte was a Swedish Red Cross official who, among other things, tried to rescue some Jews from the camps by negotiating with Schellenberg, Kaltenbrunner, and Himmler from late 1944 into 1945. The Swedish Red Cross did manage to rescue about 7,500 women from Ravensbrück, including some from France, Sweden, and Poland. See Bauer, *Jews for Sale*, 246–47.

10. The raid on Dresden in February 1945 has been the subject of much controversy. Around 50,000 people lost their lives as a result of the Allied bombing.

11. The order to evacuate all camps and prisons, and/or to kill those prisoners who could not travel, led to mass murder. For an introduction and the literature, see Gellately, *Backing Hitler*, 242–52.

## PAUL O. SCHMIDT

1. This refers to the Italian invasion and war against Ethiopia. The invasion began in October 1935, and led to Italian occupation of Addis Ababa and to complete

annexation in May 1936. The Ethiopians continued to fight on outside the capital city.

2. Yosuke Matsuoka has been described as the "hawkish Japanese foreign minister." For the context of his meetings with Hitler in April 1941 see Kershaw, *Hitler,* 2:363–64.

3. Maksim Litvinov (1876–1951), commissar for foreign affairs of the USSR, was dismissed from office in May 1939 and became ambassador to the United States (1941–43).

PHOTOGRAPHIC PERMISSIONS

The publisher would like to thank the Corbis Archive for furnishing the photographs and granting the rights to reprint the images of Sepp Dietrich, Hans Fritzsche, Alfred Jodl, Erich von Manstein, Erhard Milch, and Paul O. Schmidt; the Granger Collection for the image of Franz von Papen; the Bundesarchiv for the image of Rudolf Mildner; and the United States Holocaust Memorial Museum for the images of Erich von dem Bach-Zelewski, Kurt Daluege, Karl Doenitz, Hans Frank, Wilhelm Frick, Walther Funk, Hermann Goering, Franz Halder, Rudolf Hess, Rudolf Hoess, Wilhelm Keitel, Albert Kesselring, Constantin von Neurath, Otto Ohlendorf, Joachim von Ribbentrop, Alfred Rosenberg, Fritz Sauckel, Hjalmar Schacht, Walter Schellenberg, Baldur von Schirach, Albert Speer, and Julius Streicher.